Accumulo

Application Development,
Table Design, and Best Practices

Aaron Cordova, Billie Rinaldi, and Michael Wall

Beijing · Boston · Farnham · Sebastopol · Tokyo

Accumulo: Application Development, Table Design, and Best Practices

by Aaron Cordova, Billie Rinaldi, and Michael Wall

Copyright © 2015 Aaron Cordova, Billie Rinaldi, Michael Wall. All rights reserved.

Printed in the United States of America.

Published by O'Reilly Media, Inc., 1005 Gravenstein Highway North, Sebastopol, CA 95472.

O'Reilly books may be purchased for educational, business, or sales promotional use. Online editions are also available for most titles (*http://safaribooksonline.com*). For more information, contact our corporate/institutional sales department: 800-998-9938 or *corporate@oreilly.com*.

Editor: Marie Beaugureau	**Indexer:** WordCo Indexing Services, Inc.
Production Editor: Matthew Hacker	**Interior Designer:** David Futato
Copyeditor: Kim Cofer	**Cover Designer:** Ellie Volckhausen
Proofreader: Eileen Cohen	**Illustrators:** Aaron Cordova and Billie Rinaldi

July 2015: First Edition

Revision History for the First Edition

2015-06-30: First Release

See *http://oreilly.com/catalog/errata.csp?isbn=9781449374181* for release details.

The O'Reilly logo is a registered trademark of O'Reilly Media, Inc. *Accumulo: Application Development, Table Design, and Best Practices*, the cover image of a yak, and related trade dress are trademarks of O'Reilly Media, Inc.

While the publisher and the authors have used good faith efforts to ensure that the information and instructions contained in this work are accurate, the publisher and the authors disclaim all responsibility for errors or omissions, including without limitation responsibility for damages resulting from the use of or reliance on this work. Use of the information and instructions contained in this work is at your own risk. If any code samples or other technology this work contains or describes is subject to open source licenses or the intellectual property rights of others, it is your responsibility to ensure that your use thereof complies with such licenses and/or rights.

978-1-449-37418-1

[LSI]

Table of Contents

Foreword

Apache Accumulo burst onto the database scene in 2011 and has established itself as the highest-performance open source database in the world. This unprecedented achievement is a testament to the hard work of the many dedicated developers in the Accumulo community. Aaron Cordova, Billie Rinaldi, and Michael Wall have been leaders in the Accumulo community since its inception, and I can think of no one more qualified to write the definitive book on Accumulo.

The most distinguishing features of the Accumulo database are high performance, scalability, and flexible security. This book does a thorough job of providing the key concepts necessary for developers to utilize these features, while also making the material accessible to a wide audience.

Finally, Aaron, Billie, and Michael have taken great care in creating this text and have incorporated feedback on its development from the entire community. It has been a pleasure to watch this book grow and evolve into the impressive volume that it has become.

—Dr. Jeremy Kepner
MIT Lincoln Laboratory

Preface

Goals and Audience

We have designed this book to gather in a single place our community's collective knowledge of how best to use Apache Accumulo. This includes some history and background on the Accumulo project, how to configure and tune an Accumulo instance, and much about how to write applications using Accumulo. This book should help you get started with Accumulo, as well as provide a reference for those already familiar with it.

Those new to distributed applications will find an overview of why data stores such as Accumulo have become popular in recent years. People looking to write applications using Accumulo will find detailed information about its API as well as common design patterns and motivations behind various uses of Accumulo. Administrators of Accumulo will learn basic through advanced configuration options, including tips for tuning Accumulo for better performance. Even experienced Accumulo users are likely to find some information in these pages that they have not encountered before.

Conventions Used in This Book

The following typographical conventions are used in this book:

Italic
> Indicates new terms, URLs, email addresses, filenames, and file extensions.

`Constant width`
> Used for program listings, as well as within paragraphs to refer to program elements such as variable or function names, databases, data types, environment variables, statements, and keywords.

`Constant width bold`
> Shows commands or other text that should be typed literally by the user.

Constant width italic

Shows text that should be replaced with user-supplied values or by values determined by context.

This element signifies a tip or suggestion.

This element signifies a general note.

This element indicates a warning or caution.

Using Code Examples

Supplemental material (code examples, exercises, etc.) is available for download at *https://github.com/accumulobook*. Please also see the website we made for this book at *https://accumulobook.com*.

This book is here to help you get your job done. In general, if example code is offered with this book, you may use it in your programs and documentation. You do not need to contact us for permission unless you're reproducing a significant portion of the code. For example, writing a program that uses several chunks of code from this book does not require permission. Selling or distributing a CD-ROM of examples from O'Reilly books does require permission. Answering a question by citing this book and quoting example code does not require permission. Incorporating a significant amount of example code from this book into your product's documentation does require permission.

We appreciate, but do not require, attribution. An attribution usually includes the title, author, publisher, and ISBN. For example: "*Accumulo: Application Development, Table Design, and Best Practices* by Aaron Cordova, Billie Rinaldi, and Michael Wall (O'Reilly). Copyright 2015 Aaron Cordova, Billie Rinaldi, Michael Wall, 978-1-449-37418-1."

If you feel your use of code examples falls outside fair use or the permission given above, feel free to contact us at *permissions@oreilly.com*.

Safari® Books Online

 *Safari Books Online* is an on-demand digital library that delivers expert content in both book and video form from the world's leading authors in technology and business.

Technology professionals, software developers, web designers, and business and creative professionals use Safari Books Online as their primary resource for research, problem solving, learning, and certification training.

Safari Books Online offers a range of plans and pricing for enterprise, government, education, and individuals.

Members have access to thousands of books, training videos, and prepublication manuscripts in one fully searchable database from publishers like O'Reilly Media, Prentice Hall Professional, Addison-Wesley Professional, Microsoft Press, Sams, Que, Peachpit Press, Focal Press, Cisco Press, John Wiley & Sons, Syngress, Morgan Kaufmann, IBM Redbooks, Packt, Adobe Press, FT Press, Apress, Manning, New Riders, McGraw-Hill, Jones & Bartlett, Course Technology, and hundreds more. For more information about Safari Books Online, please visit us online.

How to Contact Us

Please address comments and questions concerning this book to the publisher:

O'Reilly Media, Inc.
1005 Gravenstein Highway North
Sebastopol, CA 95472
800-998-9938 (in the United States or Canada)
707-829-0515 (international or local)
707-829-0104 (fax)

We have a web page for this book, where we list errata, examples, and any additional information. You can access this page at *http://bit.ly/accumulo_1e*.

To comment or ask technical questions about this book, send email to *bookquestions@oreilly.com*.

For more information about our books, courses, conferences, and news, see our website at *http://www.oreilly.com*.

Find us on Facebook: *http://facebook.com/oreilly*

Follow us on Twitter: *http://twitter.com/oreillymedia*

Watch us on YouTube: *http://www.youtube.com/oreillymedia*

Acknowledgments

We would like to thank our technical reviewers, Josh Elser, Eric Newton, and Christopher Tubbs, without whom this book would have been less accurate and more difficult to read. We would also like to thank the many people who gave us feedback on this book, including but not limited to Sterling Foster, Alan Mangan, Jeremy Kepner, Tessa Cordova, David Barker, Al Krinker, Alex Moundalexis, Clint Green, David Perry, Christina Wall, and Rebecca Derry.

Thanks also to GroupLens Research at the University of Minnesota for use of the MovieLens data set for our examples.

Finally, we would like to thank the Apache Accumulo community—all the developers and users who have contributed to making Accumulo a fantastically stable, fast, and useful data store.

## CHAPTER 1

Architecture and Data Model

Apache Accumulo is a highly scalable, distributed, open source data store modeled after Google's Bigtable design (*http://bit.ly/bigtable_paper*). Accumulo is built to store up to trillions of data elements and keeps them organized so that users can perform fast lookups. Accumulo supports flexible data schemas and scales horizontally across thousands of machines. Applications built on Accumulo are capable of serving a large number of users and can process many requests per second, making Accumulo an ideal choice for terabyte- to petabyte-scale projects.

Recent Trends

Over the past few decades, several trends have driven the progress of data storage and processing systems. The first is that more data is being produced, at faster rates than ever before. The rate of available data is increasing so fast that more data was produced in the past few years than in all previous years. In recent years a huge amount of data has been produced by people for human consumption, and this amount is dwarfed by the amount of data produced by machines. These systems and devices promise to generate an enormous amount of data in the coming years. Merely storing this data can be a challenge, let alone organizing and processing it.

The second trend is that the cost of storage has dropped dramatically. Hard drives now store multiple terabytes for roughly the same price as gigabyte drives stored gigabytes of data a decade ago. Although computer memory is also falling in price, making it possible for many applications to run with their working data sets entirely in memory, systems that store most data on disk still have a big cost advantage.

The third trend is that disk throughput has improved more than disk seek times, for conventional spinning-disk hard drives. Though solid-state drives (SSDs) have altered this balance somewhat, the advantage of the sequential read performance of conventional hard drives versus random read performance is a large factor in the design of the systems we'll be discussing.

Finally, we've seen a shift from using one processor to multiple processors as increases in single-processor performance have slowed. This is reflected in a shift not only to multithreaded programs on a single server but also to programs distributed over multiple separate servers.

These trends have caused system and application developers to take a hard look at conventional designs and to consider alternatives. The question many are asking is: how should we build applications so we can take advantage of all this data, in light of current hardware trends, and in the most cost-effective way possible?

The Role of Databases

Conventional relational databases have served as the workhorse for persisting application data and as the processing engine for data analysis for many years. With the advent of the World Wide Web, web applications can be exposed to millions of concurrent users, creating the need for highly scalable data storage and retrieval technologies. Many applications begin with a single relational database as the storage engine and gradually reduce the number of features enabled on the database in order to get better performance and serve more requests per second. Eventually a single database is just not enough, and applications begin to resort to distributing data among several database instances in order to keep up with demand. All of the overhead for managing multiple databases and distributing data to them has to be handled by the application.

Similarly, databases have also played an important role in analytical applications. Often a relational database will be at the center of a data warehouse in which records from operational databases are combined and refactored to support queries that answer analytical questions. The field of Business Intelligence has grown up around the capabilities of data warehouses. As more and more data becomes available, the need for these analytical systems to scale becomes greater. Not only are organizations collecting and keeping more structured data from operational systems, but interest is also growing in other types of data that's less well-structured—such as application logs, social media data, and text documents. The ability to combine all of these data sets in one place in order to ask questions across them is a compelling use case that is driving innovation in scalable systems.

Accumulo is unlike some other new distributed databases in that it was developed with more of a focus on building analytical platforms, rather than simply as the scalable persistence layer for data generated via a web application. The flexibility of the data model and support for building indexes in Accumulo make analyzing data from a variety of sources easier. Accumulo also introduces fine-grained access control to make it possible for organizations to confidently protect data of varying sensitivity levels in the same physical cluster.

Analysis and Column Storage

Many analytical databases take advantage of column-oriented storage rather than row-oriented storage, which is the primary storage for most databases.

Row-oriented storage is useful for operational applications that need to maintain some state across multiple fields or multiple rows. When updating multiple fields in a row, perhaps as part of a transaction, it is convenient to store all the fields that need to be updated simultaneously together on disk, read them off of disk together into memory in order to change values as part of a transaction, and write them back to disk together to maintain a consistent view of the data at all times.

In contrast, analytical applications often do not require any updates to data and are instead aggregating and summarizing the data. In many cases analytical questions are designed to calculate some statistic for one or a subset of the fields across all of the rows. It is inconvenient to store data in row-oriented format because it requires all the fields of one row to be read before any fields of the next row can be accessed. As a result, analytical storage engines often store data in column-oriented formats. This way, all of the data for a particular field across all rows can be found together on disk. This drastically reduces the time required to read data to answer these types of analytical questions. Because similarity is a property that compression relies on to reduce storage size, column-oriented storage also improves the opportunities for compression because the data values within a single field are often similar to one another.

Accumulo makes it possible to group sets of columns together on disk via a feature called *locality groups* so analytical applications can gain these advantages. As part of Accumulo's additional focus on analytical applications, its support for locality groups is more powerful than in some other distributed databases because the names of columns don't have to be declared beforehand, there is no penalty for a large number of different column names, and the columns can be mapped to locality groups in any way desired. We discuss locality groups in depth in "Column Families" on page 19.

Some relational databases have adopted a distributed approach to scaling to meet demand. In all distributed systems there are trade-offs. Distributed applications introduce new complexities and failure modes that might not have existed in one-server applications, so many distributed applications also ensure that the design and APIs offered are simple to make understanding the behavior of the entire system easier. In many ways new platforms like Accumulo represent stepping back to look at the problem and building a data store from the ground up to support these larger workloads and the concise set of features they require. The goal of Accumulo, being based on Google's Bigtable, is to provide a set of features that work well even as data sizes grow into the tens of petabytes—even in the presence of the regular failures expected of cheaper, commodity-class hardware that is commonly used.

Distributed Applications

To effectively use increasing amounts of available data, a few application design patterns have emerged for automatically distributing data and processing over many separate commodity-class servers connected via a network, and that vastly prefer sequential disk operations over random disk seeks. Unlike some distributed systems, applications that implement these patterns do not share memory or storage, an approach called a *shared-nothing architecture*. These applications are designed to handle individual machine failures automatically with no interruption in operations.

Perhaps the most popular of these is Apache Hadoop (*http://hadoop.apache.org*), which can be used to distribute data over many commodity-class machines and to run distributed processing jobs over the data in parallel. This allows data to be processed in a fraction of the time it would take on a single computer. Hadoop uses sequential I/O, opening and reading files from beginning to end during the course of a distributed processing job, and writing output to new files in sequential chunks. A graphical representation of *vertical* scaling versus *horizontal* or *shared-nothing* scaling is shown in Figure 1-1.

Shared-Nothing Architectures

Some distributed applications are built to run on hardware platforms featuring many processors and large amounts of shared random-access memory (RAM), and often connect to a storage area network (SAN) via high-speed interconnects such as Fibre Channel to access shared data storage.

In contrast, shared-nothing architectures do not share RAM and do not connect to shared storage, but rather consist of many individual servers, each with its own processors, RAM, and hard drives. These systems are still connected to one another via a network such as Gigabit Ethernet. Often the individual servers are of the more inexpensive sort and often include cheaper individual components, such as Serial ATA (SATA) drives rather than Small Computer System Interface (SCSI) drives.

Technologies that increase the resilience of a single server, such as hardware Redundant Array of Independent Disks (RAID) cards, which allow several hard drives within a server to be grouped together for redundancy, are unnecessary in a shared-nothing architecture. These can be replaced with an application layer that tolerates the failure of entire servers, such as the Hadoop Distributed File System (HDFS).

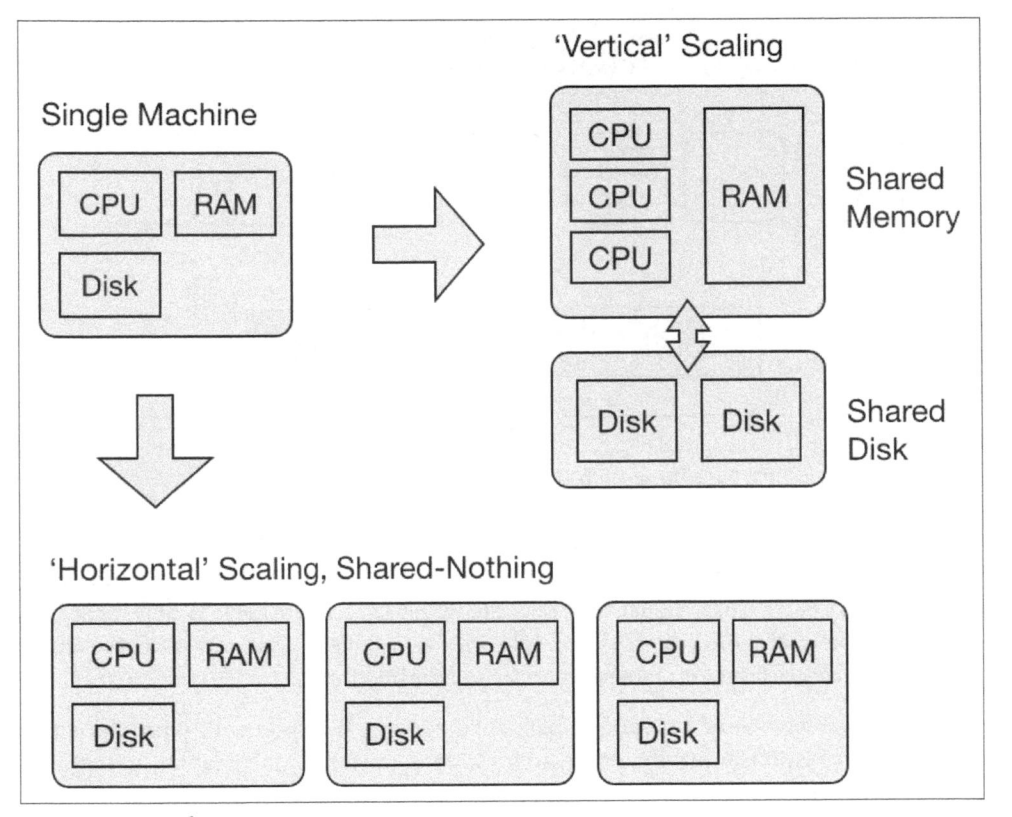

Figure 1-1. Scaling strategies

Accumulo employs this distributed approach by partitioning data across multiple servers and keeping track of which server has which partition. In some cases these data partitions are called *shards*, as in pieces of something that has been shattered. In Accumulo's case, data is stored in tables, and tables are partitioned into *tablets*. Each server hosts a number of tablets. These servers are called *tablet servers* (Figure 1-2).

Some other systems support this type of data partitioning and require that a particular field within the data be specified for the purpose of mapping a particular row to a partition. For example, a relational database may allow a table to be split into partitions based on the *Date* field. All of the rows that have a date value in January might be in one partition, and the rows with a date value in February in another. This structure is very sensitive to the distribution of values across rows. If many more rows have date values in February, that partition will be larger than the other partitions.

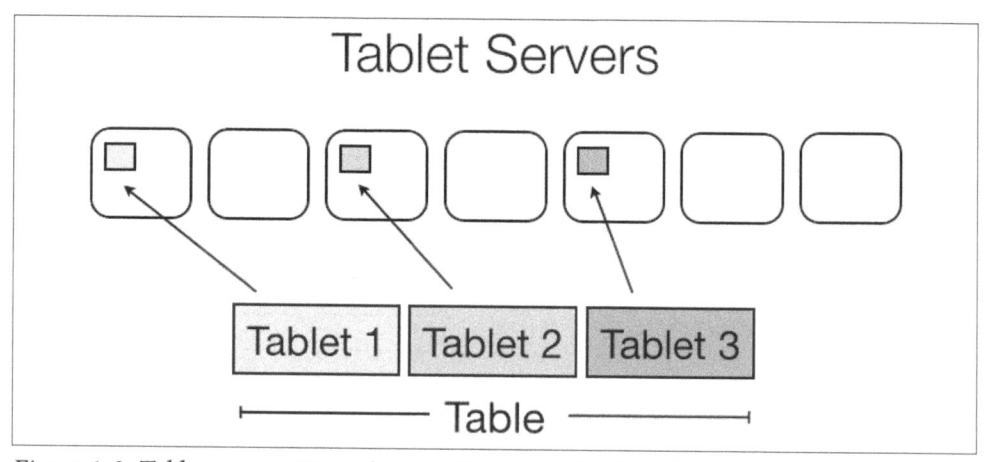

Figure 1-2. Tables are partitioned into tablets and distributed

In contrast, Accumulo does not require you to specify how to partition data. Instead, it automatically finds good points to use to split the data into tablets. As new data arrives, a particular single tablet may become larger than the others. When it reaches a configurable threshold, the tablet is split into two tablets. This way, tablets can be uniform in size without any intervention from administrators.

Partitions also have to be mapped to particular servers. If responsibility for storage is coupled with responsibility for processing requests for a particular tablet, movement of read and write processing for a tablet from one server to another also requires that the data be moved. This data movement can be expensive. So, rather than coupling responsibility for reads and writes with the storage of a tablet, Accumulo allows tablet servers to be responsible for tablets that are stored on another server, at least temporarily. Over time, tablet servers will create local copies of the data in background operations to avoid reads over the network in response to client requests.

The flexibility in assigning tablets to tablet servers allows Accumulo to be very responsive to handling individual hardware failures without requiring additional intervention from applications or administrators. This is crucial to running a large-scale cluster, because hardware failure becomes a common occurrence with hundreds or thousands of machines. Instances of Accumulo have been known to run on more than a thousand servers, hosting trillions of key-value pairs.[1]

Accumulo includes features that can be used to build a wide variety of scalable distributed applications, including storing structured or semistructured sparse and dynamic data, building rich text-search capabilities, indexing geospatial or multidi-

---

1 R. Sen, A. Farris, and P. Guerra, "Benchmarking Apache Accumulo BigData Distributed Table Store Using Its Continuous Test Suite." in IEEE International Congress on Big Data, 2013, pp. 334–341.

mensional data, storing and processing large graphs, and maintaining continuously updated summaries over raw events using server-side programming mechanisms.

Fast Random Access

Fast random access is important to many applications. *Random* access implies that even though the particular element of data that is sought is not known until the time of execution, the access time for any particular data element is roughly the same. This is in contrast to *sequential* access, in which the reads start at the beginning of a set of data and proceed to read more data until reaching the end. It's also important that that access time be fast enough to satisfy application requirements. Many web applications require that the data requested be accessible in less than one second.

There are several techniques for achieving good random-access performance. Two popular techniques are hashing and sorting. These techniques are used all the time in computer applications accessing data held in memory, but they conveniently also apply to data stored on disk, and even across multiple machines.

Unlike Hadoop jobs, where the data is often unorganized and where each job processes most or all of the data, Accumulo is designed to store data in an *organized* fashion so users can quickly find the data they need or incrementally add to or update a data set. Accumulo's role in life is to store key-value pairs, keeping the keys sorted at all times. This enables applications to achieve fast, interactive response times even when the data sizes range in the petabytes.

Accessing Sorted Versus Unsorted Data

Imagine a scenario in which you need to catch a flight, and your ticket shows your flight leaving from gate D5. Suppose that the gates are unordered; that is, gate A1 is right next to F3, which is right next to B2. If you are currently standing at gate B2, you would have no idea how close you are to D5, and no idea in which direction you should go to get closer to D5. The only strategy guaranteed to locate gate D5 is to begin visiting all the gates in the hope that you stumble across D5. This strategy is fine if you have hours and hours to spend searching. If you're in a hurry, chances are you will miss your flight. Not only is this too slow to be practical, but it is horribly inefficient. Every person trying to catch a flight will waste at least several hours and a lot of effort finding the right gate.

If the gates are sorted in a known order, such as alphabetical and numerical order so that gate A1 is physically next to gate A2 and the last A gate is next to the first B gate, finding a particular gate is much easier. You know that to find gate D5 you must skip all the A, B, and C gates, and that if you see E gates you've gone too far. Once you've found one of the D gates, say D8, you know that your gate is only three gates away. If the next gate you see is D7 or D9, you now know whether to keep going or to turn around to get to D5.

This is the same way that computers use sorted data. A computer uses an algorithm known as a *binary search* to find a key-value pair in a list sorted by key (Figure 1-3). Binary search works by looking at the key in the middle of the list and comparing that to the key it wants to find. If the key in the middle of the list is *greater than* the key sought, the computer will then search the first half of the list. If the key in the middle of the list is *less than* the key sought, the computer will search the second half of the list.

Whichever half is chosen, the computer again picks the key in the middle and compares that to the key it's looking for, and based on this comparison it decides in which direction it must continue searching. This continues until the computer finds an exact match or determines that the key sought is not in the list.

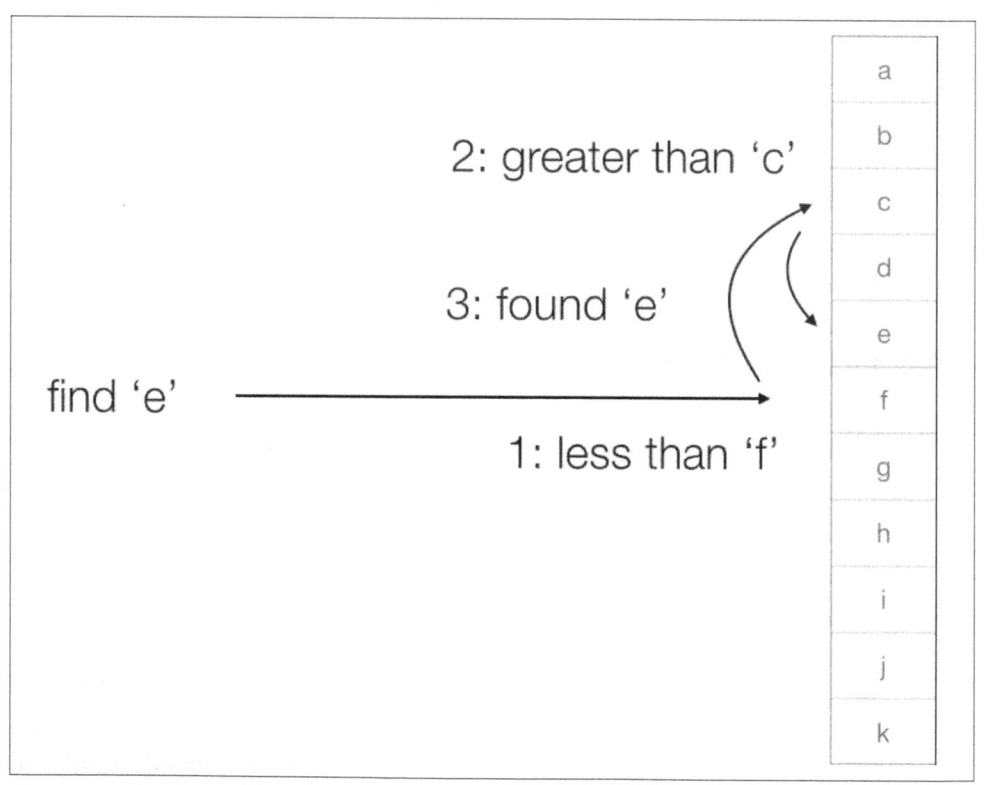

Figure 1-3. An example of binary search

This dramatically reduces the number of keys that must be examined and makes searching for a particular key faster. How much faster? If it takes 10 milliseconds to fetch and examine one key, finding a particular key in an unsorted list of a billion keys will take an average of *57 days*, because the right key could be anywhere—best case it's the first one you look at; worst case it's the last.

If the list is sorted, it only takes an average of *300 milliseconds*. If the sorted list has not a billion key-value pairs, but a trillion, it takes *400 milliseconds*—only 30 percent longer for a 1000× increase in data!

Algorithms that have this kind of performance are said to exhibit *logarithmic* access time with respect to the number of data elements, as opposed to *linear* access time, because the access time is a function not of the number of data elements but of the logarithm of the number of elements.

Hashing Versus Sorting

Hashing is a popular technique for organizing data so that a given data element can be accessed quickly. If we are storing key-value pairs, where each key is associated with a single value, a hash function applied to the key can be used to determine where a key-value pair will be stored. Good hash functions map inputs to a range of output values uniformly. When storing key-value pairs, the key is passed as the input to the hash function (called *hashing the key*) and the output hash is used as the address of the key-value pair in the storage medium. For example, we might decide to store the key-value pair *favoriteColor→red* by first hashing the key, *favoriteColor*, which produces the value 1004, and so we store that key-value pair in the 1004th slot in memory.

Lookups designed to retrieve the value of a known key consist of hashing the key, noting the hash output value and jumping to the place referenced by that hash, and retrieving the value of the key-value pair. The hash can refer to a location in memory, on disk, or on a particular machine in a cluster. If we need to look up the value for the key *favoriteColor*, we simply hash it to obtain the address 1004 and go directly to the 1004th memory slot to retrieve the key-value pair (Figure 1-4).

In distributed systems hashing is sometimes used to distribute key-value pairs across machines in a cluster. Hashing has the advantage of not requiring the system to do anything special to keep the data uniformly spread out across machines. Lookups can consist of simply hashing the key to find the server on which a key-value pair is stored, and then hashing again to find the spot within the server that contains the key-value pair.

Because these lookups consist of just one step, hashing enables very fast random access to data. However, because the hash function is designed to spread keys out uniformly across the address space, any similarity among keys is lost. For, example if we wanted to be able to access the values for not just *favoriteColor* but *favoriteIceCream* and *favoriteMovie*, we would have to do three separate lookups because these key-value pairs would end up being assigned to different places by the hash function.

Accumulo does not rely on hashing for data distribution; it uses sorting instead.

Like hashing, sorting data can enable fast random access, but unlike hashing, sorting can preserve some of the relationships among keys. This way, we can quickly find one key that we want by doing a binary search, but also any closely related keys by reading a few additional keys that appear sequentially after the first key. Because disks can read sequential data much faster than accessing data randomly, the difference between finding and returning one key versus finding one key and scanning 1,000 of the keys that follow sequentially is minimal.

This property of sorted data allows application designers to exploit any relationships, sometimes called *locality*, in their data by creating keys that group related information together when sorted (Figure 1-5).

Maintaining a sorted set of key-value pairs, especially when distributed across multiple machines, is more work than using hashing. Specifically, you have to maintain an additional mapping of which machine has which portion of the sorted set. In Accumulo, this mapping is called the *metadata table*, and Accumulo has a lot of functionality built in to handle the additional work of maintaining this information. We discuss the metadata table in depth in "Metadata Table" on page 379.

Figure 1-4. Hashing a key to an address

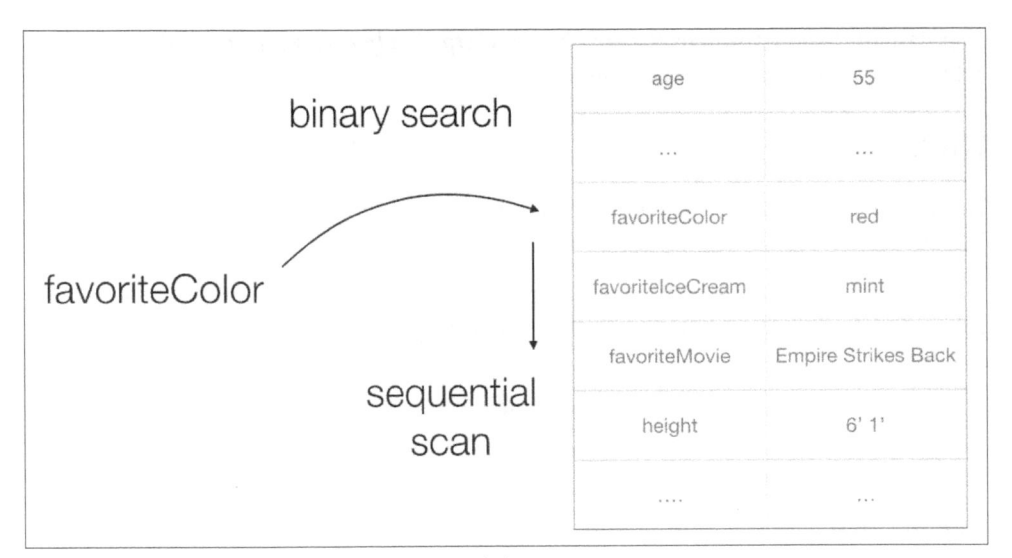

Figure 1-5. Accessing related keys in sorted data

Versions

The first public open source version of Accumulo is 1.3.

Version 1.4 has been used in production for years on very large clusters.

As of this writing, the latest stable version of Accumulo is 1.6. We will focus this book on version 1.6, pointing out differences in other versions where appropriate. Version 1.6 includes the following new features and improvements over previous versions:

- Multivolume support (running over multiple HDFS instances)
- Table namespaces
- Conditional mutations
- Partial encryption support
- Pluggable compaction strategies
- Lexicoders (tools for sorting tuples properly)
- Locality groups in memory
- Service IP addresses
- Support for ViewFS
- Maven plug-in
- Default key size constraint

You can find the complete Release Notes (*http://bit.ly/accumulo_1_6_0*) for the 1.6 release at the Apache Accumulo site.

History

Accumulo is one of several implementations based on Google's Bigtable. The others include Apache HBase, Hypertable, and Apache Cassandra.

Accumulo has been an open source project since 2011 and has since seen several releases. A brief history of the project is as follows:

2003
> Google publishes a paper describing the Google File System (GFS) (*http://bit.ly/ gfs_paper*), a distributed filesystem for storing very large files across many commodity-class servers.

2004
> Google publishes a paper describing a simplified distributed programming model and associated fault-tolerant execution framework called MapReduce (*http:// bit.ly/dean-ghemawat*).

2006
> Google publishes a paper entitled "Bigtable: A Distributed Storage System for Structured Data" (*http://bit.ly/bigtable_paper*). That same year a team from Yahoo! releases an open source version called Apache Hadoop.

Fall 2007
> An open source implementation of Google's Bigtable called HBase is started by a team at the company Powerset.

January 2008
> Hadoop becomes a top-level Apache project. HBase becomes a subproject.
>
> At the same time, a team of computer scientists and mathematicians at the US National Security Agency (NSA) are evaluating the use of various big data technologies, including Apache Hadoop and HBase, in an effort to help solve the issues involved with storing and processing large amounts of data of different sensitivity levels. Authors Billie Rinaldi and Aaron Cordova are part of this team.

July 2008
> Powerset is acquired by Microsoft.
>
> After reviewing existing solutions and comparing the stated objectives of existing open source projects to the agency's goals, the NSA team begins a new implementation of Google's Bigtable. The team focuses on performance, resilience, and access control of individual data elements. The intent is to follow the design as

described in the paper closely in order to build on as much of the effort and experience of Google's engineers as possible.

The team extends the Bigtable design with additional features that includes a method for labeling each key-value pair with its own access information, called *column visibilities*, and a mechanism for performing additional server-side functionality, called *iterators*.

May 2009
Version 1.0 of Accumulo is released, but it is not yet publicly available.

May 2010
HBase becomes a top-level Apache project.

September 2011
Accumulo becomes a public open source incubator project (*http://bit.ly/accumulo_incubation*) hosted by the Apache Software Foundation.

March 2012
Accumulo (*http://bit.ly/accumulo_project*) graduates to top-level project status. First publicly available release is 1.3.5.

April 2012
Version 1.4 is released.

May 2013
Version 1.5 is released and includes a Thrift proxy, more control over compactions, and table import and export

May 2014
Version 1.6 is released and extends the API to include conditional mutations and table namespaces.

Data Model

At the most basic level, Accumulo stores key-value pairs on disk (Figure 1-6), keeping the keys sorted at all times. This allows a user to look up the value of a particular key or range of keys very quickly. Values are stored as byte arrays, and Accumulo doesn't restrict the type or size of the values stored. The default constraint on the maximum size of the key is 1 MB.

Figure 1-6. A simple key-value pair

Rather than simple keys as shown in Figure 1-6, Accumulo keys are made up of several components. Inside the key there are three main components: a row ID, a column, and a timestamp (Figure 1-7).

Key			Value
row ID	Column	Timestamp	

Figure 1-7. Main components of the key

Rows and Columns

The row ID and column components allow developers to model their data similarly to how one might store data in a relational database, or perhaps a spreadsheet. One major difference is that relational databases often have autogenerated row IDs and rely on secondary indexes for all data access, whereas the row IDs in Accumulo can contain data that is relevant to an application.

When sorting keys, Accumulo first sorts the data by row ID, then sorts keys with the same row ID by column, and finally sorts keys with the same row ID and column by timestamp. Row IDs and columns are sorted in ascending, *lexicographical* order—which means, roughly, alphabetical order—byte-by-byte.

The row ID is used to group several key-value pairs into a logical row. All the key-value pairs that have the same row ID are considered to be a part of the same row. Row IDs are simply byte arrays. A logical row in Accumulo can consist of more data than can fit in memory. Values for multiple columns within a row can be changed atomically.

The ability to modify rows *atomically* is an important feature for application designers to keep in mind when modeling their data. This means that Accumulo will commit the changes to a particular row all at once, or not at all in the case of a failure. This allows applications always to have a consistent view of the data in a row, and not to have to handle cases in which a change is partially applied. (We discuss atomicity more in "Transactions" on page 47.)

Columns allow a row to contain multiple elements, as in a relational database table. Each column is mapped to a value. But unlike in a relational database, you don't have to declare columns before storing data in them, and not every row has to have the same columns present. Further, the type of data stored under a particular column does not have to be the same across rows. Finally, columns do not have a specified maximum length in which values must fit. (Column *names*, being part of the key, are by default limited, because the total key is constrained to be less than 1 MB. However, the values under these columns are not constrained in size by default.)

Accumulo tables can cope with missing or additional columns and changes in the underlying schema of the data because Accumulo does not make any assumptions about the schema. If rows imported every day for a month contain 10 columns and suddenly they now contain 11 columns, Accumulo will not reject a request to store the new rows; it will simply store them. Applications designed to read from the 10 known columns can continue to do so even with the new rows and simply ignore the additional column.

This departure from the relational model represents a trade-off. On the one hand, the flexibility makes storing data much easier. It is easier to store data that does not conform to a well-known schema, and it is also easier to store data whose structure changes over time.

However, whereas applications built on a relational database can rely on the database to ensure that values conform to specified types and lengths, applications built on Accumulo cannot assume that value types and lengths conform to any constraints, unless Accumulo is configured to apply specific constraints to the data. Application designers can decide whether to implement constraints to be applied by Accumulo at insert-time or whether to handle varying value types and lengths at read-time in the application.

For example, we may have a table that we use to store Wikipedia articles. The table contains some structured data, or *metadata*, about each article, along with the actual article text. Individual metadata elements may not be the same from one article to the next.

Notice that not all the rows in Figure 1-8 have data stored in every column, a property known as *sparseness*. In other systems, missing values must be indicated by storing a NULL value, which takes up space on disk. In Accumulo, the missing values simply do not appear in the list of key-value pairs. On disk, this data is laid out as a long series of sorted key-value pairs.

rowid	title	pageid	comment	text
Apache_Accumulo	Apache Accumulo	571876229	/* See also */ Added Column-oriented DBMS	Apache Accumulo is a sorted, distributed key/value store based on Google's BigTable. It is a system built on top of Apache Hadoop, Apache ZooKeeper, and Apache Thrift. ...
Apache_Hadoop	Apache Hadoop	5919308		Apache Hadoop is an open source software framework for storage and large-scale processing of data-sets on clusters of commodity hardware. Hadoop is an Apache top-level project being built ...
Apache_Thrift	Apache Thrift	10438451		Thrift is an interface definition language and binary communication protocol that is used to define and create services for numerous languages ...
BigTable	BigTable	5919973		BigTable is a compressed, high performance, and proprietary data storage system built on Google File System, Chubby Lock Service, SSTable (log-structured storage like LevelDB) ...

Figure 1-8. A table consisting of rows and columns

Note that there is no key-value pair in Figure 1-9 for the *comment* field for *Apache Thrift*, for example. Because Accumulo stores data this way, it can handle sparse data sets very efficiently. Writing a key-value pair that contains a column that doesn't appear in any other row is no different from Accumulo's perspective than storing any other key-value pair.

 If you are coming from a relational database background, it might be confusing to think of a row in Accumulo as a set of key-value pairs. Looking at data retrieved in the Accumulo shell, which we touch on first in "Demo of the Shell" on page 60, a row will actually be many lines on the screen. Figure 1-8 may be a more familiar representation of the data, and you can see how it might translate into Accumulo in Figure 1-9. In this example, a row, defined as a set of key-value pairs, is analogous to a record in a relational database. Everything with the same row ID contains information about a given record.

rowid	column	value
Apache_Accumulo	comment	/* See also */ Added Column-oriented DBMS
Apache_Accumulo	pageid	571876229
Apache_Accumulo	text	Apache Accumulo is a sorted, distributed key/value store ..
Apache_Accumulo	title	Apache Accumulo
Apache_Hadoop	pageid	5919308
Apache_Hadoop	text	Apache Hadoop is an open source software framework for storage ...
Apache_Hadoop	title	Apache Hadoop
Apache_Thrift	pageid	10438451
Apache_Thrift	text	Thrift is an interface definition language and binary ...
Apache_Thrift	title	Apache Thrift
. . .	. . .	. . .

Figure 1-9. Key-value pairs representing data for various rows and columns

Data Modification and Timestamps

Accumulo allows applications to update and delete existing information. These operations are essential to developing operational applications. Rather than modifying the data already written to disk, however, Accumulo handles modifications of this type via versioning.

The timestamp element of the key adds a new dimension to the well-known two-dimensional row-column model, and this allows data under a particular row-column pair to have more than one version (Figure 1-10). By default, Accumulo keeps only the newest version of a row-column pair, but it can be configured to store a specific number of versions, versions newer than a certain date, or all versions ever written.

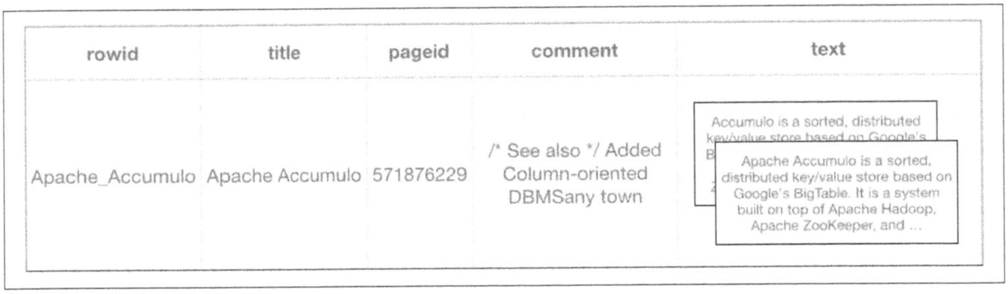

rowid	title	pageid	comment	text
Apache_Accumulo	Apache Accumulo	571876229	/* See also */ Added Column-oriented DBMSany town	Accumulo is a sorted, distributed key/value store based on Google's B Apache Accumulo is a sorted, distributed key/value store based on Google's BigTable. It is a system built on top of Apache Hadoop, Apache ZooKeeper, and ...

Figure 1-10. A table consisting of rows and columns with multiple versions

The set of key-value pairs on disk appears as in Figure 1-11.

rowid	column	timestamp	value
Apache_Accumulo	comment	20111001	/* See also */ Added Column-oriented DBMS
Apache_Accumulo	pageid	20111001	571876229
Apache_Accumulo	text	20120301	Apache Accumulo is a sorted, distributed key/value store ..
Apache_Accumulo	text	20111001	Accumulo is a sorted, distributed key/value store ..
Apache_Accumulo	title	20111001	Apache Accumulo
Apache_Hadoop	pageid	20060314	5919308
Apache_Hadoop	text	20060314	Apache Hadoop is an open source software framework for storage ...
Apache_Hadoop	title	20060314	Apache Hadoop
Apache_Thrift	pageid	20070213	10438451
Apache_Thrift	title	20070213	Apache Thrift
...	...		...

Figure 1-11. Two key-value pairs that represent two versions of data for one row-column pair

Timestamps are stored as 64-bit integers using the Java long data type. They are sorted in descending order, unlike rows and columns, so that the newest versions of a row-column pair appear first when scanning down a table. In this way, Accumulo handles updates by simply storing new versions of key-value pairs. If only the newest version is retrieved, it appears as if the value has changed.

 Timestamps that are assigned to key-value pairs by the tablet server use the number of milliseconds since midnight, January 1, 1970, also known as the Unix epoch.

Similarly, deletes are implemented using a special marker inserted in front of any existing versions. The appearance of a key-value pair with a delete marker is interpreted by Accumulo to mean "ignore all versions of this row-column pair older than this timestamp."

For example, if we wanted to remove the comment for the row identified by *Apache_Accumulo*, the Accumulo client library would insert a delete marker with the *Apache_Accumulo* row ID and the *comment* column, and that delete marker would be assigned a timestamp representing the current time by the receiving tablet server. Subsequent reads of the *Apache_Accumulo* row would encounter the delete marker and know to skip any key-value pairs for that row and column appearing after the delete marker.

To add a *comment* field back into that row we would simply write a new key-value pair, which would get a newer timestamp than the delete marker, and so it would be returned by subsequent scans.

 It is possible to specify the timestamp when inserting a new key into Accumulo, but this should only be done for advanced applications, because timestamps are used in determining the ordering of insertions and deletions. In the typical case in which the timestamp is not specified by the client, the tablet server that receives the key-value pair will use the time at which the data arrived as the timestamp.

Applications that use time information typically store that time information as the value of a separate column rather than storing it in the timestamp portion of the key.

Advanced Data Model Components

Accumulo's data model includes additional components that help applications achieve better performance and data protection. These components are extensions to the basic concept of a column.

Columns are split into three components: a *column family*, a *column qualifier*, and a *column visibility*.

Most applications will start by simply assigning the names of fields to the column qualifier. Column families and column visibilities do not have to be populated. When developers have an idea for how data will be accessed, and for the sensitivity levels of various columns, these additional components can be used to help optimize and protect information.

Column Families

Often, applications find that they will access some columns together, and not other columns. Other times they need to access all of the columns within rows. This is especially prevalent in analytical applications.

When scanning for only a subset of the columns, it can be useful to change the way groups of columns are stored on disk so that frequently grouped columns are stored together, and so that columns containing large amounts of data that are not always scanned can be isolated.

For example, we might have some columns storing relatively small, structured data, and other columns storing larger values such as text or perhaps media such as imagery, audio, or video. In the Wikipedia table, the *text* column stores long text values. Sometimes our application may need to scan just the structured details about a user or multiple users and other times will need to scan the user details and the larger columns containing media content.

To cause related columns to be stored in consecutive key-value pairs in Accumulo, application designers can place these columns in the same *column family*. To apply this to our earlier example, we can choose to put the *text* and *comment* columns under a column family called *content* and the other columns under the *metadata* column family. If we retrieve the *metadata* column family, the tablet server can do less work to read just that one column family than if the individual metadata columns were scattered throughout each row, interleaved with content columns.

Unlike Bigtable and HBase, Accumulo column families need not be declared before being used, and Accumulo tables can have a very high number of column families if necessary.

Although grouping columns into families can make retrieving a single column family within one row more efficient, it can still be inefficient to read one column family across multiple rows, because we'll still have to scan over other column families before accessing the next row. For example, it would be inefficient if we always had to read the Wikipedia content off of disk when we are only interested in the user details.

To help avoid reading data unnecessarily from disk, application designers can choose to assign column families to a *locality group*. Locality groups are stored in separate contiguous chunks of data on disk so that an application that is only scanning over column families in one locality group doesn't need to read data from any other locality groups. This gives Accumulo more of a columnar-style storage that is amenable to many analytical access patterns.

Applying locality groups to our earlier example, we can choose to put the *content* column family in one locality group and the *metadata* column family in another locality group. Before we assigned column families to locality groups, a scan configured to read only the metadata columns would still end up reading the content columns off of disk (Figure 1-12), and tablet servers would filter them out, returning only the data requested.

rowid	column family	column qualifier	timestamp	value
Apache_Accumulo	content	comment	20111001	/* See also */ Added Column-oriented DBMS
Apache_Accumulo	content	text	20120301	Accumulo is a sorted, distributed key/value store ...
Apache_Accumulo	metadata	pageid	20111001	571876229
Apache_Accumulo	metadata	title	20111001	Apache Accumulo
Apache_Hadoop	content	text	20060314	Apache Hadoop is an open source software framework for storage ...
Apache_Hadoop	metadata	pageid	20060314	5919308
Apache_Hadoop	metadata	title	20060314	Apache Hadoop
Apache_Thrift	content	text	20070213	Thrift is an interface definition language and binary ...
Apache_Thrift	metadata	pageid	20070213	10438451
Apache_Thrift	metadata	title	20070213	Apache Thrift
...	...	...	...	...

Figure 1-12. Reading over one column family still requires filtering out other column families

Once we assign the *content* column family to its own locality group, Accumulo will begin to store this textual content in a separate section on disk (Figure 1-13). Now when we read just the columns containing Wikipedia metadata, we don't have to read all of the text for each article off of disk.

Accumulo allows the assignment of column families to locality groups to change over time. New data written to Accumulo will always be written to disk according to the current assignment of column families to locality groups. Any data written prior to the change in assignment will need to be reprocessed before the benefit of the new locality groups is realized. Accumulo will reprocess data on disk automatically via a process called *compaction*, but compactions can also be forced as necessary. Using compactions to get previously written data to reflect changes in locality group assignments is described in "Locality Groups" on page 138.

Figure 1-13. Column families in different locality groups are stored together on disk

Column Visibility

Accumulo's focus on supporting analysis of data from several different sources has resulted in an additional component to the Bigtable data model called *column visibility*. The column visibility component is designed to logically isolate certain types of data based on sensitivity, by associating each value with a *security label expression*. This enables data to be protected from unauthorized access and for data sets of differing sensitivity to be stored in the same physical tables.

This feature is designed to reduce the amount of data movement that needs to occur when an organization decides that an application or an analytical process is allowed to look at two data sets. Imagine the case in which two data sets had to be stored in two physically separate systems for security reasons, called system A and system B. If one day an organization decides that it needs to join these data sets to answer an analytical question, the data from one system would have to be physically moved into the other system, say A into B, if there happens to be enough room. And the users of system B would have to be denied access to it while the data from system A resides there, if not all of them are also authorized to read data from system A. Or perhaps a third system will need to be stood up to handle the combination of this data, requiring that new hardware be acquired, software installed, and the data from both system A and system B to be copied to the new system. That process could take months.

If the data is already all stored together physically, and protected with column visibilities, then granting access of a single analytical application to both data sets is trivial. While the analytical process is running, users authorized to read only one type of data or another can continue to submit queries against the system without ever seeing anything they aren't authorized to see.

In our example, we might decide that the data residing under the *comment* and *pageid* columns does not need to be exposed to applications that allow the public to read the article text and titles (Figure 1-14), and so we can decide to protect the data in these columns using the column visibility component of the key.

rowid	metadata		content	
	title	pageid	comment	text
Apache_Accumulo	Apache Accumulo	571876229	/* See also */ Added Column-oriented DBMS	Apache Accumulo is a sorted, distributed key/value store based on Google's BigTable. It is a system built on top of Apache Hadoop, Apache ZooKeeper, and Apache Thrift. ...
Apache_Hadoop	Apache Hadoop	5919308		Apache Hadoop is an open source software framework for storage and large-scale processing of data-sets on clusters of commodity hardware. Hadoop is an Apache top-level project being built ...
Apache_Thrift	Apache Thrift	10438451		Thrift is an interface definition language and binary communication protocol that is used to define and create services for numerous languages ...
BigTable	BigTable	5919973		BigTable is a compressed, high performance, and proprietary data storage system built on Google File System, Chubby Lock Service, SSTable (log-structured storage like LevelDB) ...

Figure 1-14. Two columns are deemed viewable by internal applications and users

The way we protect these values is by populating the column visibility components with *security label expressions*, sometimes called simply *security labels*. Security label expressions consist of one or more tokens combined by logical operators &, representing logical AND, and |, representing logical OR. Subexpressions can be grouped using parentheses.

In our simple example here, we are using just single-token expressions in our column visibility. On disk these key-value pairs now look like Figure 1-15.

rowid	column family	column qualifier	column visibility	timestamp	value
Apache_Accumulo	content	text	public	20120301	Accumulo is a sorted, distributed key-value store...
Apache_Accumulo	metadata	comment	internal	20111001	/* See also */ Added Column-oriented DBMS
Apache_Accumulo	metadata	pageid	internal	20111001	571876229
Apache_Accumulo	metadata	title	public	20111001	Apache Accumulo
Apache_Hadoop	content	text	public	20060314	Apache Hadoop is an open source software framework for storage...
Apache_Hadoop	metadata	pageid	internal	20060314	5919308
Apache_Hadoop	metadata	title	public	20060314	Apache Hadoop
Apache_Thrift	content	text	public	20070213	Thrift is an interface definition language and binary...
Apache_Thrift	metadata	pageid	internal	20070213	10438451
Apache_Thrift	metadata	title	public	20070213	Apache Thrift
...	...	...	...	...	...

Figure 1-15. Individual key-value pairs are labeled with column visibilities

Column visibilities are an extremely fine-grained form of access control. Sometimes the term *cell-level* is used when discussing Accumulo's ability to allow every value to have its own security label, which is stored in the column visibility element of the key. The term *cell-level* is used to contrast the granularity of Accumulo's security model with row-level or column-level security in which one can control access to all the data in a row or all the data in a column. It is not often the case that any one raw data set requires that each column of each row to have a different column visibility. Usually some combination of row-level or column-level access control will suffice, which column visibilities can support just as well.

But because a common application on Accumulo involves building secondary indexes, perhaps across several types of data of differing sensitivity levels, each key-value pair in an index will end up needing a specific column visibility based on the row and column from which it originated. Applications that use these types of indexes are very powerful because they allow different views of the data to be composed on the fly, according to the access level of the user performing the query.

For example, a user with only the *public* access token can scan this table and will only see the data with the *public* token in the column visibility portion of the key (Figure 1-16).

rowid	column family	column qualifier	column visibility	timestamp	value
Apache_Accumulo	content	text	public	20120301	Accumulo is a sorted, distributed key/value store
Apache_Accumulo	metadata	title	public	20111001	Apache Accumulo
Apache_Hadoop	content	text	public	20060314	Apache Hadoop is an open source software framework for storage ...
Apache_Hadoop	metadata	title	public	20060314	Apache Hadoop
Apache_Thrift	content	text	public	20070213	Thrift is an interface definition language and binary
Apache_Thrift	metadata	title	public	20070213	Apache Thrift
...	...	...	...	...	...

Figure 1-16. View of only public data in the table

A user with both the *public* and *internal* access tokens will see all of the data in the table when doing a scan (Figure 1-17).

rowid	column family	column qualifier	column visibility	timestamp	value
Apache_Accumulo	content	text	public	20120301	Accumulo is a sorted, distributed key/value store ...
Apache_Accumulo	metadata	comment	internal	20111001	/* See also */ Added Column-oriented DBMS
Apache_Accumulo	metadata	pageid	internal	20111001	571876229
Apache_Accumulo	metadata	title	public	20111001	Apache Accumulo
Apache_Hadoop	content	text	public	20060314	Apache Hadoop is an open source software framework for storage ...
Apache_Hadoop	metadata	pageid	internal	20060314	5919308
Apache_Hadoop	metadata	title	public	20060314	Apache Hadoop
Apache_Thrift	content	text	public	20070213	Thrift is an interface definition language and binary
Apache_Thrift	metadata	pageid	internal	20070213	10438451
Apache_Thrift	metadata	title	public	20070213	Apache Thrift
...	...	...	...	...	...

Figure 1-17. View of all of the data in the table

A user or application with only the *internal* access token will only see the data with a column visibility containing the *internal* token (Figure 1-18).

rowid	column family	column qualifier	column visibility	timestamp	value
Apache_Accumulo	metadata	comment	internal	20111001	(* See also *) Added Column-oriented DBMS
Apache_Accumulo	metadata	pageid	internal	20111001	571876229
Apache_Hadoop	metadata	pageid	internal	20060314	5919308
Apache_Thrift	metadata	pageid	internal	20070213	10438451
...	...	...	...	...	...

Figure 1-18. View of only internal data in the table

 Because column visibilities are used to filter data after specific rows and columns have been selected for a scan, table designers should be careful not to design an application that relies too heavily on filtering, because this will impact read performance.

The assignment of access tokens to applications, individual users, or groups of users is typically handled outside of Accumulo by a central user-management system, although access tokens can be restricted in conjunction with Accumulo or using only Accumulo if desired.

We discuss using column visibilities in designing applications in depth in "Column Visibilities" on page 184.

Full Data Model

Now that we've discussed all of the components of the Accumulo data model we can show the full model containing all components of the key, with the components of the column broken out (Figure 1-19).

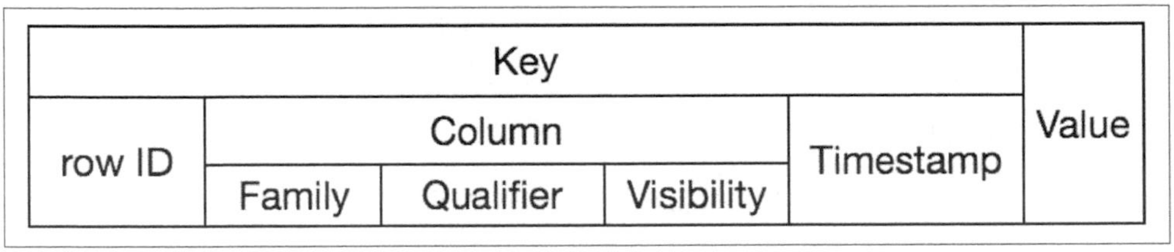

Key					Value
row ID	Column			Timestamp	
	Family	Qualifier	Visibility		

Figure 1-19. Accumulo key structure

Not all of the components must be used. At the very least, you can choose to use only the row ID and value portions of the key-value pair. In this case Accumulo will operate like a simple key-value store. Many applications start with rows and columns, and apply the use of additional components as designs are optimized.

Developers should consider carefully the components of the key that their application requires when designing tables.

Tables

When stored in Accumulo, key-value pairs are grouped into *tables*. You can apply some settings at the table level to control the behavior and management of the data. The key-value pairs within tables are partitioned into *tablets* and distributed automatically across multiple machines in a cluster.

Each table begins life as a single tablet, spanning all possible keys. Once data is written to a table and it reaches a certain size threshold, the tablet server hosting it finds a good point in the middle of the tablet and splits it into two tablets.

When a tablet server does this it always splits a tablet on a row boundary, guaranteeing that the data for each row is fully contained within one tablet and therefore resides on exactly one server. This is important to allowing consistent updates to be applied atomically to the data in an individual row.

For example, as our Wikipedia table grows, it will eventually be split along a row boundary into two tablets (Figure 1-20).

Figure 1-20. Splitting a tablet into tablets

Accumulo takes care of distributing responsibility for tablets evenly across tablet servers. A single tablet server can host several hundred tablets or more simultaneously.

We discuss the splitting process more in depth in "Splits" on page 365.

Introduction to the Client API

Accumulo provides application developers with a client library that is used to locate and communicate with tablet servers for writing data, and reading one or more key-value pairs.

Rather than providing a query language such as SQL, Accumulo provides developers with a simple API and a high degree of control over data layout, so that by designing tables carefully, many concurrent user requests can be satisfied very quickly with a minimal amount of work done at read time. Accumulo's read API is simple and straightforward.

As you would expect from a key-value store, clients can provide a key and look up the associated value, if it exists. Instead of returning one value, however, clients can opt to scan a range of key-value pairs beginning at a particular key. The performance difference between looking up and retrieving a single value versus scanning, say, a few hundred kilobytes of key-value pairs is fairly small, because the cost of reading that amount of data sequentially is dominated by the disk seek time.

This pattern allows clients to design rows such that the data elements required for a given request can be sorted near one another within the same table. Because rows may not all have the same columns, applications can be designed to take advantage of whatever data is available, potentially discovering new information in new columns along the way.

The ability to discover new information via scanning is valuable for applications that want to combine information about similar subjects from different sources that may not contain the same information about each subject.

Furthermore, it is up to the application to interpret the columns and values retrieved. Some applications store simple strings or numbers, while others store serialized programmatic objects. Some applications store map tile images in values and assemble the tiles retrieved into a user-facing web interface, the way Google Maps uses Bigtable.

Accumulo is written in Java and provides a Java client library. Clients in other languages can communicate with Accumulo via the provided Thrift proxy. All clients use three basic classes to communicate with Accumulo:

BatchWriter

All new inserts, updates, and deletes are packaged up into `Mutation` objects and given to a `BatchWriter`. A `Mutation` object contains a set of changes to be applied to a single row. The batch writer knows how the table is split into tablets and which servers the tablets are assigned to. Using this information, the batch writer efficiently groups `Mutation` objects into batches to increase write throughput. Batch writers send batches of `Mutation` objects to various tablet servers. The batch writer is multithreaded, and the trade-off between latency and throughput can be tuned. See Figure 1-21.

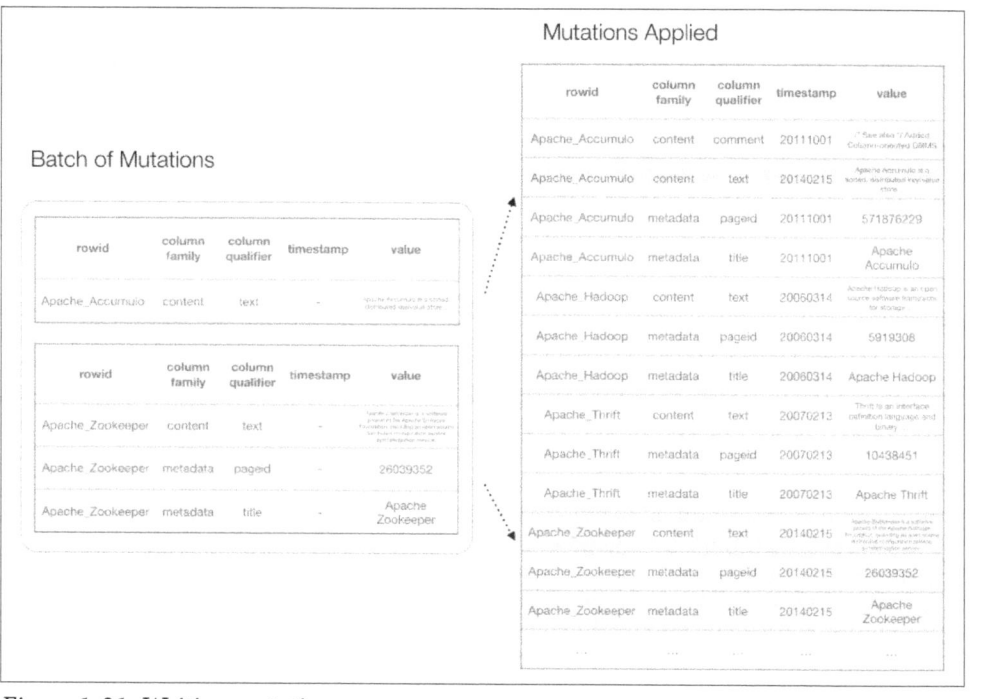

Figure 1-21. Writing mutations

Scanner

Key-value pairs are read out of a table using a `Scanner` object. A scanner can start at the beginning of a table or at a particular key, and can stop at the end of the table or a given key. After seeking to the initial key, scanners proceed to read out key-value pairs sequentially in key order until reaching the end of the table or the specified ending key. Scanners can be configured to read only certain columns. Additional configuration for a scanner can be made to apply additional logic classes called *iterators*, and specific options to iterators, to alter the set of key-value pairs returned from a particular scanner. See Figure 1-22.

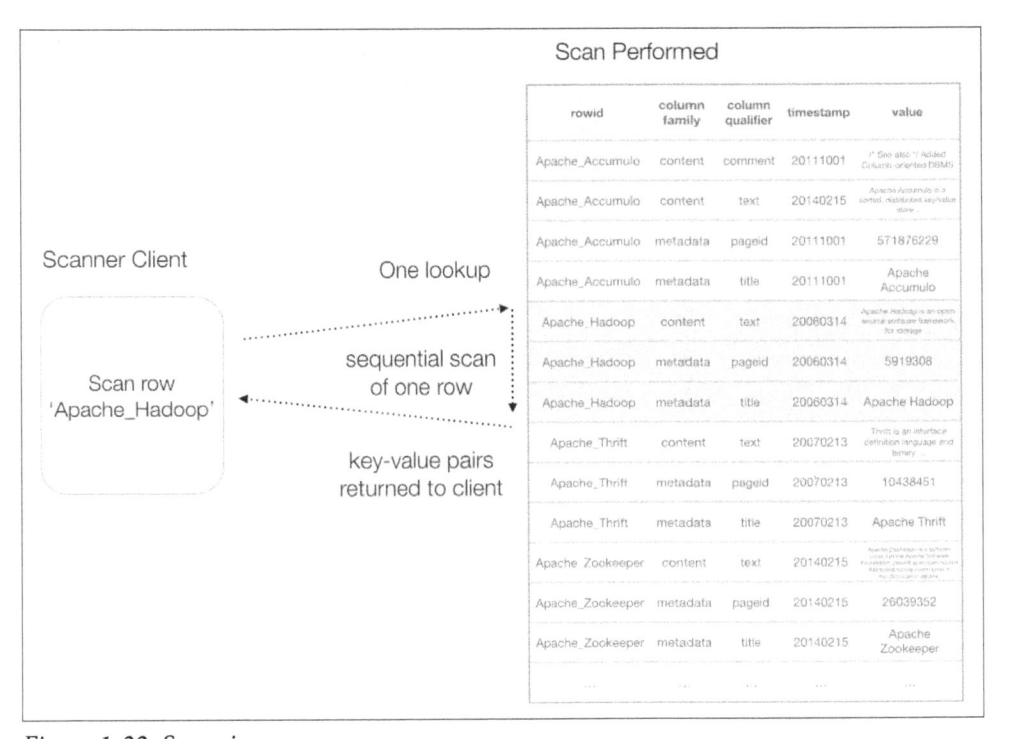

Figure 1-22. Scanning one row

BatchScanner

When multiple ranges of keys are to be read from a table, a `BatchScanner` can be used to read the key-value pairs for the ranges using multiple threads. The ranges are grouped by tablet server to maximize the efficiency of communication between threads and tablet servers. This can be useful for applications whose design requires many individual scans to answer a single question. In particular, tables designed for working with time series, secondary indexes, and complex text search can all benefit from using batch scanners. See Figure 1-23.

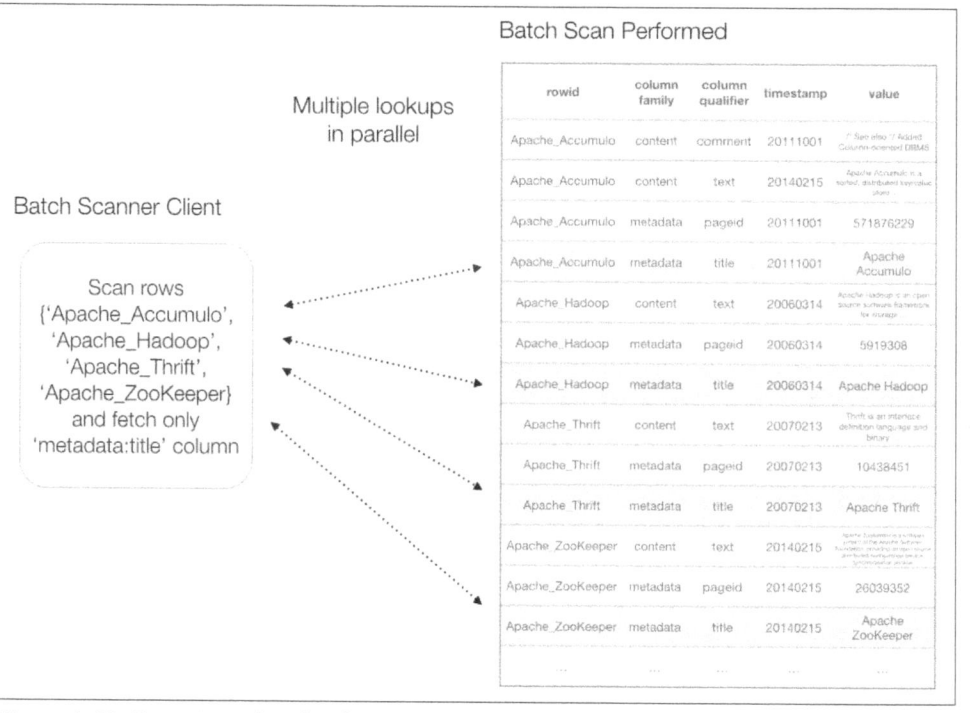

Batch Scan Performed

rowid	column family	column qualifier	timestamp	value
Apache_Accumulo	content	comment	20111001	(* See also *) Added Column-oriented DBMS
Apache_Accumulo	content	text	20140215	Apache Accumulo is a sorted, distributed key-value store
Apache_Accumulo	metadata	pageid	20111001	571876229
Apache_Accumulo	metadata	title	20111001	Apache Accumulo
Apache_Hadoop	content	text	20060314	Apache Hadoop is an open source software framework for storage
Apache_Hadoop	metadata	pageid	20060314	5919308
Apache_Hadoop	metadata	title	20060314	Apache Hadoop
Apache_Thrift	content	text	20070213	Thrift is an interface definition language and binary
Apache_Thrift	metadata	pageid	20070213	10438451
Apache_Thrift	metadata	title	20070213	Apache Thrift
Apache_ZooKeeper	content	text	20140215	Apache ZooKeeper is a Hadoop...
Apache_ZooKeeper	metadata	pageid	20140215	26039352
Apache_ZooKeeper	metadata	title	20140215	Apache ZooKeeper
...	...	...	...	...

Multiple lookups in parallel

Batch Scanner Client

Scan rows
{'Apache_Accumulo',
'Apache_Hadoop',
'Apache_Thrift',
'Apache_ZooKeeper}
and fetch only
'metadata:title' column

Figure 1-23. Scanning a batch of rows

More detail on developing applications using Accumulo's API is found in the chapters beginning with Chapter 3.

Approach to Rows

Accumulo takes a slightly different approach to rows in the client API than do some other implementations based on Bigtable, such as HBase. Accumulo's read API is designed to stream key-value pairs to the client rather than to package up all the key-value pairs for a row into a single unit before returning the data to the user.

This is often less convenient than working with data on a row-by-row basis, and applications that want to work with entire rows can do additional configuration to assist with this, as described in "Grouping by Rows" on page 110. The upside is that rows in an Accumulo table can be very large and do not need to fit in the memory of the tablet server or the client. Working with key-value pairs can come in handy when row IDs are coming from external data and the number of columns per row may be unknown or may vary widely, as can happen when building secondary indexes.

Exploiting Sort Order

The trick to taking full advantage of Accumulo's design is to exploit the fact that Accumulo keeps keys sorted. This requires application designers to determine a way to order the data such that most user queries can be satisfied with one or a small number of scans, each consisting of a lookup into a table to return one or more sequential key-value pairs.

A single scan is able to perform this lookup and return one or even hundreds of key-value pairs, often in less than a second, even when tables contain trillions of key-value pairs. Applications that understand and use this property can achieve subsecond response times for most user requests without having to worry about performance degrading as the amount of data stored in the system increases dramatically.

This sometimes requires creative thinking in order to discover a key design that works for a particular application. A good example of this is the way Google describes the row ID of its WebCrawl table in the Bigtable paper. In this table, the intent is to provide users with the ability to look up information about a given website, identified by the hostname. Because hostnames are hierarchical and because users may want to look at a specific hostname or all hostnames within a domain, Google chose to transform the hostname to support these access patterns by reversing the order in which domain name components are stored under the row ID, as shown in Table 1-1.

Table 1-1. Google's WebCrawl row design

Row ID
com.google.analytics
com.google.mail
com.google.maps
com.microsoft
com.microsoft.bing
com.microsoft.developers
com.microsoft.search
com.microsoft.www
com.yahoo
com.yahoo.mail

com.yahoo.search

com.yahoo.www

Achieving optimal performance also depends on the ability to satisfy user requests without having to filter out or ignore a large amount of key-value pairs as a part of the scan.

Because developers have such a high degree of control over how data is arranged, there are a wide variety of options for designing tables. We cover these in depth in Chapter 8.

Architecture Overview

Accumulo is a distributed application that depends on Apache Hadoop for storage and Apache ZooKeeper for configuration (Figure 1-24).

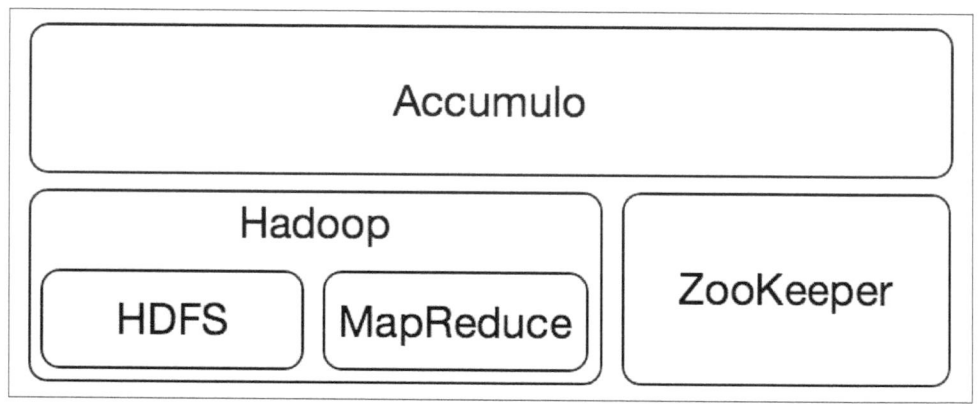

Figure 1-24. Accumulo architecture

Because Accumulo is based on Google's Bigtable, as HBase is, it uses some of the same names for components that Bigtable does, but there are some differences (Table 1-2).

Table 1-2. Accumulo and HBase Bigtable naming conventions

Apache Accumulo	Bigtable	Apache HBase
Tablet	Tablet	Region
Tablet Server	Tablet Server	Region Server
Minor Compaction	Minor Compaction	Flush

Major Compaction	Merging Compaction	Minor Compaction
(Full) Major Compaction	Major Compaction	Major Compaction
Write-Ahead Log	Commit Log	Write-Ahead Log
HDFS	GFS	HDFS
Hadoop MapReduce	MapReduce	Hadoop MapReduce
MemTable	MemTable	MemStore
RFile	SSTable	HFile
ZooKeeper	Chubby	ZooKeeper

ZooKeeper

ZooKeeper is a highly available, highly consistent, distributed application in which all data is replicated on all machines in a cluster so that if one machine fails, clients reading from ZooKeeper can quickly switch over to one of the remaining machines. ZooKeeper plays the role for Accumulo of a centralized directory and lock service that Google's Chubby (*http://static.googleusercontent.com/media/ research.google.com/en/us/archive/chubby-osdi06.pdf*) provides for Bigtable. In addition, write replication is synchronous, which means clients wait until data is replicated and confirmed on all machines before considering a write successful. In practice, ZooKeeper instances tend to consist of three or five machines.

Accumulo uses ZooKeeper to store configuration and status information and to track changes in the cluster. ZooKeeper is also used to help clients begin the process of locating the right servers for the data they seek.

Hadoop

In the same way that Google's Bigtable stores its data in a distributed filesystem called GFS, Accumulo stores its data in HDFS. Accumulo relies on HDFS to provide persistent storage, replication, and fault tolerance. Having a separate storage layer allows Accumulo to balance the responsibility for serving portions of tables independently of where they are stored, although data tends to be served from the same server on which it is stored.

Like Accumulo, HDFS is a distributed application, but one that allows users to view a collection of machines as a single, scalable filesystem. HDFS files can be very large, up to terabytes per file. HDFS automatically breaks these files into blocks—by default 64 MB or 128 MB in size depending on the version of HDFS—and distributes these blocks across the cluster uniformly. In addition, each block is replicated on multiple machines (Figure 1-25). The default replication factor is three in order to avoid losing data when one machine or even an entire rack of servers becomes unavailable. Usually, one replica is written to the local hard drive, another to another machine in the same rack, and a third to a machine in another rack. This way, even the loss of an entire rack won't cause data loss.

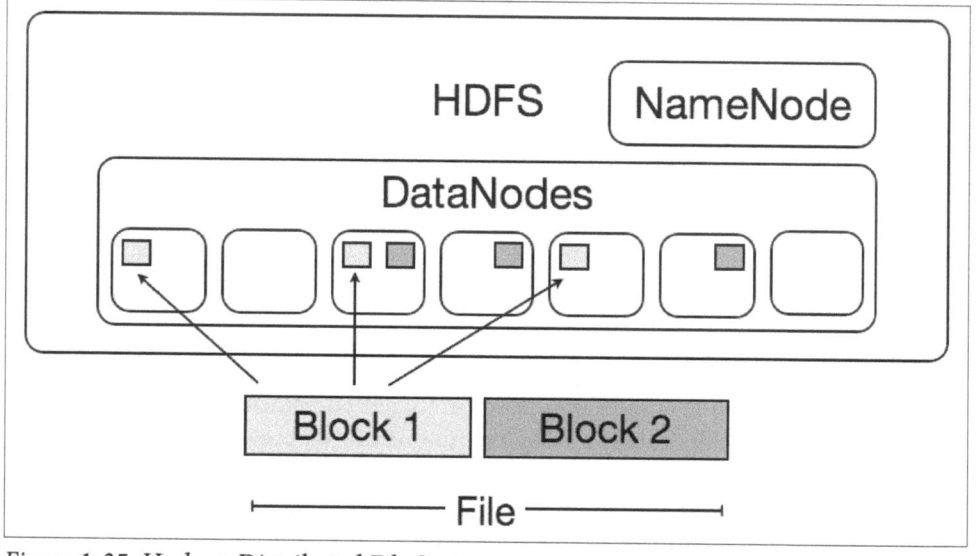

Figure 1-25. Hadoop Distributed File System

Accumulo

An Accumulo instance consists of several types of processes running on one to thousands of machines.

Analogous to HDFS files, Accumulo tables can be very large in size, up to tens of trillions of key-value pairs or more. Accumulo automatically partitions these into tablets and assigns responsibility for hosting tablets to servers called *tablet servers* (Figure 1-26).

However, unlike HDFS block replicas, Accumulo tablets are assigned to exactly one tablet server at a time. This allows one server to manage all the reads and writes for a particular range of keys, enabling reads and writes to be highly consistent because no synchronization has to occur between tablet servers. When a client writes a piece of information to a row, clients reading that row immediately after the write will see the new information.

Typically, a server will run one tablet server process and one HDFS DataNode process (Figure 1-27). This allows most tablets to have a local replica of the files they reference.

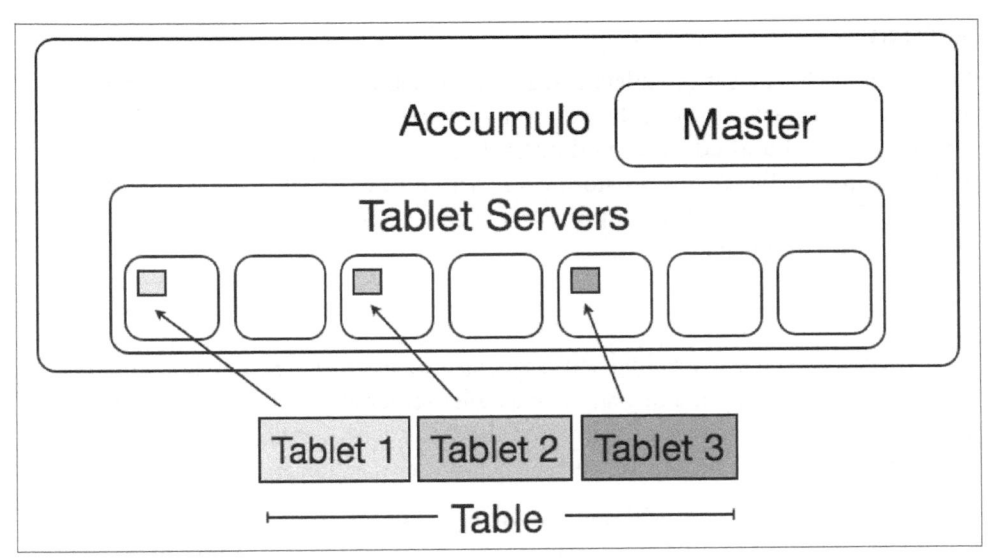

Figure 1-26. Accumulo

As a result, a tablet server can host a tablet whose file replicas are all located on other servers. This situation does not prevent the tablet's data from being read and is usually temporary, because any time a tablet server performs compaction of a tablet's files, it will by default create one local replica of each new file. Over time, a tablet tends to have one local replica for each file it references.

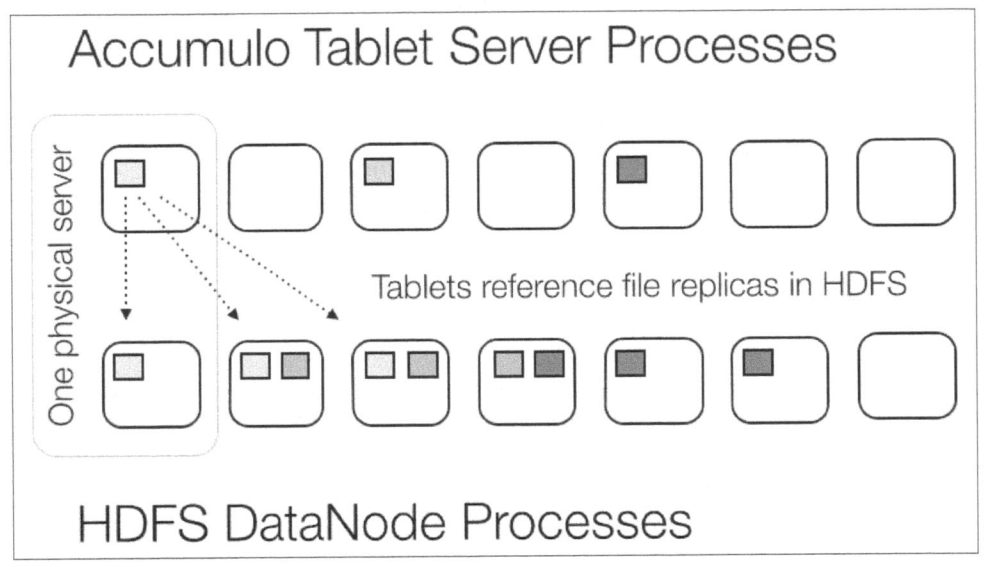

Figure 1-27. Typical process distribution

Tablet servers

Tablet servers host a set of tablets and are responsible for all the writes and reads for those tablets. Clients connect directly to tablet servers to read and write data. Tablet servers can host hundreds or even thousands of tablets, each consisting of about 1 GB of data or more. Tablet servers store data written to these tablets in memory and in files in HDFS, and handle scanning data for clients, applying any additional filtering or processing the clients request.

Master

Every Accumulo cluster has one active *master* process that is responsible for making sure all tablets are assigned to exactly one tablet server at all times and that tablets are load-balanced across servers. The master also helps with certain administrative operations such as startup, shutdown, and table and user creation and deletion.

Accumulo's master can fail without causing interruption to tablet servers and clients. If a tablet server fails while the master is down, some portion of the tablets will be unavailable until a new master process is started on any machine. When the new master process starts, it will reassign any tablets that do not have a tablet server assignment.

It is possible to configure Accumulo to run multiple master processes so that one master is always running in the event that one fails. Whichever process obtains a master ZooKeeper lock first will be the active master, and the remaining processes will watch the lock so that one of them can take over if the active master fails.

Garbage collector

The garbage collector process finds files that are no longer being used by any tablets and deletes them from HDFS to reclaim disk space.

A cluster needs only one garbage collector process running at any given time.

Monitor

Accumulo ships with an informative monitor that reports cluster activity and logging information into one web interface (Figure 1-28). This monitor is useful for verifying that Accumulo is operating properly and for helping understand and troubleshoot cluster and application performance. "Monitor Web Service" on page 429 gives descriptions of the information displayed by the monitor.

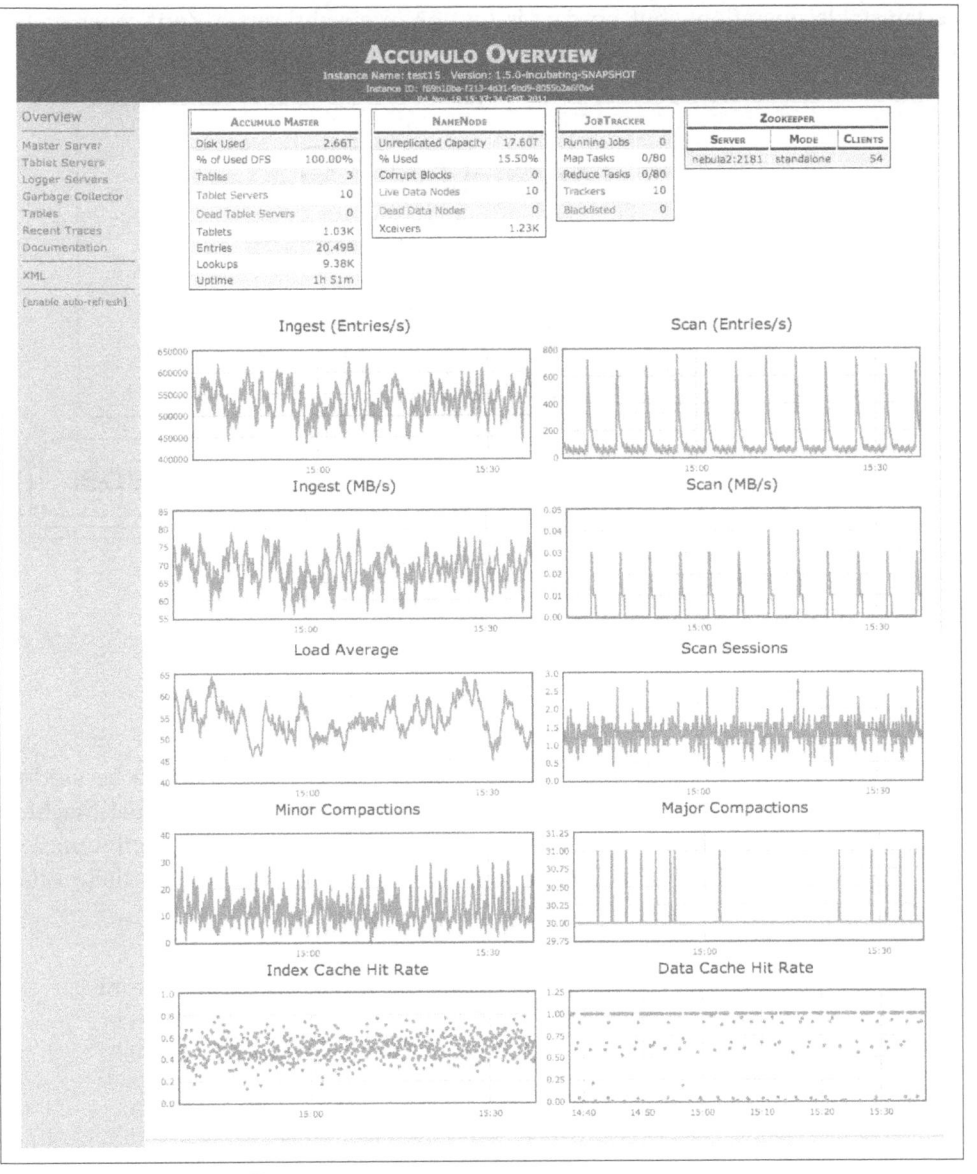

Figure 1-28. Monitor UI

Client

Accumulo provides a Java client library for use in applications. Many Accumulo clients can read and write data from an Accumulo instance simultaneously. Clients communicate directly with tablet servers to read and write data (Figure 1-29). Occasionally, clients will communicate with ZooKeeper and with the Accumulo master for certain table operations, but no data is sent or received through ZooKeeper or the master.

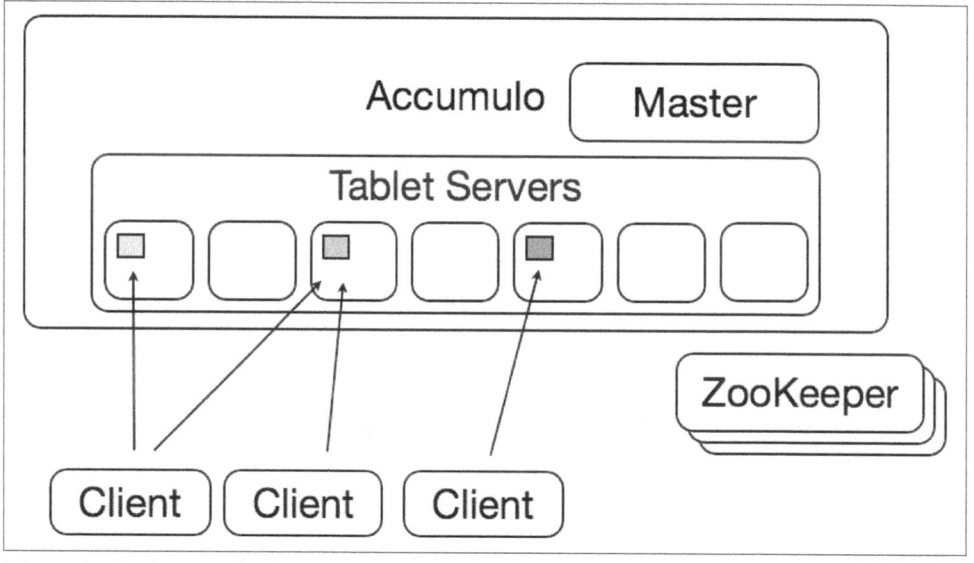

Figure 1-29. Accumulo clients

Thrift proxy

As of version 1.5, Accumulo provides an optional Thrift proxy that can be used to develop clients in languages other than those that run on the Java Virtual Machine (JVM). These other clients can connect to the Thrift proxy, which communicates with the Accumulo cluster and allows data to be read and written by these other clients.

 Accumulo versions 1.4 and older use logger processes to record each new write in an unsorted write-ahead log on disk that can be used to recover any data that was lost from the memory of a failed tablet server. Accumulo 1.5 no longer has dedicated logger processes. The write-ahead logs are written directly to files in HDFS.

A Typical Cluster

A typical Accumulo cluster consists of a few *control nodes* and a few to many *worker nodes* (Figure 1-30).

Control nodes include:

- One, three, or five machines running ZooKeeper
- Ideally, two machines running HDFS NameNode processes, one active, one for failover
- One to two machines running Accumulo master, garbage collector, and/or monitor
- For Hadoop 1, an optional machine running a Hadoop job tracker process if MapReduce jobs are required
- For Hadoop 2, an optional machine running a YARN resource manager process if MapReduce jobs are required

Each worker node typically includes:

- One HDFS DataNode process for storing data
- One tablet server process for serving queries and inserts
- For Hadoop 1, an optional Hadoop task tracker for running MapReduce jobs
- For Hadoop 2, an optional YARN node manager for running MapReduce jobs

 The logger process mentioned in Accumulo versions 1.4 and earlier would have typically run on each worker node.

In addition, applications require one to many processes using the Accumulo client library to write and read data.

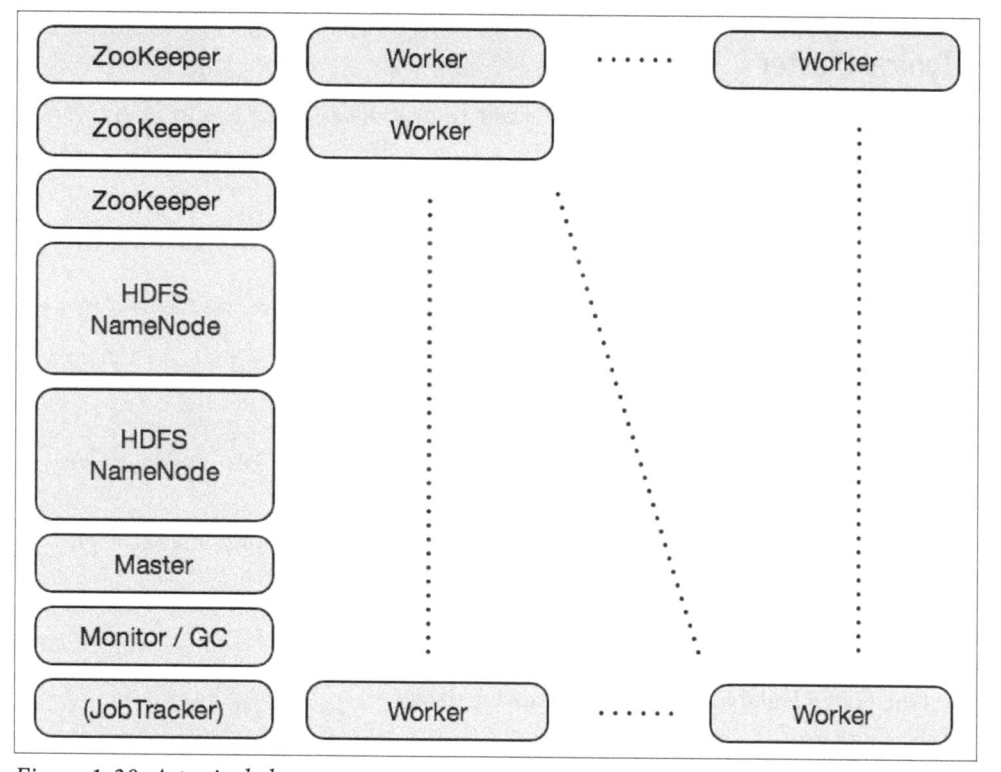

Figure 1-30. A typical cluster

Additional Features

In addition to the features already described, Accumulo provides more features to help you build scalable applications running on large clusters. Not all of these are unique to Accumulo, but the combination of these features is likely unique.

Automatic Data Partitioning

Accumulo tables can be very large, up to petabytes in size. You can tune the tablet-splitting process, but you don't have to worry about choosing a good key on which to partition because Accumulo automatically finds good split points.

High Consistency

Accumulo provides a highly consistent view of the data. Tablets are assigned to exactly one tablet server at a time. An update to a particular key's value is immediately reflected in subsequent reads because those updates and reads go to the same server.

Other NoSQL systems allow writes for a particular key to happen on more than one server, and consistency is achieved via communication between these servers. Because this communication is not instantaneous, these systems are considered *eventually consistent*. One advantage of eventually consistent systems is that a single instance of the database can run over geographically disparate data centers, and writes to some servers can continue even if those servers cannot communicate with all of the other servers participating in the cluster.

An Accumulo instance is designed to be deployed within a single data center and to provide a highly consistent view of the data. One advantage of high consistency is that application logic can be simplified.

Automatic Load Balancing

The Accumulo master automatically balances the responsibility for serving tablets across tablet servers. When one tablet server has more tablets than another, the master process will instruct the overloaded tablet server to stop serving a tablet and instruct the underloaded tablet server to begin hosting that tablet.

Massive Scalability

Accumulo is considered a *horizontally scalable* application, meaning that you can increase the capabilities of the system by adding more machines, rather than by replacing existing machines with bigger, more capable machines (vertical scaling). New machines joining an Accumulo cluster begin participating in the cluster very quickly, because no data movement is required for these new machines to start hosting tablets and the reads and writes associated with them.

Accumulo can also work well at large scale, meaning on clusters consisting of thousands of machines hosting petabytes of data.

A major benefit to building on Accumulo is that an application can be written and deployed on a small cluster when the amount of data and the number of concurrent writes and reads is low. As data or read-write demand grows, the Accumulo cluster can be expanded to handle more data and reads without an application rewrite.

Many distributed systems today are built to scale from one server to many. Accumulo may be one of the most scalable data stores out there. As of version 1.6, Accumulo is capable of running across multiple instances of HDFS with different HDFS NameNodes. This means that Accumulo can be configured to support more update operations than can be accommodated by a single HDFS instance.

Failure Tolerance and Automatic Recovery

Like Hadoop, Accumulo is designed to survive single server failures and even the failure of a single rack. If a single Accumulo tablet server fails, the master process notes this and reassigns its tablets to the remaining tablet servers. Accumulo clients automatically manage the failover from one tablet server to another. Application developers do not need to worry about retrying their operations simply because a machine fails.

In a large cluster these types of failures are commonplace, and Accumulo does a lot of work to minimize the burden on application developers as well as administrators so that a single instance running on thousands of machines is tractable.

Support for Analysis: Iterators

Storing large amounts of data and making it searchable is only part of the solution to the problem of taking full advantage of big data. Often data needs to be aggregated, summarized, or modeled in order to be fully understood and utilized. Accumulo provides a few mechanisms for performing analysis on data in tables.

One of these mechanisms, Accumulo *iterators*, enable custom aggregation and summarization within tablet servers to allow you to maintain result sets efficiently and store the data at a higher level of abstraction. They are called iterators because they iterate over key-value pairs and allow developers to alter the data before writing to disk or returning information to users.

There are various types of iterators that range from filtering to simple sums to maintaining a set of statistics. These are covered in "Iterators" on page 209.

Developers have used iterators to incrementally update edge weights in large graphs for applications such as social network analysis or computer network modeling. Others have used iterators to build complex feature vectors from a variety of sources to represent entities such as website users. These feature vectors can be used in machine-learning algorithms like clustering and classification to model underlying groups within the data or for predictive analysis.

Support for Analysis: MapReduce Integration

Beyond iterators, Accumulo supports analysis via integration with the popular Hadoop MapReduce framework. Accumulo stores its data in HDFS and can be used as the source of data for a MapReduce job or as the destination of the output from a MapReduce job. MapReduce jobs can either read from tablet servers using the Accumulo client library, or from the underlying files in which Accumulo stores data via the use of specific MapReduce input and output formats.

In either case, Accumulo supports the type of data locality that MapReduce jobs require, allowing MapReduce workers to read data that is stored locally rather than having to read it all from remote machines over the network.

We cover using MapReduce with Accumulo in depth in Chapter 7.

Data Lifecycle Management

Accumulo provides a good degree of control over how data is managed in order to comply with storage space, legal, or policy requirements.

In addition, the timestamps that are part Accumulo's key structure can be used with iterators to age data off according to a policy set by the administrator. This includes aging off data older than a certain amount of time from now, or simply aging off data older than a specific date.

Timestamps can also be used to distinguish among two or more versions of otherwise identical keys. The built-in `VersioningIterator` can be configured to allow any number of versions, or only a specific number of versions, to be stored. Google's original Bigtable paper describes using timestamps to distinguish among various versions of the Web as it was crawled and stored from time to time.

With this built-in functionality in the database, work that otherwise must be done in a batch-oriented fashion involving a lot of reading and writing data back to the system can be performed incrementally and efficiently.

We cover age-off in depth in "Data Age-off" on page 450.

Compression

Accumulo compresses data by default using several methods. One is to apply a compression algorithm such as GZip or LZO to blocks of data stored on disk. The other is a technique called *relative-key encoding*, in which the shared prefixes of a set of keys are stored only once, and the following keys only need express the changes to the initial key.

Compressing data in this way can improve I/O, because reading compressed data and doing decompression can be faster than reading uncompressed data and not doing decompression. Compression also helps offset the cost of the block replication that is performed by HDFS.

The Bigtable paper describes two types of compression. One compresses long common strings across a large window, and the other does compression over small windows of data. These types of custom compression are not implemented in Accumulo.

Robust Timestamps

When Accumulo tablet servers are assigning timestamps to key-value pairs, Accumulo ensures that the timestamps are internally consistent. Accumulo only assigns new timestamps that are later than the most recent timestamp for a given tablet. In other words, timestamps assigned by a tablet server are guaranteed to increase.

This addresses the inevitable situation in which some servers in the cluster have clocks that are off and are applying timestamps from the future to keys. If these keys were transferred to another server, newly written data would be treated as older than existing data. It would be very confusing for users not to see the data they expect. It would be an even more critical problem in the Accumulo metadata that keeps track of tablets and their files. Entire data files could be lost if this problem were allowed to occur. Thus, Accumulo only assigns new timestamps that are later than the most recent timestamp for a given tablet.

It is also possible to use a one-up counter for timestamps by configuring a table with a time type of *logical* instead of the default time type of *milliseconds* since the UNIX epoch (*http://en.wikipedia.org/wiki/Unix_time*) (Midnight UTC on January 1, 1970). In either case, tablet servers ensure that a newly written key-value pair is never stamped with a timestamp that precedes the most recent timestamp for the key's tablet. This does not, however, prevent arbitrary user-assigned timestamps from being written to a table.

Accumulo and Other Data Management Systems

Application developers and systems engineers face a wide range of choices for managing their data today. Often the differences among these options are subtle and require a deep understanding of technologies' capabilities as well as the problem domain. To help in deciding when Accumulo is or isn't a good fit for a particular purpose, we compare Accumulo to some other popular options.

Comparisons to Relational Databases

Relational databases, by far the most popular type of database in use today, have been around for several decades and serve a wide variety of uses. Understanding the relative strengths and weaknesses of these systems is useful for determining how and when to use them instead of Accumulo.

SQL

One of the strengths of relational databases is that they implement a set of operations known as *relational algebra* codified in Structured Query Language (SQL). SQL allows users to perform rich and complex operations at query time, including set intersection, joins, aggregations, and sorting. Relational databases are heavily optimized to perform these operations at query time.

One challenge of using SQL is that of performing this work at query time on a large amount of data. Relational Massively Parallel Processing (MPP) databases approach this by dividing the work to perform SQL operations among many servers. The approach taken by Accumulo is to encourage aggressive precomputation where possible, often using far more storage to achieve the space-time trade-off, in order to minimize the work done at query time and maintain fast lookups even when storing petabytes of data.

Space-Time Trade-off and Cheap Space

In computer science, the *space-time trade-off* refers to the fact that you can use more space to store the results of computation in order to reduce the time required to get answers to users. Conversely, you can save space by waiting until users ask and computing answers on the fly.

Over the past decade the cost of storage has dropped dramatically. As a result, Accumulo applications tend to precompute as much as possible, often combining into one table data that would be stored as two or more tables in a relational database.

When applications are designed to support answering analytical questions about entities of interest, it is common to precompute the answer for all entities periodically, or to update the answers via iterators when new raw data is ingested, so that queries can consist of a simple, very fast lookup.

Transactions

Many relational databases provide very strong guarantees around data updates, commonly termed ACID, for Atomicity, Consistency, Isolation, and Durability.

ACID

Atomicity
Either all the changes in a transaction are made or none is made. No partial changes are committed.

Consistency
The database is always in a consistent state. This means different things in different contexts. For databases in which some rows can refer to others, consistency means that a referenced row must exist.

Isolation
Each transaction is made independent of other transactions. Changes appear the same whether done serially or concurrently.

Durability
Changes are persistent and survive certain types of failure.

In relational databases these properties are delivered via several mechanisms. One such mechanism is a *transaction*, which bundles a set of operations together into a logical unit. Transactions are important for supporting *operational workloads* such as maintaining information about inventory, keeping bank accounts in order, and tracking the current state of business operations. Transactions can contain changes to multiple values within a row, changes to values in two or more rows in the same table, or even updates to multiple rows in multiple tables. These types of workloads are considered online transaction processing (OLTP).

Accumulo guarantees these ACID properties for a single mutation (a set of changes for a single row) but does not provide support for atomic updates across multiple rows. Nor does Accumulo maintain consistent references between rows. Row isolation for reads can be obtained by enabling the feature for a particular scanner (see "Isolated Row Views" on page 111).

Normalization

If you store multiple copies of the same data in different places, it can be difficult to ensure a high degree of consistency. You might update the value in one place but not the other. Therefore, storing copies of the same values should be avoided.

Values that don't have a one-to-one relationship to each other are often divided into separate tables that keep pointers between themselves. For example, a person typically only has one birth date, so you can store birth date in the same table as first name and other one-to-one data (Figure 1-31).

But a person may have many nicknames or favorite songs. This type of one-to-many data is stored in a separate table (Figure 1-32). There is a well-defined process, called *normalization*, for deciding which data elements to put into separate tables. There are several degrees to which normalization can be applied, but it typically involves breaking out data involved in one-to-many or many-to-many relationships into multiple tables and joining them at query time.

Another group of workloads is termed online analytical processing (OLAP). Relational databases have been used to support these kinds of workloads as well. Often analysis takes the approach of looking at snapshots of operational data, or simply may bring together reference data that doesn't require updates but requires efficient read and aggregation capabilities. Because these data snapshots are no longer updated, there is no opportunity for the data to become inconsistent, and the need for normalization is diminished.

Because OLAP workloads require fewer updates, tables are often precombined, or *denormalized*, to cut down on the operations that are carried out a query time (Figure 1-33). This is another example of the space-time trade-off, whereby an increase in storage space used reduces the time to get data in the format requested.

ID	Name	Date of Birth
1001	Bob Jones	1978-04-01
1002	Fred Smith	1965-11-02
1003	Wei Chang	1983-12-06
1004	David Garcia	1976-09-09

Figure 1-31. A table containing a one-to-one relationship

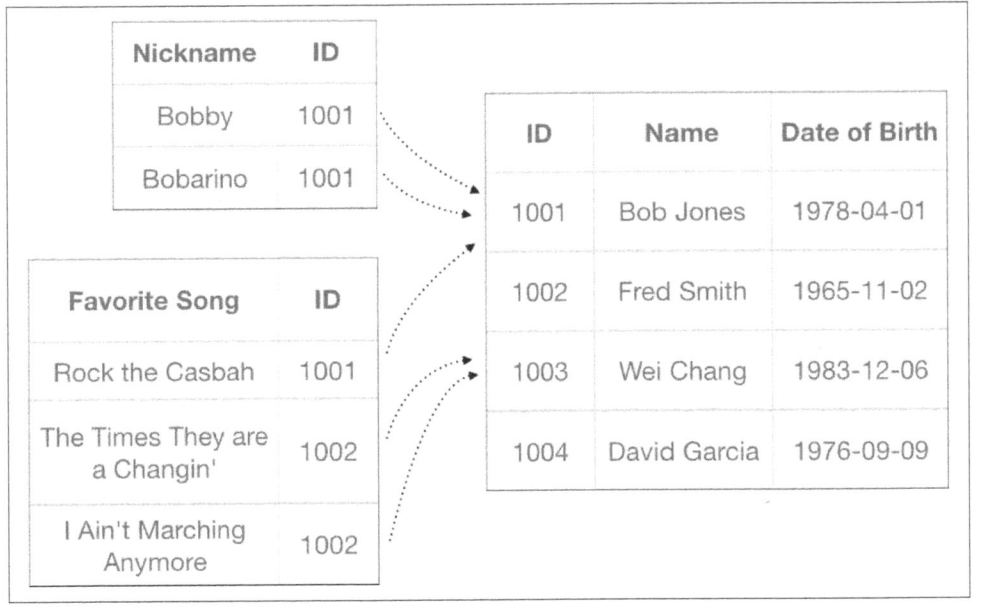

Figure 1-32. An example of normalization

ID	Name	Date of Birth	Nickname	Favorite Song
1001	Bob Jones	1978-04-01	Bobby	Rock the Casbah
1001	Bob Jones	1978-04-01	Bobarino	Rock the Casbah
1002	Fred Smith	1965-11-02		
1003	Wei Chang	1983-12-06		The Times They are a Changin'
1003	Wei Chang	1983-12-06		I Ain't Marching Anymore
1004	David Garcia	1976-09-09		

Figure 1-33. An example of denormalization

In the example in Figure 1-33 of denormalizing data for analysis, it is easy to see how you would want a system like Accumulo that is highly scalable, employs compression of redundant data, and handles sparse data well.

Accumulo does not implement relational algebra. Accumulo provides ACID guarantees, but on a more limited basis. The only transactions allowed by Accumulo are inserts, deletes, or updates to multiple values within a single row. These transactions are atomic, consistent, isolated, and durable. But a set of updates to multiple rows in the same table, or rows in different tables, do not have these guarantees.

Accumulo is therefore often used for massive operational workloads that can be performed via single-row updates, or for massive OLAP workloads.

Comparisons to Other NoSQL Databases

Accumulo belongs to a group of applications known as *NoSQL databases*. The term *NoSQL* refers to the fact that these databases support data access methods other than SQL and is short for Not SQL or Not Only SQL—although the engineer who coined the term NoSQL, Carlo Strozzi, has expressed that it may be more appropriate to call these applications nonrelational databases.[2]

---

2 "NoSQL Relational Database Management System: Home Page." Strozzi.it. 2 October 2007. Retrieved 29 March 2010.

Rather than using SQL for creating queries to fetch data and perform aggregation, Accumulo provides a simplified API for writing and reading data. Departing from the relational model and SQL has two major implications: increased flexibility in how data is modeled and stored, and the fact that some operations that other databases perform at query time are instead applied when data is written. In other words, results are precomputed so that query-time operations can consist solely of simple, fast tasks.

Compared to other NoSQL databases, Accumulo has some features that make it especially dynamic and scalable.

Data model

NoSQL it's a somewhat nebulous term, and is applied to applications as varied as Berkley DB, memcached, Bigtable, Accumulo, MongoDB, Neo4j, Amazon's Dynamo, and others.

Some folks have grouped distributed software systems into categories based on the data model supported. These categories can consist of the following:

Pure key-value
- Riak
- Dynamo
- memcached

Columnar (Bigtable)
- Bigtable
- Accumulo
- HBase
- Cassandra

Document
- MongoDB
- CouchDB

Graph
- Neo4j

Some of these applications have in common a key-value data model at a high level. Accumulo's data model consists of key-value pairs at the highest level, but because of the structure of the key it achieves some properties of conventional two-dimensional, flat-record tables, columnar and row-oriented databases, and a little bit of hierarchy in the data model via column families and column qualifiers.

Apache Accumulo, Apache Cassandra, and Apache HBase share this basic Bigtable data model.

Other NoSQL data stores, such as MongoDB and CouchDB, are considered to be document-oriented stores because they store JavaScript Object Notation (JSON)–like documents natively.

Neo4j is a graph-oriented database whose data model consists of vertices and edges.

Choosing which data model is most appropriate for an application is probably the first and foremost factor one should consider when choosing a NoSQL technology. There is some flexibility in applying the data model because, for example, a key-value store can be made to store graph data and because a document-based data model is sort of a superset of the key-value model.

Key ordering

Some NoSQL databases use hashing to distribute their keys to servers. This makes lookups simple for clients but can require some data to be moved when machines are added to or removed from the cluster. It can also make scanning across a sequential range of keys more difficult or impossible.

Because Accumulo maintains its own dynamic mapping of keys to servers it can very quickly handle machines joining or leaving the cluster, with no data movement and minimal interruption to clients. In addition, the key space is partitioned dynamically and automatically so that the data is distributed evenly throughout the cluster.

Tight Hadoop integration

Many NoSQL databases have their own storage mechanism. Accumulo uses HDFS. This offers several advantages:

- Accumulo can use the output of MapReduce jobs without having to move large amounts of data. Accumulo can also serve as the source of input data for MapReduce jobs. This allows Hadoop clusters to be used for mixed workloads.

- Accumulo benefits from the significant work done by the Hadoop community to make HDFS resilient, scalable, and stable.

- Because Hadoop is becoming the de-facto standard for large data processing in many organizations, Accumulo reduces the cost of acquiring a scalable, low-latency query capability by building on existing investment in Hadoop.

High versus eventual consistency

Some NoSQL databases are designed to run over geographically distributed data centers and allow data to be written in more than one place simultaneously. This results in a property known as *eventual consistency*, in which a value read from the database may not be the most up-to-date version.

Accumulo is designed to run within a single data center and provides a highly consistent view of the data at all times. This means that users are guaranteed to always see the most up-to-date version of the data, which simplifies application development.

When comparing NoSQL databases, you may want to consider which trade-offs have been made in the design. In particular, much attention has been paid to the CAP theorem, which states that in designing a distributed database, you can choose to provide at most two of the following properties: high Consistency, Availability, and Partition-tolerance (hence CAP). A good treatment of this concept is in "Brewer's Conjecture and the Feasibility of Consistent, Available, Partition-Tolerant Web Services" (*http://bit.ly/gilbert_lynch*) by Seth Gilbert and Nancy Lynch.

See "Accumulo and the CAP Theorem" on page 379 for a discussion on the choices made in the Accumulo design with respect to the CAP Theorem.

Column visibility and access control

Organizations are turning to Accumulo in order to satisfy stringent data-access requirements and to comply with legal and corporate requirements and policies.

Most databases provide a level of access control over the data. Accumulo's column visibilities are often more fine-grained and can be used to implement a wide variety of access-control scenarios.

HBase in particular has implemented Accumulo's column visibilities—including the same types of security label expressions as Accumulo as well as a different mode of access involving attaching access-control lists (ACLs) to cells.

One important note is that HBase includes a NOT operator (!) that can make it impossible to allow users to view the data using a subset of all their tokens, because they could remove a token used as part of a NOT expression to protect data. See the Accumulo mailing list (*http://bit.ly/accumulo_mailing_list*) for the thread "'NOT' operator in visibility string."

For example, suppose there were multiple cells with the following labels:

```
kvpair1: private
kvpair2: ( private | admin ) & !probationary
kvpair3: admin
```

To query Accumulo's key-value pairs, the user must always provide a list of authorization tokens to use for the query. Accumulo's built-in ColumnVisibilityFilter determines whether a particular set of tokens is sufficient to view a particular key-value pair. Each user has a maximum set of tokens he is allowed to use for queries. It is not uncommon for applications developed on Accumulo to allow users to issue queries with a subset of their allowed tokens in order to see data as it would be viewed at different visibility levels. For example, a user with both the *private* and *admin* tokens might choose to query the data with just the *private* token. This helps with publishing data to other groups of users that are granted different authorization tokens.

In the presence of the NOT operator, applications cannot allow users to view the data with any fewer than all of their tokens, because removing a token from a query would *increase* the number of key-value pairs visible to the user, amounting to an elevation of privilege. In the preceding example, imagine issuing a query with the *private* and *probationary* tokens versus a query with just the *private* token.

Another important note is that HBase does not consider the security label expression to be a part of the key portion of the data model, as Accumulo does. This implies a model in which a key-value pair at one visibility level can be overwritten with a different visibility level. In Accumulo's visibility model, you can store multiple values at different visibility levels for the same row and column, because the visibility is considered part of the key. It is not possible to overwrite one visibility with another less restrictive visibility.

HBase's implementation is also a bit different from Accumulo's in that it utilizes coprocessors (*http://bit.ly/hbase_cell_security*) since HBase doesn't have a construct like Accumulo iterators. There may be performance differences as a result.

MongoDB has recently added a feature called *redact* as part of its Aggregation Framework (*http://bit.ly/redact_operator*) that can be used to filter out subdocuments based on a flexible set of expressions. It appears likely that Accumulo's filtering logic could also be implemented in this framework.

Iterators

Accumulo's iterators allow application developers to push some computation to the server side, which can result in a dramatic increase in performance depending on the operations performed. HBase provides a mechanism called *coprocessors*, which execute code and can be triggered at many places. Unlike coprocessors, iterators operate in only three places, are stackable, and are an integral part of the data processing pipeline since much of the tablet server's core behavior is implemented in built-in system iterators.

 Iterators are applied at scan time, when flushing memory to disk (minor compaction), and when combining files (major compaction).

Because iterators can be used much like MapReduce map or combine functions, iterators can help execute analytical functionality in a more streamlined and organized manner than batch-oriented MapReduce jobs. Developers looking to efficiently create and maintain result sets should consider iterators as an option.

Dynamic column families and locality groups

As mentioned in "Column Families" on page 19, Accumulo can have any number of column families, and column families can be assigned arbitrarily to locality groups. Accumulo does not require column families to be declared before they can be used. Accumulo stores key-value pairs together on disk according to how their column families are mapped to locality groups within a single file, rather than using separate files or directories to separate the data, which keeps file management overhead constant. Furthermore, changes can be made to how the data is stored on disk by reconfiguring locality groups on the fly, without changing how data is modeled in the Accumulo key.

In contrast, HBase requires column families to be declared beforehand, and each column family is stored in a separate directory in HDFS, which drastically limits the flexibility of column family usage. Because column families are mapped to HDFS directories in HBase, they must consist of printable characters, whereas in Accumulo they are arbitrary byte arrays. Because every column family is a separate storage directory in HBase, in practice it is recommended that tables have fewer than 10 column families total (see Lars George's *HBase: The Definitive Guide* [O'Reilly]). Each column family in HBase is effectively in its own locality group, and multiple families cannot be grouped together.

File handle resources are limited per server, and the overall number of files and directories in HDFS is limited by the capacity of the NameNode, so having the number of files be dependent on your specific data model rather than on the overall amount of data becomes a consequence that every application must consider. Accumulo application designers do not have to consider this problem because Accumulo does not have this limitation.

HBase requires that at least one column family be declared per table, and every key-value pair inserted must specify a column family, whereas Accumulo does not require the column family portion of the key to be filled out. It can be left blank, even if column qualifiers or other parts of the key are filled out.

Support for very large rows

Accumulo does not assume that rows must fit entirely in memory. Key-value pairs are streamed back to the client in batches, and it's possible for the client to fetch a portion of a row first and to stream the rest of the row in separate batches.

An example of an application design that may require arbitrarily large rows is in the use of tables to store secondary indexes for document search, where the row ID is used to store search terms that may be mapped to many document IDs stored in column qualifiers. The row corresponding to a common search term would be especially large, because that term is likely to appear in a large number of documents.

Parallelized BatchScanners

In addition to being able to scan over a single range of key-value pairs, Accumulo provides a BatchScanner in its client API that can be used to fetch rows from multiple places in a table simultaneously in multiple threads. This is also useful for applications performing queries using secondary indexes.

Namespaces

Accumulo tables can be assigned to a namespace, which enables them to be configured and managed as a group. This makes it easier to have multiple groups of people managing tables in the same cluster. See "Table Namespaces" on page 160 for details.

Use Cases Suited for Accumulo

Accumulo's design represents a set of objectives and technical features different from those in data management systems such as filesystems and relational databases. Application and system designers need to understand how these features work together. We present here a few applications that could leverage Accumulo's strengths.

A New Kind of Flexible Analytical Warehouse

In attempts to build a system to analyze all the data in an organization by bringing together many disparate data sources, three problems can easily arise: a scalability problem, a problem managing sparse dynamic data, and security concerns.

Accumulo directly addresses all three of these with horizontal scalability, a rich key-value data model that supports efficiently storing sparse data and that facilitates discovery, and fine-grained access control. An analytical data warehouse built around Accumulo is still different from what one would build around a relational database. Analytical results would be aggressively precomputed, potentially using MapReduce. Many types of data could be involved, including semistructured JSON or XML, or features extracted from text or imagery.

Building the Next Gmail

The original use case behind Bigtable was for building websites that support massive scale in two dimensions: number of simultaneous users and amount of data managed. If your plan is to build the next Gmail, Accumulo would be a good starting point.

Massive Graph or Machine-Learning Problems

Features such as iterators, MapReduce support, and a data model that supports storing dimensional sparse data make Accumulo a good candidate for creating, maintaining, storing, and processing extremely large graphs or large sets of feature vectors for machine-learning applications.

MapReduce has been used in conjunction with Accumulo's scan capabilities to efficiently traverse graphs with trillions of edges (*http://bit.ly/big_graph_experiment*), processing hundreds of millions of edges per second.

Some machine-learning techniques, especially nonparametric algorithms such as k-nearest neighbors, are *memory-based* and require storing all the data rather than building a statistical model to represent the data. Keeping or "remembering" all the data points is what is meant by "memory-based," not that the data all lives in RAM. Accumulo is able to store large amounts of these data points and provides the basic data selection operations for supporting these algorithms efficiently. See "Machine Learning" on page 343 for more on this.

In addition, for predictive applications that use models built from slowly changing historical data, Accumulo can be used to store historical data and make it available for query, and to support building models from this data via MapReduce. Accumulo's ability to manage large tables allows users to use arbitrarily complex predictive models to score all known entities and store their results for fast lookup, rather than having to compute scores at query time.

Relieving Relational Databases

Because relational databases have performed well over the past several decades, they have become the standard place for putting all data and have had to support a wide variety of data management problems. But as database expert Michael Stonebraker and others have argued (*http://bit.ly/stonebraker_cetintemel*), trying to have only one platform can result in challenges stemming from the difficulty of optimizing a single system for many use cases.

Accumulo has been used to offload the burden of storing large amounts of raw data from relational databases, freeing them up for more specialized workloads such as performing complex runtime operations on selected subsets or summaries of the data.

Massive Search Applications

Google has used Bigtable to power parts of its primary search application (*http://bit.ly/caffeine_bigtable*). Accumulo has features such as automatic partitioning, batch scanning, and flexible iterators that can be used to support complex and large-scale text search applications.

Applications with a Long History of Versioned Data

Wikipedia is an application with millions of articles edited by people around the world. Part of the challenge of these types of massive-scale collaborative applications is storing many versions of the data as users edit individual elements. Accumulo's data model allows several versions of data to be stored, and for users to retrieve versions in several ways. Accumulo's scalability makes having to store all versions of data for all time a more tractable proposition.

CHAPTER 2

Quick Start

Now that you have a basic understanding of Accumulo, this chapter should get you up and running. We will work through a couple of different install options and then work through a few examples. The accumulo-quickstart installation should be suitable for use with examples throughout the rest of this book.

The quickest method to get started with Accumulo is to use the `MiniAccumuloCluster`. It is a minimal version of Accumulo that starts ZooKeeper and runs against the local filesystem instead of starting up HDFS. It provides a testing and experimentation environment that is close to that of a full-blown Accumulo installation, but without the initial configuration overhead. The `MiniAccumuloCluster` is great for writing automated tests and for experimenting with approaches. It will not scale to large data, but it is perfect for getting started.

The example project we will use is based on the Instamo Archetype, which is an Accumulo contrib (*http://accumulo.apache.org/contrib.html*) project.

Our example includes a maven *pom.xml* file with populated dependencies. It also contains `ShellExample`, `MapReduceExample`, and `ExampleAccumuloUnitTest` classes that illustrate running different types of client code. Code run against a `MiniAccumuloCluster` works the same as code that runs against a full Accumulo installation.

To get started, make sure you have Java 1.7 installed and Apache Maven 3.0.4 or greater. See *http://maven.apache.org/* if you need to install Maven. Now, clone the Git repository that contains all source for this book:

```
git clone https://github.com/accumulobook/examples
```

Change to the *quickstart* directory. Let's get started.

Demo of the Shell

We will begin with a look at how to use the shell. From the *quickstart* directory, run the following:

```
mvn clean compile exec:exec -Pshell
```

The shell profile that is selected with the `-Pshell` option runs the `main()` method of the `ShellExample` class. This starts a ZooKeeper process, an Accumulo master process, two Accumulo TabletServer processes, and an Accumulo shell client. You will be presented with an interactive shell that looks something like this:

```
[INFO] Scanning for projects...
[INFO]
[INFO] ------------------------------------------------------------------------
[INFO] Building Mini Accumulo Cluster Example 0.0.1-SNAPSHOT
[INFO] ------------------------------------------------------------------------
[INFO]
[INFO] --- maven-clean-plugin:2.4.1:clean (default-clean) @ mini-accumulo-
       cluster-example ---
[INFO] Deleting /Users/accumulobook/src/accumulo-book/sourcecode/chapter2/mini-
       accumulo-cluster-example/target
[INFO]
[INFO] --- maven-resources-plugin:2.5:resources (default-resources) @ mini-
       accumulo-cluster-example ---
[debug] execute contextualize
[WARNING] Using platform encoding (UTF-8 actually) to copy filtered resources,
       i.e. build is platform dependent!
[INFO] Copying 1 resource
[INFO]
[INFO] --- maven-compiler-plugin:2.0.2:compile (default-compile) @ mini-accumulo-
       cluster-example ---
[INFO] Compiling 3 source files to /Users/accumulobook//src/accumulo-book/
       sourcecode/chapter2/mini-accumulo-cluster-example/target/classes
[INFO]
[INFO] --- exec-maven-plugin:1.2.1:exec (default-cli) @ mini-accumulo-cluster-
       example ---

---- Initializing Accumulo Shell

Starting the MiniAccumuloCluster in /var/folders/2y/
    n9lzqm2x10lfxqm9n40xvfvw0000gn/T/1425610595980-0
Zookeeper is localhost:24968
Instance is miniInstance
[main] INFO  org.apache.accumulo.minicluster.impl.MiniAccumuloClusterImpl  -
    Starting MAC against instance miniInstance and zookeeper(s) localhost:24968.

Shell - Apache Accumulo Interactive Shell
-
- version: 1.6.2
- instance name: miniInstance
- instance id: de5cd0be-b63b-458a-a1eb-6cad5e360350
-
```

```
- type 'help' for a list of available commands
-
root@miniInstance>
```

The default prompt on the shell shows the current Accumulo user, *root*, and the current Accumulo instance name, *miniInstance*.

If your shell is idle for too long (60 minutes by default), you will receive an Authorization Timeout when you try to enter commands. You just need to enter the user's password again. As set in the *ShellExample.java* file, the password is *pass1234*.

The help Command

Start by running the `help` command. This command will show all available commands. To see more information about a specific command, run `help` *command* (for example, run `help delete` to learn more about the `delete` command). See Appendix A for more information on the shell commands.

The shell also supports history and tab completion.

Creating a Table and Inserting Some Data

Now that you know how to get help on shell commands, let's create a table and insert some data. Because Accumulo is a schemaless database, all you need is the table name. The schema will evolve as you insert data. So let's create a table a named *table1* by using the `createtable` command:

```
root@miniInstance> createtable table1
root@miniInstance table1>
```

Notice that the prompt changed and now shows you the current table, *table1*.

The table is currently empty, so we need to insert some data. We will use the `insert` command. We introduce the Accumulo data model in "Data Model" on page 13, so let's insert some example data using the `insert` *row column_family column_quali fier value* `-l` *column_visibility* `-ts` *timestamp* shell command:

```
insert "bob jones" "contact" "address" "123 any street" -l "billing"
insert "bob jones" "contact" "city" "anytown" -l "billing"
insert "bob jones" "contact" "phone" "555-1212" -l "billing"
insert "bob jones" "purchases" "sneakers" "$60" -l "billing&#x26;inventory"
insert "fred smith" "contact" "address" "444 main st." -l  "billing"
insert "fred smith" "contact" "city" "othertown" -l "billing"
```

```
insert "fred smith" "purchases" "glasses" "$30" -l "billing&#x26;inventory"
insert "fred smith" "purchases" "hat" "$20" -l "billing&#x26;inventory"
```

> Generally it is best to let Accumulo manage the timestamps on its keys. Setting timestamps explicitly should be left to advanced use cases, because it can result in unexpected behavior if you are not very familiar with how the key's timestamp is used in Accumulo.

Scanning for Data

Once you get data into Accumulo, you need to view it. We will use the scan command, so run:

```
scan
```

Wait, didn't we just insert data? Why did the scan not return anything? The data we entered included column visibilities with the -l switch, but the *root* user does not have authorizations to view those. A user in Accumulo can write data with any authorizations (unless it has been prohibited by configuring the VisibilityConstraint—see "Authorizations" on page 183), but viewing records requires authorization. Keep this in mind whenever you don't see data you thought you inserted.

A user's current authorizations can be viewed with the getauths command. Running getauths now will show an empty list. Assign the necessary authorizations with the following:

```
setauths -u root -s inventory,billing
```

Run another getauths. to ensure that you set them correctly. The result should be:

```
billing,inventory
```

Notice that the auths are now sorted. You should now see all records with another scan:

```
root@miniInstance table1> scan
bob jones contact:address [billing]     123 any street
bob jones contact:city [billing]     anytown
bob jones contact:phone [billing]     555-1212
bob jones purchases:sneakers [billing&#x26;inventory]     $60
fred smith contact:address [billing]     444 main st.
fred smith contact:city [billing]     othertown
fred smith purchases:glasses [billing&#x26;inventory]     $30
fred smith purchases:hat [billing&#x26;inventory]     $20
```

You may have noticed that the timestamp is not displayed. Even though we didn't add one on insert, they are there. Use the -st or --show-timestamps switch to see them:

```
bob jones contact:address [billing] 1425611200186     123 any street
bob jones contact:city [billing] 1425611200286     anytown
```

```
bob jones contact:phone [billing] 1425611200318    555-1212
bob jones purchases:sneakers [billing&#x26;inventory] 1425611200354    $60
fred smith contact:address [billing] 1425611200385    444 main st.
fred smith contact:city [billing] 1425611200417    othertown
fred smith purchases:glasses [billing&#x26;inventory] 1425611200455    $30
fred smith purchases:hat [billing&#x26;inventory] 1425611200488    $20
```

If you want to view just the records for one row ID, use the -r switch. This will limit the results to one row ID:

```
root@miniInstance table1> scan -r "bob jones"
bob jones contact:address [billing]    123 any street
bob jones contact:city [billing]    anytown
bob jones contact:phone [billing]    555-1212
bob jones purchases:sneakers [billing&#x26;inventory]    $60
```

Using Authorizations

By default, the shell scan command will use all of the current user's granted authorizations. Use the -s switch to limit the scan authorizations:

```
root@miniInstance table1> scan -s billing
bob jones contact:address [billing]    123 any street
bob jones contact:city [billing]    anytown
bob jones contact:phone [billing]    555-1212
fred smith contact:address [billing]    444 main st.
fred smith contact:city [billing]    othertown
```

We did not insert any records with only the *inventory* visibility, so you would not see any results using just that authorization.

Using a Simple Iterator

We have briefly discussed Accumulo's iterators. One built-in iterator is the GrepIterator (*http://accumulo.apache.org/1.6/apidocs/index.html?org/apache/accumulo/core/iterators/user/GrepIterator.html*), which searches the key and the value for an exact string match. The shell's grep command sets up this iterator and uses it during the scan:

```
root@miniInstance table1> grep town
bob jones contact:city [billing]    anytown
fred smith contact:city [billing]    othertown
```

Demo of Java Code

Now let's do the same things, but this time using Java code instead of shell commands. The Java code to perform these operations exists in the JavaExample class of *quickstart*. It connects to any specified running Accumulo instance and does not start up its own MiniAccumuloCluster.

For this exercise, leave the Accumulo shell example running, and we will connect to its `MiniAccumuloCluster` using Java code. If you stopped it, restart it with the following command:

```
mvn compile exec:exec -Pshell
```

You will need to know the ZooKeeper and instance information the `ShellExample` used to start up. It is output just before the shell starts up, something like this:

```
---- Initializing Accumulo Shell

Starting the MiniAccumuloCluster in /var/folders/2y/
    n9lzqm2x10lfxqm9n40xvfvw0000gn/T/1425610595980-0
Zookeeper is localhost:11272
Instance is miniInstance
```

We need this information to connect to the running Accumulo instance. To facilitate copying and pasting the following examples, set an environment variable for the Zoo-Keeper port with something like this:

```
export ZKPORT=11272
```

Be sure to use the correct port number.

Creating a Table and Inserting Some Data

Take a look at the *JavaExample.java* file in *src/main/java/com/accumulobook/macexample*. Much of the code is for parsing arguments and selecting which command to run. The relevant code that uses the Accumulo client API will be highlighted here.

All commands that will be run here need to get a reference to the Accumulo Connector (*http://bit.ly/accumulo_connector*). Using the instance name and the location of the running ZooKeeper, the code to get this `Connector` is in the `getConnection()` method of `JavaExample` class. All the `Command` classes extend the `AbstractCommand` class, which provides a `setConnection()` method that the `JavaExample` uses to set each Command's `Connector`. Here is what the code looks like for the `getConnection()` method. The `instance` and `zookeepers` fields are set based on command-line parameters when the code is executed:

```java
public Connector getConnection() throws AccumuloException,
        AccumuloSecurityException {
    Instance i = new ZooKeeperInstance(instance, zookeepers);
    Connector conn = i.getConnector(user, new PasswordToken(password));
    return conn;
}
```

Using this `Connector` inside some Java code, let's create a table. For this part of the quickstart, the table will be called *table2*. From the terminal where you started the shell, you can run the `tables` command, and you should not see a *table2* table. Let's

---

create that table now. In a new terminal window at the *quickstart* directory, run the following:

```
mvn clean compile exec:exec -Dtable.name=table2 -Dinstance.name=miniInstance \
-Dzookeeper.location=localhost:$ZKPORT -Pjava:create
```

Be sure to replace the `instance.name` and `zookeeper.location` values with what was displayed when the `ShellExample` started. If this hangs for more than 15 seconds or so after outputting "Running create command," your ZooKeeper location may be wrong. Once execution is complete, you should be able to run `tables` from the shell in the other window and see *table2*.

The `Connector` has access to `TableOperations`, which is used to perform table operations (see Chapter 4). We use the `createTable()` method to create the table. Here is the code example from the `CreateCommand` `run()` method:

```
public void run() throws AccumuloException, AccumuloSecurityException,
        TableExistsException {
    System.out.println("Creating table " + table);
    if (connection.tableOperations().exists(table)) {
        throw new RuntimeException("Table " + table + " already exists");
    } else {
        connection.tableOperations().create(table);
        System.out.println("Table created");
    }
}
```

On line 3, we check to ensure that the table does not already exist. This is not technically necessary, because a `TableExistsException` will be thrown, but this pattern of checking for existence before creating a table enables us to do something different if we wanted.

Now let's insert some data. As in the shell example, we will do this one row at time. Later, you will see how to batch up inserts, or mutations, and execute them together. Here is the first row. When copying and pasting, remember to change the `instance.name` and `zookeeper.location` values:

```
mvn clean compile exec:exec -Drow.id="bob jones" \
-Dcolumn.family=contact \
-Dcolumn.qualifier=address \
-Dauths=billing \
-Dvalue="123 any street" \
-Dtable.name=table2 \
-Dinstance.name=miniInstance -Dzookeeper.location=localhost:$ZKPORT -Pjava:insert
```

 The `-D` switches are simply setting system properties that get passed to the `JavaExample` class as arguments.

From the shell, you can now change to the *table2* table by running `table table2`, and then you can run `scan`. If your user has the *billing* authorization, you should see the record. If you don't see any records, use `getauths` and `setauths` for the *root* user as we showed earlier to ensure that the *billing* authorization is present.

We will look at how to handle authorizations with Java in the next section.

Again using the `Connector` object, here is the code that inserts data:

```
public void run() throws TableNotFoundException, MutationsRejectedException {
    System.out.println("Writing mutation for " + rowId);
    BatchWriter bw = connection.createBatchWriter(table, new BatchWriterConfig());
    Mutation m = new Mutation(new Text(rowId));
    m.put(new Text(cf), new Text(cq), new ColumnVisibility(auths), timestamp,
        new Value(val.getBytes())));
    bw.addMutation(m);
    bw.close();
}
```

A `BatchWriter` (*http://bit.ly/accumulo_batchwriter*) is created from the `Connector`. A `Mutation` (*http://bit.ly/accumulo_mutation*) is constructed with the row ID for a new key-value pair. There are multiple put methods for `Mutation` with different signatures to define the rest of the key-value pair. The `Mutation` is added to the `BatchWriter`. You could also add multiple mutation objects to a batch writer, which is a more typical usage that saves the overhead of creating a new `BatchWriter` as well as batching together data to amortize network communication overhead. When the batch writer is closed or flushed, the added mutations are sent to Accumulo.

Here are commands you can copy and paste to insert the rest of the sample data. Each of these commands needs the instance name and ZooKeeper location updated. There is also a batch script explained after these commands that may be easier to use:

```
mvn clean compile exec:exec -Drow.id="bob jones" \
-Dcolumn.family=contact \
-Dcolumn.qualifier=city \
-Dauths=billing \
-Dvalue="anytown" \
-Dtable.name=table2 \
-Dinstance.name=miniInstance -Dzookeeper.location=localhost:$ZKPORT -Pjava:insert

mvn clean compile exec:exec -Drow.id="bob jones" \
-Dcolumn.family=contact \
-Dcolumn.qualifier=phone \
-Dauths=billing \
-Dvalue="555-1212" \
-Dtable.name=table2 \
-Dinstance.name=miniInstance -Dzookeeper.location=localhost:$ZKPORT -Pjava:insert

mvn clean compile exec:exec -Drow.id="bob jones" \
-Dcolumn.family=purchases \
```

```
-Dcolumn.qualifier=sneakers \
-Dauths=billing\&inventory \
-Dvalue="\$60" \
-Dtable.name=table2 \
-Dinstance.name=miniInstance -Dzookeeper.location=localhost:$ZKPORT -Pjava:insert

mvn clean compile exec:exec -Drow.id="fred smith" \
-Dcolumn.family=contact \
-Dcolumn.qualifier=address \
-Dauths=billing \
-Dvalue="444 main st." \
-Dtable.name=table2 \
-Dinstance.name=miniInstance -Dzookeeper.location=localhost:$ZKPORT -Pjava:insert

mvn clean compile exec:exec -Drow.id="fred smith" \
-Dcolumn.family=contact \
-Dcolumn.qualifier=city \
-Dauths=billing \
-Dvalue="othertown" \
-Dtable.name=table2 \
-Dinstance.name=miniInstance -Dzookeeper.location=localhost:$ZKPORT -Pjava:insert

mvn clean compile exec:exec -Drow.id="fred smith" \
-Dcolumn.family=purchases \
-Dcolumn.qualifier=glasses \
-Dauths=billing\&inventory \
-Dvalue="\$30" \
-Dtable.name=table2 \
-Dinstance.name=miniInstance -Dzookeeper.location=localhost:$ZKPORT -Pjava:insert

mvn clean compile exec:exec -Drow.id="fred smith" \
-Dcolumn.family=purchases \
-Dcolumn.qualifier=hat \
-Dauths=billing\&inventory \
-Dvalue="\$20" \
-Dtable.name=table2 \
-Dinstance.name=miniInstance -Dzookeeper.location=localhost:$ZKPORT -Pjava:insert
```

The bash script is *quickstart/bin/insert-all.sh*. It runs all these commands for you but allows you to pass in the instance name, ZooKeeper location, and table name values once at the beginning. Run it as follows from the *quickstart* directory, replacing the parameters with the correct values for your running shell:

```
./bin/insert-all.sh miniInstance "localhost:$ZKPORT" table2
```

You can run these mutations multiple times but still end up with only eight key-value pairs. The reason is that Accumulo defaults to keep only the most recent version of each key by configuring the VersioningIterator on every new table. Even if the same data is inserted multiple times, you will only see one version of each key-value pair.

If you don't see eight key-value pairs, check your auths again with `getauths` and make sure you see billing and inventory. Assuming you didn't stop the shell after running the shell demo, *table1* and *table2* should now have exactly the same data.

Scanning for Data

Now let's use some Java code to scan all the rows. Run the following, and all the rows will be printed:

```
mvn clean compile exec:exec -Dtable.name=table2 -Dinstance.name=miniInstance \
-Dzookeeper.location=localhost:$ZKPORT -Pjava:scan
```

You will see output like the following:

```
Running scan command
Scanning table2
Scanning with all user auths
Scanning for all rows
Results ->
  bob jones contact:address [billing] 1425613612825 false 123 any street
  bob jones contact:city [billing] 1425613620377 false anytown
  bob jones contact:phone [billing] 1425613627653 false 555-1212
  bob jones purchases:sneakers [billing&#x26;inventory] 1425613634458 false $60
  fred smith contact:address [billing] 1425613640651 false 444 main st.
  fred smith contact:city [billing] 1425613646562 false othertown
  fred smith purchases:glasses [billing&#x26;inventory] 1425613652640 false $30
  fred smith purchases:hat [billing&#x26;inventory] 1425613659394 false $20
```

Here is the code that is run in the ScanCommand:

```
System.out.println("Scanning " + table);
Authorizations authorizations = null;
if ((null != auths) && (!auths.equals("SCAN_ALL"))) {
    System.out.println("Using scan auths " + auths);
    authorizations = new Authorizations(auths.split(","));
} else {
    System.out.println("Scanning with all user auths");
    authorizations = connection.securityOperations().getUserAuthorizations(user);
}
Scanner scanner = connection.createScanner(table, authorizations);
if ((null != row) && (!row.equals("SCAN_ALL"))) {
    System.out.println("Scanning for row " + row);
    scanner.setRange(new Range(row));
} else {
    System.out.println("Scanning for all rows");
}
System.out.println("Results ->");
for (Entry<Key,Value> entry : scanner) {
    System.out.println("   " + entry.getKey() + " " + entry.getValue());
}
```

On line 10, we create a `Scanner` (*http://accumulo.apache.org/1.6/apidocs/index.html? org/apache/accumulo/core/client/Scanner.html*) object from the `Connector`. This `Scan ner` is what scans Accumulo and returns an `Iterable` of results. We iterate over those results on line 18 and print out the Accumulo `Key` (*http://accumulo.apache.org/1.6/ apidocs/index.html?org/apache/accumulo/core/data/Key.html*) and `Value` (*http://accu mulo.apache.org/1.6/apidocs/index.html?org/apache/accumulo/core/data/Value.html*). The `toString()` method of the `Key` outputs the key's timestamp by default. There is also a `toStringNoTime()` method on `Key` if we want to model the shell example more closely. That is left as an exercise for the reader.

This scan does not limit the results; everything is returned just as in running the `scan` command in the Accumulo shell. Let's see how we could limit the results to just the *bob jones* row. Run the following:

```
mvn clean compile exec:exec -Dtable.name=table2 -Drow="bob jones" \
-Dinstance.name=miniInstance -Dzookeeper.location=localhost:$ZKPORT -Pjava:scan
```

The result will be something like this:

```
Running scan command
Scanning table2
Scanning with all user auths
Scanning for row bob jones
Results ->
  bob jones contact:address [billing] 1425613612825 false 123 any street
  bob jones contact:city [billing] 1425613620377 false anytown
  bob jones contact:phone [billing] 1425613627653 false 555-1212
  bob jones purchases:sneakers [billing&#x26;inventory] 1425613634458 false $60
```

Here we provide `row="bob jones"`, which is passed along to the `run()` method on the `ScanCommand`. Line 13 shows how to provide that information to the `Scanner`, using the `Range` (*http://accumulo.apache.org/1.6/apidocs/index.html?org/apache/accu mulo/core/data/Range.html*) class. Ranges can also be defined in other ways to better limit the results. Review the API documentation for more information. We also cover additional ways to construct key ranges throughout this book, in particular in "Craft-ing Ranges" on page 108.

 This example uses the `createScanner()` method on the `Connector`. This `Scanner` object runs in one thread and hits one range at a time. You can also use the `createBatchScanner()` method, which returns a `BatchScanner` and will scan multiple ranges in parallel. When your data is spread out on many tablet servers, this `BatchS canner` can return results much faster. However, the `BatchScanner` does not guarantee any ordering of the results returned. Your code will have to handle that correctly.

Using Authorizations

As we mentioned before, the shell scan command uses all of the user's authorizations by default. This is a convenience provided by the shell for interactively accessing the data. To make the Java scan example work the same way, we had to do a couple of things. First we set a default value of SCAN_ALL for the auths property used by Scan Command in the *pom.xml* file. This allows us to not pass in -Dauths=*something*. If Scan Command finds that the authorizations are set to the default SCAN_ALL value, it will look up the user's entire set of authorizations and use those for the scan, as is done in the Accumulo shell. On line 8 of the ScanCommand run() method, you see the securityOp erations() method of the Connector used to obtain a SecurityOperations (*http://bit.ly/accumulo_securityoperations*) object. From this object, we use the getUserAutho rizations() method to obtain an Authorizations (*http://bit.ly/accumulo_auths*) object that contains all the user's authorizations. Alternatively, if we explicitly pass in auths for ScanCommand, it will provide them to the string array constructor of Author izations on line 5. In either case, the Authorizations object is used when creating a Scanner on line 10.

As we did in the shell demo, let's scan for just records with the *billing* authorization. Run the following:

```
mvn clean compile exec:exec -Dtable.name=table2 -Dauths=billing \
  -Dinstance.name=miniInstance -Dzookeeper.location=localhost:$ZKPORT -Pjava:scan
```

You should get results like these:

```
Running scan command
Scanning table2
Using scan auths billing
Scanning for all rows
Results ->
  bob jones contact:address [billing] 1425613612825 false 123 any street
  bob jones contact:city [billing] 1425613620377 false anytown
  bob jones contact:phone [billing] 1425613627653 false 555-1212
  fred smith contact:address [billing] 1425613640651 false 444 main st.
  fred smith contact:city [billing] 1425613646562 false othertown
```

Here, the results are limited to records that could be viewed using only the *billing* authorization.

Using a Simple Iterator

The last thing we want to show in Java code is how to set up an iterator. The shell example used the built-in GrepIterator. We will do the same here. To run the example, use the following, again replacing the instance name and ZooKeeper location as appropriate:

```
mvn clean compile exec:exec -Dtable.name=table2 -Dterm=town \
-Dinstance.name=miniInstance -Dzookeeper.location=localhost:$ZKPORT -Pjava:grep
```

Your results should look like this:

```
Running grep command
Grepping table2
Results ->
  bob jones contact:city [billing] 1425613620377 false anytown
  fred smith contact:city [billing] 1425613646562 false othertown
```

The Java code is similar to the scan example, but instead of setting up a range, we add the GrepIterator to the Scanner. Here is the code:

```
System.out.println("Grepping " + table);
Authorizations authorizations = connection.securityOperations()
    .getUserAuthorizations(user);
Scanner scanner = connection.createScanner(table, authorizations);
Map<String, String> grepProps = new HashMap<String, String>();
grepProps.put("term", term);
IteratorSetting is = new IteratorSetting(25, "sample-grep",
    GrepIterator.class.getName(), grepProps);
scanner.addScanIterator(is);
System.out.println("Results ->");
for (Entry<Key,Value> entry : scanner) {
    System.out.println("  " + entry.getKey() + " " + entry.getValue());
}
```

The authorizations are set up on line 2 just as in the SCAN_ALL case for the ScanCom mand. The scanner is created the same way also, shown on line 3. But on line 6, we construct an IteratorSetting (*http://bit.ly/iteratorsetting*) using a GrepIterator and map of properties that set the term to be the value we passed in, *town* in this case. The 25 in the constructor is the priority of this iterator. The "sample-grep" string is a unique name for the iterator that will be used as a key to group together the iterator's configuration information in ZooKeeper (its priority, class, and options). Line 7 shows how the IteratorSetting is added to the Scanner. Looping over results is just as was shown in the ScanCommand.

Iterator names must be unique within a table and iterator scope. So must iterator priorities. More on iterator configuration can be found in "Iterators" on page 209.

A More Complete Installation

Although the quickstart example using the MiniAccumuloCluster will get you started quickly, that installation doesn't start several components, such as the monitor. The Hadoop installation is minimal, so you do not get a chance to learn any of those tools.

The `MiniAccumuloCluster` is really more suitable for starting up Accumulo and using it for testing.

So if `MiniAccumuloCluster` is not what most developers use, what is the best way to get a development environment set up? Most developers use a full installation, either on one node or in small cluster with virtual machines (VMs) or on a service like Amazon EC2. Typically that requires going through the process of installing Hadoop, ZooKeeper, and Accumulo individually. This can be a daunting task if you have no experience with any of these components.

Instead of providing a VM image for you to use, we decided to facilitate setting up a one-node install. The advantages of not using a preconfigured VM are better performance and more flexibility. A full installation, even on one node, will allow you to shut down Accumulo and save the data. The rest of this book will assume you are using a full installation.

To get a more complete installation, we are going to use the quickinstall project from the book's GitHub site (*https://github.com/accumulobook/quickinstall*). This project will download all the necessary components, install and configure them, and then start everything up for you. To use the quickinstall, you need to build it yourself or download the bundle from *http://accumulobook.com/quickinstall*. The file is over 170 MB, but includes full installs of Accumulo, Hadoop, and ZooKeeper.

 This quickinstall has only been tested on Linux and Mac OS X. Getting the full stack, particularly Hadoop, to run on Windows is more difficult.

If you would like to build it yourself, clone the project with:

```
git clone https://github.com/accumulobook/quickinstall
```

Then run:

```
mvn clean package
```

This will also download the installs of Accumulo, Hadoop, and ZooKeeper, so be patient. The resulting *tar.gz* in the target directory is what has been uploaded to *http://accumulobook.com/quickinstall*.

Open a new terminal window and extract that file with `tar tzf`. Then change into the *quickinstall-home* directory. Run the install with the following:

```
./bin/install
```

If the install fails, the error messages should be helpful for resolving issues. Follow the instructions and rerun the install script after fixing whatever was wrong. If you have previously attempted to install Hadoop, make sure there are no HADOOP_* environment variables already set up in your environment. The quickinstall and other example commands will not work otherwise.

This script configures Hadoop, formats the NameNode, and then starts HDFS and YARN. An attempt is made to use native libraries for Hadoop. It then configures Zoo-Keeper and starts it. Lastly, the script configures Accumulo, runs its initialization, and then starts it. An attempt is made to build the Accumulo native libraries using Accumulo's own script. Accumulo's manual and API documentation are also included.

Let's look at the *quickinstall-home* directory when the installation is complete:

accumulo-1.6.1
> Contains the Accumulo installation

hadoop-2.4.1
> Contains the Hadoop installation

zookeeper-3.4.6
> Contains the ZooKeeper installation

hdfs
> The directory where Hadoop stores data

zk-data
> The directory where ZooKeeper stores data

Also in *quickinstall-home* is a *bin* directory with some helper scripts:

- Quickinstall helpers

  quickinstall-env
  > Sets up the environment variables

  qi-start
  > Starts Hadoop, ZooKeeper, and Accumulo

  qi-stop
  > Stops Accumulo, Hadoop, and ZooKeeper

- Documentation helpers

  hadoop-doc
  > Opens the local copy of Hadoop's documentation

accumulo-doc
> Opens the local copy of Accumulo's documention

Both Hadoop and Accumulo as packaged contain documentation and API docs you can use. Running the `quickinstall-env` command will set up some environment variables and make sure your path contains the correct location for Hadoop, Zoo-Keeper, and Accumulo.

After the install, everything should be running. It is a self-contained environment and everything should be under the *quickinstall-home* directory. The benefit of this is that you can stop everything, remove that directory, and reinstall if needed.

You can verify everything is running with this command:

```
jps -lm
```

This command should show you processes that include the following:

- Hadoop processes

```
org.apache.hadoop.hdfs.server.datanode.DataNode
org.apache.hadoop.hdfs.server.namenode.NameNode
org.apache.hadoop.hdfs.server.namenode.SecondaryNameNode
org.apache.hadoop.yarn.server.nodemanager.NodeManager
org.apache.hadoop.yarn.server.resourcemanager.ResourceManager
```

- ZooKeeper process

```
org.apache.zookeeper.server.quorum.QuorumPeerMain
```

- Accumulo processes

```
org.apache.accumulo.start.Main gc --address localhost
org.apache.accumulo.start.Main master --address localhost
org.apache.accumulo.start.Main monitor --address localhost
org.apache.accumulo.start.Main tracer --address localhost
org.apache.accumulo.start.Main tserver --address localhost
```

To start up an Accumulo shell, first run:

```
source bin/quickinstall-env
```

 If things were not running, you could run `qi-start` to start Hadoop, ZooKeeper, and then Accumulo after sourcing *quickinstall-env*. When you want to stop everything, run `qi-stop`. Accumulo and Hadoop both include *start-all.sh* scripts, which can be confusing. The scripts provided with quickinstall start and stop all the processes you will need. Inspect `qi-start` and `qi-stop` to see how to start processes separately.

Now you need to run the main `accumulo` command, which is located in *quickinstall-home/accumulo-1.6.1/bin*. This is the main entry point for working with Accumulo from the command line. It will be on your path if you sourced the *quickinstall-env* script. Let's run the shell:

```
accumulo shell -u root -p secret
```

This will start the shell you saw in the shell example. Try out some of the commands, such as `tables`. You should only see the *accumulo.root*, *accumulo.metadata*, and *trace* tables, which are internal tables we discuss more in "Metadata Table" on page 379 and "Using Tracing" on page 481, respectively.

Let's get set up to run the `insert` and `scan` commands with Java code again. We will handle the table creation and granting authorizations to the *root* user in the shell. Create a table named *table3*:

```
createtable table3
```

Now ensure that the *root* user has *billing* and *inventory* authorizations:

```
setauths -u root -s "billing,inventory"
```

Once that is complete, we will use a script similar to the *./bin/insert-all.sh* script from the Java example. However, this script will use not use Maven to execute the `JavaExample` class; instead, it will run it directly. You will need to use Maven to build a JAR by executing the following from the *examples/quickstart* directory:

```
mvn package
```

Go back to the terminal window were you checked out the book's source code. From the *examples/quickstart* directory, source the *quickinstall-env* script from the *quickinstall-home/bin* directory where the quickinstall is running to set up the environment for the running cluster. Now run the `JavaExample` using the `accumulo` command:

```
source PATH_TO_QUICKINSTALL_HOME/bin/quickinstall-env
accumulo -add $PWD/target/mini-accumulo-cluster-example-0.0.1-SNAPSHOT.jar \
com.accumulobook.macexample.JavaExample
```

You should be presented with the default usage from the `JavaExample` class, explaining all the options:

```
Error: The following options are required: -i, --instance -z, --zookeepers -p,
  --password -u, --user
Usage: <main class> [options] [command] [command options]
  Options:
  * -i, --instance
       Accumulo instance name
  * -p, --password
       Accumulo user password
  * -u, --user
```

```
            Accumulo user
     * -z, --zookeepers
          Comma-separated list of zookeepers
    Commands:
      create        Usage: create [options]
           Options:
           * -t, --table
                 Table name to create

   insert       Usage: insert [options]
       Options:
         -a, --auths
            ColumnVisiblity expression to insert with data
       * -cf, --columnFamily
            Column Family to insert
       * -cq, --columnQualifier
            Column Qualifier to insert
       * -r, --rowid
            Row Id to insert
       * -t, --table
            Table to scan
       * -val, --value
            Value to insert

   scan        Usage: scan [options]
       Options:
         -a, --auths
            Comma separated list of scan authorizations
         -r, --row
            Row to scan
       * -t, --table
            Table to scan

   grep        Usage: grep [options]
       Options:
       * -t, --table
            Table to scan
       *     --term
            Term to grep for in table
```

Using the accumulo command along with the -add option is the easiest and cleanest way to run Java programs with a classpath already set up for your Accumulo installation.

Now let's insert the first key-value pair:

```
accumulo -add $PWD/target/mini-accumulo-cluster-example-0.0.1-SNAPSHOT.jar \
com.accumulobook.macexample.JavaExample \
-i accumulo -z localhost:2181 -u root -p secret \
insert -r "bob jones" -t table3 -cq contact -cf address \
-val "123 any street" -a billing
```

 For this example, we used the Accumulo instance name and the ZooKeeper location from the quickinstall. This is the normal way to connect to a running Accumulo instance.

From the Accumulo shell where you installed and ran the quickinstall, run the `scan` command. When you ran the `createtable table3` command, the Accumulo shell put in `table3`, which you can see in the prompt:

```
root@accumulo table3> scan
bob jones address:contact [billing]    123 any street
```

The other insert commands are in the *./bin/insert-all2.sh* file back in the *examples/ quickstart* terminal. You can either copy and paste the commands from this file into the terminal, including the variables that are set up, or you can just run the *insert- all2.sh* script:

```
./bin/insert-all2.sh
```

The output should look like this:

```
Running insert command
Writing mutation for bob jones
Running insert command
Writing mutation for bob jones
Running insert command
Writing mutation for bob jones
Running insert command
Writing mutation for bob jones
Running insert command
Writing mutation for fred smith
Running insert command
Writing mutation for fred smith
Running insert command
Writing mutation for fred smith
Running insert command
Writing mutation for fred smith
```

Once the data is inserted, let's use the shell to scan to make sure we can see all the data. This time, let's run the shell with the -e switch to pass in an Accumulo command. This will exit the shell after the command finishes and dump the output back to STDOUT. First, from the Accumulo shell window, type **exit** to get out of the shell. We will now use the -e switch to pass in a command for the shell to execute. For that reason, our `scan` command needs to use the -t switch to specify which table to scan. Using command-line execution with the Accumulo shell is a useful technique, because you can then use all the regular Unix tools such as `grep`, `sed`, and `cut`:

```
accumulo shell -u root -p secret -e "scan -t table3"
```

Assuming the data was inserted and your Accumulo user authorizations include billing,inventory, the output should look like this:

```
bob jones address:contact [billing]     123 any street
bob jones city:contact [billing]     anytown
bob jones phone:contact [billing]     555-1212
bob jones sneakers:purchases [billing&#x26;inventory]     $60
fred smith address:contact [billing]     444 main st.
fred smith city:contact [billing]     othertown
fred smith glasses:purchases [billing&#x26;inventory]     $30
fred smith hat:purchases [billing&#x26;inventory]     $20
```

Eight lines should be returned. You could count the lines manually, or you could pipe the last command though wc -l:

```
accumulo shell -u root -p secret -e "scan -t table3 -st" | wc -l
```

If you don't get all eight, revisit the previous commands and make sure the records have been inserted correctly and that your authorizations are configured properly.

Now run the following to execute the same scan with the JavaExample command. You must be either be in the terminal within the *examples/quickstart* directory or modify the location of the JAR to an absolute path:

```
accumulo -add $PWD/target/mini-accumulo-cluster-example-0.0.1-SNAPSHOT.jar \
com.accumulobook.macexample.JavaExample \
-i accumulo -z localhost:2181 -u root -p secret scan -t table3
```

The output should be:

```
Running scan command
Scanning table3
Scanning with all user auths
Scanning for all rows
Results ->
  bob jones address:contact [billing] 1425654249954 false 123 any street
  bob jones city:contact [billing] 1425654251454 false anytown
  bob jones phone:contact [billing] 1425654252921 false 555-1212
  bob jones sneakers:purchases [billing&#x26;inventory] 1425654254414 false $60
  fred smith address:contact [billing] 1425654255892 false 444 main st.
  fred smith city:contact [billing] 1425654257394 false othertown
  fred smith glasses:purchases [billing&#x26;inventory] 1425654258824 false $30
  fred smith hat:purchases [billing&#x26;inventory] 1425654260287 false $20
```

The result should be the same as from scanning in the earlier example. Try limiting the results by row:

```
accumulo -add $PWD/target/mini-accumulo-cluster-example-0.0.1-SNAPSHOT.jar \
com.accumulobook.macexample.JavaExample \
-i accumulo -z localhost:2181 -u root -p secret scan -t table3 -r "bob jones"
```

The output should be:

```
Running scan command
Scanning table3
Scanning with all user auths
Scanning for row bob jones
Results ->
  bob jones address:contact [billing] 1425654249954 false 123 any street
  bob jones city:contact [billing] 1425654251454 false anytown
  bob jones phone:contact [billing] 1425654252921 false 555-1212
  bob jones sneakers:purchases [billing&#x26;inventory] 1425654254414 false $60
```

Now try limiting the results by authorizations:

```
accumulo -add $PWD/target/mini-accumulo-cluster-example-0.0.1-SNAPSHOT.jar \
com.accumulobook.macexample.JavaExample \
-i accumulo -z localhost:2181 -u root -p secret scan -t table3 -a billing
```

The output should be:

```
Running scan command
Scanning table3
Using scan auths billing
Scanning for all rows
Results ->
  bob jones address:contact [billing] 1425654249954 false 123 any street
  bob jones city:contact [billing] 1425654251454 false anytown
  bob jones phone:contact [billing] 1425654252921 false 555-1212
  fred smith address:contact [billing] 1425654255892 false 444 main st.
  fred smith city:contact [billing] 1425654257394 false othertown
```

For a last exercise, try running the grep example:

```
accumulo -add $PWD/target/mini-accumulo-cluster-example-0.0.1-SNAPSHOT.jar \
com.accumulobook.macexample.JavaExample \
-i accumulo -z localhost:2181 -u root -p secret grep -t table3  --term town
```

The output should be:

```
Running grep command
Grepping table3
Results ->
  bob jones city:contact [billing] 1425654251454 false anytown
  fred smith city:contact [billing] 1425654257394 false othertown
```

Other Important Resources

We have seen how to interact with Accumulo both in the shell and in code. Another important tool for interacting with Accumulo is the monitor page. Assuming your quickinstall is still running, visit *http://localhost:50095*. We will not discuss the monitor page in detail here, but feel free to click around and look at the different information it provides. More details about the monitor are at "Monitor" on page 377.

Another important tool is the logfiles. For the quickinstall, these are located in *quickinstall-home/accumulo-1.6.1/logs*. The Accumulo processes we listed with the `jps` command each has its own log. The logs are prefixed with *gc, master, monitor, master,* or *tserver*. By default, Accumulo configures a *.log* and *.debug.log* for each process, with the latter logging everything at a log level of DEBUG.

One Last Example with a Unit Test

We talked about the `MiniAccumuloCluster` being good for unit testing. There is an example named *Example.java* in the *examples/quickstart/main/java/com/accumulo-book/macexample* directory. It is a bit of a contrived example, but it has no knowledge of the `MiniAccumuloCluster`. Instead it just knows about the instance name, Zoo-Keeper location, and root password, and uses those to connect to an Accumulo instance. The *ExampleTest.java* test starts up a `MiniAccumuloCluster` and then uses the instance name, ZooKeeper location, and root password from that to construct a new `Example`. Methods on this instance of `Example` are then tested against the `MiniAccumuloCluster`, as if it were a full Accumulo instance. You may have noticed that a unit test was executed when you ran `mvn package` earlier. This *ExampleTest.java* was the test that ran. Feel free to run `mvn test` and study the output.

Additional Resources

- Main Apache Accumulo page (*http://accumulo.apache.org*)
- Official Accumulo documentation (*http://bit.ly/accumulo_manual*)
- Javadocs (*http://accumulo.apache.org/1.6/apidocs*)
- Downloads (*http://accumulo.apache.org/downloads/*)
- Source code (*http://bit.ly/accumulo_source*)
- GitHub mirror (*https://github.com/apache/accumulo*)
- Mailing list information (*http://bit.ly/accumulo_lists*)
- Issues/Jira (*http://bit.ly/accumulo_jira*)
- Build server (*http://bit.ly/accumulo_build_server*)
- Latest GitHub projects (*http://bit.ly/accumulo_github*)

## CHAPTER 3

Basic API

Accumulo is designed to support building applications that support huge numbers of simultaneous users, handling a large number of write, update, and read requests by providing highly scalable, low-latency, random access to data in tables. These tables can be designed to support Internet applications that serve data to and receive data from millions of users around the world. In addition, Accumulo provides capabilities well suited to keeping a large amount of data organized for the purposes of analysis, and for delivering analytical results to many users of varying access levels.

The Java client API is the primary method of getting data into and out of Accumulo tables. Applications can be written in Java or other JVM-based languages using the provided client library or in non-JVM–based languages by using the Thrift proxy.

Applications typically need to perform three tasks: getting data into Accumulo, applying any necessary transformations to existing data to map to the Accumulo data model, and performing scans against Accumulo tables to satisfy user requests.

Many Accumulo clients are deployed as part of a web application, allowing users to perform interactive requests for information stored in Accumulo tables, although this is certainly not a requirement. Some clients provide access to information in Accumulo to other services.

When you design an application on the Accumulo API, you should consider a few questions that will assist in determining how to write the application, how the data should be organized within one or more Accumulo tables, and ideally, what level of performance to expect.

These considerations are all equally important.

The first thing to consider when creating an application on Accumulo is simply what activities the application will carry out on behalf of the user. The questions to answer include but are not limited to:

- Does the application capture information provided by the user?
- Are there semantic rules governing relationships in the information managed?
- Does data need to be updated?

In particular, attention should be paid to the *access patterns* that the application requires. The term *access pattern* refers to how the user wants to access the data. For example, users may need to retrieve information about books based on the title, and at other times, by the author, and at other times, both. Knowing what information users know and how they will use that to find out information they don't know will help guide the design of tables and rule out designs that will not perform well.

The second thing to consider are the data characteristics of the data that is managed by Accumulo, including questions such as:

- Does the data already exist or is it being created by the user via the application, or both?
- If some data already exists, in what format is it currently stored?
- Is combining two or more existing data sets required? If so, is the way they should be combined known beforehand?
- At what rate will data arrive?
- What sensitivities exist within the data?
- What groups of users will need access to which parts of the data?

The third consideration in application design is *performance*. Applications must handle requests quickly enough to satisfy business or mission requirements, in the context of large amounts of data and large numbers of users. We discuss performance in depth in Chapter 13.

Development Environment

To begin writing Java applications for Accumulo, obtain the Accumulo Java library. Information on developing applications in other languages is described in "Thrift Proxy" on page 236.

Obtaining the Client Library

The latest Accumulo Java client library can be obtained from the official site (*http://accumulo.apache.org/downloads*). If you are using Maven to manage project dependencies, no special repositories need to be added to the Maven *settings.xml* file.

Using Maven

To see if Maven is installed, type `mvn -version`. If the Maven version is not 3.0.4 or greater, download and install it from *http://maven.apache.org*. To add Accumulo as a dependency for a Maven project, add the following to the dependencies section of the *pom.xml* file:

```
<dependency>
  <groupId>org.apache.accumulo</groupId>
  <artifactId>accumulo-core</artifactId>
  <version>1.6.0</version>
</dependency>
```

Run `mvn clean package` to create a JAR, or use the appropriate Maven goals for the project.

Using Maven with an IDE

Several IDEs include built-in support for Maven that makes development easier:

Eclipse
> If you're using Eclipse, you might need to install a plug-in for Maven support (*http://maven.apache.org/eclipse-plugin.html*).

NetBeans (http://wiki.netbeans.org/Maven)
> Comes with Maven support.

IntelliJ IDEA (http://bit.ly/intellij_idea)
> Comes with Maven support.

Configuring the Classpath

Bundling up the Accumulo dependencies with a client JAR is discouraged, because it can make debugging difficult later. A better way to handle dependencies is to configure the classpath properly. The *accumulo-core*, *accumulo-trace*, and ZooKeeper JARs are ones that are likely to be needed on the classpath. Commons and log4j JARs may also be necessary. To run a MapReduce job, dependencies must be passed to the MapReduce child processes using the `-libjars` parameter. Accumulo comes with scripts that configure the classpath and libjars (if applicable) for standalone or MapReduce jobs. The usage for these scripts follows:

Standalone
```
bin/accumulo -add jarFile className args
```

MapReduce
```
bin/tool.sh jarFile className args
```

Introduction to the Example Application: Wikipedia Pages

Basic Accumulo applications often begin with a data set and some things we want to do with that data. For the purposes of introducing readers to the Accumulo API, we're going to use the data from Wikipedia. We'll write an application to load this data and to query it, with the goal of allowing users to explore the information contained within it in various ways.

Wikipedia Data

Wikipedia is a collection of over 30 million articles in 287 languages, including 4.3 million in English, written by volunteers. Articles contain free-form text and associated *metadata* including title, timestamps, contributor information, and references to other articles and sources.

You can download a snapshot (*http://dumps.wikimedia.org/enwiki/latest/*) of the English Wikipedia articles. In addition to one file containing all the articles (*enwiki-latest-pages-articles.xml.bz2*), it is possible to download files containing just a portion of the articles with filenames like *enwiki-latest-pages-articles1.xml-p000000010p000010000.bz2*. Alternatively, a specific set of pages can be downloaded via the Special Export option (*http://en.wikipedia.org/wiki/Special:Export*).

The data is stored in XML format. The body of the articles is in the MediaWiki markup format, developed specifically for Wikipedia.

An abbreviated example of an article is as follows:

```
<mediawiki xmlns="http://www.mediawiki.org/xml/export-0.10/"
  xmlns:xsi="http://www.w3.org/2001/XMLSchema-instance"
  xsi:schemaLocation="http://www.mediawiki.org/xml/export-0.10/
    http://www.mediawiki.org/xml/export-0.10.xsd" version="0.10" xml:lang="en">
<siteinfo>
<sitename>Wikipedia</sitename>
<dbname>enwiki</dbname>
<base>http://en.wikipedia.org/wiki/Main_Page</base>
<generator>MediaWiki 1.25wmf14</generator>
<case>first-letter</case>
<namespaces>
<namespace key="-2" case="first-letter">Media</namespace>
...
<namespace key="2600" case="first-letter">Topic</namespace>
```

```
</namespaces>
</siteinfo>
<page>
<title>Apache Accumulo</title>
<ns>0</ns>
<id>34571412</id>
<revision>
<id>637313466</id>
<parentid>631046295</parentid>
<timestamp>2014-12-09T12:33:13Z</timestamp>
<contributor>
<username>Frap</username>
<id>612852</id>
</contributor>
<model>wikitext</model>
<format>text/x-wiki</format>
<text xml:space="preserve" bytes="5554">
...
'''Apache Accumulo''' is a computer software project that developed a
sorted, distributed key/value store based on the [[Bigtable]] technology
from [[Google]].<ref>[http://accumulo.apache.org/ Apache Accumulo].
Accumulo.apache.org. Retrieved on 2013-09-18.</ref> It is a system
built on top of [[Apache Hadoop]], [[Apache ZooKeeper]], and [[Apache
Thrift]].
...
</text>
<sha1>dzr6dhn3hlq22aalz44g8g8abo15qm4</sha1>
</revision>
</page>
</mediawiki>
```

As an example of using the API, we'll parse these articles and write them to Accumulo. First we'll devise a way of mapping the data to the Accumulo data model into one or more tables. Next we'll ingest the data using parts of the Accumulo Java client API. Finally, we'll write some code to allow users to query these tables in various ways.

Data Modeling

Instead of formulating questions as database queries, application designers should break questions into scan operations—ideally as few of them as possible per user request. To start getting used to this way of thinking, it is a good idea to begin application design with a single table. Additional tables can be added to the application if it is determined that they are necessary to support additional access patterns.

When deciding how to represent data in Accumulo, developers face one of two challenges: either creating a new *schema* that allows them to model the data they will be creating, or mapping existing data conforming to an existing schema to the Accumulo data model in a way that supports the access patterns required.

A Quick Overview of Data Modeling

Data modeling is a task that involves identifying the structure of a concept to be represented in a system and defining its representation within the system. It is often performed at many levels and in many ways. A *schema* is a description of the structure in data.

A particular schema can be represented in various ways when stored in different systems. For example, one could define the concept of an *address* to be made up of a street number, a city name, a state, a zip code. An address such as this is composed of four named elements and has a specific meaning to a particular application. For this reason, this schema could be considered a *semantic* or *conceptual* data model. Conceptual models can be represented in several formats, or *logical* models.

For example, one might represent or *map* a particular address to the JSON format as follows:

```
{
  street: '123 any street',
  city: 'anytown',
  state: 'CA',
  zipCode: 90210
}
```

Or as XML:

```
<records>
  <address>
    <street required=true>123 any street</street>
    <city>anytown</city>
    <state>CA</state>
    <zip code>90210</zip code>
  </address>
</records>
```

In other places one might represent an address as a table, such as in a relational database.

JSON, XML, and two-dimensional tables can be thought of as logical methods of capturing a conceptual model in a particular way for a particular purpose. In fact, many applications make use of several logical data models to represent the same conceptual data in various places. For example, an application may retrieve some rows from a relational database representing a user's profile and deserialize them as a programmatic object in memory, and then convert the programmatic object to JSON before sending it to a web browser.

Accumulo has its own logical model as well, consisting of multidimensional keys and simple values. We cover the elements of the data model in "Data Model" on page 13.

The final type of data model is a *physical model*. A physical model describes how data elements are stored or transmitted in some physical medium. An example of a physical model is a B-Tree file for relational databases or the RFile file format used by Accumulo.

In some systems there are more than three levels of abstraction. The number of levels required depends on the complexity of the system. Additional levels of abstraction can help in keeping each individual level simple and manageable.

The Accumulo data model is again included in Figure 3-1 as a convenient reminder during our modeling task.

Key			Value
row ID	Column	Timestamp	

Figure 3-1. Basic Accumulo key structure

As in any key-value system, if one knows the key, the associated value can be found very quickly. With a single Accumulo table we should store the information that an application will use to perform lookups in elements within the Accumulo key, and the information to be retrieved in the value. To start, we'll create a table that allows users to specify an article title and retrieve the text or associated metadata. The way we'll map Wikipedia data to the Accumulo data model is as described in Table 3-1.

Table 3-1. One method for storing Wikipedia articles in Accumulo

Row ID	Column family	Column qualifier	Column visibility	Value
page title	contents		*contents visibility*	*page contents*
page title	metadata	id	*id visibility*	*id*
page title	metadata	namespace	*namespace visibility*	*namespace*
page title	metadata	revision	*revision visibility*	*revision*
page title	metadata	timestamp	*timestamp visibility*	*timestamp*

Here we're storing the timestamp of each Wikipedia article under a column called *timestamp*. This should not be confused with the timestamp that is part of each key, which will be provided by the tablet servers and used to keep track of when each key-value pair was written.

We'll put our code to do this in the `WikipediaIngest` class. Our client code will produce this table in Accumulo based on a Wikipedia XML dump file:

```
Alternate Olympics contents: []      refimprove \x0AIn artistic gymnasti ...
Alternate Olympics metadata:id []    15713865
Alternate Olympics metadata:namespace []
Alternate Olympics metadata:revision []    7328338
Alternate Olympics metadata:timestamp []    2013-04-09T08:05:05Z
Ancient Olympic Games contents: []      pp-protected  for \x0A pp-move  ...
Ancient Olympic Games metadata:id []    19098431
Ancient Olympic Games metadata:namespace []
Ancient Olympic Games metadata:revision []    5207008
Ancient Olympic Games metadata:timestamp []    2013-08-19T10:52:07Z
Arena X-Glide contents: []      \x0AArena X-Glide is a swimsuit made ...
Arena X-Glide metadata:id []    23781846
Arena X-Glide metadata:namespace []
Arena X-Glide metadata:revision []    7328338
Arena X-Glide metadata:timestamp []    2012-09-24T15:35:39Z
...
```

As we introduce the API we'll return to this example to illustrate how the parts of the API fit into a broader application.

Obtaining Example Code

Code for the examples we describe here can be downloaded from *https://github.com/ accumulobook/examples*.

Before building, we need to put one JAR that is not available in any public repo into our local Maven repo (see "Traversing the Example Twitter Graph" on page 326 for another example using the Ubigraph library (*http://ubietylab.net/ubigraph/*)):

```
mvn install:install-file -Dfile=lib/ubigraph-0.2.4.jar -DgroupId=org.ubiety \
    -DartifactId=ubigraph -Dversion=0.2.4 -Dpackaging=jar
```

The examples can be built via Maven:

```
mvn clean compile
```

The examples ending in *Example.java* can be run from within an IDE or from the command line without setting up an external Accumulo cluster.

To run an example from the command line, use the following:

```
mvn exec:java -Dexec.mainClass="com.accumulobook.[package].[Example]" \
    -Dexec.args="argument"
```

All of these classes use the `MiniAccumuloCluster` class discussed in Chapter 2. The `MiniAccumuloCluster` is a single process that stores data to a temporary directory on disk that is deleted when the instance is shut down.

In these classes you will see:

```
Connector conn = ExampleMiniCluster.getConnector();
```

That code can be replaced with the following code to execute against an actual Accumulo instance like the quickinstall:

```
String instanceName = "your_instance";
String zooKeepers = "your_zoo_server_1:port,your_zoo_server_2:port";

Instance instance = new ZooKeeperInstance(instanceName, zooKeepers);

Connector conn = instance.getConnector("your_username",
    new PasswordToken("your_password"));
```

Downloading Sample Wikipedia Pages

It is convenient to be able to work with a sample set of Wikipedia pages. These can be downloaded via the Special Export API.

For example, to download a set of pages from the *Hadoop* category one can use the `curl` command as follows:

```
curl -d "" "http://en.wikipedia.org/w/index.php?title=Special:Export\
&pages=Cloudera%0AApache_HBase%0AApache_ZooKeeper%0AApache_Hive\
%0AApache_Mahout%0AMapR%0AHortonworks%0AApache_Accumulo%0ASqoop\
%0AApache_Hadoop%0AOozie%0ACloudera_Impala%0AApache_Giraph%0AApache_Spark\
&action=submit" > hadoopPages.xml
```

In some of our examples we'll use the equivalent of this `curl` command in Java. The `WikipediaPagesFetcher` class will do this for us.

Downloading All English Wikipedia Articles

A dump of all e=English Wikipedia articles (*http://bit.ly/english_lang_wikipedia*) is available. The dump will consist of a single large XML file. The XML contains metadata about each article and the article contents, marked up in the WikiMedia format. The full dump can be somewhat large.

Our examples use the bliki (*https://code.google.com/p/gwtwiki*) library to parse these files.

We'll first introduce the basic API for reading and writing data. Then we'll work through an example of modeling data from Wikipedia, providing ways to add data from our application and access information.

Connect

The Accumulo client API begins with an `Instance` object, which describes a particular Accumulo cluster. An Accumulo instance is uniquely identified by a set of ZooKeeper servers and an instance name. A single set of ZooKeeper servers can manage multiple Accumulo instances, so the Accumulo instance name is required:

```
String instanceName = "accumulo_instance";
String zooKeepers = "zoo_server_1:port,zoo_server_2:port";

Instance instance = new ZooKeeperInstance(instanceName, zooKeepers);
```

Both data-specific and administrative actions are handled through an Accumulo `Connector` object. The `Connector` is obtained from an `Instance` object:

```
String principal = "user_name";
AuthenticationToken token = new PasswordToken("password");

Connector connector = instance.getConnector(principal, token);
```

For more information on providing credentials, see "Authentication" on page 176.

Connectors are used primarily to obtain other objects required to read and write data, namely, `BatchWriter`, `Scanner`, and `BatchScanner`. They can also be used to perform administrative actions through the `tableOperations()`, `securityOperations()`, and `instanceOperations()` methods. Connectors can be shared by multiple threads.

The following sections illustrate how to use the objects obtained from a `Connector` to read and write data.

Insert

Writing data into Accumulo is accomplished by creating a `Mutation` object and adding it to a `BatchWriter`.

A `Mutation` encapsulates a set of changes to a single row. The changes can be either *puts* or *deletes*. We'll address deletes later. All the changes within a single mutation can be applied atomically, meaning they either succeed or fail as a group. This is because a row is always fully contained within a single tablet, which is always assigned to exactly one tablet server.

This makes it easy for applications to make concurrent updates to a row without worrying about mutations being partially applied:

```
String rowId = "Article_Title";
String metadataColFam = "metadata";
String authorColQual = "author";
Value authorValue = new Value("Joe Jones".get());
```

```
Mutation m = new Mutation(rowId);
m.put(metadataColFam, authorColQual, authorValue);
```

Note that column families do not have to be declared to exist before they are specified in a mutation. In addition, column families and column qualifiers are allowed to be empty `String` objects or byte arrays. There are multiple incarnations of the `put()` method that allow specifying more or fewer parts of the key. For example, we could also specify a `ColumnVisibility` object as part of our put:

```
String rowId = "Article_Title";
String metadataColFam = "metadata";
String authorColQual = "author";
ColumnVisibility publicColVis = new ColumnVisibility("public");
Value authorValue = new Value("Joe Jones".get());

Mutation m = new Mutation(rowId);
m.put(metadataColFam, authorColQual, publicColVis, authorValue);
```

We can also specify a timestamp, although this is generally discouraged. They do not have to represent time and can be used to store logical version numbers of keys, but when using custom timestamps applications are entirely responsible for managing versions through insert, update, and delete operations.

Unlike all other components of the key, timestamps are stored as Java `Longs` and are sorted in descending order:

```
String rowId = "Article_Title";
String metadataColFam = "metadata";
String authorColQual = "author";
ColumnVisibility publicColVis = new ColumnVisibility("public");
Long timestamp = System.currentTimeMillis();
Value authorValue = new Value("Joe Jones".get());

Mutation m = new Mutation(rowId);
m.put(metadataColFam, authorColQual, publicColVis, timestamp, authorValue);
```

Multiple puts can be applied to a single mutation. Each of these puts will insert new data for the column specified:

```
String rowId = "Article_Title";

String metadataColFam = "metadata";
String authorColQual = "author";
Value authorValue = new Value("Joe Jones".get());

String pageIdColQual = "pageid";
Value pageIdValue = new Value("54321".get());

Mutation m = new Mutation(rowId);
m.put(metadataColFam, authorColQual, authorValue);
m.put(metadataColFam, pageIdColQual, pageIdValue);
```

A single mutation will be converted into multiple key-value pairs, one for each unique column mutated (Figure 3-2). Unless specified in the client, all the key-value pairs for a mutation will receive the same timestamp from the tablet server.

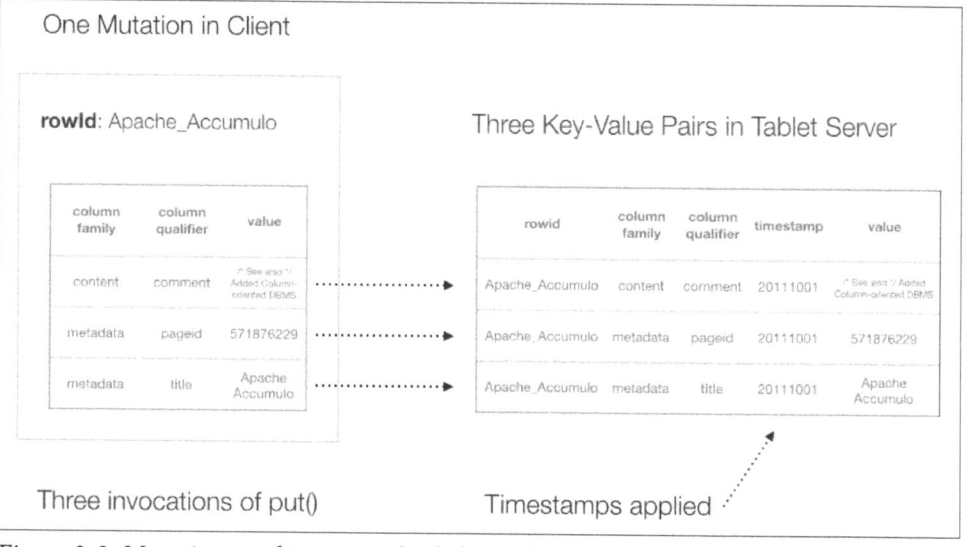

Figure 3-2. Mutation resulting in multiple key-value pairs

 put() should be called only once per column to be manipulated, because having multiple key-value pairs with the same row Id, column components, and timestamp will result in one of those key-value pairs being arbitrarily picked to be kept by the server.

Strings Versus Byte Arrays

In these examples we use String objects for elements of the key. The advantage of using String objects is that they are human-readable and the sort order is relatively apparent. However, these don't have to be Strings. When supplied with String objects the Key class automatically converts them to UTF-8–encoded byte arrays.

For some applications, other objects can be serialized to byte arrays. When doing this, keep in mind that Accumulo will compare two byte arrays by comparing one byte at a time. If this doesn't result in the sort order desired, the serialization process can be manipulated to produce byte arrays that do sort properly.

Value objects of course are not sorted and also store byte arrays. This makes it possible to store binary or other data without worrying about having to escape certain characters.

When storing serialized objects other than `Strings`, it is possible to create a custom `Formatter` for displaying the objects in a human-readable way so that key-value pairs can be inspected in the shell. We discuss custom `Formatters` in "Human-Readable Versus Binary Values and Formatters" on page 311.

In general, the elements within keys should be relatively small. Keeping the total key size under a megabyte will allow Accumulo to efficiently process many keys simultaneously during reads and writes in memory.

In Accumulo 1.6, there is a `Constraint` configured on all new tables that rejects mutations if they contain keys larger than 1 MB. We discuss configuring tables in Chapter 4.

Recall that values are stored as byte arrays and are not sorted as the elements of the key are. Values can contain more data than the elements of the key can but should still be kept within a reasonable size for tablet servers to process, because they will read data from tables on disk into memory in order to retrieve them for clients.

Values in practice can be used to store an incredibly wide variety of data. Accumulo will never interpret the bytes unless an application configures a table to do so explicitly. As such, the information contained in a value is completely up to the discretion of the application.

We discuss some best practices in techniques for creating values in "Designing Values" on page 307.

Committing Mutations

Once we have one or more mutations we want to apply to a table, we can commit them by adding them to a `BatchWriter`. `BatchWriters` will efficiently group mutations into batches based on the way tablets are assigned to tablet servers in order to minimize the network overhead involved in sending mutations to tablet servers:

```
BatchWriterConfig config = new BatchWriterConfig()
  .setMaxMemory(MAX_MEMORY)
  .setMaxLatency(LATENCY, TimeUnit.MILLISECONDS)
  .setMaxWriteThreads(THREADS);

BatchWriter bw = connector.createBatchWriter("table name", );

...
bw.addMutation(m);

...
bw.close();
```

Typical values for these parameters are:

Max Memory
> 1000000 (1 million bytes or roughly 1 MB)

Max Latency
> 1000 (1 thousand milliseconds)

Max Write Threads
> 10

 Application developers should always tune the `BatchWriter` parameters to obtain the best performance on their particular data.

The size of batches a `BatchWriter` uses is controlled via the *Max Memory* setting. Giving a `BatchWriter` more memory allows the `BatchWriter` to group more mutations together before sending them over the network.

Max Latency determines how long a `BatchWriter` will wait before sending mutations that do not comprise a full batch. This is so mutations don't end up waiting a long time for a full batch to be created.

Most clients can experiment with these parameters to achieve the throughput and maximum latency they need.

The `BatchWriter` provides a `flush()` method that can be used to ensure that all mutations that haven't been sent are sent. This usually does not need to be called and can significantly degrade performance if used extensively, because it will defeat the `BatchWriter`'s attempts to amortize network overhead. One possible use of `flush()` is to aid in synchronizing writes between two or more tables.

Here is a simple example of code in a client application that calls `flush()` on a `Batch Writer` every 1,000 mutations, in order to ensure that all writes thus far were committed successfully:

```
class MyIngestClient {

    private BatchWriter bw = connector.createBatchWriter("table name", );
    private int totalWritten = 0;
    ...

    public void writeData(Mutation m) throws MutationsRejectedException {
        bw.add(m);
        totalWritten++;

        if(totalWritten % 1000 == 0)
```

```
      bw.flush();
  }

  ...
  public void shutdown() throws MutationsRejectedException {
    bw.close();
  }
}
```

We'll talk about handling that `MutationsRejectedException` in the next section.

The `close()` method should be used to send any remaining mutations and shut down the write threads when a `BatchWriter` is no longer needed. Simply allowing Java to garbage-collect the `BatchWriter` object can cause the final batches to be sent and threads to close, but explicitly calling `close()` is a better practice.

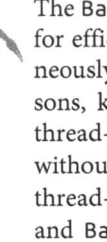 **Thread Safety**

The `BatchWriter` and `BatchScanner` create their own thread pools for efficiently communicating with multiple tablet servers simultaneously. If an application has more than one thread for other reasons, keep in mind that `Connector` and `BatchWriter` objects are thread-safe, in that they can be shared and used by multiple threads without synchronization. But `Scanner` and `BatchScanner` are *not* thread-safe—each thread should obtain and use its own `Scanner` and `BatchScanner` instances or else use them in a synchronized manner so that only one thread is accessing them at a time. `Batch Writer` and `BatchScanner` instances should be closed via `close()` when no longer needed.

Handling Errors

The Accumulo client automatically handles errors related to the automatic failover from one tablet server to another. This frees up the application designer to focus on the logic of the application rather than having to write the code to retry inserts.

Accumulo assumes that client applications do care to know that all mutations have been successfully applied. If for some reason a mutation fails, the Accumulo client will throw a `MutationsRejectedException`.

A mutation can fail for several reasons:

- Mutations contained `ColumnVisibility` instances that the submitting user was not authorized to write if configured—see "Authorizations" on page 183.
- Mutations violated one or more `Constraints` configured for the table.
- A persistent server failure prevented the write from succeeding.

- Other unknown errors.

Each of these types of failures can be *permanent* or *transient*. A permanent failure means that a particular mutation is simply not allowed to be written to the table, according to `Constraints` currently configured. Simply retrying to commit these mutations will not work, because the mutations violate some rule and will never be allowed to be written.

If `getAuthorizationFailuresMap()` or `getConstraintViolationSummaries()` returns any elements, then there are permanent failures. Applications that receive exceptions in these cases should report the situation to the user or developer, because it is likely that there is either some malformed data, a security problem, or a bug.

Transient failures, on the other hand, can succeed if the application tries to commit them again. `getErrorServers()` can return a list of servers that the automatic retries failed to write to. Applications can choose to retry indefinitely, or to fail and report the error to the user or administrators.

Finally, any other errors are simply counted and are available via `getUnknownExceptions()`.

The type of failure that caused the `MutationsRejectedException` to be thrown can be obtained from the exception object:

```
try {
  bw.addMutation(m);
  bw.close();
} catch (MutationsRejectedException ex) {

  // ---] Permanent failures [----

  // mapping of keyextent mappings to SecurityErrorCode
  Map<KeyExtent, Set<SecurityErrorCode>> authFailuresMap =
    ex.getAuthorizationFailuresMap();
  if(authFailuresMap.size() > 0) {
    // retrying will fail. log any recently added mutations
    for(Entry<KeyExtent, Set<SecurityErrorCode>> extent :
        authFailuresMap.entrySet()) {
      ...
    }
  }

  // list of constraint violations
  if(ex.getConstraintViolationSummaries().size() > 0) {
    // retrying will fail. log any recently added mutations
    for(ConstraintViolationSummary summary :
        ex.getConstraintViolationSummaries()) {
      ...
    }
  }
```

```
// ----] Transient failures [----

// A list of servers that had internal errors when mutations were written
// optionally log
// optionally retry
Collection<String> errorServers = ex.getErrorServers();
...

// the number of unknown other errors
// log and possibly retry
int numUnknown = ex.getUnknownExceptions();
...
}
```

The exact mutations that were rejected are not reported. Future versions of Accumulo may make it easier to identify particular problems with individual mutations. For now, applications can keep track of recently added mutations in order to log them in the event of persistent errors, or to retry them in the case of transient failures.

If no exceptions are thrown by a `BatchWriter` when calling `flush()` or `close()`, an application can be assured that all mutations added to that `BatchWriter` have been persisted to Accumulo's write-ahead log on disk, and at that point even a single server or single rack failure should not result in any lost data.

So far we've only covered simple inserts. Next, we'll examine reading data, and then revisit other operations possible in mutations, including updates and deletes.

Note that this application is essentially defining the structure or schema of the table. By default Accumulo does not place restrictions on what column families and column qualifiers may be used, or on the structure of the row ID. This means that clients that write data must be coupled with clients that read data. In practice they can simply be the same client, but if they are separate, care must be taken to ensure that clients reading tables are either kept in sync with clients that write, or that they can dynamically discover and handle changes to the table. This can be done, for example, by ignoring additional columns and only scanning for known columns, or by treating the contents of rows as dynamic.

Insert Example

For our Wikipedia data, we'll be creating one row per article. Our parser will give us a Java object called `WikipediaArticle` containing the information for one article.

Because we have all the information we need about an article in one object, we'll map the elements of each article to various columns in one mutation and submit them to a `BatchWriter`.

This code is from the example code provided at the GitHub repository mentioned in "Obtaining Example Code" on page 88. We include the full classnames of these examples for ease of reference:

```
Mutation m = new Mutation(article.getTitle().replace(" ", "_"));

String wikitext = article.getText();
String plaintext = model.render(converter, wikitext)
    .replace("{{", " ")
    .replace("}}", " ");

m.put("contents", "", plaintext);
m.put("metadata", "namespace", article.getNamespace());
m.put("metadata", "timestamp", article.getTimeStamp());
m.put("metadata", "id", article.getId());
m.put("metadata", "revision", article.getRevisionId());

writer.addMutation(m);
```

To run an example that creates the *WikipediaArticles* table, downloads some Wikipedia articles, and inserts them into the table, run the following command in the Accumulo example code directory:

```
$ mvn clean compile
$ mvn exec:java -Dexec.mainClass="com.accumulobook.basic.WikipediaIngestExample"
```

This will start up a `MiniAccumuloCluster`, download and ingest a set of Wikipedia articles in the *Hadoop* category into a table called *WikipediaArticles*, and start up a shell for examining the data. You should see output similar to the following:

```
$ mvn exec:java -Dexec.mainClass="com.accumulobook.basic.WikipediaIngestExample"
[INFO] Scanning for projects...
[INFO]
...

Parsing articles ...
Parsing Cloudera
Parsing Apache HBase
Parsing Apache ZooKeeper
Parsing Apache Hive
Parsing Apache Mahout
Parsing MapR
Parsing Hortonworks
Parsing Apache Accumulo
Parsing Sqoop
Parsing Apache Hadoop
Parsing Oozie
Parsing Cloudera Impala
Parsing Apache Giraph
Parsing Apache Spark
done.
starting shell ...
```

```
Shell - Apache Accumulo Interactive Shell
-
- version: 1.6.0
- instance name: miniInstance
- instance id: xxxxxxxx
-
- type 'help' for a list of available commands
-
root@miniInstance> table WikipediaArticles
root@miniInstance WikipediaArticles> scan

Apache_Accumulo contents: []      Infobox software Apache Accumulo is a computer
    software project ...
Apache_Accumulo metadata:id []     34571412
Apache_Accumulo metadata:namespace []
Apache_Accumulo metadata:revision []     6640499
Apache_Accumulo metadata:timestamp []     2014-01-22T05:32:03Z
Apache_Giraph contents: []      Infobox Software \x0AApache Giraph is an Apache
    project to perform graph processing on big data. ...
Apache_Giraph metadata:id []     37752641
Apache_Giraph metadata:namespace []
Apache_Giraph metadata:revision []     604610728
Apache_Giraph metadata:timestamp []     2014-04-17T16:12:43Z
----hit any key to continue or 'q' to quit ----
root@miniInstance WikipediaArticles> quit
```

Using Lexicoders

In our example, we are storing simple `Strings` in our key elements. It is possible to store other values as well, because key elements are simply byte arrays, but ensuring that different types sort properly can be a challenge.

Accumulo provides a set of helper classes, called Lexicoders, to aid in converting objects of various types into byte arrays that preserve the native sort order.

Lexicoders have two methods, `encode()` and `decode()`, used to process a single object of a specified type. For example, the `DateLexicoder` takes a `Date` instance and returns a byte array that will sort properly when inserted as part of a key in an Accumulo table:

```
DateLexicoder dateLexicoder = new DateLexicoder();

byte[] dateBytes = dateLexicoder.encode(new Date());
```

A Lexicoder can also decode bytes it has encoded to retrieve the original object:

```
Date date = dateLexicoder.decode(dateBytes);
```

Lexicoders can even be used to store composite types, such as lists and pairs. To store a list of three `Double` objects in a row ID, we can use the `ListLexicoder`:

```
List<Double> threeDimCoord = new ArrayList<>();
threeDimCoord.add(9.0);
threeDimCoord.add(2.0);
threeDimCoord.add(7.0);

ListLexicoder<Double> coordCoder = new ListLexicoder<>();
byte[] coordBytes = coordCoder.encode(threeDimCoord);
```

We discuss using Lexicoders when reading data in "Crafting Ranges" on page 108 and when using indexes in "Using Lexicoders in indexing" on page 290.

Writing to Multiple Tables

Often applications will want to write data to multiple tables. It is possible to simply have multiple `BatchWriters`, each writing to a different table (Figure 3-3).

In these cases, it can be more efficient to use a `MultiTableBatchWriter` to allow mutations destined for tablets that belong to different tables, but that are hosted on the same tablet server, to be combined when sent over the network (Figure 3-4). This reduces network overhead and increases throughput. It also makes memory management simpler.

Little needs to change in code to make use of the `MultiTableBatchWriter`. We first create the `MultiTableBatchWriter` and then get individual `BatchWriter` objects from it, one for each table being written to. `Mutations` are added to the `BatchWriter` corresponding to the table they belong in.

Here's an example of creating two separate `BatchWriters`:

```
BatchWriterConfig conf = new BatchWriterConfig();

writer1 = conn.createBatchWriter("table1", conf);
writer2 = conn.createBatchWriter("table2", conf);
...
writer1.close();
writer2.close();
```

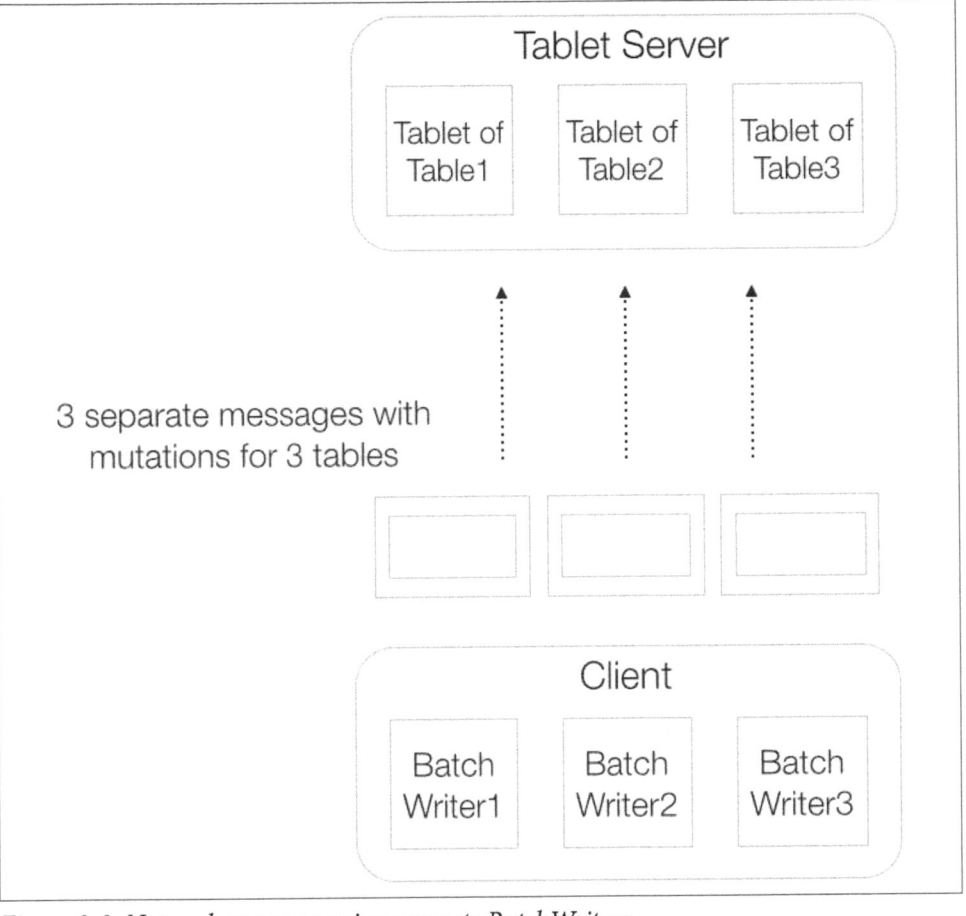

Figure 3-3. Network messages using separate BatchWriters

And here's an example using the `MultiTableBatchWriter`:

```
BatchWriterConfig conf = new BatchWriterConfig();

MultiTableBatchWriter multiTableBatchWriter =
    conn.createMultiTableBatchWriter(conf);

writer1 = multiTableBatchWriter.getBatchWriter("table1");
writer2 = multiTableBatchWriter.getBatchWriter("table2");
...
multiTableBatchWriter.close();
```

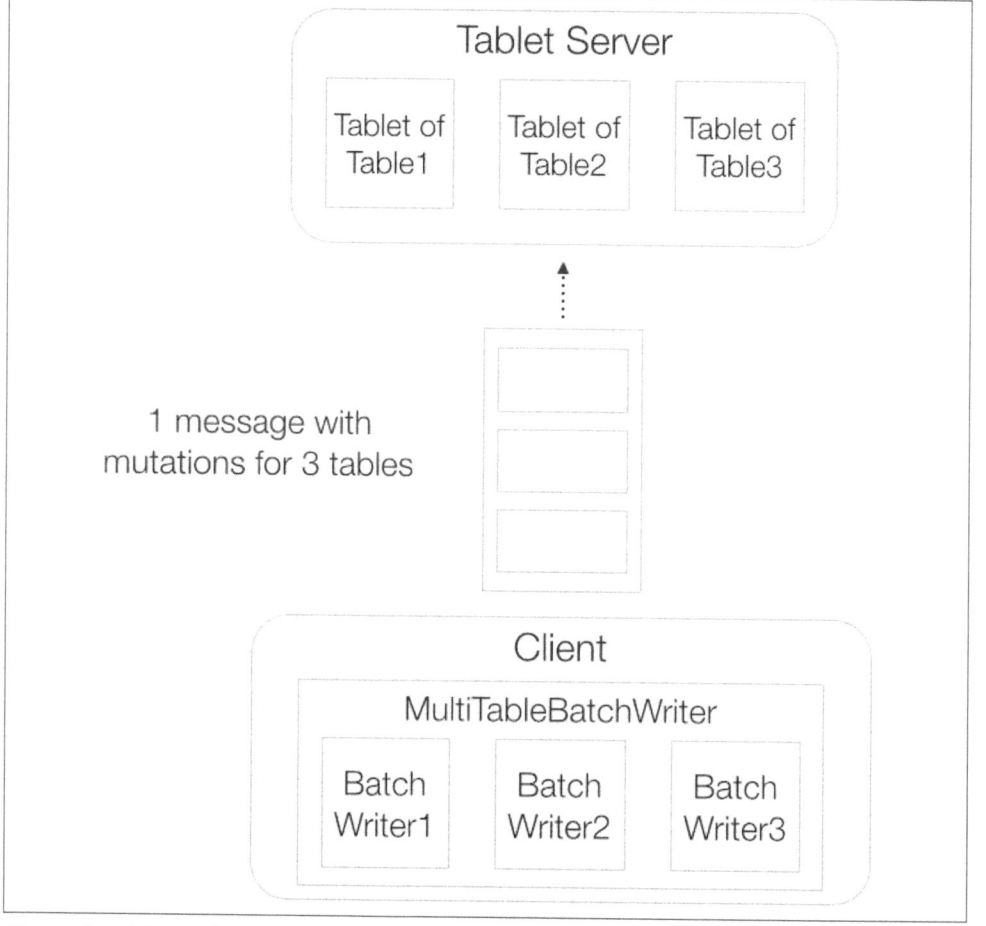

Figure 3-4. Network messages using MultiTableBatchWriter

Also note that the `MultiTableBatchWriter` has its own `flush()` and `close()` methods, which will cause any pending mutations to be written, regardless of which `Batch Writer` they were added to. This can aid in keeping two or more tables in sync by allowing the client to write a set of mutations to multiple tables and consider them all committed upon successful return, or to handle the `MutationsRejectedException` thrown by either the `flush()` or `close()` method.

We describe an example that uses the `MultiTableBatchWriter` when discussing secondary indexing in "Using MultiTableBatchWriter for consistency" on page 284.

Lookups and Scanning

Reading data from Accumulo is accomplished with a `Scanner`. A `Scanner` returns data via implementing the Java `Iterator` interface over key-value pairs. By default a `Scanner` will return key-value pairs starting at the beginning of a table and eventually will return all key-value pairs.

To create a `Scanner`, simply specify the table over which to scan and provide an `Authorizations` object representing the authorizations of the user. We discuss the `Authorizations` object in depth in "Authorizations" on page 183. For now we'll assume that all data is visible:

```
Scanner scanner = connector.createScanner("table_name", new Authorizations());
for (Entry<Key,Value> entry : scanner) {

  Key k = entry.getKey();
  Value v = entry.getValue();


  ...
}
```

All the elements of the key can be obtained from the `Key` object:

```
Key k = entry.getKey();

Text row = k.getRowID();

Text colFam = k.getColumnFamily();

Text colQual = k.getColumnQualifier();

ColumnVisibility colVis = k.getColumnVisibility();

Long ts = k.getTimestamp();
```

To specify a range of keys to scan over, use the `setRange()` method of `Scanner`:

```
Scanner scanner = connector.createScanner("table_name", new Authorizations());
Range r = new Range(startKey, endKey);
scanner.setRange(r);

for (Entry<Key,Value> entry : scanner) {
  ...
}
```

We can scan over the contents of one row by setting a `Range` on the `Scanner` consisting of one row ID (Figure 3-5):

```
Scanner scanner = connector.createScanner("table_name", new Authorizations());
Range r = new Range("Apache_Hadoop");
scanner.setRange(r);
```

```
for (Entry<Key,Value> entry : scanner) {
  ...
}
```

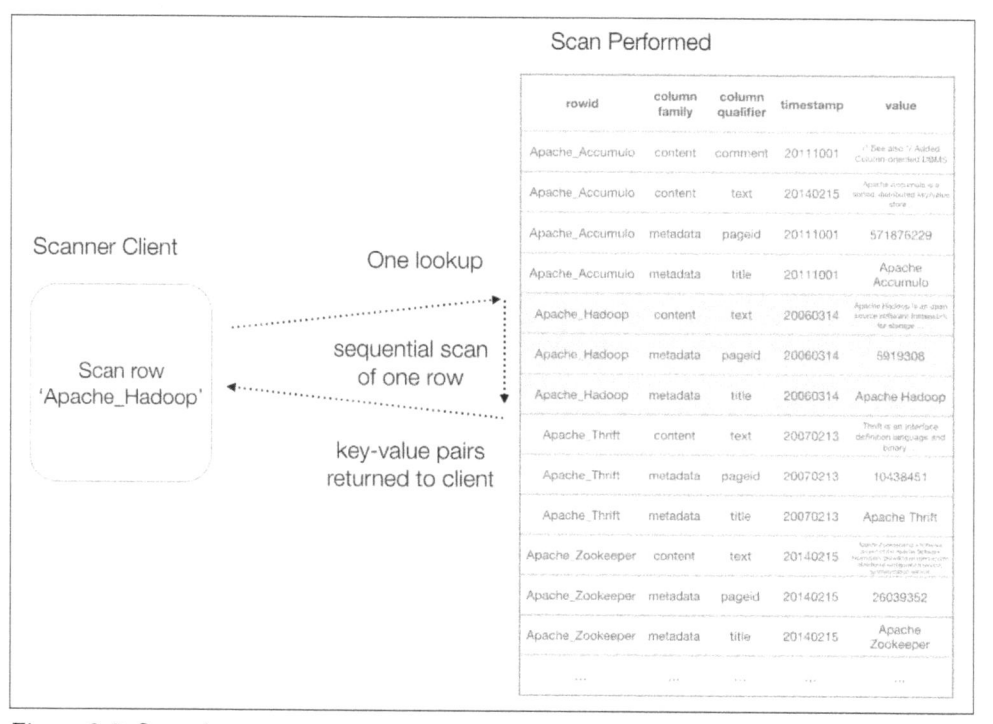

Figure 3-5. Scanning one row

We can also scan the whole table for only a particular column (Figure 3-6):

```
Scanner scanner = connector.createScanner("table_name", new Authorizations());
scanner.fetchColumn(new Text("metadata"), new Text("title"));

for (Entry<Key,Value> entry : scanner) {
  ...
}
```

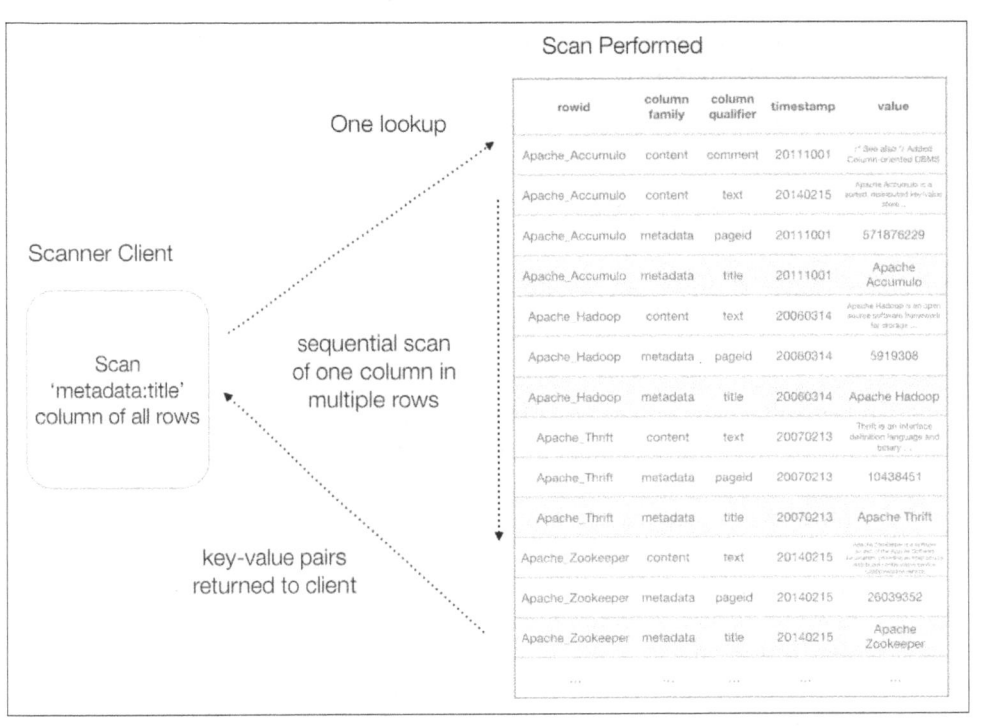

Scan Performed

rowid	column family	column qualifier	timestamp	value
Apache_Accumulo	content	comment	20111001	(* See also *) Added Column-oriented DBMS
Apache_Accumulo	content	text	20140215	Apache Accumulo is a sorted, distributed key-value store ...
Apache_Accumulo	metadata	pageid	20111001	571876229
Apache_Accumulo	metadata	title	20111001	Apache Accumulo
Apache_Hadoop	content	text	20060314	Apache Hadoop is an open source software framework for storage ...
Apache_Hadoop	metadata	pageid	20060314	5919308
Apache_Hadoop	metadata	title	20060314	Apache Hadoop
Apache_Thrift	content	text	20070213	Thrift is an interface definition language and binary ...
Apache_Thrift	metadata	pageid	20070213	10438451
Apache_Thrift	metadata	title	20070213	Apache Thrift
Apache_Zookeeper	content	text	20140215	...
Apache_Zookeeper	metadata	pageid	20140215	26039352
Apache_Zookeeper	metadata	title	20140215	Apache Zookeeper
...	...	...	...	...

One lookup

Scanner Client

Scan 'metadata:title' column of all rows

sequential scan of one column in multiple rows

key-value pairs returned to client

Figure 3-6. Scanning one column

Note that this will cause tablet servers to retrieve but skip over all the other columns present. If an application often needs to retrieve a single column or a particular subset of columns in a scan, a feature called *locality groups* can be used to minimize the data that has to be read from disk and skipped over. We discuss locality groups in "Locality Groups" on page 138.

A Scanner can have only one Range specified but can have any number of columns or column families configured. By default, if fetchColumn() and fetchColumnFamily() have not been called, a Scanner will return all columns it finds.

Calling fetchColumnFamily() will return all columns within the specified family. fetchColumn() expects both the column family and column qualifier to be specified.

> An empty String, "", or an empty byte array stored in a column family or column qualifier are treated as valid identifiers. This means we can request a key with a column family "example" and column qualifier "" and the Scanner will only return key-value pairs for which the column family is "example" and the column qualifier is "".

Here is an example of scanning for one row, returning a specific column and all columns within a specific family:

```
Scanner scanner = connector.createScanner("table_name", new Authorizations());
Range r = new Range("Apache_Hadoop");
scanner.setRange(r);
scanner.fetchColumn(new Text("metadata"), new Text("title"));
scanner.fetchColumnFamily(new Text("content"));

// returns the title and any data under the 'content' column family
for (Entry<Key,Value> entry : scanner) {
  ...
}
```

Note that key-value pairs come streaming into the client according to the Java Iterator interface design. Accumulo does not load up all the columns and values for a particular row into memory simultaneously, unless a client is configured to do so. HBase and some other data stores may present more of a row-oriented API. Accumulo does provide a wrapper for a scanner that lets the client iterate over rows (see "Grouping by Rows" on page 110), while still iterating over individual key-value pairs within each row to avoid loading an entire row into memory. For an example of how to load discrete rows into a data structure in client memory and retrieve specific columns from those structures, see "WholeRowIterator example" on page 229 on using the WholeRowIterator.

Lookup Example

In our Wikipedia example, we can retrieve all the information for a given article title via a simple scan. To do so we create a Scanner on our *WikipediaArticles* table and set it to scan over a range that encompasses one row.

We then print out components of the key-value pairs we retrieve:

```
Scanner scanner = conn.createScanner(WikipediaConstants.ARTICLES_TABLE, auths);

// attempt to read one article
scanner.setRange(new Range(articleTitle));

for (Map.Entry<Key, Value> entry : scanner) {
  Key key = entry.getKey();
  String field;
  if (key.getColumnFamily().toString().equals("contents")) {
    field = "contents";
  } else {
    field = key.getColumnQualifier().toString();
  }

  String valueString = new String(entry.getValue().get());
  System.out.println(field + "\t" + valueString);
}
```

We can also choose to scan only the *metadata:revisions* column for all articles:

```
Scanner scanner = conn.createScanner(WikipediaConstants.ARTICLES_TABLE, auths);

// scan one column from all rows
scanner.fetchColumn(new Text(columnFamily), new Text(columnQualifier));

for (Map.Entry<Key, Value> entry : scanner) {
  Key key = entry.getKey();

  String valueString = new String(entry.getValue().get());
  System.out.println(key.getRow().toString() + "\t" + valueString);
}
```

The `WikipediaClient` class contains an example of doing both of these things. It will start up a `MiniAccumuloCluster`, ingest Wikipedia articles from the Hadoop category, and perform these scans.

The example can be run in the example code directory via the following:

```
$ mvn clean compile
$ mvn exec:java -Dexec.mainClass="com.accumulobook.basic.WikipediaLookupExample"
[INFO] Scanning for projects...
...
Parsing articles ...
Parsing Cloudera
...
Parsing Apache Spark
done.

Printing out one article:
--------------
contents  Infobox software Apache Accumulo is a computer software project
    ...
id 34571412
namespace
revision 6640499
timestamp  2014-01-22T05:32:03Z

Printing out one column:
--------------
Apache_Accumulo  6640499
Apache_Giraph  604610728
Apache_HBase 5925038
Apache_Hadoop  12010884
Apache_Hive  612679440
Apache_Mahout  618938594
Apache_Spark 14011316
Apache_ZooKeeper 618486465
Cloudera 615986938
Cloudera_Impala  14508071
Hortonworks  615116461
MapR 21911013
```

```
Oozie    605458201
Sqoop    19309860
```

Crafting Ranges

The Range class has a variety of helpful constructors and utility methods to create a range covering all keys that match portions of a given key exactly.

To obtain all values in all columns for a specific row:

```
Range oneRow = Range.exact("Apache_Hadoop");
```

This is equivalent to:

```
Range oneRow = new Range("Apache_Hadoop");
```

as was used earlier to scan one row.

To get all values for a specific row and column family:

```
Range oneRowOneFamily = Range.exact("Apache_Hadoop", "metadata");
```

To get the value for a specific row, column family, and column qualifier (Figure 3-7):

```
Range oneKey = Range.exact("Apache_Hadoop", "metadata", "title");
```

This will usually return only one value unless the table's versioning settings have been altered from the default or unless there happen to be more than one column visibility for this key.

To get a key with a specific column visibility:

```
Range oneKey = Range.exact("Apache_Hadoop", "metadata", "title", "public");
```

To get the value for a fully specified key:

```
Range oneValue = Range.exact("row_0", "column_family_1", "column_qualifier_2",
    "column_visibility_3", 1234567890l);
```

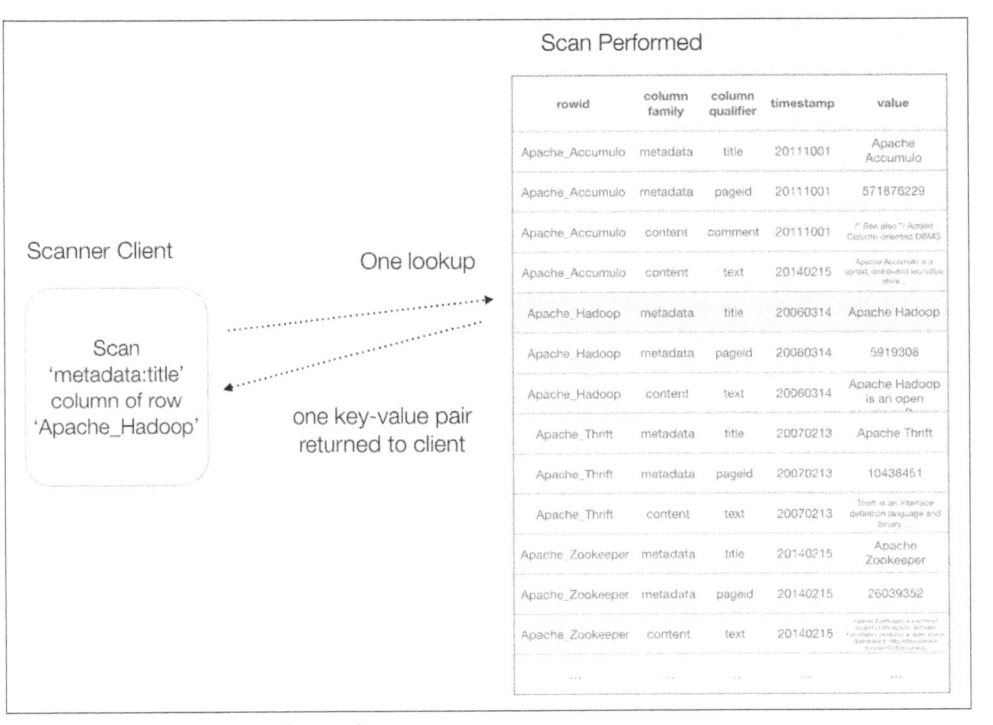

Figure 3-7. Scanning one key-value pair

Similarly, there are utility methods to create a range covering all keys that match a given prefix:

```
// all values in rows that begin with 'Apache_'
Range.prefix("Apache_");

// all values in column families in the 'Apache_Hadoop' row that begin with 'meta'
Range.prefix("Apache_Hadoop", "meta");

// all values in column qualifiers in the 'Apache_Hadoop' row
// in the 'metadata' column family that begin with 'page'
Range.prefix("Apache_Hadoop", "metadata", "page");

// all values in the 'Apache_Hadoop' row, 'metadata' column family,
// and 'pageid' column qualifier that have a column visibility
// beginning with 'pub'
Range.prefix("Apache_Hadoop", "metadata", "pageid", "pub");
```

For example, suppose our *WikipediaArticles* table contains the following keys:

```
Whitaker
White
Whitehouse
Whitewash
Whiz
```

To scan over all the keys that begin with the word *white*—sometimes signified with a wildcard in search systems as *white**—we can obtain the right Range via the following:

```
Range whiteRange = Range.prefix("White");
```

To get a set of Range instances that correspond to the way a tablet is split into tablets, the splitRangeByTablets() method can be used. This can be used to break a long range into multiple ranges according to the split points within a table. This is typically not needed but is used in situations such as a MapReduce job when various clients are assigned to process all the data per tablet:

```
int maxSplits = 100;

Set<Range> ranges = connector.tableOperations()
    .splitRangeByTablets(tableName, givenRange, maxSplits)
```

If you're using Lexicoders to encode row IDs or columns in mutations, you should use the same Lexicoders when creating Range objects for use in scanners.

For example, if we have stored our row IDs using the IntegerLexicoder, we should again use the IntegerLexicoder when specifying start or stop rows in a Range. Because Lexicoders return byte arrays, we'll wrap them in a Text object when creating a Range:

```
Integer start = -26;
Integer stop = 105;

IntegerLexicoder ilex = new IntegerLexicoder();

Range range = new Range(new Text(ilex.encode(start)),
    new Text(ilex.encode(stop)));
```

See "Using Lexicoders in indexing" on page 290 for using Lexicoders in Ranges when scanning secondary indexes.

Grouping by Rows

For scanning over a range that spans multiple rows, a Java Iterator over key-value pairs might not be the most convenient way to process those rows. The application would have to determine for itself when one row ends and another begins. To assist with this, Accumulo provides a wrapper that groups key-value pairs by row. The Row Iterator constructor takes either a Java Iterator or Iterable over Entry<Key,Value>>, so it is easy to use with an Accumulo Scanner. The RowIterator itself implements the Iterator<Iterator<Entry<Key,Value>>> interface:

```
// passing a Scanner to RowIterator
RowIterator rowIterator = new RowIterator(connector.createScanner("table_name",
    new Authorizations()));
while (rowIterator.hasNext()) {
```

```
    Iterator<Entry<Key,Value>> row = rowIterator.next();
    while (row.hasNext()) {
      Entry<Key, Value> kv = row.next();
    }
  }
}

// passing scanner.iterator() to RowIterator
Iterator<Iterator<Entry<Key,Value>>> rowIterator2 =
  new RowIterator(scanner.iterator());
```

Reusing Scanners

Scanners return a new `Iterator` when the `iterator()` method is called. The `Iterator` that is returned is a separate object from the `Scanner`, and any changes in the `Scanner` will not affect any existing `Iterators` already retrieved.

For example, we could set the range of a `Scanner` and configure it to fetch a particular column. Calling `iterator()` will instantiate the scan:

```
Scanner scanner = new Scanner("table_name", new Authorizations());
scanner.setRange(new Range("Apache_Hadoop"));
scanner.fetchColumn(new Text("metadata"), new Text("title"));

Iterator<Entry<Key,Value>> titleIter = scanner.iterator();
```

We could then change some settings on the `Scanner`, such as the set of columns to fetch, while leaving other settings intact. Calling `iterator()` again would return a new `Iterator` object, separate from the `Iterator` already retrieved:

```
...
scanner.clearColumns();
scanner.fetchColumn(new Text("metadata"), new Text("pageid"));

Iterator<Entry<Key,Value>> pageIdIter = scanner.iterator();
```

Isolated Row Views

By default, `Scanners` can retrieve key-value pairs that are parts of a mutation currently being applied. To ensure that `Scanners` see rows containing only the results of fully completed mutations, the `enableIsolation()` method can be applied to a `Scanner`:

```
Scanner scanner = new Scanner("table_name", new Authorizations());
scanner.setRange(new Range("Apache_Hadoop"));
scanner.enableIsolation();

for (Entry<Key,Value> entry : scanner) {
  ...
}
```

Note that using a `Scanner` in isolation mode is only necessary if consistent reads of multiple columns of each row are required. Scans for only one column per row will not benefit from isolation mode.

A Note on Isolation

Students of relational databases may recognize the *isolation* property as the *I* in the ACID acronym. Wikipedia defines *isolation* (*http://bit.ly/acid_isolation*) to mean: "The isolation property ensures that the concurrent execution of transactions results in a system state that would be obtained if transactions were executed serially, i.e. one after the other. Providing isolation is the main goal of concurrency control. Depending on concurrency control method, the effects of an incomplete transaction might not even be visible to another transaction." In this case, using `Scanners` in isolation mode that ensures the effects of a not yet completed mutation are not visible to readers of the table. Regardless of whether isolation mode is used with `Scanners`, tablet servers ensure that partially applied mutations are not permanently committed to a table in the event of a failure during the writing of the mutation.

To see the effect of isolation mode on `Scanners` in action, Accumulo ships with an example. The following command will apply a series of mutations to rows in one thread, while another continually scans the table looking for partial updates. The command will print out any partial updates it finds:

```
./bin/accumulo org.apache.accumulo.examples.simple.isolation.InterferenceTest \
   -i instance -z zookeepers -u username -p password -t isotest --iterations 1000
```

If you don't get any ERROR statements, run the command again. Sometimes 1,000 iterations are not enough to expose the issue. Running the command with the `--isolation` flag set will perform the same test but using isolated reads:

```
./bin/accumulo org.apache.accumulo.examples.simple.isolation.InterferenceTest \
   -i instance -z zookeepers -u username -p password -t isotest \
   --iterations 1000 --isolated
```

Tuning Scanners

Scanners handle communication with tablet servers in identifying and retrieving key-value pairs. For efficiency reasons, tablet servers return key-value pairs to `Scanners` in batches.

Scanners can be tuned to adjust the size of batches as well as when to prefetch batches.

For example, if it is known that key-value pairs are generally fairly large, perhaps over 500 KB each—or if we are mostly interested in doing very small scans over only a few key-value pairs—we can choose to reduce the batch size for a `Scanner` to avoid shipping unwanted key-value pairs from the server to the client. On the other hand, if we are often scanning over larger numbers of smaller key-value pairs, we can choose to increase the batch size.

To get the current batch size (numbered in key-value pairs) for a scanner, use the `getBatchSize()` method:

```
Scanner scanner = conn.createScanner("mytable", auths);

int size = scanner.getBatchSize();
```

To adjust the batch size, use the `setBatchSize()` method:

```
scanner.setBatchSize(size * 2);
```

When scanning over many key-value pairs, `Scanners` will wait until the end of a batch is reached before fetching another batch. This causes the client to pause for a short time until the next batch is available. If we know we are routinely going to scan over multiple batches, we can save time by having the scanner prefetch the next batch sooner.

By default, a threshold is configured for how many batches must be read from a scanner before it will start to prefetch the next batch. To see the current threshold, use the `getReadaheadThreshold()` method:

```
long numBatches = scanner.getReadaheadThreshold();
```

To change the read-ahead threshold, use the `setReadaheadThreshold()` method:

```
scanner.setReadaheadThreshold(numBatches / 2);
```

Application designers should experiment with these settings to find optimal values for various types of accesses.

Batch Scanning

Data can be retrieved for multiple ranges simultaneously using a `BatchScanner`. Rather than a single `Range` object, `BatchScanners` take a *set* of Ranges and communicate with many tablet servers in parallel threads to read all the data within the ranges specified.

`BatchScanners` do not return data in sorted order, because they retrieve data from many tablet servers at once.

 When designing applications, keep in mind that the `Scanner` will always return key-value pairs in sorted order, but the `BatchScan ner` will not.

A BatchScanner is obtained in a manner similar to that of a Scanner:

```
int numThreads = 10;
BatchScanner bscan = connector.createBatchScanner('myTable',
    new Authorizations(), numThreads);
```

The last parameter designates the number of threads to use to communicate with tab-let servers. Most clients will want to use more than one thread if there is more than one tablet server.

We'll pass the BatchScanner an ArrayList of Range objects:

```
List<Range> ranges = new ArrayList<Range>();
ranges.add(new Range("Apache_Accumulo"));
ranges.add(new Range("Apache_Hadoop"));
ranges.add(new Range("Apache_Thrift"));
ranges.add(new Range("Apache_ZooKeeper"));

bscan.setRanges(ranges);
```

Results from BatchScanner are read the same way as from Scanner:

```
for(Entry<Key,Value> entry : bscan) {
  // access the elements of the entries
  ...
}
```

A BatchScanner can be configured with many of the same options that a Scanner can. For example, we can set a BatchScanner to fetch only certain columns (Figure 3-8):

```
int numThreads = 10;
BatchScanner bscan = connector.createBatchScanner('myTable',
    new Authorizations(), numThreads);

List<Range> ranges = new ArrayList<Range>();
ranges.add(new Range("Apache_Accumulo"));
ranges.add(new Range("Apache_Hadoop"));
ranges.add(new Range("Apache_Thrift"));
ranges.add(new Range("Apache_ZooKeeper"));

bscan.setRanges(ranges);

bscan.fetchColumn(new Text("metadata"), new Text("title"));

for(Entry<Key,Value> entry : bscan) {
  // access the elements of the entries
  ...
}
```

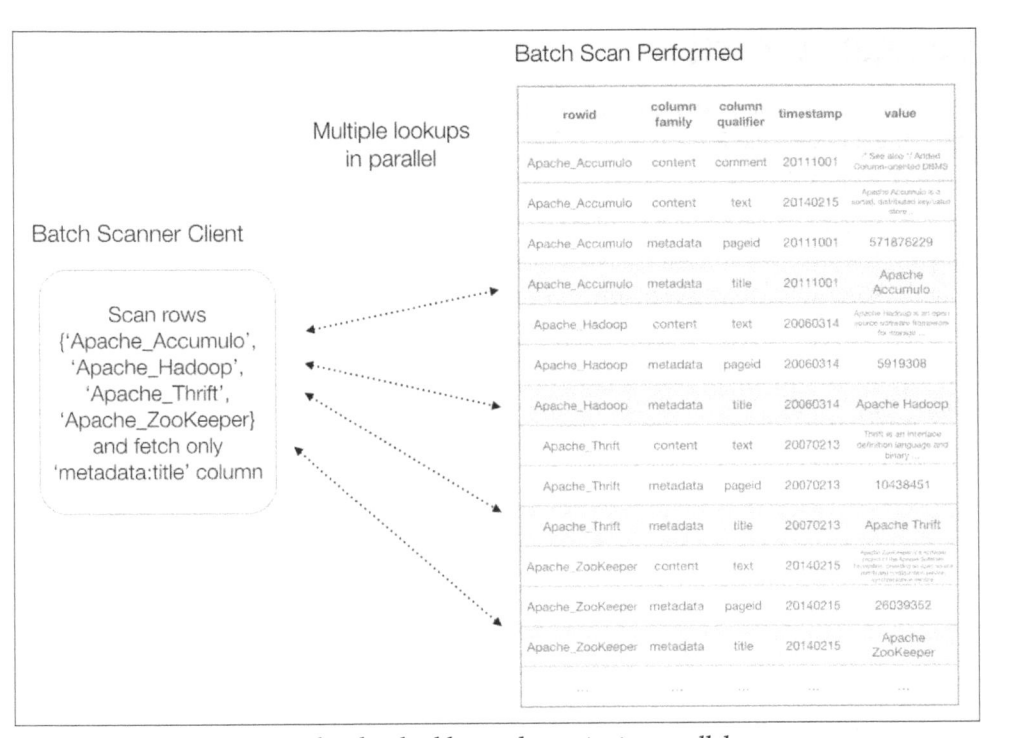

Figure 3-8. Scanning several individual key-value pairs in parallel

The ranges that are passed to a `BatchScanner` can each span many key-value pairs, but in practice the performance improvement of using `BatchScanners` versus individual `Scanners` is most pronounced when a large number of small ranges are scanned.

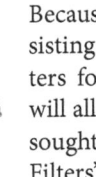

Because `BatchScanners` often look up many individual ranges consisting of a single row ID, it can be beneficial to enable bloom filters for tables that are often scanned using `BatchScanners`. This will allow tablet servers to skip files that do not contain the row IDs sought by the `BatchScanner`, improving performance. See "Bloom Filters" on page 142 for details.

Batch scanning comes in handy for looking up a set of record IDs retrieved from a secondary index or doing small joins between tables. We use `BatchScanners` for our example in "Secondary Indexing" on page 275.

Update: Overwrite

Simple updates that overwrite existing keys are straightforward in Accumulo: simply inserting a new value for an existing key will cause the old value to appear to be overwritten (Figure 3-9).

This is because Accumulo will place new versions of existing keys at the beginning, causing the first version of a key encountered by a scan to be the latest version. By default Accumulo tables keep only the latest version of each key.

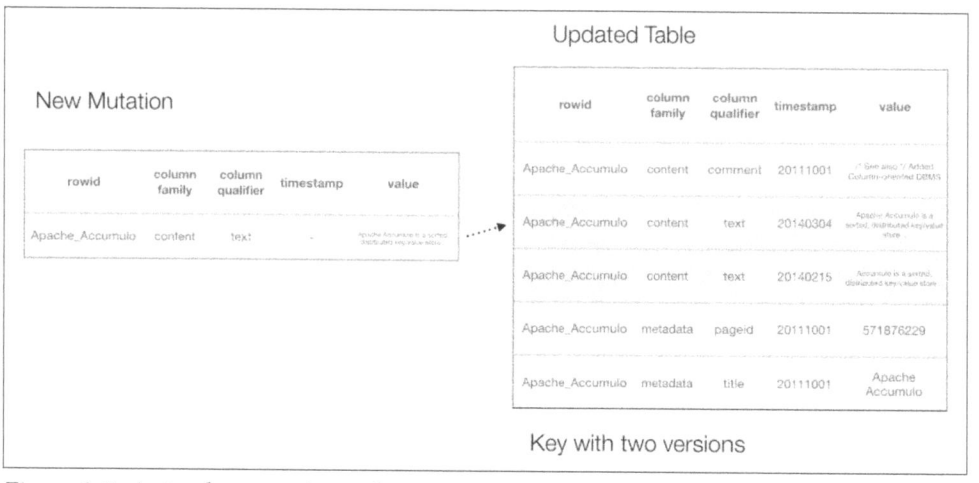

Figure 3-9. A simple overwrite update

No data has to be read in order to perform an overwrite. For this reason, simple overwrite updates have the same performance as inserts. In some databases the ability to either update or insert information in the same operation is called an *upsert*. Typically in other systems, an update to a key that doesn't exist will cause an error, unless an upsert operation is explicitly specified. In Accumulo, inserts are considered updates if there happens to be an existing version of the key being inserted, but from a mechanical standpoint there is no difference between an insert and an update, either in performance or in client usage.

Overwrite Example

In our Wikipedia application, doing an update to the metadata of an article is straightforward. We implement this method the same as for inserting new data:

```
public void updateMetadata(
        final String title,
        final String attribute,
        final String value,
        final boolean flush)
        throws MutationsRejectedException {
```

```
Mutation m = new Mutation(title);
m.put(WikipediaConstants.METADATA_FAMILY, attribute, value);

batchWriter.addMutation(m);

if(flush)
  batchWriter.flush();
}
```

This example will simply insert new information for the column specified. Unless we modify the `VersioningIterator` for this table, any old versions will be suppressed from scans and eventually eliminated from disk during the compaction process.

Allowing Multiple Versions

Accumulo can be configured to keep multiple versions of a key-value pair by changing the `maxVersions` parameter of the `VersioningIterator`.

Using the shell:

```
user@accumulo> config -t table_name -s table.iterator.majc.vers.opt.maxVersions=2
user@accumulo> config -t table_name -s table.iterator.minc.vers.opt.maxVersions=2
user@accumulo> config -t table_name -s table.iterator.scan.vers.opt.maxVersions=2
```

Or through Java:

```
connector.tableOperations().setProperty("table_name",
    "table.iterator.majc.vers.opt.maxVersions", "2");
connector.tableOperations().setProperty("table_name",
    "table.iterator.minc.vers.opt.maxVersions", "2");
connector.tableOperations().setProperty("table_name",
    "table.iterator.scan.vers.opt.maxVersions", "2");
```

You can keep all versions by removing the `VersioningIterator` entirely:

```
user@accumulo> deleteiter -t table_name -n vers -all
```

Some applications may want to keep several versions on disk, return the latest by default, and allow clients to request more than the latest version whenever necessary.

To do this, the `maxVersions` option for `minc` and `majc` should be set to something greater than 1, say 10, and the `scan` option should be set to 1. Unless they specify otherwise, clients will see only the latest version for each value. If they want to go back and view more versions, they can configure a `Scanner` to return more than one version:

```
Scanner scanner = connector.createScanner("myTable", auths);
IteratorSetting setting = new IteratorSetting(20, "vers",
    "org.apache.accumulo.core.iterators.user.VersioningIterator");
```

```
VersioningIterator.setMaxVersions(setting, 10);
scanner.addScanIterator(setting);
```

 Even if a table is configured to allow Scanners to retrieve all versions, no entries that are suppressed by delete markers will ever be returned.

For example, in our Wikipedia application, we can choose to allow multiple versions of a page to exist indefinitely, in order to preserve the history of edits to an article. For most lookups, we'll only want the latest version of an article, but editors may want to view all versions of an article to compare changes over time.

Update: Appending or Incrementing

Some updates need to add information to existing values. These are different from simple overwrites because the existing values will need to be combined with the new value in some way.

An example is adding some amount to a running total. Instead of reading the old value out, adding the new value to it, and writing the combined value back, Accumulo allows new values to be written alongside old values, and values are combined at scan time or compaction time.

Accumulo can perform these kinds of updates very efficiently through the use of Accumulo iterators, as described in "Combiners for incrementing or appending updates" on page 221. Effectively, appending or incrementing updates can be done as quickly as inserts. Applications that require these kinds of updates can simply treat them like inserts and configure iterators on the table being updated.

An example of using iterators to do efficient incrementing updates is described in "Ingesters and Combiners as MapReduce Computations" on page 264.

Update: Read-Modify-Write and Conditional Mutations

Accumulo 1.6 supports *conditional mutations* that can be used to do efficient read-modify-write operations on rows. The ability to place conditions on mutations enables applications to achieve a higher degree of consistency. These are more involved updates than simple overwrites, because they involve checking the state of an existing row. These are also only necessary when appending or incrementing updates by using iterators is insufficient.

Conditional mutations are a bit different from Constraints, as we discuss in "Constraints" on page 201, in that Constraints allow mutations to be rejected or accepted based on the information contained within just the one new mutation, whereas conditional mutations allow a mutation to be rejected or accepted based on the information in the row to be modified.

Conditional mutations are more expensive than regular mutations and constraints because they perform a read of the current data in the table, in addition to accessing the disk to persist the new mutation in the write-ahead log. Server are able to perform fewer conditional mutations than they can regular mutations.

Conditional Mutations and Percolator

Conditional mutations are especially interesting because they provide part of the foundation for a system like Google's *Percolator* (*http://bit.ly/percolator_paper*) to be built on Accumulo. Percolator is a system Google built to transition the work of updating its primary web index from a batch-oriented MapReduce-based job to a more continuous, incremental system. Percolator "provides cross-row, cross-table transactions with ACID sematics."

A project to implement an open source version of Percolator for Accumulo is called Fluo (*https://github.com/fluo-io/fluo*).

Conditional Mutation API

The `ConditionalMutation` class is used to specify a set of conditions that must be satisfied in order to apply the puts or deletes contained within the mutation. `ConditionalMutation` objects are like regular `Mutation` objects except that they can have `Condition` objects added.

A `Condition` object can be configured to check for the absence of a column or to check that a column's value is equal to a given value.

A `Condition` that checks to see if a column is absent can be created as follows:

```
Condition markedColumnAbsent = new Condition("internal", "marked");
```

One or more `Condition` objects can be added to a `ConditionalMutation`:

```
ConditionalMutation cm = new ConditionalMutation(someRow);
```

```
cm.addCondition(markedColumnAbsent);
```

Then regular puts and deletes can be applied to the mutation. These will only succeed if all conditions added are satisfied:

```
cm.put("internal", "marked", "");
cm.put("metadata", "dateMarked", new Date().toString());
```

In this example, the ConditionalMutation will first check to see if no column is identified by *internal:marked* currently in the row. If the column is absent, this Conditio nalMutation will be applied, which puts a new column, *internal:marked*, into the row that prevents future ConditionalMutations of this type to succeed, and puts another column, *metadata:dateMarked*, into the row with a value representing the current date.

Rather than just checking that a column is absent, we can check to see whether a column contains a value we expect:

```
Condition ensureColorIsBlue = new Condition("details", "color");
ensureColorIsBlue.addValue("blue");

ConditionalMutation otherCm = new ConditionalMutation(someRow);

otherCm.addCondition(ensureColorIsBlue);
```

In this case, the ConditionalMutation will only be applied if the *details:color* column contains the value blue.

To submit a ConditionalMutation, we pass it to a ConditionalWriter object via the write() method, which returns the success status of each ConditionalMutation. The success status is returned via a Result object, which can be examined to find out if the conditional mutation succeeded, or if there were problems with the mutation:

```
ConditionalWriter cwriter = new ConditionalWriter("myTable", config);

ConditionalWriter.Result result = cwriter.write(cm);

try {
  switch(result.getStatus()) {
    case ACCEPTED:
      // condition was met and mutation was applied
      ...
      break;
    case REJECTED:
      // condition was not met
      ...
      break;
    case VIOLATED:
      // mutation violated a constraint
      ...
      break;
    case UNKNOWN:
      // unknown server error
      ...
      break;
    case INVISIBLE_VISIBILITY:
      // condition involved a visibility not visible to user
      ...
      break;
```

```
      default:
        break;
    }
  }
```

Conditional Mutation Batch API

Besides just single writes, a `ConditionalWriter` can also be passed multiple `Conditio` `nalMutations`. In this case the `write()` method will return an `Iterator` over `Result` objects:

```
ArrayList<ConditionalMutation> mutations = new ArrayList<>();
// ConditionalMutations are added
...

Iterator<ConditionalWriter.Result> results = conditionalWriter.write(mutations);
```

Because there are multiple `Results`, we can ask a `Result` to which mutation it applied in order to know which `ConditionalMutations` succeeded or failed:

```
ArrayList<ConditionalMutation> mutations = new ArrayList<>();
// ConditionalMutations are added
...

Iterator<ConditionalWriter.Result> results = conditionalWriter.write(mutations);

for(ConditionalWriter.Result result : results) {
  try {
    switch(result.getStatus()) {
      case ACCEPTED:
        ...
        break;
      case REJECTED:
        System.err.println("mutation failed: " +
          result.getMutation().toString());
        ...
        break;
      ...
    }
  }
}
```

Conditional Mutation Example

347.50bIn our example application we'd like to let users submit new revisions to Wikipedia pages, but we want to avoid the following situation, in which users overwrite each other's edits:

1. Alice downloads the current version of a page, marked by revision 1.

2. Bob also downloads revision 1 of a page.

3. Alice makes her edits and submits them as revision 2.

4. Bob makes his edits and submits them as revision 2, overwriting Alice's edits.

In this scenario, multiple concurrent submissions can cause some edits to be lost. We'll use conditional mutations to avoid this situation. What we'd rather have happen is the following:

1. Alice downloads the current version of a page, marked by revision 1.
2. Bob also downloads revision 1 of a page.
3. Alice makes her edits and submits them as revision 2.
4. Bob makes his edits and submits them as revision 2, but he receives an error because the revision currently in Accumulo is not the last revision he read.
5. Bob reads revision 2, which includes Alice's edits.
6. Bob merges his edits with Alice's, resolving any conflicting edits.
7. Bob submits his edits again, this time as revision 3.
8. Because the current revision still in Accumulo is 2, Bob's edits are accepted and written.

The crucial bit of logic here is in step 4. Accumulo's conditional mutation mechanism will allow us to check that we have the latest revision right before committing a write.

Here is an example of a method that will try to write new contents of a page and fail if the current revision is not the last revision we read:

```
public boolean updateContent(
        final String title,
        final String lastRevision,
        final String contents) throws WikipediaEditException, IOException {

  if (closed)
    throw new IOException("client closed");

  final String newRevision = Integer.toString(
        Integer.parseInt(lastRevision) + 1);

  ConditionalMutation cm = new ConditionalMutation(title);
  Condition lastRevisionStillCurrent = new Condition(
        WikipediaConstants.METADATA_FAMILY,
        WikipediaConstants.REVISION_QUAL);

  // this requires that the version in the table is the last revision we read
  lastRevisionStillCurrent.setValue(lastRevision);
  cm.addCondition(lastRevisionStillCurrent);

  // add puts for our changes
  cm.put(WikipediaConstants.METADATA_FAMILY,
        WikipediaConstants.REVISION_QUAL,
```

```
        newRevision);

    cm.put(WikipediaConstants.CONTENTS_FAMILY, "", contents);

    // submit to the server
    ConditionalWriter.Result r = conditionalWriter.write(cm);
    try {
      switch (r.getStatus()) {
        case ACCEPTED:
          return true;
        case REJECTED:
          return false;
        case VIOLATED:
          throw new WikipediaEditException("constraint violated");
        case UNKNOWN: // could retry
          logger.warn("unknown error from server: {0}", r.getTabletServer());
          return false;
        case INVISIBLE_VISIBILITY:
          throw new WikipediaEditException("condition contained a visibility " +
              "the user cannot satisfy");
        default:
          throw new AssertionError(r.getStatus().name());
      }
    } catch (AccumuloException | AccumuloSecurityException ex) {
      throw new WikipediaEditException(ex);
    }
  }
```

In this example, the updateContent() method will apply the edits and return true if no one has edited the page since the caller read it. It will return false if another user has committed an edit since the caller read it, in which case the caller can read the current version, merge edits, and try to commit again. This method throws exceptions for other problems that retrying will not solve—such as violating any constraints on the table—or for problems reading data as part of the condition that the user is not authorized to see.

If a tablet server fails right after successfully applying a conditional mutation, the client will receive a status of UNKNOWN, because it cannot be known whether the mutation was applied or not. In this case the Accumulo master will assign the tablet containing the row of interest to a new tablet server, and the client can check the status of the row to be mutated to see if the mutation succeeded or not.

The example WikipediaEditExample class contains a main() method that will do a lookup of a page, commit an edit, attempt to commit an edit to an old revision, and then do a new read and commit to the latest revision. Abbreviated code that performs those steps is as follows:

```
Map<String, String> hadoopArticle = client.getContentsAndRevision(
    "Apache_Hadoop");
```

```
String originalContents = hadoopArticle.get(WikipediaConstants.CONTENTS_FAMILY);
String newContents = originalContents.toLowerCase();
String lastRevision = hadoopArticle.get(WikipediaConstants.REVISION_QUAL);


// apply our edit
if (client.updateContent("Apache_Hadoop", lastRevision, newContents)) {
  System.out.println("edit of revision " + lastRevision + " succeeded.");
} else {
  System.out.println("edit of revision " + lastRevision + " failed.");
}

// if we try again, we should fail
if (client.updateContent("Apache_Hadoop",  lastRevision, newContents)) {
  System.out.println("second edit of revision " + lastRevision + " succeeded.");
} else {
  System.out.println("second edit of revision " + lastRevision + " failed.");
}

// need to pull current revision again
hadoopArticle = client.getContentsAndRevision("Apache_Hadoop");
String nextRevision = hadoopArticle.get(WikipediaConstants.REVISION_QUAL);

// put back original contents
// now we should succeed
if (client.updateContent("Apache_Hadoop", nextRevision, originalContents)) {
  System.out.println("edit of revision " + nextRevision + " succeeded.");
} else {
  System.out.println("edit of revision " + nextRevision + " failed.");
}
```

The first edit should succeed, the second should fail because it's trying to update a revision that has already been overwritten, and the final edit should succeed because it is applied to the latest revision.

To run the example code, type the command in the first line of the following:

```
$ mvn exec:java -Dexec.mainClass="com.accumulobook.basic.WikipediaEditExample"
...
Parsing articles ...
...
done.
edit of revision 12010884 succeeded.
second edit of revision 12010884 failed.
edit of revision 12010885 succeeded.
```

These types of edits allow our table to apply only one revision at a time, which aids in deconflicting concurrent edits.

Delete

An individual key-value pair can be deleted from a table. Technically the way this is accomplished is by inserting a special *delete key* (Figure 3-10). A delete key in Accumulo is a normal key with an internal *delete flag* set to `true`.

If a delete key is inserted, all keys with the same row and column as the delete key with a timestamp the same or earlier than the delete key's timestamp will be removed, along with their values. Deletes in Accumulo do not delete a specific key-value pair; rather, they delete all earlier versions of the key.

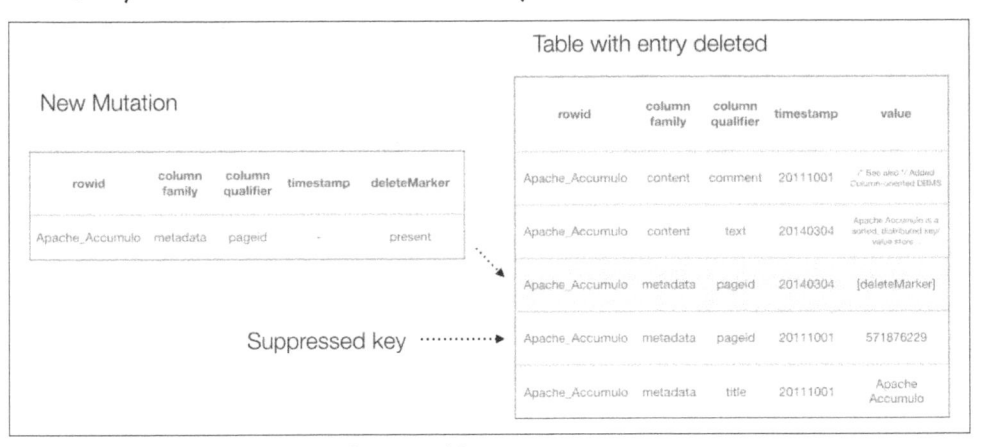

Figure 3-10. Deleting an entry from a table

In these diagrams, for convenience the delete marker is shown as appearing where the value would be, but technically the delete marker is part of the key.

Earlier we mentioned that a mutation can contain *puts* or *deletes*. As an example, perhaps we insert a column on rows that represent articles that are in dispute. When the dispute is resolved, we can remove the dispute marker from the row. The following code deletes the column identified by the family `attributes` and qualifier `dispute Marker` in the row identified by `Article Title`:

```
Mutation m = new Mutation("Article Title");
m.putDelete("attributes", "disputeMarker");
batchWriter.addMutation(m);
```

Subsequent reads of this row will no longer include the *attributes:disputeMarker* column.

Any number of deletes can be included in a mutation, and deletes can be included in a mutation along with puts, but one should avoid including a delete and put for the same column in the same mutation if timestamps are not specified by the client or if timestamps are the same. We go into more detail on this in the next section.

Deleting and Reinserting

Usually deleting a key and reinserting it with a different value is not necessary in Accumulo. The new key-value pair can just be inserted, and it will become the most recent version for that key.

However, some applications may want to delete all earlier versions of a key before creating a new version. A delete key sorts before an identical key without the delete flag set. As a result, you can't delete a key and insert the same key in a single mutation if Accumulo is managing the timestamps. Accumulo will assign the same timestamp to both keys, and the nondelete key will be deleted by the delete key. To delete a key and reinsert it, first add a mutation containing the delete key to the `BatchWriter`, flush the `BatchWriter` so the mutation is sent to Accumulo, then add a mutation containing the new key to the `BatchWriter`. This will ensure that the new key is assigned a later timestamp than the delete key (Figure 3-11).

If you are managing your own timestamps, the same effect can be achieved in a single mutation by giving the new key a later timestamp than the delete key. If the application logic requires that the timestamp on the key must stay the same, the process is more complicated. Firstly, you would not be able to replace the value for a key by inserting the key again with an identical timestamp. Versioning behavior is not well defined when rows have identical keys, to include the same timestamp.

Secondly, after a delete key is inserted, the delete key remains in Accumulo until a full major compaction has been executed on the tablet containing the key. This is the only kind of compaction that reads and rewrites all data for a tablet, thereby ensuring that none of the tablet's files contains a key that should have been deleted. To reinsert a different value for a key at the same timestamp, insert a delete entry for that key, request a compaction so that the delete key and all earlier versions of the key are purged, wait for the compaction to finish, and then insert the new key. If your table is small, you can compact the entire table, but if it is large that can take a long time and tax Accumulo's resources. Instead you can compact the row containing the desired key. Using timestamps in this manner is discouraged because it works against the key versioning inherent in Accumulo.

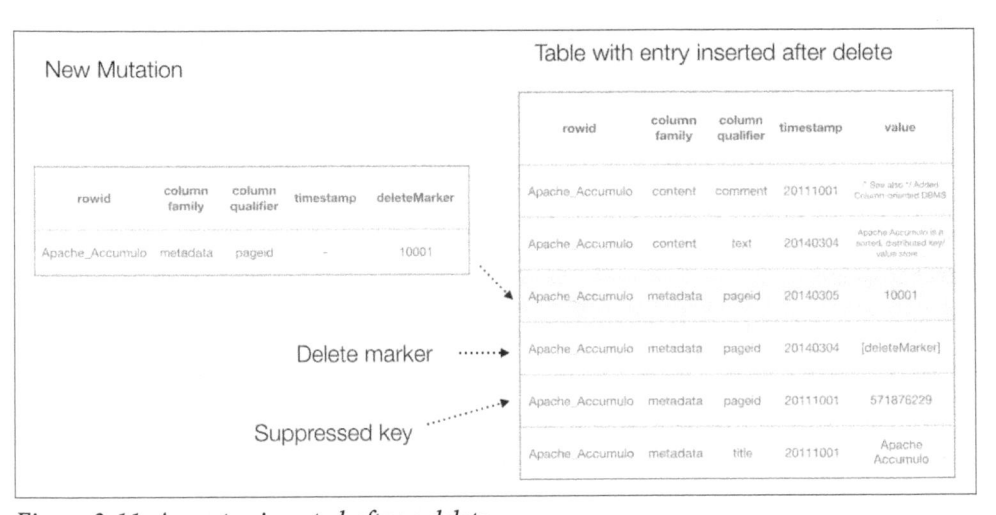

Figure 3-11. An entry inserted after a delete

Removing Deleted Data from Disk

Data masked by a delete key can still reside on disk until files have been reprocessed in compactions. For a discussion of ensuring that deleted data is removed from disk at a particular time, see "Ensuring that deletes are removed from tables" on page 450.

Batch Deleter

The Accumulo client API provides a method for deleting ranges of keys simultaneously using the `BatchDeleter`. The `BatchDeleter` is kind of a combination of a `BatchScanner` and a `BatchWriter` in that it takes multiple ranges to be deleted and simply inserts delete markers for any key-value pairs in those ranges.

This would otherwise require writing code to use a `BatchScanner` to fetch each key-value pair, convert each key-value pair returned into a mutation, put a delete into the mutation that matches the key-value pair, and then submit those mutations to a `BatchWriter`.

The `BatchDeleter` does all this for us. The `BatchDeleter` does not perform these operations more efficiently than our own code would, but it provides a clean client API for performing them.

To use a `BatchDeleter`, first instantiate it much like a `BatchWriter`:

```
BatchWriterConfig config = new BatchWriterConfig();
config.setMaxMemory(1000000L);
config.setMaxWriteThreads(10);
config.setMaxLatency(10, TimeUnit.SECONDS);
int numThreads = 10;
```

```
BatchDeleter deleter = conn.createBatchDeleter("table_name", auths, numThreads,
    config);
```

Next we add a set of ranges as we do for a BatchScanner:

```
deleter.setRanges(ranges);
```

We can optionally fetch a subset of columns or apply iterators to this scan to further refine the set of entries to be deleted. These settings are applied as they are for the BatchScanner.

Finally, we call delete() to perform the scans and insert delete markers:

```
deleter.delete();
```

We should also call close() to release the resources used by the BatchDeleter as it creates multiple threads to perform its work.

Here is an example of how a BatchDeleter might be used to delete a set of articles from our *WikipediaArticles* table:

```
public boolean deleteArticles(final String ... titles) throws IOException {

  if (closed)
    throw new IOException("client closed");

  BatchWriterConfig config = new BatchWriterConfig();
  config.setMaxMemory(1000000L);
  config.setMaxWriteThreads(10);
  config.setMaxLatency(10, TimeUnit.SECONDS);
  int numThreads = 10;

  try {
    BatchDeleter deleter = conn.createBatchDeleter(
            WikipediaConstants.ARTICLES_TABLE, auths, numThreads, config);
    deleter.setRanges(transform(newArrayList(titles), rangeConverter));
    deleter.delete();
    deleter.close();

    return true;
  } catch (TableNotFoundException | MutationsRejectedException ex) {
    logger.error(ex.getMessage());
  }
  return false;
}
```

For an efficient method of simply removing a large range of rows from a table without inserting deletion entries for each key-value pair, see the deleterows command in the Table API in "Deleting Ranges of Rows" on page 135.

Testing

Applications can be tested in several ways other than with a fully distributed Accumulo instance. These include the `MockAccumulo` and the `MiniAccumuloCluster` classes.

MockAccumulo

`MockAccumulo` is an in-memory instance that can be used to test applications without setting up an Accumulo instance.

Obtaining a new `MockInstance` is done as follows:

```
Instance instance = new MockInstance();
```

The instance can be used to write and read data, which it stores in memory. The data will disappear when the instance is destroyed or the JVM stops.

Because the `MockAccumulo` cluster operates this way, it is especially useful for unit testing.

MiniAccumuloCluster

Accumulo ships with a class called `MiniAccumuloCluster` that can be used to write unit tests for Accumulo clients without having to set up a full Accumulo cluster. It supports the full Accumulo client API so tests can write data and read it back to verify correct behavior.

Unlike the `MockInstance`, which operates entirely in memory, the `MiniAccumuloCluster` writes to a temporary directory on the local disk for the duration of the test. This allows tests to be run where a minicluster is set up and kept running while other instantiations of the JVM that operate against this minicluster can be started and stopped. For example, we can start up a cluster and obtain the instance name, Zoo-Keeper servers, and username and password from one JVM, then run a class in another JVM using those settings to write data, and a third to read data.

Setting up the Accumulo minicluster is done via:

```
import com.google.common.io.Files;

File tempDirectory = Files.createTempDir();
MiniAccumuloCluster accumulo = new MiniAccumuloCluster(tempDirectory,
    "password");
accumulo.start();
Instance instance = new ZooKeeperInstance(accumulo.getInstanceName(),
    accumulo.getZooKeepers());
```

Once an instance is started, `Connector` objects can be obtained:

```
Connector conn = instance.getConnector("root", new PasswordToken("password"));
```

The `MiniAccumuloCluster` must be explicitly stopped via the `stop()` method:

```
accumulo.stop();
```

Many of the examples in this book are run against the `MiniAccumuloCluster`.

Now that we have the basic API under our belt, we can start building basic applications for Accumulo. Use of uninitialized value within @id_list in sprintf at index-xml.pl line 407, <> chunk 2009. In the following chapters, we'll look at more API methods for managing tables, handling security, pushing application logic to the server side, and some useful table designs.

## CHAPTER 4

Table API

Although most Accumulo client code will consist of reading and writing data as we have outlined in Chapter 3, many administrative functions are also available via the client API. Accumulo requires very little setup before an application can write data. Unlike relational databases and even some other NoSQL databases, Accumulo does not require any upfront declaration about the structure of the data to be stored in tables. Row IDs and columns do not have to be specified before data is written, nor does information about the lengths or types of values. The bare minimum required to begin writing and reading data is simply to provide a name when creating a new table.

However, the Accumulo API does provide a wide array of features for configuring and tuning tables and for controlling cluster actions. We outline those features in this chapter. Most of these operations can also be carried out via shell commands. We list the API methods here and the shell commands in "Table Operations" on page 440.

Basic Table Operations

Accumulo provides an API for creating, renaming, and deleting tables. This API can be used to manage the construction and lifecycle of tables entirely within an application.

Permission to perform various table operations—such as creating, reading, writing, altering, and deleting tables—is controlled on a per-user basis. More information on these permissions can be found in "Table Permissions" on page 181.

Creating Tables

Tables can be created via the TableOperations object:

```
TableOperations ops = connector.tableOperations();
ops.createTable('myTable');
```

The `TableOperations` object allows us to check whether a table exists and to delete a table as well:

```
if(ops.exists('myTable'))
  ops.delete('myTable');
```

Tables can also be created through the Accumulo shell:

```
user@accumulo> createtable myTable
```

In our example code, we need to create a table to store Wikipedia articles. For this we'll use the following code:

```
TableOperations ops = connector.tableOperations();
if(!ops.exists("WikipediaArticles")) {
  ops.createTable("WikipediaArticles");
}
```

We can obtain a list of tables by calling the `list()` method:

```
SortedSet<String> tables = ops.list();
```

In the shell, this command is called `tables`:

```
user@accumulo> tables
accumulo.root
accumulo.metadata
```

In Accumulo 1.6, all Accumulo instances start with two tables, the *root* table and the *metadata* table. These keep track of which tablet server is hosting each tablet, and other information about the system. The use of these tables for internal operations is described in Chapter 10.

Options for creating tables

Newly created Accumulo tables have several default settings. Many of these are set at reasonable values for a range of cluster sizes and may not require changing.

Options that can be set via the API on a table at creation time are whether to enable versioning and what timestamp type is used. The `VersioningIterator` is enabled by default and configured to remove all but the latest version of each key. In addition, as of Accumulo 1.6, the `DefaultKeySizeConstraint` is also enabled, which rejects any keys that are larger than 1 MB, though values can still be larger. The constraint on key sizes is designed to help prevent performance degradation due to memory require-ments of larger keys. We discuss iterators and constraints at length in "Iterators" on page 209 and "Constraints" on page 201.

The `VersioningIterator` can be disabled with an additional parameter to the `crea teTable()` method:

```
boolean useVersioningIterator = false;
ops.createTable('myTable', useVersioningIterator);
```

Both the `VersioningIterator` and the `DefaultKeySizeConstraint` can be disabled
when you create a table in the shell with the `--no-default-iterators` flag:

```
user@accumulo> createtable myTable --no-default-iterators
```

The default time type is `TimeType.MILLIS`. This instructs tablet servers to use the current system time in milliseconds since the Unix epoch when assigning timestamps to
mutations that have no timestamps provided by the client, which is common.

The other possibility is `TimeType.LOGICAL`, which uses a one-up counter. Logical time
can be enabled through the API like this:

```
boolean useVersioningIterator = true;
ops.createTable('myTable', useVersioningIterator, TimeType.LOGICAL);
```

Or in the shell:

```
user@accumulo> createtable myTable -tl
```

 Most table settings can be changed, enabled, or disabled after a
table is created. However, the time type of a table cannot be
changed after the table is created.

When creating tables, you may want to consider placing them into their own *namespace*, which we discuss in "Table Namespaces" on page 160.

Logical Time Example

Let's observe the timestamps Accumulo sets for a simple table using `TimeType.LOGI`
`CAL`:

```
user@accumulo> createtable -tl testTable
user@accumulo testTable> addsplits m
user@accumulo testTable> insert a b c d
user@accumulo testTable> insert e f g h
user@accumulo testTable> insert w x y z
user@accumulo testTable> insert i j k l
user@accumulo testTable> scan -st
a b:c []  1    d
e f:g []  2    h
i j:k []  3    l
w x:y []  1    z
user@accumulo testTable> flush -w
```

There are two tablets. In the first tablet are entries for rows *a*, *e*, and *i*, with insert timestamps 1, 2, and 3, matching their insert order. In the second tablet there is only one entry for row *w*, with insert timestamp of 1.

Now let's take a look at some entries in the Accumulo metadata table. This is a more complex table that also uses TimeType.LOGICAL. It will be interesting to see its entries ordered by their timestamps, so let's reorder them after we retrieve them from a scan:

```
$ ./bin/accumulo shell -u user -p password -e "scan -st -t \
    accumulo.metadata" | sort -t" " -k4,4
...
3< srv:dir [] 18    hdfs://node-1.example.com:8020/apps/accumulo/tables/3/
    default_tablet
3< loc:1497335ebb20011 [] 20    node-1.example.com:9997
3< ~tab:~pr [] 21    \x01m
3;m loc:1497335ebb20011 [] 22    node-1.example.com:9997
3;m srv:dir [] 22    hdfs://node-1.example.com:8020/apps/accumulo/tables/3/
    t-0000090
3;m ~tab:~pr [] 22    \x00
3;m file:hdfs://node-1.example.com:8020/apps/accumulo/tables/3/t-0000090/
    F0000093.rf [] 26    208,3
3;m last:1497335ebb20011 [] 26    node-1.example.com:9997
3;m srv:flush [] 26    1
3;m srv:lock [] 26    tservers/node-1.example.com:9997/
    zlock-0000000001$1497335ebb20011
3;m srv:time [] 26    L3
3< file:hdfs://node-1.example.com:8020/apps/accumulo/tables/3/default_tablet/
    F0000094.rf [] 27    173,1
3< last:1497335ebb20011 [] 27    node-1.example.com:9997
3< srv:flush [] 27    1
3< srv:lock [] 27    tservers/node-1.example.com:9997/
    zlock-0000000001$1497335ebb20011
3< srv:time [] 27    L1
```

We'll focus on only those metadata entries for our test table, without going into great detail about what each entry means. More information on the contents of the metadata table can be found in Appendix B.

In examining the entries, we can see the results of six mutations, applied at timestamps 18, 20, 21, 22, 26, and 27. At time 18, the table was created and the default directory for its tablet was written in column srv:dir. At time 20, the tablet was assigned to a tablet server, whose address was written in the loc column. At times 21 and 22, a split occurred, creating tablet 3;m, assigning it a srv:dir and loc, and changing the key ranges for both tablets by setting their ~tab:~pr columns. At times 26 and 27, a flush occurred, writing a new filename for each tablet in the file column, as well as some other metadata. During this flush, the most recent timestamp for each tablet was written to the srv:time column. We can see that the 3;m tablet has most recent time 3, while the 3< tablet has most recent time 1, which agrees with the entries we have written to the test table.

Futhermore, we also know that mutations were applied at timestamps 19, 23, 24, and 25, and that the entries with those timestamps must have been overwritten by subsequent mutations.

This illustrates that analyzing what happens in an application when entries are inserted into Accumulo can be a complex task. The logical time type makes this task somewhat easier, although both time types serve the essential purpose of guaranteeing insert order into a tablet. `TimeType.LOGICAL` should only be used for applications for which the actual time of insert does not matter, only the ordering of inserts.

Renaming

Tables can be renamed via the `rename()` method. If a table is assigned to a user-defined namespace, the new name must include the same namespace as the old name (we cover naming tables within a namespace in "Creating" on page 161):

```
ops.rename("oldName", "newName");
```

In the shell this can be done via the `renametable` command:

```
user@accumulo oldname> renametable oldname newname
user@accumulo newname>
```

Deleting Tables

Tables can be deleted via the `delete()` method:

```
void delete(String tableName)
```

This will remove the table, its configuration, and all data from the system. Disk space will not be reclaimed from HDFS until the Accumulo garbage collector has a chance to identify the files that were used by the deleted table and remove them from HDFS.

Tables can be deleted in the shell via the `deletetable` command:

```
user@accumulo> deletetable myTable
deletetable { myTable } (yes|no)? yes
Table: [myTable] has been deleted.
user@accumulo>
```

Deleting Ranges of Rows

A range of rows within a table can be deleted via the `deleteRows()` method. This can be used to remove a specific range, or to eliminate all rows within a table without removing the table itself. To remove a range of rows, specify a start and end row to the `deleteRows()` method:

```
Text startRow = new Text("k");
Text endRow = new Text("r");
ops.deleteRows("myTable", startRow, endRow);
```

 When you specify start and end rows, the deleteRows() method will remove rows that sort after *but not including* the start row, and rows that sort before *and including* the end row.

To delete all rows from the beginning of the table, use null for the start row parameter. In this example, all rows from the beginning of the table to the specified end row will be deleted:

```
Text endRow = new Text("r");
ops.deleteRows("myTable", null, endRow);
```

Similarly, rows after a specific start row to the end of the table can be deleted:

```
Text startRow = new Text("k");
ops.deleteRows("myTable", startRow, null);
```

To remove all rows, use null for both the start and end row. This is equivalent to *truncating* a table in a relational database. Removing all rows will leave the table and its configuration intact:

```
ops.deleteRows("myTable", null, null);
```

These operations can be done in the shell using the deleterows command:

```
user@accumulo> deleterows --table myTable --begin-row k --end-row r
```

To delete rows beginning at the start of the table, or ending at the end of the table, or both, the --force flag must be present:

```
user@accumulo> deleterows --table myTable --begin-row k --force
user@accumulo> deleterows --table myTable --end-row r --force
```

To remove all rows (truncate), simply specify --force with no start or end row:

```
user@accumulo> deleterows --table myTable --force
```

Deleting Entries Returned from a Scan

The previous section outlined deleting a simple range of rows. All columns for all rows specified will be deleted in that case.

But we might want to delete a more complex set of entries—for example, not just all columns for all rows in a range, but perhaps just certain columns.

We cover a method for deleting entries that would be returned in a particular scan configuration with a `BatchDeleter` in "Batch Deleter" on page 127. The same functionality is available in the shell via the `deletemany` command.

Configuring Table Properties

Tables have a set of properties that control the features that are enabled and that tune table behavior. There are three main methods for setting, removing, and viewing these settings.

To list the current properties for a table, use the `getProperties()` method:

```
for(Entry<String,String> property : ops.getProperties(String tableName))
    System.out.println(property.getKey() + "\t" + property.getValue());
```

This can be done in the shell via the `config` command. The `config` command and other commands that run on a specific table can either use the default table or the table specified with the `--table` or `-t` option. The Accumulo shell displays the current table in the command prompt, if the current table is set. The following prompt shows that the current table is *myTable*, switches to another table, and runs the `config` command on *myTable*:

```
user@accumulo myTable> table otherTable
user@accumulo otherTable> config --table myTable
-----------+----------------------------------------------+--------------------
SCOPE      | NAME                                         | VALUE
-----------+----------------------------------------------+--------------------
default    | table.balancer ............................ | org.apache.accumu...
```

To set a property, use the `setProperty()` method. For example, to change the replication factor for new files associated with this table we could do the following:

```
ops.setProperty("myTable", "table.file.replication", "1");
```

This can be done in the shell via the `config` command with the `-s` or `--set` option followed by the name and value of the property to set, separated by =:

```
user@accumulo> config --table myTable --set table.file.replication=1
```

To remove a property, use the `removeProperty()` method. Removing a property causes the table to revert to the default setting for a property. For example, if we remove the table-specific setting for `table.file.replication`, the table will revert to the default setting of 0, which indicates that the HDFS default replication factor should be used:

```
ops.removeProperty("myTable", "table.file.replication");
```

This can be done in the shell via the `config` command and the `-d` or `--delete` option specifying the property to be removed:

```
user@accumulo> config --table myTable --delete table.file.replication
```

These methods can be used to set a variety of properties that enable certain features or alter table behavior as we describe in the following sections. In some cases, the TableOperations object provides additional convenience methods for setting multiple related properties simultaneously, but these can always be set using the setProperty() and removeProperty() methods.

Locality Groups

Locality groups allow application designers to direct Accumulo to store certain sets of column families together on disk. This allows some sets of column families to be read from disk without having to read data from all the other column families. Locality groups are the reason that Accumulo and other Bigtable-style systems are sometimes grouped under the *columnar NoSQL data stores* category. We introduce the concept of locality groups in "Column Families" on page 19.

Accumulo's locality groups are easy to set up and manage. Locality groups do not have to be specified during table creation, and changes to locality groups are effected via background compaction processes, so that tables can remain online and available through these changes.

A new table has only one default locality group, and all column families that might ever appear in a table are assigned to it. To assign some column families to a separate locality group from the default, the setLocalityGroups() method of TableOperations can be used:

```
Set<Text> groupOne = new HashSet<>();
groupOne.add(new Text("colFamA"));
groupOne.add(new Text("colFamB"));

Set<Text> groupTwo = new HashSet<>();
groupTwo.add(new Text("colFamC"));
groupTwo.add(new Text("colFamD"));

Map<String,Set<Text>> groups = new HashMap<>();
groups.put("localityGroupOne", groupOne);
groups.put("localityGroupTwo", groupTwo);

ops.setLocalityGroups("myTable", groups);
```

Any column families not included in this mapping will remain in the *default* locality group. If new column families appear in the table they will also be stored in the *default* locality group.

Column families can be moved to a new locality group at any time. Newly written files will group data on disk according to the locality group settings at the time the file is created. This is true for either minor compaction or major compaction.

The current assignment of column families to locality groups can be seen via the `get LocalityGroups()` method of `TableOperations`:

```
for(Map<String,Set<Text>> group : ops.getLocalityGroups("myTable").entrySet()) {
  System.out.println("\nGroup: " + group.getKey());

  for(Text colFam : group.getValue()) {
    System.out.println(colFam.toString());
  }
}
```

Locality groups example

In our Wikipedia application, we have a situation that can benefit from using locality groups. We store the article text in the *content* column along with the article metadata columns together in the same row for each article.

This is convenient for reading all the information for a particular article; we can scan a single row to get what we need.

Other times this may not be so convenient. Consider the case when we want to read out one metadata column from multiple rows. We'd have to read large chunks of text from the *content* column and filter it out as we scan from one row to the next (Figure 4-1).

Using a locality group to separate the content and metadata columns from one another on disk allows us to leave the content on disk when we're only reading metadata columns, but also preserves the ability to read content and metadata together when we need to (Figure 4-2). The trade-off is that reading out all the columns of a row will be slightly less efficient because we'll have to read from two portions of a file instead of one.

rowid	column family	column qualifier	timestamp	value
Apache_Accumulo	content	comment	20111001	/* See also */ Added Column-oriented DBMS
Apache_Accumulo	content	text	20120301	Accumulo is a sorted, distributed key/value store ...
Apache_Accumulo	metadata	pageid	20111001	571876229
Apache_Accumulo	metadata	title	20111001	Apache Accumulo
Apache_Hadoop	content	text	20060314	Apache Hadoop is an open source software framework for storage ...
Apache_Hadoop	metadata	pageid	20060314	5919308
Apache_Hadoop	metadata	title	20060314	Apache Hadoop
Apache_Thrift	content	text	20070213	Thrift is an interface definition language and binary ...
Apache_Thrift	metadata	pageid	20070213	10438451
Apache_Thrift	metadata	title	20070213	Apache Thrift
...	...	...	...	...

Figure 4-1. Reading over one column family still requires filtering out other column families

We can apply locality group assignments to our column families using the following example code:

```
public void setupLocalityGroups(final boolean compact) throws
        AccumuloException,
        AccumuloSecurityException,
        TableNotFoundException {

    Set<Text> contentGroup = new HashSet<>();
    contentGroup.add(WikipediaConstants.CONTENTS_FAMILY_TEXT);

    Set<Text> metadataGroup = new HashSet<>();
    metadataGroup.add(WikipediaConstants.METADATA_FAMILY_TEXT);

    Map<String, Set<Text>> groups = new HashMap<>();
    groups.put("contentGroup", contentGroup);
    groups.put("metadataGroup", metadataGroup);

    conn.tableOperations().setLocalityGroups(WikipediaConstants.ARTICLES_TABLE,
        groups);
    ...
```

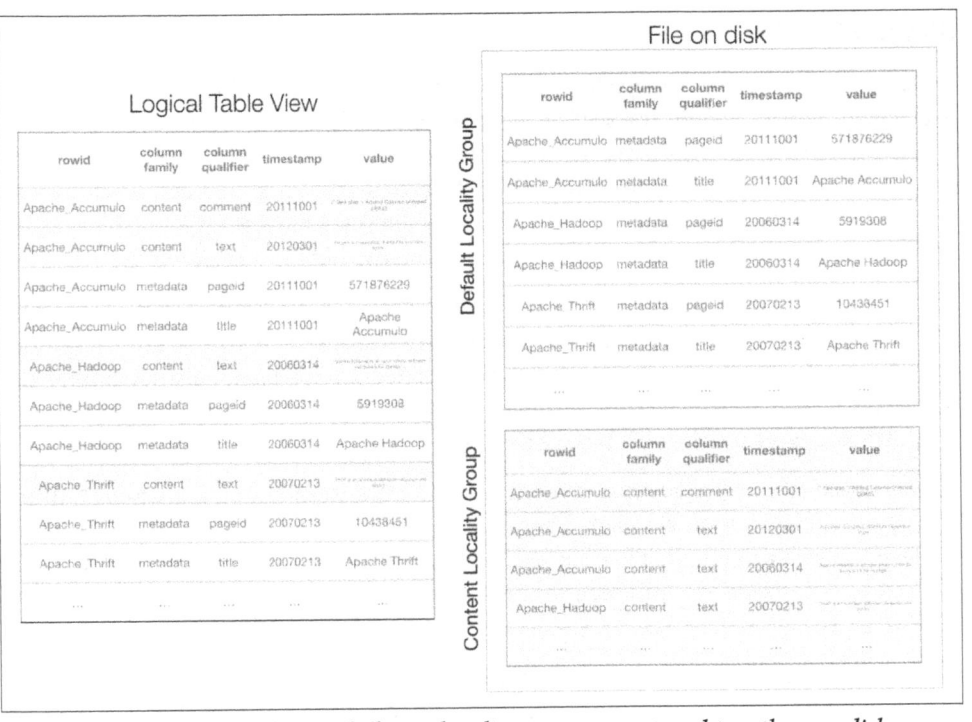

Figure 4-2. Column families in different locality groups are stored together on disk

Any newly written files will be organized according to these locality groups. To cause any existing files to be reprocessed to reflect the locality group assignment, we can compact our table (we cover the `compact` command in "Compacting" on page 149):

```
public void setupLocalityGroups(final boolean compact) throws
        AccumuloException,
        AccumuloSecurityException,
        TableNotFoundException {
    ...
    if(compact) {
      conn.tableOperations().compact(
            WikipediaConstants.ARTICLES_TABLE,
            null,
            null,
            false,
            false);
    }
}
```

Now when using our `WikipediaClient.scanColumn()` method in the example code to read a metadata column, tablet servers will not have to read out any data from the content column family, resulting in better scan performance.

Bloom Filters

A *bloom filter* (*http://en.wikipedia.org/wiki/Bloom_filter*) is a highly memory-efficient data structure for keeping track of set membership with allowed false positives but no false negatives. False positives in this situation mean that some percentage of the time, when we check a bloom filter to see if particular item is in a set, it will return the answer *yes* when the item is not actually in the set. But having no false negatives means that the bloom filter will never say *no* when the item is actually in the set.

This comes in handy in an Accumulo context when we are looking for a particular key in a table. Enabling bloom filters on a table will allow us to consult the bloom filter to see if a particular key is in a file associated with a tablet. By consulting the bloom filter, we can figure out if a file doesn't contain a key at all instead of having to seek into and read the data portion of the file.

This is especially useful because often a key will exist in only one file when multiple files are associated with a tablet. Therefore, we often only need to read one file to retrieve the key-value pair. This can reduce the time to look up a particular key-value pair from hundreds of milliseconds, if there are many files, to perhaps tens of milliseconds.

Of course, because bloom filters can return false positives, some percentage of the time the bloom filter will say that a file has a key when it doesn't. In this case we look in the file and find out that the key we want isn't there after all, but this is acceptable behavior. We sometimes search files we don't need to but are guaranteed never to skip a file that does contain our key.

 Bloom filters are most useful when an application performs lots of lookups of single rows. They are less useful when an application mostly performs scans over multiple rows. A bloom filter is only consulted for ranges containing keys from a single row.

The cost of using bloom filters is the memory they take up. When bloom filters are enabled, each file has a bloom filter generated for it when it is created. This filter is stored along with the file and is, by default, lazily loaded into memory by the tablet server.

By default bloom filters are not enabled on tables, but they can be enabled via the `TableOperations` object:

```
ops.setProperty("myTable", "table.bloom.enabled", "true");
```

These can also be enabled and other settings configured via the standard `config` command in the shell:

```
user@accumulo> config -t myTable -s table.bloom.enabled=true
```

After bloom filters are enabled, newly written files will have bloom filters generated for them. Existing files will not. Compaction of older files will cause new files to be written with bloom filters for existing data. See "Compacting" on page 149 for details on scheduling compaction operations for a table.

Additional options that can be set and their defaults are as follows:

`table.bloom.error.rate`
> This property specifies the desired acceptable error rate for the bloom filter, as a percentage. A lower error rate will require that more memory be used. The default value is 0.5%.

`table.bloom.hash.type`
> This property defines the type of hash function to use when storing and looking up items in the bloom filter. The default hash function type is murmur.

`table.bloom.load.threshold`
> Even when enabled, bloom filters are lazily loaded to keep the cost of loading a new tablet low. By default, a tablet server will wait until at least one seek that could have used a bloom filter is actually performed before loading the bloom filter from disk into memory. This behavior can be changed via the `table.bloom.load.threshold` property. Setting this property to 0 will cause a bloom filter to be loaded when the file is opened.

`table.bloom.size`
> Bloom filters are configured with a particular number of slots. The combination of this property and the desired error rate ultimately determines the amount of memory dedicated to the bloom filter. The default value is 1,048,576 bytes, or 1 MB.

Key functors

Bloom filters can be configured to use just the row ID; a combination of row ID and column family: or row ID, column family, and column qualifier when checking to see if a key exists in a file.

For example, by default bloom filters only check to see if a file contains the same row ID as a given key. If a key has the same row ID as any key store in a file, the bloom filter will return *yes* to the question of whether or not the file should be opened. This could result in more false positives, because the keys in a file can be for the same row but different columns than the one our key identifies.

On the other hand, storing more than just the row ID in the bloom filter makes the lookup more specific. But this can cause the bloom filter to use up more memory in order to maintain the desired false positive rate, because there are more possible identifiers to be stored in the bloom filter.

The portion of the key stored in a bloom filter and used for lookups is controlled by the *key functor*.

The functor used can be configured on a per-table basis via the `table.bloom.key.functor` property. Accumulo ships with three possible functors:

`org.apache.accumulo.core.file.keyfunctor.RowFunctor`
Causes only the row ID to be used when the bloom filter is consulted. This is the default setting.

`org.apache.accumulo.core.file.keyfunctor.ColumnFamilyFunctor`
Causes the row ID and the column family to be used when the bloom filter is consulted.

`org.apache.accumulo.core.file.keyfunctor.ColumnQualifierFunctor`
Causes the row ID, column family, and column qualifer to be used when the bloom filter is consulted.

Additional functors can be created by extending the `org.apache.accumulo.core.file.keyfunctor.KeyFunctor` Java interface. This can be used to make a bloom filter take advantage of an application's access patterns when deciding whether to search a file for a particular range.

Caching

Caching data in memory is extremely important to the performance of many conventional database applications. Often a separate set of processes designed to keep part or all of a database's data in memory are used to keep the operational load placed on a database low.

In contrast, Accumulo is designed to make data access fast—even when data is fetched from disk—by keeping data organized, and to scale up the number of operations that can be performed by distributing data across multiple machines. Applications can then exploit *spatial locality* by doing one seek to find a set of related key-value pairs, which are then read off of disk sequentially at a high rate.

However, Accumulo also employs its own caching mechanisms to allow applications to take advantage of *temporal locality*. Temporal locality refers to the situation in which key-value pairs that have been accessed once are more likely to be accessed again within a short period of time. With caching, key-value pairs that are fetched several times within a short period are fetched from disk once and stored in memory. Subsequent accesses to the desired key-value pairs are fast because they can read from memory instead of going to disk again.

In particular, Accumulo provides two types of caches. The first is an *index cache*, which stores the internal key-to-data block mapping for each file of a tablet. These indexes are used to identify which block of a file should be read from disk to satisfy a read request. By default the index cache is enabled.

Another cache, the *data block cache*, is used to store data blocks read from files. By default the data block cache is disabled.

 Whether or not temporal locality exists for a particular table depends on the access patterns of an application. For applications that tend to fetch the same sets of key-value pairs several times in a short period, enabling the data block cache can improve performance considerably, depending on the memory resources available.

Applications that don't perform multiple fetches of the same sets of key-value pairs within a short time will not see a benefit from enabling the data block cache. Having the data block cache enabled for applications that scan large swaths of a table will not provide a benefit and can cause data blocks for other tables to be evicted from memory, decreasing the benefit of caching data blocks for those other tables.

Application designers can enable or disable either cache for a particular table in the usual manner, via the `setProperty()` method. The data block cache property is called `table.cache.block.enable`, and the index cache property is `table.cache.index.enable`:

```
ops.setProperty("myTable", "table.cache.block.enable", "true");
```

The page for an individual table in the Accumulo monitor will show the index cache hit rate and the block or data cache hit rate.

Tablet Splits

Accumulo automatically splits tablets when they reach a certain size threshold and tends to create uniformly sized tablets that are load-balanced evenly across the cluster. Many applications have no need to alter the split points of a table.

However, in some instances applications might want to control the split points for a table, or to obtain a list of splits.

One scenario for splitting a tablet manually is when you are preparing to stream a large volume of writes to a new table or a new set of tablets within a table. For example, let's say we have an application that wants to keep track of user interactions on a daily basis. We can choose to organize our table by defining row IDs consisting of the day followed by a user ID:

```
2015-03-14_usernameK
```

So each day, all of our writes will be sorted toward the end of the table, because the date portion of the row ID begins with the date. This is a problem, because the tablet that spans from the last known row to positive infinity is only hosted by one tablet server. Our ingest will be limited to the write throughput of one server, no matter how many servers we have.

User IDs may be somewhat randomly distributed throughout the day. We can improve the distribution of our writes each day by strategically presplitting the table with a new set of split points starting with tomorrow's date, and a user ID portion based on perhaps the distribution of user IDs from the previous day or several days.

So if the previous day's tablets ended up getting split automatically by Accumulo into the following split points:

```
2015-03-14_usernameC
2015-03-14_usernameF
2015-03-14_usernameJ
...
2015-03-14_usernameQ
2015-03-14_usernameV
```

We might opt, at the end of the day on March 14, to generate the following split points for the next day:

```
2015-03-15_usernameC
2015-03-15_usernameF
2015-03-15_usernameJ
...
2015-03-15_usernameQ
2015-03-15_usernameV
```

To add splits to a table, use the addSplits() method:

```
SortedSet<Text> partitionKeys = new TreeSet<>();

// add splits
partitionKeys.add(new Text("f"));
partitionKeys.add(new Text("j"));
partitionKeys.add(new Text("r"));
...

ops.addSplits("myTable", partitionKeys);
```

Adding split points, either manually or automatically, will not cause data to be unavailable or files to be changed right away. Newly split tablets will share files for a period of time, each owning nonoverlapping ranges of keys in the files. For example, one tablet might use keys from the beginning of the file up until some midpoint key, with another tablet using keys after that midpoint through the end of the file. The files will continue to be shared until a major compaction writes out new files, one for each tablet. Creating new splits is primarily a matter of adding some entries to the metadata table.

We might want to take the splits from one table and apply them to a new table. A list of splits within a table can be obtained via the listSplits() method:

```
Collection<Text> splits = ops.listSplits("myTable");
// note: in earlier versions of Accumulo this was called getSplits()
```

It is possible to obtain a sample of the splits of a table by specifying the maximum number of splits to return. The splits will be sampled uniformly:

```
Collection<Text> sampleSplits = ops.listSplits("myTable", 10);
// note: in previous versions this methods was called getSplits()
```

Quickly and automatically splitting

Applications can control how aggressively tablet servers automatically split tablets by setting the table.split.threshold property.

Instead of adding specific split points, applications can temporarily lower the split threshold while live ingest is happening until a table has as many or more tablets as there are tablet servers.

Creating splits this way can result in many tablets sharing RFiles in HDFS initially. It is not until a major compaction is run for a tablet that an RFile can be created that belongs exclusively to a tablet.

Shared Rfiles are not typically a problem but can cause "chop" compactions to occur when later merging tablets. When merging tablets that may have been created using the split threshold lowering process, consider running the compact command on the table first.

To change the table split threshold, use the handy setProperty() method and specify a new threshold in terms of bytes:

```
ops.setProperty("table.split.threshold", "500k");

int numTablets = 0;
int numServers = conn.instanceOperations().getTabletServers().size(); ❶

while(numTablets < numServers) {
```

```
    // wait a while
    ...
    numTablets = ops.listSplits("myTable", 10);
}

ops.setProperty("table.split.threshold", "1G");
```

❶ See "Instance Operations" on page 165 for details on the instance-level operations API.

We discuss splitting tablets for performance reasons more in "Splitting Tables" on
page 498.

Merging tablets

Tablets can become empty over time, as data is aged off, or as data is deleted from a
table, or as the result of adding splits that don't end up reflecting the actual distribution of the keys.

Empty tablets don't generally cause serious problems for tables. Perhaps the biggest
issue with empty tablets is that they can cause the distribution of actual data within a
table to be uneven across servers, because the default table load balancer only looks at
the number of tablets, not the amount of data within each tablet.

Empty tablets or even just smaller tablets can be merged into larger tablets to achieve
a more uniform distribution of data across tablets.

To merge tablets in a given range, use the merge() method:

```
    ops.merge("myTable", new Text("ja"), new Text("jd"));
```

There is a utility class, org.apache.accumulo.core.util.Merge, that will loop over
small tablets, merging until there are no more tablets smaller than a given size:

```
    long goalSize = AccumuloConfiguration.getMemoryInBytes("500M");
    boolean force = true;
    Merge merge = new Merge();

    Text start = null; // begin at the start of the table
    Text end = null; // go to the end of the table

    merge.mergomatic(conn, "myTable", start, end, goalSize, force);
```

A few other methods relating to tablets can be useful: getMaxRow() to find out the last
existing row within a range; and splitRangeByTablets(), which can be used to split
a range according to how tablets are currently split. splitRangeByTablets() is used,
for instance, in Accumulo's MapReduce integration to align MapReduce input splits
to tablets:

```
Text getMaxRow(String tableName, Authorizations auths, Text startRow,
    boolean startInclusive, Text endRow, boolean endInclusive)

Set<Range> splitRangeByTablets(String tableName, Range range, int maxSplits)
```

Compacting

New writes to Accumulo tables are sent to two places by the tablet server: a sorted in-memory data structure, called the *in-memory map*, and an unsorted log on disk, called the *write-ahead log*. When the in-memory map reaches a certain size, it is flushed to a new file in HDFS, a process called a *minor compaction*.

Applications can direct tablet servers to flush all the recent mutations from memory to disk for a particular table via the TableOperations.flush() method. This is different from the BatchWriter.flush() method, which sends all of the mutations from a client to tablet servers.

Flushing a table can make it easier to perform certain operations, such as shutting down a tablet server, because a flushed table's tablets require no recovery if a tablet server is shut down:

```
ops.flush(String tableName, Text start, Text end, boolean wait)
```

Over time, the number of files associated with each tablet increases, up to the maximum number of files per tablet specified for the table. Tablet servers automatically decide when to combine two or more files into one new file in a process called *major compaction*. Lookups on tablets with fewer files can be carried out more quickly because fewer disk seeks are involved in locating the start key of interest.

By default, Accumulo is tuned to allow each tablet to have several files. This has the effect of balancing the resources dedicated to ingest with those dedicated to lookups.

Applications can choose to compact a table on demand to improve lookup performance via the compact() method. Unlike the periodic compactions that a tablet server performs in the background, an application-initiated compaction will always merge all files associated with a tablet into one file. This can also help when you are attempting to remove deleted data from disk, or with ensuring that changes in configured options or iterators are immediately reflected in a table's files.

Major compactions scheduled from the API or the shell will always cause the data for each tablet to be rewritten to one new file, even when a tablet already has only one file.

This is useful for ensuring that changes in table configuration—affect all of the table's data on disk.

Compactions can be scheduled over a particular range, or over an entire table. It is also possible to request that the compact method perform a minor compaction before starting the major compaction, and/or to make the method wait until the compactions are complete:

```
boolean flush = true;
boolean wait = false;

Text startRow = new Text("ja");
Text endRow = new Text("jd");

ops.compact("myTable", startRow, endRow, flush, wait);
```

To compact the entire table, set the start and end row parameters to null:

```
ops.compact("myTable", null, null, flush, wait) ;
```

Compacting an entire table or a range within a table can be a useful way of ensuring that changes in table configuration are reflected in all the data stored on disk.

To configure iterators to be used just for the duration of a compaction, applications can pass in a list of IteratorSetting objects:

```
List<IteratorSetting> iterators = new ArrayList<>();
...
boolean flush = true;
boolean wait = false;
void compact("myTable", start, end, iterators, flush, wait);
```

If compactions are already taking place, the requested compaction of a table will be queued up and performed as soon as resources become available. A set of queued compactions for a table can be cancelled via the cancelCompaction() method:

```
ops.cancelCompaction("myTable");
```

Compaction properties

Compactions require precious I/O and CPU resources. As such, how often compactions take place can have a large effect on query and ingest performance. The following are the available compaction properties and their behavior:

table.compaction.major.ratio
: This property controls how aggressively tablet servers automatically compact files. By default the setting is 3, which instructs tablet servers to compact a set of files if their combined size is at least three times the size of the largest tablet in the set. For example, if there were three or more files of the same size, they would be compacted into a single file. Setting this ratio higher makes tablet servers wait longer before combining files.

`table.compaction.major.everything.idle`

This property controls how long after the last write to a tablet to wait before considering the tablet to be idle. A tablet server sometimes chooses to compact idle tablets, because compacting a tablet's files into a single file can improve query performance. Idle compactions might never happen if the tablet server is busy. The default idle time is one hour. Tablets that already only have one file will not be compacted in this way.

`table.compaction.minor.idle`

This property tells the tablet server how long after receiving the last mutation to leave a tablet's data in the in-memory map before flushing to disk. Typically a tablet server waits until the available memory is close to being used up, but in this case, if a tablet has not seen any mutations for this period of time, the tablet server can opt to flush the data to disk. The default is 5 minutes.

`table.compaction.minor.logs.threshold`

This is the maximum number of write-ahead logs that will be associated with a tablet before the tablet server will perform a minor compaction. After the minor compaction takes place, the tablet will no longer need the data previously written to those logs, which will reduce recovery time if the tablet server goes down. The default setting is 3.

Additional Properties

Several other settings can be controlled on a per-table basis. Application designers should at least be aware of these options, because their configuration can depend on access patterns and data used as part of the application. These include the following:

`table.balancer`

This controls the way that a table's tablets are distributed throughout the cluster. By default, a table's tablets are spread across tablet servers so that each tablet server has close to the same number of tablets using the `DefaultLoadBalancer` class. This does not take into account the number of entries per tablet or the number of bytes per tablet, just the number of tablets. Some tables call for a different strategy of distributing tablets across servers.

To implement a custom load balancer, create a Java class that extends `org.apache.accumulo.server.master.balancer.TabletBalancer`, implementing the following methods:

```
public abstract class TabletBalancer {

    ...

    /**
     * Assign tablets to tablet servers. This method is called
```

```
 * whenever the master finds tablets that are unassigned.
 * ...
 */
abstract public void getAssignments(
      SortedMap<TServerInstance,
      TabletServerStatus> current,
      Map<KeyExtent,TServerInstance> unassigned,
      Map<KeyExtent,TServerInstance> assignments);

/**
 * Ask the balancer if any migrations are necessary.
 * ...
 */
public abstract long balance(
      SortedMap<TServerInstance,
      TabletServerStatus> current,
      Set<KeyExtent> migrations,
      List<TabletMigration> migrationsOut);
...
}
```

table.classpath.context

This property allows the Java CLASSPATH used for a particular table to be specified. Iterators and other custom classes can be loaded for a particular table
without affecting the classes loaded for other tables.

tserver.memory.maps.max

This controls the amount of memory dedicated to holding newly written data in
memory before flushing to disk.

table.failures.ignore

If part of a table is unavailable for some reason—for example, if there is a problem with HDFS data nodes serving a particular block of a file associated with a
tablet—a scan over that part of a tablet will result in an Exception. It is possible
to allow scans to proceed and return any data that is available, even in the presence of some unavailable data by setting table.failures.ignore to true. By
default this setting is false.

table.file.blocksize

This property controls the size of HDFS file blocks used for a table. Setting this
value to be close to the split threshold means that a file can consist of just one
block and therefore can be retrieved from a single HDFS data node, which can
increase query performance.

table.file.compress.blocksize

When Accumulo writes key-value pairs to disk, they are first grouped into blocks
and, by default, compressed. The default setting is 100K, which groups 100 KB of

key-value pairs before compression. This means that a compressed block that decompressed to about 100 KB will be retrieved from disk when even only a single key-value pair is read. If an application will mostly retrieve one, or few, small key-value pairs, setting this property lower can result in better query performance. If an application will regularly scan larger ranges of key-value pairs, setting this value higher will reduce file storage overhead slightly and result in prefetching more data from disk, which will be faster for these applications than having files that have more, smaller blocks.

`table.file.compress.blocksize.index`

The files Accumulo uses to store sorted key-value pairs on disk include a section for indexes. These indexes help a tablet server find which block or blocks of a file to load for a particular range of keys. This property controls the size of the blocks used to store index entries for a file. The default is 128 KB, represented as 128K.

`table.file.compress.type`

This property allows tables to be compressed with the specified algorithm. Accumulo ships with Gzip and LZO compression libraries. The default compression algorithm is Gzip. Compression can be turned off by setting this property to none, which is not recommended for most apps. In general, choosing a compression algorithm involves a trade-off between resources needed to perform compression and the amount of compression.

`table.file.max`

This property sets the maximum number of files that can be associated with a tablet. If a new file needs to be written to this tablet and the maximum number of files is already reached, a tablet server will perform a *merging minor compaction* in which one data file is rewritten along with data from memory into a new file, so that the maximum number of files is not exceeded. Merging minor compactions are slower than compactions that simply flush out data in memory to a new file, because they involve reading an existing file and performing a merge-sort with data from memory to create a new file. This has the effect of slowing down ingest while keeping the number of files that a tablet server may need to open down to a reasonable number for any given query.

Setting this property to a value less than the value for `tserver.scan.files.open.max` will prevent a tablet server from having more files than it is willing to open all at once. This property can be set to 0, in which case it will default to the value of `tserver.scan.files.open.max` - 1.

Increasing this value will allow more new files to be flushed to disk before merging minor compactions kick in, effectively tuning a table for faster ingest at the expense of queries. Conversely, setting this value lower will end up throttling ingest and will make queries faster. The default value is 15 files.

`table.file.replication`

Controls the number of file block replicas associated with this table. A table that requires more fault tolerance can set this number higher. Tables that store data that can be restored from another source can set this property lower. Fewer replicas will result in faster ingest rates. Setting this property to 0 will cause tablet servers to use the HDFS default replication setting. 0 is the default setting.

`table.file.type`

Older versions of Accumulo use a file type known as the *map* file type. Newer versions use a format called an *RFile*. The default setting for this property is `rf`, meaning that new files will be written in the RFile format. See "File formats" on page 369 for more information on these formats.

`table.formatter`

Some tables can have complex data elements stored in keys or values. For example, a table can contain a serialized Avro object. Anything that is not a Java `String` will likely show up in the shell as a jumble of characters. Specifying a custom table formatter can cause a table's values to be printed out in a human-readable representation. Custom `Formatter` classes are discussed in "Human-Readable Versus Binary Values and Formatters" on page 311.

`table.interepreter`

When scans are performed in the shell, arguments are interpreted as strings. This may not result in the type of range desired if a table's rows or columns are not stored as strings. For example, a table may have serialized Java `Long` objects as row IDs.

When row IDs or columns that are not Java `Strings` are used, an alternative interpreter can be used for performing scans within the shell. Custom interpreters can be created by extending `org.apache.accumulo.core.util.interpret.ScanInterpreter`:

```
public interface ScanInterpreter {

    Text interpretRow(Text row);

    Text interpretBeginRow(Text row);

    Text interpretEndRow(Text row);

    Text interpretColumnFamily(Text cf);

    Text interpretColumnQualifier(Text cq);
}
```

The methods defined by the `ScanInterpreter` interface can be used to transform a given start row, end row, or column name into the right format for a particular table. The default scan interpreter is `org.apache.accumulo.core.util.inter pret.DefaultScanInterpreter`. Setting a custom interpreter can be done by setting the `table.interepreter` property to the fully qualified class name of the custom interpreter.

`table.scan.max.memory`

This is the maximum amount of memory that a server will use to batch results of a scan before sending them to a client. For applications with typically larger scans, setting this property higher can improve performance. The default is 512 KB (512K).

`table.security.scan.visibility.default`

This setting allows key-value pairs in a table that have a blank column visibility to be considered to have a default column visibility. For example, we can store key-value pairs with no column visibility set but have the `table.security.scan.vis ibility.default` property set to `public`, which will have the effect of requiring that all users performing scans against these key-value pairs in the table at least possess the *public* authorization token.

> When a scanner returns key-value pairs that have no column visibility set, they will appear to have blank column visibilities when returned to the client, even though a default visibility can be in place. That is, the tablet server does not fill in the column visibilities of key-value pairs returned with the default visibility for the table.
>
> Also, this is a scan-time setting only. It will not cause the default column visibility to be persisted to disk within any of the keys. This is convenient because it allows the default visibility to be changed without rewriting all the data already stored thus far.

Key-value pairs without a column visibility set can be seen by anyone when there is no default visibility configured. See the discussion in "Using a Default Visibility" on page 190 for more on using the default visibility setting.

`table.walog.enabled`

This property controls whether to persist new writes to a log on disk before considering a write to be successful. By default all new mutations are persisted to the write-ahead log on disk before a tablet server reports to a client that the write succeeded. This setting is `true` by default. The write-ahead log only applies to writes written to a table via mutations added to a `BatchWriter`. The write-ahead log is not involved in bulk-loading new files to a table. This setting does not need to be set to `false` when using bulk loading; the write-ahead log is simply not used. See "MapReduce and Bulk Import" on page 268 for more on bulk import.

 Tables that have the write-ahead log disabled can lose data if live writes are being streamed to servers and a server dies. The write-ahead log should only be disabled in cases where data is backed up elsewhere and where tables are regularly checkpointed, so that a consistent view of the table can be created from replaying live writes to data from the last complete checkpoint after a server failure.

Online Status

Accumulo tables can be brought *offline*, meaning they will be unavailable for queries and writes, and they will not utilize any system resources other than disk storage.

This can be useful for tables that do not need to be available at all times but occasionally can be brought online for some queries and then taken offline again to free up system resources for other tables. We cover another use case for taking tables offline when discussing cloning and exporting tables in "Importing and Exporting Tables" on page 158.

To take a table offline using the `TableOperations` object, use the `offline()` method:

```
ops.offline("myTable");
```

This will instruct all tablet servers to begin unloading all tablets for the table specified, flushing any data in memory to disk and releasing any system resources dedicated to those tablets, such as open file handles. Because this can take some time, depending on the size of the table, this call is asynchronous.

Applications can call this method with an additional parameter that causes the call to wait until a table is offline:

```
ops.offline("myTable", true);
```

 The *accumulo.root* and *accumulo.metadata* tables cannot be taken offline. To operate on the files associated with these tables, Accumulo would need to be shut down.

The */tables* section of the Accumulo monitor shows the online status of all tables. A table that is offline can be brought online again with the `online()` method:

```
ops.online("myTable");
// or
ops.online("myTable", true);
```

This will instruct tablet servers to be assigned responsibility for all the tablets of the table specified.

Tables can be taken offline and back online in the shell as well. See "Changing Online Status" on page 444 for shell methods relating to the online status of tables.

Cloning

Tables can be cloned via the `clone()` method. Because all underlying files of Accumulo tables are immutable, cloning can be performed very efficiently.

When a table is cloned, it can also be optionally flushed to ensure that a consistent view of the table is cloned at a specific point in time, via the Boolean `flush` parameter. A cloned table will inherit all the configuration of the original table. Some properties of the original table can be excluded when the cloned table is created, and properties can be optionally set to specified values as well.

A cloned table will not inherit the table *permissions* of the original. The user that created the cloned table will be the only user authorized to read and alter the table at first:

```
boolean flush = true;
Map<String,String> propsToSet = new HashMap<>();
// set any properties to be different for the cloned table
...

Set<String> propsToExclude = new HashSet<>();
// identify any properties not to be copied from the original table
// defaults will be used instead unless set in propsToSet
...

ops.clone("originalTable", "newTable", flush, originalProps, propsToExclude);
```

Cloning is a good option when the need arises for a consistent copy of a table that can be manipulated without affecting the original.

Using cloning as a snapshotting mechanism

Cloning can also be thought of as a way of taking a snapshot of a table at a particular time. If something corrupts a table that is outside the fault-tolerant measures of Accumulo—such as a bug in a client writing new data to a table or a user accidentally deleting data—being able to restore a table from a recent snapshot can save a lot of data and time.

Making a snapshot can be done as in this example:

```
...
// clone the table as a snapshot
System.out.println("Creating snapshot");

boolean flush = true;

Map<String,String> propsToSet = new HashMap<>();

Set<String> propsToExclude = new HashSet<>();

String timestamp = Long.toString(System.currentTimeMillis());

String snapshot = "myTable_" + timestamp;
ops.clone("myTable", snapshot, flush, propsToSet, propsToExclude);
...
```

Cloned tables as snapshots can be named with a unique identifier, such as the time they were cloned. Restoring a snapshot could be as simple as stopping clients, deleting or renaming the primary table, and cloning the snapshot table using the original table name as the name of the newly cloned table.

An example is as follows:

```
...
System.out.println("Restoring from snapshot");
ops.delete("myTable");
ops.clone(snapshot, "myTable", flush, propsToSet, propsToExclude);

// any existing scanners will no longer work
// get a new one
scan = conn.createScanner("myTable", new Authorizations());
for(Map.Entry<Key, Value> kv : scan) {
  System.out.println(
    kv.getKey().getRow() + "\t" +
        new String(kv.getValue().get()));
}
...
```

Importing and Exporting Tables

Accumulo tables can be exported to a directory in HDFS, or other HDFS-compatible filesystems, and also imported.

For a table to be exported, it must be taken offline and stay offline for the duration of the export. This ensures that there is a consistent set of files in HDFS for all tablets in the table, and that the garbage collector process will not delete any files in the initial list created by the export command before the files can be copied to another place. Because offline tables are unavailable for new writes and reads, applications can choose to clone the table instead, take the clone offline, and export the clone instead of the original table.

Exporting a table will include information such as the table configuration, the split points, and the logical time information, if any, so that when the table is imported, the destination table will resemble the original.

To export a table, you must specify a path to a directory in HDFS in which table information can be written:

```
ops.offline("myTable");
ops.exportTable("myTable", "/exports/myTable/");
```

The */exports/myTable* directory now contains metadata information and a file containing commands for Hadoop's `distcp` feature that can be used to copy the files from our table to another HDFS instance. For instructions on doing this, see "Import, Export, and Backups" on page 446.

Tables exported in this way can be programmatically imported into Accumulo, but the data files must be copied first:

```
hadoop distcp -f /exports/myTable/distcp.txt /exports/myTable_contents
```

Once the files have been copied, the table can be imported with the following methods. The files can only be imported once. To import the same table again, the `distcp` command must be repeated:

```
ops.createTable("anotherTable");
ops.importTable("anotherTable", "/exports/myTable_contents")
```

Exporting and importing a table can facilitate moving a table from one Accumulo namespace to another, because simply renaming a table to move it into a different namespace is not possible.

Newly imported tables will have the same table configuration applied and split points as the exported table.

Additional Administrative Methods

There are a few additional features in the administrative API.

The `clearLocatorCache()` method can be used to cause a client to forget the mapping of tablets to servers and to learn the mapping anew by reading the metadata table:

```
void clearLocatorCache(String tableName)
```

The `tableIdMap()` method will return a Java `Map` of table names to IDs that are used to identify table resources in HDFS and in the metadata table. Looking up a table's ID can be helpful for locating files in HDFS or entries in the metadata table.

```
Map<String,String> tableIdMap();
```

The `getDiskUsage()` command is useful for seeing how many bytes on disk are used by a table. The method can be used for multiple tables simultaneously:

```
Set<String> tables = new HashSet<>();
tables.add("testTable");

List<DiskUsage> usages = ops.getDiskUsage(tables);

System.out.println(usages.get(0).getUsage() + " bytes");
```

The `testClassLoad()` method is useful for testing whether a class can be correctly loaded for a given table—for example, a custom iterator or constraint or other user-defined class.

If a specific `CLASSPATH` is set for the table, it will be used to attempt to load the class. The class can be tested for whether it implements a given interface:

```
String className = "org.my.ClassName";
String asTypeName = "org.my.Interface";
boolean canLoad = ops.testClassLoad("testTable", className, asTypeName);
```

To configure iterators or constraints on a table, see "Iterators" on page 209 and "Constraints" on page 201, respectively.

Table Namespaces

A new feature in Accumulo 1.6 is that tables can be grouped using a namespace. For example, one department of an organization can have a set of tables that it can name without worrying about using the same name for a table as another department.

Here is an example of a set of tables in separate namespaces, perhaps supporting separate applications. There are three namespaces, `intranet`, `wiki`, and `sensor`, perhaps each storing data from different sources, but doing similar things such as storing records imported, and storing index entries:

```
intranet.index
intranet.records
intranet.stats
wiki.index
wiki.docPartIndex
wiki.articles
wiki.audit
sensor.records
sensor.index
sensor.trends
```

Each namespace can use any names for their tables. In addition, some settings can be applied at the namespace level and will affect all tables in that namespace. Namespaces provide a convenient way for configuring and managing tables in groups.

In a table name, the portion preceding a single dot (.) constitutes the namespace, and the portion following the dot represents the specific table within the namespace. For example, the metadata and root tables live within the system namespace, accumulo, so they appear as *accumulo.metadata* and *accumulo.root*. Tables without a namespace portion and a dot are assigned to the default namespace.

Namespaces can be controlled via the NamespaceOperations class, obtained from a Connector object:

```
NamespaceOperations nsOps = conn.getNamespaceOperations();
```

Creating

A namespace must be created explicitly before a new table can be created within that namespace. A namespace can only consist of letters, numbers, and underscore characters. We can also check for the existence of a namespace:

```
if(!nsOps.exists("myNamespace"))
  nsOps.create("myNamespace");
```

Now we can create tables within this namespace. To assign a table to a namespace simply prepend the name of the namespace and a dot before the name of the table:

```
conn.getTableOperations().create("myNamespace.myTable");
```

Attempting to assign a table to a namespace, that doesn't exist will result in an exception.

These actions can also be done in the shell:

```
user@accumulo> createnamespace myNamespace
user@accumulo> createtable myNamespace.myTable
```

 Once a table has been created in a namespace it cannot be moved to another namespace simply by renaming. Tables can be renamed as long as the namespace portion of the name is unchanged.

You can move a table to a namespace by exporting it to a directory in HDFS and then importing it into a table in a different namespace. See "Importing and Exporting Tables" on page 158.

To obtain a list of namespaces, use the list() method:

```
for(String namespace : nsOps.list())
  System.out.println(namespace);
```

To list namespaces in the shell, use the namespaces command:

```
user@accumulo> namespaces
accumulo
myNamespace
```

To get the name of the system namespace, use the `systemNamespace()` method. For the name of the default namespace, use the `defaultNamespace()` method.

It is possible to set properties on the default namespace, and all tables in the default namespace will be affected (we cover setting properties on namespaces in "Setting Namespace Properties" on page 162):

```
String systemNS = nsOps.systemNamespace();
String defaultNS = nsOps.defaultNamespace();
```

Renaming

Namespaces can be renamed. In this case all the tables within the namespace will appear under the new namespace:

```
nsOps.rename("myNamespace", "myNewNamespace");
```

In the shell this is achieved via the `renamenamespace` command:

```
user@accumulo> createnamespace ns

user@accumulo> createtable ns.test

user@accumulo ns.test> tables
accumulo.metadata
accumulo.root
ns.test

user@accumulo ns.test> renamenamespace ns newns
user@accumulo newns.test> tables

accumulo.metadata
accumulo.root
newns.test
```

Setting Namespace Properties

Any properties configured on a namespace will be applied to all the tables within it. This makes changing the properties for a group of tables easy. Tables can still have individual properties too, in which case they will override any corresponding namespace properties.

The only properties that should be applied to namespaces are those properties that are normally applied to individual tables. These typically begin with the `table` prefix. For a list of table properties, see "Configuring Table Properties" on page 137.

To set a property, use the `setProperty()` method on a `NamespaceOperations` object:

```
nsOps.setProperty("myNamespace", "table.file.replication", "2");
```

The property will be propagated to all tablet servers via ZooKeeper and may take a few seconds to affect all tables within the namespace.

Similarly, to remove a property, use the removeProperty() method. This will also be propagated within a few seconds to tablet servers. When a property has been removed from a namespace, the tables within the namespace inherit the system setting if it exists, or the default setting:

```
nsOps.removeProperty("myNamespace", "table.file.replication");
```

Properties of a namespace can be listed via the getProperties() method:

```
for(Entry<String,String>> e : getProperties("myNamespace"))
    System.out.println(e.getKey() + "\t" + e.getValue());
```

Setting and viewing namespace properties in the shell can be done with the -ns option to the config command:

```
user@accumulo> config -ns myNamespace -s property=setting
user@accumulo> config -ns myNamespace -d property
user@accumulo> config -ns myNamespace
```

Deleting

Before a namespace can be deleted, all the tables within the namespace must be deleted. Once a namespace is empty, the delete() method can be used to remove it:

```
nsOps.delete("myNamespace");
```

A NamespaceNotEmptyException will be thrown if the namespace still contains any tables.

In the shell this can be done via the deletenamespace() command:

```
user@accumulo newns.test> deletenamespace newns
deletenamespace { newns } (yes|no)? yes
2014-08-23 12:14:37,297 ERROR [main] shell.Shell (Shell.java:logError(1139)) -
    org.apache.accumulo.core.client.NamespaceNotEmptyException: Namespace newns
    (Id=1) it not empty, contains at least one table

user@accumulo newns.test> deletetable newns.test
deletetable { newns.test } (yes|no)? yes
yes
Table: [newns.test] has been deleted.

user@accumulo> deletenamespace newns
deletenamespace { newns } (yes|no)? yes
yes
user@accumulo>
```

Configuring Iterators

Similarly to the way Accumulo iterators can be configured for individual tables as described in "Iterators" on page 209, iterators can be configured for a namespace, which will apply the iterator to all tables within the namespace.

Iterators can be configured to be applied at all scopes (scan-time, minor compaction, and major compaction) or specific scopes. To add an iterator on all scopes:

```
IteratorSetting iterSet = new IteratorSetting(10, "myIter",
    com.examples.Iterator.class);
nsOps.attachIterator("myNamespace", iterSet);
```

Iterators can also be applied to specific scopes. For example, you can set an iterator to be applied at only minor compaction and major compaction times:

```
IteratorSetting iterSet = new IteratorSetting(10, "myIter",
    com.examples.Iterator.class);
EnumSet<IteratorScope> scopes =
    EnumSet.of(IteratorScope.MINC, IteratorScope.MAJC);
nsOps.attachIterator("myNamespace", iterSet, scopes);
```

The same methods available for working with iterators on individual tables can also be used for namespaces. These include:

- checkIteratorConflicts()
- getIteratorSetting()
- listIterators()
- removeIterator()

See "Iterators" on page 209 for details on using these methods.

Configuring Constraints

Constraints can be applied to namespaces in order to control the mutations allowed to be written to any tables within the namespace. Like the methods for configuring iterators, these methods are identical to their table-specific counterparts and include:

- addConstraint()
- listConstraints()
- removeConstraint()

See "Constraints" on page 201 for details on using these methods.

Testing Class Loading for a Namespace

The `testClassLoad()` method can be used to check whether a class can be loaded for a particular namespace. This is similar to the table-specific method, described in "Additional Administrative Methods" on page 159.

Instance Operations

An Accumulo instance consists of all the processes that are participating in the same cluster. It is possible to set instance-wide properties, and obtain information about the instance, via the `InstanceOperations` object:

```
InstanceOperations instOps = conn.instanceOperations();
```

Setting Properties

Properties can be set on an instance-wide basis. Setting a property will override the setting in *accumulo-site.xml*; or if a property doesn't appear in the *accumulo-site.xml* file, it will override the default.

Any type of property can be set here, whether it applies to the instance, to a namespace, or to an individual table:

```
instOps.setProperty("property", "value");

instOps.removeProperty("property");
```

Configuration

To retrieve a list of property settings as they appear in the *accumulo-site.xml* file, use the `getSiteConfiguration()` method:

```
Map<String, String> siteConfig = instOps.getSiteConfiguration();
for(Map.Entry<String, String> setting : siteConfig.entrySet()) {
  System.out.println(setting.getKey() + "\t" + setting.getValue());
}
```

To retrieve a list of properties as they are currently configured in ZooKeeper, use `getSystemConfiguration()`. Properties set via the shell or programmatically will be reflected here, in addition to any set in *accumulo-site.xml*, as well as the defaults:

```
Map<String, String> sysConfig = instOps.getSystemConfiguration();
for(Map.Entry<String, String> setting : sysConfig.entrySet()) {
  System.out.println(setting.getKey() + "\t" + setting.getValue());
}
```

Cluster Information

The `InstanceOperations` object can be used to obtain current information about the instance. To obtain a list of currently active tablet servers, use the `getTabletServ ers()` method:

```
List<String> servers = instOps.getTabletServers();
```

To get a list of active scans for a particular tablet server, specify the tablet server in the form *IP address* : *port*:

```
List<ActiveScan> scans = instOps.getActiveScans(tserver);
for(ActiveScan s : scans) {
  System.out.println(
    "age:\t" + s.getAge() + "\n"
    + "auths:\t" + s.getAuthorizations() + "\n"
    + "client:\t" + s.getClient() + "\n"
    + "columns:\t" + s.getColumns() + "\n"
    + "extent:\t" + s.getExtent() + "\n"
    + "idle:\t" + s.getIdleTime() + "\n"
    + "last contact:\t" + s.getLastContactTime() + "\n"
    + "scan id:\t" + s.getScanid() + "\n"
    + "server side iterator list:\t" + s.getSsiList() + "\n"
    + "server side iterator options:\t" + s.getSsio() + "\n"
    + "state:\t" + s.getState() + "\n"
    + "table:\t" + s.getTable() + "\n"
    + "type:\t" + s.getType() + "\n"
    + "user:\t" + s.getUser() + "\n");
}
```

An `ActiveScan` object will contain several pieces of information:

age
  The time in seconds since the scan began on this server

auths
  A list of authorizations to apply to this scan

client
  The IP address and port number of the client process

columns
  A list of columns fetched as part of the scan, or blank for all

extent
  The tablet being scanned

idle
  The amount of time in seconds since the scan has returned any data

last contact
: The amount of time in seconds since the client last contacted the server

scan id
: An identifier for the scan

server side iterator list
: A list of iterators applied on the server side

server side iterator options
: Any options applied to server-side iterators

state
: One of:

  - RUNNING when the scan is being performed

  - IDLE when waiting for the client to request more data

  - QUEUED when waiting for system resources to become available to start the scan

table
: The name of the table being scanned

type
: One of:

  - SINGLE for a regular Scanner

  - BATCH for a BatchScanner

user
: The name of the user performing the scan

Here is a sample of the information returned:

```
age: 3507
auths:
client:  192.168.10.70:56689
columns: []
extent:  f<<
idle:  27
last contact:  27
scan id: 0
server side iterator list: []
server side iterator options:  {}
state: RUNNING
table: table8
```

```
type:   SINGLE
user:   root

age: 1941
auths:
client:   192.168.10.70:56619
columns: []
extent:   6<<
idle:   27
last contact:   27
scan id: 0
server side iterator list: []
server side iterator options:   {}
state: QUEUED
table: table9
type:   SINGLE
user:   root

age: 135
auths:
client:   192.168.10.70:56716
columns: []
extent:   7<<
idle:   1
last contact:   1
scan id: 0
server side iterator list: []
server side iterator options:   {}
state: IDLE
table: table1
type:   SINGLE
user:   root
```

To list active compactions scheduled or running on a tablet server, specify the server using a string consisting of *IP address* : *port*:

```
List<ActiveCompaction> compactions = instOps.getActiveCompactions(tserver);
  for(ActiveCompaction c : compactions) {
    System.out.println(
      "age:\t" + c.getAge() + "\n"
      + "entries read:\t" + c.getEntriesRead() + "\n"
      + "entries written:\t" + c.getEntriesWritten() + "\n"
      + "extent:\t" + c.getExtent() + "\n"
      + "input files:\t" + c.getInputFiles() + "\n"
      + "iterators:\t" + c.getIterators() + "\n"
      + "locality group:\t" + c.getLocalityGroup() + "\n"
      + "output file:\t" + c.getOutputFile() + "\n"
      + "reason:\t" + c.getReason(). + "\n"
      + "table:\t" + c.getTable() + "\n"
      + "type:\t" + c.getType(). + "\n");
}
```

The ActiveCompaction object will consist of the following information:

age
> The length of time in seconds that the compaction has been running or scheduled

`entries read`
> The number of entries read from input files or from memory

`entries written`
> The number of entries written to the output file

`extent`
> An identifier for the tablet being compacted

`input files`
> A list of input files

`iterators`
> A list of iterators applied to the compaction

`locality group`
> Any locality groups involved

`output file`
> The path of the output file

reason
> The originator of the compaction. Either:
>
> - CHOP when part of a merge operation
> - CLOSE as is done before unloading a tablet
> - IDLE when a compaction is triggered by the setting `tablet.compaction.idle`
> - SYSTEM when automatically triggered by the tablet server's internal resource manager due to data in memory, or number of files
> - USER when requested by the user

table
> The name of the table

type
> One of:
>
> - FULL resulting in one file for the tablet
> - MAJOR combining several files into one

- MERGE combining in-memory data with the tablet's smallest file
- MINOR flushing in-memory data to a new file

An example of some active compactions from the test program *com.accumulo-book.tableapi.InstanceOpsExample.java* are as follows:

```
==== tserver.local:56481 ====
age: 914
entries read:  43008
entries written: 43008
extent:  j<<
input files: []
iterators: []
locality group:
output file: file:/var/folders/ks/ltzkjxtn5t9cb302mrgzxldm0000gn/T/
    1409356659029-0/accumulo/tables/j/default_tablet/F000002a.rf_tmp
reason:  SYSTEM
table: table15
type:  MINOR

age: 4519
entries read:  186368
entries written: 93184
extent:  6<<
input files: [file:/var/folders/ks/ltzkjxtn5t9cb302mrgzxldm0000gn/T/
    1409356659029-0/accumulo/tables/6/default_tablet/F000001l.rf, file:/var/
    folders/ks/ltzkjxtn5t9cb302mrgzxldm0000gn/T/1409356659029-0/accumulo/tables/
    6/default_tablet/F000001x.rf, file:/var/folders/ks/
    ltzkjxtn5t9cb302mrgzxldm0000gn/T/1409356659029-0/accumulo/tables/6/
    default_tablet/A000000f.rf, file:/var/folders/ks/
    ltzkjxtn5t9cb302mrgzxldm0000gn/T/1409356659029-0/accumulo/tables/6/
    default_tablet/F000001v.rf]
iterators: []
locality group:
output file: file:/var/folders/ks/ltzkjxtn5t9cb302mrgzxldm0000gn/T/
    1409356659029-0/accumulo/tables/6/default_tablet/A0000021.rf_tmp
reason:  USER
table: table9
type:  FULL
```

To check whether a tablet server is reachable, use the ping() method:

```
String ipAddress = "10.0.0.1";
String port = "9997";

try {
  instOps.ping(ipAddress + ":" + port)
} catch(AccumuloException ae) {
  System.out.println("server " + ipAddress + ":" + port + " unreachable.");
}
```

You can also test whether a class is loadable from the instance-wide classpath by calling the `testClassLoad()` method:

```
String className = "org.my.ClassName";
String asTypeName = "org.my.Interface";

boolean loadable = instOps.testClassLoad(className, asTypeName);
```

Precedence of Properties

Properties that are applied more specifically take precedence over those applied more generally. For example, an instance-wide property can be overridden by a namespace-specific property, which itself can be overridden by a table-specific property (Figure 4-3).

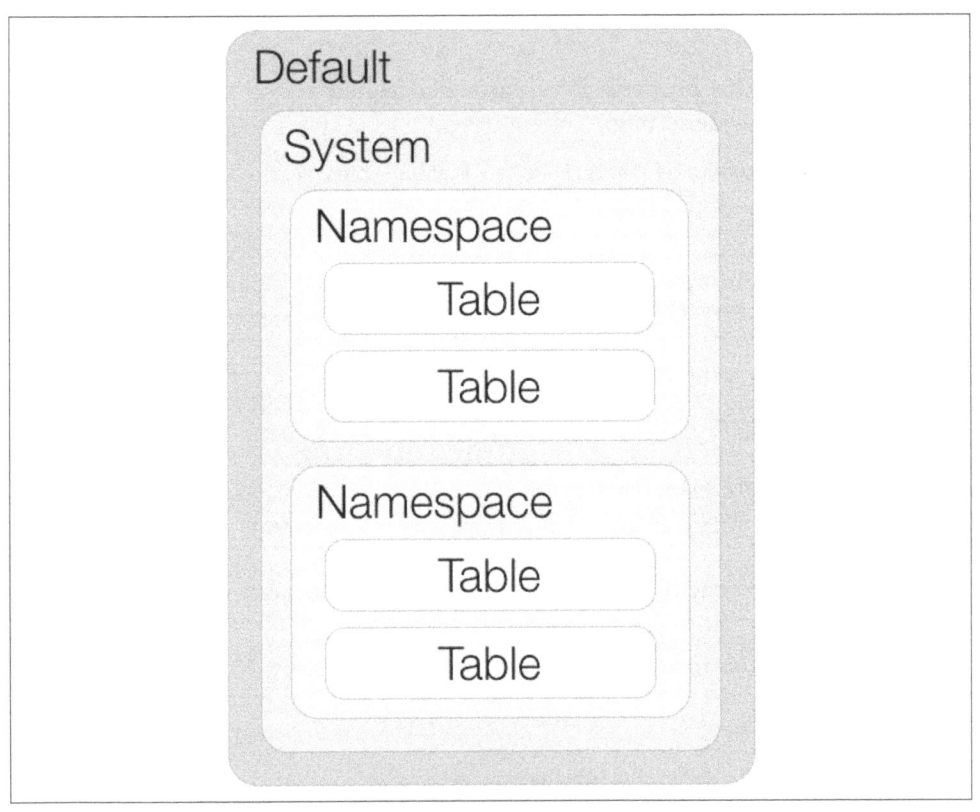

Figure 4-3. Precedence of properties

For example, we might choose to change a property across all tables from the default to a specific setting we choose. First, we'll look at the default setting:

```
user@accumulo> config -f table.file.replication
-----------+-----------------------------------------------------------+---------
```

```
SCOPE       | NAME                                                  | VALUE
------------+-------------------------------------------------------+---------
default     | table.file.replication .................................. | 0
------------+-------------------------------------------------------+---------
```

The value, 0, means to use whatever the default replication setting is in HDFS.

We can change the table file replication property for all tables in all namespaces by not specifying a namespace or table when we apply the property change:

```
user@accumulo> config -s table.file.replication=1
user@accumulo> config -f table.file.replication
------------+-------------------------------------------------------+---------
SCOPE       | NAME                                                  | VALUE
------------+-------------------------------------------------------+---------
default     | table.file.replication .................................. | 0
system      |    @override .......................................... | 1
------------+-------------------------------------------------------+---------
```

If we now look at this property for a particular namespace or table, we see that it inherits the system-wide setting:

```
user@accumulo> config -f table.file.replication -t ns.test
------------+-------------------------------------------------------+---------
SCOPE       | NAME                                                  | VALUE
------------+-------------------------------------------------------+---------
default     | table.file.replication .................................. | 0
system      |    @override .......................................... | 1
------------+-------------------------------------------------------+---------

user@accumulo> config -f table.file.replication -ns ns
------------+-------------------------------------------------------+---------
SCOPE       | NAME                                                  | VALUE
------------+-------------------------------------------------------+---------
default     | table.file.replication .................................. | 0
system      |    @override .......................................... | 1
------------+-------------------------------------------------------+---------
```

We can override the system-wide property by setting the property for a namespace:

```
user@accumulo> config -ns ns -s table.file.replication=2
user@accumulo> config -f table.file.replication -t ns.test
------------+-------------------------------------------------------+---------
SCOPE       | NAME                                                  | VALUE
------------+-------------------------------------------------------+---------
default     | table.file.replication .................................. | 0
system      |    @override .......................................... | 2
------------+-------------------------------------------------------+---------

user@accumulo> config -f table.file.replication -ns ns
------------+-------------------------------------------------------+---------
SCOPE       | NAME                                                  | VALUE
------------+-------------------------------------------------------+---------
default     | table.file.replication .................................. | 0
```

```
system      |     @override ........................................... | 2
------------+---------------------------------------------------------+---------
```

The system-wide property is still in effect for tables outside the ns namespace:

```
user@accumulo> config -f table.file.replication
------------+---------------------------------------------------------+---------
SCOPE       | NAME                                                    | VALUE
------------+---------------------------------------------------------+---------
default     | table.file.replication ................................ | 0
system      |     @override ........................................... | 1
------------+---------------------------------------------------------+---------
```

Finally, if we set a property for a particular table, it will override the namespace setting:

```
user@accumulo> config -t ns.test -s table.file.replication=3
user@accumulo> config -f table.file.replication -t ns.test
------------+---------------------------------------------------------+---------
SCOPE       | NAME                                                    | VALUE
------------+---------------------------------------------------------+---------
default     | table.file.replication ................................ | 0
system      |     @override ........................................... | 3
------------+---------------------------------------------------------+---------

user@accumulo> config -f table.file.replication -ns ns
------------+---------------------------------------------------------+---------
SCOPE       | NAME                                                    | VALUE
------------+---------------------------------------------------------+---------
default     | table.file.replication ................................ | 0
system      |     @override ........................................... | 2
------------+---------------------------------------------------------+---------

user@accumulo> config -f table.file.replication
------------+---------------------------------------------------------+---------
SCOPE       | NAME                                                    | VALUE
------------+---------------------------------------------------------+---------
default     | table.file.replication ................................ | 0
system      |     @override ........................................... | 1
------------+---------------------------------------------------------+---------
```

## CHAPTER 5

Security API

Accumulo controls access to data in its tables in a number of ways: *authentication*, *permissions*, and *authorizations*.

These can be thought of as applying at two levels: authentication and permissions at the higher application and table level, and authorizations—which are used along with *column visibilities*—at the lower, key-value–pair level. Authentication relates to Accumulo users and how a user confirms its identity to Accumulo. Permissions control what operations Accumulo users are allowed to perform. Authorizations control which key-value pairs Accumulo users are allowed to see.

Accumulo provides the ability to create accounts, grant permissions, and grant authorizations. All of these mechanisms are pluggable, with their defaults being to store and retrieve user information in ZooKeeper. Custom security mechanisms are discussed in "Custom Authentication, Permissions, and Authorization" on page 195.

High-level security-related operations such as creating users and granting permissions and authorizations are carried out via the `SecurityOperations` object, obtained from a `Connector` object:

```
SecurityOperations secOps = conn.securityOperations();
```

Security operations can be logged to an audit log if Accumulo is configured to do so (see "Auditing Security Operations" on page 194).

Low-level key-value–pair security occurs naturally whenever `ColumnVisibility` and `Authorizations` objects are used when reading and writing data.

For any given set of security mechanisms, there are essentially two ways to manage access control: create an account for every user using Accumulo's security mechanisms, or create accounts for each application and delegate authentication, permissions, and authorization for each user to the application. In the latter case, it is the application's job to authenticate individual users, look up their permissions and authorization tokens, and pass their authorizations faithfully onto Accumulo when data is read or written. This is discussed further in "Using an Application Account for Multiple Users" on page 198.

Authentication

Accumulo user accounts are used to limit the permissions that an application or an individual user can carry out, and to limit the set of authorization tokens that can be used in lookups. Some basic instance information such as instance ID, locations of master processes, and location of the root tablet can be retrieved from the Instance object itself. This information is available to anyone.

To retrieve any additional information from Accumulo, an application must *authenticate* as a particular user.

Before authenticating, the user must exist and have an AuthenticationToken associated with it. The default type of AuthenticationToken is the PasswordToken that simply wraps a password for the user. AuthenticationToken can be extended to support other authentication methods such as Lightweight Directory Access Protocol (LDAP).

To create a new user, use the createLocalUser() method:

```
String principal = "myApplications";
PasswordToken password = new PasswordToken("appSecret");

secOps.createLocalUser(principal, password);

// in version 1.4 and earlier
Authorizations initialAuthorizations = new Authorizations();
secOps.createUser(principal, "password".getBytes(), initialAuthorizations);
```

 After initialization Accumulo only has one user, the *root* user, with a password set at initialization time. The *root* user can be used to create other user accounts and grant privileges. See "Initialization" on page 410 for more details on setting up the root account.

To authenticate as a user, provide a username, or *principal*, and an AuthenticationToken when obtaining a Connector object from an Instance:

```
String principal = "myApp";
AuthenticationToken token = new PasswordToken("appSecret");

Connector connector = instance.getConnector(principal, token);
```

In addition, the following methods will simply return whether a particular principal and `AuthenticationToken` are valid:

```
String principal = "myApp";
AuthenticationToken token = new PasswordToken("appSecret");

boolean authenticated = authenticateUser(principal, token);

// deprecated since 1.5
boolean authenticated = authenticateUser(String user, byte[] password);
```

To set a user's password, use `changeLocalUserPassword()`:

```
String principal = "myUser";
PasswordToken token = new PasswordToken("newPassword");
secOps.changeLocalUserPassword(principal, token);

// in 1.5 and older
secOps.changeUserPassword(principal, "newPassword".getBytes());
```

To obtain a list of users, use the `listLocalUsers()` method:

```
Set<String> users = secOps.listLocalUsers();

// in 1.4 and earlier
Set<String> users = secOps.listUsers();
```

To remove a user from the system, use the `dropLocalUser()` method:

```
secOps.dropLocalUser("user");

// in 1.4 and earlier
secOps.dropUser("user");
```

Permissions

Once a user is authenticated to Accumulo, the types of operations allowed are governed by the permissions assigned to the Accumulo user.

There are system permissions, which are global; namespace permissions assigned per namespace; and table permissions assigned per table. Some permission names are repeated in more than one scope. For example, there are `DROP_TABLE` permissions for the system, namespace, and table scopes. These three permissions allow a user to delete any table, delete a table within a namespace, and delete a specific table, respectively. The `CREATE_TABLE` permissions only appear in system and namespace, because it does not make sense to create a specific table that already exists.

The user that creates a table is assigned all table permissions for that table. Users must be granted table permissions manually for tables they did not create, with the exception that all users can read the root and metadata tables.

If a user tries to perform an operation that is not allowed by the user's current permissions, an exception will be thrown.

System Permissions

System permissions allow users to perform the following actions:

GRANT
> Grant and revoke permissions for users

CREATE_TABLE
> Create and import tables

DROP_TABLE
> Remove tables

ALTER_TABLE
> Configure table properties, perform actions on tables (compact, merge, online/offline, rename, and split), and grant or revoke permissions on tables

CREATE_USER
> Create users and check permissions for users

DROP_USER
> Remove users and check permissions for users

ALTER_USER
> Change user authentication token or authorizations, and check permissions for users

CREATE_NAMESPACE
> Create namespaces

DROP_NAMESPACE
> Remove namespaces

ALTER_NAMESPACE
> Rename namespaces, configure namespace properties, and grant or revoke permissions on namespaces

SYSTEM
> Perform administrative actions including granting and revoking the SYSTEM permission, checking authentication for users, checking permissions and authorizations for users, and performing table actions (merge, online/offline, split, and delete a range of rows)

To grant a system permission to a user, use the `grantSystemPermission()` method. For example:

```
String principal = "user";

secOps.grantSystemPermission(principal, SystemPermission.CREATE_TABLE);
```

To see whether a user has a particular system permission, use the `hasSystemPermission()` method:

```
boolean hasPermission = secOps.hasSystemPermission(principal,
    SystemPermission.CREATE_TABLE);
```

Permissions can be revoked for users via the `revokeSystemPermission()` method:

```
secOps.revokeSystemPermission(principal, SystemPermission.CREATE_TABLE);
```

An example of granting a user system-wide permissions is as follows:

```
// get a connector as the root user
Connector adminConn = instance.getConnector("root", rootPasswordToken);

// get a security operations object as the root user
SecurityOperations adminSecOps = adminConn.securityOperations();

// admin creates a new user
String principal = "testUser";
PasswordToken token = new PasswordToken("password");
adminSecOps.createLocalUser(principal, token);

// get a connector as our new user
Connector userConn = instance.getConnector(principal, token);

// ...

// user tries to create user table in default namespace
String userTable = "userTable";

try {
  userConn.tableOperations().create(userTable);
} catch (AccumuloSecurityException ex) {
  System.out.println("user unauthorized to create table in default namespace");
}

adminSecOps.grantSystemPermission(principal, SystemPermission.CREATE_TABLE);

userConn.tableOperations().create(userTable);
System.out.println("table creation in default namespace succeeded");
```

Namespace Permissions

Permissions can apply to namespaces as well. Namespace permissions are granted for a particular namespace. Some of the permissions apply to actions performed on the namespace itself, and some apply to all tables within the namespace:

ALTER_NAMESPACE
: Grant and revoke table permissions for tables in the namespace, and alter the namespace

ALTER_TABLE
: Alter tables in the namespace

BULK_IMPORT
: Import into tables in the namespace

CREATE_TABLE
: Create tables in the namespace

DROP_NAMESPACE
: Delete the namespace

DROP_TABLE
: Delete a table from the namespace

GRANT
: Grant and revoke namespace permissions on a namespace, and alter the namespace

READ
: Read tables in the namespace

WRITE
: Write to tables in the namespace

To check whether a user has a permission for a given namespace, use the `hasNamespacePermission()` method:

```
String namespace = "myNamespace";
boolean hasNSWritePermission = secOps.hasNamespacePermission(principal,
    namespace, NamespacePermission.WRITE);
```

To grant a user a permission for a namespace, use the `grantNamespacePermission()` method. The permission will apply to all tables within the namespace:

```
secOps.grantNamespacePermission(principal, namespace, NamespacePermission.WRITE);
```

To revoke a permission from a user for a namespace, use the `revokeNamespacePermission()` method:

```
secOps.revokeNamespacePermission(principal, namespace,
    NamespacePermission.WRITE);
```

A short example:

```
String adminNS = "adminNamespace";
adminConn.namespaceOperations().create(adminNS);

try {
  userConn.tableOperations().create(adminNS + ".userTable");
} catch (AccumuloSecurityException ex) {
  System.out.println("user unauthorized to create table in adminNamespace");
}

// allow user to create tables in the root NS
adminSecOps.grantNamespacePermission(principal, adminNS,
    NamespacePermission.CREATE_TABLE);

userConn.tableOperations().create(adminNS + ".userTable");
System.out.println("table creation in adminNamespace succeeded");
```

Table Permissions

Table permissions are granted per table, allowing users to perform actions on specific tables:

READ
> Scan and export the table

WRITE
> Write to the table, including deleting data, and perform some administrative actions for the table including flushing and compaction

BULK_IMPORT
> Import files to the table

ALTER_TABLE
> Configure table properties, perform actions on the table (compact, flush, merge, online/offline, rename, and split), and grant or revoke permissions on the table

GRANT
> Grant and revoke permissions for the table

DROP_TABLE
> Remove the table

Some actions require a combination of permissions. These include:

Write conditional mutations
> `TablePermission.READ` and `TablePermission.WRITE`

Clone a table

> `SystemPermission.CREATE_TABLE` or `NamespacePermission.CREATE_TABLE` and `TablePermission.READ` on table being cloned

To grant a table permission to a user for a table, use the `grantTablePermission()` method:

```
String table = "myTable";

secOps.grantTablePermission(principal, table, TablePermission.WRITE);
```

To check whether a user has a specific permission on a table, use the `hasTablePermission()` method:

```
boolean canWrite = secOps.hasTablePermission(principal, table,
    TablePermission.WRITE);
```

To revoke a permission from a user for a given table, use the `revokeTablePermission()` method:

```
secOps.revokeTablePermission(principal, table, TablePermission.WRITE);
```

These actions can be carried out in the shell as well, as detailed in "Application Permissions" on page 424.

An example of using table permissions is as follows:

```
String adminTable = "adminTable";
adminConn.tableOperations().create(adminTable);

// user tries to write data
BatchWriterConfig config = new BatchWriterConfig();
BatchWriter writer = userConn.createBatchWriter(adminTable, config);
Mutation m = new Mutation("testRow");
m.put("", "testColumn", "testValue");

try {
  writer.addMutation(m);
  writer.close();
} catch (Exception ex) {
  System.out.println("user unable to write to admin table");
}

// admin grants permission for user to write data
adminSecOps.grantTablePermission(principal, adminTable, TablePermission.WRITE);

writer = userConn.createBatchWriter(adminTable, config);

writer.addMutation(m);
writer.close();
System.out.println("user can write to admin table");
```

See the full listing of *PermissionsExample.java* for more detail.

Authorizations

Once a user is authenticated to Accumulo and is given permission to read a table, the user's authorizations govern which key-value pairs can be retrieved.

Authorizations are applied to `Scanners` and `BatchScanners`. The set of authorizations that can be used for a particular scan is limited by the set of authorizations associated with the user account. If a user attempts to scan with an authorization that is not already associated with the user account specified in the `Connector`, an exception will be thrown.

To see the list of authorizations associated with a user, use the `getUserAuthorizations()` method:

```
Authorizations auths = secOps.getUserAuthorizations(principal);
```

To associate authorizations with a user, use the `changeUserAuthorizations()` method. This will replace any existing authorizations associated with the user:

```
Authorizations auths = new Authorizations("a","b","c");
secOps.changeUserAuthorizations(principal, auths);
```

> Be sure to include existing authorizations when using the `changeUserAuthorizations()` method to add new authorization tokens, or else previous tokens will be lost. Existing tokens can be retrieved with the `getUserAuthorizations()` method.

A user's authorizations encapsulate a set of strings, sometimes referred to as authorization *tokens*. These strings have no intrinsic meaning for Accumulo, but an application can assign its own meaning to them, such as groups or roles for its users.

For a user to be able to read data from Accumulo, a table name and a set of authorization tokens must be provided to either the `createScanner()` or the `createBatchScanner()` method of the `Connector`:

```
Scanner scan = conn.createScanner("myTable", new Authorizations("a", "b", "c"));
```

Because the `Connector` is associated with a specific user, the authorizations provided when a `Scanner` or `BatchScanner` is obtained must be a subset of the authorizations assigned to that user. If they are not, an exception will be thrown.

 Passing in a set of authorizations at scan time allows a user to act in different roles at different times. It also allows applications to manage their own users apart from Accumulo. You can choose to have one Accumulo user account for an entire application and to let the application set the authorizations for each scan based on the current user of the application.

Although this requires the application to take on the responsibility for managing accurate authorizations for their users, it also prevents users from having to interact with Accumulo or the underlying Hadoop system directly, allowing more strict control over access to your data.

See "An Example of Using Authorizations" on page 185 for an example of using less than all of the possible authorizations associated with a user.

Column Visibilities

To determine which key-value pairs can be seen given a particular set of authorizations, each key has a *column visibility* portion. A column visibility consists of a Boolean expression containing *tokens*, & (and), | (or), and parentheses—such as (a&bc)|def. Evaluation of the Boolean expression requires each string to be interpreted as true or false. For a given set of authorizations, a string is interpreted as true if it is contained in the set of authorizations.

The visibility (a&bc)|def would evaluate to true for authorization sets containing the string def or containing both of the strings a and bc. When the visibility evaluates to true for a given key and a set of authorizations, that key-value pair is returned to the user. If not, the key-value pair is not included in the set of key-value pairs returned to the client. Thus it isn't possible to find out that a particular key-value pair exists, or to see the full key or value, without satisfying the column visibility.

Tokens used in column visibilities can consist of letters, numbers, underscore, dash, colon, and as of Accumulo version 1.5, can contain periods and forward slashes. As of version 1.5, tokens can also contain arbitrary characters if the token is surrounded by quotes, as in "a?b"&c. The corresponding authorizations do not need to be quoted, so the minimum set of authorizations needed to view this example visibility would contain a?b and c.

Limiting Authorizations Written

By default, if users have write permission for a table, they can write keys that they do not have authorization to retrieve. You can change this behavior by configuring a constraint on the table. With the VisibilityConstraint, users cannot write data they are not allowed to read:

```
connector.tableOperations().addConstraint(tableName,
    VisibilityConstraint.class.getName());
```

This can also be accomplished through the Accumulo shell. When the table is created, add an `-evc` flag to the `createtable` command:

```
user@accumulo> createtable -evc tableName
```

To add the constraint to an existing table, use the `constraint` command instead:

```
user@accumulo> constraint -t tableName \
    -a org.apache.accumulo.core.security.VisibilityConstraint
```

An Example of Using Authorizations

We'll illustrate bringing the concepts of users, permissions, authorizations, and column visibilities together in a quick example. Let's say we are writing an application to keep track of the information associated with a safe in a bank. The safe contains a set of safety deposit boxes that are used by bank employees and customers to store objects securely.

There is an outer door to the safe that is protected by a combination known only to a few bank employees. Other bank employees can see privileged information about the safe, but not information about the contents of customers' boxes.

Customers can write down and read information about safety deposit boxes they rent but cannot see any information privileged to bank employees or other customers.

First we'll create a table as an administrator and write initial information about a particular safe:

```
// get a connector as the root user
Connector adminConn = instance.getConnector("root", rootPasswordToken);

// get a security operations object as the root user
SecurityOperations secOps = adminConn.securityOperations();

// admin creates a new table and writes some data
// protected with Column Visibilities
System.out.println("\n--- creating table ---");
String safeTable = "safeTable";
adminConn.tableOperations().create(safeTable);
```

The admin writes the initial information about a safe, including the name, location, and combination:

```
// admin writes initial data
System.out.println("\n--- writing initial data ---");
BatchWriterConfig config = new BatchWriterConfig();
BatchWriter writer = adminConn.createBatchWriter(safeTable, config);
Mutation m = new Mutation("safe001");
```

```
// write information about this particular safe
m.put("info", "safeName", new ColumnVisibility("public"),
    "Super Safe Number 17");
m.put("info", "safeLocation", new ColumnVisibility("bankEmployee"),
    "3rd floor of bank 2");
m.put("info", "safeOuterDoorCombo",
    new ColumnVisibility("bankEmployee&safeWorker"), "123-456-789");

// store some information about bank owned contents stored in the safe
m.put("contents", "box001",
    new ColumnVisibility("bankEmployee"), "bank charter");

// commit mutations
writer.addMutation(m);
writer.close();
```

Next the administrator will need to create user accounts for customers. In this example we're using one account per individual user.

Each customer gets a unique user ID and authorization token, in addition to the public token:

```
// admin creates a new customer user
String customer = "customer003";
PasswordToken customerToken = new PasswordToken("customerPassword");
secOps.createLocalUser(customer, customerToken);

// set authorizations for user and grant permission to read and write
// to the safe table
Authorizations customerAuths = new Authorizations("public", "customer003");
secOps.changeUserAuthorizations(customer, customerAuths);
secOps.grantTablePermission(customer, safeTable, TablePermission.READ);
```

Now the newly created customer can log in and is prevented from seeing any information privileged to bank employees:

```
// get a connector as our customer user
Connector customerConn = instance.getConnector(customer, customerToken);

// user attempts to get a scanner with
// authorizations not associated with the user
System.out.println("\n--- customer scanning table for bank employee " +
    "privileged information ---");
Scanner scanner;
try {
  scanner = customerConn.createScanner(safeTable,
      new Authorizations("public", "bankEmployee"));

  for(Map.Entry<Key, Value> e : scanner) {
    System.out.println(e);
  }
} catch (Exception ex) {
```

```
    System.out.println("problem scanning table: " + ex.getMessage());
  }
```

This results in the output:

```
--- customer scanning table for bank employee privileged information ---
problem scanning table:
    org.apache.accumulo.core.client.AccumuloSecurityException:
Error BAD_AUTHORIZATIONS for user customer003 on table safeTable(ID:1) -
The user does not have the specified authorizations assigned
```

If the customer scans the table with all the authorizations associated with his account, she will see the information marked as public:

```
// user reads data with authorizations associated with the user
System.out.println("\n--- customer scanning table for allowed information ---");
scanner = customerConn.createScanner(safeTable, customerAuths);
for(Map.Entry<Key, Value> e : scanner) {
  System.out.println(e);
}
```

The output is:

```
--- customer scanning table for allowed information ---
safe001 info:safeName [public] 1409424734681 false Super Safe Number 17
```

The customer must be granted write access to the table before writing any information. The customer can then write information protected with a column visibility consisting of just his own unique authorization token. Subsequent scans will return this information along with the public safe information:

```
// admin grants write permission to user
secOps.grantTablePermission(customer, safeTable, TablePermission.WRITE);

// user writes information only she can see to the table
// describing the contents of a rented safety deposit box
System.out.println("\n--- customer writing own information ---");
BatchWriter userWriter = customerConn.createBatchWriter(safeTable, config);
Mutation userM = new Mutation("safe001");
userM.put("contents", "box004", new ColumnVisibility("customer003"),
    "jewelry, extra cash");
userWriter.addMutation(userM);
userWriter.flush();

// scan to see the bank info and our own info
System.out.println("\n--- customer scanning table for allowed information ---");
scanner = customerConn.createScanner(safeTable, customerAuths);
for(Map.Entry<Key, Value> e : scanner) {
  System.out.println(e);
}
```

The output is:

```
--- customer writing own information ---
--- customer scanning table for allowed information ---
safe001 contents:box004 [customer003] 1409424734828 false jewelry, extra cash
safe001 info:safeName [public] 1409424734681 false Super Safe Number 17
```

Now the administrator will create an account for a bank employee. The bank employee will have access to bank privileged information, public information, but not any information associated with any customer:

```
// admin creates a new bank employee user
String bankEmployee = "bankEmployee005";
PasswordToken bankEmployeeToken = new PasswordToken("bankEmployeePassword");
secOps.createLocalUser(bankEmployee, bankEmployeeToken);

// admin sets authorizations for bank employee
// and grants read permission for the table
Authorizations bankEmployeeAuths = new Authorizations("bankEmployee", "public");
secOps.changeUserAuthorizations(bankEmployee, bankEmployeeAuths);
secOps.grantTablePermission(bankEmployee, safeTable, TablePermission.READ);

// connect as bank employee
Connector bankConn = instance.getConnector(bankEmployee, bankEmployeeToken);
```

If the bank employee attempts to scan for customer information, an exception will be thrown:

```
// attempt to scan customer information
System.out.println("\n--- bank employee scanning table for customer " +
    "information ---");
Scanner bankScanner;
try {
  bankScanner = bankConn.createScanner(safeTable,
      new Authorizations("customer003"));

  for(Map.Entry<Key, Value> e : bankScanner) {
    System.out.println(e);
  }
} catch (Exception ex) {
  System.out.println("problem scanning table: " + ex.getMessage());
}
```

Resulting in the output:

```
--- bank employee scanning table for customer information ---
problem scanning table:
    org.apache.accumulo.core.client.AccumuloSecurityException:
Error BAD_AUTHORIZATIONS for user bankEmployee005 on table safeTable(ID:1) -
The user does not have the specified authorizations assigned
```

Now we'll have the bank employee scan for all information she is allowed to see. Because this employee has a set of authorizations different from the customer's, this view of the table will be different than the view the customer gets when doing the same scan:

```
// bank employee scans all information they are allowed to see
System.out.println("\n--- bank employee scanning table for allowed " +
    "information ---");
bankScanner = bankConn.createScanner(safeTable, bankEmployeeAuths);

for(Map.Entry<Key, Value> e : bankScanner) {
  System.out.println(e);
}
```

Here is the output:

```
--- bank employee scanning table for allowed information ---
safe001 contents:box001 [bankEmployee] 1409424734681 false bank charter
safe001 info:safeLocation [bankEmployee] 1409424734681 false 3rd floor of bank 2
safe001 info:safeName [public] 1409424734681 false Super Safe Number 17
```

It is also possible to perform a scan using less than all the authorizations we possess. In this case, the bank employee will generate a view of the table that is viewable by users with only the public token:

```
// bank employee scans using a subset of authorizations
// to check which information is viewable to the public
System.out.println("\n--- bank employee scanning table for only public " +
    "information ---");
bankScanner = bankConn.createScanner(safeTable, new Authorizations("public"));

for(Map.Entry<Key, Value> e : bankScanner) {
  System.out.println(e);
}
```

Here is the view generated:

```
--- bank employee scanning table for only public information ---
safe001 info:safeName [public] 1409424734681 false Super Safe Number 17
```

Finally, we may want to protect the table against attempts to write information to a key-value pair that is protected with a visibility that the writing user cannot satisfy. This prevents confusing situations in which a user writes data but then cannot read it out:

```
// admin protects table against users writing new data they cannot read
adminConn.tableOperations().addConstraint(safeTable,
    "org.apache.accumulo.core.security.VisibilityConstraint");

// customer attempts to write information protected with a bank authorization
// which would erase the combination for the outer door of the safe
System.out.println("\n--- customer attempting to overwrite bank " +
    "information ---");
try {
  userM = new Mutation("safe001");
  userM.put("info", "safeOuterDoorCombo",
      new ColumnVisibility("bankEmployee&safeWorker"), "------");
  userWriter.addMutation(userM);
```

```
    userWriter.flush();
} catch (Exception e) {
    System.out.println("problem attempting to write data: " + e.getMessage());
}
```

This results in the error:

```
--- customer attempting to overwrite bank information ---
problem attempting to write data: # constraint violations :
1  security codes: {}  # server errors 0 # exceptions 0
```

 Even if users are able to write a new key-value pair using the same row ID and column as an existing key, they can only cause the newly written key-value pair to obscure the old key-value pair, via Accumulo's VersioningIterator, which by default returns only the newest version of a key-value pair. It would be possible in this case to configure a scan to read more than one version for a key, which would allow authorized users to see the old key-value pair. But it would not be possible for the new key-value pair to cause the value of the old key-value pair to become visible. According to the column visibility of the new key-value pair, it would simply be obscured.

This inability to expose information this way, by writing new key-value pairs, makes it possible to build highly secure applications more easily, because applications do not have to explicitly prevent this issue.

Using a Default Visibility

You may have noticed in our example application that all key-value pairs were protected with at least one token in a column visibility. We used the public token to denote information that everyone was able to read, and distributed the public authorization token to all users.

It is possible to have a table in which some key-value pairs have column visibilities and others do not. The default behavior for unlabeled data is to allow any user to read it. This can be changed by applying a default visibility to a table.

When the default visibility is specified, unlabeled key-value pairs will be treated as if they are labeled with the default column visibility.

To specify the default visibility for a table, set the `table.security.scan.visibil ity.default` property to the desired column visibility expression.

For example:

```
ops.setProperty("table.security.scan.visibility.default", "public");
```

When key-value pairs with empty labels are scanned, if they are returned as part of the scan they are displayed as having a blank column visibility, even when a default visibility is set.

Here is an example of the way a view of a table will change after the default visibility is set. First we'll create a table that has a key-value pair with a blank column visibility and see it show up in all scans:

```
// get a connector as the root user
Connector conn = instance.getConnector("root", rootPasswordToken);

// create an example table
String exampleTable = "example";
conn.tableOperations().create(exampleTable);

// write some data with col vis and others without
BatchWriterConfig config = new BatchWriterConfig();
BatchWriter writer = conn.createBatchWriter(exampleTable, config);
Mutation m = new Mutation("one");

m.put("", "col1",  "value in unlabeled entry");
m.put("", "col2",  new ColumnVisibility("public"), "value in public entry");
m.put("", "col3",  new ColumnVisibility("private"), "value in private entry");

writer.addMutation(m);
writer.close();

// add auths to root account
conn.securityOperations().changeUserAuthorizations("root",
    new Authorizations("public", "private"));
// scan with no auths
System.out.println("\nno auths:");
Scanner scan = conn.createScanner(exampleTable, Authorizations.EMPTY);
for(Map.Entry<Key, Value> e : scan) {
  System.out.println(e);
}

// scan with public auth
```

```
System.out.println("\npublic auth:");
scan = conn.createScanner(exampleTable, new Authorizations("public"));
for(Map.Entry<Key, Value> e : scan) {
  System.out.println(e);
}

// scan with public and private auth
System.out.println("\npublic and private auths:");
scan = conn.createScanner(exampleTable,
    new Authorizations("public", "private"));
for(Map.Entry<Key, Value> e : scan) {
  System.out.println(e);
}
```

The output of this is as follows:

```
no auths:
one :col1 [] 1409429068159 false value in unlabeled entry

public auth:
one :col1 [] 1409429068159 false value in unlabeled entry
one :col2 [public] 1409429068159 false value in public entry

public and private auths:
one :col1 [] 1409429068159 false value in unlabeled entry
one :col2 [public] 1409429068159 false value in public entry
one :col3 [private] 1409429068159 false value in private entry
```

Now we'll add a default visibility:

```
// turn on default visibility
System.out.println("\nturning on default visibility");
conn.tableOperations().setProperty(exampleTable,
    "table.security.scan.visibility.default", "x");

// scan with no auths
System.out.println("\nno auths:");
scan = conn.createScanner(exampleTable, Authorizations.EMPTY);
for(Map.Entry<Key, Value> e : scan) {
  System.out.println(e);
}

// scan with public auth
System.out.println("\npublic auth:");
scan = conn.createScanner(exampleTable, new Authorizations("public"));
for(Map.Entry<Key, Value> e : scan) {
  System.out.println(e);
}

// scan with public and private auth
System.out.println("\npublic and private auths:");
scan = conn.createScanner(exampleTable,
    new Authorizations("public", "private"));
for(Map.Entry<Key, Value> e : scan) {
```

```
        System.out.println(e);
    }
```

The output for this now appears as:

```
turning on default visibility
no auths:

public auth:
one :col2 [public] 1409429068159 false value in public entry

public & private auths:
one :col2 [public] 1409429068159 false value in public entry
one :col3 [private] 1409429068159 false value in private entry
```

Making Authorizations Work

For authorizations to be effective in protecting access to data in Accumulo, applications and users must:

1. Properly apply column visibilities to data at ingest time.

2. Apply the right authorizations at scan time.

Often Accumulo applications will rely on using specially vetted libraries for creating the proper column visibilities. If not, then ingest clients can be individually reviewed and trusted.

For retrieving authorizations, a separate service can be employed to manage the association of individual users to their sets of authorizations. This service is trusted by the application, and the application itself is trusted to faithfully pass along the authorizations retrieved from such a service to Accumulo.

A typical deployment can be like that shown in Figure 5-1.

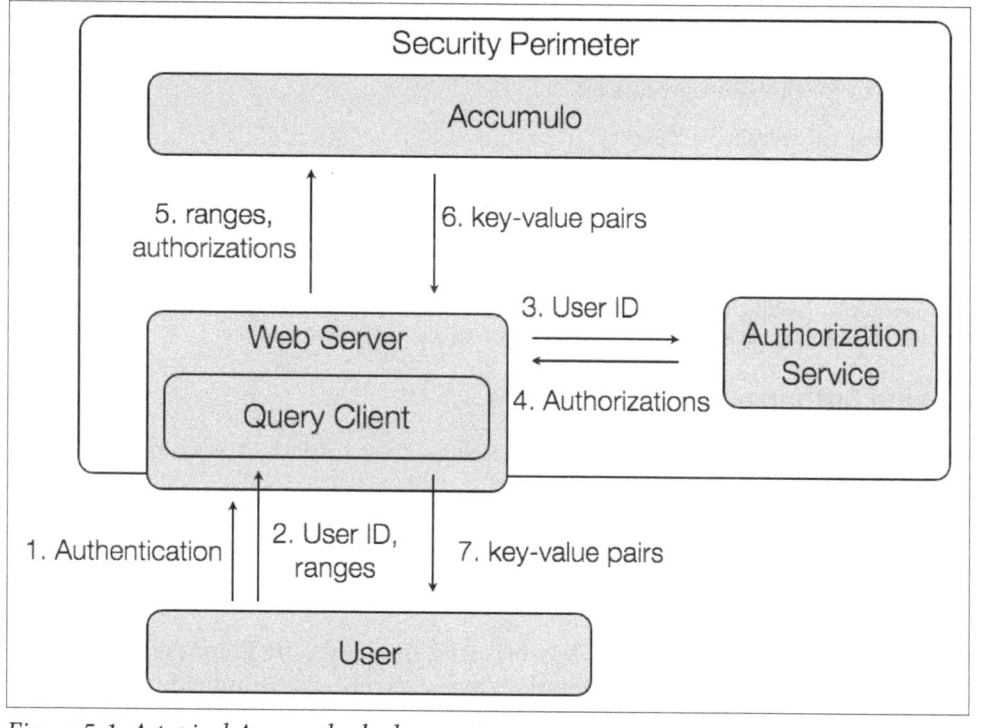

Figure 5-1. A typical Accumulo deployment

Auditing Security Operations

Accumulo can be configured to log security operations. Auditing is configured in the *auditLog.xml* file in the Accumulo *conf/* directory. The logging is done via the Java log4j package and by default is configured to log via a DailyRollingFileAppender to a local file named *<hostname>.audit* in the Accumulo log directory. The following section of the *auditLog.xml* file configures the logging level:

```
<logger name="Audit" additivity="false">
  <appender-ref ref="Audit" />
  <level value="OFF"/>
</logger>
```

By default, logging is turned off. To enable logging security operations that fail due to lack of permissions, set the level to WARN:

```
<level value="WARN"/>
```

To log all security operations, set the level to INFO. This will include successful security operations logged as *operation: permitted* as well as unsuccessful operations logged as *operation: denied*. Scanning with an authorization the user does not possess is an example of an operation that would be logged as denied at the INFO level:

```
<level value="INFO"/>
```

Custom Authentication, Permissions, and Authorization

The authentication, permissions, and authorization tasks for Accumulo accounts are handled in ZooKeeper by default. These tasks are handled by three classes: ZKAuthen ticator for authenticating users, ZKAuthorizor for associating users with authorizations, and ZKPermHandler for determining what actions a user can carry out on the system and tables.

As of Accumulo version 1.5 developers can provide custom classes that override these default security mechanisms. This allows organizations that manage users and their authorizations in a centralized system to integrate those existing systems with Accumulo. In these cases, the custom classes must be available to server processes and specified in the *accumulo-site.xml* configuration file.

Not all of the three mechanisms must be overridden at the same time. For example, you can choose to rely on ZooKeeper for permissions handling and authentication, while using a custom authorization mechanism.

The default configuration of these mechanisms' properties is shown in Table 5-1.

Table 5-1. Accumulo authentication and authorization properties

Setting name	Default	Purpose
instance.security.authorizor	org.apache.accu mulo.server.security.han dler.ZKAuthorizor	Associate users with authorization tokens
instance.security.authenticator	org.apache.accu mulo.server.security.han dler.ZKAuthenticator	Authenticate users
instance.security.permissionHandler	org.apache.accu mulo.server.security.han dler.ZKPermHandler	Manage users' system and table-level permissions

These settings cannot be changed in ZooKeeper on a running cluster. They must be changed in the *accumulo-site.xml* file and require a restart of Accumulo for the changes to take effect.

Creating a custom mechanism is done by implementing the Authenticator, Authori zor, or PermissionHandler interface. These interfaces define the methods required by Accumulo to determine the access restrictions for user requests.

Custom Authentication Example

Here we'll implement a trivial authenticator that uses only one hardcoded username and password. This would be impractical for any real-world deployment because no changes to the initial settings are possible, but it will help us illustrate the process of configuring and deploying a custom authentication scheme.

For this incredibly simple example we'll implement only a few methods, shown in the following code. The rest of the methods of the interface that must be implemented we will leave empty:

```
public class HardCodedAuthenticator implements Authenticator {

    @Override
    public boolean authenticateUser(String principal, AuthenticationToken token)
        throws AccumuloSecurityException {
      return principal.equals("onlyUser") &&
        new String(((PasswordToken)token).getPassword()).equals("onlyPassword");
    }

    @Override
    public Set<String> listUsers() throws AccumuloSecurityException {
      HashSet<String> users = new HashSet<String>();
      users.add("onlyUser");
      return users;
    }

    @Override
    public boolean userExists(String user) throws AccumuloSecurityException {
      return user.equals("onlyUser");
    }

    @Override
    public Set<Class<? extends AuthenticationToken>> getSupportedTokenTypes() {
      return (Set)Sets.newHashSet(PasswordToken.class);
    }

    @Override
    public boolean validTokenClass(String tokenClass) {
      return tokenClass.equals(PasswordToken.class.toString());
    }
    ...
}
```

We can build and deploy our example code JAR as described in "Deploying JARs" on page 407.

Next we need to stop Accumulo if it's running and configure it to use our `Authentica tor`. In practice, custom security mechanisms like this should most likely be configured before Accumulo is initialized, so that the proper authorizations and permissions can be coordinated with the creation of the initial *root* user.

We'll only change the authenticator in *accumulo-site.xml* in this example:

```
<property>
  <name>instance.security.authenticator</name>
  <value>com.accumulobook.tableapi.HardCodedAuthenticator</value>
</property>
```

Once configuration is done, we can start up Accumulo and attempt to authenticate using the username onlyUser and password onlyPassword:

```
[centos@centos]$ bin/accumulo shell -u onlyUser
Password: ************

Shell - Apache Accumulo Interactive Shell
-
- version: 1.6.0
- instance name: test
-
- type 'help' for a list of available commands
-
onlyUser@test> tables
accumulo.metadata
accumulo.root
trace
```

Any attempt to use our previous root account will fail:

```
[centos@centos]$ bin/accumulo shell -u root
[shell.Shell] ERROR: org.apache.accumulo.core.client.AccumuloSecurityException:
    Error BAD_CREDENTIALS for user root - Username or Password is Invalid
[centos@centos]$
```

Our hardcoded user account will not have permissions to manipulate anything, or any authorizations, so it is not very practical. In practice, these custom mechanisms will need to store information in a centralized location accessible to all processes, as the default ZooKeeper implementation does. For example, you could use a simple relational database or an LDAP service.

Custom authorizers and permissions handlers can be created and deployed similarly.

Other Security Considerations

In addition to column visibilities being properly applied at ingest time and the proper authorizations retrieved and used in scans, there are some other things to consider when building a secure application on the Accumulo API:

- Direct access to tablet servers must be limited to trusted applications—because the application is trusted to present the proper authorizations at scan time. A rogue client may be configured to pass in authorizations the user does not have.

- Access to the underlying HDFS instance must not be allowed. Otherwise an HDFS client could open and read all the key-value pairs stored in Accumulo's files without presenting the proper authorizations.

- Similarly, access should be disallowed to the underlying Linux filesystem on machines on which tablet server and HDFS DataNode processes run.

- Access to ZooKeeper should be restricted because Accumulo uses it to store configuration information about the cluster, including the list of Accumulo accounts and passwords.

Using an Application Account for Multiple Users

Many Accumulo applications do not create accounts through Accumulo for each individual user. This is because some clients choose to do their own authentication and authorization of individual users via a centralized service within an organization. Clients are therefore trusted to present user credentials properly.

When applications are deployed this way, client *applications* must still authenticate themselves to Accumulo before performing any reads or writes. Administrators and application designers can restrict the privileges that a client has to particular tables, as well as the maximal set of authorizations the client is allowed to pass for any of the users it is serving. This way, even though users can have more authorizations granted to them than an application requires, a client application's account can be restricted to those authorizations deemed necessary to carry out the actions of that particular application.

Network

The network that Accumulo uses to communicate between nodes and to HDFS and ZooKeeper should be protected against unauthorized access. Most Accumulo deployments do not use Secure Socket Layer (SSL) between nodes, but rather use SSL between user browsers and trusted web applications.

See "Network Security" on page 417 for more information on securing the network for an Accumulo deployment.

Disk Encryption

Disks can be encrypted to prevent unauthorized reading of the data should a physical hard drive be stolen. But if those with physical access to the cluster are not trusted, then the operating system and memory of the machines participating in the Accumulo cluster would have to be similarly protected. When running Accumulo in multitenant environments, such as a cloud infrastructure-as-a-service provider like Amazon's EC2 or Rackspace, consideration should be given to the security precautions implemented by the service provider.

For both situations—running in a cluster without trusting those with physical access or running in the cloud—it may be feasible to employ application-level encryption of values and to devise keys that are not sensitive. This is problematic when it comes to building a secondary index, which can rely on the ordering of values to perform scans.

If scans across ranges of terms in an index can be foregone, then using a strategy involving hashes of values as keys can still provide fast simple lookups. Ranges of terms could no longer be scanned because secure hashes of index terms would, by virtue of the design of hash functions, no longer have any meaningful sort order. In this case, adjacent keys would have no relationship to each other.

Accumulo also supports encryption of data at rest via modules that implement the `org.apache.accumulo.core.security.crypto.CryptoModule` interface, which consists of the following methods:

```
CryptoModuleParameters getEncryptingOutputStream(CryptoModuleParameters params)

CryptoModuleParameters getDecryptingInputStream(CryptoModuleParameters params)

CryptoModuleParameters generateNewRandomSessionKey(CryptoModuleParameters params)

CryptoModuleParameters initializeCipher(CryptoModuleParameters params)
```

The `DefaultCryptoModule` class is an example that can be used to encrypt data stored in HDFS. This implementation stores the master key along with files in HDFS, which may not meet security requirements. For details on configuring Accumulo to use this or other modules, see "Encryption of Data at Rest" on page 422.

## CHAPTER 6

Server-Side Functionality and External Clients

Beyond reading and writing data, configuring tables, and securing data, Accumulo has a few additional concepts that can be used to add functionality to tables, and for performing some computation on the server side. These mechanisms are optional but can have a drastic impact on application performance, depending on the access patterns and updates that an application requires.

Constraints

Tables can apply logic to data that is about to be written to determine if a given mutation should be allowed. This logic is implemented by creating a *constraint*. Constraints are classes that implement a simple filtering function that is applied to every mutation before writing it to a table.

Constraints can be used to ensure that all data in a table conforms to some specification. This helps simplify applications, because they can then assume that the data read from this table has already been checked for conformity.

For example, we can choose to constrain the values inserted into a table to be of a certain type, such as a number. This allows applications to avoid having to check the type of values returned.

If a mutation fails a constraint's criteria, the mutation will be rejected and a code returned, indicating which criterion was violated. For example:

```
try {
  writer.addMutation(m);
}
catch (MutationsRejectedException e) {
```

```
List<ConstraintViolationSummary> violations =
  e.getConstraintViolationSummaries();

for(ConstraintViolationSummary v : violations) {
  System.out.println(v.getConstrainClass() +
  "\n" + v.getNumberOfViolatingMutations() +
  "\n" + v.getViolationDescription());
}
}
```

If a constraint is violated, we only see how many mutations were involved and which criterion failed. Applications will need to examine the mutations submitted to determine which mutations failed and which did not and were submitted successfully. Retrying the mutations that violate constraints will result in another exception.

Constraints can be used to help debug new clients without the chance for corrupting data in the table, or for limiting dynamic data inserted to that which conforms to the constraints—perhaps saving off the data that fails to another place for inspection.

For example, if we are ingesting data from another database and we expect it to conform to a specific schema but the schema has since changed, our constraint that enforces the expected schema will immediately detect the change. This will halt our ingest process until we can figure the situation out. Relational databases operate this way and some applications may want to do this.

Other applications can take advantage of Accumulo's flexibility in storing any type of value and any set of columns to write data that is not well understood to a table where it can be explored.

Constraint Configuration API

To add a constraint to a table, use the addConstraint() method of the TableOpera tions object:

```
TableOperations ops = conn.tableOperations();

ops.addConstraint("myTable", MyConstraint.class.getName());
```

A table can have several constraints applied. To see the list of constraints for a table, use the listConstraints() method:

```
Map<String,Integer> constraints = ops.listConstraints("myTable");
```

This will return the name of the constraint as well as a unique ID number assigned to the constraint. This number can be used to remove a constraint via the removeCon straint() method:

```
ops.removeConstraint("myTable", 2);
```

By default, tables in Accumulo 1.6 have the `DefaultKeySizeConstraint` enabled. This constraint rejects mutations that contain keys larger than 1MB in size. This can prevent a tablet server from running out of memory when loading RFile indexes containing very large keys.

Constraint Configuration Example

In this example, we'll create a mutation that violates the `DefaultKeySizeConstraint`. It will fail. Then we'll disable the constraint and apply the mutation successfully.

First, we'll look at the table constraint configuration:

```
Connector conn = ExampleMiniCluster.getConnector();

TableOperations ops = conn.tableOperations();
ops.create("testTable");

for(Map.Entry<String, Integer> c : ops.listConstraints("testTable").entrySet()) {
  System.out.println(c);
}
```

This shows the constraint and its ID number:

```
org.apache.accumulo.core.constraints.DefaultKeySizeConstraint=1
```

Now we'll try to insert a key with a 5 MB column qualifier, which exceeds the constraint's criterion of all keys being under 1 MB. When we try to flush to the table, an exception will be thrown and we can see what constraint violations occurred:

```
// create a column qualifier that is 5MB in size

StringBuilder sb = new StringBuilder();
for(int i=0; i < 1024 * 1024; i++) {
  sb.append("LARGE");
}

String largeColQual = sb.toString();

BatchWriter writer = conn.createBatchWriter("testTable",
    new BatchWriterConfig());
Mutation m = new Mutation("testRow");

m.put("", largeColQual, "");

try {
  writer.addMutation(m);
  writer.flush();
  System.out.println("successfully written");
}
catch (MutationsRejectedException ex) {

  List<ConstraintViolationSummary> violations =
```

```
    ex.getConstraintViolationSummaries();

  for(ConstraintViolationSummary v : violations) {
    System.out.println(v.getConstrainClass() +
    "\n" + v.getNumberOfViolatingMutations() +
    "\n" + v.getViolationDescription());
  }
}
```

The output is:

```
org.apache.accumulo.core.constraints.DefaultKeySizeConstraint
1
Key was larger than 1MB
```

Now we'll disable the constraint and try again.

 In particular, it is a good idea to leave the DefaultKeySizeCon
straint enabled, because it will help prevent large data elements
from causing memory issues in tablet servers. Data elements larger
than 1 MB are likely best suited for storage as the value of a key-
value pair and not in the key.

```
// remove constraint and try again
ops.removeConstraint("testTable", 1);

for(Map.Entry<String, Integer> c : ops.listConstraints("testTable").entrySet()) {
  System.out.println(c);
}

writer = conn.createBatchWriter("testTable", new BatchWriterConfig());

try {
  writer.addMutation(m);
  writer.flush();
  System.out.println("successfully written");
} catch (MutationsRejectedException ex) {

  List<ConstraintViolationSummary> violations =
    ex.getConstraintViolationSummaries();

  for(ConstraintViolationSummary v : violations) {
    System.out.println(v.getConstrainClass() +
    "\n" + v.getNumberOfViolatingMutations() +
    "\n" + v.getViolationDescription());
  }
}
```

Now we see that there are no constraints on the table when we list them, and the output shows:

```
successfully written
```

Creating Custom Constraints

To create a constraint, create a class that implements the `Constraint` interface:

```
public interface Constraint {

    String getViolationDescription(short violationCode);

    List<Short> check(Environment env, Mutation mutation);
}
```

Next we'll show a custom constraint example.

Custom Constraint Example

Let's say we have an application that keeps track of personal information, such as age, height, and weight. We'd like to make sure that every time we track weight, we track height too, and vice versa. Further, height and weight should be restricted to sensible values. At the very least they should be nonnegative.

We can create a constraint to apply these restrictions to all mutations before they are committed to the table. Any application that reads our table is then guaranteed that if it finds a *height* column in a row, the *weight* column can also be found. Applications also don't have to check whether the values are negative, because our constraint will have done that for us.

The code for our example constraint consists primarily of two methods. One is for checking a new mutation, and the other is for mapping violation codes to human-readable explanations. First, we'll implement our `check()` method:

```
private static final short INVALID_HEIGHT_VALUE = 1;
private static final short INVALID_WEIGHT_VALUE = 2;
private static final short MISSING_HEIGHT = 3;
private static final short MISSING_WEIGHT = 4;

final static List<Short> NO_VIOLATIONS = new ArrayList<>();
final static byte[] heightBytes = "height".getBytes();
final static byte[] weightBytes = "weight".getBytes();

@Override
public List<Short> check(Environment env, Mutation mutation) {

    List<Short> violations = null;

    List<ColumnUpdate> updates = mutation.getUpdates();

    boolean haveHeight = false;
    boolean haveWeight = false;

    for(ColumnUpdate update : updates) {
```

```
        // check height update
        if(equalBytes(update.getColumnQualifier(), heightBytes)) {
          haveHeight = true;
          if(!isNonNegativeNumberString(update.getValue())) {
            if(violations == null)
              violations = new ArrayList<>();
            violations.add(INVALID_HEIGHT_VALUE);
          }
        }

        // check weight update
        if(equalBytes(update.getColumnQualifier(), weightBytes)) {
          haveWeight = true;
          if(!isNonNegativeNumberString(update.getValue())) {
            if(violations == null)
              violations = new ArrayList<>();
            violations.add(INVALID_WEIGHT_VALUE);
          }
        }
      }

    // if we have height, we must also have weight
    if(haveHeight && ! haveWeight) {
      if(violations == null)
        violations = new ArrayList<>();
      violations.add(MISSING_WEIGHT);
    }

    // if we have weight, we must also have height
    if(haveWeight && !haveHeight) {
      if(violations == null)
        violations = new ArrayList<>();
      violations.add(MISSING_HEIGHT);
    }

    return violations == null ? NO_VIOLATIONS : violations;
  }
```

Next we'll implement getViolationDescription() to map violation codes to strings:

```
@Override
public String getViolationDescription(short violationCode) {
  switch(violationCode) {
    case INVALID_HEIGHT_VALUE:
      return "Invalid height value";
    case INVALID_WEIGHT_VALUE:
      return "Invalid weight value";
    case MISSING_HEIGHT:
      return "Missing height column";
    case MISSING_WEIGHT:
      return "Missing weight column";
  }
```

```
      return null;
  }
```

We have a few helper methods, too. In particular, when looking for a column qualifier, we want to compare byte arrays rather than converting byte arrays to strings. We also write a method for checking the type and range of values:

```
private boolean equalBytes(byte[] a, byte[] b) {
  return Value.Comparator.compareBytes(a, 0, a.length, b, 0, b.length) == 0;
}

// return whether the value is a string representation of a non-negative number
private boolean isNonNegativeNumberString(byte[] value) {
  try {
    double val = Double.parseDouble(new String(value));
    return val >= 0.0;
  } catch(NumberFormatException nfe) {
    return false;
  }
}
```

Now we can test our constraint by writing some mutations to a test table. First, we'll create a table and enable our constraint on it (see "Deploying JARs" on page 407 for information on deploying a JAR in production):

```
TableOperations ops = conn.tableOperations();
ops.create("testTable");

// add our custom constraint
ops.addConstraint("testTable", ValidHeightWeightConstraint.class.getName());

for(Map.Entry<String, Integer> c : ops.listConstraints("testTable").entrySet()) {
  System.out.println(c);
}
```

We can see our constraint in the list of table constraints printed out:

```
com.accumulobook.advanced.ValidHeightWeightConstraint=2
org.apache.accumulo.core.constraints.DefaultKeySizeConstraint=1
```

Now we'll try to write a mutation that we know will fail—a row with just a *height* column and no *weight* column:

```
BatchWriter writer = conn.createBatchWriter("testTable",
    new BatchWriterConfig());

// create an invalid mutation with only a height update
Mutation m = new Mutation("person");
m.put("", "height", "6.0");

writeAndReportViolations(writer, m);
```

We get an exception with the information:

```
com.accumulobook.advanced.ValidHeightWeightConstraint
1
Missing weight column
```

Now we'll add a *weight* column, but give it a negative value:

```
// create a mutation with a valid height but
// an invalid weight value
m = new Mutation("person");
m.put("", "height", "6.0");
m.put("", "weight", "-200.0");

// try to write
writer = conn.createBatchWriter("testTable", new BatchWriterConfig());
writeAndReportViolations(writer, m);
```

This results in the output:

```
com.accumulobook.advanced.ValidHeightWeightConstraint
1
Invalid weight value
```

Finally, we create a sensible mutation, with both *height* and *weight*, and valid values for both:

```
// create a valid mutation this time
m = new Mutation("person");
m.put("", "height", "6.0");
m.put("", "weight", "200.0");

writer = conn.createBatchWriter("testTable", new BatchWriterConfig());
writeAndReportViolations(writer, m);
```

Our output now shows:

```
successfully written
```

We can also check to make sure mutations that are missing both *height* and *weight* can succeed:

```
// write a mutation that has nothing to do with weight or height
m = new Mutation("person");
m.put("", "name", "Joe");

writer = conn.createBatchWriter("testTable", new BatchWriterConfig());
writeAndReportViolations(writer, m);
```

Our mutation succeeded:

```
successfully written
```

Iterators

Accumulo provides a server-side programming framework called *iterators*, which can be used to customize a table's behavior. An iterator is a simple function applied on the server that can apply logic to one or more key-value pairs. Because Accumulo is doing work to ensure that key-value pairs are always kept in sorted order, there is a convenient opportunity to apply additional logic to these key-value pairs.

An iterator can be applied to filter out certain key-value pairs based on some criteria, or to combine, aggregate, or summarize the values of several related key-value pairs. Some iterators transform the value of a key-value pair into a new value.

Imagine the case in which we have several versions of the same key-value pair. We can configure an iterator to choose the version with the maximum numerical value. Or we can choose to sum across or append the values to produce a composite value. We'll get into the specifics of these types of iterators in the following sections.

Iterators and Coprocessors

Iterators are a feature unique to Accumulo. They are not described in the original Bigtable paper from Google (*http://bit.ly/bigtable_paper*). The opportunity to apply user-defined functions on the server side for a variety of useful reasons became apparent to the Accumulo developers as a consequence of implementing the internal logic of sorting key-value pairs from multiple sources such as files and in-memory structures, and filtering based on visibilities.

A later paper from Google about a project called Percolator (*http://bit.ly/percolator_paper*) describes additional processes that run alongside tablet servers, called coprocessors, but these are different from iterators in that coprocessors are separate processes that do not run in the same memory space as tablet servers.

Other Bigtable implementations have adopted various server-side programming mechanisms. HBase employs coprocessors that run in region server memory. (For more on HBase, see *HBase: The Definitive Guide* [O'Reilly].) placing them somewhere between Accumulo's iterators and Google's coprocessors.

There is also a young project called Fluo (*https://github.com/fluo-io*) that is implementing coprocessors for Accumulo.

Iterators are applied in succession so that each iterator uses, as its source data, another iterator's output. Each iterator's output consists of sorted key-value pairs. To determine the order in which the iterators are applied, each iterator is assigned a priority. In each scope, the iterators are applied successively from the lowest priority to the highest.

Tablet servers apply several iterators by default to all key-value pairs for functions such as basic merge-sorting, selecting key-value pairs based on column family and column qualifiers specified in scanner options, skipping deleted data, and filtering out key-value pairs that the user is not authorized to see (Figure 6-1).

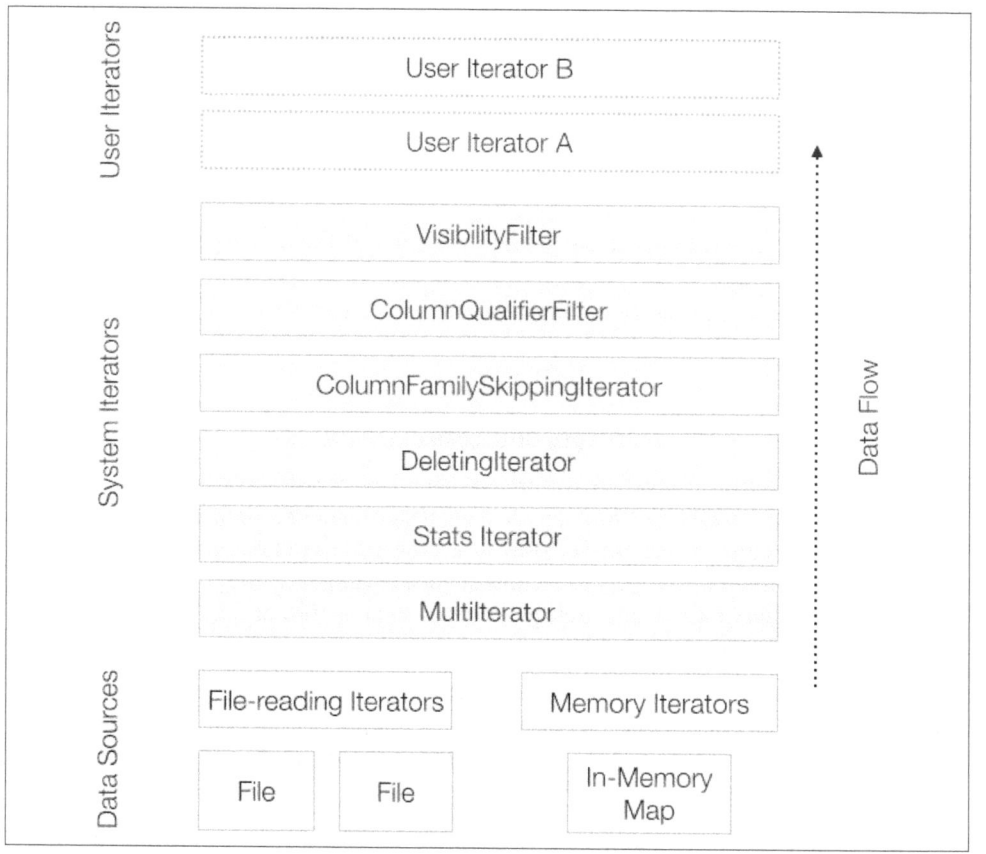

Figure 6-1. Iterators are applied in a stack

Each iterator has an opportunity to filter out key-value pairs, collect information, or transform values. User-configured iterators are applied after all the system iterators have processed key-value pairs.

A series of iterators is applied in the three scopes in which a tablet server processes data:

Minor compaction
When flushing the sorted in-memory map to a sorted file on disk

Major compaction
When combining some number of sorted files into a single file

Scan

When reading all of its sorted in-memory and on-disk structures to answer a scan query

These scopes are labeled *minc*, *majc*, and *scan*, respectively.

Iterators applied at *minc* and *majc* time permanently change the data stored in Accumulo. Scan-time iterators can be applied for all scans of a table, or on a per-scan basis.

Iterator Configuration API

To configure an iterator through the Java API, create an `IteratorSetting` object. At a minimum, provide the iterator's priority and its class. The priority determines the order in which iterators are applied; the lower the number, the earlier the iterator is applied.

You can also provide a shorthand name for the iterator. If this isn't provided, the simple name for the class will be used as its name.

Once the object is created, the convention is for parameters specific to a given iterator to be set via static methods of that iterator. Then the iterator can be added to the table or to a particular scanner.

For example, to configure an age-off filtering iterator, we could use the following code:

```
int priority = 15;
IteratorSetting setting = new IteratorSetting(priority, AgeOffFilter.class);
AgeOffFilter.setTTL(setting, 3600000);

TableOperations ops = connector.tableOperations();
ops.attachIterator(tableName, setting);
```

By default, this adds the iterator to all scopes, but which scopes to use can be supplied with an `EnumSet` passed to the `attachIterator()` method. The following would apply the iterator to all future scans of the table:

```
ops.attachIterator(tableName, setting, EnumSet.of(IteratorScope.scan));
```

To configure the iterator to be used only for a particular scanner, use the following:

```
scanner.addScanIterator(setting);
```

Before adding an iterator to a table, we can use the `checkIteratorConflict()` method to check if there are any potential conflicts with the way we've set up our iterator. This will report whether any existing iterators have the same name or priority as the iterator described in the `IteratorSetting` object:

```
ops.checkIteratorConflicts(tableName, setting, scopes)
```

 Iterator priorities determine the order in which they are applied. The lower the priority value, the earlier the iterator is applied to a key-value pair.

The VersioningIterator, for example, is enabled by default at priority 20, so any iterator added with a priority less than 20 will be applied before the VersioningIterator and will see all versions of key-value pairs that might exist. An iterator with a priority value higher than 20 will be applied after the VersioningIterator and so will only see key-value pairs that have passed through the VersioningIterator filter logic.

The checkIteratorConflicts() method just described will help avoid adding an iterator with the same priority as an existing iterator.

We can use the listIterators() method to see which iterators are configured on a given table. This will list the names and scopes of all iterators configured on the table:

```
Map<String,EnumSet<IteratorScope>> iterators = ops.listIterators(tableName);
```

To see specific options for a configured iterator, use the getIteratorSetting() method:

```
IteratorSetting setting = ops.getIteratorSetting(tableName, name, scope);
```

Iterators configured on a table can be removed via the removeIterator() method. The iterator will only be removed for the scopes specified:

```
conn.tableOperations().removeIterator(tableName, name, scopes);
```

For details on configuring iterators via shell commands, see "Configuring iterators" on page 441.

We'll now look at an example of setting up the VersioningIterator.

VersioningIterator

The VersioningIterator is the only programmable iterator that is configured for all Accumulo tables by default. Each Accumulo key has a timestamp that is used for versioning.

Let's say you insert a key with value *a*. If you insert the same key at a later time with value *b*, Accumulo considers the second key-value pair to be a more recent version of the first. By default, only the latest timestamped version will be kept.

The VersioningIterator can be configured to keep a different number of versions, or you can remove it to keep all versions. Here we look at the effects of configuring the VersioningIterator on a table.

Iterator Configuration Example

In this example we'll create a table, which will have the `VersioningIterator` configured by default. Then we'll alter the configuration to see the effects of iterators on our
example data.

First we'll insert several versions of the same key and see how the `VersioningItera`
`tor` applies:

```
Connector conn = ExampleMiniCluster.getConnector();
TableOperations ops = conn.tableOperations();

ops.create("testTable");

// insert some data
BatchWriter writer = conn.createBatchWriter("testTable",
    new BatchWriterConfig());
Mutation m = new Mutation("row");
m.put("", "col", "1");
writer.addMutation(m);

m = new Mutation("row");
m.put("", "col", "2");
writer.addMutation(m);

m = new Mutation("row");
m.put("", "col", "3");
writer.addMutation(m);
writer.flush();

// look at the key-value pair we inserted
System.out.println("\nview with versioning iterator on");
Scanner scanner = conn.createScanner("testTable", Authorizations.EMPTY);
for(Map.Entry<Key, Value> e : scanner) {
  System.out.println(e.getKey() + ":\t" + e.getValue());
}
```

Our output looks like this:

```
view with versioning iterator on
row :col [] 1409449409924 false: 3
```

Note that there is only one version, the last one we inserted. The others are being suppressed by the `VersioningIterator`.

If we were to flush this table, the other versions would disappear completely. As it is
now, they are all still lurking in memory, and the `VersioningIterator` is filtering out
all but the latest when we do a scan.

Now we'll look at how the `VersioningIterator` is set up:

```
// list all iterators
System.out.println("\niterators");
Map<String, EnumSet<IteratorUtil.IteratorScope>> iters =
  ops.listIterators("testTable");
for(Map.Entry<String, EnumSet<IteratorUtil.IteratorScope>> iter :
    iters.entrySet()) {
  System.out.println(iter.getKey() + ":\t" + iter.getValue());
}

// look at the settings for the versioning iterator
IteratorSetting setting = ops.getIteratorSetting("testTable", "vers",
    IteratorScope.scan);

System.out.println("\niterator options");
for(Map.Entry<String, String> opt : setting.getOptions().entrySet()) {
  System.out.println(opt.getKey() + ":\t" + opt.getValue());
}
```

Our output is:

```
iterators
vers:  [majc, minc, scan]

iterator options
maxVersions: 1
```

This shows that the VersioningIterator is the only one configured, and that it applies to all three scopes: major compaction, minor compaction, and scans.

The options show that it is configured to keep one version of each key-value pair.

Now we'll disable the VersioningIterator and see if we can retrieve all versions we inserted:

```
// disable the versioning iterator for all scopes
ops.removeIterator("testTable", "vers", EnumSet.allOf(IteratorScope.class));

// look at our table again
System.out.println("\nview with versioning iterator off");
for(Map.Entry<Key, Value> e : scanner) {
  System.out.println(e.getKey() + ":\t" + e.getValue());
}
```

Now we see all versions:

```
view with versioning iterator off
row :col [] 1409449409924 false: 3
row :col [] 1409449409924 false: 2
row :col [] 1409449409924 false: 1
```

Finally, we'll enable a different kind of iterator, the SummingCombiner, which will add up the values of all versions of our key and return the sum:

```
// enable the SummingCombiner iterator on our table
IteratorSetting scSetting = new IteratorSetting(15, "sum",
```

```
        SummingCombiner.class);

    // apply combiner to all columns
    SummingCombiner.setCombineAllColumns(scSetting, true);

    // expect string representations of numbers
    SummingCombiner.setEncodingType(scSetting, SummingCombiner.Type.STRING);

    ops.checkIteratorConflicts("testTable", scSetting,
        EnumSet.of(IteratorScope.scan));

    // attach the iterator
    ops.attachIterator("testTable", scSetting, EnumSet.of(IteratorScope.scan));

    // look at our table now
    System.out.println("\nview with summing combiner iterator on");
    for(Map.Entry<Key, Value> e : scanner) {
      System.out.println(e.getKey() + ":\t" + e.getValue());
    }
```

Now we only see one version, but the value represents the sum of all three versions
we inserted :

```
view with summing combiner iterator on
row :col [] 1409449409924 false:  6
```

Adding Iterators by Setting Properties

Iterators are configured like all other table options: by setting properties specific to a
table.

To configure an iterator via properties, use the `setProperty()` method. Doing this
requires knowing what properties exist and what their acceptable settings are. Also,
iterator conflicts are not checked when properties are set directly. For these reasons,
setting iterators with `IteratorSetting` objects through the API described in the pre‐
vious section is preferable and recommended. However, it is good to be aware of the
table properties associated with your iterators:

```
connector.tableOperations().setProperty("table.iterator.majc.ageoff.opt.ttl",
    "3600000");
connector.tableOperations().setProperty("table.iterator.majc.ageoff",
    "10,org.apache.accumulo.core.iterators.user.AgeOffFilter");
```

When setting up iterators this way it is a good idea to set the options first, to keep the
iterator from being instantiated before it is properly configured.

Filtering Iterators

Filters are iterators that simply decide whether or not to include existing key-value
pairs. They do not alter the key-value pairs in any way.

We'll look at the filters supplied with Accumulo and then how to create our own.

Built-in filters

Some useful filters are provided with Accumulo:

AgeOffFilter
> Removes keys when their timestamps differ from the current time by more than a specified parameter (in milliseconds).

ColumnAgeOffFilter
> Stores a separate age-off parameter for each column, to age off columns at different rates.

TimestampFilter
> Only keeps keys with timestamps earlier and/or later than given start and end parameters.

RegExFilter
> Returns key-value pairs that match a Java regular expression in a particular portion of the key or value (the row, column family, column qualifier, or value). Regular expressions can be provided for any subset of these four, and matches can be determined by ORing or ANDing together the results of each individual regular expression.

GrepIterator
> An iterator that matches exact strings to all key-value pairs scanned. This is great for doing one-time scans of a table. If you find yourself using this iterator frequently you might want to look into secondary indexes, as described in "Secondary Indexing" on page 275.

ReqVisFilter
> Removes keys with empty column visibilities.

LargeRowFilter
> Suppresses entire rows that have more than a configurable number of columns. It buffers the row in memory when determining whether or not it should be suppressed, so the specified number of columns should not be too large.

RowFilter
> An abstract iterator that decides whether or not to include an entire row. Subclasses of RowFilter must implement an acceptRow() method that takes as a parameter a SortedKeyValueIterator<Key,Value> (which will be limited to the row being decided upon) and returns a Boolean. This allows you to decide to include a row based on several features of the row, such as the presence of two or more columns or a relationship between values.

All filters can be configured to reverse their logic by using the `setNegate()` method:

```
IteratorSetting setting;
boolean negate = true;

MyFilter.setNegate(setting, negate);
```

Custom filters

Custom filters can be written by extending `org.apache.accumulo.core.itera` `tors.Filter`. Subclasses of `Filter` must implement an `accept()` method that takes `Key` and `Value` as parameters and returns a `boolean`.

The interface is as follows:

```
public abstract class Filter extends WrappingIterator
    implements OptionDescriber {
  ...
  /**
   * @return <tt>true</tt> if the key/value pair is accepted by the filter.
   */
  public abstract boolean accept(Key k, Value v);

}
```

We'll walk through an example next to see how to make our own custom filter.

Custom filtering iterator example

Here we'll create a custom filtering iterator that returns key-value pairs only if the value, interpreted as a number, is greater than a user-provided threshold.

First we create our filter class by extending `Filter` and defining our `accept()` method:

```
public class GreaterThanFilterExample extends Filter {

    private static final String GREATER_THAN_CRITERION = "greaterThanOption";

    private long threshold = 0;

    @Override
    public boolean accept(Key k, Value v) {
      try {
        long num = Long.parseLong(new String(v.get()));
        return num > threshold;
      } catch(NumberFormatException ex) {
        // continue and return false
      }

      return false;
    }
```

```
      ...
}
```

We need to write a few other methods to make users aware of the required `threshold` setting:

```
@Override
public IteratorOptions describeOptions() {
  IteratorOptions opts = super.describeOptions();
  opts.addNamedOption(GREATER_THAN_CRITERION,
      "Only return values greater than given numerical value");
  return opts;
}

@Override
public boolean validateOptions(Map<String,String> options) {
  if(!super.validateOptions(options) ||
      !options.containsKey(GREATER_THAN_CRITERION)) {
    return false;
  }

  String gtString = options.get(GREATER_THAN_CRITERION);
  try {
    Long.parseLong(gtString);
  }
  catch (NumberFormatException e) {
    return false;
  }

  return true;
}
```

Also, the convention is for iterators to provide static methods for filling out options on `IteratorSetting` objects. We'll add one for our threshold:

```
public static void setThreshold(
        final IteratorSetting setting,
        final int threshold) {

  setting.addOption(GREATER_THAN_CRITERION, Integer.toString(threshold));
}
```

Next we want to fetch the threshold from the iterator options whenever our iterator is used. Iterator classes are set up and torn down at the discretion of the tablet server. The `init()` method will allow us to perform some setup before the `accept()` method is called:

```
@Override
public void init(SortedKeyValueIterator<Key,Value> source,
    Map<String,String> options, IteratorEnvironment env) throws IOException {
  super.init(source, options, env);
  if (options.containsKey(GREATER_THAN_CRITERION)) {
    String gtString = options.get(GREATER_THAN_CRITERION);
```

```
        threshold = Long.parseLong(gtString);
    }
}
```

Finally, we can test our filter. We'll use the `ExampleMiniCluster` to create a test table and apply our iterator to it:

```
Random random = new Random();

Connector conn = ExampleMiniCluster.getConnector();
TableOperations ops = conn.tableOperations();

ops.create("testTable");

// insert some data
BatchWriter writer = conn.createBatchWriter("testTable",
    new BatchWriterConfig());

for(int i=0; i < 30; i++) {

  int rowNum = random.nextInt(100);
  int colNum = random.nextInt(100);
  int value = random.nextInt(100);

  Mutation m = new Mutation("row" + rowNum);

  m.put("", "col" + colNum, Integer.toString(value));
  writer.addMutation(m);
}

writer.flush();
```

Now that our test table is full of values with random numbers between 0 and 100, we'll add our iterator and scan:

```
IteratorSetting setting = new IteratorSetting(15, "gtf",
    GreaterThanFilterExample.class.getName());
GreaterThanFilterExample.setThreshold(setting, 80);

conn.tableOperations().attachIterator("testTable", setting);

// we could, instead, set our iterator just for this scan
//scanner.addScanIterator(setting);

// check for the existence of our iterator
for(Map.Entry<String, EnumSet<IteratorUtil.IteratorScope>> i :
    conn.tableOperations().listIterators("testTable").entrySet()) {
  System.out.println(i);
}
```

Checking for our iterator on the table shows:

```
gtf=[majc, minc, scan]
vers=[majc, minc, scan]
```

The only thing left to do is to scan our table and check the output:

```
// scan whole table ❶
Scanner scanner = conn.createScanner("testTable", Authorizations.EMPTY);
for(Map.Entry<Key, Value> e : scanner) {
  System.out.println(e);
}
```

❶ Note that using an iterator to scan an entire table is not scalable to large tables, but is good enough for our test here.

The output we get should show no values under our threshold, 80:

```
row0  :col1 [] 1409452474218 false 95
row13 :col94 [] 1409452474218 false 91
row32 :col70 [] 1409452474218 false 84
row34 :col56 [] 1409452474218 false 92
row49 :col94 [] 1409452474218 false 95
row59 :col86 [] 1409452474218 false 92
row93 :col60 [] 1409452474218 false 91
```

 It may be tempting to write complicated filtering iterators to apply arbitrary query logic. Keep in mind that filtering data is expensive, especially in a big data context. An application that requires good performance at scale will limit filtering to the absolute minimum.

To deploy this iterator to a production cluster, we'll need to build a JAR that contains our class and place it where server processes can load it. See "Deploying JARs" on page 407 for details.

Combiners

Combiners are iterators that combine all the versions of a key-value pair into a single key-value pair, instead of keeping the most recent versions of a key-value pair as the VersioningIterator does. Combiners work on sets of keys that only differ in their timestamp. If you want to combine key-value pairs that do not all have the same row, column family, qualifier, and visibility, you'll have to write a different custom iterator.

All combiners can be set to run on one or more particular columns or all columns:

```
int priority = 35;
IteratorSetting setting = new IteratorSetting(priority, "mycombiner",
    MyCombiner.class);

List<IteratorSetting.Column> columns = new ArrayList<>();
```

```
// can be applied to all columns in a family
columns.add(new IteratorSetting.Column("attributes"));

// and a specific column
columns.add(new IteratorSetting.Column("orders", "amount"));

MyCombiner.setColumns(setting, columns);
```

To set a combiner to apply to all columns, use the setCombineAllColumns() method:

```
MyCombiner.setCombineAllColumns(setting, true);
```

If a combiner is configured to apply to all columns, any columns passed to the setColumns() method are ignored.

Combiners for incrementing or appending updates

Combiners can help when an application calls for doing updates in which new values should be appended or otherwise combined with existing values. In many systems this requires reading the existing values first, applying the combination logic, and writing back the combined value. Accumulo can combine updates very efficiently by allowing multiple partially combined values to coexist until the finalized answer is needed—for example when a value is read by a client performing a scan. This allows these types of updates to be applied to a table with the same performance as simple inserts or overwriting updates.

For example, if we would like to update a numerical value by adding a new amount to the existing value, we don't have to somehow lock the row and column, read out the old value, add our new amount to it, and write it back. We can simply insert the amount to be added and instruct the server to add up all the existing values for that row and column. When the server writes values to disk it always writes the combined value to cut down on the partial values that are stored.

Being able to perform inserts without reading data can mean the difference between a few hundred insert operations per second and potentially hundreds of thousands of insert operations per second. It is certainly worth the effort to investigate the possibility of using combiners to help your application carry out updates.

To illustrate the difference, consider the following scenario. Let's say we are maintaining a summary of the number of times we have seen each word in a corpus. When we would like to update results we have two choices. One approach is to have the application read the old value, add the new value, and write the combined value back (Figure 6-2).

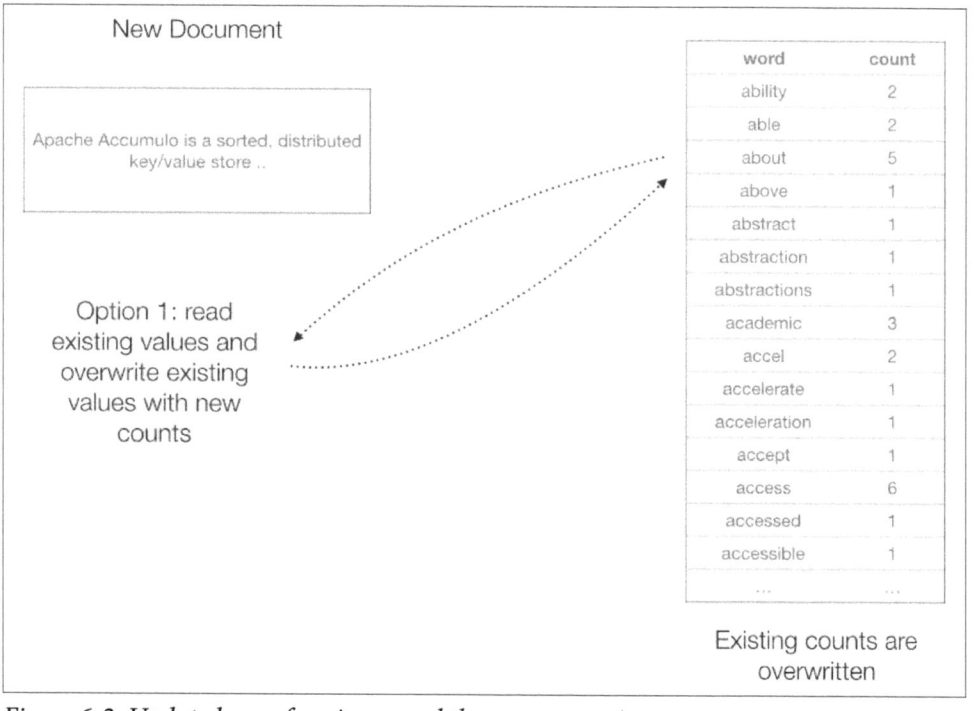

Figure 6-2. Update by performing a read then an overwrite

Another, much faster approach is to do a simple insert of the additional counts, and let a combiner do the final summation (Figure 6-3).

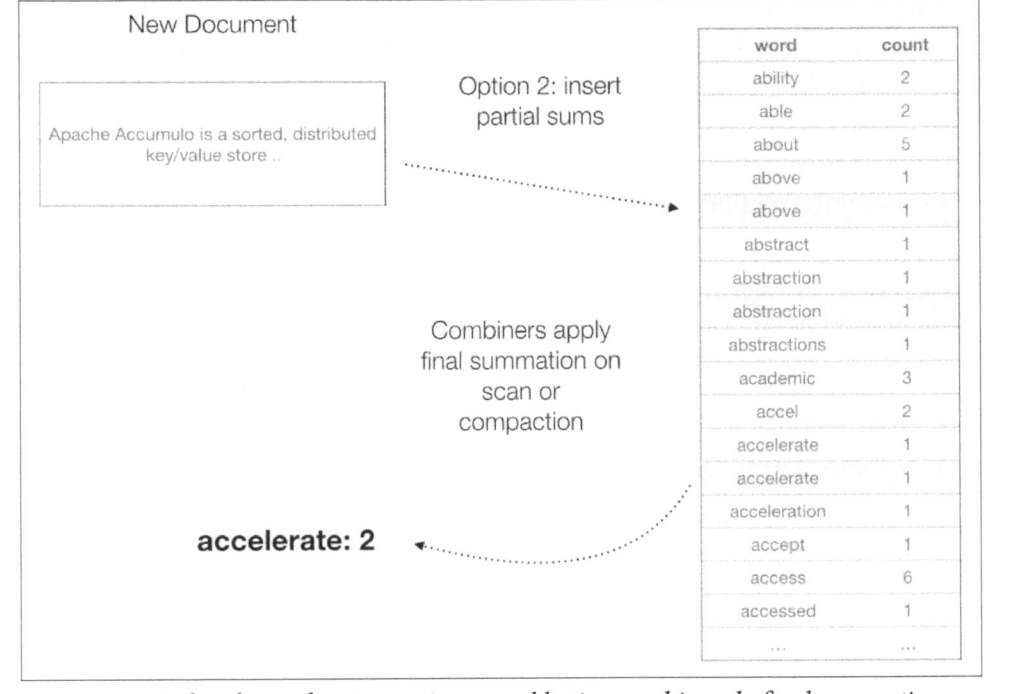

Figure 6-3. Update by performing an insert and letting combiner do final summation

Built-in combiners

Accumulo comes with a number of combiners. These are in the `org.apache.accu mulo.core.iterators.user` package:

LongCombiner

    An abstract combiner that interprets Accumulo `Value`s as Java `Long` objects. It comes with three possible encoding types: `STRING`, which prints and parses the number as a string; `LONG`, which encodes the number in exactly 8 binary bytes; and `VARNUM`, which uses a variable-length binary encoding.

MaxCombiner

    Extends the `LongCombiner`, interpreting values as `Long`s, and returns the maximum `Long` for each set of values.

MinCombiner

    Extends the `LongCombiner`, interpreting values as `Long`s, and returns the minimum `Long` for each set of values.

SummingCombiner

    Extends the `LongCombiner`, interpreting values as `Long`s, and returns the sum of the set of values.

`SummingArrayCombiner`
> Interprets `Values` as an array of `Longs`, and returns an array of sums. If the arrays are not the same length, the shorter arrays are padded with zeros to equal the length of the largest array.

`BigDecimalCombiner`
> An abstract combiner that interprets Accumulo values as `BigDecimals`.

An additional example combiner is the `StatsCombiner` in the `org.apache.accu` `mulo.examples.simple.combiner` package. Use of this combiner is illustrated in Accumulo's *README.combiner* example.

We saw an example of setting up the `SummingCombiner` via the API in "Iterator Configuration Example" on page 213.

Next we'll look at writing our own combiner.

Custom combiners

Custom combiners can be written by extending `org.apache.accumulo.core.itera` `tors.Combiner`. Subclasses of `Combiner` must implement a `reduce()` method that takes `Key` and `Iterator<Value>` as parameters and returns a `Value`:

```
public abstract Value reduce(Key key, Iterator<Value> iter);
```

If the values are always interpreted as a particular Java type, the `TypedValue` `Combiner<V>` can be used. This combiner uses an `Encoder` to translate the type V to and from a byte array. Subclasses of `TypedValueCombiner` implement a `typedRe` `duce()` method that takes `Key` and `Iterator<V>` as parameters and returns an object of type V:

```
public abstract class TypedValueCombiner<V> extends Combiner {
  ...
  public abstract V typedReduce(Key key, Iterator<V> iter);

}
```

A combiner that extends `TypedValueCombiner` should also have a class implementing the `Encoder` interface for converting values to byte arrays and back:

```
public abstract class TypedValueCombiner<V> extends Combiner {
  ...
  public interface Encoder<V> {
    byte[] encode(V v);

    V decode(byte[] b) throws ValueFormatException;
  }
  ...
}
```

Custom combiner example

We'll implement a combiner that keeps track of the number of items seen and the sum of the items seen in order to produce an average. We can't simply store the average because we'll lose information about the number of items seen so far and won't know how much relative weight to apply to new items.

First, we'll implement an Encoder to store a Long and a Double, for the number of items seen, and the partial total:

```java
public class RunningAverageCombiner
    extends TypedValueCombiner<Pair<Long,Double>> {

  ...
  public static class LongDoublePairEncoder
      implements Encoder<Pair<Long,Double>> {

    @Override
    public byte[] encode(Pair<Long, Double> v) {
      String s = Long.toString(v.getFirst()) + ":" +
        Double.toString(v.getSecond());

      return s.getBytes(StandardCharsets.UTF_8);
    }

    @Override
    public Pair<Long, Double> decode(byte[] b) throws ValueFormatException {
      String s = new String(b, StandardCharsets.UTF_8);
      String[] parts = s.split(":");
      return new Pair<>(Long.parseLong(parts[0]), Double.parseDouble(parts[1]));
    }
  }
  ...
}
```

This class will allow us to write string values representing a count and a running total to be averaged.

Now we'll define our reduce() function, which will tell tablet servers how to combine multiple versions of values for a key. In our case, we simply keep track of the number of items we've seen, and a running total. At any given time, a client can divide the running total by the number of items seen to get the current average:

```java
  ...
  @Override
  public void init(SortedKeyValueIterator<Key,Value> source,
      Map<String,String> options, IteratorEnvironment env) throws IOException {
    super.init(source, options, env);
    setEncoder(new LongDoublePairEncoder()); ❶
  }

  @Override
```

```
public Pair<Long,Double> typedReduce(Key key,
    Iterator<Pair<Long,Double>> iter) {

  Long count = 0L;
  Double sum = 0.0;

  while(iter.hasNext()) {
    Pair<Long,Double> pair = iter.next();

    count += pair.getFirst();
    sum += pair.getSecond();
  }

  return new Pair<>(count, sum);
}
...
```

❶ Be sure to initialize the encoder to be used here.

Now we can test our combiner on a table. First we'll create a table, remove the Versio ningIterator so that our combiner receives all versions of each key, and set our custom combiner:

```
Connector conn = ExampleMiniCluster.getConnector();

TableOperations ops = conn.tableOperations();
ops.create("testTable");

// remove versioning iterator
ops.removeIterator("testTable", "vers", EnumSet.allOf(IteratorScope.class));

// configure our iterator
IteratorSetting setting = new IteratorSetting(10, "rac",
    RunningAverageCombiner.class); ❶
RunningAverageCombiner.setCombineAllColumns(setting, true); ❷
RunningAverageCombiner.setLossyness(setting, false); ❸

// attach to table for all scopes
ops.attachIterator("testTable", setting);
```

❶ Give our combiner a priority of 10, name it rac, and provide the class.

❷ Set our combiner to operate on all columns.

❸ Instruct the combiner to throw exceptions when values fail to decode with the given encoder, instead of silently discarding those values.

Now we can insert some test data. We'll generate random numbers in a particular range and insert them as multiple versions of the same key. This means the row ID, column family, column qualifier, and column visibility must be the same. Values in

---

different keys will not be combined together, only values representing multiple versions of the same key.

We'll generate numbers uniformly at random between 4.5 and 6.5. Our average should be somewhere around 5.5:

```
BatchWriter writer = conn.createBatchWriter("testTable",
    new BatchWriterConfig());

// begin writing numbers to our table
Random random = new Random();

for(int i = 0; i < 5; i++) {
  Mutation m = new Mutation("heights");
  m.put("", "average", "1:" + (random.nextDouble() * 2 + 4.5));
  writer.addMutation(m);
}
writer.flush();
```

Now we'll perform a scan on our table. This will cause our combiner to examine the key-value pairs we've written and give it a chance to combine them before returning any to our client.

We'll use the same LongDoublePairEncoder to decode values into our count and running total. Then we'll divide the total by the count and print out the average:

```
LongDoublePairEncoder enc = new LongDoublePairEncoder();

Scanner scanner = conn.createScanner("testTable", Authorizations.EMPTY);
for(Map.Entry<Key, Value> e : scanner) {
  Pair<Long,Double> pair = enc.decode(e.getValue().get());

  double average = pair.getSecond() / pair.getFirst();
  System.out.println(average);
}
```

Our output consists of one number:

```
5.975622642042859
```

Next we write one hundred more versions of our key. After scanning again our average is a little closer to 5.5:

```
5.329055520715937
```

To load this combiner into tablet servers in a production cluster we'll need to package our combiner class and encoder class into a JAR file and deploy it to all the servers. See "Deploying JARs" on page 407 for details. Be sure to compile your combiner against the same version of Accumulo that is running on your cluster.

Other Built-in Iterators

Accumulo provides a few other built-in iterators for doing things other than simple filtering and combining:

IndexedDocIterator

    This is an iterator for doing indexing by *document-based partitioning*. This iterator allows a query to scan the first half of a row, which contains a term index, for document IDs that contain particular terms; to combine sets of matching document IDs together logically in set operations; and finally to scan the second half of the row to retrieve the full documents that satisfy all query criteria. We cover this iterator in depth in "Index Partitioned by Document" on page 284.

IntersectingIterator

    The base class extended by IndexedDocIterator, the IntersectingIterator performs the operations to find selected document IDs without returning the documents themselves. It will scan a term index within a row to find document IDs containing search terms, and intersect sets of matching document IDs to find documents that contain all the search terms.

RowDeletingIterator

    Uses a special marker to indicate that an entire row should be deleted. The marker consists of a row ID, empty column family, qualifier and visibility, and a value of DEL_ROW.

TransformingIterator

    Typically an iterator will only read key-value pairs and decide to filter some out, as in filters, or to combine the values some way, as in combiners. The transforming iterator is an abstract iterator that allows parts of the keys to be transformed also. In implementing a transforming iterator, care should be taken to ensure that sorted key order is preserved.

WholeColumnFamilyIterator

    The WholeColumnFamily iterator bundles up key-value pairs within the same column family in a row together and returns them to the client as a single key-value pair. The client can then decode the key-value pair into the constituent key-value pairs within that one row and column family.

WholeRowIterator

    This iterator encodes all the key-value pairs within one row into a single key-value pair and sends it to the client as a coherent object. Clients can then decode the key-value pair to restore the original key-value pairs in the row. This is convenient for processing sets of columns and values one row at a time. It is possible to fetch a subset of the columns and still get the set of columns per row returned to the client bundled together. See the example in the next section.

WholeRowIterator example

When a table is scanned, key-value pairs are streamed back to the client in sorted order, one after another. Sets of key-value pairs with the same row ID are considered to be the same row. Clients must examine the row ID to determine which key-value pairs belong in which row, unless they are grouped using the RowIterator described in "Grouping by Rows" on page 110.

If all the key-value pairs in a row can fit in memory comfortably, we can choose to use the WholeRowIterator to get a set of key-value pairs for one row grouped together in a convenient data structure.

For this example, we'll create a test table with 100 rows containing 100 columns each. Each row will be read into client memory completely, and we can decode it into separate columns and access them in any order we choose:

```
Connector conn = ExampleMiniCluster.getConnector();

TableOperations ops = conn.tableOperations();
ops.create("testTable");

BatchWriter writer = conn.createBatchWriter("testTable",
    new BatchWriterConfig());

for(int i=1; i <= 100; i++) {
  Mutation m = new Mutation("row" + String.format("%02d", i));

  for(int j = 1; j <= 100; j++) {
    m.put("", "col" + j, Integer.toString(i * j));
  }

  writer.addMutation(m);
}
writer.flush();
```

Next we'll create a scanner and add the WholeRowIterator to it:

```
Scanner scanner = conn.createScanner("testTable", Authorizations.EMPTY);
scanner.setRange(new Range("row50", "row60"));

IteratorSetting setting = new IteratorSetting(30, "wri", WholeRowIterator.class);

scanner.addScanIterator(setting);
```

The WholeRowIterator has a decode() method that will unpack one row's worth of data for us into a SortedMap<Key,Value> object. We'll use some convenience methods for grabbing the row ID and creating a map of just column names to values:

```
private static byte[] getRow(SortedMap<Key,Value> row) {
  return row.entrySet().iterator().next().getKey().getRow().getBytes();
}
```

```
private static SortedMap<String,Value> columnMap(SortedMap<Key,Value> row) {

    TreeMap<String,Value> colMap = new TreeMap<>();
    for(Map.Entry<Key, Value> e : row.entrySet()) {

        String cf = e.getKey().getColumnFamily().toString();
        String cq = e.getKey().getColumnQualifier().toString();

        colMap.put(cf + ":" + cq, e.getValue());
    }
    return colMap;
}
```

Now we can perform our scan and operate on one row's worth of data at a time, grabbing columns in whatever order we want:

```
Scanner scanner = conn.createScanner("testTable", Authorizations.EMPTY);
scanner.setRange(new Range("row50", "row60"));
// we could choose a subset of columns via fetchColumn() too

IteratorSetting setting = new IteratorSetting(30, "wri", WholeRowIterator.class);
scanner.addScanIterator(setting);

for(Map.Entry<Key, Value> e : scanner) {
  SortedMap<Key, Value> rowData =
    WholeRowIterator.decodeRow(e.getKey(), e.getValue()); ❶

  byte[] row = getRow(rowData);
  SortedMap<String, Value> columns = columnMap(rowData);

  System.out.println("\nrow\t" + new String(row));
  System.out.println(":col31\t" + columns.get(":col31"));
  System.out.println(":col15\t" + columns.get(":col15"));
}
```

❶ Decode the key-value pair to get the row's columns.

Running our code produces the following output, showing the out-of-order access of columns within each row:

```
row   row50
:col31 1550
:col15 750

row   row51
:col31 1581
:col15 765

...

row   row60
:col31 1860
:col15 900
```

Low-level iterator API

Filtering iterators and combiners are special cases of general iterators. There is a low-level iterator API that can be used to create new types of iterators. It is much more complicated than the API for implementing new filters and combiners, however.

Lower-level iterators at the very least implement the `SortedKeyValueItera tor<Key,Value>` interface:

```
public interface SortedKeyValueIterator<K extends WritableComparable<?>,
    V extends Writable> {

  void init(SortedKeyValueIterator<K,V> source, Map<String,String> options,
      IteratorEnvironment env) throws IOException;

  boolean hasTop();

  void next() throws IOException;

  void seek(Range range, Collection<ByteSequence> columnFamilies,
      boolean inclusive) throws IOException;

  K getTopKey();

  V getTopValue();

  SortedKeyValueIterator<K,V> deepCopy(IteratorEnvironment env);
}
```

Some iterators choose to extend the `WrappingIterator` or `SkippingIterator` classes.

Some developers have been tempted to write iterators that don't simply alter the data read as it is returned to the client but also write out data, potentially to other tablet servers. Although this is theoretically possible, a few issues make it difficult.

First, tablet servers build up and tear down the iterator stack at their own discretion, and it is not guaranteed that iterator classes will be long-lived, or able to maintain state for a particular amount of time. The other issue is that Accumulo client classes can use a lot of resources, and lifecycle management of these resources would need to be altered for use within a tablet server context.

Google implemented a different solution, called coprocessors, for allowing some writes or reads to tablet servers to trigger writes to other tablet servers. Coprocessors are described in the paper "Large-scale Incremental Processing Using Distributed Transactions and Notifications" (*http://bit.ly/percolator_paper*).

Some Accumulo developers are working on a similar implementation called Fluo (*https://github.com/fluo-io/fluo*).

We'll implement a simple iterator that takes advantage of one of the features of the lower-level API: the ability to seek ahead to a new key-value pair. Our iterator will simply return the first column and its value for each row we scan. After reading the first column for a row, it will seek to the next row.

Accumulo already has an implementation of an iterator that performs this same function and includes some additional optimization: the FirstEntryInRowIterator.

Scan Versus Seek

When an application is scanning key-value pairs in Accumulo and is ready to skip ahead to the next row, this question arises: is it more efficient to keep scanning keys one-by-one until the next row is reached (performing a string comparison on the row portion of each key), or to seek ahead directly to the next row?

Seeks are fairly expensive. On spinning commodity-class disks you can typically only do 100 to 250 seeks per second, whereas doing a sequential scan can read and perform comparisons on thousands of key-value pairs per second.

If the rarity of key-value pairs of interest is sufficiently high, such that scanning would take longer than doing a seek, then seeking to the next key-value pair is more efficient.

For an example of an iterator that tries to balance these options, see *org.apache.accumulo.core.iterators.FirstEntryInRowIterator.java* in the Accumulo code base.

The code for our iterator will begin at the WrappingIterator, rather than simply implementing SortedKeyValueIterator. This will help guarantee that we don't call methods out of order.

We'll first create our class:

```
public class FirstColumnIterator extends WrappingIterator  {

    private Range range;
    private boolean inclusive;
    private Collection<ByteSequence> columnFamilies;
    private boolean done;

    public FirstColumnIterator() {} ❶

    public FirstColumnIterator(FirstColumnIterator aThis,
        IteratorEnvironment env) { ❷
      super();
      setSource(aThis.getSource().deepCopy(env));
    }

    @Override
```

```
public void init(SortedKeyValueIterator<Key,Value> source,
    Map<String,String> options, IteratorEnvironment env) throws IOException {
  super.init(source, options, env);
}
...
```

❶ We need a public default constructor because this is the constructer Accumulo will use to instantiate the iterator.

❷ Additional constructors are optional but may be helpful in implementing the deepCopy method.

Next we'll implement just the seek(), next(), hasTop(), and deepCopy() methods. seek() is called first by the tablet server, and we'll use it to store off some variables we'll need to do our seeking later. It will also handle the case in which a seek is made to the middle of a row. next() is called to prepare the next key-value pair for retrieval by getTopKey() and getTopValue(), if the key-value pair exists. hasTop() indicates whether a key-value pair exists for retrieval.

We call on our superclass, the WrappingIterator, to seek to the next row in our source iterator. Every iterator has a source that ultimately goes back to files and in-memory data structures holding key-value pairs. Our iterator simply advances the source iterator past all but the first column of each row and notes when the end of the range is reached:

```
@Override
public void next() throws IOException {
  if(done) {
    return;
  }

  // create a new range to seek to
  Key nextKey = getSource().getTopKey().followingKey(PartialKey.ROW); ❶
  if(range.afterEndKey(nextKey)) { ❷
    done = true;
  }
  else {
    Range nextRange = new Range(nextKey, true, range.getEndKey(),
        range.isEndKeyInclusive()); ❸
    getSource().seek(nextRange, columnFamilies, inclusive); ❹
  }
}

@Override
public boolean hasTop() {
  return !done && getSource().hasTop(); ❺
}

@Override
```

```
public void seek(Range range, Collection<ByteSequence> columnFamilies,
    boolean inclusive) throws IOException {
  this.range = range;
  this.columnFamilies = columnFamilies;  ❻
  this.inclusive = inclusive;

  done = false;

  Key startKey = range.getStartKey();
  Range seekRange = new Range(
      startKey == null ? null : new Key(startKey.getRow()), true,
      range.getEndKey(), range.isEndKeyInclusive());
  super.seek(seekRange, columnFamilies, inclusive);  ❼

  if (getSource().hasTop()) {
    if (range.beforeStartKey(getSource().getTopKey()))  ❽
      next();
  }
}

@Override
public SortedKeyValueIterator<Key,Value> deepCopy(IteratorEnvironment env) {
  return new FirstColumnIterator(this, env);
}
```

❶ This method will get a key that has the first possible row ID after the current key.

❷ Check to see if we've reached the end of the range requested by the user and return if so.

❸ Create a range almost exactly like the one that was first given to us by the seek() method.

❹ Advance the source iterator past all the columns of this row to the first column of the next row.

❺ Return false if next() determined the end of the range has been reached, or if there is no more data in the source iterator.

❻ Save these seek parameters off for doing seeks in our next method.

❼ Construct a range that starts at the beginning of the row containing our start key, and seek our superclass, which will seek the source iterator.

❽ Skip to the next row if the top key is before our start key, meaning that we received a seek to the middle of a row.

 Handling a seek to the middle of a row is an important condition every iterator must address. Even if an application always seeks to the beginning of a row, Accumulo can internally seek to the middle of row when performing a long scan that involves pulling multiple batches of key-value pairs from tablet servers to a client.

Now we can apply our iterator to data in a table. First, we'll create a simple table of 100 rows with 100 columns each. This will make it easy to see if our iterator is working:

```
Connector conn = ExampleMiniCluster.getConnector();

TableOperations ops = conn.tableOperations();
ops.create("testTable");

BatchWriter writer = conn.createBatchWriter("testTable",
    new BatchWriterConfig());

for(int i=0; i < 100; i++) {
  Mutation m = new Mutation("row" + String.format("%02d", i));

  for(int j = 0; j < 100; j++) {
    m.put("", String.format("col%02d", j), i + " " + j);
  }

  writer.addMutation(m);
}
writer.flush();
```

Now we'll scan the table and just count the key-value pairs without our iterator so we'll have something to compare our iterator results to:

```
Scanner scanner = conn.createScanner("testTable", Authorizations.EMPTY);

// count items returned
int returned = 0;
for(Map.Entry<Key, Value> e : scanner)
  returned++;

System.out.println("items returned: " + returned);
```

Our output shows:

```
items returned: 10000
```

Now we'll apply our iterator and see if we only see the first column for every row:

```
IteratorSetting setting = new IteratorSetting(30, "fci",
    FirstColumnIterator.class);
scanner.addScanIterator(setting);

returned = 0;
```

```
for(Map.Entry<Key, Value> e : scanner) {
  System.out.println(e);
  returned++;
}

System.out.println("items returned: " + returned);
```

Now our output shows the rows and columns returned, with only the first column of each row, and a total count of 100:

```
row00 :col00 [] 1409608777713 false 0 0
row01 :col00 [] 1409608777713 false 1 0
row02 :col00 [] 1409608777713 false 2 0
...
row98 :col00 [] 1409608777713 false 98 0
row99 :col00 [] 1409608777713 false 99 0
items returned: 100
```

Thrift Proxy

In addition to the standard Accumulo processes, there is an option to start up a proxy service (Figure 6-4). This service provides an Apache Thrift API (*http:// thrift.apache.org/*) for interacting with Accumulo. Accumulo comes compiled with C ++, Python, and Ruby clients for interacting with the Thrift API.

Thrift provides a compiler to generate serialization code and remote procedural call (RPC) clients and servers in a particular language. The structures and services are defined in files in an *interface description language* (IDL). Clients for other languages can be generated, as we describe in "Generating Client Code" on page 240. The details of the API can be found in the Accumulo IDL file at *accumulo/proxy/thrift/ proxy.thrift*.

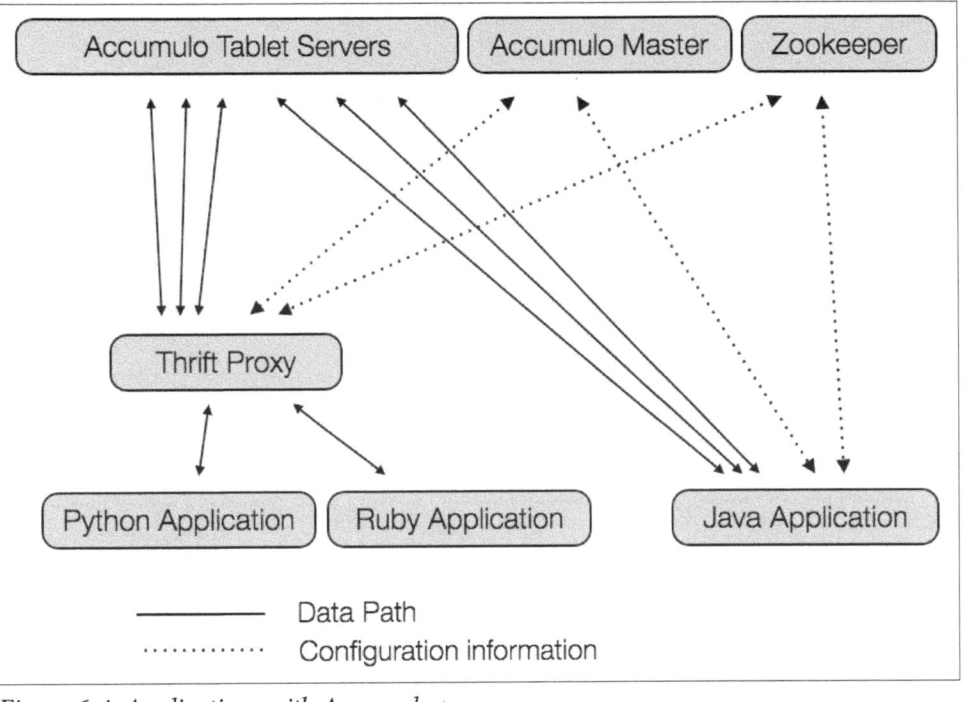

Figure 6-4. Applications with Accumulo proxy

Starting a Proxy

You must pass a configuration file to the proxy process when starting it up. An example configuration file is included with Accumulo at *accumulo/proxy/proxy.properties*. To start the proxy service, run:

```
accumulo proxy -p /path/to/proxy.properties
```

When using Thrift proxies, it is common to run one proxy process per proxy client (Figure 6-5). The proxy could be run on the same machine as the proxy client to eliminate network usage between proxies and their clients.

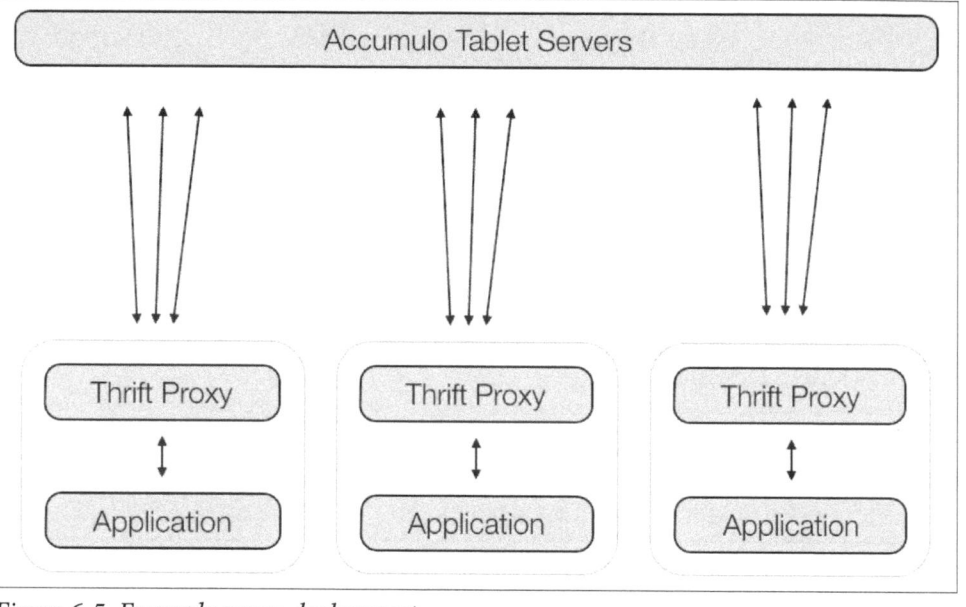

Figure 6-5. Example proxy deployment

Python Example

For this example we'll write some example code in Python (*https://www.python.org*). Python is a popular cross-platform, high-level, interpreted, object-oriented language. It ships with some operating systems and runs on Linux, Mac OS X, and Microsoft Windows.

We'll use the precompiled Python bindings that ship with Accumulo 1.6 in the *accumulo/proxy/gen-py* directory. We've included the Thrift libraries for Python in the example code, at *src/main/python*.

In this example, we'll generate a simple REST API for talking to Accumulo using Python and the Flask library (*http://flask.pocoo.org/*).

To connect to the Accumulo Thrift proxy, we'll use the following code:

```python
from thrift import Thrift
from thrift.transport import TSocket
from thrift.transport import TTransport
from thrift.protocol import TCompactProtocol

from accumulo import AccumuloProxy
from accumulo.ttypes import *


def connect():
  global client
```

```
global login

transport = TSocket.TSocket('localhost', 42424)  ❶
transport = TTransport.TFramedTransport(transport)
protocol = TCompactProtocol.TCompactProtocol(transport)
client = AccumuloProxy.Client(protocol)
transport.open()

login = client.login('root', {'password':'password'})
```

❶ This port is defined in the *proxy.properties* file.

Next we'll use the Flask notations to define some REST methods on our service. Our simple REST service will include the following methods:

```
http://host/tables GET List existing tables
http://host/tables/_tableName_ POST Creates a table
http://host/tables/_tableName_ DELETE Deletes a table
http://host/tables/_tableName_/rows POST Insert a mutation
http://host/tables/_tableName_/rows?range=_startRow_:_stopRow_
    &cols=_FamA:QualA,FamB:QualB_ GET Scan a portion of the rows of a table
```

In Python and Flask syntax, our methods will look like the following:

```
@app.route('/tables', methods=['GET'])
def listTables():

    tables = client.listTables(login)
    return json.dumps({'tables': list(tables)})


@app.route('/tables/<table>/rows', methods=['POST'])
def insert(table):

    row = request.form.get('row', '')
    colFam = request.form.get('colFam', '')
    colQual = request.form.get('colQual', '')
    colVis = request.form.get('colVis', '')
    value = request.form.get('value', '')

    m = {row: [ColumnUpdate(colFam, colQual, colVis, value=value)]}
    try:
      client.updateAndFlush(login, table, m)
    except Exception as e:
      return json.dumps({'success': False, 'message': str(e)})

    return json.dumps({'success': True})
```

Notice how when we're inserting a single value we simply create a Python dict with a single field name, representing the row ID, and a list of ColumnUpdate objects:

```
m = {row: [ColumnUpdate(colFam, colQual, colVis, value=value)]}
```

See the *src/main/python/restapi.py* file for more details.

The Thrift proxy can be started as described previously, or for this example we can run the `ExampleMiniThriftProxy.java` class included in the example code.

With the Thrift proxy running, we can start our REST service (HTTP response codes have been removed from the following transcript for readability):

```
$ python restapi.py &
 * Running on http://127.0.0.1:5000/
 * Restarting with reloader

$ curl "http://127.0.0.1:5000/tables"
{"tables": ["accumulo.root", "accumulo.metadata"]}

$ curl -d "" "http://127.0.0.1:5000/tables/test"
{"success": true}

$ curl "http://127.0.0.1:5000/tables"
{"tables": ["accumulo.root", "testTable", "accumulo.metadata"]}

$ curl -d "row=title&colFam=metadata&colQual=author&value=Joe%20Jones" \
    "http://127.0.0.1:5000/tables/test/rows"
{"success": true}

$ curl -d "row=title&colFam=content&value=This%20is%20an%20example%20article" \
    "http://127.0.0.1:5000/tables/test/rows"
{"success": true}

$ curl "http://127.0.0.1:5000/tables/test/rows"
{"results": [
  ["title", "content", "", 1407815024740, "This is an example article"],
  ["title", "metadata", "author", 1407814986048, "Joe Jones"]
]}

$ curl "http://127.0.0.1:5000/tables/test/rows?cols=content:"
{"results": [["title", "content", "", 1407815024740,
 "This is an example article"]]}

$ curl "http://127.0.0.1:5000/tables/test/rows?cols=metadata:author"
{"results": [["title", "metadata", "author", 1407814986048, "Joe Jones"]]}

$ curl -X DELETE "http://127.0.0.1:5000/tables/test"
{"success": true}

$ curl "http://127.0.0.1:5000/tables"
{"tables": ["accumulo.root", "accumulo.metadata"]}
```

Generating Client Code

The Thrift compiler can generate client code for many languages that will allow applications to communicate with the Accumulo proxy.

As of this writing Thrift supports the following languages (*http://thrift.apache.org/ docs/features*):

- C++
- C#
- Cocoa
- D
- Delphi
- Erlang
- Haskell
- Java
- JavaScript
- OCaml
- Perl
- PHP
- Python
- Ruby
- Smalltalk

If, for example, we want to develop a new application in PHP, we can run the Thrift compiler on the Accumulo IDL file:

```
thrift-0.9.0/compiler/cpp/thrift -gen php accumulo/proxy/thrift/proxy.thrift
```

This will create a directory called *gen-php* that contains the code a PHP application would need to connect and talk to the Accumulo Thrift proxy.

Language-Specific Clients

Accumulo provides an Apache Thrift proxy that enables clients to be written in any language that Thrift supports. For details on running the proxy, see "Thrift Proxy" on page 236.

A few developers have created language-specific client libraries to make it easier to use Accumulo in these languages. This list will likely become out of date very quickly, so we encourage you to search GitHub (*http://bit.ly/github_accumulo*) and follow the Accumulo blog (*https://blogs.apache.org/accumulo/*):

Python
    Python is a popular scripting language. The pyaccumulo project (*http://bit.ly/ pyaccumulo*) supports language bindings for Python.

Erlang

Erlang is a functional programming language that is popular for building distributed systems. The erlaccumulo project (*https://github.com/chaehb/erlaccumulo*) provides the client code for Erlang.

C++

C++ is a popular high-performance object-oriented language. The accumulo-cpp project (*http://bit.ly/accumulo-cpp*) provides the C++ client code.

Clojure

Clojure is a functional programming language that runs on the JVM. The clojure-accumulo project (*http://bit.ly/clojure-accumulo*) uses Clojure on top of the Java API.

Scala

Scala, another JVM language, combines object-oriented and functional programming. You can evaluate a couple of Scala wrappers around the Java API for your use. One is available from the scala-accumulo project (*http://bit.ly/scala-accumulo*) and the other from the accumulo-scala project (*http://bit.ly/accumulo-scala*).

Node.js JavaScript

The nodeulo project (*http://bit.ly/nodeulo*) provides a JavaScript client suitable for inclusion in code meant to run in a Node.js server.

Integration with Other Tools

A rich and quickly evolving ecosystem surrounds big data technologies. Many of these other software projects can be used with Accumulo as a part of a broader solution. In this section we touch on best practices for using Accumulo with some of these technologies.

Apache Hive

Apache Hive (*http://hive.apache.org*) is a popular tool for executing SQL queries on distributed applications within the Apache Hadoop ecosystem. Hive can execute a subset of the SQL specification, which is sometimes referred to as the Hive Query Language (HQL) to distinguish it from the full capabilities of SQL.

Hive queries can be executed as MapReduce jobs, and recent efforts allow Hive queries to be carried out in more low-latency execution frameworks such as Apache Tez (*http://tez.apache.org*).

Hive integration with Accumulo was first added in Hive version 0.14 and is designed to work with Accumulo 1.6. To configure Hive to work with Accumulo, you must specify four configuration parameters:

```
accumulo.instance.name
accumulo.zookeepers
accumulo.user.name
accumulo.user.pass
```

These can be applied to a Hive session via `-hiveconf` options:

```
hive -hiveconf accumulo.instance.name=accumulo \
  -hiveconf accumulo.zookeepers=zoo1 -hiveconf accumulo.user.name=hive \
  -hiveconf accumulo.user.pass=hive
```

Table options

The columns of Hive tables are mapped to columns in Accumulo when an Accumulo table is created. One of the original columns of the Hive table can be used as the row ID of the Accumulo table. This will enable queries over ranges of values for this column to be performed efficiently.

If a Hive table is to be created with columns named *name*, *age*, and *height*, we might choose to map these to Accumulo by storing the *name* column as the row ID, and the other columns in a common column family. This can be specified via the `WITH SERDE PROPERTIES()` function during table creation. Our use of this function can look like the following:

```
CREATE TABLE people(name STRING, age INT, height INT)
STORED  BY 'org.apache.hadoop.hive.accumulo.AccumuloStorageHandler'
WITH SERDEPROPERTIES('accumulo.columns.mapping' =
                 ':rowid,attributes:age,attributes:height');
```

The column mapping relies on the order of fields in the Hive table specification, assigning the first Accumulo column name to the first Hive table column and so on.

By default the Accumulo table name is the same as the Hive table name. This can be overridden via the `WITH TBLPROPERTIES()` function:

```
WITH TBLPROPERTIES ("accumulo.table.name" = "hive_people")
```

A table created with `CREATE TABLE` will be considered *managed* by Hive, meaning it will be created and destroyed along with the Hive table. To map a Hive table to an existing Accumulo table without tying the lifecycle of the Accumulo table to the Hive table, use the `EXTERNAL` keyword.

If we simply want to inform Hive of a table we have already created in Accumulo, we can do something like the following:

```
CREATE EXTERNAL TABLE people(name STRING, age INT, height INT)
STORED  BY 'org.apache.hadoop.hive.accumulo.AccumuloStorageHandler'
WITH SERDEPROPERTIES('accumulo.columns.mapping' =
                 ':rowid,attributes:age,attributes:height');
```

Serializing values

Values in Hive tables can be of various types. By default, values are serialized as strings when stored in Accumulo. Values can also be stored using a binary serialization by adding #b to the end of a field name in the mapping.

For example, if we want to store the age field using binary serialization we can specify it as `attributes:age#b`. To explicitly specify string serialization, #s can be used.

Additional options

Additional behavior can be controlled via the following options:

`accumulo.iterator.pushdown`
> Use iterators to execute filter predicates. True by default.

`accumulo.default.storage`
> Set the serialization method to be used by default when no method is specified. The default is `string`.

`accumulo.visibility.label`
> A visibility label to be applied to records written to Accumulo. By default this is empty.

`accumulo.authorizations`
> A list of authorizations, separated by commas, to be applied when scanning Accumulo tables. Blank by default.

`accumulo.composite.rowid.factory`
> The name of a Java class that can be used to customize behavior when constructing `LazyObjects` from the row ID without changing the `ObjectInspector`.

`accumulo.composite.rowid`
> Apply custom parsing of the row ID column into a `LazyObject`.

`accumulo.table.name`
> The name of the Accumulo table to use. By default this is the same as Hive table name.

`accumulo.mock.instance`
> Use an instance of `MockAccumulo` for testing instead of an actual Accumulo instance. Default is `false`.

Hive example

To explore how Hive and Accumulo can be used together, we'll import some data about storm fatalities from the National Oceanic and Atmospheric Administration's (NOAA) National Climatic Data Center website (*http://www.ncdc.noaa.gov*) into a

---

table in Accumulo and manipulate the data using HQL queries to answer ad-hoc questions:

```
$ wget http://www1.ncdc.noaa.gov/pub/data/swdi/stormevents/csvfiles/\
  StormEvents_fatalities-ftp_v1.0_d2014_c20141022.csv.gz
$ gunzip StormEvents_fatalities-ftp_v1.0_d2014_c20141022.csv.gz
```

We can start Hive with the options that allow it to connect to a local Accumulo instance. In this example we're using Hortonworks' HDP 2.1 sandbox VM (*http://bit.ly/hortonworks_sandbox*):

```
$ hive -hiveconf accumulo.instance.name=hdp \
  -hiveconf accumulo.zookeepers=localhost -hiveconf accumulo.user.name=root \
  -hiveconf accumulo.user.pass=secret
```

We'll create a regular Hive table for loading the storm fatalities data from the comma-separated value (CSV) file we downloaded. Hive does not yet support loading data directly into a *native* table like Accumulo, so we'll populate a Hive table and then transfer it into Accumulo:

```
hive> CREATE TABLE storm_fatalities(fat_yearmonth INT, fat_day INT, fat_time INT,
      fatality_id STRING, event_id STRING, fatality_type STRING,
      fatality_date DATE, fatality_age int, fatality_sex STRING,
      fatality_location string, event_yearmonth int) row format delimited fields
      terminated by ',' stored as textfile;

hive> load data local inpath
      './StormEvents_fatalities-ftp_v1.0_d2014_c20141022.csv'
      into table storm_fatalities;
Copying data from
    file:/home/hive/StormEvents_fatalities-ftp_v1.0_d2014_c20141022.csv
Copying file: file:/home/hive/StormEvents_fatalities-ftp_v1.0_d2014_c20141022.csv
Loading data to table default.storm_fatalities

Table default.storm_fatalities stats: [numFiles=1, numRows=0, totalSize=28337,
    rawDataSize=0]
OK
Time taken: 1.72 seconds
```

We can run a query to check our data against the Accumulo table after loading:

```
hive> select avg(fatality_age) from storm_fatalities;
OK
44.875
Time taken: 13.12 seconds, Fetched: 1 row(s)
```

Now we'll set up the Accumulo table, similar to the Hive table, but also specifying the mapping:

```
hive> CREATE TABLE acc_storm_fatalities(fat_yearmonth INT, fat_day INT,
      fat_time INT, fatality_id STRING, event_id STRING, fatality_type STRING,
      fatality_date DATE, fatality_age int, fatality_sex STRING,
      fatality_location string, event_yearmonth int)
      STORED BY 'org.apache.hadoop.hive.accumulo.AccumuloStorageHandler'
```

```
WITH SERDEPROPERTIES('accumulo.columns.mapping' =
    'time:yearmonth,time:day,time:time,:rowid,event:id,fatality:type,
        time:date,person:age,person:sex,fatality:location,event:yearmonth');

hdfs://sandbox.hortonworks.com:8020/user/hive/warehouse/acc_storm_fatalities
OK
Time taken: 1.542 seconds
```

Let's copy our storm data into the Accumulo table:

```
hive> INSERT OVERWRITE TABLE acc_storm_fatalities SELECT * FROM storm_fatalities;
OK
Time taken: 8.082 seconds
```

Looking in the Accumulo shell we can see the data in our table:

```
accumulo shell -u user
Password: ******

Shell - Apache Accumulo Interactive Shell
-
- version: 1.5.1.2.1.5.0-695
-
user@hdp> tables
!METADATA
acc_storm_fatalities
test
trace

user@hdp> table acc_storm_fatalities

user@hdp acc_storm_fatalities> scan
21149 event:id []      482017
21149 event:yearmonth []    201401
21149 fatality:location []    "Vehicle/Towed Trailer"
21149 fatality:type []     "D"
21149 person:sex []    "F"
21149 time:day []    6
21149 time:time []    0
21149 time:yearmonth []    201401
21186 event:id []      482572
21186 event:yearmonth []    201401
21186 fatality:location []    "Vehicle/Towed Trailer"
21186 fatality:type []    "I"
21186 person:age []    2
21186 person:sex []    "M"
21186 time:day []    6
21186 time:time []    0
21186 time:yearmonth []    201401
```

We can now perform queries over our Accumulo table as we would with a regular
Hive table:

```
hive> SELECT AVG(fatality_age) FROM acc_storm_fatalities;

Total MapReduce CPU Time Spent: 3 seconds 260 msec
OK
44.875
Time taken: 30.656 seconds, Fetched: 1 row(s)

hive> SELECT count(1),fatality_location FROM acc_storm_fatalities
    GROUP BY fatality_location;
Total MapReduce CPU Time Spent: 3 seconds 160 msec
OK
1   "Boating"
1   "Business"
4   "Camping"
1   "Golfing"
2   "Heavy Equipment/Construction"
58  "In Water"
1   "Long Span Roof"
18  "Mobile/Trailer Home"
9   "Other"
87  "Outside/Open Areas"
45  "Permanent Home"
6   "Permanent Structure"
5   "Under Tree"
100  "Vehicle/Towed Trailer"
1   FATALITY_LOCATION
Time taken: 29.797 seconds, Fetched: 15 row(s)
```

Optimizing Hive queries

Hive works best for ad-hoc analytical queries on data stored in a columnar format. This allows Hive to only read the columns involved in a query and leave other columns unread on disk. Because Accumulo supports locality groups, we can achieve the same performance gains as other columnar storage formats (see "Column Families" on page 19 and "Locality Groups" on page 138).

In our example, we might want to put the data about personal details and time into their own locality groups, leaving all other columns in the *default* locality group:

```
user@hdp acc_storm_fatalities> getgroups
user@hdp acc_storm_fatalities> setgroups person=person time=time
user@hdp acc_storm_fatalities> getgroups
time=time
person=person
```

We can compact to apply our changes to the files on disk:

```
user@hdp acc_storm_fatalities> compact
user@hdp acc_storm_fatalities>
```

Enabling block caching for our tables can also assist in keeping frequently accessed data blocks in memory:

```
user@hdp acc_storm_fatalities> config -s table.cache.block.enable=true
```

A query involving the field stored in the Accumulo row ID will use a `Scanner` configured only over the range specified. For example, the following query scans over a single row, so it would return much faster than an entire table scan:

```
hive> SELECT * FROM acc_storm_fatalities where event_id=500101;
OK
201404 3 0 22298 500101  "I" NULL  2 "M"
    "Permanent Home" 201404
Time taken: 0.041 seconds, Fetched: 1 row(s)
```

Additional notes on the Accumulo-Hive integration are available online (*http://bit.ly/ accumulointegration*):

Apache Pig

Apache Pig is a high-level data-processing language that compiles scripts down to a series of MapReduce jobs that can be executed on data in Accumulo tables. As of Pig 0.13, Accumulo can be used as a `Storage` (*http://bit.ly/accumulostorage*) option.

Pig can use Accumulo as the source of data in `LOAD` statements and the destination in `STORE` statements.

To load data from an Accumulo table, use the following syntax:

```
dataset = LOAD 'accumulo://tableName?instance=myInstance&user=myUser
    &password=myPassword&zookeepers=myZooKeeperServers'
    USING org.apache.pig.backend.hadoop.accumulo.AccumuloStorage(
    'column specification') AS
    ('pig schema definition');
```

A column specification is a comma-separated list of column identifiers. A column identifier can be *, meaning all columns, a specific column family such as *myFamily:*, or a specific column such as *myFamily:myColumnQualifier*. A column prefix can also be specified, such as *myFamily:col**.

Specifying just a column family, or a prefix followed by a wildcard, requires that the columns be represented as a `map[]` in the associated Pig schema definition. Individual columns in the specification can be represented as particular data types in the Pig schema definition. Pig will load row IDs from the Accumulo table into the first element of tuples read, as a `chararray` by default.

In `STORE` statements, use the following syntax:

```
STORE dataset
INTO 'accumulo://tableName?instance=myInstance&user=myUser&password=myPassword
    &zookeepers=myZooKeeperServers'
USING org.apache.pig.backend.hadoop.accumulo.AccumuloStorage(
    'column specification', 'options');
```

The column specification is the same as for the LOAD statement. Options to be specified include the following:

-c|--caster
> The class name that implements LoadStoreCaster to use when serializing types to and from Accumulo tables. Default is UTF8StringConverter. AccumuloBinary Converter is an alternative.

-auths|--authorizations
> A comma-separated list of authorizations to apply when loading data from Accumulo.

-s|--start
> Specifies the inclusive start row at which to begin reading when loading data.

-e|--end
> Specifies the inclusive row at which to stop reading.

-buff|--mutation-buffer-size
> The number of bytes to use when buffering data to be written to Accumulo.

-wt|--write-threads
> The number of threads to use when writing to Accumulo.

-ml|--max-latency
> The maximum number of milliseconds to wait before flushing a set of writes to Accumulo.

-sep|--separator
> A character used to separate column names when parsing the column specification. The default is a comma.

-iw|--ignore-whitespace
> Whether to strip whitespace from the column specification. The default is true.

We'll run through an example to make these ideas more clear.

Pig example

To communicate with Accumulo, Pig needs to know the location of the Accumulo JARs:

```
export PIG_CLASSPATH="$ACCUMULO_HOME/lib/*:$PIG_CLASSPATH"
```

We'll use the example data provided for exploring Pig in *Programming Pig* by Alan Gates (O'Reilly):

```
wget -O NYSE_daily https://github.com/alanfgates/programmingpig/blob/master/\
    data/NYSE_daily?raw=true
```

Let's start Pig and load this file into a schema:

```
$ pig
grunt> daily = load 'NYSE_daily' as (exchange:chararray, symbol:chararray,
            sdate:chararray, open:float, high:float, low:float, close:float,
            volume:int, adj_close:float);
```

We'll use Pig to generate a field that we can use as a row ID in an Accumulo table; in this case we'll use the symbol name followed by the date. This will give us a table that supports efficiently looking up all information for a particular symbol in chronological order. We'll also generate a new field representing the closing price times the volume:

```
grunt> daily_by_symbol_date = foreach daily generate CONCAT(symbol, sdate), open,
            high, low, close, volume * close;
```

Now we can tell Pig to store this data in a table in our local Accumulo instance:

```
grunt> store daily_by_symbol_date
        INTO 'accumulo://daily?instance=hdp&user=root&password=secret
        &zookeepers=localhost'
        USING org.apache.pig.backend.hadoop.accumulo.AccumuloStorage('prices:open,
        prices:high,prices:low,prices:close,calculated:voltimesclose');
```

Note that we didn't mention the first element of the tuples in `daily_by_symbol_date` in our column specification, because that element will be written to Accumulo as the row ID:

```
Success!

Job Stats (time in seconds):
JobId  Alias Feature Outputs
job_local1392295495_0002 daily,daily_by_symbol_date  MAP_ONLY
  accumulo://daily?instance=hdp&user=root&password=secret&zookeepers=localhost,

Input(s):
Successfully read records from: "file:///root/pig-0.13.0/NYSE_daily"

Output(s):
Successfully stored records in: "accumulo://daily?instance=hdp&user=root
  &password=secret&zookeepers=localhost"

Job DAG:
job_local1392295495_0002
```

Now we should have some data in a table in Accumulo:

```
root@hdp daily> scan
CA1988-07-25 calculated:voltimesclose []    5.329194E7
CA1988-07-25 prices:close []    26.52
CA1988-07-25 prices:high []    26.88
CA1988-07-25 prices:low []    26.16
CA1988-07-25 prices:open []    26.16
CA1990-12-20 calculated:voltimesclose []    1.526916E7
CA1990-12-20 prices:close []    7.6
```

```
CA1990-12-20 prices:high []    7.6
CA1990-12-20 prices:low []     7.24
CA1990-12-20 prices:open []    7.24
```

We can continue to work with this data in Pig via LOAD statements. We'll use the ability to scan a particular range to limit our data set to information for all dates for a single stock. We can also select just a subset of the columns available. In this example, we'll look at only the stock *CSX*, and the *close* and *voltimesclose* columns:

```
csxinfo = LOAD 'accumulo://daily?instance=hdp&user=root&password=secret
        &zookeepers=localhost'
        USING org.apache.pig.backend.hadoop.accumulo.AccumuloStorage(
        'prices:close,calculated:voltimesclose', '-s CSX -e CSY') AS
        (symdate:chararray, close:float, voltimesclose:float);

dump csxinfo;

(CSX1988-02-18,30.12,6.0517104E7)
(CSX1988-03-02,29.25,5.87691E7)
...
(CSX2009-12-30,49.12,6.65576E7)
(CSX2009-12-31,48.49,8.255908E7)
```

This is much more efficient than having to read all the data and use Pig's `filter` operator to limit the data.

If we want to allow Pig to use an irregular set of columns in Accumulo rows, we can use Pig maps to store whatever columns we happen to find in an Accumulo row:

```
csxinfo = LOAD 'accumulo://daily?instance=hdp&user=root&password=secret
        &zookeepers=localhost'
        USING org.apache.pig.backend.hadoop.accumulo.AccumuloStorage(
        '*', '-s CSX -e CSY') AS
        (symdate:chararray, allcolumns:map[]);
```

We can also limit the map to just those columns in a particular family:

```
csxinfo = LOAD 'accumulo://daily?instance=hdp&user=root&password=secret
        &zookeepers=localhost'
        USING org.apache.pig.backend.hadoop.accumulo.AccumuloStorage(
        'prices:', '-s CSX -e CSY') AS
        (symdate:chararray, prices:map[]);
```

As we did with Hive, we can use Accumulo's locality groups feature to partition groups of columns into separate files on disk to make reading a particular subset of columns more efficient. Carefully generating row IDs can make accessing a subset of rows as Pig tuples dramatically more efficient.

Apache Kafka

Apache Kafka (*http://kafka.apache.org*) is a scalable, fast, distributed queue developed originally at LinkedIn. For this reason it is attractive as part of a larger data workflow as a way to connect different systems together. For example, a variety of applications can be made to publish their data to topics in Kafka, and a different set of other systems can be configured to read data from the topics on the Kafka queue. The applications publishing and the applications reading don't have to be configured to talk to one another, just to talk to Kafka.

This was one powerful idea behind the push a few years ago for organizations to move to a service-oriented architecture, including a centralized queue serving as a message bus for the entire organization. Because Kafka is distributed it is a good candidate for inclusion in a big data workflow.

Accumulo clients can read from Kafka topics and write the data read to Accumulo tables. This provides other applications with the capability to push data to Accumulo tables simply by publishing data to a Kafka topic. Accumulo clients can of course be configured to listen for data pushed from other applications directly, but using a queue allows multiple consumers to read the same data without configuring complicated pipelines.

Kafka provides some guarantees around the data consumed from its topics:

- Messages sent by a producer to a particular topic partition will be appended in the order in which they are sent. That is, if a message M1 is sent by the same producer as a message M2, and M1 is sent first, then M1 will have a lower offset than M2 and appear earlier in the log.

- A consumer instance sees messages in the order in which they are stored in the log.

- For a topic with replication factor N, we will tolerate up to N–1 server failures without losing any messages committed to the log.

One thing that is important for many applications is to process each message once, or sometimes at least once. Kafka can partition a topic and allow multiple consumers to be grouped within a common group ID in order for the partitions to be consumed in parallel. Each message will be delivered to a consumer group only once. Within the consumer group, individual consumers can tell a broker that they have consumed a message from a particular partition of a topic by updating an offset. From the Kafka documentation (*http://bit.ly/kafka_getting_started*):

> Our topic is divided into a set of totally ordered partitions, each of which is consumed by one consumer at any given time. This means that the position of consumer in each partition is just a single integer, the offset of the next message to consume. This makes the state about what has been consumed very small, just one number for each partition. This state can be periodically check-pointed. This makes the equivalent of message acknowledgements very cheap.

When using Accumulo to store messages read from Kafka, you can get closer to achieving this property of writing each message once in the presence of individual machine failures by synchronizing the updating of the Kafka consumer offsets with flushing batches successfully to Accumulo.

An example of code that acts as a Kafka consumer and Accumulo ingest client is as follows:

```
package com.accumulobook.integration;

import com.google.common.base.Function;
import com.google.common.collect.Iterables;
import java.util.ArrayList;
import java.util.HashMap;
import java.util.List;
import java.util.Map;
import java.util.Properties;

import kafka.consumer.ConsumerConfig;
import kafka.consumer.KafkaStream;
import kafka.javaapi.consumer.ConsumerConnector;
import kafka.message.MessageAndMetadata;

import org.apache.accumulo.core.client.BatchWriter;
import org.apache.accumulo.core.client.BatchWriterConfig;
import org.apache.accumulo.core.client.Connector;
import org.apache.accumulo.core.client.MutationsRejectedException;
import org.apache.accumulo.core.client.TableNotFoundException;
import org.apache.accumulo.core.data.Mutation;

public class KafkaIngestClient {
  private final ProblemMessageSaver saver;

  public interface ProblemMessageSaver {

    void save(final List<byte[]> messages);
  }

  private final KafkaStream<byte[], byte[]> stream;
  private final BatchWriter batchWriter;
  private final int batchFlushSize;
  private final Function<byte[], Mutation> messageConverter;
  private final ConsumerConnector consumerConnector;
  private final ArrayList<byte[]> messageBuffer;

  public KafkaIngestClient(
      final String zookeeper,
      final String consumerGroup,
      final String topic,
      final String table,
      final BatchWriterConfig bwc,
      final Connector conn,
      final int batchFlushSize,
      final Function<byte[], Mutation> messageConverter,
```

```
       final ProblemMessageSaver saver) throws TableNotFoundException {

    // create kafka consumer
    Properties props = new Properties();
    props.put("zookeeper.connect", zookeeper);
    props.put("auto.offset.reset", "smallest");
    props.put("autocommit.enable", "false");
    props.put("group.id", consumerGroup);


    ConsumerConfig consumerConfig = new ConsumerConfig(props);
    consumerConnector =
        kafka.consumer.Consumer.createJavaConsumerConnector(consumerConfig);

    Map<String, Integer> topicCountMap = new HashMap<>();
    topicCountMap.put(topic, new Integer(1));
    Map<String, List<KafkaStream<byte[],byte[]>>> consumerMap =
        consumerConnector.createMessageStreams(topicCountMap);

    stream = consumerMap.get(topic).get(0);


    // create Accumulo batch writer
    batchWriter = conn.createBatchWriter(table, bwc);
    this.batchFlushSize = batchFlushSize;
    this.messageConverter = messageConverter;
    this.messageBuffer = new ArrayList<>();
    this.saver = saver;
  }

  public void run() {

    for(MessageAndMetadata<byte[], byte[]> mm : stream) {

      byte[] message = mm.message();
      messageBuffer.add(message);

      if(messageBuffer.size() >= batchFlushSize) {
        while (true) {
          try {
            batchWriter.addMutations(Iterables.transform(messageBuffer,
                messageConverter));
            batchWriter.flush();
            consumerConnector.commitOffsets();
            messageBuffer.clear();
            break;
          } catch (MutationsRejectedException ex) {

            // constraint violations and authorization failures
            // will not be solved simply by retrying
            if (ex.getConstraintViolationSummaries().size() > 0
                || ex.getAuthorizationFailuresMap().size() > 0) {
```

```
        // save off these messages for examination and continue
        saver.save(messageBuffer);
        consumerConnector.commitOffsets();
        messageBuffer.clear();
        break;
      }
      // else will retry until success
    }
   }
  }
 }
}
```

In the event that a machine dies, some of the messages read from the Kafka queue and batched in memory by the Accumulo client library will not yet have been written to Accumulo. Another machine starting up to take over consumption of the partition from which the failed machine was reading (or perhaps an existing client allowed by Kafka to take over consumption of the partition from the failed machine) will start reading messages from the offset of the last message known to have been written to Accumulo successfully, so that no messages will fail to be written to Accumulo.

Because it is possible for the `BatchWriter` to flush messages to Accumulo on its own in the background, this strategy provides *at-least-once* processing semantics, meaning each message will be processed once, or in the case of failure, perhaps more than once. If the mapping of Kafka messages to key-value pairs written to Accumulo is deterministic, Accumulo's `VersioningIterator` can be configured to eliminate any duplicates by keeping only the latest version of a particular row and column within a key. This is the default configuration for all tables in Accumulo.

Integration with Analytical Tools

Many use cases call for processing data with additional analytical tools on a separate machine outside of Accumulo or on additional processes colocated with Accumulo tablet servers, such as R or OpenTDSB.

R is a popular analytical tool that implements a wide variety of statistical algorithms. Some work has gone into integrating R with Accumulo (*http://bit.ly/raccumulo*). This adapter makes it possible for R to function as an Accumulo client and to pull data into R for further analysis.

OpenTSDB is a project for storing time series in scalable databases such as Accumulo. An adapter for OpenTSDB onto Accumulo (*http://bit.ly/accumulo-opentsdb*) is also available.

MapReduce API

One advantage of Accumulo's integration with Hadoop is that MapReduce jobs can be made to read input from Accumulo tables and also to write results to Accumulo tables. This can be done for ingesting a large amount of data quickly, for analyzing data in Accumulo tables, or for outputting data from Accumulo tables to HDFS.

Formats

Accumulo provides MapReduce input and output formats that read from Accumulo and write to Accumulo directly. There are input and output formats for both MapReduce APIs: org.apache.hadoop.mapred and org.apache.hadoop.mapreduce.

A MapReduce job can read input from an Accumulo table, write output to an Accumulo table, or both.

To configure a MapReduce job to read input from an Accumulo table, use code similar to the following:

```
job.setInputFormatClass(AccumuloInputFormat.class);

AccumuloInputFormat.setInputTableName(job, "table_name");

ClientConfiguration zkiConfig = new ClientConfiguration()
        .withInstance("myInstance")
        .withZkHosts("zoo1:2181,zoo2:2181");

AccumuloInputFormat.setZooKeeperInstance(job, zkiConfig);
AccumuloInputFormat.setConnectorInfo(job, "username",
    new PasswordToken("password"));

List<Pair<Text,Text>> columns = new ArrayList<>();
columns.add(new Pair(new Text("colFam"), new Text("colQual")));
AccumuloInputFormat.fetchColumns(job, columns); // optional
```

```
List<Ranges> ranges = new ArrayList<Range>();
ranges.add(new Range("a", "k"));
AccumuloInputFormat.setRanges(job, ranges); // optional

AccumuloInputFormat.setScanIsolation(job, true); // optional

AccumuloInputFormat.setScanAuthorizations(job, auths); // optional
```

The `AccumuloInputFormat` class takes care of configuring `Scanner` objects within map workers to deliver the key-value pairs specified in the options.

Internally, each `Mapper` has a `Scanner` over a particular range, which provides key-value pairs to the map function. Accumulo will assign each tablet as an `InputSplit` to a map worker. In addition, Accumulo tries to assign a tablet to a map worker that is running on the same machine that is currently hosting the tablet. This tends to provide the kind of physical data locality that map workers expect for efficient processing.

This behavior can be disabled via the `InputFormatBase.setAutoAdjustRanges()` method, in which case the MapReduce job will assign one map worker to each `Range` configured on the input format. If these ranges span tablets, a map worker will end up reading information from more than one tablet, which makes it harder to assign map tasks to machines that have a local copy of tablet data:

```
InputFormatBase.setAutoAdjustRanges(job, false);
```

To configure a MapReduce job to output data to an Accumulo table, use the `Accumu loOutputFormat` class:

```
job.setOutputFormatClass(AccumuloOutputFormat.class);

ClientConfiguration zkiConfig = new ClientConfiguration()
            .withInstance("myInstance")
            .withZkHosts("zoo1:2181,zoo2:2181");

AccumuloOutputFormat.setZooKeeperInstance(job, zkiConfig);
AccumuloOutputFormat.setConnectorInfo(job, "username",
    new PasswordToken("password"));

BatchWriterConfig config = new BatchWriterConfig();

AccumuloOutputFormat.setBatchWriterOptions(job, config);
AccumuloOutputFormat.setDefaultTableName(job, "table_name");
AccumuloOutputFormat.setCreateTables(job, true); //optional ❶
```

❶ `setCreateTables()` tells Accumulo whether or not to create any output tables that may not exist.

Writing Worker Classes

Mappers over Accumulo tables receive a `Key` object and a `Value` object for each `map()` call:

```
public static class WordCountMapper extends Mapper<Key,Value,K2,V2> {

  @Override
  public void map(Key k, Value v, Context context) {

  }
}
```

Accumulo's `InputFormatBase` can be extended to provide arbitrary objects of type K,V to a mapper, where K,V can be derived from any number of `Key`, `Value` pairs.

MapReduce jobs that write to Accumulo tables emit a `Text` object and a `Mutation` object. When a job writes to just one table, the `Text` object can be omitted and `null` passed instead:

```
public static class WordCountReducer extends Reducer<K,V,Text,Mutation> {

  @Override
  public void reduce(K k, Iterable<V> values, Context context) {
    // process input

    Mutation m = new Mutation(row);
    m.put(colFam, colQual, value);

    context.write(null, m);

  }
}
```

Each `Reducer` has a `BatchWriter` that sends data to Accumulo via `Text` (table name), `Mutation` pairs.

MapReduce Example

We'll run the ubiquitous Word Count example over our Wikipedia articles.

First we'll create our mapper, combiner, and reducer worker classes, starting with the mapper. Our mapper will read the value of the *contents* column from our original *WikipediaArticles* table and break the article text up into individual words, counting the appearance of each word within the document along the way:

```
public static class WordCountMapper extends Mapper<Key,Value,Text,IntWritable> {

  @Override
  public void map(Key k, Value v, Context context) throws IOException,
```

```
            InterruptedException {

        String text = new String(v.get());

        // count words in article
        HashMap<String, Integer> wordCounts = new HashMap<>();
        for (String word :
            text.replaceAll("[^a-zA-Z ]", " ").toLowerCase().split("\\s+")) {
          if (!wordCounts.containsKey(word)) {
            wordCounts.put(word, 0);
          }
          wordCounts.put(word, wordCounts.get(word) + 1);
        }

        for (Map.Entry<String, Integer> e : wordCounts.entrySet()) {
          context.write(new Text(e.getKey()), new IntWritable(e.getValue()));
        }
      }
    }
```

Next, we'll apply a combiner that will sum over the words seen in the documents processed by an individual map worker. This cuts down on the number of key-value pairs that have to be shuffled, sorted, and read by reduce workers. Specifically, this combiner takes a word and a set of partial sums and produces the word and one partial sum:

```
    public static class WordCountCombiner
        extends Reducer<Text,IntWritable,Text,IntWritable> {

      @Override
      public void reduce(Text k, Iterable<IntWritable> values, Context context)
          throws IOException, InterruptedException {
        int sum = 0;
        for(IntWritable v : values) {
          sum += v.get();
        }

        context.write(k, new IntWritable(sum));
      }
    }
```

Finally, our reducer will take all the partial sums from all the map workers and calculate the final count for each word. We will emit a single mutation, which will be written to the output table by AccumuloOutputFormat using an internal BatchWriter. We'll store the final count as a String representation of an integer in our output table:

```
    public static class WordCountReducer
        extends Reducer<Text,IntWritable,Text,Mutation> {

      @Override
      public void reduce(Text k, Iterable<IntWritable> values, Context context)
```

```
      throws IOException, InterruptedException {
    int sum = 0;
    for(IntWritable v : values) {
      sum += v.get();
    }

    Mutation m = new Mutation(k.toString());
    m.put("count", "", Integer.toString(sum));

    context.write(null, m);
  }
}
```

Now we need to make a driver to configure and run our job. For this job, this will consist of setting up the worker classes, and configuring AccumuloInputFormat and AccumuloOutputFormat:

```
@Override
public int run(String[] args) throws Exception {

    Job job = Job.getInstance(new Configuration());
    job.setOutputKeyClass(Text.class);
    job.setOutputValueClass(IntWritable.class);

    job.setMapperClass(WordCountMapper.class);
    job.setCombinerClass(WordCountCombiner.class);
    job.setReducerClass(WordCountReducer.class);

    // input
    job.setInputFormatClass(AccumuloInputFormat.class);

    ClientConfiguration zkiConfig = new ClientConfiguration()
            .withInstance(args[0])
            .withZkHosts(args[1]);

    AccumuloInputFormat.setInputTableName(job, WikipediaConstants.ARTICLES_TABLE);
    List<Pair<Text,Text>> columns = new ArrayList<>();
    columns.add(new Pair(WikipediaConstants.CONTENTS_FAMILY_TEXT, new Text("")));

    AccumuloInputFormat.fetchColumns(job, columns);
    AccumuloInputFormat.setZooKeeperInstance(job, zkiConfig);
    AccumuloInputFormat.setConnectorInfo(job, args[2], new PasswordToken(args[3]));

    // output
    job.setOutputFormatClass(AccumuloOutputFormat.class);

    BatchWriterConfig config = new BatchWriterConfig();

    AccumuloOutputFormat.setBatchWriterOptions(job, config);
    AccumuloOutputFormat.setZooKeeperInstance(job, zkiConfig);
    AccumuloOutputFormat.setConnectorInfo(job, args[2],
        new PasswordToken(args[3]));
```

```
AccumuloOutputFormat.setDefaultTableName(job,
    WikipediaConstants.WORD_COUNT_TABLE);
AccumuloOutputFormat.setCreateTables(job, true);

job.setJarByClass(WordCount.class);

job.submit();
return 0;
}
```

We can run this from within our IDE, or by packaging this up as a JAR and submitting via the `mapred` command:

```
mapred -jar wordCount.jar
```

When the job is done we can examine the word counts in the shell:

```
root@miniInstance> table WikipediaWordCount
table WikipediaWordCount

root@miniInstance WikipediaWordCount> scan -b accumulo
scan -b accumulo
accumulo count: []    20
achieve count: []     1
achieved count: []    1
achieves count: []    1
```

MapReduce over Underlying RFiles

Typically, Accumulo uses HDFS to store all data that's stored in tables. The format of these files is RFile, described in "File formats" on page 369.

By design, Accumulo's files are *immutable*, meaning their contents cannot be changed. Writing new data and combining old files is done by creating new files. This makes it possible to easily process a consistent snapshot of a table by reading the underlying RFiles.

MapReduce jobs can be run over a set of RFiles for a table. Doing MapReduce in this way not only provides a consistent view of a table, which could also be done by reading over a clone of a table, but it also allows the MapReduce job to avoid using resources of tablet servers by reading directly from data nodes. The jobs can be more efficient for that reason.

To run MapReduce over a set of RFiles for a table, typically users will clone the table beforehand and take the cloned table offline. This will keep the set of RFiles static throughout the time the MapReduce job is running.

The API for cloning a table and taking it offline is as follows:

```
TableOperations ops = conn.tableOperations();
```

```
boolean flush = true;
Map<String,String> propertiesToSet = Collections.EMPTY_MAP;
Set<String> propertiesToExclude = Collections.EMPTY_SET;

ops.clone(originalTable, cloneTable, flush, propertiesToSet,
    propertiesToExclude);
```

When we configure the MapReduce job, we simply use the `setOfflineTableScan()` method when configuring our `AccumuloInputFormat`:

```
AccumuloInputFormat.setOfflineTableScan(job, true);
```

Example of Running a MapReduce Job over RFiles

We'll run through an example of running a MapReduce job over RFiles using the `WordCount` class from our previous example.

Our job setup code is almost identical to the previous example, but this time we'll clone our articles table first, take it offline, then configure our job to use the cloned table's underlying RFiles:

```
// clone the articles table
ZooKeeperInstance inst = new ZooKeeperInstance(args[0], args[1]);
Connector conn = inst.getConnector(args[2], new PasswordToken(args[3]));

conn.tableOperations().clone(
  WikipediaConstants.ARTICLES_TABLE,
  WikipediaConstants.ARTICLES_TABLE_CLONE,
  true,
  Collections.EMPTY_MAP,
  Collections.EMPTY_SET);

// take cloned table offline, waiting until the operation is complete
boolean wait = true;
conn.tableOperations().offline(WikipediaConstants.ARTICLES_TABLE_CLONE, wait);

ClientConfiguration zkiConfig = new ClientConfiguration()
  .withInstance(args[0])
  .withZkHosts(args[1]);

// input
job.setInputFormatClass(AccumuloInputFormat.class);
AccumuloInputFormat.setInputTableName(job,
    WikipediaConstants.ARTICLES_TABLE_CLONE);
List<Pair<Text,Text>> columns = new ArrayList<>();
columns.add(new Pair(WikipediaConstants.CONTENTS_FAMILY_TEXT, new Text("")));

AccumuloInputFormat.fetchColumns(job, columns);
AccumuloInputFormat.setZooKeeperInstance(job, zkiConfig);
AccumuloInputFormat.setConnectorInfo(job, args[2], new PasswordToken(args[3]));
```

```
// configure to use underlying RFiles
AccumuloInputFormat.setOfflineTableScan(job, true);
```

We run this job as we did our previous example, either from within the IDE, or by building a JAR and using the mapred command:

```
mapred jar mapReduceFilesExample.jar
```

Delivering Rows to Map Workers

In our previous examples, it was only necessary for us to receive one key-value pair in each map task. It may be necessary for each call to the map method to receive a row containing multiple columns instead. To configure a MapReduce job to deliver rows to the map method we could set the WholeRowIterator on our AccumuloInputFormat and then decode each row into multiple key-value pairs inside our map function definition, but there is another input format we can use that will do this work for us.

AccumuloRowInputFormat will deliver a row ID as the key to a mapper, and a PeekingIterator<Entry<Key,Value>> as the value. The peeking iterator will contain the key-value pairs within this row, in sorted order.

Our mapper can then process individual columns within a row like this:

```
public void map(Text rowID, PeekingIterator<Entry<Key,Value>> value,
    Context context) {
  Entry<Key,Value> entry = value.next();
  // process this column

  entry = value.next();
  // process this column, etc
}
```

Ingesters and Combiners as MapReduce Computations

The MapReduce programming model is designed for batch computation rather than incremental computation. For example, when calculating word counts over a set of 10,000 documents, a MapReduce job would read all the documents and calculate how many times each word appears. If we then add a *single* new document to the corpus, we either must read in all the original 10,000 documents again along with the new document, or read all the previous word counts and add the counts from the one new document to the existing counts (Figure 7-1).

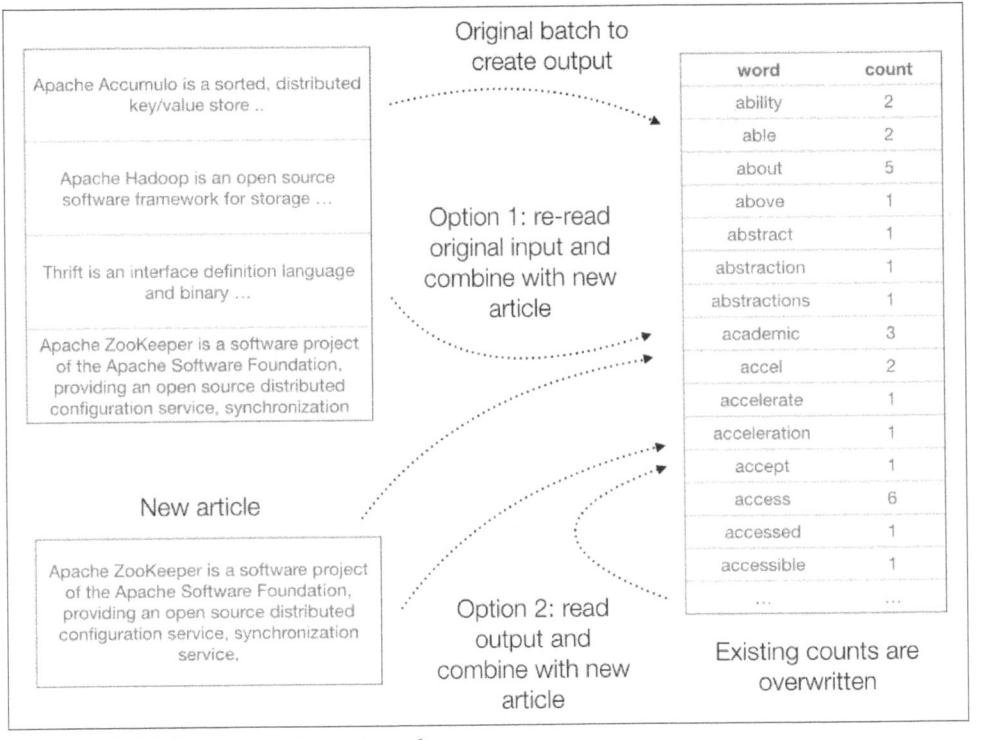

word	count
ability	2
able	2
about	5
above	1
abstract	1
abstraction	1
abstractions	1
academic	3
accel	2
accelerate	1
acceleration	1
accept	1
access	6
accessed	1
accessible	1
...	...

Figure 7-1. Updating word count results

Either option is a lot of work to add just one document.

As a result, incrementally updating a result set such as this in an efficient way tends to be done by waiting until there are a substantial number of new documents before updating the result set, the cost of which is that the result set is not updated very often.

In contrast, Accumulo's combiners can be used to incrementally update a result set much more efficiently. In MapReduce, you can specify a combiner class that will be used to combine together intermediate output from the map phase before it is sent to the reduce phase. You can think of Accumulo's combiners as performing a similar function.

In the word count example, the MapReduce job maps over documents and outputs word,1 for each word in the document. A combiner sums up the word counts for each mapper and sends those intermediate counts to a reducer, which tallies the final counts. In this simplest MapReduce use case, the same class is used for the reducer and the combiner. To perform a word count in Accumulo, you can configure a LongCombiner on the table and insert entries with row *word* and value 1 (Figure 7-2). After the data is written into Accumulo, the computation is complete.

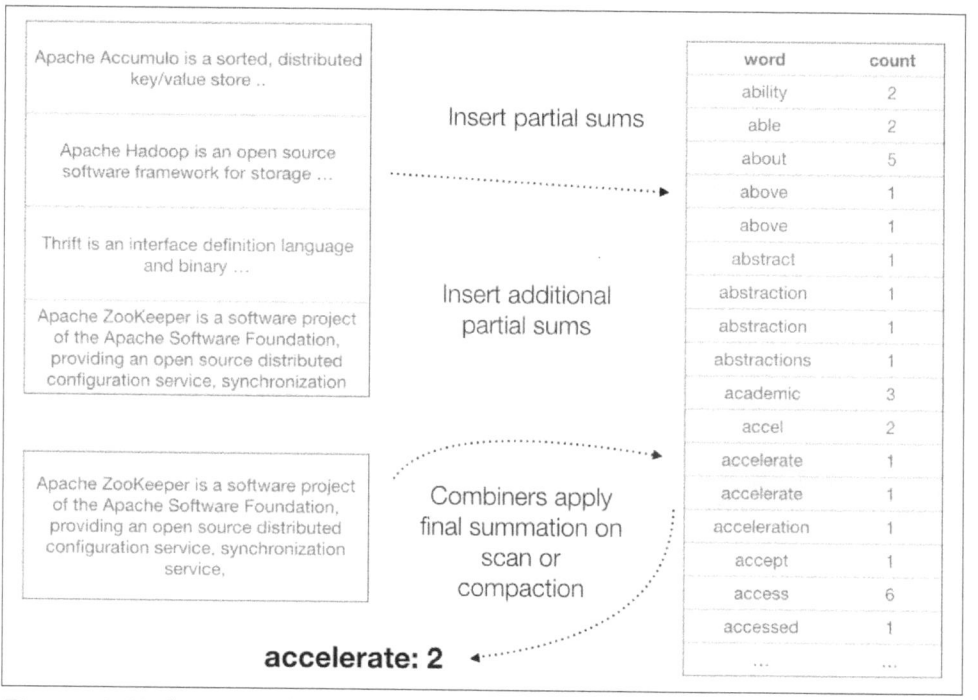

word	count
ability	2
able	2
about	5
above	1
above	1
abstract	1
abstraction	1
abstraction	1
abstractions	1
academic	3
accel	2
accelerate	1
accelerate	1
acceleration	1
accept	1
access	6
accessed	1
...	...

Insert partial sums

Insert additional partial sums

Combiners apply final summation on scan or compaction

accelerate: 2

Figure 7-2. Updating word count results incrementally

An example of configuring a table this way is as follows:

```
IteratorSetting iterSet = new IteratorSetting(
    10,
    "summingCombiner",
    org.apache.accumulo.core.iterators.user.SummingCombiner.class.getName());

SummingCombiner.setEncodingType(iterSet, SummingCombiner.Type.LONG);

List<IteratorSetting.Column> columns = new ArrayList<>();
columns.add(new IteratorSetting.Column(new Text("colFam"), new Text("colQual")));
SummingCombiner.setColumns(iterSet, columns);

// or instead, to apply combiner to all columns
// SummingCombiner.setCombineAllColumns(iterSet, true);

conn.tableOperations().attachIterator("table_name", iterSet);
```

In the class WordCountIngester we can perform the work our previous WordCount Mapper performed:

```
String wikitext = article.getText();
String plaintext = model.render(converter, wikitext)
    .replace("{{", " ")
    .replace("}}", " ");
```

```
// count words in article
HashMap<String, Integer> wordCounts = new HashMap<>();
for(String word :
    plaintext.replaceAll("^[a-zA-Z]"," ").toLowerCase().split("\\s+")) {
  if(!wordCounts.containsKey(word)) {
    wordCounts.put(word, 0);
  }

  wordCounts.put(word, wordCounts.get(word) + 1);
}

try {
  for (Map.Entry<String, Integer> e : wordCounts.entrySet()) {
    Mutation m = new Mutation(e.getKey());
    m.put("counts", "", e.getValue().toString());

    batchWriter.addMutation(m);
  }
} catch (MutationsRejectedException e) {
  e.printStackTrace();
}
```

The `SummingCombiner` will perform the final reduce function for us. We set up the table as follows:

```
if (!conn.tableOperations().exists(WikipediaConstants.WORD_COUNT_TABLE)) {
  conn.tableOperations().create(WikipediaConstants.WORD_COUNT_TABLE);

  // configure combiner
  IteratorSetting iterSet = new IteratorSetting(
    10,
    "summingCombiner",
    org.apache.accumulo.core.iterators.user.SummingCombiner.class.getName());

  SummingCombiner.setEncodingType(iterSet, SummingCombiner.Type.STRING);

  List<IteratorSetting.Column> columns = new ArrayList<>();
  columns.add(new IteratorSetting.Column(new Text("counts"), new Text("")));
  SummingCombiner.setColumns(iterSet, columns);

  conn.tableOperations().attachIterator(WikipediaConstants.WORD_COUNT_TABLE,
      iterSet);
}
```

The final results of a reduce computation that assumes it has seen all the values for a particular key would typically be performed by a scan-time iterator and are not persisted in the table. An example of a computation that might be performed at scan time is the final divide in a running average.

MapReduce and Bulk Import

In some cases, rather than writing data to Accumulo incrementally, an application will want to provide a set of new files to Accumulo all at once. A MapReduce output format, the `AccumuloFileOutputFormat`, is provided for creating a set of files in the RFile format for bulk import into Accumulo. See "File formats" on page 369 for details on the RFile format.

The most efficient way to create these RFiles is for them to each contain one continuous range of key-value pairs that doesn't overlap with any other RFile's key-value pairs. This is so that when these files are introduced to existing tablets in an Accumulo table, only one or maybe two tablets will require data in each RFile. Using the `RangePartitioner` is important to ensuring this property of the output RFiles.

To configure a job to use the `RangePartitioner`:

```
job.setPartitionerClass(RangePartitioner.class);
RangePartitioner.setSplitFile(job, "/jobconfig/splitsFile.txt"); ❶
```

❶ The splits file should be a file in HDFS that contains one Base64-encoded split point per line.

Each `Reducer` will create a separate RFile, and data must be output from the reduce method in sorted order. For example, a `Reducer` take the following form:

```
public static class ReduceClass extends Reducer<Text,Text,Key,Value> {

  public void reduce(Text key, Iterable<Text> values, Context output) ❶
    throws IOException, InterruptedException {

    for (Text value : values) {
      // create outputKey and outputValue
      output.write(outputKey, outputValue);
    }
  }
}
```

❶ We're not emitting a `Text` and `Mutation` object, as is done with the `AccumuloOut putFormat`, but rather, `Key` and `Value` objects.

If the for loop does not create output keys in sorted order, you can instead insert the `Key`, `Value` pairs into a `TreeMap` in the for loop, and then iterate over the `TreeMap` to do the output writes at the end of the reduce method.

Once our job is finished we can import the RFiles via the `importDirectory()` method:

```
boolean setTimestamps = true;
importDirectory("table_name", "/inputFiles", "/failedFiles", setTimestamps);
```

This will move the files into directories associated with the table specified and introduce them to existing tablets.

Bulk Loading and Split Points

The split points used in a MapReduce job don't need to be perfect. Accumulo can handle a mismatch in the split points used in files for bulk loading versus the current distribution of split points in a table by allowing tablets to share access to files that span their split points temporarily. The major compaction process will allow tablets to obtain a new set of files that only contain the data that falls within the range of the tablet.

However, because major compaction is required to get data from bulk imported files into the right ranges if the split points are misaligned, using split points in bulk files that differ significantly from the split points in a table means that the cluster will pay a high price in terms of I/O, in order to assimilate the data from a bulk import.

In addition, using a pathological set of split points (e.g., an unnecessarily large number of them) is a good way to cause a cluster to grind to a crawl if a high enough load is placed on the HDFS NameNode for delete and rename operations associated with bulk import.

See "Bulk-loading files from a MapReduce job" on page 448 for details on using the Accumulo shell to bulk-load files created from MapReduce jobs.

Bulk Ingest to Avoid Duplicates

Another reason to use bulk import is to avoid writing duplicate entries into Accumulo tables when a large number of clients are used to write data. The more clients involved in writing data, the higher the chance that one can fail. If clients are simply writing data to Accumulo in response to individual user write requests, this may not be much of a problem. Applications can use conventional load balancers to find a live client and write their data.

However, in a scenario in which clients are writing information from a set of files, for example, the loss of a client makes it likely that only a portion of a file was ingested. If another client is directed to reingest the file, there is a chance that it will create duplicate entries in the table.

One way to avoid this is to make the key-value pairs written for each piece of input data deterministic. That is to say, each input record is converted into the same set of key-value pairs no matter when or which client is ingesting the record. This can still result in the same key-value pair getting written more than once, but the `Versionin gIterator` can be configured to ignore all but the latest version of a key-value pair, effectively eliminating duplicates.

Sometimes creating deterministic key-value pairs is not an option. For example, an application may want to create key-value pairs for an input record that use the time-stamp of when the data was ingested as part of the row ID. This would allow data to be read from Accumulo roughly in the order in which it arrived. For more discussion on storing data in time order, see Chapter 9.

In this case, reloading some input records from a partially processed input file would result in duplicate records with different row IDs. Using MapReduce and bulk loading would avoid loading in any key-value pairs from a file that was partially processed when the machine processing it suffered a failure. This can also allow for loading some set of key-value pairs all together as an atomic unit as each RFile is either completed and loaded or discarded, so that another worker can produce a complete file.

Table Design

Accumulo provides application developers with a high degree of control over data layout, which has a large effect on the performance of various access patterns. Here we discuss some table designs for various purposes and address particular issues in designing keys, values, and authorizations.

Single-Table Designs

Some applications require looking up values based on a few specific pieces of data most of the time. In these cases it is convenient to identify any hierarchies that may exist in the data and to build a single table that orders the data according to the hierarchy.

For example, if we are writing an application to store messages, such as email, we might have a hierarchy that consists of user accounts identified by unique email addresses. Within a user account we have folders, and each folder contains zero or more email messages (Figure 8-1).

In addition to natural hierarchies in the data, we also need to consider access patterns. A common query will be to access a list of messages to or from a user within a particular folder, preferably in time order from most recent to oldest.

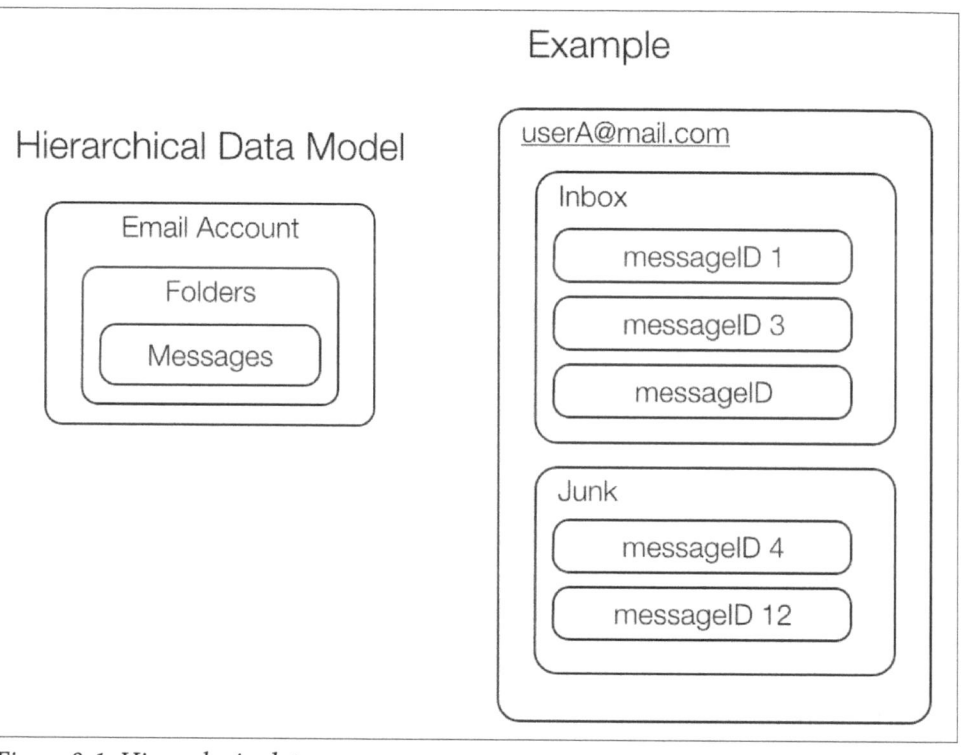

Figure 8-1. Hierarchy in data

An example application method for fetching this data can look like the following:

```
listMessages(emailAddress, folder, offset, num)
```

where *emailAddress* is the user's email address, *folder* indicates which mail folder to access, and *offset* and *num* together indicate which set of messages to fetch for the purposes of displaying email addresses in pages. The first page would have an *offset* of 0 and could have a *num* of 100 to show the first (most recent) 100 email messages.

To support reading this data efficiently, we could store all the messages that belong to a user under a row ID consisting of the user's email address, followed by the folder, and finally, the date and time at which the email was created or arrived. We may also want to store a unique identifier for this email at the end, to distinguish messages that arrive at the same time. Our row IDs then would look something like this:

```
alice@accumulomail.com_inbox_20110103051745_AFBBE
```

where `alice@accumulomail.com` is the email address, followed by the folder name (`inbox`), followed by a zero-padded date and time representation that is designed to sort dates properly, followed by a hash of some part of the email or perhaps an ID that is delivered in the email header.

This works, except that using the human-readable representation of the data would order our keys in ascending time order, rather than descending as most email applications do. To change this, we can transform the representation of the date in the row ID so that they sort in reverse time order. One way to do this is to subtract the date from a number larger than the largest date we expect to ever store. For example, the date element could be subtracted from the number 99999999999999. We could store the actual date in a value in this row.

Note that we're using an underscore as the delimiter here. A different delimiter may be required depending on whether we ever need to parse the row ID and whether underscores are valid characters for the elements of the row ID.

We then need to determine how to store each part of the message. We can decide to break out the subject and body into different columns so that users can quickly get a list of messages showing the subject without having to read all of the bodies of those messages. Other times, a user will need to retrieve an entire message, including the body and subject. The application method to retrieve all the data for a single message can look like the following:

```
getMessage(emailAddress, folder, date, emailId)
```

So we can have one column family for small amounts of data like the subject, and another column family for the email bodies. This will allow us to store those two column families in different locality groups, which means we can efficiently read one from disk without reading the other, and other times we can still read them both fairly efficiently.

Now a message in our table may look like Table 8-1.

Table 8-1. Email message table

Row	Column family	Column qualifier	Value
alice@accumulo mail.com_inbox_79889896948254_AFBBE	details	subject	Re: meeting fri
alice@accumulo mail.com_inbox_79889896948254_AFBBE	details	from	bob@othermail.com
alice@accumulo mail.com_inbox_79889896948254_AFBBE	content		Alice, can we meet Monday instead?

This one table can now fulfill both types of requests. The implementation of listMes sages() without paging would involve creating a single scan such as:

```
public Iterator<Entry<Key,Value>> listMessages(
    String emailAddress,
```

```
            String folder,
            Authorizations auths) {

        Scanner scanner = inst.createScanner("emailMessagesTable", auths);

        // we only want to scan over the 'details' column family
        scanner.fetchColumnFamily("details");
        scanner.setRange(Range.prefix(emailAddress + "_" + folder));

        return scanner.iterator();
    }
```

Similarly, the implementation of getMessage() would involve creating a single scan such as:

```
    public Iterator<Entry<Key,Value>> listMessages(
        String emailAddress,
        String folder,
        String date,
        String emailID,
        Authorizations auths) {

        String transformedDate = (99999999999999-Integer.parseInt(date)).toString();

        Scanner scanner = inst.createScanner("emailMessagesTable", auths);
        // we want all column families, and so we don't fetch a particular family
        scanner.setRange(Range.exact(emailAddress + "_" + folder + "_" +
            transformedDate + "_" + emailID));

        return scanner.iterator();
    }
```

In this example, our table exploits natural hierarchies in the data and addresses the two most common access patterns for retrieving information for an application. There are any number of variations on this theme, but a design involving a single table is limited in the number of ways the data can be accessed. For example, this table would not support finding email messages that contain one or more search terms. For those access patterns, additional tables for secondary indexes are necessary.

Implementing Paging

By default, scanners return key-value pairs until the set of results is exhausted. Applications that want to enable users to page through results have several options.

For example, we can create a method that takes a start row ID, a set of columns, a page offset, and a page size:

```
    public List<Entry<Key,Value>> getResults(String startRow, List<Text> columns,
        int offset, int pageSize)
```

We can choose to create brand-new `Scanner` objects every time this method is called, and skip over the previous page until we reach the specified offset. This has the disadvantage of having to read more and more results off of disk and transfer them to the client as the page offset increases. If users will typically only look at the first few pages this might be acceptable.

An example of using Google's Guava library (*https://github.com/google/guava*) to modify a Java iterator returned from a `Scanner` is as follows:

```
import com.google.common.collect.FluentIterable;

public List<Entry<Key,Value>> getResults(String startRow, List<Text> columns,
    int offset, int pageSize) {

  // ... after the scanner has been setup
  FluentIterable<Entry<Key, Value>> fiter = FluentIterable.from(scanner);
  fiter.skip(offset);
  fiter.limit(pageSize);

  return Lists.newArrayList(fiter);
}
```

Another option is to cache recently created scanners and associate them with individual queries. When users request the next page in a set of results, we can simply retrieve the scanner and continue fetching the next page of key-value pairs. Scanners do not have the ability to seek backward, but if the primary method of paging through results is to start at the first and move through the pages sequentially, this method may work well. This has the disadvantage of having to keep scanners around and expire them after a certain amount of time or until the user closes the session.

Another option for paging forward is to, instead of caching `Scanner` objects, cache the last key-value pair seen and then create a new scanner, seeking to the next logical key that appears after the last key-value pair seen. This has the advantage of not requiring scanner resources to be kept open, but it can incur more overhead by creating a new scanner for every page requested.

When paging is implemented in the context of secondary indexes, we need to process record IDs retrieved from the index table that match the query criteria to identify the page of records requested, and then fetch only matching actual records for that page.

Secondary Indexing

Applications that use a single table and employ a simple access pattern are among the most scalable, consistent, and fast. This type of design can serve in a wide variety of applications. When storing records in an Accumulo table, we can store them in sorted order but can only sort them one way.

In the previous example we stored emails in order of the recipient's email address, then by the date, and finally by a unique email ID. In this case the *record ID* used is a concatenation of those three elements. If we want to look up records based on other criteria, we have to scan the entire table. For these other access patterns, building a *secondary index* can provide a solution. These applications still need to minimize the work done at query time, to ensure high performance as the amount of data and the number of concurrent users increase.

Secondary indexes are tables that allow users to quickly identify the record IDs that contain a value from a particular field. Those record IDs can then be used to retrieve the full record from the primary table containing records. We'll next discuss two types of secondary indexes: a *term-partitioned* index and a *document-partitioned* index.

Index Partitioned by Term

One way to build a secondary index is by storing individual terms to be queried in the row ID. For example, we can retrieve Wikipedia pages that contain a given word by building a table storing the words found in article text in the Accumulo row ID and the article title as the column qualifier.

Table 8-2 recalls our *WikipediaArticles* table from "Data Modeling" on page 85, which used article titles as the row ID.

Table 8-2. Wikipedia article contents

Row	Column family	Column qualifier	Column visibility	Value
page title	contents		contents visibility	*page contents*
page title	metadata	id	id visibility	*id*
page title	metadata	namespace	namespace visibility	*namespace*
page title	metadata	revision	revision visibility	*revision*
page title	metadata	timestamp	timestamp visibility	*timestamp*

Now we create a secondary index that maps words appearing in Wikipedia pages to the page titles, shown in Table 8-3. An index organized by storing words or terms as the row ID is referred to as a *term-partitioned* index.

Table 8-3. Wikipedia index of contents

Row	Column family	Column qualifier	Column visibility	Value
word	contents	*page title*	*page visibility*	

The entries for an index on a subset of Wikipedia articles are as follows:

```
white contents:Friendship_Games []
white contents:Olympic_Games []
white contents:Olympic_Games_ceremony []
whitfield, contents:Cotswold_Olimpick_Games []
whitsun, contents:Cotswold_Olimpick_Games []
whitsun. contents:Cotswold_Olimpick_Games []
who contents:Alternate_Olympics []
who contents:Ancient_Olympic_Games []
who contents:Arena_X-Glide []
```

Because in a secondary index table we're swapping the order of the row IDs and values from the original table, an index like this is sometimes called an *inverted index*. However, note that we don't store the title from the *WikipediaArticles* table in the value portion of the secondary index, but rather we store titles in the column qualifier. This is because a term can appear in more than one article. We don't want article titles to be different versions of values for the terms, and we could envision wanting to scan a range of titles within a term, so we simply store the titles under the column qualifier and leave the value blank.

This technique also works for indexing the article metadata fields. It is possible to store the index entries for all fields in the same table if we want (see Table 8-4). We'll store the concatenated column family and qualifier from the original table in the column family of the index so that a client can fetch values from a particular column, if they so choose. By not specifying the column family, a client can find the rows in which a given value appears in any field.

Table 8-4. Wikipedia index of all fields

Row	Column family	Column qualifier	Column visibility	Value
word	contents	*page title*	*page visibility*	
id	metadata:id	*page title*	*page visibility*	
namespace	metadata:namespace	*page title*	*page visibility*	
revision	metadata:revision	*page title*	*page visibility*	
timestamp	metadata:timestamp	*page title*	*page visibility*	

When we build a secondary index table, one value from the original table can become many key-value pairs if we are *tokenizing* the text of the original values and storing a key-value pair for every individual word in the index. Index tables are a good example of using up more disk space to gain speed when doing searches.

In this case, we're using roughly twice the disk space of our original table in order to avoid doing expensive table scans. Developers of relational databases will recognize this trade-off, because relational database indexes are also stored on disk. Accumulo's default compression techniques can help mitigate the additional disk space used.

Not only does this require additional disk space, but it will also take longer to write this data from clients because we're now writing not only the original record, but also some number of index entries. Application designers should consider the impact on ingest speed versus the speed up gained for queries and choose which fields, if any, to write to a secondary index based on the types of queries required.

The horizontal scalability of Accumulo's design makes accommodating additional precomputation such as this a matter of simply adding more hardware resources.

An example of an ingest client that writes data to the *WikipediaArticles* table and the *WikipediaIndex* table at the same time is as follows:

```
// write article data to articles table as before
String wikitext = page.getText();
String plaintext = model.render(converter, wikitext);
plaintext = plaintext
.replace("{{", " ")
.replace("}}", " ");

Mutation m = new Mutation(page.getTitle()); ❶
m.put(WikipediaConstants.CONTENTS_FAMILY, "", plaintext);
m.put(WikipediaConstants.METADATA_FAMILY, WikipediaConstants.NAMESPACE_QUAL,
    page.getNamespace());
m.put(WikipediaConstants.METADATA_FAMILY, WikipediaConstants.TIMESTAMP_QUAL,
    page.getTimeStamp());
m.put(WikipediaConstants.METADATA_FAMILY, WikipediaConstants.ID_QUAL,
    page.getId());
m.put(WikipediaConstants.METADATA_FAMILY, WikipediaConstants.REVISION_QUAL,
    page.getRevisionId());

writer.addMutation(m);

// write index entries as well

// tokenize article contents on whitespace and punctuation and set to lowercase
```

```
HashSet<String> tokens = Sets.newHashSet(plaintext.replace("\"", "")
    .toLowerCase().split("\\s+"));
for (String token : tokens) {
  if (token.length() < 2) { // skip single letters
    continue;
  }

  Mutation indexMutation = new Mutation(token); ❶
  indexMutation.put(WikipediaConstants.CONTENTS_FAMILY, page.getTitle(),
      BLANK_VALUE); ❷

  indexWriter.addMutation(indexMutation);
}
```

❶ Create a new `Mutation` with the term that users can query as the row ID.

❷ Designate this index entry as being from the article contents by specifying a column family. Store the page title in the column qualifier so that we use it to perform a subsequent lookup on the primary articles table.

We're only indexing simple words here, by tokenizing the original text on whitespace. We talk about how to index other types of values in "Indexing Data Types" on page 288.

Now we have a table containing original articles, with the article title as the key, and another table containing index entries of words found in articles with pointers to the article titles from which they came.

Querying a Term-Partitioned Index

With this term-partitioned secondary index we can now look up article titles by the value of any metadata field, or by any word appearing in the article body. Once we have some article titles retrieved from the index table, we can retrieve the information about the articles by doing lookups against the original *WikipediaArticles* table using a `BatchScanner`:

```
public void querySingleTerm(String term) throws TableNotFoundException {

  Scanner scanner = conn.createScanner(WikipediaConstants.INDEX_TABLE, auths);
  // lookup term in index
  scanner.setRange(Range.exact(term));

  // store all article titles returned
  HashSet<Range> matches = new HashSet<>();
  for (Entry<Key, Value> entry : scanner) {
    matches.add(new Range(entry.getKey().getColumnQualifier().toString()));
  }

  if(matches.isEmpty()) {
    System.out.println("no results");
```

```
        return;
    }

    for (Entry<Key, Value> entry : retrieveRecords(conn, matches)) {
      System.out.println("Title:\t" + entry.getKey().getRow().toString()
            + "\nRevision:\t" + entry.getValue().toString() + "\n");
    }
  }

  private Iterable<Entry<Key,Value>> retrieveRecords(Connector conn,
      Collection<Range> matches) throws TableNotFoundException {
    // retrieve original articles
    BatchScanner bscanner = conn.createBatchScanner(
        WikipediaConstants.ARTICLES_TABLE, auths, 10);
    bscanner.setRanges(matches);

    // fetch only the article contents
    bscanner.fetchColumn(new Text(WikipediaConstants.METADATA_FAMILY),
          new Text(WikipediaConstants.REVISION_QUAL));

    return bscanner;
  }
```

Note that our query code is coupled with our ingest code. If we change our ingest code, the schema of our index or original articles table will change and our query code will have to be updated in order to query these tables properly.

The query we just performed is an example of a *point query*, in which we find all records containing an exact term. We can also use this index to perform *range queries*, in which we retrieve all records matching a range of terms. See "Using Lexicoders in indexing" on page 290 for an example.

Dealing with the nuances of secondary indexing in applications will be new to developers accustomed to working with relational databases, which do the work of building secondary indexes for applications. The trade-off for having to do this work is an incredible amount of flexibility in how data is indexed and retrieved.

This level of control is appropriate for Accumulo because the large data volumes Accumulo is designed to manage make it imperative for data to be organized in ways that are optimized for specific access patterns; otherwise performance will quickly degrade.

A suboptimal query on even a few gigabytes of data, such as a simple linear scan, can still be done quickly because that much data will fit comfortably in the main memory a single server and even a single desktop or notebook computer. But sub-optimal queries on hundreds of terabytes of data will be too slow for users to tolerate.

One way to view indexing is as a way to precompute views of the data that are optimal for the required access patterns. The scalability of the system and the relatively low cost of storage makes materializing these views feasible.

Combining query terms

In the previous example we were only querying for a single term or a single range of terms at a time. If we needed to look up records that satisfy more than one criterion—say, for example, all Wikipedia articles containing the word *baseball* with a timestamp newer than a year ago—we would need to do separate scans for each criterion and combine the article titles returned to get articles that match both criteria. To be specific, each scanner returns a set of titles matching the scan criterion applied, and the intersection of those sets of titles represents articles that match all criteria. The union of those sets of titles would represent articles that match at least one criterion.

A simple implementation that uses one `HashSet` to determine records that match any term is as follows:

```
// returns records matching any term
public void queryMultipleTerms(String ... terms) throws TableNotFoundException {

  HashSet<String> matchingRecordIDs = new HashSet<>();

  for(String term : terms) {

    Scanner scanner = conn.createScanner(WikipediaConstants.INDEX_TABLE, auths);
    // lookup term in index
    scanner.setRange(Range.exact(term));

    for (Entry<Key, Value> entry : scanner) {
      matchingRecordIDs.add(entry.getKey().getColumnQualifier().toString());
    }
  }

  if(matchingRecordIDs.isEmpty()) {
    System.out.println("no results");
    return;
  }

  // convert to Ranges
  List<Range> ranges = Lists.newArrayList(
        Iterables.transform(matchingRecordIDs, new StringToRange()));

  for (Entry<Key, Value> entry : retrieveRecords(conn, ranges)) {
    System.out.println("Title:\t" + entry.getKey().getRow().toString()
          + "\nRevision:\t" + entry.getValue().toString() + "\n");
  }
}

private class StringToRange implements Function<String,Range> {

  @Override
  public Range apply(String f) {
    return new Range(f);
```

```
    }
  }
```

For multiple single-term lookups—such as all articles that contain both the word *baseball* and *record*—we can take advantage of the fact that the article titles, which are stored in the column qualifier, are sorted within a single row and column family. We can combine the titles returned from two single-term scans by simply comparing the titles as they are returned from each scan to find matches, rather than having to load all the titles in memory and perform set intersection using something like Java collections. This is important because we often can't predict how many records will match a given criterion.

Problems can arise when queries become more complex than this. Some of these can be better addressed via a *document-partitioned* index, as described in "Index Partitioned by Document" on page 284.

Querying for a term in a specific field

In our previous example, we were looking for index entries that match our query term, regardless of the field in which our term may have appeared in the original record. We can execute a more focused query by specifying a field in which our term must appear, presuming we've stored this field information in the key of our index.

For example, if we want only articles in which the term *wrestling* appears in the body of the article, we can limit the range of our initial scanner to entries representing an appearance of the word *wrestling* within the body of the article. When we created our index, we used the column family to store information about the field from which an index term originated. So we can simply construct a range covering the exact row and column we want when configuring our scanner. When scanning only one row, this is more efficient than using the fetchColumn() method, because no key-value pairs in other columns will be iterated over and rejected.

Modifying our query from the previous example, we have:

```
Scanner scanner = conn.createScanner(WikipediaConstants.INDEX_TABLE, auths);
// lookup term and field in index
scanner.setRange(Range.exact(term), WikipediaConstants.CONTENTS_FAMILY); ❶

// store all article titles returned
HashSet<Range> matches = new HashSet<>();
for (Entry<Key, Value> entry : scanner) {
    matches.add(new Range(entry.getKey().getColumnQualifier().toString()));
}

if(matches.isEmpty()) {
    System.out.println("no results");
    return;
}
```

```
for (Entry<Key, Value> entry : retrieveRecords(conn, matches)) {
  System.out.println("Title:\t" + entry.getKey().getRow().toString()
          + "\nRevision:\t" + entry.getValue().toString() + "\n");
}
```

❶ Now we include the column family in range, which identifies the field in which the search term appears.

It is even possible to build an index across tables this way, by storing the table name in the key. For example, we could choose to build our index to store information as in Table 8-5.

Table 8-5. Index across multiple tables

Row	Column family	Column qualifier	Column visibility	Value
value	originalTable-field	record ID	page visibility	

This type of index would allow queries to be performed across multiple data sets simultaneously. The flexibility of index tables allows for options such as this.

Maintaining Consistency Across Tables

Term-based secondary indexes must be maintained along with the original table so that inconsistencies do not arise. Even though Accumulo does not provide multirow transactions or cross-table transactions, this consistency can often be managed in the application.

One strategy for managing consistency between the original table and the secondary index table is to carefully order read and write operations. You can choose to wait until new rows are written to the original table first, and then write the corresponding entries to the secondary index. If for some reason a write to the original table fails, it can be retried before any index entries are written. This way clients aren't referred by the index to a row in the original table that doesn't exist.

Inversely, when data is deleted from the original table, the index entries should be removed first, and then the row from the original table. These strategies will prevent any clients from looking up data in the index that has not yet been written or that has been removed from the original table.

More complicated strategies may be required if an application involves concurrent updates to indexed data. One potential way to address updating secondary indexes is to look to higher-level abstractions built on top of Accumulo, such as the Fluo (*https://github.com/fluo-io*) framework, which allows writes to be triggered to index tables from updates to a primary record table.

Using MultiTableBatchWriter for consistency

We introduce the `MultiTableBatchWriter` in "Writing to Multiple Tables" on page 100.

The `MultiTableBatchWriter` has `close()` and `flush()` methods that allow applications to push new data to multiple tables and verify that they were written successfully. This can help when synchronizing writes to secondary indexes while writing to original tables.

To use a `MultiTableBatchWriter` in our indexing example, we'll first create a `Multi TableBatchWriter` and use it to obtain the individual `BatchWriter` objects for our index and record table:

```
BatchWriterConfig conf = new BatchWriterConfig();
MultiTableBatchWriter multiTableBatchWriter =
    conn.createMultiTableBatchWriter(conf);

writer = multiTableBatchWriter.getBatchWriter(WikipediaConstants.ARTICLES_TABLE);
indexWriter =
    multiTableBatchWriter.getBatchWriter(WikipediaConstants.INDEX_TABLE);
```

Our application can keep track of mutations and call `flush()` periodically to determine when a batch has been written successfully or that a set of mutations should be retried.

Instead of calling `flush()` on individual `BatchWriter` objects, we instead call it on our `MultiTableBatchWriter` like this:

```
try {
  multiTableBatchWriter.flush();
} catch (MutationsRejectedException mre) {
  // report or retry
}
```

Also, when we are done writing data, we call `close()` on our `MultiTableBatch Writer` instead of individual `BatchWriter`s:

```
try {
  multiTableBatchWriter.close();
  System.out.println("done.");
} catch (MutationsRejectedException mre) {
  // report or retry
}
```

See the full listing of *WikipediaIngestMultiTableExample.java* for details.

Index Partitioned by Document

A basic term-partitioned index is useful for retrieving all the data containing a particular word or having a specific value for a field. If we need to find all the data contain-

---

ing two different words, the client code would have to issue two scans to the basic index, bringing the document IDs for both back to the client side and intersecting the two lists. This can be inefficient if one or both of the terms appears in many documents, requiring many IDs to be retrieved. One solution to this problem is to build a *document-partitioned index*. In such an index, sets of documents are grouped together into partitions, and each partition is assigned an ID. The index is organized first by partition ID, then by word. Table 8-6 shows an example.

Table 8-6. Document-partitioned table

Row	Column family	Column qualifier	Column visibility	Value
partition ID	doc \0 wikiDoc	*page title*	*page visibility*	*page contents*
partition ID	ind	*word* \0 wikiDoc \0 *page title* \0 *info*	*page visibility*	

Document-Based Partitioning

Document-based partitioning is a concept employed by other systems. Google describes a kind of document-based partitioning in a 2003 paper on the main indexes backing the famous Google search application, entitled "Web Search for a Planet: The Google Cluster Architecture." (*http://bit.ly/1N9v47T*)

In this paper Google says that "the search is highly parallelizable by dividing the index into pieces (index shards), each having a randomly chosen subset of documents from the full index" and that "each query goes to one machine (or a subset of machines) assigned to each shard."

Similarly, some distributed relational databases, sometimes called massive parallel processing (MPP) databases, employ this type of strategy for distributing data across machines and executing queries across partitions.

The partition ID is the row portion of the key. The page contents are stored in one column family of the row, and the index is stored in another column family. To retrieve all the pages containing the words "wrestling" and "medal" in this partition, we can read over and merge the sorted lists of page titles obtained by scanning over the keys starting with `partition ID_ :` index : wrestling and starting with `partition ID :` index : medal.

This intersection can be accomplished on the server side with an appropriate Accumulo iterator. We discuss iterators in more depth in "Iterators" on page 209. An iterator that seeks to multiple starting points and intersects the results is called an *intersecting iterator*.

To use this method, a data set should be divided into an appropriate number of partitions so that the partitions are not too large or too small, and there are enough of them that they are spread over the desired number of servers. Ideally each partition will fill an entire tablet, so its size should be somewhere between 256 MB and tens of gigabytes. For the Wikipedia data, we'll use 32 partitions.

Example code for building this table is as follows:

```
private static final int NUM_PARTITIONS = 10;
private static final Value BLANK_VALUE = new Value("".getBytes());

@Override
public void process(WikiArticle article, Siteinfo info) throws SAXException {

  String wikitext = article.getText();
  String plaintext = model.render(converter, wikitext);
  plaintext = plaintext.replace("{{", " ").replace("}}", " ");

  Mutation m = new Mutation(Integer.toString(Math.abs(
      article.getTitle().hashCode()) % NUM_PARTITIONS));
  m.put("doc" + '\0' + "wikiDoc", article.getTitle(), plaintext);

  // tokenize article contents on whitespace and punctuation and set to lowercase
  HashSet<String> tokens = Sets.newHashSet(plaintext.toLowerCase()
      .split("\\s+"));
  for (String token : tokens) {
    m.put("ind", token + '\0' + "wikiDoc" + '\0' + article.getTitle() + '\0',
        BLANK_VALUE);
  }

  try {
    writer.addMutation(m);
  } catch (MutationsRejectedException e) {
    throw new SAXException(e);
  }
}
```

Unlike term-partitioned indexes, in a document-partitioned table Accumulo can make all the inserts for a given document atomically because they are all inserted into the same row. The trade-off is that all partitions must be searched when performing queries.

Key-value pairs in this table look as follows:

```
root@miniInstance> table WikipediaPartitioned
table WikipediaPartitioned
root@miniInstance WikipediaPartitioned> scan
scan
0 doc\x00wikiDoc:Sqoop []    Infobox software Sqoop is a ...
0 ind:\x00wikiDoc\x00Sqoop\x00 []
```

```
0  ind:2012.\x00wikiDoc\x00Sqoop\x00 []
0  ind:a\x00wikiDoc\x00Sqoop\x00 []
0  ind:accumulo\x00wikiDoc\x00Sqoop\x00 []
0  ind:also\x00wikiDoc\x00Sqoop\x00 []
0  ind:and\x00wikiDoc\x00Sqoop\x00 []
0  ind:apache\x00wikiDoc\x00Sqoop\x00 []
0  ind:application\x00wikiDoc\x00Sqoop\x00 []
0  ind:archives\x00wikiDoc\x00Sqoop\x00 []
```

Querying a Document-Partitioned Index

When querying the data, we will use a `BatchScanner` along with an intersecting iterator, the `IndexedDocIterator`, to find relevant pages in each of the partitions. To scan
all partitions, we give the `BatchScanner` a special range that covers the entire table.

Code to query our document-partitioned index is as follows:

```java
BatchScanner scanner = conn.createBatchScanner(
    WikipediaConstants.DOC_PARTITIONED_TABLE, auths, 10);
scanner.setTimeout(1, TimeUnit.MINUTES);
scanner.setRanges(Collections.singleton(new Range()));

Text[] termTexts = new Text[terms.length];
for (int i = 0; i < terms.length; i++) {
  termTexts[i] = new Text(terms[i]);
}

// lookup all articles containing the terms
IteratorSetting is = new IteratorSetting(50, IndexedDocIterator.class);
IndexedDocIterator.setColfs(is, "ind", "doc");
IndexedDocIterator.setColumnFamilies(is, termTexts);
scanner.addScanIterator(is);

for (Entry<Key, Value> entry : scanner) {
  String[] parts = entry.getKey().getColumnQualifier().toString().split("\0");
  System.out.println(
          "doctype: " + parts[0] +
          "\ndocID:" + parts[1] +
          "\ninfo: " + parts[2] +
          "\n\ntext: " + entry.getValue().toString());
}
```

See the *WikipediaQueryMultiterm.java* file for more detail.

 Be aware than when you use the document-partitioned index strategy with a BatchScanner, a single query is sent to all tablets involving all tablet servers in the query, whereas queries against term-partitioned indexes typically involve only a few machines. This reduces the number of concurrent queries that the cluster can support. By involving more machines, Accumulo can process more complex queries in a fairly bounded time frame.

The document-partitioned indexing strategy described minimizes the network usage involved in these queries as well as round trips between the client and tablet servers. It does this by performing all intersections within the server memory and by storing the full record alongside the index entries for that record.

Applications that utilize a document-partitioned index don't necessarily need to query all partitions for every user request. For example, an application designer might choose to use partitions to implement paging and to return the first page or pages to users by scanning a subset of the partitions. Users can then request additional pages, which are populated via scans of the remaining partitions.

The mapping of documents to partitions is typically done via hashing or round-robin, but it can be done in other ways, depending on the needs of the application. For example, the value of a particular field within a document or record—such as the document type—might be chosen to determine in which partition a document or record belongs. However, care should be taken to ensure partitions are all about the same size, so that tablet servers are evenly loaded.

Term-partitioned and document-partitioned indexes are two of the more popular table designs for addressing a wide variety of access patterns with a minimum number of tables.

Indexing Data Types

Values in the original table can be just about anything. Accumulo will never interpret a value and doesn't sort them. When building a secondary index, sort order of these items must be considered. For values to sort properly, they may need to be transformed. Here are a few examples of how the human-readable string representations of these values may not be the right way to store values in the keys of an index table.

String representations of numbers, when sorted lexicographically as Accumulo sorts them, do not end up in numerical order. These must be transformed in order to sort properly. One way to make lexicographic sorting match numeric sorting is to pad the numbers to a fixed width with zeros on their left. For example:

```
0
1
```

```
11
2
```

might be stored as:

```
00
01
02
11
```

Another example is IP addresses, which consist of four 8-bit numbers called octets, each of which ranges between 0 and 255, separated by a period. Because the string representation of an octet can be either one, two, or three characters, IP addresses do not sort well lexicographically:

```
192.168.1.1
192.168.1.15
192.168.1.16
192.168.1.2
192.168.1.234
192.168.1.25
192.168.1.3
192.168.1.5
192.168.1.51
192.168.1.52
```

To avoid this situation, the octets can simply be zero-padded to sort IP addresses properly:

```
192.168.001.001
192.168.001.002
192.168.001.003
192.168.001.005
192.168.001.015
192.168.001.016
192.168.001.025
192.168.001.051
192.168.001.052
192.168.001.234
```

Fortunately, there is a human-readable way to store dates that sorts them in the proper order using the longest time periods first and zero-padding:

```
YYYYMMDD

20120101
20120102
20120201
20120211
20120301

YYYYMMDDHHmmSS
```

Including dashes, spaces, and colons will not change this basic order:

```
YYYY-DD-MM HH:mm:SS
```

Dates could also be converted to a value such as milliseconds since midnight January 1, 1970 or some other convention and stored as numbers with appropriate padding or encoding.

In the original BigTable paper the authors describe a method for storing domain names so that subdomains that share a common domain suffix sort together:

```
com.google.appengine
com.google.mail
com.google.www
com.msdn
com.msdn.developers
com.yahoo
com.yahoo.mail
com.yahoo.search
```

It may be preferable to simply transform strings from the natural output of the toString() representation to a string that sorts values properly. If at all possible, the Lexicoder framework (described in the next section) should be used to help do this sorting, but in general knowing how to sort values is important to developing tables that allow for range queries.

Using Lexicoders in indexing

Accumulo 1.6 provides a set of Lexicoders to aid in converting various types to byte arrays so that they sort properly. Lexicoders are provided for the following types in the org.apache.accumulo.core package:

- BigInteger
- Bytes
- Date
- Double
- Integer
- List
- Long
- Pair
- String
- Hadoop Text Object
- Unsigned Integer
- Unsigned Long

- UUID

Lexicoders come in especially handy in creating a secondary index. When various types appear as values in original records, the Lexicoders can convert them to properly sorted byte arrays suitable to use in the row ID of an inverted index.

An example of using Lexicoders to index dates appears in our `WikipediaIngestWithIndexExample` class:

```
Date d = dateFormat.parse(page.getTimeStamp());

byte[] dateBytes = dateLexicoder.encode(d);

Mutation dateIndexMutation = new Mutation(dateBytes);
dateIndexMutation.put(WikipediaConstants.TIMESTAMP_QUAL, page.getTitle(),
    BLANK_VALUE);
indexWriter.addMutation(dateIndexMutation);
```

We will also want to use the same Lexicoder when converting query terms to index entries. Lexicoders return byte arrays, which we can wrap in a `Text` object and pass to the `Range` constructor:

```
public void queryDateRange(
        final Date start,
        final Date stop) throws TableNotFoundException {

    DateLexicoder dl = new DateLexicoder();

    Scanner scanner = conn.createScanner(WikipediaConstants.INDEX_TABLE, auths);

    // scan over the range of dates specified
    scanner.setRange(
            new Range(
                new Text(dl.encode(start)),
                new Text(dl.encode(stop))));

    // store all article titles returned
    HashSet<Range> matches = new HashSet<>();
    for (Entry<Key, Value> entry : scanner) {
      matches.add(new Range(entry.getKey().getColumnQualifier().toString()));
    }

    if(matches.isEmpty()) {
      System.out.println("no results");
      return;
    }

    for (Entry<Key, Value> entry : retrieveRecords(conn, matches)) {
      System.out.println("Title:\t" + entry.getKey().getRow().toString()
              + "\nRevision:\t" + entry.getValue().toString() + "\n");
    }
}
```

We can now query for articles with timestamps appearing within a range of dates:

```
SimpleDateFormat df = new SimpleDateFormat("yyyy-MM-dd");
System.out.println("querying for articles from 2015-01-01 to 2016-01-01");
query.queryDateRange(df.parse("2015-01-01"), df.parse("2016-01-01"));
```

We'll get several results in the output:

```
querying for articles from 2015-01-01 to 2016-01-01
...
Title: Apache Hadoop
Revision:  11630810

Title: Apache Hive
Revision:  18882023
```

Custom Lexicoder example: Inet4AddressLexicoder

Developers can write custom Lexicoders for encoding new types into byte arrays. To create a custom Lexicoder, a class must implement the `Lexicoder` interface and specify the type targeted. This will require that two methods be defined: `encode()` and `decode()`:

```
byte[] encode(V v);

V decode(byte[] b) throws ValueFormatException;
```

Because IP addresses were not listed in the types of Lexicoders that are distributed with Accumulo, we'll write our own. We'll use the byte representation that `Inet4Address` returns, because it will sort the way we want. Here is a list of IP addresses we'll store in the order in which we want them to be sorted:

```
192.168.1.1
192.168.1.2
192.168.11.1
192.168.11.11
192.168.11.100
192.168.11.101
192.168.100.1
192.168.100.2
192.168.100.12
```

Here's the implementation of our Lexicoder:

```
public class Inet4AddressLexicoder implements Lexicoder<Inet4Address> {

    @Override
    public byte[] encode(Inet4Address v) {
        return v.getAddress();
    }

    @Override
    public Inet4Address decode(byte[] b) throws ValueFormatException {
```

```
      try {
        return (Inet4Address) Inet4Address.getByAddress(b);
      } catch (UnknownHostException ex) {
        throw new ValueFormatException(ex.getMessage());
      }
    }
  }
}
```

Now we'll run an example, first encoding by the string representation, then using our
Lexicoder:

```
Connector conn = ExampleMiniCluster.getConnector();

List<String> addrs = new ArrayList<>();

addrs.add("192.168.1.1");
addrs.add("192.168.1.2");
addrs.add("192.168.11.1");
addrs.add("192.168.11.11");
addrs.add("192.168.11.100");
addrs.add("192.168.11.101");
addrs.add("192.168.100.1");
addrs.add("192.168.100.2");
addrs.add("192.168.100.12");

conn.tableOperations().create("addresses");

BatchWriter writer = conn.createBatchWriter("addresses",
    new BatchWriterConfig());

// ingest using just address strings
for(String addrString : addrs) {

  Mutation m = new Mutation(addrString);
  m.put("", "address string", addrString);

  writer.addMutation(m);
}

writer.flush();

System.out.println("sort order using strings");
Scanner scanner = conn.createScanner("addresses", Authorizations.EMPTY);
for(Map.Entry<Key, Value> e : scanner) {
  System.out.println(e.getValue());
}
```

This will output the following list:

```
sort order using strings
192.168.1.1
192.168.1.2
192.168.100.1
```

```
192.168.100.12
192.168.100.2
192.168.11.1
192.168.11.100
192.168.11.101
192.168.11.11
```

Notice how the addresses in the 192.168.100 network appear before the addresses in the 192.168.11 network. This ordering would prevent us from doing range scans properly.

Now we'll ingest this same list using our Lexicoder:

```
// delete rows
conn.tableOperations().deleteRows("addresses", null, null);


// ingest using lexicoder
Inet4AddressLexicoder lexicoder = new Inet4AddressLexicoder();

for(String addrString : addrs) {

  InetAddress addr = InetAddresses.forString(addrString);

  byte[] addrBytes = lexicoder.encode((Inet4Address)addr);

  Mutation m = new Mutation(addrBytes);
  m.put("", "address string", addrString);

  writer.addMutation(m);
}

writer.close();

// scan again
System.out.println("\nsort order using lexicoder");
for(Map.Entry<Key, Value> e : scanner) {
  System.out.println(e.getValue());
}
```

The output of this code is the following:

```
sort order using lexicoder
192.168.1.1
192.168.1.2
192.168.11.1
192.168.11.11
192.168.11.100
192.168.11.101
192.168.100.1
192.168.100.2
192.168.100.12
```

Now our addresses are sorted properly. We can implement range scans for not just individual addresses, but also for addresses within an IP network.

Full-Text Search

Searching a corpus of documents for items matching a set of search terms is more complicated than simple key-value lookups, but it can still be addressed in several ways using specific table designs. In "Secondary Indexing" on page 275 we discuss strategies for querying with multiple terms by using a term-partitioned index and a document-partitioned index, which can be used to perform full-text searches, if the index entries consist of individual words.

There is a contributed project called *wikisearch* (*http://bit.ly/accumulo_wikisearch*) that illustrates a few techniques for going beyond the document-partitioned index design outlined in "Index Partitioned by Document" on page 284.

The wikisearch example calculates some statistics on terms and uses them to optimize queries. Like the document-partitioned index, this table design employs iterators to perform additional work on the server side.

There are four tables in this project.

wikipediaMetadata

The *wikipediaMetadata* table (Table 8-7) keeps track of the fields that are indexed. It is consulted in order to determine if a query requires searching fields that are not indexed. If so, the query will proceed without trying to consult the index entries in the other tables.

This table has a `SummingCombiner` iterator configured to add up the values of the f column family.

Table 8-7. WikiSearch metadata

Row	Column family	Column qualifier	Column visibility	Value
field name	e	*language id* \0 LcNoDiacriticsNormalizer	all | *language id*	
field name	i	*language id*	all | *language id*	

wikipediaIndex

The *wikipediaIndex* table (Table 8-8) serves as a global index, identifying which partitions contain articles that have a specified field value for a specified field name. This is so that partitions that don't contain any information about a particular search term can be omitted from the set of partitions to query in the second step.

Table 8-8. WikiSearch index

Row	Column family	Column qualifier	Column visibility	Value
field value	*field name*	*partition id \0 language id*	all | *language id*	Uid.List object

This table has an additional iterator configured, the `GlobalIndexUidCombiner`. This iterator maintains a list of article IDs that are associated with a search term and a count of how many times this search term has been written to this table. If the list of IDs grows over 20 by default, then it stops keeping track of individual UIDs and only keeps the count.

This table is queried to obtain information on the number of articles in which a search term appears and optionally, if the number of articles is low enough, the actual list of article IDs in which a search term appears. In these cases, this saves us an additional lookup against the *wikipedia* table.

Once the information about all the search terms in a query has been obtained from this table, the query logic determines whether to do additional scans against the *wikipedia* table, and what type of scans to do—whether an *optimized* scan including the index within each partition searched or a full table scan.

wikipedia

The *wikipedia* table (Table 8-9) contains the full text of each article and a set of index entries. The set of documents within a partition appears first, under the *d* column family. Then there are a set of index entries consisting of a column family beginning with the prefix *fi* and containing the field name in which a term appears, a column qualifier containing the word found in the field, the language ID, and the article ID.

This is organized to allow a server-side iterator to scan over the index entries and determine which articles satisfy all of the query criteria specified. Once a set of articles is obtained the iterator can then return either the content for the set of matching documents or simply the article IDs.

Table 8-9. WikiSearch document

Row	Column family	Column qualifier	Column visibility	Value
partition id	d	*language id \0 article id*	all | *language id*	*Base64 encoded Gzip'ed document*
partition id	fi \0 *field name*	*field value \0 language id \0 article id*	all | *language id*	

This table doesn't have any iterators configured after ingest, but when the query code determines that an *optimized* query plan can be executed, the `OptimizedQueryItera` tor class or `EvaluatingIterator` class can be applied to `BatchScanner` objects and configured for the duration of a particular query.

wikipediaReverseIndex

The *wikipediaReverseIndex* table (Table 8-10) is the reverse of the *wikipediaIndex* table. It is used to perform index lookups using leading wildcards—instead of the *wikipediaIndex* table, which supports exact term matches and those with trailing wildcards.

Table 8-10. WikiSearch reverse index

Row	Column family	Column qualifier	Column visibility	Value
reversed field value	*field name*	partition id \0 language id	all | *language id*	Uid.List object

Ingesting WikiSearch Data

We'll work through installing and using the wikisearch project and examine the tables created:

```
[accumulo@host ~]$ git clone \
    https://git-wip-us.apache.org/repos/asf/accumulo-wikisearch.git
```

 The accumulo-wikisearch has not been updated since the Accumulo 1.5.0 release. You will need to install Accumulo 1.5.0 with Hadoop 1.0.4 to run these examples.

Next we'll copy the example configuration file and edit it to work with our Accumulo instance:

```
[accumulo@host ~]$ cd accumulo-wikisearch
[accumulo@host accumulo-wikisearch]$ mvn
[accumulo@host accumulo-wikisearch]$ cp ingest/conf/wikipedia.xml.example \
    conf/wikipedia.xml
[accumulo@host accumulo-wikisearch]$ vi ingest/conf/wikipedia.xml
```

The configuration file should be filled in with the information about our Accumulo cluster:

```
<configuration>
  <property>
    <name>wikipedia.accumulo.zookeepers</name>
    <value>your-zookeeper:2181</value>
  </property>
  <property>
    <name>wikipedia.accumulo.instance_name</name>
```

```
      <value>your-instance</value>
    </property>
    <property>
      <name>wikipedia.accumulo.user</name>
      <value>your-username</value>
    </property>
    <property>
      <name>wikipedia.accumulo.password</name>
      <value>your-password</value>
    </property>
    <property>
      <name>wikipedia.accumulo.table</name>
      <value>wikipedia</value>
    </property>
    <property>
      <name>wikipedia.ingest.partitions</name>
      <value>5</value>
    </property>
</configuration>
```

 The current version of this project is built against Accumulo 1.5.0 and Hadoop 1.0 but can be modified by editing the *pom.xml* files.

With the configuration file set up the way we want it, we need to install the project's iterators to a location where the tablet servers can access and load them. In this case we'll use the *$ACCUMULO_HOME/lib/ext/* directory on the local filesystem of each of the tablet servers:

```
[accumulo@host accumulo-wikisearch]$ scp ingest/lib/wikisearch-ingest-1.5.0.jar \
    accumulo@tserver1:/opt/accumulo/accumulo-1.5.0/lib/ext/
[accumulo@host accumulo-wikisearch]$ scp ingest/lib/protobuf-java-2.3.0.jar \
    accumulo@tserver1:/opt/accumulo/accumulo-1.5.0/lib/ext/
```

Now we'll place a file containing some Wikipedia articles into HDFS so they can be loaded into Accumulo via a MapReduce job. See "Wikipedia Data" on page 84 for details on obtaining Wikipedia files:

```
[accumulo@host ~]$ mv enwiki-latest-pages-articles1.xml-p000000010p000010000.bz2\
    wiki.xml.bz2
[accumulo@host ~]$ hdfs dfs -mkdir /input
[accumulo@host ~]$ hdfs dfs -mkdir /input/wiki
[accumulo@host ~]$ hdfs dfs  -put wiki.xml.bz2 /input/wiki/
```

Now we're ready to run the script that loads this data into tables in Accumulo:

```
[accumulo@host accumulo-wikisearch]$ cd ingest/bin
[accumulo@host bin]$ ./ingest.sh /input/wiki/

INFO zookeeper.ClientCnxn: Session establishment complete on server
```

```
    zookeeper:2181
Input files in /input/wiki: 1
Languages:1

INFO input.FileInputFormat: Total input paths to process : 1
INFO mapred.JobClient: Running job: job_201410202349_0007
INFO mapred.JobClient:  map 0% reduce 0%
INFO mapred.JobClient:  map 100% reduce 0%
INFO mapred.JobClient: Job complete: job_201410202349_0007
```

When the job is complete we can examine the tables. The import code applies security tokens for the language of an article to the key-value pairs imported, so we need to grant these tokens to our Accumulo user:

```
[accumulo@host ~]$ accumulo shell -u accumulo
password:

accumulo@host> setauths -u <user> -s all,enwiki,eswiki,frwiki,fawiki
accumulo@host> tables
!METADATA
trace
wikipedia
wikipediaIndex
wikipediaMetadata
wikipediaReverseIndex
```

We'll set up an application to query these tables in the next section.

Querying the WikiSearch Data

This example project ships with a web application that we can use to query the wikisearch tables we created in the preceding section.

First, we'll configure the app for our Accumulo instance:

```
[accumulo@host query]$ cp src/main/resources/META-INF/ejb-jar.xml.example \
    src/main/resources/META-INF/ejb-jar.xml
[accumulo@host query]$ vi src/main/resources/META-INF/ejb-jar.xml

<enterprise-beans>
    <session>
      <ejb-name>Query</ejb-name>
      <env-entry>
        <env-entry-name>instanceName</env-entry-name>
        <env-entry-type>java.lang.String</env-entry-type>
        <env-entry-value>your-instance</env-entry-value>
      </env-entry>
      <env-entry>
        <env-entry-name>zooKeepers</env-entry-name>
        <env-entry-type>java.lang.String</env-entry-type>
        <env-entry-value>your-zookeepers</env-entry-value>
      </env-entry>
      <env-entry>
```

```
      <env-entry-name>username</env-entry-name>
      <env-entry-type>java.lang.String</env-entry-type>
      <env-entry-value>your-username</env-entry-value>
    </env-entry>
    <env-entry>
      <env-entry-name>password</env-entry-name>
      <env-entry-type>java.lang.String</env-entry-type>
      <env-entry-value>your-password</env-entry-value>
    </env-entry>
    <env-entry>
      <env-entry-name>tableName</env-entry-name>
      <env-entry-type>java.lang.String</env-entry-type>
      <env-entry-value>wikipedia</env-entry-value>
    </env-entry>
    <env-entry>
      <env-entry-name>partitions</env-entry-name>
      <env-entry-type>java.lang.Integer</env-entry-type>
      <env-entry-value>5</env-entry-value>
    </env-entry>
    <env-entry>
      <env-entry-name>threads</env-entry-name>
      <env-entry-type>java.lang.Integer</env-entry-type>
      <env-entry-value>8</env-entry-value>
    </env-entry>
  </session>
</enterprise-beans>
```

Next, we'll build the query project:

```
[accumulo@host accumulo-wikisearch]$ mvn install
[accumulo@host accumulo-wikisearch]$ cd query
[accumulo@host query]$ mvn package assembly:single
```

Now we'll install it in a JBoss AS 6.1 server (*http://download.jboss.org/jbossas/6.1/ jboss-as-distribution-6.1.0.Final.zip*). In our case JBoss lives in */opt*:

```
[accumulo@host query]$ cd /opt/jboss/server/default
[accumulo@host default]$ tar -xzf ~/accumulo-wikisearch/query/target/\
    wikisearch-query-1.5.0-dist.tar.gz
```

Copy over the WAR file to the *deploy* directory:

```
[accumulo@host default]$ cp ~/accumulo-wikisearch/query-war/target/\
    wikisearch-query-war-1.5.0.war deploy/
```

Now we can start JBoss:

```
[accumulo@host deploy]$ /opt/jboss/bin/run.sh -b 0.0.0.0 &
```

Finally, we'll copy some JAR files from JBoss's directories into the *lib/ext/* directories of our tablet servers:

```
[accumulo@host lib]$ sudo cp kryo-1.04.jar \
    /opt/accumulo/accumulo-1.5.0/lib/ext/
[accumulo@host lib]$ sudo cp minlog-1.2.jar \
```

```
            /opt/accumulo/accumulo-1.5.0/lib/ext/
[accumulo@host lib]$ sudo cp commons-jexl-2.0.1.jar \
            /opt/accumulo/accumulo-1.5.0/lib/ext/
[accumulo@host lib]$ cd ..
[accumulo@host default]$ sudo cp deploy/wikisearch-query-1.5.0.jar \
            /opt/accumulo/accumulo-1.5.0/lib/ext/
```

We can bring up the user interface for this application by going to *http://<hostname>:*
8080/accumulo-wikisearch/ui/ui.jsp in a web browser (Figure 8-2).

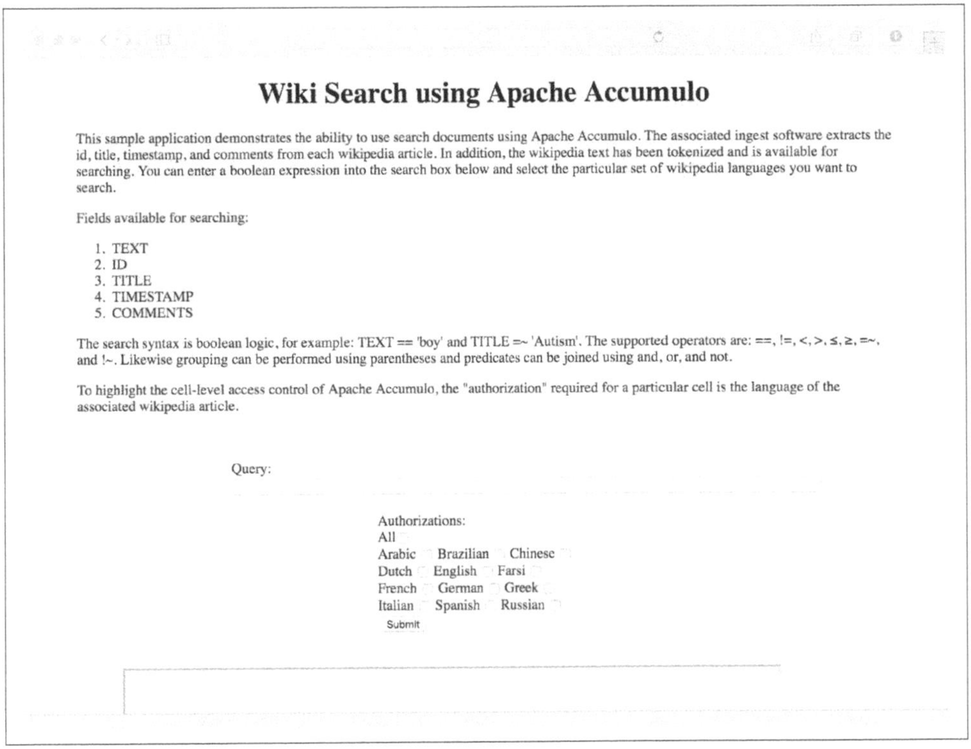

Figure 8-2. The Wikisearch UI

This example uses the Apache Commons JEXL library to create a query language.
The supported JEXL operators include:

- ==

- !=

- <

- <=

- >

- >=

- =~
- !~
- and
- or

We'll do a search for documents that contain both the words *old* and *man*:

```
TEXT == 'old' and TEXT == 'man'
```

This returns the results in Figure 8-3.

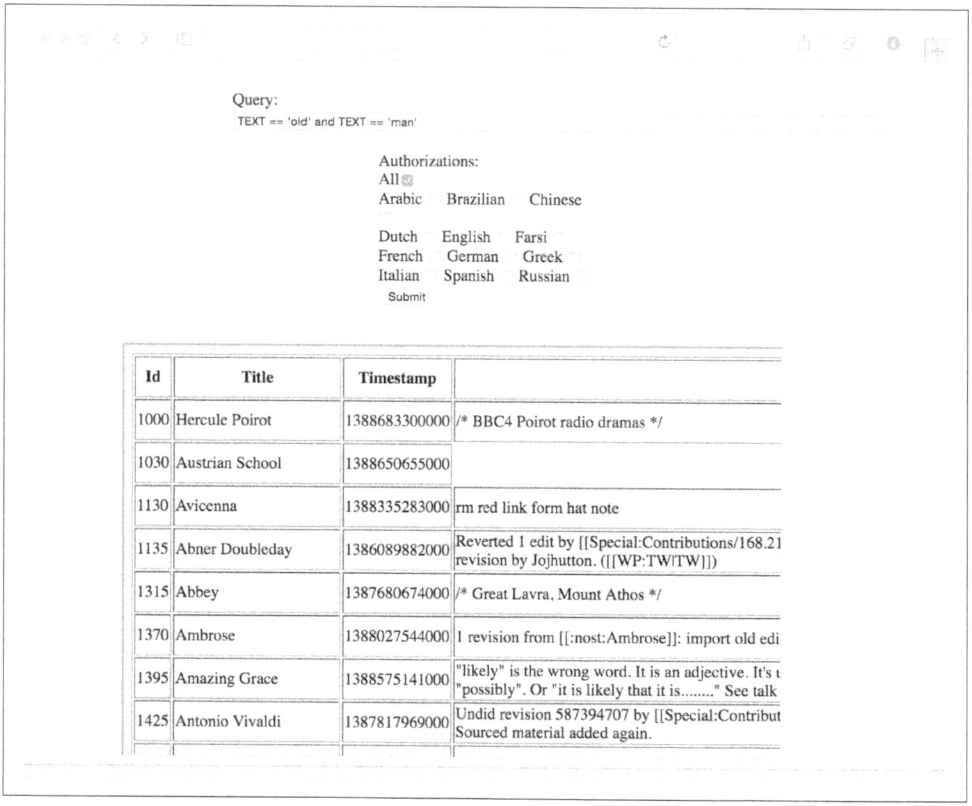

Query:
TEXT == 'old' and TEXT == 'man'

Authorizations:
All ☑
Arabic   Brazilian   Chinese

Dutch   English   Farsi
French   German   Greek
Italian   Spanish   Russian
Submit

Id	Title	Timestamp	
1000	Hercule Poirot	1388683300000	/* BBC4 Poirot radio dramas */
1030	Austrian School	1388650655000	
1130	Avicenna	1388335283000	rm red link form hat note
1135	Abner Doubleday	1386089882000	Reverted 1 edit by [[Special:Contributions/168.21 revision by Jojhutton. ([[WP:TW|TW]])
1315	Abbey	1387680674000	/* Great Lavra, Mount Athos */
1370	Ambrose	1388027544000	1 revision from [[:nost:Ambrose]]: import old edi
1395	Amazing Grace	1388575141000	"likely" is the wrong word. It is an adjective. It's ι "possibly". Or "it is likely that it is........" See talk
1425	Antonio Vivaldi	1387817969000	Undid revision 587394707 by [[Special:Contribut Sourced material added again.

Figure 8-3. Search results

The logs show that there were 986 matching entries for this query:

```
HTML query: TEXT == 'old' and TEXT == 'man'
Connecting to [instanceName = koverse, zookeepers = koversevm:2181,
    username = root].
986 matching entries found in optimized query.
AbstractQueryLogic: TEXT == 'old' and TEXT == 'man' 2.63
    1) parse query 0.00
```

```
    2) query metadata 0.01
    3) full scan query 0.00
    3) optimized query 2.62
    1) process results 0.14
        1) query global index 0.02
1976233182 Query completed.
```

We'll try adding another search term, *sea*:

```
TEXT == 'old' and TEXT == 'man' and TEXT == 'sea'
```

This returns the results in Figure 8-4.

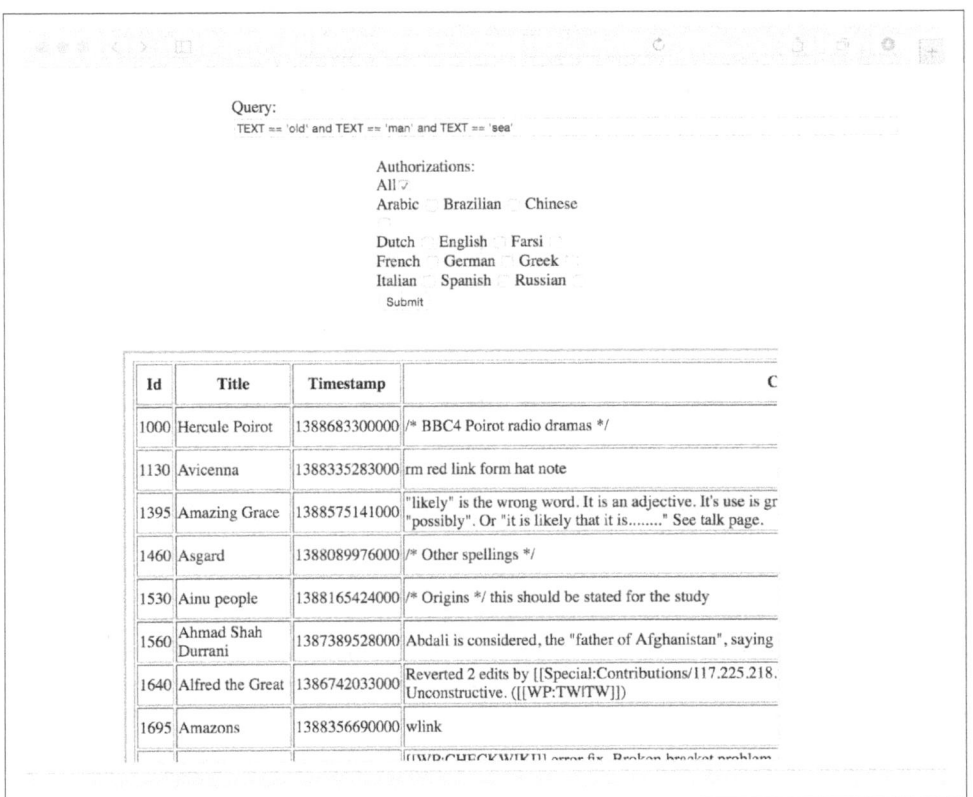

Figure 8-4. Refined search results

This cuts down the matching entries to only 339:

```
HTML query: TEXT == 'old' and TEXT == 'man' and TEXT == 'sea'
Connecting to [instanceName = koverse, zookeepers = koversevm:2181,
    username = root].
339 matching entries found in optimized query.
```

Designing Row IDs

Row IDs are the most powerful elements of the Accumulo data model because they determine the primary sort order of all the data. Here we discuss considerations for designing good row IDs, along with a few issues that can arise and methods for addressing them.

Lexicoders

The first place to look for help in designing row IDs that sort properly is Lexicoders. Lexicoders are a set of classes designed to help convert a variety of object types into byte arrays that preserve the native sort order of the objects. We introduce Lexicoders in "Using Lexicoders in indexing" on page 290 for helping sort various types of objects.

Composite Row IDs

When you construct row IDs that consist of multiple elements, it is necessary to use delimiters in order to have rows sorted hierarchically, such that all of the rows that begin with one element are sorted before the first row of the next first-place element appears.

For example, if we want to sort data by first name then secondarily by last name, we need a delimiter to ensure that if we read only first names we see them all in order regardless of what last names might follow each first name. Without a delimiter we can run into the following situation:

```
bobanderson
bobbyanderson
bobjones
```

In this case "bob anderson" should be followed by "bob jones," but because we are missing a delimiter, "bobby anderson" appears between them. Using a delimiter we get the desired sort order:

```
bob_anderson
bob_jones
bobby_anderson
```

Because the delimiter, in this case an underscore, sorts before the third *b* in "bobby," all first names with four or more letters are sorted after all the appearances of "bob."

An effective delimiter should be a character that sorts before any characters that are likely to appear in the elements of a row ID. The null character 0 can be used if necessary.

Composite row IDs may be human-readable enough as-is. If not, custom `Formatters` can be written to make viewing them easier. See "Human-Readable Versus Binary Values and Formatters" on page 311.

The `ListLexicoder` and `PairLexicoder` can help in designing composite row IDs.

Key Size

As mentioned in "Constraints" on page 201, Accumulo 1.6 has a constraint added to new tables that the complete key be smaller than 1 MB. Keep in mind that the complete key includes the row ID, column family, column qualifier, visibility, and timestamp. Keeping the key under 1 MB is a best practice for all versions of Accumulo.

Avoiding Hotspots

In many table designs, hotspots can arise as the result of uneven distribution of row IDs, which often arises from skew in the source data. A common example is that of time-ordered row IDs, which we addressed by introducing a fixed number of bucket IDs as prefixes to spread newly written data across multiple parts of the table. We discuss avoiding hotspots in that we discuss in "Time-Ordered Data" on page 317.

Other examples include frequently appearing items in data sets, such as very frequent words appearing in textual data, highly populated areas in geospatial data, and temporal spikes in time series data. These can all cause an inordinate amount of data to be sent to one server, undermining the effectiveness of the distributed system.

Hotspots can involve simply one server being many times busier than all the others. They also can involve contention over individual rows and the creation of very large rows, due to Accumulo's control over concurrent access to each individual row. In either case, the general approach is to alter the row IDs to either spread them over a larger portion of the table and therefore over a larger number of servers, or to simply break up highly contested rows into multiple rows to eliminate contention and overly large rows.

In the case of many writes ending up going to one server, introducing some sort of prefix in front of the row ID can cause the writes to be sent to as many servers as there are unique prefixes. An example of this is the fixed buckets that we discuss in "Time-Ordered Data" on page 317 and also in document-partitioned indexes in "Index Partitioned by Document" on page 284.

An example of breaking up contentious rows is to append a suffix to the row ID. Multiple writes to the same data then end up going to different row IDs while keeping the rows next to each other, preserving scan order. One example is in indexing the word *the*, which appears more than any other word in English documents. Instead of simply indexing the word *the*, you can attach a random suffix to the word *the* like this:

```
the_023012
the_034231
the_323133
the_812500
```

This way multiple writers can still index the word *the* and avoid contention because they are technically writing to different rows. In addition, the tablet containing the word *the* can now be split into multiple tablets hosted on multiple servers, which would not be possible if all instances of the word *the* were indexed into the same row.

Scanners only need to be modified to begin at the first random suffix and end at the last:

```
'the_' to 'the`'
```

Other strategies for avoiding hotspots in indexed data involve indexing pairs of words when one word is very frequent. Instead of indexing *the* we would index *the_car*, *the_house*, etc. This has the advantage of making it easier to find records containing two words when one word is very frequent, while preserving the ability to retrieve all records containing just the frequent word.

Sometimes, very frequent items are not of interest to an application and can simply be omitted from the index. Apache Lucene and other indexing libraries often employ *stop lists*, which contain very frequent words that can be skipped when individual words in a document are indexed.

Some users have used Accumulo combiners to keep track of how many times a term appears in an index using a separate column family and cease to store additional terms after seeing a given number of them, as in the *wikisearch* example in "Full-Text Search" on page 295. This strategy is useful because it doesn't require knowing the frequent terms beforehand, as a stop list does. However, by itself it doesn't prevent clients from continuing to write frequent terms that will be ignored. An index like this could be scanned periodically (perhaps using a MapReduce job) to retrieve only the highly frequent terms for the purpose of creating a stop list that clients can use.

Designing Row IDs for Consistent Updates

Accumulo is designed to split tables into tablets on row boundaries. Tablet servers will not split a row into two tablets, so each row is fully contained within one tablet. The Accumulo master ensures that exactly one tablet server will be responsible for each tablet, and therefore each row. As a result, applications can make multiple changes to the data in one row simultaneously or, in database parlance, *atomically*, meaning that the server will never apply a portion of the changes. If something goes wrong while some changes are applied, the mutation will simply fail, the row will revert to the last consistent state, and the client process can try it again.

Applications that need to make updates to several data elements simultaneously can try to use the row construct to gather the data that needs to be changed simultaneously together under one row ID. An example is perhaps changing all of the elements of a customer address simultaneously so that the address is always valid and not some combination of an old and new address.

Sometimes grouping data that needs to be changed under a common row ID is not possible. An example is an application that needs to transfer amounts of money between accounts. This involves subtracting an amount from one account and adding it to the other account. Either both or neither of these actions should succeed. If only one succeeds, money is either created or destroyed. The pair of accounts that needs to be modified is not known beforehand and is impractical for use as a row ID.

It is possible to achieve this capability in a system based on BigTable as evidenced by Google's Percolator paper (*http://bit.ly/percolator_paper*), which describes an application layer implemented over BigTable that provides distributed atomic updates, or *distributed transactions*. The Fluo (*https://github.com/fluo-io/fluo*) project is developing a framework for distributed transactions on top of Accumulo.

Also see "Transactions" on page 47.

Designing Values

Values in Accumulo are stored as byte arrays. As such they can store any type of data, but it is up to the application developer to decide how to serialize data to be stored. Many applications store Java `String` objects or other common Java objects. There is no reason, however, that more complicated values cannot be stored.

Some developers use custom serialization code to convert their objects to values. Technologies such as Google's Protocol Buffers (*http://bit.ly/protocol_buffers*), Apache Thrift, or Apache Avro (*http://avro.apache.org*) have been used to generate code for serializing and deserializing complex structures to byte arrays for storage in values. Kryo (*http://bit.ly/kryo_esoteric*) is another good, Java-centric, technology for serializing Java objects extremely quickly, although the support across different versions of Kryo is limited.

Iterators can also be made to deserialize and operate on these objects.

Here we present an example using Apache Thrift. Thrift uses an IDL to describe objects and services. The IDL files are then compiled by the Thrift compiler (*http://bit.ly/apache_thrift*) to generate code in whatever languages are desired for implementing servers and clients. The Thrift compiler will generate serialization and deserialization code in a variety of on-the-wire formats for any data structures declared in the IDL files and will generate RPCs for any services defined. Then it is up to the application developer to implement the logic behind the RPCs.

It is possible to implement the client in one language and the server in another. This is a primary advantage to using Thrift.

In our example, we won't create any Thrift services but will simply use Thrift to define a data structure and generate code to serialize it for storage in an Accumulo table.

Thrift structs and services are written in the IDL and are stored in a simple text file. We'll design a *struct* in the Thrift IDL to store information about an order:

```
struct Order {
    1:i64 timestamp
    2:string product
    3:string sku
    4:float amount
    5:optional i32 discount
}
```

In our Order struct, we have five elements. The first four are required and the last is optional. The elements are numbered to support the ability to add and remove elements without breaking services that are built against older versions of these structs.

Next we'll use the Thrift compiler to generate Java classes to serialize and deserialize this struct:

```
laptop:~ cd thrift
laptop:thrift compiler/cpp/thrift -gen java order.thrift
```

This will create a directory called *gen-java* that will contain our Java classes—in our case just one, *Order.java*. The generated file for even this simple structure is fairly long so we won't include it here.

We can then use our newly generated class to serialize Java objects to byte arrays and back when writing to and reading from Accumulo tables:

```
public class OrderHandler {

    public void takeOrder(
        final long customerID,
        final String product,
        final Double amount,
        final int discount,
        final String sku,
        final BatchWriter writer) throws TException, MutationsRejectedException {

        // fill out the fields of the order object
        Order order = new Order();
        order.timestamp = new Date().getTime();
        order.product = product;
        order.sku = sku;
        order.amount = amount;
        if (discount > 0) {
```

```
      order.discount = discount;
    }

    // we use a TMemoryBuffer as our Thrift transport to write to
    // when serializing
    TMemoryBuffer buffer = new TMemoryBuffer(300);

    // we use the efficient TBinaryProtocol to store a compact
    // representation of this object.
    // other options include TCompactProtocol and TJSONProtocol
    TBinaryProtocol proto = new TBinaryProtocol(buffer);

    // this serialized our structure to the memory buffer
    order.write(proto);

    byte[] bytes = buffer.getArray();

    // we'll store this order under a row identified by the customer ID
    Mutation m = new Mutation(Long.toString(customerID));

    // we generate a UUID based on the bytes of the order to distinguish
    // one order from another in the list of orders for each customer
    m.put("orders", UUID.nameUUIDFromBytes(bytes).toString(), new Value(bytes));
    writer.addMutation(m);
  }

  ...
}
```

When reading from this table we can use similar code to deserialize a list of `Order` objects from values found in the *orders* table:

```
...
public class OrderHandler {

  ...

  public List<Order> getOrders(
    final long customerId,
    final Authorizations auths,
    final Connector connector) throws TableNotFoundException, TException {

    // instantiate a scanner to fetch this data from the table
    Scanner scanner = connector.createScanner("orders", auths);

    // create a range to restrict this scanner to read the given customer's info
    scanner.setRange(new Range(Long.toString(customerId)));
    scanner.fetchColumnFamily(new Text("orders"));

    ArrayList<Order> orders = new ArrayList<>();

    for(Entry<Key,Value> entry : scanner) {
      // use a TMemoryInputTransport to hold serialized bytes
```

```
TMemoryInputTransport input =
    new TMemoryInputTransport(entry.getValue().get());

// need to use the same protocol to deserialize
// as we did to serialize these objects
TBinaryProtocol proto = new TBinaryProtocol(input);

Order order = new Order();

// deserialize the bytes in the protocol
// to populate fields in the Order object
order.read(proto);
orders.add(order);
  }

  return orders;
  }
}
```

When you use an object-serialization framework, a programmatic object is converted into a byte array and stored as a single value in a table. This strategy is convenient in cases when the entire object is always retrieved.

When an application requires retrieving only a portion of an object, the fields within an object can be mapped to one key-value pair each. The advantage of splitting up the fields of an object into separate key-value pairs is that individual fields can be retrieved without having to retrieve all the fields. Locality groups can be used to further isolate groups of fields that are read together from those that are not read. See the section in "Locality Groups" on page 138 on configuring locality groups.

Storing Files and Large Values

Accumulo is designed to store structured and semistructured data. It is not optimized to serve very large values, such as those that can arise from storing entire files in Accumulo. The practical limit for a value size depends on available memory, because Accumulo loads several values into memory simultaneously when servicing client requests.

When storing larger values than what comfortably fits in memory, users typically do one of two things: store the files in HDFS or some other scalable filesystem or blob store such as Amazon's S3, or break up files into smaller chunks.

When storing files in an external filesystem or blob store, Accumulo only needs to store a pointer, such as a URL, to where the actual file can be retrieved from the external store. This has the advantage of allowing users to search and find files using Accumulo. It also inherits all the benefits of security and indexing while not having to store that actual data in Accumulo, which frees up resources for just doing lookups.

If users are more interested in retrieving specific parts of files, breaking up files into chunks and storing them in Accumulo may work better, because Accumulo can then provide the chunk of the user-requested file in one request rather than looking up the file pointer in Accumulo and fetching the file it from an external system. Files broken up into chunks can still cause problems when many chunks are retrieved simultaneously, because they can overwhelm available memory.

The Accumulo documentation (*http://bit.ly/accumulo_docs*) includes an example of storing files as well as some discussion.

Users have contributed some example techniques (*http://bit.ly/accumulo_blob_store*) for doing this.

All of this logic is managed in an application or service layer implemented above Accumulo.

Human-Readable Versus Binary Values and Formatters

In some cases it is convenient to store values in a format that is readable by humans. For example, debugging becomes easier, and viewing data in the Accumulo shell is possible.

In some cases, values are stored in human-readable form, such as UTF8 strings, and are converted to binary on the fly for operations, then converted back to human-readable values before they're written back to the table. One example is that of storing numbers as strings in a table configured to sum the numerical values in those strings. In this case, the iterator that performs the summation is responsible for converting strings into Long or Double objects before summing them together, and then converting them back into String objects before outputting them to be sent either to the user or to the disk for storage. The provided SummingCombiner can be configured to do this for strings, or to simply treat values as Long objects.

Many applications can be made more efficient by using binary values. In this case, however, values are no longer easily read in the shell. To make debugging and viewing binary values easier, users can create a custom Formatter by implementing org.apache.accumulo.core.util.format.Formatter. This will allow the shell to display otherwise unreadable keys and values using some human-readable representation:

```
package org.apache.accumulo.examples;

/**
 * this is an example formatter that only shows a deserialized value
 * and not the key
 */

public class ExampleFormatter implements Formatter {
```

```
        private Iterator<Entry<Key,Value>> iter;

        @Override
        public void initialize(Iterable<Map.Entry<Key, Value>> scanner,
                    boolean includeTimestamps) {
          iter = scanner.iterator();
        }

        @Override
        public boolean hasNext() {
          return iter.hasNext();
        }

        @Override
        public String next() {
          Entry<Key,Value> n = iter.next();
          byte[] bytes = n.getValue().getBytes();
          // deserialize
          String s = myDeserializationFunction(bytes);
          return s;
        }

        @Override
        public void remove() {
        }

        private String myDeserializationFunction(byte[] bytes) {
          ...
        }
      }
```

Formatters can be configured on a per-table basis by setting the `table.formatter` option. Customer formatters only need to be included on the CLASSPATH when you run the shell.

The shell also makes it easy to configure formatters via the `formatter` command.

To add a formatter:

```
user@accumulo> table myTable
user@accumulo myTable> scan

user@accumulo> formatter -f org.apache.accumulo.examples.ExampleFormatter \
    -t myTable
user@accumulo> scan
```

To remove a formatter:

```
user@accumulo> formatter -r -t myTable
```

Designing Authorizations

Authorization tokens can represent any attribute or class of the data or of users. A short example of a token based on the data may be useful.

In many industries some data needs to be stored that represents information that can be used to identify an individual. This kind of data is typically referred to as Personally Identifiable Information (PII). There are guidelines and laws (*http://bit.ly/protecting_pii*) in the United States and other countries for how to protect PII. Other fields related to this individual might be less sensitive if the fields containing PII are omitted. Often groups such as analysts and researchers need access to these other fields but not the PII, so that they can find relationships and causes in activities and conditions.

Information such as a name, home address, and date of birth are just a few of the types of fields that are deemed PII. It could be useful to label data in these fields with the fact that it is considered PII. We could simply define a token called *pii* and require that users possess this token in order to read PII data. The definition of information considered PII may change, but it is not likely to change quickly. The set of users that are authorized to see PII data may change quickly, so we keep this mapping in an external system.

Besides attributes of the data to create tokens like PII, a common pattern is to label data based on the general purpose of its existence. Some fields may exist only to express how data travels within the organization, which may be sensitive and is only useful for internal debugging or auditing. This data can be labeled as for internal use only or that it exists only for auditing. We can create tokens for each of these, perhaps *debug* and *audit*.

Finally, it is common to label data based on a well-defined role in an organization that represents a group of people who need to work with it. The relationship of data to these groups is often slow-changing, though the membership of individual users in each group is often highly dynamic. Tokens that represent groups such as these may include such things as *administration*, *billing*, or *research* to denote the role that requires access to the data.

When a field has more than one characteristic, we can combine these tokens using & or |, which are Boolean operators representing that both tokens are required (logical AND) or that just one or both are required (logical OR), respectively.

 If you are upgrading to Accumulo 1.5 or later, the API for authorizations has changed slightly. The `toString()` method no longer calls the `serialize()` method. The `serialize()` method now Base64-encodes the `auths` array. Be sure to test these changes thoroughly as you upgrade.

When you consider granting authorizations to users, it is suggested that you do not use the *root* for anything other than table manipulation—such as creating tables and granting privileges—and that you do not give the *root* user any security labels. By following this suggestion, you force developers and system admins to log in as the correct user to access data.

For more on the relationship between user accounts and authorizations, see "An Example of Using Authorizations" on page 185.

Designing Column Visibilities

Once the notion of which authorization tokens might be needed is addressed, we next need to decide how to apply those tokens in column visibilities. Recall that the Accumulo data model allows a security label to be stored as part of each key. Security labels are stored in the part of the key called the *column visibility* (Figure 8-5).

Key				Value
row ID	Column		Timestamp	
	Family	Qualifier	**Visibility**	

Figure 8-5. Accumulo data model

Accumulo's security labels are designed to be flexible to meet a variety of needs. However, a result of this flexibility is that the way to define tokens and combine them into labels isn't always obvious.

There are several things to keep in mind when designing security labels. First is which attributes of the data define the sensitivity thereof:

- Is every record as sensitive as every other?
- Are some fields more sensitive than others?

Second is what requirements relate to accessing the data:

- Do users need to be granted permission before being able to read particular data elements?
- Is access based on job role?
- How quickly do access control needs change?

Column visibilities are designed to not be changed often. In fact, it is impossible to actually change the column visibility stored in the key. Rather, users have to delete the old key and write a new key and value with a different column visibility. The

`VersioningIterator` does not help us here, because two keys that differ only by their column visibility are considered to be different keys by the `VersioningIterator`.

Keys That Differ Only in Column Visibility

Because two keys that differ only in column visibility are considered two separate keys, those keys can coexist and won't be deduplicated by the `Versioning Iterator`. This can be desirable if there are multiple representations of values at different sensitivity levels. A facetious example is that one's age with the *public* column visibility can be 29, when one's *private* age is really 34.

A better application of this concept is to use representations of values at different resolutions. For example, a person's full address can be more sensitive than just the address limited to zip code. In practice, the zip code is a different field and can be labeled separately.

Imagine a satellite image that is very high-definition and reveals potentially private details such as the contents of an individual's backyard. We might choose to down-sample this image to a lower resolution to obscure sensitive details and make that representation of the image more widely accessible.

It is of course easy for application designers to choose to store these representations under different columns, but the option for multiple representations of a value that only differ in sensitivity should be understood.

A bigger issue in trying to change column visibilities is that there can be many billions or trillions of key-value pairs, and if regular changes in column visibilities are required to support changes in access control, many new-key value pairs must be written to suppress older versions of the data. For a nontrivial amount of data, this is not tractable.

For this reason it is generally recommended to label data with attributes of the data or long-standing use cases of the data, using tokens that describe attributes of the data or groups of users that are not likely to change frequently, if ever, and then to assign tokens to individual users in order to grant access. This mapping of users to tokens is always stored in some external system such as an LDAP server. As such, the user-token mappings can be changed rapidly without the need to rewrite any data in Accumulo.

Advanced Table Designs

After covering the basics of table design in the previous chapter, here we discuss advanced design considerations for storing some commonly encountered types of data in Accumulo. Examples include time series, graph, geospatial, feature vector, and other data.

Time-Ordered Data

Reading and writing data in time order is a common requirement. In a previous example, we ordered email messages in reverse time order within a particular folder belonging to a particular user account. Some applications want to access data primarily in time order. That is, the first and most important element of the data is the time component. Examples include time series such as stock data, application logs, and series of events captured by sensors.

We could simply use a timestamp as the row ID of a table. Rows will be sorted in increasing time order, and retrieving the data for one timestamp or a range of timestamps is straightforward.

But using a simple timestamp as the row ID of a table can be problematic when it comes to writing the data. This is because often new data arrives with timestamps that only ever increase. If we simply order our data this way, all new data will always be written to the end of the table, specifically to the last tablet, which spans some timestamp we've already seen up to positive infinity (Figure 9-1).

Figure 9-1. Hotspot in time-ordered table

Because each tablet is hosted by exactly one tablet server, data will always be written to one server. This might be acceptable if one tablet server can cope with the rate of incoming data. If not, that last tablet on one tablet server will become a bottleneck in the overall ingest process.

To avoid this, some users have resorted to partitioning their table into several buckets and storing ideally uniform partitions of the data in each bucket. One way to do this is to prefix the timestamps with an integer as shown in Figure 9-2.

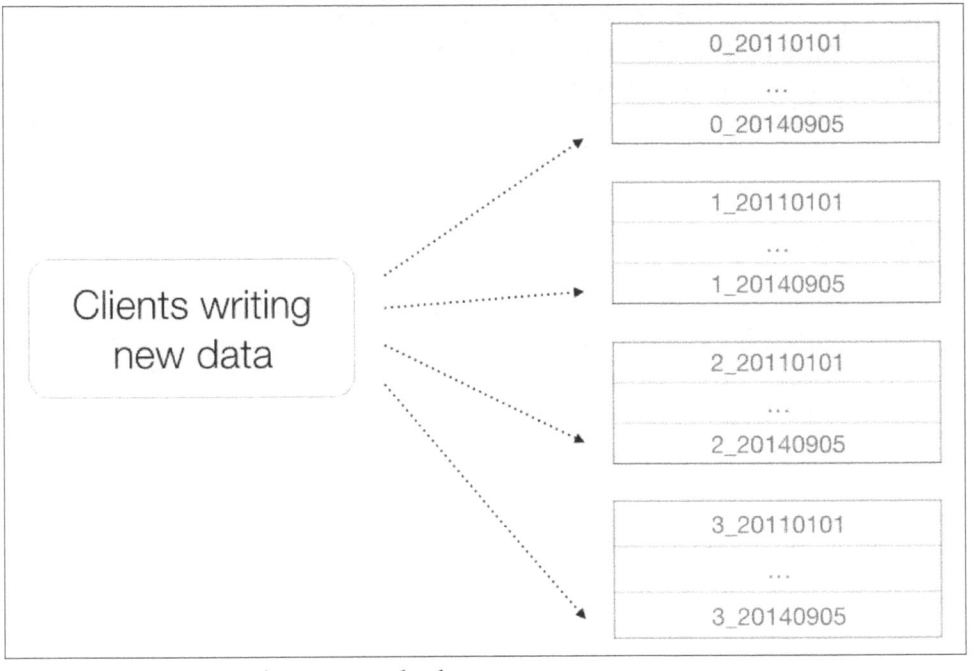

Figure 9-2. Alternative layout using buckets

Then new key-value pairs can be uniformly written to each of these buckets. This allows new data to be ingested in time order into several servers at once. The trade-off is that each bucket must be queried in order to retrieve all the data for a particular time range. In this case we can elect to use a BatchScanner configured with a Range for the desired time range within each bucket. This is especially useful if the intent is to perform MapReduce jobs over time ranges of data.

Drawbacks include the fact that the number of buckets must be chosen ahead of time and that the table will be limited to being hosted by as many servers as there are buckets.

Graphs

Graphs are incredibly useful for representing data for a wide variety of problems.

 In this section we are using the computer science definition of a graph: a set of *vertices* or *nodes*, and a set of *edges* representing connections between nodes. This is in contrast to the notion of a graph as a visual representation of the data, sometimes called a *chart*, such as a *bar graph*.

Graphs representing many real-world phenomena can present challenges for some other data storage systems because they can exhibit some difficult properties, depending on the representation. These include *sparseness*, in which most nodes connect to few other nodes, and *skew* in the distribution of node degrees, meaning that while most nodes connect to few other nodes, a small number of nodes connect to many other nodes, or even all of them.

Consider a graph that represents words and the documents in which they appear. Such a graph could be considered an inverted index of a set of documents, if we were to store the graph by listing pairs of nodes that represent words in sorted order. This graph would exhibit the properties of sparseness and skew because a large number of words would appear in only a few documents, and some words—such as *the*, *a*, and *or*—would appear in all or almost all of the documents.

Figure 9-3 shows a small example of a social network. A real social network would also exhibit skew, because most people will have connections to a number of friends or colleagues likely numbering in the low hundreds, while some famous people will be followed or friended by many thousands or even millions of other users.

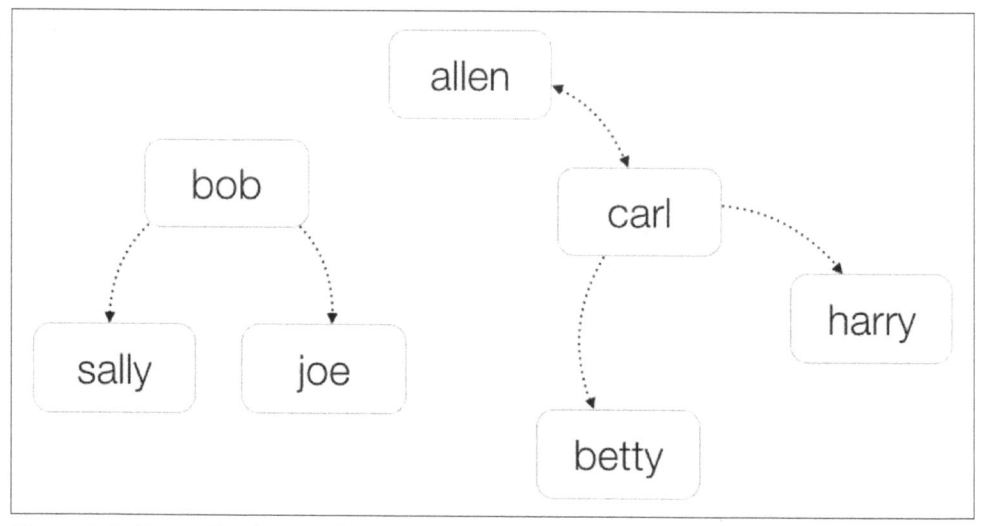

Figure 9-3. Example of a graph representing a social network

Of the two most common ways to represent graphs—as a *matrix* or as an *edge-list*—the edge-list representation is best suited to these types of graphs because no storage is required to represent the pairs of nodes that are not connected. Accumulo is especially well-suited to handling an edge-list when pairs of nodes are mapped to rows and columns, because Accumulo handles sparse rows efficiently, and because rows in Accumulo can be large and are not assumed to fit into the memory of a single machine.

An example of how we might store a graph in Accumulo is as follows:

```
row ID  column family column qualifier  value
allen friends   carl
bob friends   joe
bob friends   sally
carl  friends   allen
carl  friends   betty
carl  friends   harry
```

We can even store multiple types of edges by using the column family to describe the type of edge:

```
row ID  column family column qualifier  value
allen family    jared
allen family    michael
allen friends   carl
bob friends   joe
bob friends   sally
carl  friends   allen
carl  friends   betty
carl  family    susan
carl  friends   harry
```

This allows applications to efficiently look up all of the nodes connected to a given node, and to select nodes connected via all or a subset of the types of edges present. Technically, a graph of this type with multiple types of edges is called a *multigraph*. It is possible in a multigraph to have two or more edges of different types between the same two nodes.

Some graphs feature directed edges, in which the relationship between two nodes flows in a particular direction. For example, one user of a social messaging app may follow the status updates of another user but not vice versa. In our table, the first node, represented by the row ID, can signify the originating node and the second node the destination node.

Graph edges can also be weighted in order to represent some feature of the edge such as strength, distance, or cost. Accumulo is especially well suited to maintaining large graphs whose edges, nodes, and weights are updated over time. This is because, in addition to the ability to add new columns at ingest time, Accumulo's iterators offer an extremely efficient way to aggregate contributions to edge weights.

We can choose to store the edge weight in the value of our table and configure our table to use an iterator, such as the built-in SummingCombiner, in order to add up the weights for each unique row-column pair. We may want to store the number of messages two users of a messaging application have sent to each other over time. Our table can then look like this:

```
row ID  column family  column qualifier  value
allen   family         jared             2
allen   family         michael           55
allen   friends        carl              6
bob     friends        joe               17
bob     friends        sally             1
carl    friends        allen             3
carl    friends        betty             20
carl    family         susan             4
carl    friends        harry             2
```

Whenever a user sends another user a message, we can update the graph simply by inserting a new mutation with a count of one:

```
user@accumulo friendGraph> insert allen family jared 1
```

Accumulo will automatically sum up the inserts for each row-column pair and return the aggregated result whenever it is read:

```
user@accumulo friendGraph> scan -b allen family:jared
allen family:jared [] 3
```

Because Accumulo applies iterators at scan time and during compactions, *updates* to this graph table are as inexpensive as simple inserts. A large number of individual update/inserts can be sent to this table.

Tables like these have some interesting properties. One is that the number of key-value pairs will reflect the number of existing edges in the graph. The number of key-value pairs in this table then grows with the number of real-world relationships that exist, but not with the number of individual interactions that are aggregated to represent the weight of these relationships. Also, often graphs built to reflect real-world relationships have many fewer edges than they could have. A graph with N nodes can have up to N^2 edges, but the number of edges in many real-world graphs is on the order of N—that is, simply some multiple of N.

So a summarized graph representation of a large number of events will end up having many fewer key-value pairs than there are raw events. In addition, the number of new nodes in real-world graphs often grows relatively slowly over time.

A table design that builds a graph from several different data sources and aggregates the interactions in relationships observed is a powerful method of combining data and allowing natural patterns to emerge. For example, consider a table supporting an analytical application that combines sources of data such as interactions between customers, customers check-ins at store locations, and products customers have rated. All the information for a particular customer would be organized under one row so looking up everything that a company knows about that customer can be found quickly by doing a single scan.

Applications can be written to handle the appearance of new columns and present whatever information is available to analysts.

Building an Example Graph: Twitter

To illustrate the concepts of the graph table we've outlined, we'll build a graph from information in the public Twitter stream. Tweets can include mentions of users, replies to other users, and mentions of hashtags. We can build a graph from these relationships by inserting edges into a graph table as we process the stream.

First we'll set up our table to store edges and increment the weight of the edge each time we insert it:

```java
public static BatchWriter setupTable(
        final Connector conn,
        final String name,
        boolean deleteIfPresent) throws Exception {

  TableOperations ops = conn.tableOperations();

  // create table
  if (ops.exists(name) && deleteIfPresent) {
    ops.delete(name);
  }

  ops.create(name);

  // remove versioning iterator
  ops.removeIterator(name, "vers",
      EnumSet.allOf(IteratorUtil.IteratorScope.class));

  // setup summing combiner
  IteratorSetting iterSet = new IteratorSetting(10, "sum",
      SummingCombiner.class);
  SummingCombiner.setCombineAllColumns(iterSet, true);
  SummingCombiner.setEncodingType(iterSet,
      SummingCombiner.STRING_ENCODER.getClass().getName());

  ops.attachIterator(name, iterSet);

  return conn.createBatchWriter(name, new BatchWriterConfig());
}
```

Next, we'll parse the Twitter stream, inserting edges for the relationships we care about as we go. We'll use the Twitter4j library and set up a StatusListener that can write to our graph table:

```java
private static class TGStatusListener implements StatusListener {

  private final BatchWriter writer;
```

```
  public TGStatusListener(final BatchWriter writer) {
    this.writer = writer;
  }

  @Override
  public void onStatus(Status status) {

    String user = status.getUser().getScreenName();

    // keep track of replies
    Graph.writeEdge(user, status.getInReplyToScreenName(), "reply", 1, writer,
        true);

    // track mentions
    for(UserMentionEntity mention : status.getUserMentionEntities()) {
      Graph.writeEdge(user, mention.getScreenName(), "mention", 1, writer, true);
    }

    // treat hashtags as nodes
    for(HashtagEntity ht: status.getHashtagEntities()) {
      Graph.writeEdge(user, ht.getText(), "hashtag", 1, writer, true);
    }
  }
  ...
}
```

The implementation of the writeEdge() method is as follows. We treat each edge as a single key-value pair. Inserting an edge multiple times will cause their weights to be summed using the SummingCombiner:

```
public static void writeEdge(
        final String nodeA,
        final String nodeB,
        final String edgeType,
        int weight,
        final BatchWriter writer,
        boolean storeReverseEdge) {
  try {
    Mutation forward = new Mutation(nodeA);
    forward.put(edgeType, nodeB, new Value(Integer.toString(weight).getBytes()));
    writer.addMutation(forward);

    if (storeReverseEdge) {
      Mutation reverse = new Mutation(nodeB);
      reverse.put(edgeType, nodeA,
          new Value(Integer.toString(weight).getBytes()));
      writer.addMutation(reverse);
    }
  } catch (MutationsRejectedException ex) {
    Logger.getLogger(TwitterGraph.class.getName()).log(Level.SEVERE, null, ex);
  }
}
```

Next we'll discuss traversing graphs and return to this example to explore the graph we've created.

Traversing Graph Tables

Tables as described previously make it easy to do some types of graph traversal.

Retrieving all of a given node's directly connected neighbors (the *one-hop* neighbors) is particularly easy. It involves a simple scan of one row of the table and extraction of the connected neighbors by reading the column qualifiers:

```
import com.google.common.base.Function;
import com.google.common.collect.Iterables;

public Iterable<String> getNeighbors(
        final String node,
        final Scanner scanner,
        final String edgeType) {

  scanner.setRange(Range.exact(node));

  if(!edgeType.equals("ALL"))
    scanner.fetchColumnFamily(new Text(edgeType));

  return Iterables.transform(scanner, new Function<Entry<Key,Value>,String>() {

    @Override
    public String apply(Entry<Key, Value> f) {
      return f.getKey().getColumnQualifier().toString();
    }
  });
}
```

Further traversing the graph and retrieving all the neighbors of the one-hop neighbors can be done using a `BatchScanner`. If we are careful to remove all the neighbors we've already visited from the set of neighbors we pass to the `BatchScanner`, we can continue to do this until we have visited the entire graph, in breadth-first order:

```
import com.google.common.base.Function;
import com.google.common.collect.Iterables;
import com.google.common.collect.Sets;

public Iterable<String> neighborsOfNeighbors(
        final Iterable<String> neighbors,
        final BatchScanner batchScanner,
        final String edgeType) {

  List<Iterable<String>> nextNeighbors = new ArrayList<>();

  // process given neighbors in batches of 100
  for (List<String> batch : Iterables.partition(neighbors, 100)) {
```

```
      batchScanner.setRanges(Lists.transform(batch, new Function<String, Range>() {
        @Override
        public Range apply(String f) {
          return Range.exact(f);
        }
      }));

      if (!edgeType.equals("ALL"))
        batchScanner.fetchColumnFamily(new Text(edgeType));

      nextNeighbors.add(Iterables.transform(batchScanner,
          new Function<Entry<Key, Value>, String>() {
        @Override
        public String apply(Entry<Key, Value> f) {
          return f.getKey().getColumnQualifier().toString();
        }
      }));
    }

    return Sets.newHashSet(Iterables.concat(nextNeighbors));
  }
```

We can run into some limitations around the amount of data we can keep in memory as we do this, but we can elect to store some of the state of our traversal back into the table in Accumulo.

Higher-level traversals and algorithms can be built using sequences of scans and batch scans. Some work (*http://bit.ly/big_graph_experiment*) has been done at the National Security Agency to process some very large graphs using MapReduce over Accumulo tables.

Traversing the Example Twitter Graph

Using our previous example, we'll use the methods described earlier to explore the Twitter graph. For this example, we'll visualize some data from our graph using Ubigraph (*http://ubietylab.net/ubigraph*), a free graph visualization tool.

A copy of the Ubigraph JAR is included in the *lib/* directory of the example code. Install it into your local Maven repository if you haven't done so already:

```
[accumulo@host lib]$ mvn install:install-file -Dfile=ubigraph-0.2.4.jar \
    -DgroupId=org.ubiety -DartifactId=ubigraph -Dversion=0.2.4 -Dpackaging=jar
```

Next we'll start the Ubigraph server, which will listen for requests to visualize nodes and edges of our graph. You must accept the license and download the server (*http://bit.ly/ubigraph*) to run this example:

```
[accumulo@host ubigraph]$ bin/ubigraph_server
8 processors
Using single-level layout.
Running Ubigraph/XML-RPC server.
```

We'll use our graph methods to retrieve a few nodes and their neighbors:

```java
// visualize our graph, one node at a time
System.out.println("visualizing graph ...");
UbigraphClient client = new UbigraphClient();

for (String startNode :
    new String[]{"a", "b", "c", "d", "e", "f", "g", "h", "i"}) {

  Scanner startNodeScanner = conn.createScanner(TWITTER_GRAPH_TABLE,
      Authorizations.EMPTY);
  Optional<String> node = Graph.discoverNode(startNode, startNodeScanner);
  startNodeScanner.close();

  if (node.isPresent()) {

    // visualize start node
    int nodeId = client.newVertex();
    client.setVertexAttribute(nodeId, "label", node.get());

    Scanner neighborScanner = conn.createScanner(TWITTER_GRAPH_TABLE,
        Authorizations.EMPTY);
    for (String neighbor :
        Graph.getNeighbors(node.get(), neighborScanner, "ALL")) {

      // visualize neighbor node
      int neighborId = client.newVertex();
      client.setVertexAttribute(neighborId, "label", neighbor);

      // visualize edge
      client.newEdge(nodeId, neighborId);
    }
    neighborScanner.close();
  }
}
```

To run this example, you'll need to obtain the API keys necessary to access Twitter programmatically from our example application by visiting *http://dev.twitter.com* and registering a new application. Once your application is registered you can obtain the Access Token, Access Token Secret, Consumer Key, and Consumer Secret to use as arguments to the TwitterGraph class:

```
$ mvn exec:java -Dexec.mainClass="com.accumulobook.designs.graph.TwitterGraph" \
  -Dexec.args="access token, access token secret consumer key \
  consumer secret"

processing twitter stream ...

2785 [Twitter Stream consumer-1[initializing]] INFO twitter4j.TwitterStreamImpl
    - Establishing connection.
3642 [Twitter Stream consumer-1[Establishing connection]] INFO
    twitter4j.TwitterStreamImpl - Connection established.
```

```
3642 [Twitter Stream consumer-1[Establishing connection]] INFO
    twitter4j.TwitterStreamImpl - Receiving status stream.

shutting down twitter stream.

visualizing graph ...
```

After this message, the Ubigraph window will display a few clusters of nodes representing a Twitter user and his connections to other users or hashtags he has mentioned (Figure 9-4).

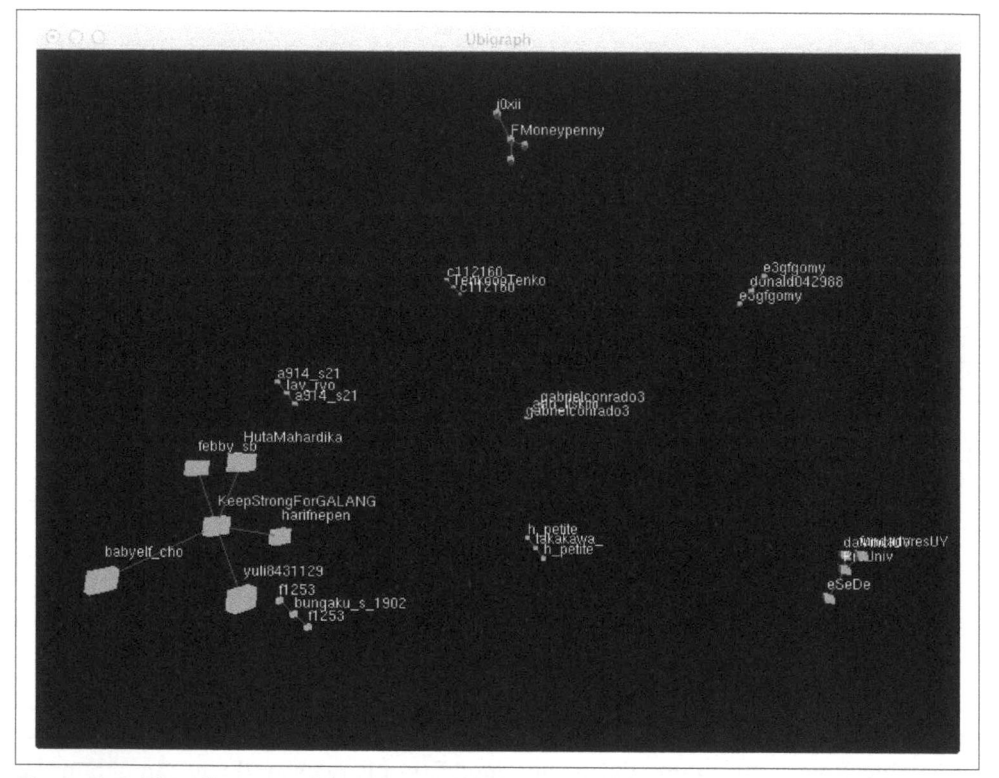

Figure 9-4. Visualization of the Twitter graph

A few other projects are designed to process graphs that have been adapted for use
with Accumulo, including the two we describe next.

Blueprints for Accumulo

Blueprints is part of the TinkerPop (*http://www.tinkerpop.com/*) graph toolkit. The
AccumuloGraph project (*https://github.com/JHUAPL/AccumuloGraph*) implements
the Blueprints API on Accumulo, enabling Blueprints-enabled applications to run on
Accumulo. The implementation involves a table to store the graph that is similar to

the design described previously but includes a few more features as well as a separate optional table as an index on vertex and edge properties.

Titan

Titan (*http://thinkaurelius.github.io/titan/*) is "a scalable graph database optimized for storing and querying graphs containing hundreds of billions of vertices and edges distributed across a multi-machine cluster. Titan is a transactional database that can support thousands of concurrent users executing complex graph traversals."

A few efforts have been started to begin allowing Accumulo to be used as the backend storage layer, but some changes in the Titan API may be required before this can be done efficiently. The most mature effort is the titan-accumulo (*http://bit.ly/titan-accumulo*) project. be found at

Semantic Triples

The Semantic Web and related natural-language–processing technologies have created significant interest in representing *triples* consisting of a subject, predicate, and object. Such triples can conform to the Resource Description Framework (*http://www.w3.org/RDF/*) (RDF) Semantic Web model. Accumulo can be used to store and access triples efficiently, and even support higher-level query languages such as SPARQL (*http://www.w3.org/TR/rdf-sparql-query/*).

The general strategy is to store each *subject*, *object*, and *predicate* three times, ordering the triples differently each time so that a scan can be performed to retrieve one, two, or three elements efficiently. One table stores elements in SPO order (subject, predicate, object), another in OSP order, and the third in POS. This way any query for all three elements can be done on any table, a query for any two elements can be done on the table in which those to elements appear first, and a query for a single element can be done on the table in which the element appears first.

This strategy is described in the paper "Rya: A Scalable RDF Triple Store for the Clouds" (*http://bit.ly/rdf_triple_store*). These three tables can be used, along with the appropriate query logic, to satisfy SPARQL queries on RDF triples.

This table design is a good example of how multiple orderings of elements can support a wide range of queries.

Semantic Triples Example

We'll use the Freebase API to explore building a table to hold semantic triples.

The Freebase data set (*http://bit.ly/freebase_data*) contains a set of facts, each containing three items: a *subject*, a *predicate*, and an *object*. Students of English grammar may recognize these as basic parts of one type of sentence. The facts are curated from a variety of sources including wikis. In many cases the facts are extracted using machine-learning techniques from free-text sentences.

We'll pull all the information about several topics from Freebase into a table holding semantic triples (Table 9-1). First, we need a method for constructing all the ways we'll need to store a triple. Our strategy will be to store the first element of a triple in the row ID, the next in the column family, and the third in the column qualifier.

Table 9-1. Storing triples

Row	Column family	Column qualifier	Column visibility	Value
spo_ subject	predicate	object		
osp_ object	subject	predicate		
pos_ predicate	object	subject		

For each triple, we'll store three key-value pairs, one for each permutation of S, P, and O. We'll prefix the row ID with the ordering of the triple elements so we know which element is which for any given triple:

```
public static void insertTriples(
        final String subject,
        final BatchWriter writer) throws Exception {

    final List<Pair<String,String>> properties = getProperties(subject);

    // for SPO triple
    Mutation spo = new Mutation("spo_" + subject);

    for(Pair<String, String> prop : properties) {

        String predicate = prop.getFirst();
        String object = prop.getSecond();

        spo.put(predicate, object, BLANK);

        Mutation pos = new Mutation("pos_" + predicate);
        pos.put(object, subject, BLANK);
        writer.addMutation(pos);

        Mutation osp = new Mutation("osp_" + object);
        osp.put(subject, predicate, BLANK);
        writer.addMutation(osp);
    }

    writer.addMutation(spo);
```

```
    writer.flush();
  }
```

We'll request information from the API about a few topics and load them into our table:

```
Connector conn = ExampleMiniCluster.getConnector();

if(conn.tableOperations().exists("triples"))
  conn.tableOperations().delete("triples");

conn.tableOperations().create("triples");

BatchWriter writer = conn.createBatchWriter("triples", new BatchWriterConfig());

System.out.println("loading data ...");

FreebaseExample.insertTriples("darth_vader", writer);
FreebaseExample.insertTriples("jedi", writer);
FreebaseExample.insertTriples("luke_skywalker", writer);
FreebaseExample.insertTriples("yoda", writer);
FreebaseExample.insertTriples("obi_wan_kenobi", writer);

System.out.println("done.");
```

Now we can ask questions by querying this table using one or two elements of a triple and retrieve the remaining one or two elements per associated triple. For example, we can ask to see everything about Darth Vader:

```
System.out.println("\n=== Darth Vader ===");

for(String s : query(
        "darth_vader",  ❶
        null,  ❷
        null,  ❸
        conn.createScanner("triples", Authorizations.EMPTY))) {
  System.out.println(s);
}
```

❶ Subject

❷ Predicate

❸ Object

Our query function will figure out which elements of a triple are present in the query and scan the proper rows accordingly. When only one element of a triple is provided, our query function will return both of the remaining two elements for every triple that matches the element provided. When two elements are provided, our query function returns a list of the one remaining element in all matching triples. For our query about Darth Vader as a subject, we'll get back a list of predicates and objects for all triples containing *darth_vader* as the subject. Our implementation of these types of queries is as follows:

```java
public static Iterable<String> query(
        final String subject,
        final String predicate,
        final String object,
        final Scanner scanner) throws Exception {

    if(subject == null && predicate == null && object == null)
        throw new IllegalArgumentException("Must specify at least one of subject,
            predicate, object");

    if(subject != null) {
        if(predicate != null) { // SP_ get all objects for subject and predicate
            scanner.setRange(Range.prefix("spo_" + subject));
            scanner.fetchColumnFamily(new Text(predicate));

            return Iterables.transform(scanner, cqSelector);
        }
        else {
            if(object != null) { // S_O get all predicates for subject and object

                scanner.setRange(Range.prefix("osp_" + object));
                scanner.fetchColumnFamily(new Text(predicate));

                return Iterables.transform(scanner, cqSelector);
            }
            else { // S__ get all predicates and objects for subject
                scanner.setRange(Range.prefix("spo_" + subject));
                return Iterables.transform(scanner, cfqSelector);
            }
        }
    }
    else {
        if(predicate != null) {
            if(object != null) { // _PO get all subjects for predicate and object
                scanner.setRange(Range.prefix("pos_" + predicate));
                scanner.fetchColumnFamily(new Text(object));

                return Iterables.transform(scanner, cqSelector);
            }
            else { // _P_ get all subjects and objects for predicate
                scanner.setRange(Range.prefix("pos_" + predicate));
                return Iterables.transform(scanner, cfqSelector);
            }
        }
        else { // __O get all subjects and predicates for object
            scanner.setRange(Range.prefix("osp_" + object));
            return Iterables.transform(scanner, cfqSelector);
        }
```

```
    }
  }
```

The `cqSelector` and `cfqSelector` classes return the remaining one or two elements of matching triples, respectively:

```
// returns just the last element of a matching triple
private static final Function<Entry<Key,Value>,String> cqSelector =
        new Function<Entry<Key,Value>,String>() {

  @Override
  public String apply(Entry<Key, Value> e) {
    return e.getKey().getColumnQualifier().toString();
  }
};

// returns the last two elements of a matching triple
private static final Function<Entry<Key,Value>,String> cfqSelector =
        new Function<Entry<Key,Value>,String>() {

  @Override
  public String apply(Entry<Key, Value> e) {
    return e.getKey().getColumnFamily().toString() + "\t"
            + e.getKey().getColumnQualifier().toString();
  }
};
```

Our query for `subject:darth_vader` returns a list of predicate and object results:

```
=== Darth Vader ===
/award/ranked_item/appears_in_ranked_lists AFI's 100 Years
/book/book_character/appears_in_book Path to Truth
/book/book_character/appears_in_book The Changing of the Guard
/book/book_character/appears_in_book The Dangerous Games
...
/common/topic/alias  Anakin Skywalker
/common/topic/alias  Lord Vader
...
/fictional_universe/fictional_character/character_created_by George Lucas
/fictional_universe/fictional_character/children Leia Organa
/fictional_universe/fictional_character/children Luke Skywalker
```

We can also get just a list of objects for a given subject and predicate. For example, to see all the jobs Darth Vader has held:

```
System.out.println("\n=== Darth Vader's Jobs ===");
for(String s : query(
        "darth_vader",
        "/fictional_universe/fictional_character/occupation",
        null,
        conn.createScanner("triples", Authorizations.EMPTY))) {
  System.out.println(s);
}
```

This returns the results:

```
=== Darth Vader's Jobs ===
Assassin
Dark Lord of the Sith
Jedi
Martial Artist
```

We can search for subjects and objects associated with just a given predicate. For example, to see a list of organizations and their members:

```
System.out.println("\n=== Memberships ===");
for(String s : query(
        null,
        "/fictional_universe/fictional_character/organizations",
        null,
        conn.createScanner("triples", Authorizations.EMPTY))) {
    System.out.println(s);
}
```

And we get:

```
=== Memberships ===
Jedi    darth_vader
Jedi    luke_skywalker
Jedi    yoda
Rebel Alliance    luke_skywalker
```

Spatial Data

In addition to numerical and textual data, Accumulo has been used to store, index, and retrieve spatial data consisting of geographical coordinates. Spatial data is challenging because each point is two-dimensional and Accumulo's tables, as well as any data stored in memory or on disk, can only be sorted in one way. Naive implementations might choose to index latitude separately from longitude and use set operations to identify data that falls within a given box on Earth, but this strategy often requires retrieving and then filtering out many more points than lie within the box.

There are several strategies for storing spatial data in Accumulo that try to avoid heavy reliance on filtering.

Open Source Projects

GeoMesa (*http://geomesa.github.io/*) is an open source project to support storing spatio-temporal data (a combination of geographical and time-based information) in Accumulo. GeoMesa makes use of a technique called *geohashing* (*http://bit.ly/geomesa_geohashing*), which is described as "a binary string in which each character indicates alternating divisions of the global longitude-latitude rectangle."

The GeoMesa project (*http://geomesa.github.io/*) is also designed to work with Geo-Server (*http://geoserver.org/about/*), an open source server for sharing geospatial data that can allow many popular mapping applications to connect to it, including Google Earth and ArcGIS.

Another project is GeoWave (*http://bit.ly/geowave*), which provides multidimensional indexing and support for geographic objects and geospatial operators. GeoWave includes a GeoServer plug-in that is compatible with the Open Geospatial Consortium (OGC) standard—a set of MapReduce input and output formats for bulk analysis of geospatial data in Hadoop.

Space-Filling Curves

Space-filling curves (*http://bit.ly/space-filling_curve*) are another technique for mapping higher-dimensional data to a single dimension. They work by imposing an order in which points in the higher-dimensional space are visited. Listing these points in order is how these points are written to a one-dimensional index.

Any ordering could be used, but space-filling curves are designed to maintain good locality after the points are mapped to one dimension. The points that are close together in high-dimensional space tend to be close together in the one-dimensional list. The locality-preserving property is useful for indexing data in Accumulo because the goal of our tables is to answer most user requests with one or a small number of scans.

Several popular space-filling curves have been used in Accumulo tables. The easiest to implement and understand is the Z-order curve, which visits points in higher-dimensional space in a Z-like pattern (*http://bit.ly/z-order_curve*). Others include the Hilbert Curve (*http://bit.ly/hilbert_curve*) and Peano Curve (*http://bit.ly/peano_curve*).

For two-dimensional geospatial data, we simply need to convert the points by using the instructions for creating a space-filling curve and then write the transformed points to Accumulo.

For the Z-order curve, suppose we have the decimal-degree coordinates:

```
Lat: 033.11 Lon: 044.22
```

These are transformed into row ID by simply interleaving the digits from each number:

```
0034341212
```

When scanning for the points that fall within a user-provided range, we similarly convert the starting and stopping points (i.e., the lower lefthand point and upper righthand point) to points on the curve and scan the table to retrieve all the points that lie within that range.

For our Z-order curve example, we might query from (30.00, 40.00) to (35.00, 45.00). These query points are translated to 33050000 and 44050000. We set up our scan to range from 0033050000 to 0044050000.

In this example we're using human-readable strings to store our Z-order coordinates, but in practice a more compact representation can be used. Here is an example of code that implements the common pattern for scanning tables containing Z-order coordinates:

```
Double startLat = 30.0;
Double stopLat = 35.0;
Double startLon = 40.0;
Double stopLon = 45.0;

// assuming we've stored our points as human-readable strings
String startZPoint = "0034000000";
String stopZPoint = "0034550000";

Range range = new Range(startZPoint, stopZPoint);
Scanner scanner = new Scanner("myGeoTable");
scanner.setRange(range);

ArrayList<Value> results = new ArrayList<>();

for(Entry<Key,Value> entry : scanner) {
 // unscramble the point returned
   String zPoint = entry.getKey().getRow().toString();
 StringBuilder latStr = new StringBuilder();
 StringBuilder lonStr = new StringBuilder();

 for(int i=0; i < zPoint.length(); i+=2) {
   latStr.append(zPoint.charAt(i));
   lonStr.append(zPoint.charAt(i+1));
 }

 Double lat = Double.parse(latStr.build());
 Double lon = Double.parse(lonStr.build());

 // filter points outside our box
 if(lat >= startLat && lat <= stopLat
    && lon >= startLon && lon <= stopLon) {

   results.add(entry.getValue());
 }
}
```

We are guaranteed to receive all points within the requested area, but we can get points that lie outside the requested range. These points can be filtered out, either by the client or by a filtering iterator configured on the table.

The Z-order curve will sometimes return a large number of points outside the requested area, particularly around the middle of the indexed area. Other curves can perform better but at the cost of increased complexity of implementation.

Multidimensional Data

Some of the strategies for storing two-dimensional spatial data in Accumulo can be generalized to store higher-dimensional data. For example, in addition to latitude and longitude, an index can be built that stores altitude and other numerical data. Textual data can also be combined with numerical data in these indexes.

For example, to store points consisting of latitude, longitude, and altitude, we can choose to zero-pad our points and combine them using the Z-order curve:

```
Lat: 00033.11 Lon: 00044.22 Altitude (feet): 11555.00
```

This would be combined in the Z-curve to produce the point:

```
001001005345345120120
```

To query for a cube in this space we pick two three-dimensional corners of the cube on opposite sides, transform these points as before, and perform a scan, filtering out any points that fall outside the cube.

D4M and Matlab

The Dynamic Distributed Dimensional Data Model (*http://www.mit.edu/~kepner/D4M/*) (D4M) was developed by Dr. Jeremy Kepner and others at MIT Lincoln Labs to take advantage of data stores like Accumulo. It has been used for a wide variety of applications and has been shown to have extremely good performance characteristics (*http://bit.ly/kepner_et_al*). D4M is a technique for applying linear algebra to databases that simplifies the creation of new analytics using parallel computation tools such as pMatlab (Parallel Matlab Toolkit), MatlabMPI, and gridMatlab.

The Accumulo tables used by D4M involve storing associative arrays in a table and also storing its logical transpose so that rows and columns can both be searched efficiently.

The D4M schema (*http://bit.ly/d4m_schema*) as used with Accumulo consists of four tables.

If we ingest records, each consisting of a unique ID and a set of fields and values, the D4M schema can be described as follows.

The *TEdgeTxt* table is used to store any original text found in records. It is used to retrieve the full text of any records found by searching other tables, or to simply retrieve records by ID if the ID is known.

Table 9-2. TEdgeTxt

row ID	column	value
record ID	field	full text

The *Tedge* table (Table 9-3) is used to store any metadata found in records. It can also store tokenized words from the text in the *TedgeTxt* table.

Table 9-3. Tedge

row ID	column	value
record ID	field|value	1

The transpose of the *Tedge* table is stored in the *TedgeT* table (Table 9-4) and is used to look up record IDs by the values of specific fields.

Table 9-4. TedgeT

row ID	column	value
field|value	record ID	1

The *TedgeDeg* table (Table 9-5) stores a count of the number of times a field-value pair has been seen. It can be used to answer simple questions and to provide statistics for queries involving more than one field-value pair.

Table 9-5. TedgeDeg

row ID	column	value
field|value	"degree"	count

Linear algebra operations can then be performed by fetching arrays using either the row-oriented or column-oriented tables and by executing operations in parallel using one of the parallel Matlab frameworks mentioned.

The D4M software (*http://bit.ly/d4m_software*) is available for download. The ZIP files include an eight-lecture course on how to use D4M.

D4M Example

We'll walk through an example.

First we'll start up an Accumulo instance running locally. For testing we'll just start up a `MiniAccumuloCluster` instance using the Accumulo quickstart project from "Demo of the Shell" on page 60.

After cloning the examples project and changing into the *quickstart* directory, start up a shell via:

```
mvn clean compile exec:exec -Pshell
```

This will start a shell and a `MiniAccumuloCluster` that we can use just for the duration of this example. This program will generate a different ZooKeeper port each time it runs, so we'll take note of the ZooKeeper port that is printed out and use it in the following examples to connect to this instance:

```
...
---- Initializing Accumulo Shell

Starting the MiniAccumuloCluster in /var/folders/...
Zookeeper is localhost:25641
Instance is miniAccumulo

Shell - Apache Accumulo Interactive Shell
...
```

We'll leave the shell running in a terminal window while we run these other steps.

Adding D4M to Octave or Matlab

To load and analyze data we need GNU Octave or Matlab. Octave (*http://bit.ly/ octave_language*) is an open source high-level computing language similar to Matlab.

 Make sure you have a version of Octave with the Java interface. If you see "error: javaObject: Octave was not compiled with Java interface," follow the `java` package installation instructions (*http:// bit.ly/java_pkg_install*).

Next we'll download the D4M libraries:

```
$ wget http://www.mit.edu/~kepner/D4M/d4m_api_2.5.1.zip
$ wget http://www.mit.edu/~kepner/D4M/libext_2.5.1.zip
```

Unzip both and place the *libext* folder inside the *d4m_api* folder. This folder will be our *D4M_HOME*:

```
$ unzip d4m_api_2.5.1.zip
$ unzip libext_2.5.1.zip
$ mv libext d4m_api
```

We'll also need to create a file called *classpath.txt* in our home directory so Octave can find the Java classes D4M needs. Add one line for each JAR file in *d4m_api/lib* and *d4m_api/libext*:

```
/home/user/d4m_api/libext/accumulo-core-1.5.0.jar
/home/user/d4m_api/libext/commons-jci-core-1.0.jar
/home/user/d4m_api/libext/jtds-1.2.5.jar
/home/user/d4m_api/libext/accumulo-fate-1.5.0.jar
/home/user/d4m_api/libext/commons-jci-fam-1.0.jar
/home/user/d4m_api/libext/libthrift-0.9.1.jar
/home/user/d4m_api/libext/accumulo-server-1.5.0.jar
/home/user/d4m_api/libext/commons-lang-2.4.jar
/home/user/d4m_api/libext/log4j-1.2.15.jar
/home/user/d4m_api/libext/accumulo-trace-1.5.0.jar
/home/user/d4m_api/libext/commons-logging-1.0.4.jar
/home/user/d4m_api/libext/slf4j-api-1.6.1.jar
/home/user/d4m_api/libext/commons-collections-3.2.jar
/home/user/d4m_api/libext/hadoop-core-1.1.2.jar
/home/user/d4m_api/libext/slf4j-log4j12-1.6.1.jar
/home/user/d4m_api/libext/commons-configuration-1.5.jar
/home/user/d4m_api/libext/hadoop-tools-1.1.2.jar
/home/user/d4m_api/libext/zookeeper-3.3.5.jar
/home/user/d4m_api/libext/commons-io-1.4.jar
/home/user/d4m_api/libext/json.jar
/home/user/d4m_api/lib/D4M_API_JAVA_AC.jar
/home/user/d4m_api/lib/D4M_API_JAVA.jar
```

Loading example data

We'll use an example of ingesting data via Matlab scripts from *https://github.com/denine99/d4mBB/*. Clone this Git repository:

```
$ git clone https://github.com/denine99/d4mBB/

$ cd d4mBB
```

Edit the *d4m_Baseball_Demo.m* script with the information for our `MiniAccumu loCluster` instance. The top of the file should look like this:

```
%% Demonstrates D4M's capabilities on a small Baseball statistic data set by
% (1) Parsing data into a form ready for ingestion
% (2) Ingesting data into memory or an Accumulo Table
% (3) Querying data to answer several questions of interest

% User Parameters:
doDB = 1;   % Use an Accumulo Database instead of in-memory Associative Arrays
DB = DBserver('localhost:[your-zookeeper-port]','Accumulo','miniInstance',
    'root','pass1234');
```

This shows us how to connect to Accumulo from Matlab or Octave.

Now we'll start up Matlab or Octave and add the D4M libraries to our path:

```
[user@hostname d4mBB]$ octave
GNU Octave, version 3.8.1
...
octave:1> addpath('../d4m_api/matlab_src')
```

Next we'll run the demo script, which will load data from a CSV file into Accumulo tables and perform some commands to fetch the data:

 This script loads data into memory to organize the information and then writes to Accumulo. If data does not fit in memory it can be loaded into memory and written to Accumulo in parts.

```
octave:2> d4m_Baseball_Demo
INGEST time (sec) = 0.731
INGEST time (sec) = 0.494
...
INGEST time (sec) = 0.147
INGEST time (sec) = 0.094
INGEST time (sec) = 0.064
Creating baseballMaster in localhost:12953 Accumulo
Creating baseballMasterT in localhost:12953 Accumulo
Creating baseballMasterDeg in localhost:12953 Accumulo
Creating baseballSalaries in localhost:12953 Accumulo
Creating baseballSalariesT in localhost:12953 Accumulo
Creating baseballSalariesDeg in localhost:12953 Accumulo
Creating baseballMaster in localhost:12953 Accumulo
Creating baseballMasterT in localhost:12953 Accumulo
Creating baseballMasterDeg in localhost:12953 Accumulo
Creating baseballSalaries in localhost:12953 Accumulo
Creating baseballSalariesT in localhost:12953 Accumulo
Creating baseballSalariesDeg in localhost:12953 Accumulo
...
```

This script will run a series of queries and display the results in a paginated screen. Type **q** to exit that screen.

Let's take a look at what the script is doing. The D4M API uses the concept of a table and a table-pair. The script uses the following commands to create tables and table pairs in Accumulo:

```
Tm = DB('baseballMaster', 'baseballMasterT');
Tmd = DB('baseballMasterDeg');
```

Next the demo script performs some queries. The first is "Find all stored information about a specific player: zobribe01 (Ben Zobrist)":

```
octave:3> Tm('playerID|zobribe01,',:)
(playerID|zobribe01,bats|B)        1
(playerID|zobribe01,birthCountry|USA)       1
(playerID|zobribe01,birthState|IL)       1
```

```
(playerID|zobribe01,birthYear|1981)      1
(playerID|zobribe01,height|75)        1
(playerID|zobribe01,nameFirst|Ben)       1
(playerID|zobribe01,nameLast|Zobrist)      1
(playerID|zobribe01,weight|200)        1
```

A few lines down we find a query to "Find how many players weigh < 200 lb. and bat with left hand or both hands." First the script finds out how many players meet each criterion separately:

```
octave:4> A = sum(str2num(Tmd('weight|000,:,weight|199,',:)),1);
octave:5> B = str2num(Tmd('bats|L,bats|B,',:));
octave:6> A
(1,degree)       13182
octave:7> B
(bats|B,degree)     1106
(bats|L,degree)     4629
```

Now the script will find those that meet both criteria. "A > B, so we will first query for all the rows of players that bat L or B" and "Then, within those rows, we will find the players that weigh < 200 lb":

```
octave:8> A_LB = Tm(:,'bats|L,bats|B,');
octave:9> A_LB_all = Tm(Row(A_LB),:);
octave:10> A_LB_light = A_LB_all(:,'weight|000,:,weight|199,');
octave:11> NumStr(Row(A_LB_light))
ans = 4463
```

Help reference for the D4M Matlab scripts is available via:

```
>> help D4M
```

The D4M libraries ship with some built-in examples in *D4M_HOME/examples/*.

Load example data using Java

To load some example data using Java, we'll use the *D4M_Schema* project:

```
git clone https://github.com/medined/D4M_Schema.git
```

Open up the *D4M_Schema/schema* project in Netbeans or Eclipse. Edit the file in *src/main/resources/d4m.properties* to contain the following settings:

```
accumulo.instance.name=miniInstance
accumulo.zookeeper.ensemble=localhost:your-zookeeper-port
accumulo.user=root
accumulo.password=pass1234
```

Run the *com.codebits.example.d4m.TaxYear2007ToAccumulo.java* file.

This will create the D4M tables and load a CSV file containing tax information into those tables. This code does not use any libraries from the previous D4M example; it simply knows how to create tables of the structure that the D4M API understands.

These tables can be used to perform queries in Matlab as in the preceding examples and can also be seen in the shell when you start the *RunShell.java* program:

```
root@miniInstance> tables
!METADATA
Tedge
TedgeDegree
TedgeMetadata
TedgeText
TedgeTranspose

root@miniInstance> table TedgeDegree

root@miniInstance TedgeDegree> scan
adjusted gross income (in thousands)|$-1 :degree []    1
adjusted gross income (in thousands)|$10007290 :degree []    1
adjusted gross income (in thousands)|$100192 :degree []    1
adjusted gross income (in thousands)|$1002480 :degree []    1
adjusted gross income (in thousands)|$10025 :degree []    1
adjusted gross income (in thousands)|$100273 :degree []    1
...
```

After you run these examples, quitting the shell and stopping the `MiniAccumuloClus` `ter` will shut down the Mini Accumulo instance and erase the data used.

These examples use a single machine to process data retrieved from Accumulo. You can perform these operations in parallel on multiple machines by using the Parallel Matlab Toolbox (*http://bit.ly/pmatlab*). This will enable these analytics to scale along with the size of the data machines.

Machine Learning

Large-scale data storage and retrieval are two challenges that are directly addressed by Accumulo. But often simply storing raw data and delivering subsets to users as the results of queries can still be overwhelming, if even subsets consist of more results than users can understand.

Data mining, knowledge discovery, and machine-learning techniques help address the problem of transforming an overwhelming amount of raw data into higher-level representations that are more amenable for making decisions. Because Accumulo is often a part of decision processes based on big data, some techniques for doing machine learning in Accumulo have emerged.

Storing Feature Vectors

Some techniques for storing graphs that we mentioned earlier can be used in machine-learning methods. Machine learning often involves the construction of *feature vectors*, which are used to describe entities of interest. For example, users of a video rental application can be the entities that are described by feature vectors consisting of all the movies they have ever watched or rated. A *feature* can be any measure that might be informative for determining a property of interest about an entity, such as whether a user might want to watch a new movie, or whether a particular location might be a good place to build a new store, etc. Features can be binary (either an entity has a feature or it doesn't), or features can be weighted with a real number. The construction of features is not always obvious and often involves the application of domain expertise to help come up with likely useful features.

An example feature vector is as follows:

```
actionMoviesWatched: 28
dramasWatched: 3
...
raidersOfLostArkRating: 4
flightOfTheNavigatorRating: 3
...
```

A feature vector consists of all the features that apply to a particular entity. These vectors can be very large (i.e., high dimensional) and can vary widely from one entity to another. For this reason, storing feature vectors can be challenging for many traditional databases. Accumulo is particularly well suited for storing a feature vector as a set of columns in a row because of its support for dynamic columns, large rows, and sparse rows.

In addition, Accumulo iterators can be used to efficiently increment feature weights as new raw observations arrive. For example, each time a user watches a film we might add a new feature describing the fact that the user watched this movie, as well as incrementing the weight for the number of films the user has watched in the genre of this movie:

```
Movie:
  Casablanca

Features:
  watchedCasablanca: true
  dramasWatched: +1
```

Using an iterator to update the *dramasWatched* feature allows us to increment the value without reading out the old value first.

We can store an entity's feature vector in a single row in an Accumulo table. The row ID is the name of the entity, and the columns are named after the feature. Either the value can be ignored when the presence of the column is taken to mean that the entity has that feature and absent columns are taken to mean the entity doesn't, or the value can be used to store the weight of the feature:

```
user123  watchedCasablanca -
user123  dramasWatched     3
```

We might also elect to put different types of features into their own locality groups so that we can efficiently select different types of features in case we don't always want to use them all.

Once we've built a table to store feature vectors, we might also want to create another table that stores the names of features in the row ID and the names of entities in columns so we can quickly look up all the entities that have a particular feature:

```
watchedCasablanca  user123
watchedCasablanca  user234
watchedGattaca     user123
```

This table can be considered an index on features.

A Machine-Learning Example

These tables make it possible to perform a variety of machine-learning tasks. For example, there is a classifier called the k-Nearest-Neighbors Classifier that works by finding some number, k, of entities in the database that are most similar or nearest to an entity of interest based on a similarity metric that compares two feature vectors. These entities are the nearest neighbors. Once the k nearest neighbors are found, we can get an estimate for some property of the entity of interest by averaging the value of that property across the nearest neighbors.

K nearest neighbors is an example of a *nonparametric* method, or *instance-based* learning, because it requires storing information about every previous instance seen, rather than building a representative model. Accumulo is well suited to such a task because of its scalability.

To illustrate this, we'll use the MovieLens data set (*http://bit.ly/movielens_data*), which can be downloaded in sizes of 100 KB, 1 MB, or 10 MB ratings. For example, the 100 KB data set consists of:

- 100,000 ratings (1–5) from 943 users on 1,682 movies.
- Each user has rated at least 20 movies.
- Simple demographic information for the users (age, gender, occupation, zip).

We'll ingest the *u.data* file, which contains the values for the *userId*, *movieId*, *rating*, and *timestamp* fields, per line. The *u.item* file contains the *movieId*, *title*, *release date*, *video release date*, *IMDB url*, and information on which genres it belongs to.

This example is written in Python and uses the Accumulo Thrift proxy. Details on using the Thrift proxy can be found in "Thrift Proxy" on page 236. To run this example using the Thrift proxy connecting to a MiniAccumuloCluster, simply run the ExampleMiniThriftProxy class from the examples:

```
mvn exec:java -Dexec.mainClass="com.accumulobook.ExampleMiniThriftProxy"
```

First we'll import the ratings file (*u.data*) and the file describing movies (*u.item*). The code for parsing these files and storing the data in Accumulo is as follows:

```python
#!/usr/bin/python

import sys
import csv
import math
import uuid

import common
from accumulo.ttypes import *

client = None
login = None

def loadMLFile(filename):
    if client.tableExists(login, 'ml'):
        client.deleteTable(login, 'ml')
    client.createTable(login, 'ml', True, TimeType.MILLIS)

    opts = WriterOptions(1000000, 5000, 30000, 10)
    writer = client.createWriter(login, 'ml', opts)

    print 'loading file ...'
    with open(filename,'r') as f:
        reader = csv.reader(f,delimiter='\t')

        for userId, itemId, rating, timestamp in reader:

            # entity to feature
            m = {'user_' + userId: [ColumnUpdate('movie', 'item_' + itemId,
                value=rating)]}
            client.update(writer, m)

            # write feature to entity
            im = {'item_' + itemId: [ColumnUpdate('movie', 'user_' + userId,
                value=rating)]}
            client.update(writer, im)

    client.closeWriter(writer)


def loadMoviesFile(filename):
    if client.tableExists(login, 'movies'):
        client.deleteTable(login, 'movies')
    client.createTable(login, 'movies', True, TimeType.MILLIS)

    opts = WriterOptions(1000000, 5000, 30000, 10)
    writer = client.createWriter(login, 'movies', opts)

    # movie id | movie title | release date | video release date |
```

```
# IMDb URL | unknown | Action | Adventure | Animation |
# Children's | Comedy | Crime | Documentary | Drama | Fantasy |
# Film-Noir | Horror | Musical | Mystery | Romance | Sci-Fi |
# Thriller | War | Western |

print 'loading file ...'
with open(filename,'r') as f:
    reader = csv.reader(f,delimiter='|')

    for rec in reader:
        # entity to feature
        m = {'item_' + rec[0] : [ColumnUpdate('movie', 'title',
            value='movie_' + rec[1])]}
        client.update(writer, m)

        # write feature to entity
        im = {'movie_' + rec[1] : [ColumnUpdate('movie', 'id',
            value='item_' + rec[0])]}
        client.update(writer, im)

    client.closeWriter(writer)
```

We'll run these interactively using the Python interpreter:

```
python -i recommendedMovies.py
>>>
>>> loadMLFile('/Data/movielens-100k/u.data')
loading file ...
>>> loadMoviesFile('/Data/movielens-100k/u.items')
loading file ...
>>>
```

This will populate our tables, *ml* and *movies*.

We can now scan to see all the ratings for a particular movie or user:

```
>>> common.printScan('ml','item_1','item_10')
item_1 movie user_1   5
item_1 movie user_10 4
item_1 movie user_101  3
item_1 movie user_102  3
item_1 movie user_106  4
item_1 movie user_108  4
...
>>> common.printScan('ml','user_1','user_10')
user_1 movie item_1   5
user_1 movie item_10 3
user_1 movie item_100  5
user_1 movie item_101  2
user_1 movie item_102  2
user_1 movie item_103  1
user_1 movie item_104  1
user_1 movie item_105  2
```

Now we can find the nearest users. Our implementation is as follows. First we retrieve all the movies a given user has rated. These constitute the user's *feature vector*. Because we have organized our table so that a user's ratings are all stored in the same row, we can fetch a user's feature vector using a single scan:

```
def kNearestNeighbors(table, rowId, k):

    topK = [(0.0,None)] * k

    # get features of rowId
    features = getFeatures(table, rowId)
    # print out movie titles
    print 'got features', \
        '\n'.join(['\t'.join((lookupMovie(x[0]),x[1])) for x in features.items()])
```

Next we'll get all the other users that have rated one of the movies rated by our given user. We rely on the fact that we've also stored movie-to-user relationships in our *ml* table. For this we'll use a `BatchScanner` and give to it all the movie IDs from our user's feature vector:

```
    # get other entities with at least one feature in common
    others = set([e.key.colQualifier for e in common.batchScan(table,
        features.keys())])
    others.remove(rowId)

    print 'got ', len(others), 'others'
```

We'll use *cosine similarity* to compare two users. This will return a value between 0 and 1. A 0 value means that two users have nothing in common, and 1 means that their feature vectors are identical.

Cosine similarity for two vectors A and B is defined as $\cos(\theta) = \dfrac{A \cdot B}{\|A\| \, \|B\|}$

A dot B is defined as:

$$A \cdot B = \sum_{i=1}^{n} A_i \times B_i$$

And $\|A\|$ is defined as:

$$\sqrt{\sum_{i=1}^{n} A_i^2}$$

Here's our implementation:

```
def cosineSim(a, b):

    maga = math.sqrt(sum([x * x for x in map(float, a.values())]))
```

```
        magb = math.sqrt(sum([x * x for x in map(float, b.values())]))
        d = 0.0

        for k,v in a.items():
            d += float(b.get(k, 0.0)) * float(v)

    return d / (maga * magb)
```

Now we'll get the full feature vector for each of the users returned. Once we have those, we can calculate the similarity score to our given user. We sort the other users in descending order of score and keep only the top *k*:

```
    # grab each entity's feature vector
    processed = 0
    for other in others:
        otherFeatures = getFeatures(table, other)

        d = cosineSim(features, otherFeatures)
        #print d, other

        topK.append((d,other,otherFeatures))
        processed += 1
        if processed % 100 == 0:
            print 'sorting topk'
            topK.sort(reverse=True)
            topK = topK[:k]

    topK.sort(reverse=True)
    topK = topK[:k]
    return topK
```

We'll run the kNearestNeighbors() method:

```
>>> neighbors = kNearestNeighbors('ml', 'user_456', 10)
got features movie_To Die For (1995) 3
movie_Better Off Dead... (1985)  3
movie_Speed (1994) 2
movie_Young Frankenstein (1974)  4
movie_Maltese Falcon, The (1941) 4
...
got  940 others
sorting topk
```

Now we have our nearest neighbors, their similarity scores, and their feature vectors. We'll print out just the list of scores and neighbor names:

```
>>> for n in neighbors:
...     print n[0], n[1]
...
0.507011769831 user_59
0.484341141469 user_276
0.472683044333 user_846
0.467597644954 user_916
```

```
0.464106214554 user_339
0.46275022327 user_561
0.46052254186 user_94
0.457961659774 user_429
0.452115992772 user_387
0.450752649362 user_870
```

This is an example of *nearest neighbor search*, simply finding the nearest neighbors. This might be useful in itself; for example, if we were building a social network for movie lovers, this algorithm would help us build a *recommendation engine* that recommends similar users with whom we might want to communicate, because they appear to rate movies similarly.

If we were interested in predicting a particular attribute or property of a user, we could use the nearest neighbors to make our prediction by averaging the attribute or property values of the nearest neighbors and using that average as our prediction for the entity of interest. This is known as *nearest neighbor classification*.

We can go further and use a variation of this nearest neighbor classifier to build a different recommendation engine that suggests movies to our given user, by predicting the rating our given user would give a movie based on the ratings her nearest neighbors gave to the movie.

For example, if we want to estimate the rating that a new user, user_456, will give to the movie *Pulp Fiction*, having not watched it yet, we use the top k entities that are most similar to user_456 and average the rating that those users gave to the movie to come up with our estimate:

```python
def recommendedScore(nearest, movie):
    item = lookupMovieId(movie)  ❶
    score = 0.0
    matched = 0
    for n in nearest:
        items = n[2]
        if items.has_key(item):
            matched += 1
            score += float(items[item])
    # average
    if matched > 0:
        score = score / matched
    return score
```

❶ Convert the movie name to movie ID.

If the average rating that the top k most similar users gave to a movie was 4 stars out of 5, we might elect then to recommend to a user that she watch the movie:

```
>>> recommendedScore(neighbors, 'movie_Pulp Fiction (1994)')
4.9
```

user_456 actually rated *Pulp Fiction* a 5. Let's look at a movie user_456 rated low, Jaws 2:

```
>>> recommendedScore(neighbors, 'movie_Jaws 2 (1978)')
3.0
```

These scan operations are designed to be fast enough to return answers in time for some interactive applications. Depending on the data set, features will likely need to be tuned to minimize the number of candidates examined at query time. We could also decide to simply update this table throughout the day and at night precalculate a list of movies to recommend to each user by using a MapReduce job, storing this list of recommendations in Accumulo for fast lookup as users visit our web application.

Similar operations can be used to cluster users into natural groups, again using similarity metrics to compare feature vectors. Other types classifiers can also be trained on these feature vectors to produce models appropriate for scoring new instances in real time to predict class or some value of interest.

In machine-learning applications in which Accumulo is already a part of the architecture, it could be used to provide low-latency, high-throughput access to static global resources, even though some other more lightweight distributed key-value stores may perform better.[1] In this case Accumulo could be used to store and update model probabilities, especially when the model is larger than fits comfortably in memory even in a distributed cache such as memcached.

Accumulo may be more suitable than some other key-value stores because the use of iterators could make incrementing model weights very efficient, as long as the application is more interested in incrementing weights more often than reading weights. If any locality is associated with weights, it could be exploited to write and scan weights in batches, resulting in better throughput than reading and writing each individually.

Approximating Relational and SQL Database Properties

Accumulo is a nonrelational database, meaning it doesn't provide built-in support for joins, cross-row or cross-table transactions, or referential integrity. Similarly, Accumulo does not implement SQL operations over tables. However, Accumulo can be made to behave more like a relational or SQL database in some ways if desired.

Schema Constraints

One thing that some other databases do is to enforce a schema on inserted data. If a particular row doesn't conform to the specified schema of a table, the insert fails. In

---

1 See Jimmy Lin et al., "Low-Latency, High-Throughput Access to Static Global Resources within the Hadoop Framework" (*http://bit.ly/lin_et_al*), 2009.

contrast, Accumulo is designed to support building tables with widely varying structure across rows. The set of columns and value types in a table are defined only by the actual data. This requires applications to handle missing columns and values of any type or size. In practice the code used to insert data is therefore more closely coupled with the code used to query the data.

By requiring that inserts conform to a particular schema, applications can be less closely coupled and can be simplified. Accumulo can be made to apply constraints to tables that are examined at insert time. Users can write a `Constraint` class that requires each column name to be one of a specified set, and can also apply type and size limitations to values stored. Mutations that fail these constraints will be rejected.

See "Constraints" on page 201.

SQL Operations

Although Accumulo doesn't support SQL, a few SQL operations are trivial to implement using the Accumulo API. Besides implementing these capabilities in your own client, Accumulo also integrates with Apache Pig and Apache Hive, which can perform some SQL operations. See "Apache Pig" on page 248 on how to do operations like joins, group by, and order by on Accumulo using the Apache Pig scripting language and "Apache Hive" on page 242 for using Apache Hive with Accumulo to execute SQL queries.

SELECT

Also known as *projection*, the SQL `SELECT` clause is used to select a set of columns from a table. By default, scanners retrieve all available columns, even those the user may not know about. Scanners can be configured to retrieve only a particular set of columns using the `fetchColumn()` and `fetchColumnFamily()` methods.

WHERE

Also known as *selection*, the SQL `WHERE` clause is used to select a subset of rows from a table. Accumulo scanners can be configured to scan over only a subset of rows by specifying a range of row IDs. Similarly, applications can use secondary indexes to identify sets of row IDs that can be combined using set operations to identify a final set of row IDs that satisfy the logic of a `WHERE` clause. This set of row IDs can be passed to a `BatchScanner` to retrieve the full rows from a record table.

Projection and selection can be combined by calling the `fetchColumn()` or `fetchColumnFamily()` methods on the `BatchScanner` used to retrieve the final set of original records.

Most relational databases generate statistics about indexes and data in tables as the data is inserted. These statistics are used by query planners to optimize data retrieval.

For example, if we were querying for records containing the value *book* in one field and the value *$10* in another field, we could consult the statistics table to see which value appears less frequently. If the value *book* appears in only a small number of records and the value *$10* appears in many, we can plan our query out by first fetching those record IDs that contain the value *book*, and then filtering that subset to find records that match the second criterion.

There is no reason that similar statistics could not be stored in Accumulo. The `Sum mingCombiner` can come in handy for updating counts in a statistics table.

JOIN, GROUP BY, and ORDER BY

Because Accumulo is designed to answer user requests in subsecond times, and to scale to very large amounts of data, the operations that can be performed at query time are limited to things that can be done very quickly, despite the size of the data. `SELECT` and `WHERE` operations are among those.

`JOIN`, `GROUP BY`, and `ORDER BY` are more complex and require significant resources to perform on large amounts of data. Recently, several new systems have emerged to aid in performing these operations at scale, namely MPP databases such as Vertica, Greenplum, and Asterdata, as well as Cloudera's Impala (*http://bit.ly/clou dera_impala*) and Facebook's Presto (*http://prestodb.io/*), which are based in part on Google's Dremel (*http://bit.ly/dremel_paper*) and Tenzing (*http://bit.ly/tenzing_paper*) projects. These work by performing SQL operations in parallel quickly enough to be interactive.

Accumulo keeps data in tables sorted by keys at all times but does not sort data on the fly. Users of Accumulo tend to materialize transformations of original data sets in several tables and perform simple lookups on these tables in subsecond times, rather than computing new transformations on the fly while users wait. In general, operations that require sorting and transforming all the data tend to be performed using MapReduce.

Accumulo doesn't provide built-in support for joins, but there are several strategies for joining two tables.

Strategies for Joins

Although Accumulo doesn't provide SQL support, there are a few ways in which tables can be joined on the fly. This may not be tractable for very large tables, but in some cases it is feasible.

Joins and sorts are expensive operations. Relational databases are optimized to perform this kind of work on tables at query time. Accumulo tables can be very large, so rather than performing joins and alternate sort orders at query time, you may consider trying to precompute these joined or sorted tables ahead of time, maintaining them as the original table is updated so users aren't waiting for results.

Of course not all types of joins and sorts can be anticipated. For truly ad-hoc joins, sorts, and aggregations, frameworks like Apache Hive or Cloudera's Impala can be used. See "Apache Hive" on page 242 for details on using Hive with Accumulo tables. There is work taking place to make Impala work with Accumulo also.

The trade-off when using these tools is that, in order to make these operations fast enough to be used interactively, as many of the machines as possible are involved in the operation. This reduces the number of concurrent users that can be querying the system at any given time when compared to the number of users that can be performing scans against precomputed Accumulo tables.

The cost of performing a join at query time depends on which parts of the Accumulo key are being joined. Estimates of the cost of joining two tables in different ways follow:

RowID to RowID

When two tables are to be joined based on the row ID of each table, performing a join is a simple matter of scanning both tables once simultaneously and returning rows that appear in both.

The number of comparisons that needs to be done to accomplish this is on the order of the size of the two tables, or O(a+b) in algorithm performance parlance.

When we write O(something) we are using *big-O* notation. The definition of big-O is that the big-O of a particular function is the number of steps required to accomplish the function expressed in terms of n where n is the number of input items, times a constant factor. The term representing the constant factor is omitted when big-O notation is written.

So, for example, if a function for finding an item in a list requires $2*n$ steps (which would be a slow search algorithm), we would simply write O(n) when using big-O notation. The constant factor 2 is omitted.

This helps computer scientists focus on the relative efficiency of an algorithm as the number of input items increases. The effect of the constant factors tends to diminish as the other parts of the function apply to input data.

We should note here too that big-O notation describes the worst-case runtime complexity of an algorithm. Other letters are used to describe best-time and expected or average-time complexity.

Value to row ID

When joining the values from one table, *A*, with the row IDs of another table, *B*, it is best to scan the values of *A* and to look up whether *B* contains a row ID for that value.

The number of comparisons required to perform this join is O(a * log2(b)), where a is the size of table *A* and b is the size of table *B*.

Value to value

If two tables are to be joined on their values, it is more efficient to build an index of one of the tables and perform a value-to–rowID join by scanning the values of one and doing lookups for each value in the other. This is because the number of comparisons required to join two tables' unsorted values is O(a*b), whereas the comparisons it takes to build an index of one is O(b*log2(b)) and building the index and doing the join, O(b*log2(b) + a*log2(b)), is less than O(a*b).

These runtime estimates make it clear that it is not infeasible to perform the occasional join of two tables even when data sets are large, but that these joins are often still too slow to be performed interactively while users wait. The tools mentioned in the previous section are specifically designed to perform SQL operations at scale with the goal of being fast enough for interactive queries, typically from seconds to a few minutes.

GROUP BY and ORDER BY

GROUP BY and ORDER BY can be performed often in one MapReduce job.

In some cases, Accumulo can apply the functions typically used in a GROUP BY query using iterators, provided that the data is already sorted in the desired fashion in a table. Accumulo supports applying iterators at scan time, allowing aggregated views of the data to be created on the fly as data is read from disk and sent to clients.

An example of this is when a table contains a record of individual events stored under some set of identifiers and a scan applying a combining iterator combines the individual events into an aggregated value. Such events might be individual orders, with the product name stored in the key and the amount of the order in the value.

Internals

This chapter describes the internal workings of Accumulo. Although Accumulo can be used without a knowledge of its internals, developing an increased understanding of how Accumulo works will make it easier to understand and make decisions about how best to interact with Accumulo.

Tablet Server

Accumulo tables are split into contiguous ranges called *tablets*. Each tablet is assigned to a *tablet server*, also known as a *tserver*, that is responsible for all reads and writes for the tablet. Each tablet server can be assigned hundreds or even thousands of tablets. If an Accumulo instance reaches well over 1,000 tablets per server, it is time to start making adjustments: merging tablets, deleting old data, rethinking the table design, or increasing the size of the cluster.

An Accumulo instance typically runs one tablet server per slave node (for example, each server that is running an HDFS DataNode). A tablet server registers with an Accumulo instance by obtaining a lock in ZooKeeper. If a tablet server loses or is unable to monitor its lock, it will kill itself. It is important for Accumulo to be able to keep track of properly functioning tablet servers and to automatically shut down unresponsive tablet servers in order to ensure that a tablet is never assigned to more than one tablet server. ZooKeeper locks assist this process.

The following sections describe many of the operations tablet servers perform on their tablets.

Discussion of Log-Structured Merge Tree

The reading and writing for an individual tablet are governed by a log-structured merge-tree approach[1] as interpreted in the BigTable design. This technique is designed to take best advantage of hardware that performs fast sequential writes and is most useful when much more data is written than is read.

When reading or writing new data, the Accumulo client library first locates which tablet should contain the data and which tablet server is hosting that tablet. This is accomplished by looking up the location of the root table, which contains information about the tablets of the metadata table. Once the desired metadata tablet and its location are read from the root tablet, the desired data tablet and its location are looked up in the metadata tablet. The client library caches tablet locations that it has found previously, so when data is looked up again it may be able to skip one or more of these steps.

Starting in Accumulo 1.6, the root tablet is considered to be in a separate root table that is never split. In earlier versions, the root tablet is considered to be part of the metadata table. This change does not affect how the client interacts with Accumulo, but it simplifies Accumulo's internal implementation.

Write Path

Within a tablet, incoming writes are committed to an on-disk write-ahead log. (Write-ahead logging can optionally be disabled per table, at the risk of losing data if a single tablet server goes down with data in memory that has not made it onto disk.) The write-ahead log is not sorted by key, because new data is appended to it. In Accumulo 1.5.0 and later, the write-ahead log is stored directly in HDFS. The number of replicas required for the write-ahead logfiles can be configured. In Accumulo 1.4 a custom logging process writes to local disk instead. The write-ahead logs are manually replicated onto the disk of one remote server in addition to local disk.

---

1 See Patrick O'Neil, Edward Cheng, Dieter Gawlick, and Elizabeth O'Neil. "The log-structured merge-tree (LSM-tree)." *Acta Inf.* 33, 4 (1996), 351–385.

Once the new data is confirmed to be on disk, it is inserted into a sorted in-memory structure. At this point, the write is successful and the data will available for reads (Figure 10-1).

When the resource manager determines that a tablet server's allocated memory is becoming full, it selects some tablets for *minor compaction*, which means flushing data from memory to disk. Successful minor compaction results in a new sorted HDFS file associated with the tablet.

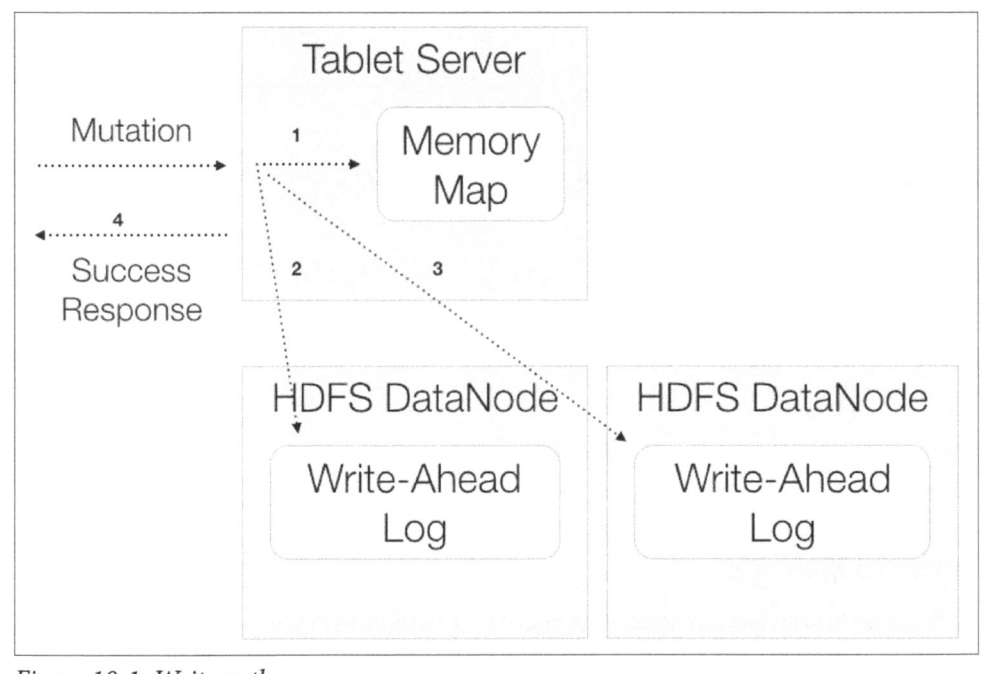

Figure 10-1. Write path

Read Path

Within a tablet, reads consist of constructing a merged view of sorted in-memory and on-disk structures (Figure 10-2). The on-disk structures are HDFS files associated with the tablet and do not include write-ahead logfiles, which are unsorted.

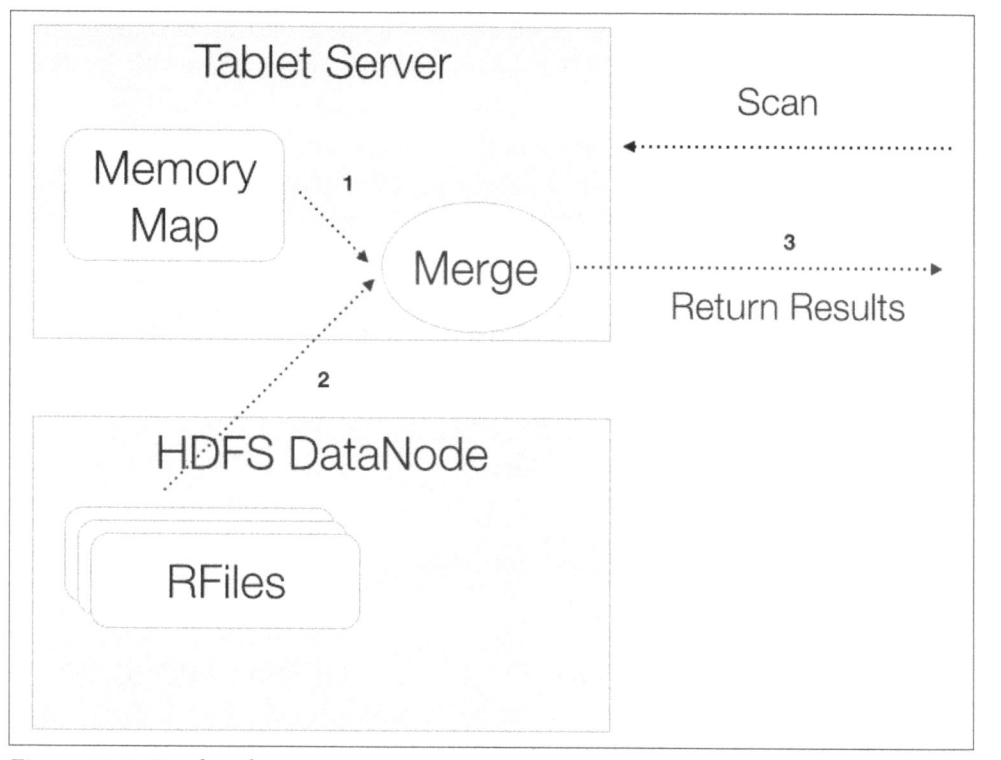

Figure 10-2. Read path

Resource Manager

Each tablet server has a resource manager that maintains thread pools for minor and major compaction, tablet splits, migration and assignment, and a read-ahead pipeline. The sizes of these thread pools are configurable via appropriate properties, with the exception of the split and assignment thread pools, which each contain a single thread:

```
tserver.compaction.major.concurrent.max
tserver.compaction.minor.concurrent.max
tserver.migrations.concurrent.max
tserver.readahead.concurrent.max
tserver.metadata.readahead.concurrent.max
```

Minor compaction

Minor compaction is the process of flushing data that is sorted in memory onto a sorted file on disk (Figure 10-3).

The resource manager includes a memory manager that periodically evaluates the current states of the server's assigned tablets and returns a list of tablets that should be minor-compacted. The memory manager is pluggable, with its class being configured by `tserver.memory.manager`.

The default memory manager is the `LargestFirstMemoryManager`. If the total memory usage of all the tablets on the tablet server exceeds a dynamic threshold, or if the time of a tablet's last write is far enough in the past, a tablet will be selected for minor compaction. The threshold is adjusted over time so that the highest memory usage before a minor compaction is between 80 and 90 percent of the maximum memory allowed for the tablet server, `tserver.memory.maps.max`. If too many minor compactions are already queued, it will not select additional tablets for minor compaction until the queue has decreased. The number of minor-compaction tasks allowed in the queue is twice the number that can be executed concurrently, which is controlled by the global `tserver.compaction.minor.concurrent.max` configuration property . The per-table `table.compaction.minor.idle` property controls how long a tablet can be idle before becoming a candidate for minor compaction. The memory manager selects the tablet with the highest combination of memory usage and idle time— memory * 2^(minutes idle / 15)—or, if memory is not too full, the idle tablet with the highest combination of these.

If a tablet has more than a specified number of write-ahead logfiles (`table.compaction.minor.logs.threshold`), it will be minor compacted outside of the memory management system. This is to reduce recovery time in the case of tablet server failure.

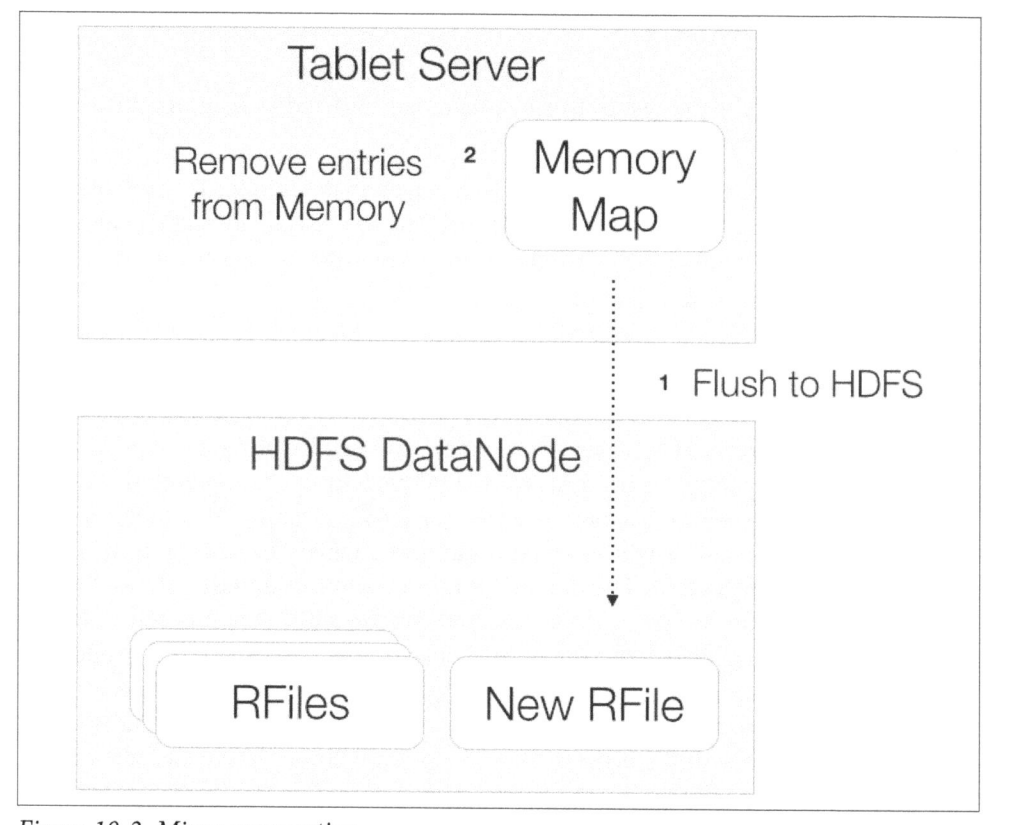

Figure 10-3. Minor compaction

Major compaction

When there are too many files for a tablet, read performance will suffer because each lookup must perform a merged read of all the sorted files and in-memory structures for the tablet. For this reason, each tablet server has a thread pool devoted to merging together files within a tablet. This process of merging together some or all of a tablet's files is called *major compaction* (Figure 10-4). If all of a tablet's files are merged into a single file, it is called a *full major compaction*. The full major compaction is noted as a special case because additional cleaning up of obsolete data is possible when all of a tablet's existing data is being rewritten.

You can request a full major compaction for a table through the shell or the API. The compaction can be restricted to a range of tablets specified by start and end rows. A user-initiated compaction can also be canceled.

Major compactions are also initiated automatically by tablet servers. Tablet servers evaluate whether files need to be merged periodically. How long the tablet servers wait between evaluations is controlled by the global `tserver.compac tion.major.delay` property.

In Accumulo 1.6 and later, the strategy for performing major compactions is pluggable and is configured per table with the `table.majc.compaction.strategy` property.

The per-table `table.compaction.major.ratio` property influences the tablet server's decision whether to merge files and which files are merged. To determine whether a tablet's files are in need of major compaction, the tablet server first sorts the files by size. If the size of the largest file times the compaction ratio is less than or equal to the sum of the sizes of all the files, the set of files is merged into a single file. If this is not true, the largest file is removed from the set and the remaining files are evaluated. This is repeated until a set of files is selected for compaction or until there is only one file left in the set. This algorithm is chosen to reduce the number of times data is rewritten through major compaction. Effectively, it tries to compact small files into significantly larger files that won't need to be compacted as often.

There is a maximum for the number of files a single major compaction thread is allowed to open, `tserver.compaction.major.thread.files.open.max`. If a set of files selected for major compaction contains more files than this maximum, the compaction will merge the N-smallest files, where N is the number of files that are allowed. The remaining uncompacted files will eventually be compacted in multiple passes.

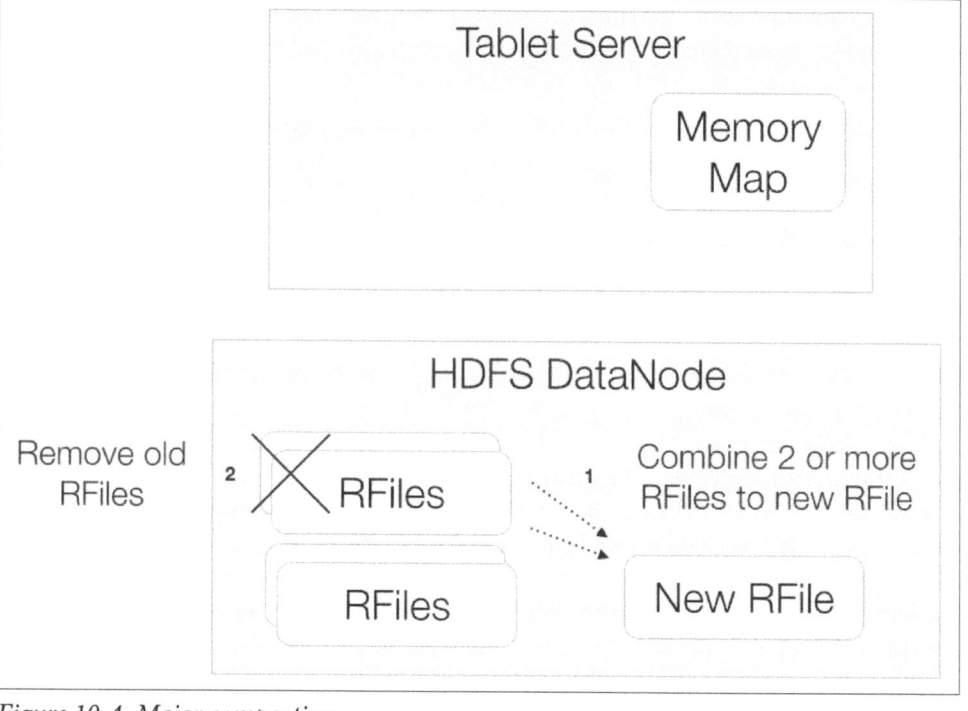

Figure 10-4. Major compaction

Merging minor compaction

The major compaction algorithm can result in a large number of files as the tablet size grows. This can reduce read performance and increase memory usage requirements for the tablet server. There is a per-table property that provides a hard maximum on the number of files per tablet, `table.file.max`. When a tablet reaches this number of files, the tablet server will not create new files via minor compaction. Instead, the tablet server will choose the tablet's smallest file, and merge the data from this file and the in-memory structure into a new file (Figure 10-5). This process is called a *merging minor compaction*.

 Consider adjustments to the `table.file.max` property carefully. Making it low can increase read performance while decreasing write performance. The performance of bulk-loading data is not affected.

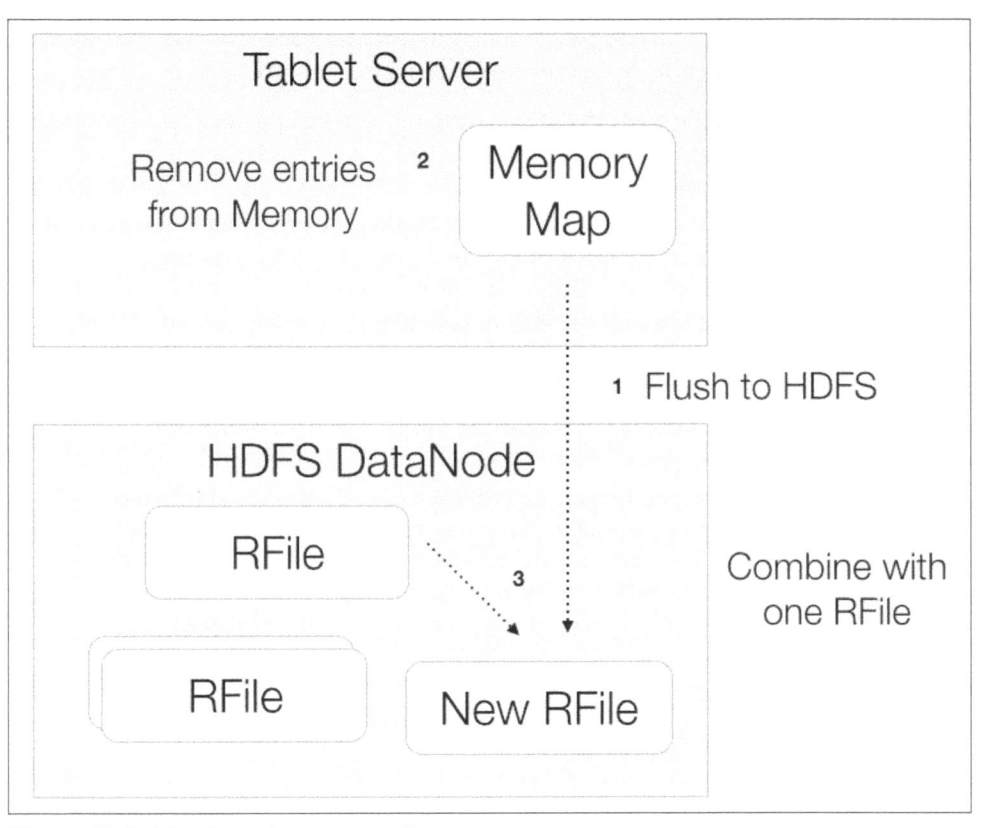

Figure 10-5. Merging minor compaction

Splits

When a tablet's size reaches a configurable threshold, the tablet server will decide to split it into two tablets (Figure 10-6). Splitting tablets into smaller pieces allows Accumulo to spread load more evenly across tablet servers. Tablets are split on row boundaries only, so that a row is never spread across more than a single tablet. The threshold for tablet size is set in bytes via `table.split.threshold`. Conceptually, the server must create two new tablets, split the original tablet's data appropriately between the two new tablets, and update the metadata table with information about the two new tablets, removing information about the original tablet as needed.

To make splitting a lightweight metadata operation that does not require rewriting the original tablet's data, the names of a tablet's files are stored in the metadata table. This allows files to be associated with more than one tablet. When reading data from its files, a tablet restricts its reads to the range of keys in its own domain. When a tablet is split into two new tablets, both of the new tablets will use the files of the original tablet. Splitting takes priority over compaction so that a tablet that is growing very quickly can be split into as many tablets as needed before the new tablets start compacting their files, which would otherwise be an ingest bottleneck.

Splitting requires multiple rows in the metadata table to be updated. This means that it is not inherently an atomic operation. To achieve fault tolerance during splitting, the tablet server performs the following process. First the tablet is closed so that no new writes are accepted. Then three writes are made to the metadata table: the tablet is made smaller and is marked as splitting; a new tablet is added; and the original tablet's splitting marks are removed. The tablet server swaps the new tablets for the old tablet in its online tablet list, and the master is informed of the new tablets. If the tablet server goes down during the splitting process, a new tablet server will pick up the splitting process where it left off. The new server determines that splitting must be continued if a tablet it is assigned has splitting marks in the metadata table.

 Splitting a table into enough tablets is essential to being able to take advantage of the parallelism of the system. By default, a table's tablets will be spread evenly across the tablet servers. For some applications it is better not to leave the split points to chance. Split points can be specified when a table is created, or added to an existing table.

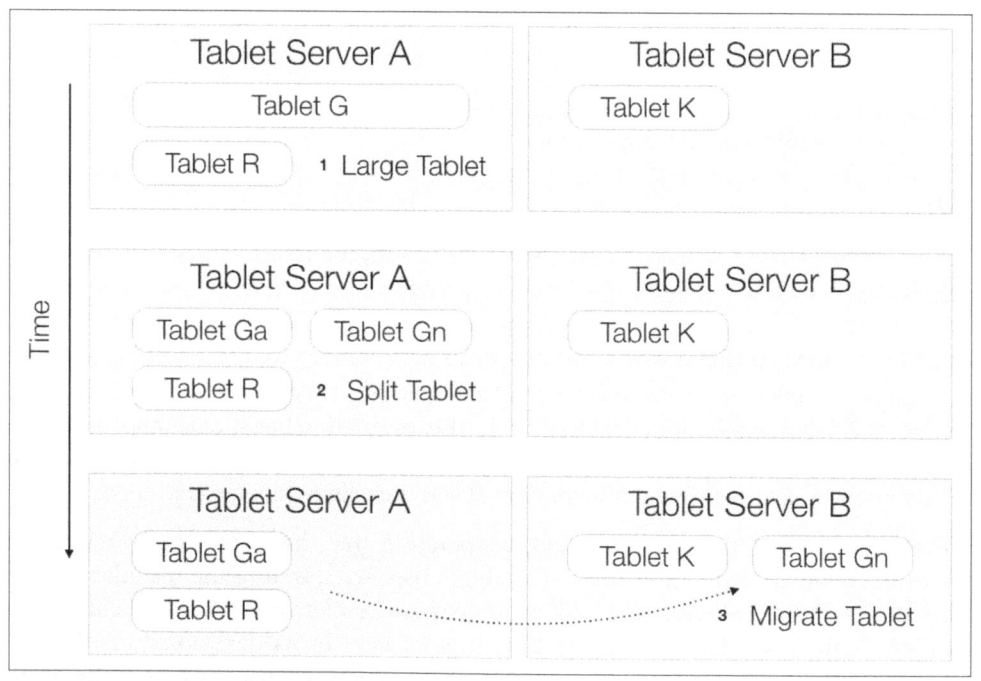

Figure 10-6. Tablet splitting process

Write-Ahead Logs

Write-ahead logs are used to guarantee data integrity in the presence of hardware or software failures. Because each tablet contains an in-memory map that stores recently written data, this data must be persisted to disk first to ensure that it isn't lost. A single write-ahead logfile is only written to by a single tablet server, but log entries for all tablets assigned to that server can be intermingled in the same logfile. Bulk ingest does not utilize the write-ahead log or the in-memory map for a tablet, because this involves introducing new sorted files to a tablet.

The logging mechanisms are different in different versions of Accumulo. Accumulo 1.4 and earlier used custom logging processes. Each slave node would typically be configured to run one tablet server process and one logger process. When a tablet server received new data, it would log the data to the local logger process, if present, and to one remote logger process. It would send data to two remote loggers if a local logger was not present.

In Accumulo 1.5 and later, data is logged directly to a file in HDFS, so that separate logger processes are not needed. The tablet server waits until the data is replicated appropriately by HDFS, and then it proceeds with inserting the data into the in-memory map for the appropriate tablet. The HDFS replication of write-ahead logfiles is controlled with the `tserver.wal.replication` property. If this property is set to 0, the HDFS default replication is used. Setting this property to 2 will provide similar performance and data protection to Accumulo 1.4. Setting it to 3 will provide even better data protection, ensuring that data is written to three different disks before it is committed to Accumulo. However, this will use more disk I/O resources when writing and can affect ingest performance. It is not recommended that the replication of write-ahead logfiles be set to 1, because a single server failure could result in data loss.

Recovery

Like regular data files, the write-ahead logfiles containing data for a given tablet are written to the metadata table row for that tablet. If a tablet server is assigned a tablet that has write-ahead log entries in the metadata table, the tablet server will conduct a log recovery before bringing the tablet online (Figure 10-7). Because the logs contain unsorted data for multiple tablets, the files are first sorted so that servers don't need to read through irrelevant data to recover the data for a single tablet. Sorting of logfiles is done by a work queue managed in ZooKeeper. The master submits files to this work queue when it reassigns tablets that have write-ahead log entries. Each tablet server monitors the work queue for new files that need to be sorted and maintains a thread pool for sorting tasks. The size of the thread pool is controlled with the `tserver.recovery.concurrent.max` property.

A single tablet server will win the race to grab a file from the work queue and begin sorting it. It reads a large chunk of the file into memory and writes it out sorted by entry type, tablet, and original order in the file. It repeats this process, creating a new file for each chunk that fits in memory, until the entire file is sorted. The size of the sorted chunks defaults to 200 MB and can be adjusted by changing the `tser ver.sort.buffer.size` property. A typical write-ahead logfile size is 1 GB, controlled by `tserver.walog.max.size`. Under normal circumstances a tablet will only have one or two write-ahead logfiles, so with the default settings there may be 5 to 10 sorted file chunks to read during data recovery.

In addition to logged data, the file contains minor compaction start and finish markers and specifies a concise tablet ID for each tablet referenced. The usual identifier for a tablet is its key extent (start row exclusive, end row inclusive), but a short ID is assigned in the write-ahead logs so that it can be specified in fewer bytes. Once the sorting is completed, the tablet server that will host the tablet begins recovering the data for that tablet. It conducts a merged read of all the sorted log chunks that can contain data for the tablet. First it finds the tablet ID, then it uses the ID to find the last minor compaction that succeeded for the tablet. This determines which log entries must be replayed. Once the tablet server has replayed the log entries, it minor-compacts the tablet. Currently, a tablet server only recovers one tablet at a time, because newly assigned tablets are only loaded one at a time.

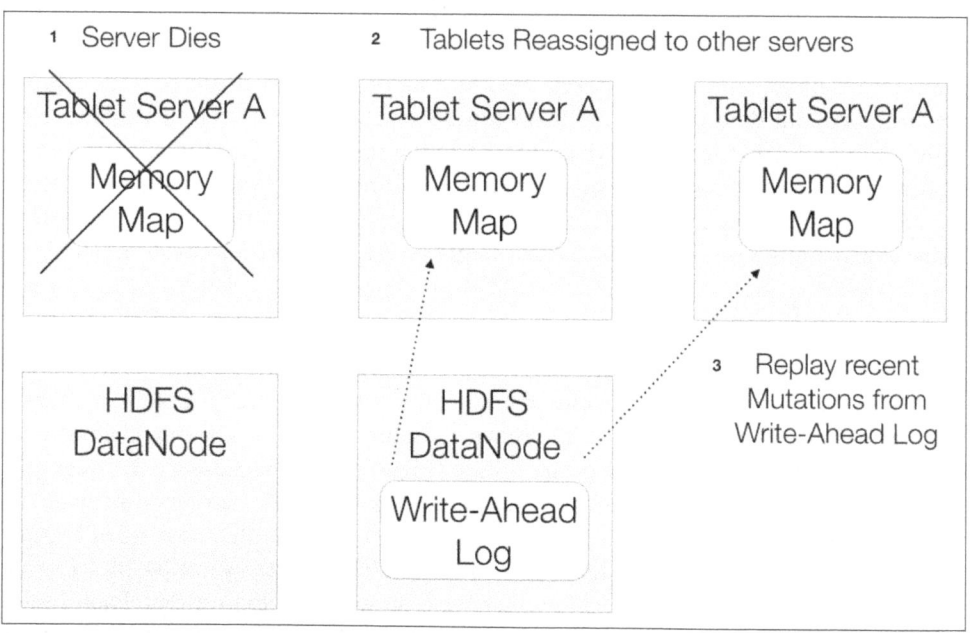

Figure 10-7. Recovery from tablet server failure

File formats

BigTable's SSTable file format (*http://bit.ly/bigtable_paper*) is described as a sequence of compressed data blocks followed by a block index. Both the data blocks and the index consist of key-value pairs sorted by key, with the index containing the first key of each data block (or perhaps a smaller equivalent key) paired with the location in the file of the beginning of that data block. When the file is opened, the index is read into memory. To locate a key in the file, a binary search is performed on the index to find the location of the data block containing the desired key. Then this data block is read from disk and scanned sequentially until the desired key is reached.

The file format used by Accumulo is the RFile, which stands for relative key file. RFiles have a similar structure to SSTables with a few additional optimizations. The size of the compressed blocks in an RFile is controlled per table with the `table.file.compress.blocksize` property, which defaults to 100 KB. This size is prior to compression.

 Note that compressed blocks (~100 KB) are not the same as HDFS blocks (128 MB or more). There are many compressed blocks per HDFS block.

RFile optimizations

A single-index approach doesn't work well for very large files because as the file size grows, so must the size of the index. Because the index is read into memory when the file is opened, it will take longer to open larger files. This can be mitigated somewhat by increasing the compressed block size to decrease the size of the index, but then lookup times will also increase because the data blocks are scanned sequentially when looking up keys. To support very large files, Accumulo 1.4 introduces a multilevel index. The `table.file.compress.blocksize.index` property, defaulting to 128 KB prior to compression, sets the maximum size of an index block. When a file is written, the index to the beginnings of the compressed data blocks is accumulated in memory. When the index reaches its maximum size, a *level 0* index block is written out, a *level 1* index is started with a pointer to the level 0 index block, and a new level 0 index block is started with pointers to data blocks. When all the data has been written out, any remaining index blocks are written to the file. When the file is opened, only the highest level index must be read into memory. There is no limit to the number of index levels, but a two-level index is sufficient for files in the tens of gigabytes with the default settings. See Figure 10-8 for an illustration of the on-disk data layout for a two-level index.

Accumulo 1.5 features an additional optimization to reduce the time needed to sequentially scan a data block. Once a given data block has been accessed once, it is cached in memory. When the data block has been accessed twice, the RFile begins building a dynamic, ephemeral index by storing the key and pointer corresponding to the midpoint of the block. As the block continues to be used, when it is accessed 2^N times, N additional keys will be added to the ephemeral index.

Relative key encoding

Within a compressed block, Accumulo performs compression of identical portions and identical prefixes of portions of consecutive keys. A single byte is used to encode whether the row, column family, column qualifier, column visibility, and/or timestamp match those of the previous key. Of the remaining three bits in that byte, one is used to indicate whether any prefix compression is present for the key, another is used as the deletion flag for the key, and the last is unused. Prefix compression is only available in Accumulo 1.5 and later. If prefix compression is present, an additional byte is used to indicate whether the row, column family, column qualifier, and/or column visibility have a common prefix as the previous key, and whether the timestamp is expressed as a difference from the previous timestamp. A common prefix must be at least two bytes. The remaining three bits of the prefix compression byte are unused.

If a portion of the key matches that portion of the previous key identically, as indicated in the first byte, no additional information needs to be written for that portion. If a portion of the key has a common prefix with that portion of the previous key, the length of the prefix is written followed by the remaining bytes for that portion of the key. In the case of the timestamp, there is no prefix length, but the difference from the previous key is written. If a portion of the key has no common prefix with the previous key, the entire portion is written.

Locality groups

To enable greater intermingling of different types of data in a single Accumulo table, RFiles also support locality groups. This feature allows sets of column families to be grouped together on disk, which can result in better compression. It also allows applications to tune a table's disk layout to better suit its access patterns. For example, if two columns are always queried together, the columns could be put in a locality group. Alternatively, if one column contains very large data, such as image files, and another column contains much smaller data, such as text, these columns could be put in different locality groups to improve the lookup times when only text data is retrieved.

BigTable maintains separate SSTables for each locality group, whereas RFiles store locality groups in different sections of the same file. This makes the number of files Accumulo must manage independent of the number of locality groups or column families.

Unlike BigTable, Accumulo does not require column families to be specified before data can be inserted into those families. To accommodate the use of unspecified column families, Accumulo introduces the concept of a default locality group. All columns are stored in the default locality group unless configured otherwise. Locality group mappings can be added or changed at any time, but will only take effect for new files written. RFiles are immutable, so files remain in the locality groupings that were in effect when the files were created. When new files are created through minor or major compaction, they will use the newest locality group configuration.

Figure 10-8 illustrates how the file layout is modified to make accessing data within a locality group efficient.

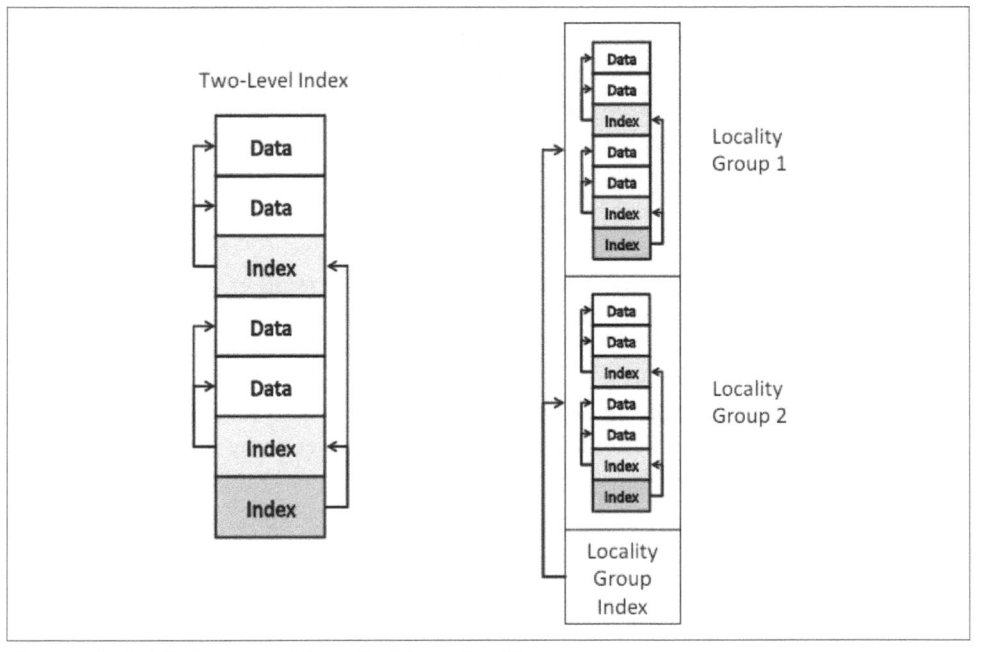

Figure 10-8. File layout with and without locality groups

Bloom filters

Bloom filters are data structures used to help determine whether a set of elements contains a given element. Accumulo can use bloom filters to determine whether a given key might be found in a file, or whether that file does not need to be searched for the key.

Bloom filters can optionally be enabled per table. The properties governing the bloom filter configuration are of the form `table.bloom.*`.

If enabled, a bloom filter layer maintains a set of bloom filters for each file. Each key in a file is hashed with a number of hash functions, and the resulting hashes are represented as a bit vector. A bloom filter is the OR of the bit vectors for each key in a file.[1]

When looking up a key in the file, the bloom filter can be used to determine if the file can contain the key, or definitively does not contain the key (Figure 10-9). This check can be performed more efficiently than seeking for the key in the file, especially if the bloom filter has already been loaded into memory.

By default, the bloom filter layer hashes the row portion of the key, so it can be used to determine if a particular row appears in the file. However, it can be configured to hash the row and column family, or the row, column family, and column qualifier. This is controlled by setting `table.bloom.key.functor` to one of the three classes one of three classes from the `org.apache.accumulo.core.file.keyfunctor` package: `RowFunctor`, `ColumnFamilyFunctor`, and `ColumnQualifierFunctor`.

 Because seeks are specified for Accumulo in terms of a `Range` of keys, and not a specific key, the bloom filter layer will only provide improvements when the `Range` seeked only covers a single row in the case of the default `RowFunctor`, or a single row and column family in the case of the `ColumnFamilyFunctor`, or a single row, column family and column qualifier in the case of the `ColumnQualifierFunctor`.

---

1 For general information about bloom filters, see Burton H. Bloom, "Space/time trade-offs in hash coding with allowable errors" (*http://bit.ly/bloom_cacm_1970*), *Communications of the ACM* 13, 7(July 1970), 422-426.

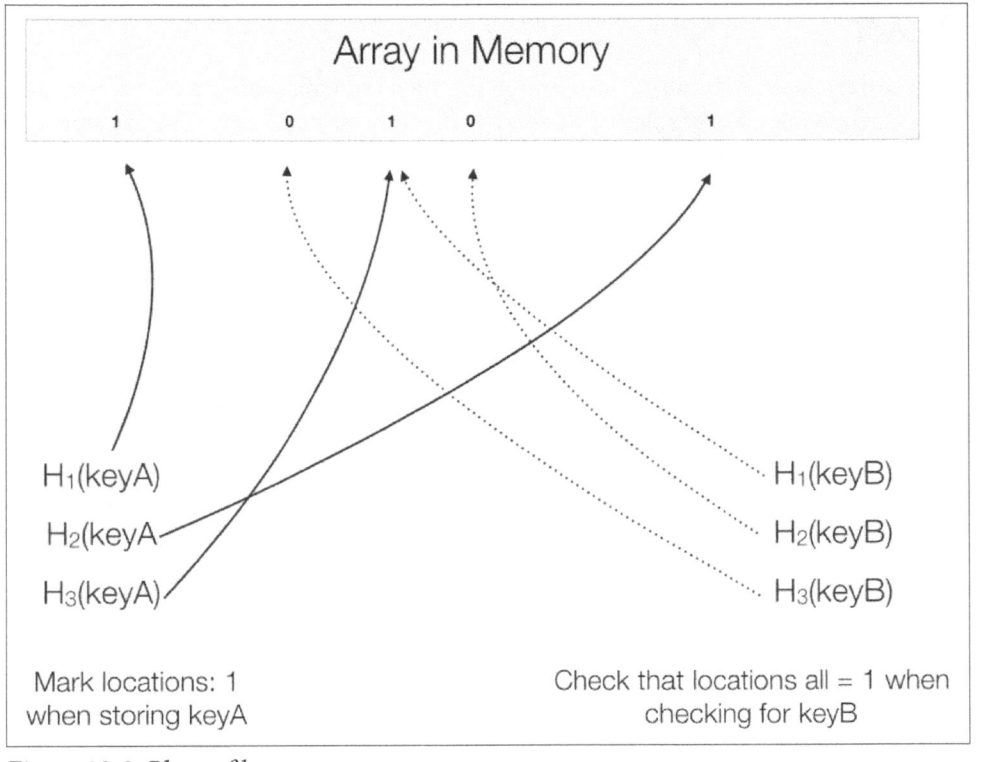

Figure 10-9. Bloom filter

Caching

Each tablet server process holds two `BlockCache` instances, one for data blocks and one for index blocks. These are caches in memory of individual compressed blocks of Accumulo RFiles. Though compressed on disk, the blocks are cached uncompressed in memory and take up JVM heap. The size of each cache is specified in bytes with the `tserver.cache.data.size` and `tserver.cache.index.size` properties.

When the amount of data stored in a cache exceeds its specified maximum size, the cache will evict its least recently accessed blocks. The cache roughly reserves a third of its size for blocks that have been accessed a single time and two-thirds of its size for blocks that have been accessed more than once. Blocks never need to be invalidated in a cache, because Accumulo's RFiles are immutable.

The caches maintain counts including number of cache hits (block reads where the block was found in the cache) and total number of block reads, and Accumulo tracks this information and displays it on its monitor page.

Master

The master's main function is to monitor the status of tablet servers and tablets and to perform tablet assignment and load balancing as necessary. The master can remove the ZooKeeper locks of unresponsive tablet servers, forcing those tablet server processes to stop. The master also handles administrative operations requested by users, such as creating tables or altering system or table configuration.

To find tablets that need to be assigned, the master continuously scans the metadata table. Each tablet's state is determined based on the loc, future, and last entries for that tablet in the metadata table. If a tablet is not in its desired state—for example, if it is unassigned or is assigned to a dead tablet server—the master will assign the tablet by setting its future entry in the metadata table and by telling a selected tablet server that it should host the tablet. A load balancer is used to select a server for the tablet.

The master uses tablet server status information to balance the load of tablets across tablet servers. If there are active tablet servers that cannot be contacted, or there are unhosted tablets, or either the master or any tablet servers are in the process of shutting down, the master will not perform load balancing. See "Load Balancer" on page 375 for more information on how tablets are balanced.

The status information collected from each tablet server includes the last contact time and some tablet server–wide information such as OS load, hold time (the amount of time the tablet server has been stuck waiting for minor compaction resources), number of lookups, cache hits, and write-ahead logs that are being sorted. Per-table information is also provided, including number of entries; entries in memory; number of tablets; number of online tables; ingest, query, and scan information; and number of minor and major compactions. If the master cannot obtain the status of a tablet server repeatedly, the master will request that the tablet server process halt.

The master is not a single point of failure, because Accumulo can continue running without it. However, if the master is down for too long, the tablets can become unbalanced, and if tablet server processes go down while the master is down, their tablets will not be reassigned.

Multiple masters can be configured, and they will create a queue of locks in Zoo-Keeper. If the active master goes down, losing its ZooKeeper lock, the next master having a lock in the queue will obtain the master lock and become the active master.

FATE

The master performs a number of administrative actions on behalf of a user. These actions can involve multiple steps, such as communicating with a tablet server, reading or writing data in ZooKeeper, and reading or writing data to the metadata table. If the master fails without completing all the steps needed for a particular action, Accumulo and the client process could be left in an undesired state. For this reason, Accumulo introduced a fault-tolerant execution system, FATE, to ensure that multistep administrative operations are made atomically—either all the steps succeed, or the original state of the system is restored.

A FATE operation breaks down an administrative action into a set of repeatable, persisted operations—objects that implement the Repo interface. Each Repo must have the same end state when executed more than once, even if it has been partially executed previously. It also should be able to undo any changes it has made. On successful execution, a Repo returns the next Repo needed to continue the action. Before a Repo is executed, it is stored in ZooKeeper along with a transaction ID associated with the FATE operation.

If the master goes down in the middle of performing a FATE operation, the next master that takes over will be able to continue the operation or roll it back based on the information recorded in ZooKeeper. The actions currently managed as FATE operations include bulk import, compact range, cancel compaction, create table, clone table, delete table, import table, export table, rename table, and shutdown tablet server.

Load Balancer

The load balancer that the Accumulo master uses to assign tablets to tablet servers is controlled by the master.tablet.balancer property. The load balancer is responsible for finding assignments for tablets that are unassigned, at start time or any other time unassigned tablets are discovered (such as when a tablet server process goes down). It is also responsible for determining when the tablet load across tablet servers is out of balance, and determining which tablets should be moved from one server to another. This is called *migration* or *reassignment*. If the default TableLoadBalancer is used, you can set a different balancer for each table by changing the table.balancer property, which defaults to the DefaultLoadBalancer. Balancing each table independently is important, because otherwise a table's tablets might not be evenly distributed, even if each tablet server is hosting the same number of tablets.

The DefaultLoadBalancer attempts to assign a tablet to the last server that hosted it, if possible. If there is no last location, it will assign the tablet to a random server. When determining whether tablets need to be reassigned to keep the tablet servers evenly loaded, the DefaultLoadBalancer looks at the number of online tablets for each server. If there are tablet servers that have more and less than the average number of online tablets, this load balancer will move tablets from overloaded servers to underloaded servers. It picks a pair of tablet servers, starting with the most loaded and least loaded, and moves the smallest number of tablets necessary to bring one of the two servers to average load. When the DefaultLoadBalancer decides to move a tablet, it first decides which table the tablet should come from. If the higher-loaded server has more tablets from any given table than the less-loaded server, the balancer picks the most out-of-balance table. If none of the tables are out of balance, the balancer picks the busiest table (as defined by ingest rate plus query rate). Once a table is chosen, the balancer selects the most recently split tablet from that table. It repeats the tablet selection process until it selects the desired number of tablets for migration.

Garbage Collector

The garbage collector is a process that deletes files from HDFS when they are no longer used by Accumulo. This is a complex operation because a file can be used by more than one tablet. Early incarnations of the garbage collector compared the files in HDFS with the files listed in the metadata table. Prior to 1.6, the garbage collector still has the option to be run this way if Accumulo is not running and has been shut down cleanly. However, when Accumulo is running this method is not sufficient because files must be put in place before their metadata entries are inserted, with the result that the metadata table is expected to be slightly behind what exists on disk.

To address this issue, there is a section of the metadata table that records candidates for deletion. If a tablet doesn't need a file anymore, it writes a deletion entry for that file to the appropriate section of the metadata table. A tablet no longer needs a file if it has performed a compaction that rewrites that file's data into a new file. Major compaction, full major compaction, and merging minor compactions all result in files that can be deleted.

The garbage collector reads the deletion section of the metadata table to identify candidates for deletion. Then the garbage collector looks to see if the deletion candidates are still in use elsewhere, if they appear as file or scan entries for any tablets, or if they are in a batch of files that are currently being bulk imported. After confirming the candidates that are no longer in use, the garbage collector removes those files from HDFS and removes the files' deletion entries from the metadata table.

The garbage collector also deletes write-ahead logfiles that are no longer being used. Rather than using deletion entries to find candidate write-ahead logs for deletion, the garbage collector finds files in the write-ahead log directories, then determines if they are still in use.

Accumulo can run without the garbage collector. However, when the garbage collector is not running, Accumulo will not reclaim disk space used by files that are no longer needed. As with the master, multiple garbage collectors can be configured, and the inactive garbage collectors will monitor a ZooKeeper lock, waiting to obtain the lock in case the active garbage collector fails.

Monitor

The Accumulo monitor process provides a web service and UI for observing Accumulo's state. It connects to the master and the garbage collector processes via Thrift RPC.

The monitor is not essential for running Accumulo, but it is a useful tool for observing Accumulo's status and learning about any issues that Accumulo may be having. Currently Accumulo only works with a single active monitor process. If a second monitor is started, it will wait to take over in the event the first monitor fails.

One of the most useful features of the monitor is that it can aggregate log messages from all Accumulo processes. By default, WARN and ERROR messages from all processes are forwarded to the monitor, which displays them under Recent Logs in its UI. This behavior is configurable in the *generic_logger* log4j configuration files.

Tracer

Accumulo includes a distributed tracing functionality based on the Google Dapper paper (*http://bit.ly/dapper_paper*) that makes it possible to understand why some operations take longer than expected. This tracing functionality captures time measurements for different parts of the system across components and different threads.

Tracing is optional. To enable tracing, one or more tracing processes are started to capture tracing information from Accumulo client and server processes using Apache Thrift RPC. If no Accumulo tracer processes are running, tracing will be disabled. The start-all script will launch one tracer process for each host defined the *ACCU-MULO_CONF_DIR/tracers* file. Usually one tracer is sufficient to handle the tracing data for even a substantial Accumulo instance.

One trace is defined as a series of spans that have timing information for a specific operation. In addition to start and stop times, each span has a description and IDs for itself, its trace, and its parent span if one exists. Clients that want to use tracing must enable it for an application and then start and stop traces for individual operations (see "Using Tracing" on page 481 for an example of enabling tracing and retrieving the results). When tracing is started, or turned on, each span associated with a trace is sent to a tracer process chosen at random from the list of tracers that have registered in ZooKeeper. Spans are received by each tracer asynchronously using Thrift RPC and inserted into the *trace* table in Accumulo. When the client operation being analyzed is complete, the client should turn tracing off, at which point any remaining spans from previous asynchronous calls will be inserted into the *trace* table. The complete trace information can then be retrieved from the *trace* table through the Accumulo shell or monitor page.

Accumulo server processes also use tracing to obtain and log information about their internal operations. Operations traced by Accumulo include every minor and major compaction, as well as 1 out of every 100 garbage-collection rounds.

Client

Accumulo clients communicate with Accumulo server processes in a variety of ways. Information such as the instance ID, instance name, master locations, tablet server locations, and root tablet location are retrieved by the client directly from ZooKeeper. Whenever the client retrieves information from ZooKeeper, that information is cached in the ZooCache. If the same information is looked up again, the client will first check the cache.

When the client obtains a connection to Accumulo, it reads the available tablet servers from ZooKeeper and connects to a tablet server to authenticate. The Connector can then be used to retrieve various types of scanner or writer objects for reading from or writing to Accumulo. It can also be used to retrieve objects that can perform table operations, instance operations, and security operations. The operations that can be performed with these objects are covered in detail in Chapter 4.

Locating Keys

When a Range is scanned, the tablet or tablets that overlap the Range must be located. When a Mutation is written, there will always be a single tablet containing the row ID of the Mutation, and that tablet must be located. The *location* of a tablet is the IP address and port of the tablet server that hosts the tablet. Tablet locations are stored in the metadata table, which itself is split into multiple tablets. So, the metadata tablet containing information about the desired tablet must also be located. The locations of metadata tablets are stored in the root tablet.

 Before Accumulo 1.6, the root tablet was a special tablet in the metadata table. In 1.6, the root tablet is in a separate table called the root table.

In fact, all the information about the metadata tablets is stored in a single root tablet that is never split. The root tablet location is retrieved from ZooKeeper, while all other tablet locations (metadata and not) are retrieved from the tablet servers hosting the root and metadata tablets. The client looks up tablet locations by conducting appropriate scans of the metadata table, but the tablet server's Thrift API is used directly rather than going through the client scan API.

The location of the root tablet is cached in the ZooCache, while the locations of other tablets are cached separately. The separate tablet location cache is not invalidated when a tablet is moved to a different server, but if the client looks for a tablet by contacting a tablet server that is not hosting the tablet, the client will remove the location from the cache and retry.

Metadata Table

The metadata table (along with the root tablet/table) is the authoritative source of information on the tablets and files for an Accumulo instance. The files for the metadata table are typically stored at a higher replication: the default is five replicas, rather than the default of three for other tables' files.

See Appendix B for details on the contents of the metadata table.

Uses of ZooKeeper

ZooKeeper is used heavily by Accumulo for determining liveness of processes, coordinating tasks, ensuring fault tolerance of administrative operations, and storing configuration that can be modified on the fly without restarting Accumulo.

See Appendix C for details on the data stored in ZooKeeper.

Accumulo and the CAP Theorem

It has been well-argued that it is basically impossible not to choose to be partition-tolerant (*http://bit.ly/cap_confusion*) when designing a distributed system because, in a distributed system, some messages between servers will inevitably be lost (which is the definition of a partition in this context).

With respect to the CAP Theorem, Accumulo is a CP system, choosing consistency over availability during a network partition. Accumulo is designed to only allow writes for a particular key to one and only one machine. Some other distributed databases allow writes for a particular key to happen at multiple machines, and they choose to replicate these writes between servers as fast as they can.

Accumulo is also designed to run within a single data center, which means it operates over a local area network (LAN) rather than a wide area network (WAN) spanning multiple data centers that are geographically distributed. In a LAN, network partitions can still occur in which some tablet servers cannot talk to other tablet servers or—more importantly—to ZooKeeper. However, when this happens the tablet servers that cannot talk to ZooKeeper cannot guarantee that they are the only server hosting a given tablet, and so they exit to avoid receiving writes and creating an inconsistent view of a tablet.

From Accumulo's perspective, if a server isn't responding to ZooKeeper (meaning it has let its tablet server lock expire), then the server may be down or it may be running and just unable to talk to ZooKeeper. So the master has a dilemma. Because the server might be running, Accumulo could allow any clients that can talk to the tablet server to continue to read from and write to it. Because there is no other place accepting changes to the tablets hosted by this tablet server, there is no problem with consistency per se. But because it is impossible to distinguish between the server being down and being unable to communicate with the ZooKeeper and master servers, tablet servers are designed to exit so the master can assign their tablets to other tablet servers that can still talk to ZooKeeper. This ensures that the tablets are available to clients and that there is only one place where a particular key can be modified.

This process takes only a few seconds or less depending on how the cluster is configured.

Any clients that cannot talk to ZooKeeper will be unable to perform any reads or writes. This amounts to a lack of availability. In a single data center, populations of client processes will not have much difference in how well they can connect to servers, as compared to client processes around the world talking to servers in multiple geographically distributed data centers. Many installations perform load balancing across clients and if for some reason some population of clients is unable to service requests, the load balancers will try to redirect requests to healthy clients.

This is different from systems that choose availability and partition-tolerance (AP) but not consistency. These systems are often designed to be run over machines in multiple data centers, separated by WAN links. These links may cease functioning for some period of time, resulting in a network partition. Even when they are functioning, the difference in latency between connecting to a machine in a near data center versus a machine in a faraway data center can result in clients attempting to talk only to machines in the near data center.

In this scenario clients can write a value to a particular key in *either* data center, whether the WAN link is functioning or not, and can read the value of the key from either data center. The values of these keys can be the same, but if the WAN link is down or if a read occurs after a client has written a new value in the far data center but before that value has been replicated to the near data center, the client talking to the near data center may read a stale value. Eventually, when the WAN link is back up or when enough time has passed for the new value to be replicated to the near data center, all clients will see the newest versions of values for all keys, giving rise to the term *eventual consistency*.

Because clients can write to the same key at multiple data centers, and because these databases are frequently distributed across data centers with high-latency WAN links between them, even when the WAN links are up some stale reads are possible because replication latency is always present and limited by the speed of light.

Because there is essentially no opportunity for data to get out of sync in Accumulo, it chooses consistency. Therefore we call Accumulo a CP system, because it can continue to operate in the presence of partitions, but not all clients can perform writes to machines on either side of a partition.

The crucial decision for distributed database designers is whether to design their databases to be globally distributed or highly consistent. Accumulo is a highly consistent, single–data center application.

Administration: Setup

Accumulo is designed to run on a large number of servers and includes several features designed to make administrating and maintaining large clusters tractable for administrators.

In particular, dynamic load balancing and automatic recovery from common types of hardware failure help keep Accumulo healthy even in clusters of over a thousand machines, in which hardware failures are common.

Preinstallation

Here are the ways in which the software environment should be set up to support installing Accumulo. For suggestions on selecting appropriate types of hardware and sizing a cluster, see "Hardware Selection" on page 473.

Operating Systems

Accumulo is regularly run and tested on several versions of Linux:

- Red Hat Enterprise Linux
- CentOS 6
- Ubuntu 12 and above

Development platforms include Linux and Mac OS X.

Kernel Tweaks

A few low-level kernel settings that can dramatically impact the responsiveness of the cluster might need to be tuned for scaling up the per-machine resources allowed when more than 100 machines are in a cluster.

Swappiness

Tablet servers should be given enough operational memory to avoid swapping. Swapping is bad because it can cause a tablet server to have to wait while the kernel retrieves from disk some page of memory that was swapped out. This delay can interfere with Accumulo's ability to determine the responsiveness of the tablet servers and to keep all the data online.

To help avoid swapping, it is recommended that the Linux vm.swappiness setting be set low to instruct the kernel to not be eager at all when it comes to swapping pages from memory out to disk.

 In Linux kernels prior to version 3.5, setting vm.swappiness to 0 would instruct the kernel to avoid swapping except when not swapping would cause an out-of-memory error. In kernel 3.5 and later, setting vm.swappiness to 0 instructs the kernel not to swap ever and to allow the out-of-memory errors to occur. Setting the value to 1 instructs the kernel to behave the same way kernels previous to 3.5 did with swappiness set to 0.

To set swappiness low temporarily, do the following:

```
echo 1 > /proc/sys/vm/swappiness
```

And to make the setting persist across system reboots, do:

```
echo "vm.swappiness = 1" >> /etc/sysctl.conf
```

If it is undesirable to set swappiness to 1 on a system, ensure that it is set to a low enough value to avoid tablet servers swapping.

Number of open files

Accumulo needs to be able to create enough threads, network sockets, and file descriptors to respond to user requests. All of these require resources from the kernel, which are limited by the number of open files allowed.

To set this, edit */etc/security/limits.conf* or add a specific file under */etc/security/limits.d/* and add the following lines:

```
accumulo  nofile  soft  65536
accumulo  nofile  hard  65536
```

Native Libraries

Because Java garbage collection can cause pauses that make it difficult to determine the status of a process, Accumulo employs its own memory management for newly written entries. This requires the use of binary libraries compiled for the specific architecture on which Accumulo is deployed. In older versions of Accumulo, binary libraries for the Linux x86-64 architecture were provided in the distributed files. If you are deploying to another architecture, or using version 1.6, these libraries must be built after installation.

If the binary libraries are not available, Accumulo will fall back on a pure-Java implementation, but at the cost of decreased performance and stability.

User Accounts

Many distributions of Hadoop configure a *mapred* and a *hdfs* user. Accumulo can be configured to use its own *accumulo* account.

If Accumulo will be installed from RPM or Debian packages, the package scripts can create the *accumulo* user account.

Linux Filesystem

Accumulo stores data in HDFS, which in turn stores blocks of data in the underlying Linux filesystem. Popular Linux filesystems include ext3, ext4, and XFS.

Accumulo 1.4 and earlier versions required the ability to write to a local directory to store write-ahead logs. A directory must be created for this purpose and must be writeable by the *accumulo* user. It can improve performance to put write-ahead logs on separate disks from disks storing HDFS data. These directories are specified in the *accumulo-site.xml* file described in "Server Configuration Files" on page 402.

Accumulo 1.5 and later versions store these files in HDFS so no additional directories need to be created.

System Services

Accumulo relies on several system services to operate properly:

Domain Name Service (DNS)
> Hadoop requires that domain names of machines be resolvable from domain to IP address and from IP address to domain name.

Network Time Protocol (NTP)
> When an Accumulo table is configured to use a TimeType of milliseconds (MIL LIS), Accumulo's tablet servers rely on system time for applying timestamps to mutations that do not otherwise have a timestamp provided. With many

machines in a cluster, some machines are bound to have clocks that are off. Running NTP daemons can help keep clocks closer in sync and avoid situations in which assigned timestamps jump forward as tablets are migrated from one server to the next. Tablet servers ensure that the timestamps they assign never decrease for any given tablet.

Secure Shell (SSH)

Accumulo ships with scripts that use SSH to start and stop processes on all machines in a cluster from a single node. This is not required, however, if another means of starting and stopping processes is used, such as *init.d* scripts.

To keep your Accumulo data secure, you also need to ensure that these services are secure just like any other system built on top of Hadoop. For the scope of this book, we cover a few important details in "Security" on page 416.

Software Dependencies

Accumulo depends on several software packages. First, Accumulo is written in Java. Java versions 1.6 and 1.7 have been tested and are known to work. The Sun/Oracle JDK is used more often in production, although OpenJDK is often used for development.

Apache Hadoop

Accumulo 1.6 binaries are built against Apache Hadoop 2.2.0, and should work with Hadoop versions 2.2.x and 1.2.x with little to no modification. To build against a different version see "Building from Source" on page 399.

Depending on the version of HDFS that is installed, different HDFS settings need to be configured in order to ensure that Accumulo can flush write-ahead logs to HDFS safely. The append or sync directive should be set to true. This setting requires that HDFS clients confirm that data has been transferred to DataNode processes successfully before returning.

Necessary settings for different versions of HDFS are summarized in Table 11-1.

Table 11-1. Hadoop durability options

Hadoop version	Setting	Default
0.20.205	dfs.support.append	must be configured
0.23.x	dfs.support.append	defaults to true
1.0.x	dfs.support.append	must be configured
1.1.x	dfs.durable.sync	defaults to true

Hadoop version	Setting	Default
2.0.0-2.0.4	dfs.support.append	defaults to true

Setting `dfs.datanode.synconclose` to `true` will help avoid data loss in the event of catastrophic failure, such as losing power to all nodes at once. This setting causes the write-ahead log to ask disks to sync writes to disk before returning, which is safe but also incurs a performance penalty. If an uninterruptible power supply is used so that machines can be shut down safely in the event of total power loss, `dfs.datanode.syn conclose` can be set to `false`.

This should be set in the *hdfs-site.xml* configuration file, and HDFS should be restarted afterwards.

Apache ZooKeeper

Apache ZooKeeper (*http://zookeeper.apache.org*) is a distributed directory service designed to keep information completely replicated and synchronized across a small number of machines. Hence it is a highly available system for keeping small amounts of data. Accumulo uses ZooKeeper to store configuration information and to coordinate actions across the cluster. See Appendix C for additional information on Accumulo's use of ZooKeeper.

ZooKeeper version 3.3.0 or later should be used.

The only configuration option of ZooKeeper that is regularly changed is the number of connections per client machine. The default is 10. Changing this is a matter of adding the line:

```
maxClientCnxns=250
```

to the *zoo.cfg* file. Versions of ZooKeeper 3.4.0 or later do not require this change.

Installation

After Hadoop and ZooKeeper are installed, Accumulo can be installed. Accumulo versions prior to 1.6 provided precompiled RPM and deb packages. For version 1.6.0 and later, the development team made the decision to no longer officially support these.

Tarball Distribution Install

Accumulo can be downloaded as a Gzipped TAR file from a mirror at *http://accu mulo.apache.org/downloads/*.

Extract the tarball to the desired location and ensure that the files are owned by the user that Accumulo processes will run as. As of Accumulo 1.6, native libraries must be built from source. Follow the instructions in "Building native libraries" on page 400 for building these and proceed to "Configuration" on page 401.

Installing on Cloudera's CDH

Cloudera provides a popular commercial distribution of Hadoop called CDH (the Cloudera Distribution for Hadoop) that ships Accumulo 1.6 as part of CDH version 5. Accumulo is packaged as an optional *parcel* in the Cloudera Manager that can be installed as part of the general installation process (Figure 11-1).

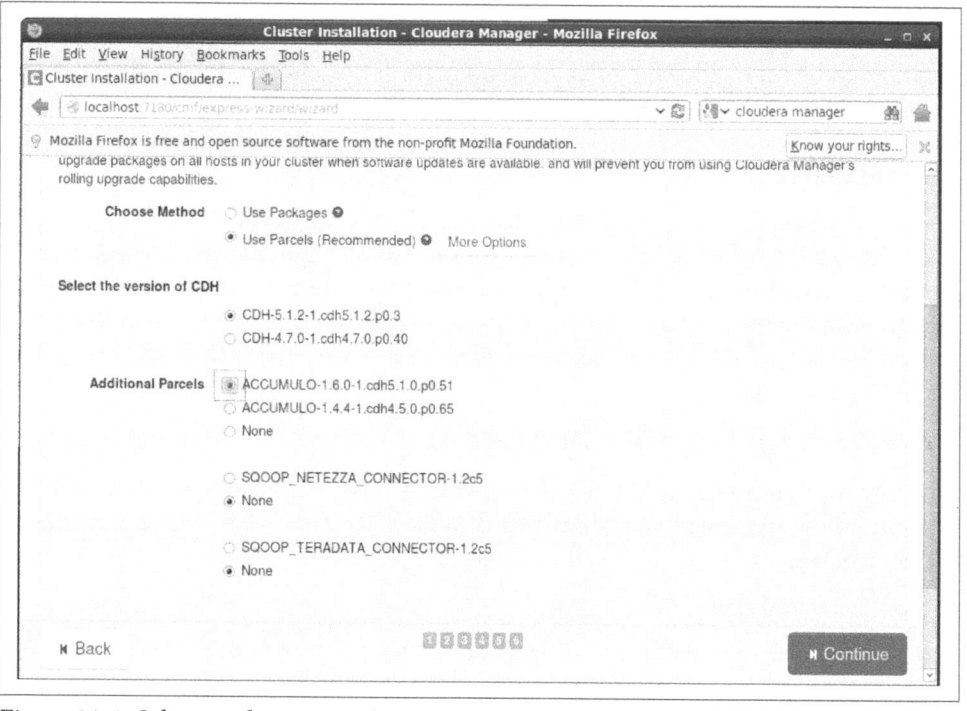

Figure 11-1. Selecting the Accumulo parcel during CDH5 install

Selecting Accumulo from the list of additional parcels and clicking Continue will begin the installation process (Figure 11-2).

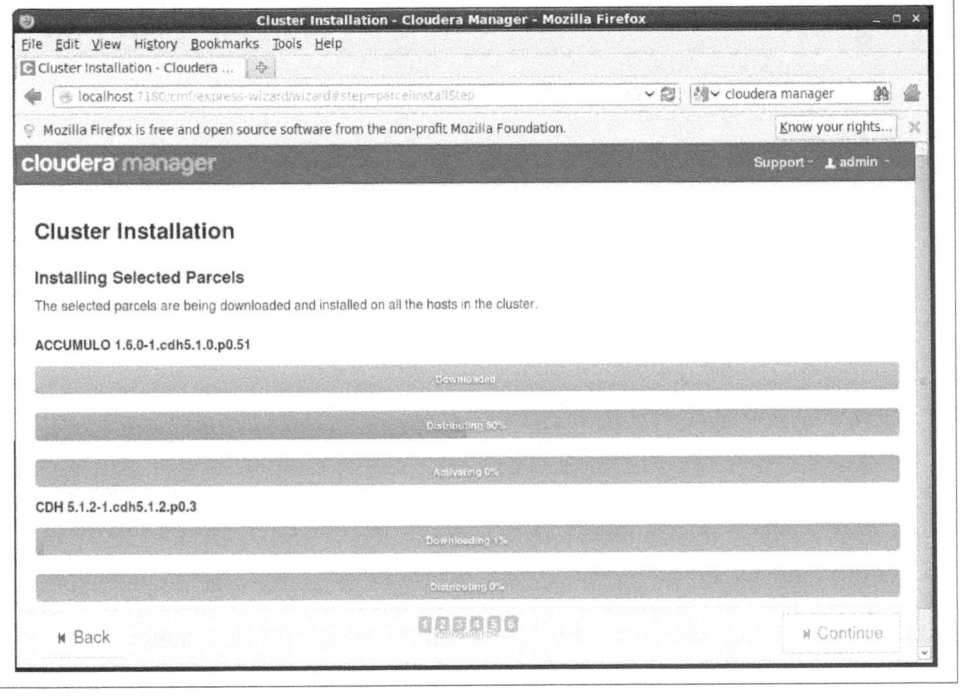

Figure 11-2. Installing the Accumulo parcel

Accumulo is now an available service. Next we need to add the service to our cluster, which will configure and start up Accumulo. From the main Cloudera Manager page, select the Add Service option. This will show a list of services to be installed (Figure 11-3). Selecting Accumulo will install Accumulo and all its dependent services, including HDFS and ZooKeeper.

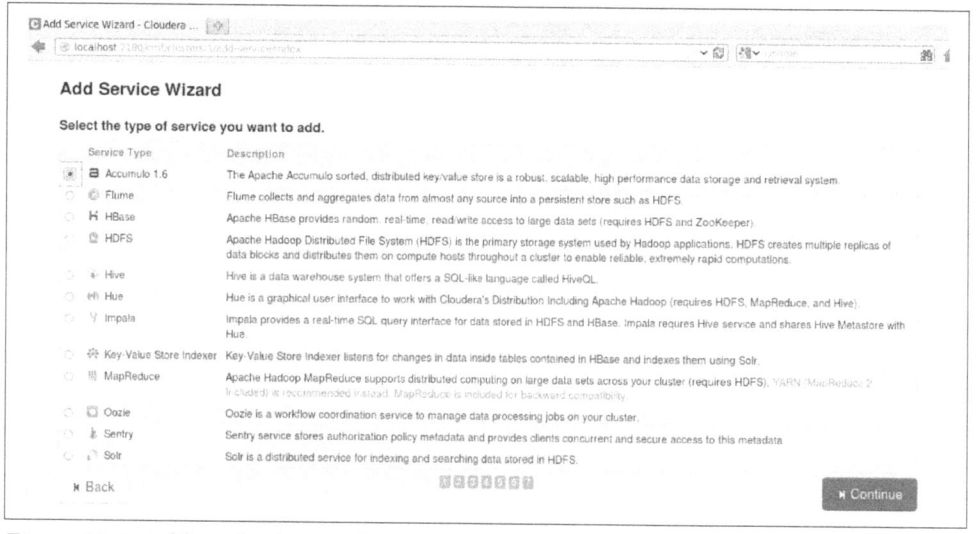

Figure 11-3. Adding the Accumulo service to the cluster

The Add Service Wizard will prompt you to assign roles to various machines in the cluster. These include which machines will run the master process, tablet server processes, etc. (Figure 11-4).

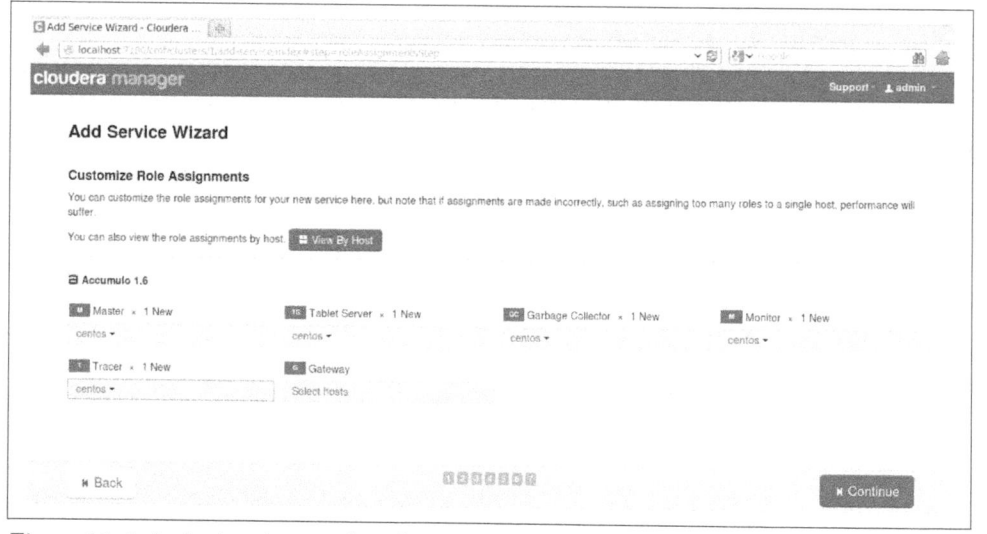

Figure 11-4. Assigning Accumulo roles to machines

Next the wizard will prompt for any configuration options that should be set before starting the service (Figure 11-5). This is a good opportunity to set things like the `Instance Secret`. Other options have good starting defaults.

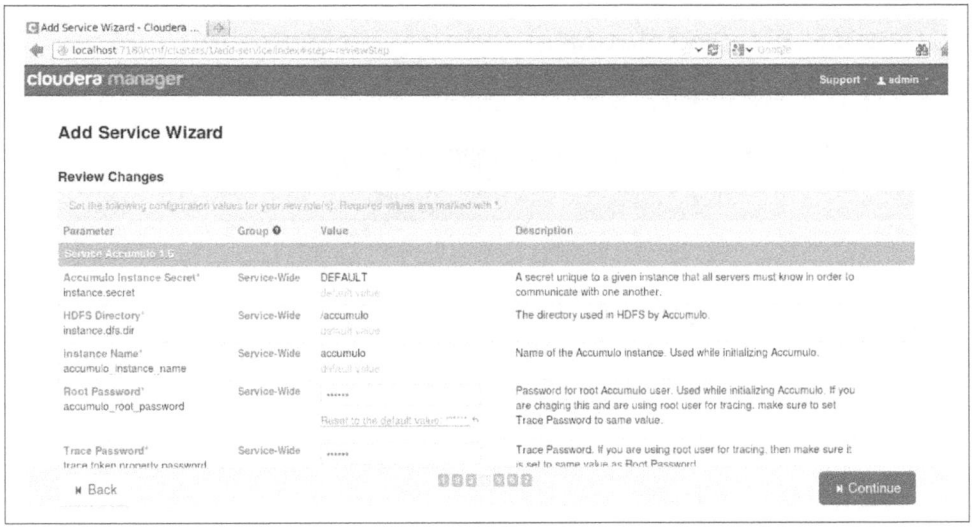

Figure 11-5. Setting configuration options before installing the Accumulo service

Finally, the wizard will start Accumulo and dependent services, if any are not already started (Figure 11-6).

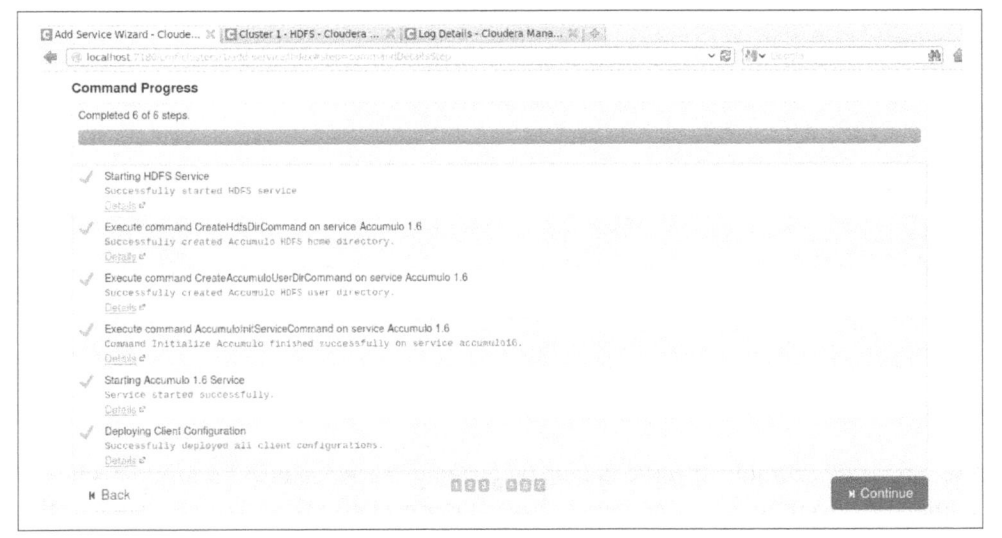

Figure 11-6. Services are started by the Add Service Wizard

After installation Accumulo will show up as a service on the main view of a cluster in the Cloudera Manager (Figure 11-7).

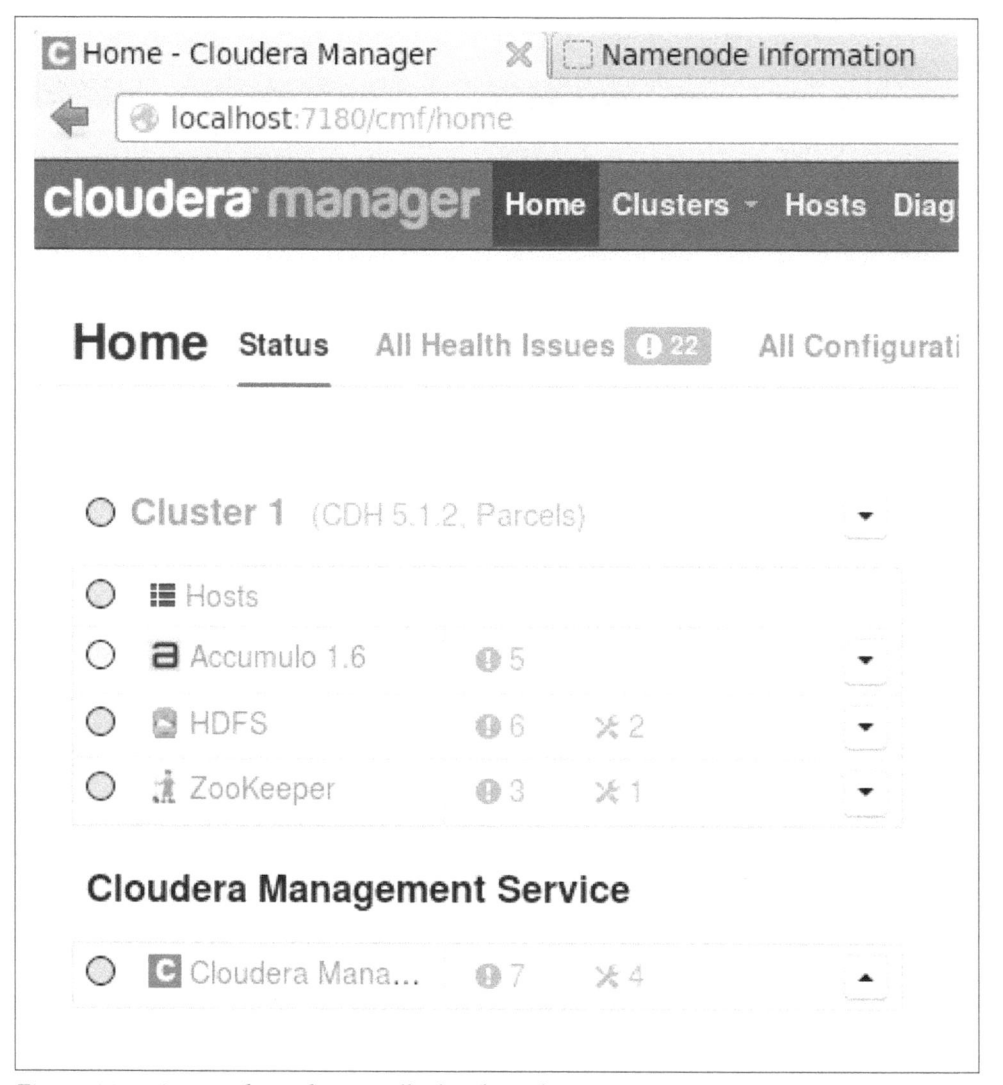

Figure 11-7. Accumulo in the overall Cloudera cluster view

You can see Accumulo-specific details by clicking the *Accumulo 1.6* link, which will display the Accumulo Service details page (Figure 11-8). There is also a link to the Accumulo monitor.

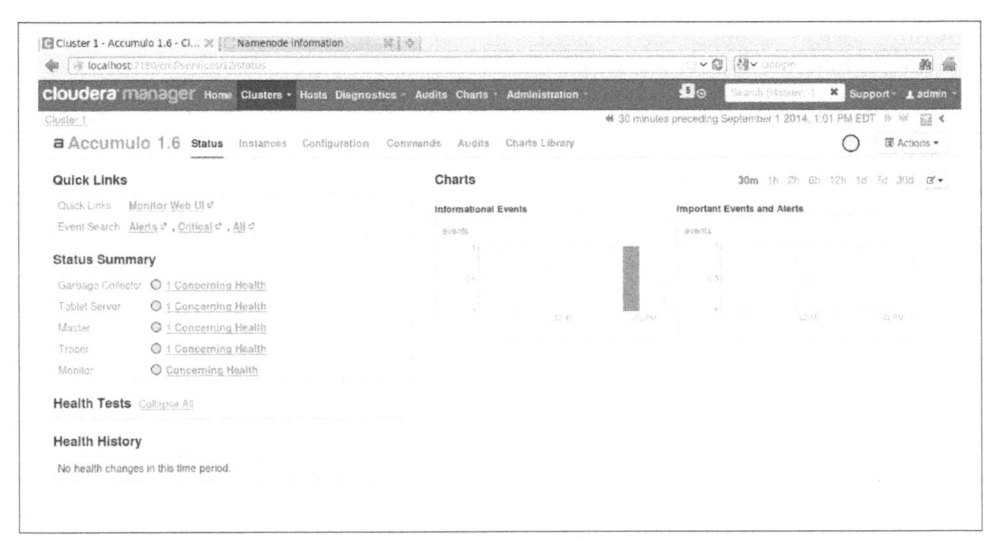

Figure 11-8. Viewing the Accumulo service in Cloudera Manager

Further configuration of the Accumulo service can be done via the Configuration tab at the top of the service details page (Figure 11-9).

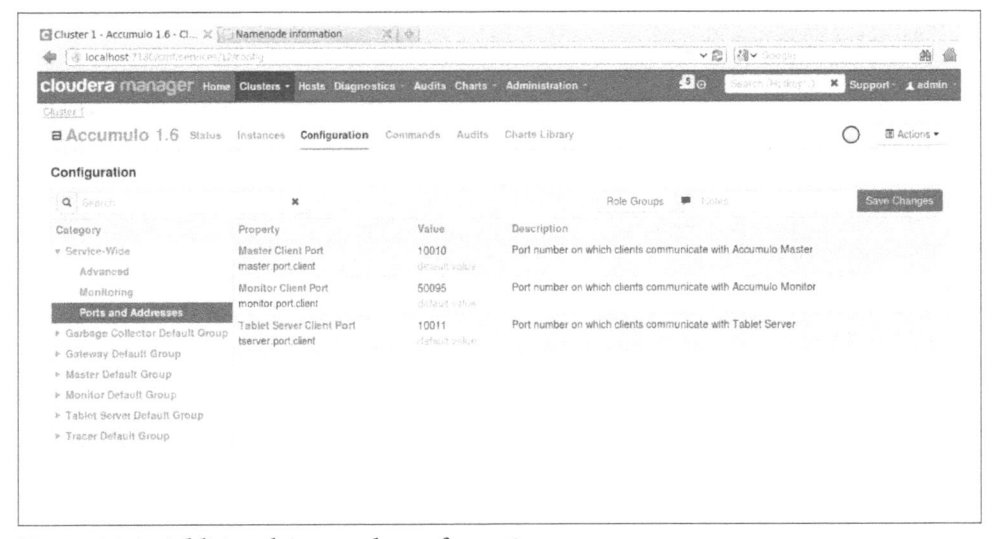

Figure 11-9. Additional Accumulo configuration

After installation, the Accumulo files are located in */opt/cloudera/parcels/ACCU-MULO*. The commands in the *bin/* directory will be part of the PATH.

Configuration files are in */etc/accumulo/conf*.

Custom JARs should be placed in */opt/cloudera/parcels/ACCUMULO/lib/ accumulo/lib/ext/* if you're not using HDFS to distribute files, as detailed in "Using HDFS" on page 408.

Installing on Hortonworks' HDP

The Hortonworks Data Platform (HDP) is a distribution of Hadoop and other scalable data processing technologies that emphasizes open source contribution. HDP 2.1 ships with Accumulo 1.5.1 as an optional RPM.

On each machine to participate in the accumulo cluster, run:

```
# yum install accumulo
```

This will install the Accumulo JARs and configuration files customized for use with HDP:

```
Setting up Install Process
Resolving Dependencies
--> Running transaction check
---> Package accumulo.x86_64 0:1.5.1.2.1.5.0-695.el6 will be installed
--> Finished Dependency Resolution
...
Total download size: 11 M
Installed size: 13 M
Is this ok [y/N]: y
Downloading Packages:
...
accumulo-1.5.1.2.1.5.0-695.el6.x86_64.rpm
Running rpm_check_debug
Running Transaction Test
Transaction Test Succeeded
Running Transaction
  Installing : accumulo-1.5.1.2.1.5.0-695.el6.x86_64
  Verifying  : accumulo-1.5.1.2.1.5.0-695.el6.x86_64
Installed:
  accumulo.x86_64 0:1.5.1.2.1.5.0-695.el6
Complete!
```

The RPM will install Accumulo in */usr/lib/accumulo*, and put configuration files in */etc/accumulo/conf*. Configuration files appropriate for the memory available on servers can be copied from */etc/accumulo/conf/examples*. For example, to copy the files that configure Accumulo to use 3 GB of RAM we would do:

```
# cp /etc/accumulo/conf/examples/3GB/standalone/* /etc/accumulo/conf/
```

The *accumulo-site.xml* and *accumulo-env.sh* files can be adjusted according to the instructions in "Configuration" on page 401, but the directory references are already set up according to the HDP layout.

Next we need to make the directory in HDFS that our configuration files expect:

```
# hdfs dfs -mkdir -p /usr/accumulo/data
```

HDP instructions recommend changing permissions on the data directory to grant access to all users. This should be restricted to only the *accumulo* user for production environments:

```
# hdfs dfs -chmod -R 777 /usr/accumulo/data
```

Next we'll change the ownership of the Accumulo data directory:

```
# sudo -u hdfs hdfs dfs -chown -R accumulo:hdfs /usr/accumulo/data
```

We can now initialize Accumulo. We need to do this only once and from one machine:

```
# /usr/lib/accumulo/bin/accumulo init
[util.Initialize] INFO : Hadoop Filesystem is hdfs://sandbox.hortonworks.com:8020
[util.Initialize] INFO : Accumulo data dir is /user/accumulo/data
[util.Initialize] INFO : Zookeeper server is localhost:2181
[util.Initialize] INFO : Checking if Zookeeper is available. If this hangs, then
    you need to make sure zookeeper is running

Instance name : hdp
Enter initial password for root (this may not be applicable for your security
    setup): ******
Confirm initial password for root: ******
[Configuration.deprecation] INFO : dfs.replication.min is deprecated. Instead,
    use dfs.namenode.replication.min
[Configuration.deprecation] INFO : dfs.block.size is deprecated. Instead, use
    dfs.blocksize
[master.Master] INFO : Loaded class :
    org.apache.accumulo.server.security.handler.ZKAuthorizor
[master.Master] INFO : Loaded class :
    org.apache.accumulo.server.security.handler.ZKAuthenticator
[master.Master] INFO : Loaded class :
    org.apache.accumulo.server.security.handler.ZKPermHandler
[security.AuditedSecurityOperation] INFO : Initialized root user with username:
    root at the request of user !SYSTEM
```

Accumulo can be started with the *start-all.sh* script. See Chapter 12 for more details on this process:

```
[root@sandbox conf]# /usr/lib/accumulo/bin/start-all.sh
Starting monitor on localhost
Starting tablet servers .... done
Starting tablet server on localhost
[server.Accumulo] INFO : Attempting to talk to zookeeper
[server.Accumulo] INFO : Zookeeper connected and initialized, attemping to talk
    to HDFS
[server.Accumulo] INFO : Connected to HDFS
Starting master on localhost
Starting garbage collector on localhost
Starting tracer on localhost

[root@sandbox conf]#
```

The default RPM may not ship with native libraries built. See "Building native libraries" on page 400 for more information on building native libraries, which will provide better performance.

Installing on MapR

MapR is a distribution of Hadoop that includes a completely redesigned, proprietary, distributed filesystem, called MapR-FS, that takes the place of HDFS. The MapR distribution includes additional features for security and enterprise integration such as NFS compatibility.

Accumulo 1.6 can be installed on MapR version 3.1 or 3.0 using the following steps (also see these instructions (*http://bit.ly/accumulo_on_mapr*)):

```
# wget http://mirror.cc.columbia.edu/pub/software/apache/accumulo/1.6.1/\
  accumulo-1.6.1-bin.tar.gz
# tar -xzf accumulo-1.6.1-bin.tar.gz

# mkdir /opt/accumulo
# mv accumulo-1.6.1 /opt/accumulo/
```

Create a volume for storing Accumulo data. This volume will take the place of the */accumulo* directory in HDFS and has additional capabilities, such as snapshots, mirroring, and quotas:

```
# maprcli volume create -name project.accumulo -path /accumulo
```

We'll disable the MapR filesystem's compression because Accumulo compresses data by default:

```
# hadoop mfs -setcompression off /accumulo
```

We'll create a configuration directory containing mostly links to the original MapR configuration files, with the exception of *core-site.xml*, so we can alter it without affecting other services:

```
[accumulo-1.6.1]# mkdir hadoop
[accumulo-1.6.1]# mkdir hadoop/hadoop-0.20.2
[accumulo-1.6.1]# cd  hadoop/hadoop-0.20.2
[hadoop-0.20.2]# ln -s /opt/mapr/hadoop/hadoop-0.20.2/* .
[hadoop-0.20.2]# rm conf
rm: remove symbolic link `conf'? y
[hadoop-0.20.2]# mkdir conf
[hadoop-0.20.2]# cd conf
[conf]# ln -s /opt/mapr/hadoop/hadoop-0.20.2/conf/* .
[conf]# cp core-site.xml t
[conf]# mv t core-site.xml
mv: overwrite `core-site.xml'? y
```

Adding the following properties to *core-site.xml* will tell the MapR filesystem to disable read/write caching, because Accumulo does its own caching:

```
<property>
  <name>fs.mapr.readbuffering</name>
  <value>false</value>
</property>
<property>
  <name>fs.mapr.aggregate.writes</name>
  <value>false</value>
</property>
```

Edit the following lines of */opt/mapr/conf/warden.conf* to allow Accumulo to use up to 2 GB of memory:

```
service.command.os.heapsize.max=2750   (from 750)
service.command.os.heapsize.min=2256 (from 256)
```

Next we'll configure Accumulo. Follow the instructions in "Server Configuration Files" on page 402 for copying configuration files and "Building native libraries" on page 400 on building native libraries. Then return here for MapR-specific configuration.

Edit *accumulo-env.sh* to point to the proper Hadoop and ZooKeeper directories:

```
test -z "$HADOOP_PREFIX" && \
export HADOOP_PREFIX=/opt/accumulo/accumulo-1.6.1/hadoop/hadoop-0.20.2/

test -z "$ZOOKEEPER_HOME" && \
export ZOOKEEPER_HOME=/opt/accumulo/accumulo-1.6.1/hadoop/hadoop-0.20.2/lib
```

Edit *accumulo-site.xml* with following properties:

```
<property>
  <name>instance.zookeeper.host</name>
  <value>maprdemo:5181</value>
  <description>comma separated list of zookeeper servers</description>
</property>

<property>
  <name>tserver.port.client</name>
  <value>9996</value>
</property>

<property>
  <name>master.walog.closer.implementation</name>
  <value>org.apache.accumulo.server.master.recovery.MapRLogCloser</value>
</property>

<property>
  <name>tserver.wal.blocksize</name>
  <value>562M</value>
</property>
```

Now Accumulo can be initialized as described in "Initialization" on page 410.

Running via Amazon Web Services

Amazon Web Services (AWS) provide a set of scripts (*http://bit.ly/accumulo_on_emr*) for spinning up an Accumulo cluster that runs on virtual machines in Amazon's EC2 (Elastic Compute Cloud).

This involves first setting up a ZooKeeper cluster using Apache Whirr, and then using the Elastic MapReduce command-line tools.

To setup a ZooKeeper cluster using Apache Whirr, use the following commands:

```
$ ssh-keygen -t rsa -P '' -f ~/.ssh/id_rsa_whirr

$ bin/whirr launch-cluster --cluster-name=zookeeper
--instance-templates='1 zookeeper'
--provider=aws-ec2
--identity=$AWS_ACCESS_KEY_ID
--credential=$AWS_SECRET_ACCESS_KEY
```

The Security Groups must be configured to allow the Accumulo machines to connect to ZooKeeper processes on these machines. See the AWS documentation on EC2 security groups for Linux instances (*http://bit.ly/ec2_security_groups*).

Obtain the EMR CLI tools (*http://amzn.to/1ftU927*):

```
$ elastic-mapreduce --create --alive --name "Accumulo" --bootstrap-action
s3://elasticmapreduce/samples/accumulo/accumulo-install.sh
--args "IP,DBNAME,PASSWORD" --bootstrap-name "install Accumulo"
--enable-debugging --log-uri s3://BUCKETNAME/accumulo-logs/
--instance-type m1.large --instance-count 4 --key-pair KEY
```

Use your own values for *IP*, *DBNAME*, *PASSWORD*, *BUCKETNAME*, and *KEY*:

IP
: The IP address of one of the ZooKeeper nodes.

DBNAME
: The name that will be used as the Accumulo instance name.

PASSWORD
: The password to use for the Accumulo *root* account.

BUCKETNAME
: The name of an S3 bucket that will be used store Accumulo logs.

KEY
: The name of an EC2 SSH key-pair.

The `--instance-type` parameter describes the type of Amazon virtual machine to be used. m1.large machines work well because they have local storage disks and a modest amount of memory and CPU. m1.xlarge instance types have also been used to build Accumulo clusters in EC2 but may not be completely configured for these scripts.

Once the script starts running, you will see a line of output similar to:

```
Created job flow j-1XIYVOM2PGH3R
```

This identifier can be used to obtain the address of the Accumulo master node:

```
$ elastic-mapreduce --list j-1XIYVOM2PGH3R

j-1XIYVOM2PGH3R     Waiting  ec2-23-22-183-67.compute-1.amazonaws.com
  Accumulo
  PENDING           Setup Hadoop Debugging

$ ssh hadoop@ec2-23-22-183-67.compute-1.amazonaws.com
```

The Accumulo instance is running at this point.

Building from Source

Accumulo is distributed under the Apache open source license, so the source code can be downloaded and modified to suit a particular need. Any modifications to the source code, or to use options different from those that were used to create the binary distributions, will require building Accumulo from source.

Several tools make this process easier. Specifically, the Java SDK and Maven build tool should be installed. Java JDK version 1.6 or 1.7 and Maven version 3.0.4 will work.

To build from source, first download the source packages (*http://accu mulo.apache.org/downloads/*) from a mirror listed on the Apache Accumulo website.

Source code is found in the file ending in *src.tar.gz*. Once downloaded it can be unpacked via:

```
tar -xzf accumulo-1.6.x-src.tar.gz
```

This will create a directory containing all the source files.

Building a tarball distribution

To compile the source into binaries, change into this directory via:

```
cd accumulo-1.6.x
```

Type:

```
mvn package -P assemble
```

This will build a distribution compiled against Hadoop 2.2.0. The distribution should run with any supported version of Hadoop without being recompiled. However, if desired it is possible to compile with a different version by supplying appropriate options. To build for a different version compatible with Hadoop-2, for example Hadoop 0.23.5, use the option:

```
mvn -Dhadoop.version=0.23.5 package -P assemble
```

To build for Hadoop 1, use the profile option and also specify the version of Hadoop. For example:

```
mvn -Dhadoop.profile=1 -Dhadoop.version=1.1.0 package -P assemble
```

Once the build process is complete, there will be a TAR file distribution in *accumulo-1.6.x/assemble/target/accumulo-1.6.x-bin.tar.gz* similar to the binary distributions available from the Accumulo website.

This tarball can be copied into the appropriate location and the instructions in "Tarball Distribution Install" on page 387 can be followed to complete installation. Most installations will also want to use the native libraries, described in the next section.

Building native libraries

Native libraries are written in C++ and must be built for a specific architecture. The binary distributions come with native libraries prebuilt for the GNU Linux x86-64 architecture. If you are building from scratch or simply for a different platform, the native libraries can be built as follows.

Before building the native libraries, install the appropriate build tools. These include *make* and *g++*. Make sure these are installed.

For CentOS, g\++ is installed via the gcc-c++ package.

The Java development kit packages should also be installed. On CentOS this requires *java-1.7.x-openjdk-devel* or *java-1.6.x-openjdk-devel*, where *x* is the latest minor version number.

JAVA_HOME may need to be set appropriately. For example:

```
export JAVA_HOME=/usr/lib/jvm/java-1.7.0-openjdk.x86_64/
```

Once these packages are installed, the native libraries can be built via a script distributed with Accumulo:

```
[centos@centos accumulo-1.6.0]$ bin/build_native_library.sh
g++ -m64 -g -fPIC -shared -O2 -fno-omit-frame-pointer -fno-strict-aliasing -Wall
-I/usr/lib/jvm/java-1.7.0-openjdk-1.7.0.65.x86_64/include
-I/usr/lib/jvm/java-1.7.0-openjdk-1.7.0.65.x86_64/include/linux -Ijavah
-o libaccumulo.so nativeMap/org_apache_accumulo_tserver_NativeMap.cc
Successfully installed native library
[centos@centos accumulo-1.6.0]$
```

In older versions of Accumulo, after downloading the source code as outlined in the previous section, type:

```
cd server/src/main/c++
make
```

The native libraries will be found in the Accumulo install directory under *lib/native/*:

```
[centos@centos accumulo-1.6.0]$ ls lib/native/
libaccumulo.so
```

Accumulo will attempt to use these if they are present. If they are not, messages will appear in the logs warning that the native libraries could not be found. If Accumulo is configured to run using native libraries, and they are not available, Accumulo may fail to start, because the nonnative Java-based libraries will cause the JVM to use more memory than is allocated.

The following section provides more information on configuring Accumulo.

Configuration

Configuring Accumulo is a process similar to configuring Hadoop, involving editing several files and distributing them across all the machines participating in an Accumulo cluster. In addition, after initialization and startup there are quite a few settings that are stored in ZooKeeper that can be modified to affect changes across the cluster without restarting.

File Permissions

Accumulo stores primary data in HDFS, including its write-ahead logs. In HDFS the user that runs Accumulo processes must have the ability to read and write to files and directories under the directory specified as `instance.dfs.dir` in *accumulo-site.xml*, which defaults to */accumulo*. The user must also be able to create this directory, which means writing to the HDFS root directory if the default directory is unchanged. It is recommended to create a directory that the *accumulo* user has permission to write to (e.g., */user/accumulo*), and to make the `instance.dfs.dir` a subdirectory of this directory (e.g., */user/accumulo/accumulo*).

For example:

```
hdfs dfs -mkdir /user/accumulo/accumulo
```

As of Accumulo version 1.6, the `instance.volumes` setting should be used instead of `instance.dfs.dir`. The `instance.volumes` property expects a comma-separated list of HDFS URIs in which it will store data.

This setting can be set to reference your NameNode with a value like `hdfs://namenode:9001/accumulo` to configure Accumulo similarly to the default `instance.dfs.dir` configuration.

Accumulo needs to be able to write application logfiles for debugging and monitoring. If you use the *accumulo* user to start Accumulo processes, these directories should be writable by the *accumulo* user.

For a Debian-based system these logs are in the */var/log* and */var/lib* directories:

```
sudo mkdir /var/log/accumulo
sudo mkdir /var/lib/accumulo
sudo chown -R accumulo:accumulo /var/log/accumulo
sudo chown -R accumulo:accumulo /var/lib/accumulo
```

Server Configuration Files

Accumulo ships with some examples based on various memory configurations. To start with these example files, copy the files into Accumulo's *conf* directory (such as */etc/accumulo/conf/*):

```
cd /etc/accumulo/conf
sudo cp -r examples/3GB/native-standalone/* .
```

Accumulo needs to know how to talk to HDFS and ZooKeeper in order to start up. Two files, *accumulo-env.sh* and *accumulo-site.xml*, control most of Accumulo's startup settings. These two files should be copied to each machine that will run Accumulo processes and should be kept in sync if anything changes.

 If you copy configuration files from a directory called *native-standalone/*, the native libraries must be built or Accumulo can fail to start. This is because the native libraries will handle their own memory allocation, and if they are not found, Accumulo reverts to using Java data structures, which will require more memory than the JVM is configured to provide. See "Building native libraries" on page 400 for details on building these libraries.

You can configure Accumulo to run without the native libraries by allocating more memory to the JVM in which the tablet server runs, so that it exceeds the amount of memory specified for the `tserver.memory.maps.max` property, set in the *accumulo-site.xml* file. The memory dedicated to the tablet server JVM is specified in the *accumulo-env.sh* file on the line that defines ACCUMULO_TSER VER_OPTS. Specifically, the -Xmx option should be set higher than `tserver.memory.maps.max`.

Beware, however, that tablet servers will not perform as well as they would when using native libaries, and if tablet servers are configured to use several gigabytes of memory, JVM garbage-collection pauses can interfere with the tablet servers' ability to respond quickly enough to requests.

Heterogeneous clusters made of machines with differing hardware can have configuration files that differ in their memory settings, for example. However, properties such as the instance secret and hostnames of ZooKeeper must be the same.

accumulo-env.sh

Set the following system variables in the *accumulo-env.sh* file to the appropriate values for your system. If you are using Debian packages this file will be mostly configured already. The only setting you may need to change is the HADOOP_CONF_DIR if you're using Hadoop 2.0 or later:

JAVA_HOME
> Should be the directory that contains *bin/java*.

HADOOP_HOME
> Should contain Hadoop JARs and a *lib/* directory.

HADOOP_CONF_DIR
> Should contain the files *core-site.xml*, *hdfs-site.xml*, etc.
>
> For Hadoop 2.0, comment out the line:
>
> ```
> # test -z "$HADOOP_CONF_DIR" && export
> HADOOP_CONF_DIR="$HADOOP_PREFIX/conf"
> ```
>
> and uncomment:
>
> ```
> test -z "$HADOOP_CONF_DIR" && export
> HADOOP_CONF_DIR="$HADOOP_PREFIX/etc/hadoop"
> ```

ZOOKEEPER_HOME
> Should contain a *zookeeper.jar* file.

Memory settings
> Settings for various hardware configs. Also see "Tablet Server Tuning" on page 488:

4 GB RAM

> *Tablet server*
> > ```
> > -Xmx1g  -Xms1g
> > ```
>
> *Master*
> > ```
> > -Xmx1g  -Xms1g
> > ```
>
> *Monitor*
> > ```
> > -Xmx1g  -Xms256m
> > ```
>
> *GC*
> > ```
> > -Xmx256m  -Xms256m
> > ```

Logger
```
-Xmx1g  -Xms256m
```
(1.4 and below only)

General options
```
-XX:+UseConcMarkSweepGC  -XX:CMSInitiatingOccupancyFraction=75
```

Other processes
```
-Xmx1g  -Xms256m
```

16 GB RAM

Tablet server
```
-Xmx4g  -Xms4g
```

Master
```
-Xmx4g  -Xms4g
```

Monitor
```
-Xmx1g  -Xms256m
```

GC
```
-Xmx1g  -Xms1g
```

Logger
```
-Xmx1g  -Xms256m (1.4 and below only)
```

General options
```
-XX:+UseConcMarkSweepGC  -XX:CMSInitiatingOccupancyFraction=75
```

Other processes
```
-Xmx1g  -Xms256m
```

64 GB RAM

Tablet server
```
-Xmx16g  -Xms16g
```

Master
```
-Xmx8g  -Xms8g
```

Monitor
```
-Xmx1g  -Xms256m
```

GC
```
-Xmx2g  -Xms2g
```

Logger
```
-Xmx1g  -Xms256m
```
(1.4 and below only)

General options
```
-XX:+UseConcMarkSweepGC -XX:CMSInitiatingOccupancyFraction=75
```

Other processes
```
-Xmx1g -Xms256m
```

96 GB RAM

Tablet server
```
-Xmx32g -Xms32g
```

Master
```
-Xmx8g -Xms8g
```

Monitor
```
-Xmx1g -Xms256m
```

GC
```
-Xmx2g -Xms2g
```

Logger
```
-Xmx1g -Xms256m (1.4 and below only)
```

General options
```
-XX:+UseConcMarkSweepGC -XX:CMSInitiatingOccupancyFraction=75
```

Other processes
```
-Xmx1g -Xms256m
```

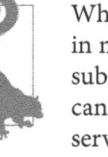 When you're allocating memory to tablet servers, you should keep in mind the memory allocated to other processes so as not to oversubscribe the available memory on a machine. Oversubscription can lead to memory pages being swapped out, which can cause servers to be so unresponsive as to be unfit to participate in an Accumulo instance.

Also see "Kernel Tweaks" on page 384 for the *swappiness* setting.

accumulo-site.xml

This XML file contains properties, each with a name and a value. Hadoop uses similar files for its configuration. This file tells Accumulo processes which ZooKeeper instance to use for configuration information and the values of various settings to use when starting up. The file should only be readable by the *accumulo* user when it contains the instance secret. A separate site file without sensitive information can be created for client use.

If you are using Debian packages or RPMs, this file should be mostly configured already.

`instance.zookeeper.host`

    Write the list of ZooKeeper servers, separated by commas, such as:

        `zk1.mycluster.com:2181,zk2.mycluster.com,zk3.mycluster.com`

`instance.secret`

    This is a shared secret among processes in a single Accumulo instance. It prevents processes that do not know the secret from joining the instance. It should be changed to a unique value for each installation.

    The instance secret is used to control the membership of the cluster, but it is not used to enforce confidentiality.

`general.classpaths`

    If you are using Hadoop 2.0 or later, make sure all the HDFS and Hadoop common JARs are added to the `general.classpaths` property. Some systems place HDFS 2.0 JARs in */usr/lib/hadoop-hdfs/* and MapReduce JARs in */usr/lib/hadoop-0.20-mapreduce* or */usr/lib/hadoop-mapreduce*.

`tserver.port.client` *and* `tserver.port.search`

    Some installations will require changing the default port number on which some processes listen, if the ports are already taken by other processes. In particular, the default tablet server port, 9997, may be taken by a Java Management Extensions (JMX) listener or other process. If so, the tablet server can be configured to listen on a different port by setting `tserver.port.client` to a specific port number or by setting `tserver.port.search` to `true`, in which case the tablet server will try the successively higher port numbers until finding an open port.

Be sure to reference "Tablet Server Tuning" on page 488 for other properties that could be configured in *accumulo-site.xml* when you tune tablet servers.

Client Configuration

In addition to inheriting settings from *accumulo-site.xml*, Accumulo clients can be configured via a Java properties file in the home directory of the user that Accumulo client processes run as. Typically this will be *accumulo*. This properties file allows each Accumulo client to be configured separately, rather than having them all inherit the same settings from server configuration files or settings stored in ZooKeeper.

The properties file is located at *$HOME/.accumulo/config*. Each line of the properties file can specify one property and one value, separated by a tab character. Lines beginning with an octothorp (#) are ignored.

For example:

```
# turn on SSL
instance.rpc.ssl.enabled true
```

We'll look at an example using this configuration file when we discuss SSL in "Configuring SSL" on page 418.

Deploying JARs

Accumulo processes are started from JAR files distributed as part of the installation. These live in *$ACCUMULO_HOME/lib*.

In addition, any Java classes that customize Accumulo, such as iterators and constraints must be distributed to servers across the cluster so that tablet servers and clients can load them.

There are several ways to get the Accumulo JARs and custom JARs onto servers.

Using lib/ext/

In *$ACCUMULO_HOME/lib/* there is a directory called *ext/* that Accumulo processes monitor for custom JARs. Accumulo has its own Java class loader that can reload updated classes without restarting the JVM. Simply placing new JARs into this directory will allow processes to load them, and to update them if they've been loaded already.

This requires copying the custom JARs onto every server, using a command such as scp. An alternative is to have Accumulo look in HDFS, which allows JARs to be uploaded once into HDFS and then retrieved by all processes that need them.

Custom JAR loading example

The code examples that are described in this book can be built into a JAR file via the following Maven commands:

```
[user@host accumulo-examples]$ mvn compile package
...
[INFO]
[INFO] --- maven-jar-plugin:2.3.2:jar (default-jar) @ accumulo-examples ---
[INFO] -----------------------------------------------------------------
[INFO] BUILD SUCCESS
[INFO] -----------------------------------------------------------------
[INFO] Total time: 2.954s
[INFO] Finished at: Mon Sep 01 13:49:33 EDT 2014
```

```
[INFO] Final Memory: 24M/310M
[INFO] -----------------------------------------------------------------------
```

Now there is a JAR file in the *target/* directory that can be deployed to tablet servers in order to load custom filters, combiners, etc. We'll copy it into *$ACCU-MULO_HOME/lib/ext/* next:

```
cp accumulo-examples-0.0.1-SNAPSHOT.jar lib/ext/
```

Now we can use any class in that JAR. For example, we can add the custom constraint defined in our example code:

```
[centos@centos accumulo-1.6.0]$ bin/accumulo shell -u root
Password: ******

Shell - Apache Accumulo Interactive Shell
-
- version: 1.6.0
- instance name: test
-
- type 'help' for a list of available commands
-
root@test test> createtable test
root@test test> constraint -a -t test \
        com.accumulobook.advanced.ValidHeightWeightConstraint
Added constraint com.accumulobook.advanced.ValidHeightWeightConstraint
        to table test with number 2
root@test test>
```

 Accumulo does not have to be stopped in order for processes to begin using the classes in new JAR files in *lib/ext/*. Accumulo deploys its own Java class loader to manage loading newer versions of classes when they become available. This is not the case for JAR files in *lib*.

Using HDFS

In addition to *lib/ext/*, Accumulo can load JARs from HDFS by using the Apache VFS class loader. The advantage of using HDFS is that administrators can manage custom JARs by uploading them once to HDFS from where all Accumulo processes can access them, instead of copying JAR files to the local filesystem of each server.

The relevant configuration option is:

```
<property>
  <name>general.vfs.classpaths</name>
  <value></value>
</property>
```

Administrators can provide a comma-separated list of HDFS paths that contain JAR files.

For example, to add classes from our example code to a path in HDFS, we would first upload the JAR file to a directory in HDFS that Accumulo processes can read:

```
[centos@centos ~]$ hdfs dfs -mkdir /accumulo/ext
[centos@centos ~]$ hdfs dfs -put accumulo-examples-0.0.1-SNAPSHOT.jar \
                  /accumulo/ext/
```

Next we would add the path to the *accumulo-site.xml* file:

```
<property>
  <name>general.vfs.classpaths</name>
  <value>hdfs://centos:8020/accumulo/ext/.*.jar</value>
</property>
```

> The general.vfs.classpaths property cannot be modified by updating the property in ZooKeeper. It must be set in *accumulo-site.xml*.

After starting Accumulo, we should be able to use classes from our uploaded JAR:

```
root@test> constraint -a -t test \
    com.accumulobook.advanced.ValidHeightWeightConstraint
Added constraint com.accumulobook.advanced.ValidHeightWeightConstraint to table
    test with number 2
root@test>
```

Setting Up Automatic Failover

Essential to running a large cluster is Accumulo's ability to tolerate certain types of failure. When certain processes fail, their workload is automatically reassigned to remaining worker nodes or backup processes on other machines. In general, setting up automatic failover for Accumulo processes is simply a matter of running an instance of a process on more than one server.

Tablet servers

The master process ensures that any tablets that were being served by a failed machine are reassigned to remaining tablet servers, which perform any recovery necessary by reading from write-ahead logs. For more on this process see "Recovery" on page 367.

Masters

A master process must be running in order for tablet server failover to happen. If no master is running, most client operations can proceed, but if any tablet server fails while the master is down, some tablets will be unavailable until a master process is started.

To avoid a situation in which tablets can become unavailable, multiple masters processes can be run to ensure that at least one master is running at all times. For this purpose, the *$ACCUMULO_HOME/conf/masters* file should contain the hostnames of the machines on which master processes are run.

The master processes use ZooKeeper to coordinate electing an active master and to elect a new active master in the event that the active master fails.

Garbage collectors

The garbage collector process is not critical to client operations but must run to ensure aged-off, deleted, and redundant data is removed from HDFS.

Initialization

Before Accumulo is started for the first time, an Accumulo instance must be initialized. This can be done on a machine that can connect to both ZooKeeper and HDFS, via the command:

```
accumulo init
```

This command should be run under the user account under which later Accumulo processes will be run, such as the *accumulo* user.

Be sure to verify that the init script is using the correct values for ZooKeeper servers and the Hadoop filesystem:

```
INFO: Hadoop Filesystem is hdfs://[your-namenode]:8020
INFO: ZooKeeper server is [your-zookeeper]:2181
```

If an error occurs, such as "java.io.IOException: No FileSystem for scheme: hdfs," check that the path to the Hadoop HDFS JARs are included in the `general.class paths` setting in the *accumulo-site.xml* file.

This script will create an entry in ZooKeeper that will be used to coordinate all configuration information for this Accumulo instance. In addition, the script will create a directory called */accumulo* in HDFS, in which all table data will be stored.

If the *accumulo* user cannot write to the root directory of HDFS, an error will be thrown. Ensure that the *accumulo* user can create the */accumulo* directory in HDFS, or create it beforehand and grant ownership to *accumulo*. Alternatively, configure Accumulo to use a different directory that the *accumulo* user has permission to write to by changing the `instance.dfs.dir` property in *accumulo-site.xml* as described in "File Permissions" on page 401.

After initialization, there will be three tables in Accumulo: *accumulo.root*, *accumulo.metadata*, and the *trace* table. See Chapter 10 for more information on how Accumulo makes use of those tables.

To reinitialize

If for some reason you want to reinitalize an Accumulo cluster, the */accumulo* directory (or whichever directory is specified as `instance.dfs.dir`) in HDFS must be moved or deleted first. Deleting */accumulo* will erase all data in any existing Accumulo tables. This can be done via the command:

```
hadoop fs -rmr /accumulo
```

Or you can simply move the directory:

```
hadoop fs -mv /accumulo /new path
```

After this is done, the *accumulo init* script can be run again. Accumulo processes should be stopped before you run the init script. The script will prompt for an instance name. If the instance name has ever been used before, the script will prompt to delete the existing entry from ZooKeeper. Answering **Y** will remove any information previously associated with that instance name, at which point initialization will proceed normally.

Multiple instances

An Accumulo instance is a logical grouping of processes into one cooperative application. It is possible for multiple Accumulo instances to share a ZooKeeper cluster and an HDFS cluster. The instances must have unique instance names and they must be configured to use different directories in HDFS.

Additionally, if processes that belong to two different Accumulo instances are located on the same server, they must be configured to use different TCP ports to communicate. The port properties to configure depend on the type of process, and include `master.port.client`, `tserver.port.client`, `gc.port.client`, `monitor.port.client`, `monitor.port.log4j`, and `trace.port.client`.

Running Very Large-Scale Clusters

Accumulo is designed to run on clusters of up to thousands of machines. There are some things to consider when running at very large scale that may not be an issue on smaller clusters.

Networking

As a distributed application, Accumulo relies heavily on the network that connects servers to one another. Like Apache Hadoop, Accumulo does not require exotic networking hardware, and it is designed to operate well on commodity-class networking components such as Gigabit Ethernet and 10 Gigabit Ethernet. Modern Hadoop configuration recommendations include considering 10 Gigabit Ethernet for reduced latency.

Limits

The largest clusters begin to be bottlenecked not by any component of Accumulo but by the underlying subsystems on which it runs. In particular, a single HDFS Name-Node becomes a bottleneck in terms of the number of update operations that the entire cluster can perform over time. This limit can be observed by looking at the time that the Accumulo garbage collector takes to complete one pass. If the garbage collector is taking over five minutes to run, the NameNode is likely a bottleneck.

Accumulo 1.6 introduces the ability to run Accumulo over multiple NameNodes to overcome this limitation. See "Using Multiple HDFS Volumes" on page 413.

Metadata Table

Accumulo's metadata table (called *accumulo.metadata* in Accumulo 1.6) is a special table designed to store the current location and other information about each tablet of every other table. As such it plays an important role in the operation of every Accumulo application.

By default, the metadata table is configured to be scalable and to provide good performance for even large clusters. Understanding how the configuration of the metadata table affects performance and scalability can help you fine-tune your cluster. In large Accumulo clusters the metadata table can be split and hosted by additional tablet servers in order to scale with the number of clients performing metadata lookups.

The default configuration for the metadata table is different from that of other tables. It is tuned for high performance and availability, and to take advantage of its relatively small size.

To improve query performance, the size of compressed file blocks is reduced from 100 K to 32 K, the data block cache is enabled so that the frequent reads by clients are serviced very quickly from data cached in memory, and the major compaction ratio is set to 1.

To increase availability and decrease the possibility of data loss, the file replication is increased to 5 (or the maximum replication defined in HDFS if that is less than 5, or the minimum replication defined in HDFS if that is greater than 5).

The split threshold is decreased from 1 GB to 64 MB because the metadata table is so much smaller than data tables, and because we want the metadata tablets spread onto multiple tablet servers for better read and write throughput.

Two locality groups are configured, so that columns that are accessed together frequently can be read more efficiently.

The metadata table configuration generally does not need to be adjusted. If your metadata table is heavily taxed early on, before it has gotten large enough for it to naturally split onto a desired number of tablet servers, you could lower the split threshold temporarily to obtain more metadata tablets.

The metadata table's design is not a limiting factor in the scalability of Accumulo. Going by the following simple calculation in the Bigtable paper (*http://bit.ly/bigtable_paper*), the metadata table can address more data than can be stored in HDFS:

Each METADATA row stores approximately 1KB of data in memory. With a modest limit of 128 MB METADATA tablets, our three-level location scheme is sufficient to address 2^{34} tablets (or 2^{61} bytes in 128 MB tablets).

Tablet Sizing

Having fewer, larger tablets can reduce the overhead of managing a large-scale cluster. This can be achieved by increasing the split threshold for splitting one tablet into two. Tablets that are tens of gigabytes in size are not unreasonable.

To increase the tablet split threshold, change the `table.split.threshold` in the shell:

```
user@accumulo myTable> config -t myTable -s table.split.threshold=20GB
```

File Sizing

For the same reason that larger tablet sizes can reduce overhead, it can be useful to increase the block size in HDFS to a value closer to the size of tablets. This reduces the amount of information the NameNode has to manage for each file, allowing the NameNode to manage more overall files.

To increase the block size for a table, set `table.file.blocksize`:

```
user@accumulo> config -t mytable -s table.file.blocksize=1GB
```

Be careful not to confuse `table.file.blocksize`, which controls the size of HDFS blocks for a given table, with `tserver.default.blocksize`, which controls the size of blocks to cache in tablet server memory.

Using Multiple HDFS Volumes

Accumulo version 1.6 and later can store files using multiple HDFS volumes, potentially on multiple NameNodes. There are several options for doing this. One is to configure Accumulo to run over two or more separate HDFS instances, each with a NameNode and a set of DataNodes, and DataNodes each store data for only one

NameNode (Figure 11-10). In this case, DataNodes are not shared between NameNodes and they operate without any knowledge of one another. Accumulo simply keeps track of which files live in which HDFS instance.

 Support for using multiple HDFS volumes is new and tooling for controlling distribution and customization is limited.

Accumulo does this by using full path names to all the files under management, including the hostname of the NameNode of the HDFS cluster in which each file lives. After Accumulo is informed of the list of NameNodes to use in the configuration file, no other configuration is necessary. Accumulo will automatically distribute files across HDFS clusters evenly.

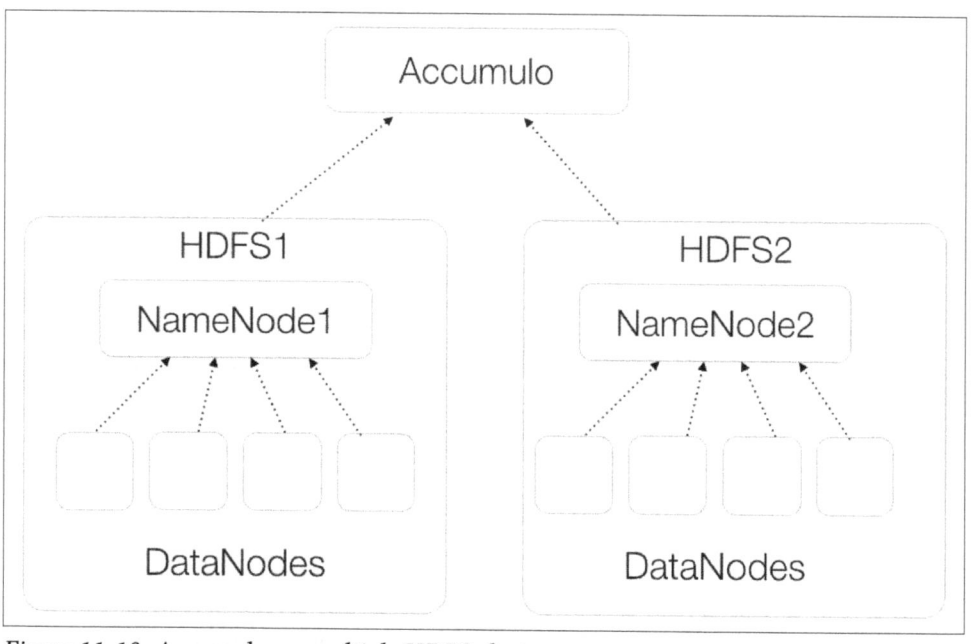

Figure 11-10. Accumulo on multiple HDFS clusters

Another option is to use NameNode *federation*, in which a set of DataNodes are shared between two or more NameNodes (Figure 11-11). Federation can make it easier to keep the data in HDFS balanced because each NameNode can see the information on every DataNode and place data based on the load of all the DataNodes.

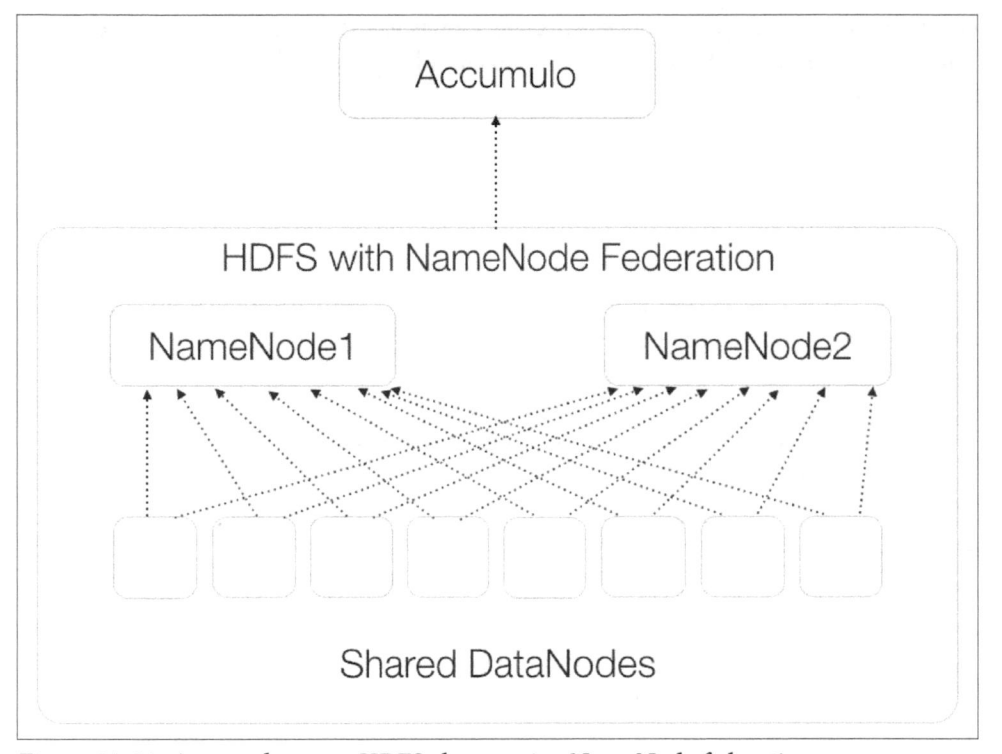

Figure 11-11. Accumulo on an HDFS cluster using NameNode federation

In either of these cases, the configuration of Accumulo is the same. A list of NameNodes to use is specified in the *accumulo-site.xml* file under the `instance.volumes` property:

```
<property>
  <name>instance.volumes</name>
  <value>hdfs://namenode1:9001/accumulo,hdfs://namenode2:9001/accumulo</value>
</property>
```

Accumulo instances that utilize multiple NameNodes are capable of scaling to extremely large sizes, beyond a few thousand nodes to ten thousand or more. With modern hard drives each server could have up to 30 TB raw, 10 TB after replication, and a cluster of 10,000 servers could store up to 100 PB. Accumulo provides a single unified view of all of this data, and lookups remain fast because of the ordering of the keys in each table.

Handling NameNode hostname changes

Because Accumulo keeps track of the hostname of the NameNode when using multiple NameNodes, special care must be taken when moving a NameNode to a new hostname. If a NameNode is moved from *namenodeA* to *namenode1*, an additional configuration property, `instance.volumes.replacements`, must be added and Accumulo must be restarted in order for Accumulo to be able to talk to the new NameNode:

```
<property>
   <name>instance.volumes.replacements</name>
   <value>hdfs://namenodeA:9001/accumulo hdfs://namenode1:9001/accumulo</value>
</property>
```

If more than one NameNode changes hostnames this way, each pair of NameNode hostnames should be listed, with commas separating pairs of hostnames and spaces separating individual hostnames:

```
<property>
  <name>instance.volumes.replacements</name>
  <value>hdfs://namenodeA:9001/accumulo hdfs://namenode1:9001/accumulo,
         hdfs://namenodeB:9001/accumulo hdfs://namenode2:9001/accumulo</value>
</property>
```

Security

Accumulo works to protect data from unauthorized access. Like any security measures, the features Accumulo provides must be coordinated with other system security measures in order to achieve the intended protection.

There are three requirements for Accumulo to guarantee that no data is exposed in an unauthorized manner:

- Data is properly labeled when inserted by Accumulo clients.
- Accumulo clients present the proper authorization tokens when reading data.
- Supporting systems listed in "System Services" on page 385 and supporting software are secured.

Column Visibilities and Accumulo Clients

Accumulo will authenticate a user according to the user's credentials (such as a password), and authorize that user to read data according to the column visibilities present within that data and the authorizations granted to the user. All other means of accessing Accumulo table data must be restricted.

Supporting Software Security

Because Accumulo stores data in HDFS, access to these files must be restricted. This includes access to both the RFiles, which store long-term data, and Accumulo's write-ahead logs, which store recently written data. Accumulo should be the only application allowed to access these files in HDFS.

Similarly, HDFS stores blocks of files in an underlying Linux filesystem. Users who have access to blocks of HDFS data stored in the Linux filesystem would also bypass data-level protections. Access to the file directories on which HDFS data is stored should be limited to the HDFS daemon user.

Unnecessary services should be turned off.

The *accumulo-site.xml* file should not be readable except by the *accumulo* user, because it contains the instance secret and the trace user's password. A separate *conf/* directory with files readable by other users can be created for client use, with an *accumulo-site.xml* file that does not contain those two properties.

Network Security

IPTables or other firewall implementations can be used to help restrict access to TCP ports.

Accumulo uses the port numbers listed in Table 11-2 by default. These should be reachable by Accumulo clients as well as by one another.

Table 11-2. Accumulo network ports

Setting name	Port number	Purpose
monitor.port.log4j	4560	The listening port for the monitor's log4j logging collection
tserver.port.client	9997	The port used for handling client connections on the tablet servers
master.port.client	9999	The port used for handling client connections on the master
trace.port.client	12234	The listening port for the trace server.
n/a	42424	Accumulo proxy server port
gc.port.client	50091	The listening port for the garbage collector's monitor service
monitor.port.client	50095	The listening port for the monitor's HTTP service

Accumulo tablet servers must be able to communicate with HDFS DataNodes and the NameNode.

Only trusted client applications should be allowed to connect to ZooKeeper and Accumulo tablet servers.

Configuring SSL

As of Accumulo 1.6.0, the Secure Sockets Layer (SSL) cryptographic protocol can be configured to secure communications among Accumulo server processes and among server and client processes. This prevents anyone with access to the network devices from reading data as it is passed from servers to clients or servers to other servers.

To configure Accumulo to communicate over SSL, each client and server should have:

- Cryptographic x.509 certificates generated
- Certificates stored in Java KeyStore files
- SSL properties configured in *accumulo-site.xml* for servers and in the client *config* file for clients

The SSL configuration properties are described in Table 11-3. The client *config* file is described in "Client Configuration" on page 406.

The Java *truststore* should contain the public certificate of the authority that has signed all of the server certificates.

Table 11-3. Accumulo SSL properties

Setting name	Default	Purpose
instance.rpc.ssl.enabled	false	Enable SSL
instance.rpc.ssl.clientAuth	false	Require clients to present SSL certs as well as servers
rpc.javax.net.ssl.keyStore	$ACCUMULO_CONF_DIR/ssl/keystore.jks	Path to keystore
rpc.javax.net.ssl.keyStorePassword	[empty]	Keystore password (if empty, uses Accumulo instance.secret)
rpc.javax.net.ssl.keyStoreType	jks	Keystore type
rpc.javax.net.ssl.trustStore	$ACCUMULO_CONF_DIR/ssl/truststore.jks	Path to truststore
rpc.javax.net.ssl.trustStorePassword	[empty]	Truststore password (if empty, uses no password)
rpc.javax.net.ssl.trustStoreType	jks	Truststore type

If Accumulo is configured to require clients to present certificates, each client must also have a *keystore* and *truststore* file. Configuring clients to use a keystore is not done in the *accumulo-site.xml* file, because clients typically should not have access to this file. Client configuration properties can be specified in a properties file (each line containing a "name-value" pair) in the user's home directory in a file named ~/.accumulo/config or in the file $ACCUMULO_CONF_DIR/client.conf.

An example client configuration is:

```
instance.rpc.ssl.clientAuth true
instance.rpc.ssl.enabled true
rpc.javax.net.ssl.keyStore path_to_keystore
rpc.javax.net.ssl.keyStorePassword keystore_password
```

If you are using your own Certificate Authority (CA), a separate truststore file containing the public key of the CA can be distributed to servers and clients as well, specified by the following:

```
rpc.javax.net.ssl.trustStore path_to_truststore
rpc.javax.net.ssl.trustStorePassword truststore_password
```

Separately, Accumulo's monitor web page can be configured to use HTTPS instead of HTTP. This is independent of whether Accumulo is using SSL for RPC. This is done by configuring the monitor to use a keystore and truststore with the following properties, similar to setting the RPC properties:

```
monitor.ssl.keyStore
monitor.ssl.keyStorePassword
monitor.ssl.trustStore
monitor.ssl.trustStorePassword
```

An example of creating a set of certificates from our own CA is as follows. First we'll create a Certificate Authority and place its public key in a keystore file, which will call the truststore:

```
[centos@centos ~]$ openssl genrsa -des3 -out root.key 4096
Generating RSA private key, 4096 bit long modulus
.............................++
..................................................................................
      ......++
e is 65537 (0x10001)
Enter pass phrase for root.key:
Verifying - Enter pass phrase for root.key:

[centos@centos ~]$ ls
root.key
```

Next we'll create a certificate request:

```
[centos@centos ~]$ openssl req -x509 -new -key root.key  -days 365 \
                        -out root.pem
Enter pass phrase for root.key:
You are about to be asked to enter information that will be incorporated
into your certificate request.
What you are about to enter is what is called a Distinguished Name or a DN.
There are quite a few fields but you can leave some blank
For some fields there will be a default value,
If you enter '.', the field will be left blank.
```

```
-----
Country Name (2 letter code) [XX]:US
State or Province Name (full name) []:DC
Locality Name (eg, city) [Default City]:Washington
Organization Name (eg, company) [Default Company Ltd]:Accumulo Corp
Organizational Unit Name (eg, section) []:Developers
Common Name (eg, your name or your server's hostname) []:Cert Auth
Email Address []:certs@accumulocorp.com
[centos@centos ~]$ ls
root.key  root.pem
```

Now we can generate a Base-64 encoded version of our PEM file:

```
[centos@centos ~]$ openssl x509 -outform der -in root.pem -out root.der
```

The Base-64 encoded certificate now can be imported into our Java keystore:

```
[centos@centos ~]$ keytool -import -alias root-key -keystore truststore.jks \
                        -file root.der
Enter keystore password:
Re-enter new password:
Owner: EMAILADDRESS=certs@accumulocorp.com, CN=Cert Auth, OU=Developers,
        O=Accumulo Corp, L=Seattle, ST=Washington, C=US
Issuer: EMAILADDRESS=certs@accumulocorp.com, CN=Cert Auth, OU=Developers,
        O=Accumulo Corp, L=Seattle, ST=Washington, C=US
Serial number: abd68bf897fcf631
Valid from: Sun Sep 14 15:57:19 GMT-05:00 2014 until: Mon Sep 14 15:57:19
        GMT-05:00 2015
...
Trust this certificate? [no]:  yes
Certificate was added to keystore
[centos@centos ~]$ ls
root.der  root.key  root.pem  truststore.jks
```

The *root.der* file can be deleted. The *root.key* file should be protected because it is used to authorize client and server certificates.

The *truststore.jks* file should be copied to servers and clients that will communicate using certificates generated by this CA's keys. This way, processes can verify that the certificates presented are authentic.

With our new CA, we can generate certificates for all the machines that will participate in our Accumulo cluster, including servers and clients.

First, we'll generate a server key:

```
[centos@centos ssl]$ openssl genrsa -out server.key 4096
Generating RSA private key, 4096 bit long modulus
..............................................................................
        ..............................................................................
        ...................++
..............................................................................++
e is 65537 (0x10001)
```

Next we'll create a certificate request that we can use with our CA to create a server certificate:

```
[centos@centos ssl]$ openssl req -new -key server.key -out server.csr
You are about to be asked to enter information that will be incorporated
into your certificate request.
What you are about to enter is what is called a Distinguished Name or a DN.
There are quite a few fields but you can leave some blank
For some fields there will be a default value,
If you enter '.', the field will be left blank.
-----
Country Name (2 letter code) [XX]:
State or Province Name (full name) []:
Locality Name (eg, city) [Default City]:
Organization Name (eg, company) [Default Company Ltd]:
Organizational Unit Name (eg, section) []:
Common Name (eg, your name or your server's hostname) []:
Email Address []:

Please enter the following 'extra' attributes
to be sent with your certificate request
A challenge password []:
An optional company name []:
[centos@centos ssl]$ ls
root.key  root.pem  server.csr  server.key  truststore.jks
```

Now we'll use our CA keys to generate a server certificate from the certificate request:

```
[centos@centos ssl]$ openssl x509 -req -in server.csr -CA root.pem \
                     -CAkey root.key -CAcreateserial -out server.pem -days 365
Signature ok
subject=/C=XX/L=Default City/O=Default Company Ltd
Getting CA Private Key
Enter pass phrase for root.key:
[centos@centos ssl]$
[centos@centos ssl]$ ls
root.key  root.pem  root.srl  server.csr  server.key  server.pem  truststore.jks
```

Next we'll make a PKCS12 file from our server certificate that we can use to import into our keystore:

```
[centos@centos ssl]$ openssl pkcs12 -export -in server.pem -inkey server.key \
                     -certfile server.pem -name 'server-key' -out server.p12
Enter Export Password:
Verifying - Enter Export Password:
[centos@centos ssl]$ ls
root.key  root.pem  root.srl  server.csr  server.key  server.p12  server.pem
    truststore.jks
```

Let's import the PKCS12 file into our keystore:

```
[centos@centos ssl]$ keytool -importkeystore -srckeystore server.p12 \
                     -srcstoretype pkcs12 -destkeystore server.jks \
                     -deststoretype JKS
```

```
Enter destination keystore password:
Re-enter new password:
Enter source keystore password:
Entry for alias server-key successfully imported.
Import command completed:  1 entries successfully imported, 0 entries failed
            or cancelled
```

We can remove the *.p12* file because it's no longer needed:

```
[centos@centos ssl]$ rm server.p12
```

The *server.jks*, *server.key*, and *truststore.jks* files should be moved to the Accumulo server and protected by changing ownership of the files to the user that Accumulo processes run as, and restricting access to only that user. The absolute local filesystem paths to and pass phrases for the *truststore.jks* and *server.jks* files should be put into the *accumulo-site.xml* file, as described in Table 11-3.

After this configuration process, Accumulo will employ SSL in communications between clients and servers, and between servers.

Encryption of Data at Rest

Accumulo controls access to data for client programs that are configured to pass user authorizations as part of scan operations. Cryptography can be used to secure data from those with physical access to storage components in which data is stored.

As of Accumulo version 1.6.0, data stored on disk can be encrypted via pluggable modules, with the exception of data stored in HDFS as part of the tablet server recovery process. An example implementation ships with Accumulo, although it stores the master key for all encryption keys in HDFS along with encrypted files.

To configure Accumulo to use encryption when storing files, add the following properties to *accumulo-site.xml*:

```
<property>
  <name>crypto.module.class</name>
  <value>org.apache.accumulo.core.security.crypto.DefaultCryptoModule</value>
</property>

<property>
  <name>crypto.cipher.suite</name>
  <value>AES/CFB/NoPadding</value>
</property>

<property>
  <name>crypto.cipher.algorithm.name</name>
  <value>AES</value>
</property>

<property>
  <name>crypto.cipher.key.length</name>
```

```
    <value>128</value>
  </property>

  <property>
    <name>crypto.secure.rng</name>
    <value>SHA1PRNG</value>
  </property>

  <property>
    <name>crypto.secure.rng.provider</name>
    <value>SUN</value>
  </property>

  <property>
    <name>crypto.secret.key.encryption.strategy.class</name>
    <value>org.apache.accumulo.core.security.crypto.
                CachingHDFSSecretKeyEncryptionStrategy</value>
  </property>

  <property>
      <name>crypto.default.key.strategy.cipher.suite</name>
      <value>AES/ECB/NoPadding</value>
  </property>
```

Kerberized Hadoop

Apache Hadoop can be deployed using Kerberos to control the processes that are allowed to participate in the cluster. To use Accumulo with a kerberized HDFS instance, you must create an Accumulo principal:

```
kadmin.local -q "addprinc -randkey accumulo/[hostname]"
```

Principals can then be exported to a *keytab* file. There can be a separate keytab file for each server, or all principals can be globbed into a single keytab file as follows:

```
kadmin.local -q "xst -k accumulo.keytab -glob accumulo*"
```

The keytab file for a server must be stored locally on that server, owned by the *accumulo* user with file permissions 400. A suggested location for the keytab file is the *$ACCUMULO_HOME/conf* directory. The absolute local path to the the keytab file on each server must be specified in the *accumulo-site.xml* file, as well as the principal. The placeholder _HOST can be used for the hostname, but the realm must be specified:

```
  <property>
    <name>general.kerberos.keytab</name>
    <value>$ACCUMULO_CONF_DIR/accumulo.keytab</value>
  </property>

  <property>
    <name>general.kerberos.principal</name>
    <value>accumulo/_HOST@[realm]</value>
  </property>
```

Application Permissions

Accumulo has the concept of a user permission, but more often these are associated with a particular application that may provide access to multiple users. Accumulo clients can do their own authentication of multiple users and also look up any associated authorization tokens, which they then faithfully pass to Accumulo tablet servers when doing scans.

Before any user can read any data, however, an account must be created, authorization tokens assigned, and access to tables granted. Administrators can work with application developers to determine the right level of access for the account and how to determine the set of authorization tokens to grant to the account.

To create an account in the shell, run the `createuser` command:

```
root@accumulo> createuser myapp
Enter new password for 'myapp': *****
Please confirm new password for 'myapp': *****
```

To allow this account to read a particular table, run:

```
root@accumulo> grant Table.READ -t mytable -u myapp
root@accumulo> System permissions:

Table permissions (!METADATA): Table.READ
Table permissions (mytable): Table.READ
```

To grant authorizations to an account, run:

```
root@accumulo> setauths -u myapp -s myauth
root@accumulo> getauths -u myapp
myauth
```

To see what permissions a user account has, run:

```
root@accumulo> userpermissions -u myapp
```

Once this has been done, an Accumulo client identified by the *myapp* account can connect to Accumulo, passing in the password specified, and perform scans against the *mytable* table and pass in the *myauth* authorization token . If a client tries to read from another table, or tries to write to *mytable*, or tries to pass in a different authorization token, it will receive an Authorization exception.

A list of available permissions can be seen via the `systempermissions` and `tablepermissions` commands.

See "Permissions" on page 177 for more on permissions.

Administration: Running

Before Accumulo is started, HDFS and ZooKeeper must be running.

Accumulo can either be managed from a single control node using scripts provided in the *bin/* directory, or using *init.d* scripts.

A running instance can be verified using the monitoring methods described in "Monitoring" on page 429.

Starting Accumulo

This section describes two types of scripts you can use to start Accumulo.

Via the start-all.sh Script

The *start-all.sh* script will SSH into all the machines listed in *masters*, *slaves*, *gc*, *monitor*, and *tracers* and start the associated processes. Password-less SSH is required to do this without having to type passwords for each machine.

 In each of these files, the hostname of machines should be listed, rather than IP address. In addition, each hostname should resolve to an IP address that can be resolved back to the same hostname.

Here is additional detail on each of the host files:

slaves

> The *conf/slaves* file is used by the *start-all.sh* script to start Accumulo processes on worker nodes, namely tablet server and, in the case of Accumulo 1.4 and

earlier, logger processes. The hostnames of all machines that should run tablet server processes should be listed in this file.

In cases in which a tablet server will run on the same machines that will host master processes, the hostname of those machines should be listed here too.

masters

The *conf/masters* file contains a list of the machines that will run a master process. There should be at least one machine, but more than two or three is generally not necessary. If more than one machine is listed here, the master processes will choose an active master, and the others will serve as failover masters in the case that the active master fails. Unlike tablet servers, only a few machines need to run master processes.

gc

This file contains a list of the machines that will run garbage collector processes. Like the master, only one will be active at any given time and any machines beyond the first will only take over should the active garbage collector fail.

monitor

This file contains a list of the machines that will run monitor processes. Like the master, only one will be active at any given time and any machines beyond the first will only take over should the active monitor fail.

tracers

This file contains a list of the machines that will run tracer processes. Like the master, only one will be active at any given time and any machines beyond the first will only take over should the active tracer fail.

Via init.d Scripts

Some distributions of Hadoop include *init.d* scripts for Accumulo.

The `ACCUMULO_HOME` environment variable may need to be set in the script.

Accumulo can then be started by running:

```
sudo service accumulo start
```

Depending on the *masters*, *slaves*, etc. files, processes will be started based on the files in which a machine's hostname appears.

Accumulo processes can be started at boot time and stopped at shutdown by adding the *accumulo* script to one or more Linux *runlevels*.

Stopping Accumulo

Accumulo clusters can be stopped gracefully, flushing all in-memory entries before exiting so that the next startup can proceed without having to recover any data from write-ahead logs. The Accumulo master orchestrates this shutdown.

Via the stop-all.sh Script

If using the *start-all.sh* and *stop-all.sh* scripts, Accumulo can be shut down via the *stop-all.sh* script. This script will attempt to talk to the master to orchestrate the shutdown. If the master is not running, the *stop-all.sh* script will hang. Hitting Ctrl-C will prompt the user to hit Ctrl-C again to cancel shutdown or else the script will forcefully kill all tablet servers and other Accumulo processes. If Accumulo is stopped this way, the next time the system is started tablet servers must recover any writes that were in memory at shutdown time from the write-ahead logs.

Usually this is not necessary. If the master is down, bringing up a new master process, perhaps on another machine, before attempting to shut down will help reduce the need for recovery on startup.

The `accumulo admin` command can also be used to stop the cluster:

```
accumulo admin stopAll
```

If a `ClassNotFoundException` occurs when using the *stop-all.sh* script, ensure that the MapReduce and HDFS JARs are correctly specified in the `general.classpaths` property in the *accumulo-site.xml* file.

Via init.d scripts

To stop all Accumulo processes on a particular node, run:

```
sudo service accumulo stop
```

Stopping Individual Processes

Individual processes can also be stopped gracefully to avoid recovery from write-ahead logs.

To stop an individual tablet server:

```
accumulo admin stop hostname
```

To stop the master:

```
accumulo admin stopMaster
```

Starting After a Crash

If tablet server processes crash or exit due to a temporary network partition, they can simply be restarted and the Accumulo master will start assigning tablets to them.

If a cluster was shut down without allowing tablet servers to flush, (e.g., if processes were all killed with a `kill -9` or if power was lost to the cluster), the cluster can be restarted and the process of recovery will begin.

For each tablet on a tablet server that was killed before it could flush the entries in memory to HDFS, the Accumulo master will coordinate a recovery process. See "Recovery" on page 367 for details.

During the recovery process, tablet servers will be assigned a tablet and will attempt to replay the mutations written to the write-ahead log to re-create the state that was in the memory of the machines that were killed. This process can take from a few seconds to a few minutes depending on the size of the write-ahead logs. The master will display the status of this process on the monitor page.

Clients can begin to read and write to tablets that aren't involved in recoveries while recoveries are taking place. As soon as a tablet's recovery is complete, clients can again read and write key-value pairs to it.

For additional information on steps to recover a cluster in cases when automatic recovery is insufficient, see "Failure Recovery" on page 456.

Now that Accumulo is installed, configured, and running, clients can connect, create tables, and read and write data.

The primary administrative concerns at this point are monitoring system usage and health, and adding or removing machines from the cluster as a result of failure or response to changes in usage. Accumulo is designed to operate on large clusters, and most individual failures do not require immediate administrative attention. Otherwise, keeping up would quickly become infeasible. Accumulo automatically detects certain types of machine failures and automatically recovers from them, reassigning work to remaining healthy machines in some cases.

For many maintenance operations it is not necessary to stop an Accumulo instance. This allows clients to continue to operate as machines fail, are added, or are removed.

One notable exception to this is in the case of upgrades. Accumulo does not yet support *rolling upgrades*, a practice in which some machines are brought down, upgraded, and introduced to the cluster while machines that have not been upgraded are still participating in the cluster.

Monitoring

Accumulo provides several methods of monitoring system health and usage. These include the monitor web service, logging, and JMX metrics.

Monitor Web Service

Accumulo provides a monitor process that gathers information from a running cluster and presents it in one place for convenience. The monitor makes it relatively simple to determine system health and performance.

Overview

The default view in the monitor presents an overview of activity in the cluster (Figure 12-1). Particularly useful are the various graphs on this page. Administrators and developers can quickly gain an idea of how well the cluster is operating, spot issues, and analyze application performance.

The main section of this page shows two tables, followed by 10 graphs, all in two columns. The two tables show information from the Accumulo master and about the ZooKeeper cluster.

An attempt is made to draw attention to any known problems with the cluster in the form of a red background that appears behind information that indicates a severe problem. This includes things such as the master being down, unassigned tablets, and log warnings and errors.

On the left are links to all the other views, described next.

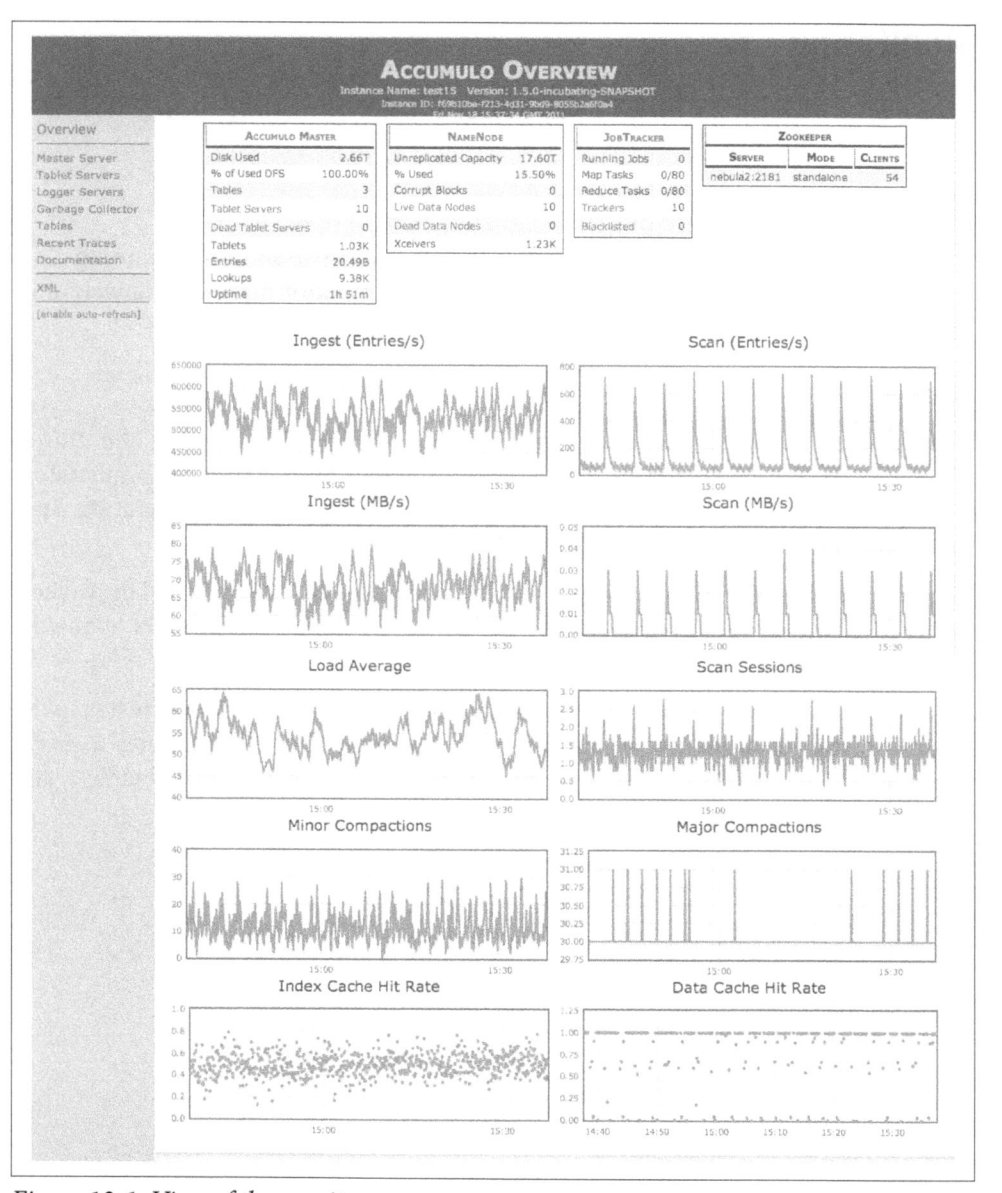

Figure 12-1. View of the monitor

Master Server View

The Master Server View provides information on the instance overall, as well as a list of tables.

A legend is provided of the meaning of the columns in the first table:

 # Online Tablet Servers
    Number of tablet servers currently available.

 # Total Tablet Servers
    The total number of tablet servers configured.

Last GC
    The last time files were cleaned-up from HDFS.

Entries
    The total number of key-value pairs in Accumulo.

Ingest
    The number of key-value pairs inserted, per second. (Note that deleted records are counted as "inserted" and will make the ingest rate increase in the near-term.)

Entries Read
    The total number of key-value pairs read on the server side. (Not all may be returned because of filtering.)

Entries Returned
    The total number of key-value pairs returned as a result of scans.

Hold Time
    The maximum amount of time that ingest has been held across all servers due to a lack of memory to store the records.

Load
    The one-minute load average on the computer that runs the monitor web server.

This view is where active recoveries from any tablet server failures are displayed.

Tablet Servers View

The Tablet Servers View shows a list of active tablet servers and activity per server.

Here, an administrator can quickly see if tablets are evenly distributed across servers, how many key-value pairs (entries) per second are being ingested, and how many entries are being read for each server. This view is particularly useful for determining whether the entire cluster is being utilized evenly, or whether there are *hotspots* (i.e., a few servers that are handling the majority of the load).

Note that this view does not show which tablets belong to which tables.

Clicking the hostname of a tablet server will show a list of tablets currently hosted by that server. Statistics about server activities such as compactions and splits are also shown.

Server Activity View

This view is a graphical representation of various aspects of server activity across the cluster.

Each circle or square in the grid represents a tablet server. Various dimensions of each server can be displayed as color or motion, according to the selections from the drop-down menus across the top of the view.

The intent of this view is to provide a high density of information at a quick glance. For example, you can choose to monitor load to see which servers may be overloaded, including by work from other processes running alongside tablet servers. Or you can choose to show queries to try to highlight any hotspots and reveal flaws in table design.

You can show information for an individual server by hovering the mouse cursor over a particular square or circle.

Garbage Collector View

The Garbage Collector View shows recent activity performed by the garbage collector. Administrators will want to check this view to make sure the garbage collector is running. Without it, the cluster could run out of disk space as files are combined in compaction operations, creating new files and making old files obsolete.

Tables View

The Tables View shows activity on a per-table basis.

Of particular interest here is the number of tablets per table. The aggregate ingest rate and number of concurrent queries will increase as the number of servers hosting a table's tablets increases, up until all servers have at least one of the table's tablets.

To see which servers are hosting a table's tablets, administrators can click the name of the table. A list of servers and the number of tablets from this particular tablet is shown.

Recent Traces View

This view shows information about recent traces, which are a sample of operations that are timed to indicate performance.

For more on tracing, see "Tracing" on page 436.

Documentation View

This view shows links to various types of documentation, including:

- User Manual
- Administration
- Combiners
- Constraints
- Bulk Ingest
- Configuration
- Isolation
- Java API
- Locality Groups
- Timestamps
- Metrics
- Distributed Tracing

Recent Logs View

This view collects log messages at the warn and error level from across the cluster. This can be very useful as clusters get larger and going out to each individual server becomes more cumbersome.

Logs are listed in ascending time order, so the latest messages appear at the bottom. You can dismiss messages that have been read and acknowledged by clicking Clear All Events.

JMX Metrics

Metrics can be enabled for measuring several operations throughout an Accumulo cluster. These include metrics such as:

- Number of minor or major compactions currently running
- Number of entries in memory
- Minimum and maximum times for scan operations
- Average time for commit preparation

The collection of these is controlled via the *$ACCUMULO_HOME/conf/accumulo-metrics.xml* file. This file allows metrics to be enabled and logged. When logging is enabled, files will be created by default in *$ACCUMULO_HOME/metrics*.

To allow servers to accept JMX connections, we may have to first modify *accumulo-env.sh* by adding the following lines:

```
export ACCUMULO_TSERVER_OPTS="-Dcom.sun.management.jmxremote.port=9006 \
    -Dcom.sun.management.jmxremote.authenticate=false \
    -Dcom.sun.management.jmxremote.ssl=false $ACCUMULO_TSERVER_OPTS"
export ACCUMULO_MASTER_OPTS="-Dcom.sun.management.jmxremote.port=9002 \
    -Dcom.sun.management.jmxremote.authenticate=false \
    -Dcom.sun.management.jmxremote.ssl=false $ACCUMULO_MASTER_OPTS"
export ACCUMULO_MONITOR_OPTS="-Dcom.sun.management.jmxremote.port=9003 \
    -Dcom.sun.management.jmxremote.authenticate=false \
    -Dcom.sun.management.jmxremote.ssl=false $ACCUMULO_MONITOR_OPTS"
export ACCUMULO_GC_OPTS="-Dcom.sun.management.jmxremote.port=9004 \
    -Dcom.sun.management.jmxremote.authenticate=false \
    -Dcom.sun.management.jmxremote.ssl=false $ACCUMULO_GC_OPTS"
export ACCUMULO_LOGGER_OPTS="-Dcom.sun.management.jmxremote.port=9005 \
    -Dcom.sun.management.jmxremote.authenticate=false \
    -Dcom.sun.management.jmxremote.ssl=false $ACCUMULO_LOGGER_OPTS"
```

If we modify this file, Accumulo processes will need to be restarted before these settings will take effect.

Next we can enable the metrics we want. For example, to turn on metrics collection for scans on tablet servers, we can simply change a `boolean` value in the metrics XML file:

```
<tserver>
  <enabled type="boolean">true</enabled>
  <logging type="boolean">false</logging>
  <update>
    <enabled type="boolean">false</enabled>
    <logging type="boolean">false</logging>
  </update>
  <scan>
    <enabled type="boolean">true</enabled>
    <logging type="boolean">false</logging>
  </scan>
```

These configuration files must be distributed throughout the cluster. We can now connect to the JMX port on processes to view the metrics. For example, we can use the `jconsole` command to view metrics for a tablet server by specifying the hostname and port:

```
jconsole
```

This opens the connection window in Figure 12-2.

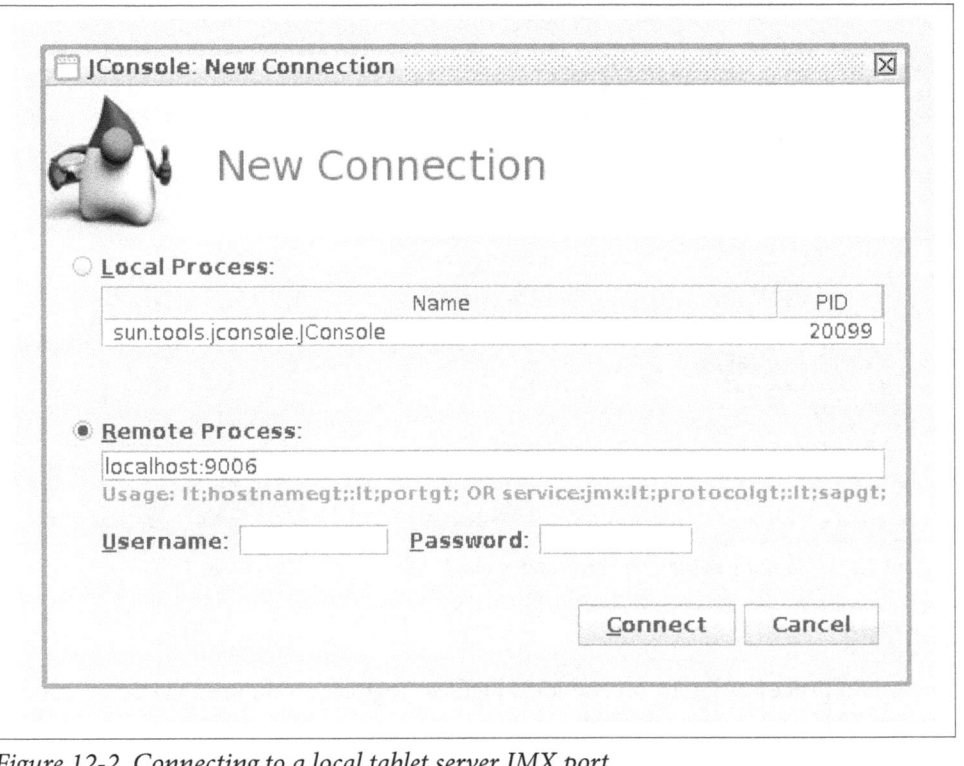

Figure 12-2. Connecting to a local tablet server JMX port

After connecting, we can navigate to the MBean tab and expand the tablet server–related metrics from the options in the left-hand pane (Figure 12-3).

We can also see metrics as they are logged to files in the *metrics/* directory:

```
accumulo@host metrics]$ ls
tserver.scan-20141025.log
```

Alex Moundalexis has written a helpful tutorial (*http://bit.ly/enabling_JMX*) on enabling JMX for use with Ganglia written.

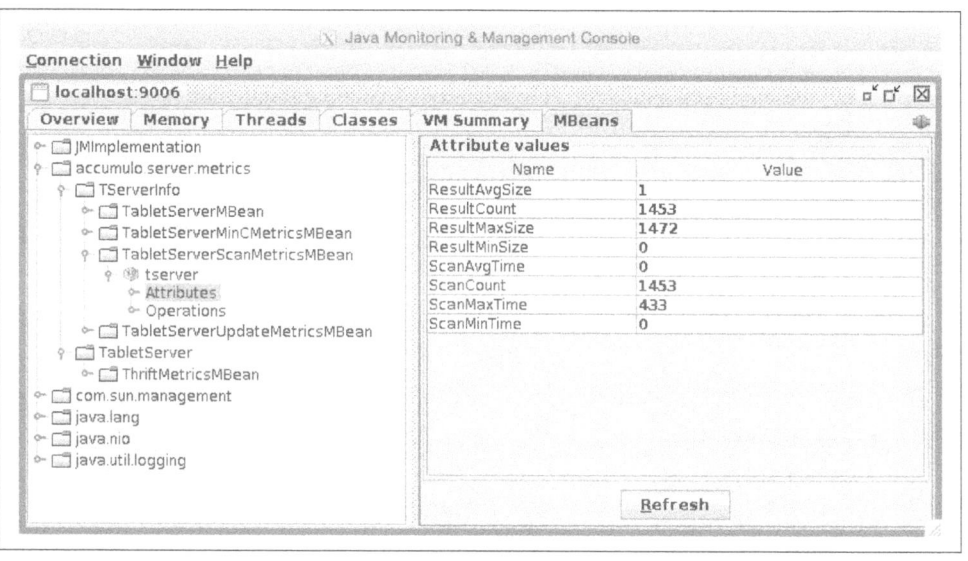

Figure 12-3. Viewing tablet server metrics via JMX

Logging

Accumulo processes log to several local logfiles. Logs are configured via Log4j configuration XML and properties files.

By default, DEBUG-level events are written to a separate debug logfile, INFO and higher-level events are written to the regular log, and WARN and higher-level events are forwarded to the monitor for consolidation. You can modify this behavior by editing the *$ACCUMULO_HOME/conf/generic_logger.xml* file and the *$ACCUMULO_HOME/conf/monitor_logger.xml* file.

You can suppress some types of messages and configure them separately by editing the *log4j.properties* file.

Tracing

In a distributed system, diagnosing application performance and errors can be difficult. This is because operations can span several machines as clients call remote procedure calls on servers and servers call other servers.

In Accumulo, clients talk primarily to tablet servers, which in turn talk to HDFS DataNode processes, all of which can be on different physical servers.

Tracing is a way of following an operation as it moves from server to server in order to get a holistic view of the timing of each stage of the operation. Clients can enable tracing explicitly, and Accumulo also traces some of its internal operations. If an Accumulo tracer process is running, trace information is collected and stored in a *trace* table in Accumulo. The Accumulo shell has a special formatter configured to display this information.

Tracing in the shell

To trace individual shell commands, you can enable tracing with the `trace on` command. Subsequent operations are traced until the `trace off` command is used to disable tracing. After tracing is disabled, trace information will be gathered and printed to the screen:

```
root@accumulo> table test
root@accumulo test> trace on
root@accumulo test> insert g g g g
root@accumulo test> scan
a b:c []    d
e f:g []    h
g g:g []    g
row f:q []     v
root@accumulo test> trace off
Waiting for trace information
Trace started at 2013/12/12 04:33:52.602
Time  Start  Service@Location      Name
14108+0       shell@ubuntu shell:root
   28+10122     shell@ubuntu close
    2+10122      shell@ubuntu binMutations
   28+10127      shell@ubuntu org.apache.accumulo.core.client.impl.
                     TabletServerBatchWriter$MutationWriter 1
   22+10127      shell@ubuntu org.apache.accumulo.core.client.impl.
                     TabletServerBatchWriter$MutationWriter 1
   22+10127       shell@ubuntu sendMutations
    2+10135        shell@ubuntu client:update
   10+10138        tserver@localhost update
    9+10138         tserver@localhost wal
    6+10140          tserver@localhost update
    6+10140           tserver@localhost wal
    2+10142            tserver@localhost update
    2+10142             tserver@localhost wal
    1+10147         tserver@localhost commit
    1+11998     tserver@localhost getTableConfiguration
    1+12003     tserver@localhost getTableConfiguration
    6+12012     shell@ubuntu scan
    6+12012      shell@ubuntu scan:location
    4+12013       tserver@localhost startScan
    4+12013        tserver@localhost tablet read ahead 7
    1+12020     tserver@localhost listLocalUsers
root@accumulo test>
```

See "Using Tracing" on page 481 for more information on enabling tracing in applications and interpreting the trace results.

Cluster Changes

Accumulo is designed to withstand regular occurrences of machine failure, so adding and removing machines from a cluster configuration can be done easily. Machines can be added to or removed from a running Accumulo instance without causing interruption to clients.

Adding New Worker Nodes

A major advantage of the shared-nothing, horizontal scale-out architecture of Accumulo and Hadoop is that adding more hardware resources can increase the aggregate performance of a cluster in a near-linear fashion. Clusters can be increased in size quite a few times and still realize a significant increase in performance rather than sharply diminishing returns.

When additional storage, increased ingest rate, or increased concurrent query performance is required, worker nodes can be added. Empirically, some clusters have been shown to yield an increase of roughly 85 percent in write and query capabilities when a cluster is doubled in size.

To add a new worker machine to a cluster, simply install the Hadoop and Accumulo software (most workers run Hadoop DataNode and tablet server processes), and copy the Hadoop and Accumulo configuration files to the new machines. Upon starting, the DataNode process will contact the HDFS NameNode and let it know that the new machine is available for storing new HDFS data blocks. When the tablet server starts it will register itself in ZooKeeper. The Accumulo master will notice that it is available and has no tablets assigned, and will begin the process of migrating responsibility for hosting several tablets to the new machine.

If the *start-all.sh* and *stop-all.sh* scripts are being used to start and stop the cluster, the new machine should be added to the *conf/slaves* file on the machine from which the start/stop scripts are run.

Removing Worker Nodes

Removing a live worker node from the cluster can be done as simply as turning off the machine. However, this will cause the cluster to have to recover the entries that were in the memory of the machine from write-ahead logs. It can take a while before all the entries are again available for query. In addition, if the worker node is running a DataNode process, the replicas on that node must be rereplicated.

To avoid the recovery process, tablet server processes can be shut down gracefully, in which they flush in-memory entries before exiting. This allows the machines that take over responsibility for its tablets to begin hosting them immediately.

The `accumulo admin` command can be used to shut down a specific tablet server:

```
accumulo admin stop [hostname]
```

If you are using the *start-all.sh* and *stop-all.sh* scripts to control the cluster, the machine's hostname should be removed from the *conf/slaves* file.

If you are removing several machines at once, care must be taken to avoid taking all of the replicas of any particular HDFS data block offline simultaneously. To avoid this, HDFS provides the ability to decommission a DataNode, which will cause HDFS to replicate all the blocks hosted by decommissioning nodes elsewhere. When this process is complete, the nodes can be turned off.

Decommissioning HDFS DataNodes can be done by adding their hostnames to the *conf/excludes.xml* file (or another file defined by the setting dfs.hosts.exclude from *$HADOOP_HOME/conf/hdfs-site.xml*) and running the command:

```
hadoop dfsadmin -refreshNodes
```

This will start the decommissioning process. The HDFS monitor page at *http:// <namenode>:50070* can be used to monitor the process for completion. When the number of decommissioning nodes is 0 and the number of decommissioned nodes reaches the correct number, the DataNode processes can be stopped.

Adding New Control Nodes

Normally control nodes do not need to be added to the cluster in order to improve performance—they don't participate in most client operations such as reading or writing data. From time to time a control node may fail and may need to be restored or replaced.

A new inactive master process can be started at any time provided it has the configuration files for a particular cluster. It will register itself in ZooKeeper and stand by until the active master process fails.

A new garbage collector process can be added if the previous garbage collector has failed. Because the garbage collector runs periodically in the background, it is not configured to perform automatic failure the way the master process is.

Removing Control Nodes

Control node processes do not maintain any persistent state and can simply be killed to remove them from the cluster. The hostnames should also be removed from the masters, monitor, gc, and tracers files to avoid trying to start processes on removed machines the next time start scripts are run.

Before stopping the active master process, an inactive master process should be started in order to ensure a master process is always running in case a tablet server fails. Once the inactive master process is started, the active master can be brought down and the inactive master will automatically take over responsibility.

Table Operations

Administrators can perform various operations on tables through the shell. These functions are also available to applications via the Table API described in Chapter 4.

Changing Settings

Accumulo allows administrators to configure a large number of settings that govern the behavior of Accumulo processes.

Besides the configuration controlled by the files in the Accumulo *conf/* directory, additional settings are stored in ZooKeeper. These settings allow changes to be made that in some cases can be reflected immediately across the cluster without having to restart processes.

The shell can be used to view current settings:

```
accumulo@hostname:~$ accumulo shell -u root
Password: ******

Shell - Apache Accumulo Interactive Shell
-
- version: 1.5.0
- instance name: accumulo
- instance id: xxxxxxxx-xxxx-xxxx-xxxx-xxxxxxxxxxxx
-
- type 'help' for a list of available commands
-
root@accumulo> config
---------+------------------------------------------+----------------------
SCOPE    | NAME                                     | VALUE
---------+------------------------------------------+----------------------
default  | gc.cycle.delay ......................... | 5m
default  | gc.cycle.start ......................... | 30s
...
default  | instance.dfs.uri ....................... |
default  | instance.security.authenticator ........ | org.apache.accumulo.
    server.security.handler.ZKAuthenticator
default  | instance.security.authorizor ........... | org.apache.accumulo.
    server.security.handler.ZKAuthorizor
default  | instance.security.permissionHandler ..... | org.apache.accumulo.
    server.security.handler.ZKPermHandler
default  | instance.zookeeper.host ................ | localhost:2181
...
default  | master.bulk.threadpool.size ............ | 5
default  | master.bulk.timeout .................... | 5m
default  | master.fate.threadpool.size ............ | 4
default  | master.lease.recovery.interval ......... | 5s
default  | master.port.client ..................... | 9999
```

To view a specific setting, use the -f flag:

```
root@accumulo> config -f table.compaction.major.everything.idle
----------+-------------------------------------------+------------------------
SCOPE     | NAME                                      | VALUE
----------+-------------------------------------------+------------------------
default   | table.compaction.major.everything.idle ... | 1h
system    |     @override ........................... | 2h
----------+-------------------------------------------+------------------------
root@accumulo>
```

You can also view settings that match a given prefix:

```
root@accumulo> config -f tserver.bulk
----------+-------------------------------------------+------------------------
SCOPE     | NAME                                      | VALUE
----------+-------------------------------------------+------------------------
default   | tserver.bulk.assign.threads ............. | 1
default   | tserver.bulk.process.threads ............ | 1
default   | tserver.bulk.retry.max .................. | 5
default   | tserver.bulk.timeout .................... | 5m
----------+-------------------------------------------+------------------------
root@accumulo>
```

The config shell command can also be used to change configuration settings.

In some cases this change will be reflected across the cluster immediately:

```
root@accumulo> config -s table.compaction.major.everything.idle=2h
```

Altering load balancing

Tablets should always be balanced evenly across tablet servers, using the default load balancer. The particular load balancer in use can be controlled on a per-table basis via the table.balancer property.

Information about configuring load balancers and how the load balancers work can be found in "Additional Properties" on page 151.

Configuring iterators

At times administrators will find it useful to enable, configure, or disable iterators for a particular table. We talk about a specific example in "Data Lifecycle" on page 449. Here we describe how to configure iterators.

Iterators that implement the OptionDescriber interface can be configured through the shell via the setiter or setscaniter commands. Iterators can also be configured through the Java API via the IteratorSetting object. Configuring iterators amounts to setting a number of string properties on a table, which are stored in ZooKeeper.

Iterators can also be configured manually by setting the appropriate properties, but this is not recommended because it can be more error-prone. To change the parameters of an existing iterator, the easiest method is to change the string property through Accumulo's API or the shell.

To configure an iterator on a given table, use the `setiter` command. The command requires a number of parameters. The iterator class can be specified with `-class` where the class name is fully qualified. Some iterators have built-in flags, so you can use those as shortcuts instead of specifying `-class` with the entire class name. These are:

- The `AgeOffFilter` (`-ageoff`)
- The `RegExFilter` (`-regex`)
- The `ReqVisFilter` (`-reqvis`)
- The `VersioningIterator` (`-vers`)

In addition to the class name, specify between one and three scopes—the `-minc`, `-majc`, and/or `-scan` scope—signifying that the iterator should be applied at minor compaction time, major compaction time, and scan time, respectively.

Configuring an iterator for the scan scope applies the iterator to all scans of the table by all users. To configure an iterator through the shell for the current scan session only (i.e., all scans issued in the shell by the current user on a given table), use the `setscaniter` command instead.

The syntax is the same as for the `setiter` command, except that the iterator scope does not need to be specified.

You must also specify the iterator's priority, which controls the order in which the iterators are applied. Specifying a shorthand name for the iterator is optional with the `-n` parameter. Iterator configuration is stored in ZooKeeper under parameter names of the form `table.iterator.scope.name.*`.

If the shell is in a table context (which can be obtained with the `table` command), the iterator will be applied to the current table. A different table can be specified with the `-t` option.

For example, to configure an `AgeOffFilter` that ages off data older than one hour, do the following:

```
user@accumulo tablename> setiter -ageoff -scan -p 10
AgeOffFilter removes entries with timestamps more than <ttl> milliseconds old
----------> set AgeOffFilter parameter negate, default false keeps k/v that pass
    accept method, true rejects k/v that pass accept method:
----------> set AgeOffFilter parameter ttl, time to live (milliseconds): 3600000
----------> set AgeOffFilter parameter currentTime, if set, use the given value
```

```
as the absolute time in milliseconds as the current time of day:
user@accumulo tablename>
```

After you have configured an iterator on a table, type `config -t table name` in the shell to see the actual properties. `config -t table name -f iterator` reduces the list to the iterator-related properties. You could set these properties manually on the table using the shell or the Java API. To add the `AgeOffFilter` to the `majc` scope in addition to the scan scope, run the following commands:

```
config -t tableName -s table.iterator.majc.ageoff.opt.ttl=3600000
config -t tableName -s table.iterator.scan.ageoff=\
    10,org.apache.accumulo.core.iterators.user.AgeOffFilter
```

Safely deploying custom iterators

Newly developed iterators can be challenging to deploy. This is because you are effectively allowing some application logic to be hosted inside tablet servers, where bugs can cause problems that affect data. One especially bad scenario is one in which a bug in an iterator causes data to be lost as it is compacted to disk.

To help avoid losing data, or experiencing other issues when deploying new custom iterators, it can be helpful to enable an iterator to be applied at scan time only, at least at first.

This can be done via the shell as follows:

```
user@accumulo> setiter -class com.company.MyIterator -n myiterator -scan \
    -t myTable -p 40
```

This allows administrators to view the effects of an iterator in a way that isn't permanent. Scanning an entire table with an iterator applied can help expose any bugs that can arise from running real data through the iterator.

If no issues are observed, an iterator can also be applied at minor and major compaction times, making the changes permanent on disk. In the shell this would be done like this:

```
user@accumulo> setiter -class com.company.MyIterator -n myiterator -minc -majc \
    -t myTable -p 40
```

If issues are observed, an iterator can be disabled in the shell via the `deleteiter` command:

```
user@accumulo> deleteiter -n myiterator -minc -majc -scan -t myTable
```

In particular, shutting down a system with a faulty iterator configured to be applied at minor compaction time can cause special havoc because tablet servers will perform minor compactions at shutdown and may prevent safe shutdown. It is preferable to disable any such iterators and attempt to correct the situation while the system is running.

Another strategy for testing out new iterators is to configure them on a clone of a table. This has the advantage of allowing the logic to be tested through scan, minor compaction, and major compaction without affecting the original table. See "Cloning" on page 444 for details on cloning tables.

Custom constraints can cause similar issues and can be similarly disabled if issues arise, but these are usually not as egregious as those with iterators.

Changing Online Status

A table can be brought *offline*, a state in which the table is no longer available for queries or writes and also no longer uses system resources.

All tables are online upon creation. The `offline` shell command can be used to take a table offline:

```
root@accumulo> offline mytable
```

The monitor's tables view will show the online/offline status of each table.

Taking tables offline can allow a cluster that is heavy on storage to store more tables than administrators would want to be available at any given time. This could be useful if tables need to be kept around for archival purposes, and can be brought online in the event that they need to be queried. Offline tables will not be affected by compactions.

To bring a table back online for queries and writes, use the `online` command:

```
root@accumulo> online mytable
```

Cloning

Accumulo tables can be *cloned* at very low cost in terms of system resources. This allows applications to operate on a version of a table without making permanent changes. As soon as a table is cloned, its clone can be written to and read from without affecting the original table.

Cloning works by copying just the configuration information for an original table to a new table. This configuration information is stored in Accumulo's metadata table. Cloning tables is fast because Accumulo's files are all immutable, meaning they can be shared between several logical tables for reads. If new entries are written to a cloned table, they will be written to a separate set of files in HDFS.

Cloned and offline tables can be considered a consistent *snapshot* of a table as it existed at the time it was cloned. Tables that are offline can be exported for the purpose of backing up data or moving a table to another cluster.

To clone a table, use the `clonetable` command in the shell, specifying the name of the original table followed by the name of the table to create as a clone of the first. In this example we create a test table and clone it:

```
root@accumulo> createtable testtable
root@accumulo testtable> insert a b c d
root@accumulo testtable> scan
a b:c [] d
root@accumulo testtable> clonetable testtable testtableclone
root@accumulo testtable> table testtableclone
root@accumulo testtableclone> scan
a b:c [] d
```

In order to get a consistent view of a table before cloning, the `clonetable` command will first flush the original table. Flushing a table will ensure that all key-value pairs that currently only live in the memory of tablet servers (and write-ahead logs) are written to HDFS. Otherwise, these key-value pairs will not show up in the newly cloned table.

It is possible to clone a table without flushing first by using the `-nf` option when creating a clone. In this case, any entries that are still in the memory of tablet servers when the `clonetable` command is run will be excluded from the newly cloned table:

```
root@accumulo testtable> insert e f g h
root@accumulo testtable> scan
a b:c [] d
e f:g [] h
root@accumulo testtable> clonetable -nf testtable testtablenoflush
root@accumulo testtable> table testtablenoflush
root@accumulo testtablenoflush> scan
a b:c [] d
root@accumulo testtablenoflush>
```

To export a snapshot of a table elsewhere, for backup or other purposes, see "Import, Export, and Backups" on page 446.

Altering cloned table properties

Table properties can be excluded from or added to the cloned table before it is brought online. For example, if the original table has an age-off iterator configured that is designed to remove data older than a given date, we may want to exclude that iterator from our cloned table, if the intent of the cloned table is to serve as an archive of the original for some time beyond the age-off date.

Possible reasons to add a property to the cloned table before it is brought online include testing out an experimental iterator or modifying the behavior of the cloned table.

For example, to modify the cloned table to keep the latest three versions of each key-value pair:

```
root@accumulo testtable> clonetable testtable testtableclone \
    -s table.iterator.majc.vers.opt.maxVersions=3,\
      table.iterator.minc.vers.opt.maxVersions=3,
      table.iterator.scan.vers.opt.maxVersions=3
root@accumulo testtable> config -t testtableclone -f table.iterator
---------+----------------------------------------------+----------------------
SCOPE    | NAME                                         | VALUE
---------+----------------------------------------------+----------------------
table    | table.iterator.majc.vers ................... | 20,org.apache.accumulo.
    core.iterators.user.VersioningIterator
table    | table.iterator.majc.vers.opt.maxVersions .. | 3
table    | table.iterator.minc.vers ................... | 20,org.apache.accumulo.
    core.iterators.user.VersioningIterator
table    | table.iterator.minc.vers.opt.maxVersions .. | 3
table    | table.iterator.scan.vers ................... | 20,org.apache.accumulo.
    core.iterators.user.VersioningIterator
table    | table.iterator.scan.vers.opt.maxVersions .. | 3
---------+----------------------------------------------+----------------------
```

Cloning for MapReduce

One use case for cloning is to create a copy of a table whose files can be used as the input to a MapReduce job. Tables that are online can receive new inserts of data, and Accumulo can perform a compaction in which the set of files that comprises a table changes. Each file Accumulo stores in HDFS is immutable once closed, but the set of files associated with a table at any given time can change. To avoid a situation in which a table's set of files changes, a table can be cloned and then taken offline:

```
root@accumulo> clonetable mytable mytablecopy
root@accumulo> tables
!METADATA
mytable
mytablecopy
trace
root@accumulo> offline mytablecopy
```

Once the table is offline, its set of files will not change and a MapReduce job can be run over them. The MapReduce job must be configured to read over a table's files instead of reading data through tablet servers. See "MapReduce over Underlying RFiles" on page 262 for details on how to configure a MapReduce job to run over files of an offline table.

Import, Export, and Backups

Accumulo stores all its data in HDFS, which features full-data replication to prevent data loss in the event that one or more machines fail. Although HDFS replication is often sufficient for maintaining data availability for applications, there are a few remaining reasons to back up data to places other than the HDFS.

The most obvious is that an Accumulo instance is designed to run within a single data center. Data centers can suffer catastrophic failure, such as in the event of a widespread power failure or natural disaster. The ability to back up data to data centers in other geographic locations is important if data is to survive one of these catastrophic failures.

Another reason to create a backup is to create a copy of the data to be used for purposes other than those of the original cluster. Servers are often powerful enough to support mixed workloads on a single cluster, and many Accumulo clusters do double duty, managing data for low-latency requests for applications and performing indepth or historical bulk analysis via MapReduce. Nevertheless, the ability to copy data to another cluster can be useful for supporting a wider variety of workloads on the same data set.

Exporting a table

Creating a backup of Accumulo data, as in other systems, involves copying the data to be backed up to another storage medium and restoring that data at some future point to recover from a disaster, or simply loading it into another Accumulo instance. To back up a table, administrators should first flush, clone, then offline the newly cloned table and leave it offline while the export is taking place. The export command will write information about a table's files to a directory in HDFS. This information can be used to copy table files to another cluster or other storage medium:

```
root@accumulo> clonetable mytable mytable_backup1
root@accumulo> offline mytable_backup1
root@accumulo> exporttable -t mytable_backup1 /table_backups/mytable
```

To use Hadoop's distcp (distributed copy) utility to move the files, reference the *distcp.txt* file like this:

```
hadoop distcp -f hdfs://namenode/backups/mytable/distcp.txt \
  hdfs://othernamenode/tmp/mytable_backup1
```

Hadoop Distributed Copy

Hadoop provides a mechanism for moving large amounts of data between HDFS instances, or other distributed filesystems, called *Distributed Copy* or *distcp* after the command name for short. Rather than pulling data out of HDFS to a single machine and then uploading it to another HDFS cluster, Distributed Copy sets up a MapReduce job that will stream files from where they are stored in HDFS DataNodes to DataNodes in another HDFS instance. This operation will attempt to use as much network bandwidth as is available and minimizes the chance for bottlenecks to occur while the data is copied.

Of course HDFS can also be used to copy data within the same HDFS instance if that is required.

Importing an exported table

To import a table that has been exported via the exporttable command, Accumulo provides an importtable command. The importtable command tables two parameters: the name of the table to create into which the files will be imported, and the directory in HDFS where exported information is stored:

```
root@accumulo> importtable importedtable /tmp/mytable_backup1
```

If the Linux *accumulo* user doesn't have permission to read the files in the import directory, this command will fail as it moves files from the import directory.

The imported table will have the same split points and configuration information as the table that was exported.

Bulk-loading files from a MapReduce job

MapReduce jobs can be used to write data into files that Accumulo understands. (See Chapter 7 for details on how this is done.) These files can then be *bulk-loaded* into Accumulo without the need to write each key-value pair to tablet servers. The advantage of bulk loading is that users can take advantage of the efficiency of MapReduce to sort data the way Accumulo would if key-value pairs were written to its tablet servers one at a time, or one batch at a time as via the BatchWriter. Another advantage of using MapReduce to create files for bulk import is that a consistent set of files can be created without the chance of creating duplicates in the event that one or more machines fail during the MapReduce job. See "Bulk Ingest to Avoid Duplicates" on page 269 for scenarios in which bulk-importing files can help avoid creating duplicate rows in Accumulo tables.

To import files created from a MapReduce job, use the importdirectory command. This command will import files into the current table set in the shell, so administrators should first set the current table via the table command before running the importdirectory command.

importdirectory expects three parameters—the name of the HDFS directory that contains files to be imported, the name of a directory to which to store any files that fail to import cleanly, and whether to set the timestamp of imported key-value pairs:

```
user@accumulo> table myTable
user@accumulo mytable> importdirectory /newFiles /importFailures true
```

Bulk Loading and Timestamps

An important consideration for bulk-loading files created via MapReduce is whether to accept the timestamps of key-value pairs in the files as valid, or to set new time-stamps for all imported key-value pairs based on the time the files are imported.

If the clock in any machine participating in the MapReduce job used to create these RFiles is set to a future time—and if the MapReduce job simply used system time to timestamp key-value pairs—then those key-value pairs—then those key-value pairs will create problems when they are bulk-imported. Specifically, if a key-value pair has a timestamp that is set to a future time, inserts and deletes that use the current time as the timestamp will appear to not have any effect, because the `VersioningIterator` uses timestamps to determine the order of operations. A key-value pair with a future timestamp will appear to be the latest mutation to a row, until time catches up with whatever future timestamp the key-value pair has.

If it is not reasonable to assume that the timestamps of key-value pairs created via MapReduce are valid (i.e., that there is a chance that some timestamps are set in the future), administrators should specify the last parameter of the `importdirectory` command as `true`.

Data Lifecycle

Managing large amounts of data creates new challenges for long-running systems. Not only can data be large to begin with, but also—as data is continually ingested over time—the amount of data under management can get to be extremely large. Applications can be designed to look after the data under their management. Accumulo can automatically apply policies set by applications and applies background compaction processes and garbage collection to maintain the data lifecycle.

System designers can elect to allow administrators to address data lifecycle issues without making changes to an application's logic. Accumulo provides some features to help address data lifecycle management even when dealing with very large-scale data, by leveraging and coordinating resources across the cluster.

Versioning

It may be the case that the data stored in Accumulo is written once and never upda-ted. If not, the first consideration in data lifecycle management is how to deal with multiple versions of data. Applications can choose to store one, some, or all versions of data. It can be useful to be able to view previous versions of data to see how data changes over time, for debugging, or simply to make reverting an application to a previous state easier.

Accumulo handles versions by examining the timestamp element of keys that are otherwise identical. That is to say, when two or more keys have the same row ID, column family, column qualifier, and column visibility, the timestamp is the only thing left that can vary between keys. Keys that only vary in timestamp are considered to be different *versions*. Each version has a unique timestamp and potentially different values. The built-in but optional `VersioningIterator` can be configured to keep one, some, or all versions.

The `VersioningIterator` is configured by default on new tables to key at most one version of a key-value pair. This policy can be changed via the following options:

```
table.iterator.majc.vers.opt.maxVersions
table.iterator.minc.vers.opt.maxVersions
table.iterator.scan.vers.opt.maxVersions
```

These options' settings apply at major compaction, minor compaction, and scan time, respectively.

Whatever the setting, the `VersioningIterator` will prefer more recent versions—the versions with the highest-numbered timestamps—over older versions.

Data Age-off

Many times data needs to be kept for a certain period of time, after which it should be deleted or archived. Accumulo's timestamps and `AgeOffFilter` support automatically removing data with timestamps that are beyond a certain date.

When the `ttl` parameter is set, the `AgeOffFilter` is set to remove key-value pairs that are older than the specified number of milliseconds:

```
setiter -ageoff -majc -minc -scan -n ageoff -p 30
-> set AgeOffFilter parameter negate, default false keeps k/v that pass accept
    method, true rejects k/v that pass accept method: false
-> set AgeOffFilter parameter ttl, time to live (milliseconds): 10000
-> set AgeOffFilter parameter currentTime, if set, use the given value as the
    absolute time in milliseconds as the current time of day:
```

Ensuring that deletes are removed from tables

The delete operation is implemented through the insertion of special delete markers that suppress earlier versions. As a result, deleted data—meaning key-value pairs suppressed by a delete marker—are not immediately removed from files belonging to a table. Key-value pairs are only really removed during the compaction processes, when data is transferred from memory to a file on disk or when two or more files are combined into a merged file.

During the minor compaction process, when data in memory is flushed to a file on disk, any key-value pairs in memory that are suppressed by a delete marker are not written to disk, but the delete marker is. This eliminates some of the deleted data that was in memory. Delete markers are kept around in order to suppress any older versions of key-value pairs that may exist in other files.

During a major compaction when multiple files are combined, any existing versions of key-value pairs that are suppressed by a delete marker found in any of the files as part of the compaction are not written to the newly merged file. This eliminates more of the deleted data, but the delete marker is still written to the newly merged file.

Only when a tablet server performs a full major compaction, merging all files for a particular tablet into one new file, is it guaranteed that all deleted data is removed and the delete marker can also be omitted from the newly merged file.

Tablet servers do not typically merge all files for a tablet into one unless there is an idle period. The `table.compaction.major.everything.idle` setting controls how long a tablet server will wait after a table receives a mutation before compacting all of its files into one. But this is not guaranteed to happen. The tablet server can be busy with other tables.

To guarantee that all deleted data has been removed from a table at a particular time, schedule a full major compaction via the shell:

```
user@accumulo table> compact
```

If the intent is not simply to remove deleted entries from a table but also to remove them from disk and reclaim space, the Accumulo garbage collector process and HDFS trash must be involved. The Accumulo garbage collector will ensure that files no longer used by Accumulo are deleted in HDFS, which can simply move them to the HDFS trash, depending on the version of HDFS.

The `hdfs dfs -expunge` command can be used to empty the HDFS trash. HDFS DataNodes must then ultimately delete blocks for those files from the Linux filesystem.

Compactions

All of Accumulo's files are immutable. Data is only removed during the compaction process, when one or more files are combined—omitting any key-value pairs that fail to pass the `VersioningIterator` and `AgeOffFilter` tests—and new files are written out. After compaction, the old files containing old key-value pairs that should be removed sit around in HDFS until the garbage collector removes them.

One thing to keep in mind is that some files may never be automatically compacted if there is no need to cut down on the number of files per tablet. To ensure that all extraneous versions and all aged-off data is removed, administrators can periodically schedule compactions of all files in a table, ensuring that all files are compacted at least once. The `compact` shell command will do this:

```
user@accumulo> compact
```

After a compaction in which key-value pairs are removed, the existing split points may no longer be appropriate. For example, the distribution of the data may have shifted, and the table can have some tablets that are empty. The `merge` shell command can be used to eliminate empty tablets, as described in "Merging Tablets" on page 453.

Using major compaction to apply changes

Because a major compaction scheduled from an application will effectively cause all the data in a table to be reprocessed, compactions are a convenient way of affecting a change in configuration for a range within a table or over the entire table. In particular, occasionally it can be useful to apply an iterator to a table just for the duration of the compaction.

For example, we can choose not to have an age-off filter configured on a table all the time, but from time to time we might choose to aggressively prune old data, perhaps within areas of a table that are known to contain data that is not considered as important anymore.

We can choose to change a configuration option on a table, such as the compression algorithm used or the replication factor for files in HDFS, and compact the entire table to ensure that the effects of those changes are realized.

Or we can choose to simply compact to ensure that all data marked for deletion is actually removed from disk.

In this example we'll demonstrate how to turn off compression for a test table. The `du` command shows how many bytes the table is using:

```
root@accumulo testtable> du
                    239 [testtable]
root@accumulo testtable> config -t testtable -s table.file.compress.type=none
root@accumulo testtable> config -t test -f table.file.compress.type
---------+-----------------------------------------------+----------
SCOPE    | NAME                                          | VALUE
---------+-----------------------------------------------+----------
default  | table.file.compress.type .................... | gz
table    |     @override ............................... | none
---------+-----------------------------------------------+----------

root@accumulo testtable> du
                    239 [testtable]
```

Note that our table has not yet changed in size. Any new files created or merged in a merging compaction will not be compressed. To change the files already on disk, we can schedule a compaction manually:

```
root@accumulo testtable> compact -t testtable
root@accumulo testtable> du
                    270 [testtable]
```

The -w option can be used to cause the shell wait for the compaction to complete before returning.

If the -t option is not specified, Accumulo will compact the current table in the shell.

If a compaction has been scheduled but has not yet begun and you want to cancel it, the --cancel option can be specified to cancel the compaction.

The --noflush option can be used to avoid flushing entries still in memory on tablet servers to disk before compacting.

Tables that are offline will not be affected by compactions.

Compacting specific ranges

It is possible to compact only a portion of a table by specifying a range of rows to the compact command.

The -b or --begin-row option and -e or --end-row options will cause the compaction to affect only the key-value pairs between the begin and end rows, inclusively.

This can be used to alter sections of a table. For example, if a table's rows are based on time, we might want to allow for more versions of each key-value pair for more recent data, and only keep one version of each key-value pair around for the oldest data.

To affect this change, we can temporarily change the VersioningIterator options for our table, and schedule a compaction for a range comprising our oldest data. We can then restore the original configuration.

Accumulo 1.6 allows administrators to specify specific iterators and options to use for a particular compaction.

See "Compacting" on page 149 for details on the compaction API.

Merging Tablets

A table's key distribution could change over time, which could even result in empty tablets due to data age-off. Even the AgeOffFilter isn't used, over time data may be deleted from tables during the normal course of an application. In this case a table can have empty tablets (Figure 12-4).

Tablet	Entries	I
[KqZmRN6CGZX5Eji7wwBBfg==]	23.78M	
[duYkPOon7RI52pDWBTbLMQ==]	0	
[9Qgn33cieSCTM8Hcy6AtqQ==]	14.22M	
[1RY/432kqWXN9XMJGOls4A==]	16.80M	
[xUd9elum5++jeodj4h+ezw==]	0	
[NTt4+crE2Kz9zV6kfSWGLg==]	0	
[UpUnpwlYLpPu43b/5CcNsQ==]	0	
[pS5RGoAecnoVWrr4NQWJmA==]	0	
[/zGeSqJjUmIiMv01ShvARw==]	0	
[uWe7xX8cCnGaCfTtyOA1sA==]	42.47M	
[1M91DvuTZkD8zygGOI1zxw==]	0	
[LuXDvyIRm7+WT5ei4PK6eQ==]	0	
[V1DWmAgemp4T6FVk1JW4tg==]	0	
[b49XcVCQ2iYyRTmI2aFQGw==]	53.38M	
[k9NvKinX5ItPBqpK3fh6MA==]	0	
[5pXbfe1/SvLWWgXypnl7Zg==]	0	
[1n8WJPMYh9cCVXbj+lhXfQ==]	0	
[MbgMiLt9zMTM9qi+oS3ePQ==]	0	
[ssEoDGtaxsvA63pRhpuBrQ==]	210.53K	
[62nmbqI17AoOIMqEufoOZu==]	0	

Figure 12-4. Empty tablets listed in the tablet server view of the monitor

Empty tablets are not a big problem per se, but they are basically wasted overhead in the metadata table. They can also cause balancing to be a bit off, because the default load balancer only looks at tablets per server and not necessarily key-value pairs per server.

Tablet merging can be used to reduce the number of tablets in the table. In a tablet merge, two or more tablets are combined to form one tablet.

Unlike tablet splitting and compaction, tablet merging is not an automatic operation performed by tablet servers, as of version 1.6.

As such, tablets will not be merged unless these commands are applied.

The merge command in the Accumulo shell has two modes: merging a range of tablets into a single tablet, or merging consecutive tablets until a given minimum size is reached. To merge tablets to a given size in bytes:

```
user@accumulo> merge -s 100M -t mytable
```

If the minimum size is chosen appropriately, this will result in fewer, larger tablets (Figure 12-5).

TABLET	ENTRIES	]
[KqZmRN6CGZX5Eji7wwBBfg==]	23.78M	
[9Qgn33cieSCTM8Hcy6AtqQ==]	14.22M	
[1RY/432kqWXN9XMJGOls4A==]	16.80M	
[uWe7xX8cCnGaCfTtyOAlsA==]	42.47M	
[96eY3RGC8E/EGijLluAtAw==]	9.11M	
[b49XcVCQ2iYyRTmI2aFQGw==]	53.38M	

Figure 12-5. Empty tablets are eliminated after merging

To merge tables beginning at a given row and ending at a given row:

```
user@accumulo> merge -b j -e o -t mytable
```

This can also be done via the Java API:

```
Instance inst = new ZooKeeperInstance(myInstance, zkServers);
Connector conn = inst.getConnector(principal, passwordToken);
conn.tableOperations().merge("mytable", new Text("e"), new Text("o"));
```

See "Merging tablets" on page 148 for details on the merging tablets via the Administrative API.

Garbage Collection

With both `VersioningIterator` and `AgeOffFilter`, as well as individual deletes, the garbage-collection process is ultimately responsible for getting rid of data permanently.

The garbage collector works by scanning the metadata table to determine which files can be removed and issuing delete commands to the HDFS NameNode. The garbage collector competes with the other processes in the cluster for HDFS NameNode resources, and so long-running garbage-collection times can be an indicator of a NameNode under stress.

Failure Recovery

With clusters of up to thousands of relatively unreliable commodity-class machines, hardware failures are commonplace. Many types of failure, however, are automatically managed and clients and administrators do not need to take any action.

Typical Failures

Here we outline the types of failures Accumulo is designed to tolerate gracefully and without immediate administrative intervention, and the actions to be taken.

Single machine failure

By far the most common occurrence—the failure of a single Accumulo server, including the master—will not cause any data to become unavailable, or even any interruption in client service.

If the Accumulo master is down, clients can continue to communicate with tablet servers, and one inactive master process will automatically be chosen to become the new active master. However, if a tablet server fails while there are no operational masters, the tablets that were being hosted by the failed tablet server will not be reassigned and hence will be unavailable for writes or reads by clients until a new master process is started again.

If a process is only temporarily crashed, as can happen if some other process uses up all available memory and a tablet server is forced to exit, the failed process can simply be restarted, as outlined in "Starting After a Crash" on page 428.

Any permanently failed machines can be replaced or removed. No configuration information needs to be changed, except perhaps to remove the hostname of a machine that you don't intend to replace from the *conf/slaves* file.

Single machine unresponsiveness

Sometimes a tablet server continues to respond to ZooKeeper requests but fails to respond to Accumulo client requests. In this scenario clients may be caused to wait indefinitely, because the master will not reassign the stalled tablet server's tablets if it still holds its ZooKeeper lock. The process may eventually exit on its own and lose its lock, allowing the Accumulo master to reassign its tablets so clients can continue.

Before that happens an administrator can elect to examine the logs on the monitor for any indication of a problem, or else simply shut down the tablet server process so that its tablets can be served by other healthy tablet servers. This way clients can continue more quickly.

Accumulo clients are designed to wait indefinitely for a cluster to become healthy in terms of all of the tablets being online and available. For example, MapReduce jobs that are stalled because of an unresponsive server may well simply continue after a stalled tablet server process is killed.

Network partitions

Accumulo does not allow clients on both sides of a network partition to continue to write data. In the event of a network partition, in which messages are lost between nodes in a cluster, some tablet servers will find themselves on a side of the partition that can continue to talk to the ZooKeeper cluster, and others will not. Rather than allowing clients that can talk to tablet servers that are disconnected from ZooKeeper to continue writing and reading data, Accumulo tablet servers will exit upon discovering that they can no longer communicate with ZooKeeper.

Because all Accumulo tablet servers and often all clients are in the same data center, it's often the case that load balancers in front of clients can redirect requests to clients that can still talk to ZooKeeper during the network partition.

For additional details, see "Accumulo and the CAP Theorem" on page 379 for a discussion of Accumulo and the CAP Theorem.

More-Serious Failures

These types of failures can result in data loss or unavailability.

All NameNodes failing simultaneously

Running a single NameNode used to be a big risk to Hadoop and Accumulo clusters because its failure meant some or all the mappings of filenames to data blocks in HDFS were lost or at least temporarily unavailable. Now HDFS can be configured to automatically failover from one NameNode to a hot standby that is kept in sync with the active NameNode.

Care must be taken to ensure the NameNodes don't share a common resource that, in the event of failure, would cause both NameNodes to go offline. There are limits to this, of course, because both NameNodes could be destroyed in a disaster affecting a data center. Accumulo is not designed to run over multiple geographically distributed data centers, though work is being done to allow Accumulo instances to replicate data to another data center in future versions of Accumulo.

All ZooKeeper servers failing simultaneously

Many of the same considerations for high-availability multiple NameNodes apply to ZooKeeper servers. At least one needs to be operating in order for Accumulo to function.

Power loss to the data center

Accumulo is designed to run within a single data center, with low-latency networking between nodes. If power is lost to the data center, none of the machines in the Accumulo cluster will be operational. The hsync setting should true to avoid data loss if no uninterruptible power supply can be used to bring down the cluster gracefully in the case of a sudden power outage.

Loss of all replicas of an HDFS data block

HDFS replicates data blocks so that the loss of any one block will not cause an interruption in service. HDFS clients will simply find another remaining replica. If all replicas of a given block are unavailable, Accumulo operations will fail.

To avoid the scenario in which a single hardware failure causes all replicas to become unavailable, HDFS provides the ability to specify the number of replicas, and also allows the specification of which machines live on which rack. The assumption here is that all machines within the same rack share a common power supply or network switch. So, not all replicas should be stored on machines in that rack; rather, at least one should be stored on a machine in another rack. This capability is known as HDFS *rack-awareness*.

Tips for Restoring a Cluster

In the more serious failures outlined previously, additional action may be required to restore the cluster to a healthy state.

The first thing is to run hadoop fsck on the HDFS */accumulo* folder to make sure there are no missing or corrupt blocks. If there are problems in HDFS, the grep command in the Accumulo shell can be used to scan the metadata table to see if any of the files affected by missing blocks are RFiles currently referenced in the metadata table. RFiles that are no longer referenced can be deleted from HDFS. If the RFiles are still referenced but are not part of the Accumulo metadata table, those RFiles will need to be put into a known good state.

If corrupt RFiles are part of the metadata table, you must rebuild the metadata by creating a new instance and importing all the data. Usually that known good state is from some time in the past, which will mean data is missing. To account for the missing data, you will need to replay all the changes since that known good state, unless you can figure out exactly what changes to replay.

It is not recommended to modify the Accumulo metadata table to get to a good state. Following are some things you can do to help yourself with these steps.

Replay data

Provide yourself with the ability to replay incoming data. This can mean saving off the ingest source files for some period. It can also mean creating a change log of updates that can be replayed. Ensure that you have timestamps for when this data was originally pushed to Accumulo.

Back up NameNode metadata

This is especially important for Hadoop 1.0 because the NameNode is a single point of failure. Back up NameNode's *fsimage*, *edits*, *VERSION*, and *fstime* files so you can recover HDFS. Doing so will allow you get Accumulo into a good state from a point in the past, and then you can do things like replay all updates since that point.

Back up table configuration, users, and split points

If the Accumulo metadata table went away or got corrupted, you could bulk-import the existing RFiles to recover. But to get your cluster to the same state, you would need to re-create the existing table configuration, table splits, and users. Some of this information is stored in ZooKeeper but is tricky to pull out. Some of this information is not saved anywhere outside the metadata table, which is why you should back it up yourself.

Accumulo 1.6 includes a command for dumping the configuration information to a file:

```
accumulo admin dumpconfig
```

Otherwise, the following commands can help gather information to help restore configuration:

config -t tablename
: This command will show you the current table configuration.

getsplits
: This command in the Accumulo shell can be used to store the current splits.

`users`
> This command in combination with the `getauths -u username` command will show you users and authorization tokens.

`systempermission, tablepermission,` *and* `userpermission`
> These commands will show permission information.

Use these commands to dump text files with information. Having this information can also help in the case when ZooKeeper information has been deleted due to user error or catastrophic failure.

Turn on HDFS trash

Turning on the HDFS trash makes a copy of every deleted file. Configuration is done by setting `fs.trash.interval` to a number of minutes greater than zero in *core-site.xml*. The trash interval should based on how much your Accumulo data changes and how much storage you have. For example, lots of HDFS storage or a higher rate of change in Accumulo would mean a longer trash interval.

Create an empty RFile

If you can't find a known good copy of an RFile, you can create an empty RFile that gets copied to that expected location.

 An empty RFile is not simply an empty file; it contains header information.

This procedure should only be used to allow an Accumulo table to be partially recovered and brought online without error.

Accumulo versions 1.5.2 and later have a utility to create an empty RFile:

```
accumulo org.apache.accumulo.core.file.rfile.CreateEmpty /some/path/to/empty.rf
```

Prior to those versions, you can use the following shell commands to create an empty RFile that will serve the same purpose:

```
createtable foo
delete "" "" ""
flush -t foo
```

Now you can find the RFile that was created with something like the following and then copy or move it:

```
tables -l # look for id of the foo table, 22 for example
hadoop fs -ls /accumulo/tables/22/default_tablet
```

Take Hadoop out of safe mode manually

When Accumulo restarts, it will begin compacting and flushing write-ahead logs. Additionally, any client will be able to write data, which could get flushed to an RFile. You can set up Hadoop to not come out of safe mode automatically, which will prevent any changes from happening to RFiles. Setting `dfs.namenode.safemode.threshold-pct` to a value greater than 1 in the Hadoop `hdfs-site.xml` config file will require human intervention to take HDFS out of safe mode.

Troubleshooting

If Accumulo clients are experiencing issues such as errors or timeouts, several things should be checked as part of the troubleshooting process.

Ensure that processes are running

If any of the services on which Accumulo depends is not healthy, Accumulo will experience issues. Make sure HDFS is running and healthy. The HDFS monitor page at *http://<namenode host>:50070* will show the status of HDFS. If any blocks are missing, Accumulo will be unable to serve the data from the files those blocks belong to. If DataNode processes have crashed, it may be possible to restart them and for their blocks to become available again.

ZooKeeper should also be running and healthy. Administrators can check this by connecting to a ZooKeeper process via Telnet (to port 2181 by default) and typing `ruok`, short for *are you ok?* The server should respond with `imok` (*I am ok*) and close the connection. If ZooKeeper is down, it should be restarted before you attempt to start any Accumulo processes.

Finally, Accumulo processes should be checked to make sure they are running and operating properly. The Accumulo monitor page will indicate problems by highlighting issues in red. For example, if you have zero running tablet servers, if any tablets are unassigned, or if the Accumulo master is unreachable, the monitor page will show red boxes behind text.

Check log messages

The Accumulo monitor also gathers error log messages from tablet servers and displays them in one place for convenience. Checking for these can help explain issues.

If the monitor is not showing any errors or if it is down, logs are still written to local files on each machine running Accumulo processes.

Understand network partitions

If for some reason a tablet server is unable to reach ZooKeeper (a condition known as a network partition), within a period of time it will lose its tablet server lock. At this point the Accumulo master will attempt to obtain the tablet server's lock. If the attempt is successful, the tablet server is no longer considered to be part of the cluster and the master will reassign its tablets to remaining healthy servers. The tablet server that lost its lock will then exit to prevent clients from sending any more writes to it.

This procedure is designed to guarantee that each tablet is hosted by only one tablet server at a time. If ZooKeeper or tablet servers are not responsive enough to network requests, tablet server processes may terminate because they can't distinguish between arbitrarily delayed requests and a network partition. If tablet servers are exiting regularly due to a loss of a ZooKeeper lock, they or ZooKeeper may not have sufficient resources.

Causes of this can include swapping to disk if available memory is insufficient, the Java garbage collector pauses when not using native libraries, or hardware for the application is insufficient.

Exception when scanning a table in the shell

When scanning a table in the shell results in an exception, the cause could be a bad formatter. Use the following to show which formatter is being used:

```
config -t tablename
```

Use the following to remove the formatter:

```
formatter -r
```

Graphs on the monitor are "blocky"

"Blocky" means that the lines are completely horizontal for a period, then there is an increase or decrease, then more horizontal lines, then an increase or decrease, and so on. This means that tablet servers are having delays in reporting information back to the monitor. Tablet servers report information back every 5 seconds. If data for two or more periods is late, the monitor uses the prior value. Usually this is an indication that one or more tablet servers are having trouble. You can look on the tablet server monitor page and sort by last update time to get an idea of which servers are having trouble. Another way to find the server is to start up a shell, run debug on, then scan accumulo.metadata. It will take some time, but you should see messages repeated with the IP address of problem servers. Once you find out which tablet server or tablet servers are having problems, you can go there and look at system monitoring tools and the logs to diagnose the cause.

Tablets not balancing across tablet servers

It is safe to stop and start the master if needed. Sometimes error messages show that tablets are not balancing, but there are no failed tablet servers and no other indication. Or the master is having problems communicating, but there is no other apparent cause. Accumulo will gracefully handle stopping the master service and restarting.

Calculate the size of changes to a cloned table

Sometimes it is useful to see how much a table has changed since it was cloned. We talk about cloning in "Table Operations" on page 440 and why it might be useful as a *snaphot* of the original table. But the original table is going to continue to change as data is inserted and deleted.

The du command in the Accumulo shell can be used to see the size in bytes of a table. When passed in multiple arguments, it also shows how much space is shared.

Here is an example run in the shell:

```
du table1Clone table1

 1,232,344 [table1]
51,212,424 [table1, table1Clone]
   723,232 [table1Clone]
```

This is showing that 51.2 MB are still shared between the tables, 723 KB have been removed from *table1*, and 1.2 MB have been added to *table1*, since the clone.

Unexpected or unexplained query results

If you get unexpected results when running a query, be sure to consider all the iterators being applied. This includes both iterators configured on the table and iterators being applied programmatically to the scanner. Having a scan iterator at the same priority as a table iterator is allowed. This is so that table iterator options can be overridden at scan time by configuring an identical iterator at scan time with different options.

But having different iterators at the same priority will cause unexpected behavior, because only one is applied and it is nondeterministic which one. Two scans that appear exactly the same may use different iterators and return different results. Additionally, consider the logic of lower-numbered iterators that may remove or alter a record before it gets to iterator you are expecting.

Slow queries

If queries are running more slowly than usual, the first thing to look for is hotspots. This is an indication that tablets or data are not balanced and Accumulo is not distributing the workload very well. Other things you might look at include:

- Is disk space filling up on tablet servers?

- Are there extra-large logfiles? Be sure to check logfiles for other services running on the node as well, such as DataNode logs.

- Are scans in the shell slow too? This is an indication of system problems instead of problems with your code.

- Is there contention on the tablet server with another Accumulo process such as garbage collection, compaction, or even MapReduce tasks?

Look at ZooKeeper

Sometimes it is useful to see what is stored in ZooKeeper. Extreme caution should be used, because changing data in ZooKeeper could cause serious issues for Accumulo. First, you need to know the instance ID, which is displayed when you log in via the shell. You can also find the instance ID by looking in */accumulo/instance_id* in HDFS or in the header of the monitor page. Use the `zkCli.sh` command included with Zoo-Keeper and any of the ZooKeeper hosts defined in *accumulo-site.xml* under the `instance.zookeeper.host` property:

```
zkCli.sh -server host:port
```

While in the command-line client, use commands like the following to see what Zoo-Keeper has stored:

```
ls /accumulo/replace with instance_id
```

The `get` command will display information about each entry.

Accumulo 1.4, some of the entries in ZooKeeper are protected. Once the CLI comes up, use a command like the following to authenticate:

```
addauth digest accumulo:SECRET
```

Replace the *SECRET* passphrase with whatever is defined in the `instance.secret` property in the *accumulo-site.xml* file.

Use the listscans command

The `listscans` command is very useful for finding out what is happening currently in your cluster. It will show you information about scans running on every tablet server. There is a lot of information, though, so it is common to dump this information to a file:

```
accumulo shell -u username -p password -e 'listscans -np' > /path/to/file.txt
```

As a developer, you can add information to what is displayed in the `listscans` command by setting options on any `IteratorSetting` object you add to your `Scanner`. This can be useful for debugging long-running queries.

Look at user-initiated compactions

When looking for long-running processes on your cluster, sometimes you may want to see what user-initiated compactions are happening. These will show up as FATE operations, and you can run the following to see what is currently in progress:

```
accumulo org.apache.accumulo.server.fate.Admin print
```

To get a sense for these over time, you can loop this command as in the following:

```
while true; do
  date;
  accumulo/bin/accumulo org.apache.accumulo.server.fate.Admin print;
  sleep 60;
done
```

There is also a `fate` command that you can run in an Accumulo shell to get information. Note that system-initiated compactions are not managed by `fate` transactions. For those, you will need to go to the tablet server logs and filter or search for the lines with `Starting MajC` or use the `listcompactions` command, which is similar to the `listscans` command.

 The Accumulo documentation has a section on troubleshooting (*http://bit.ly/accumulo_troubleshooting*) that has more troubleshooting tips not covered in this book.

Inspect RFiles

Invariably, during the development phase a situation can arise wherein key-value pairs are being labeled incorrectly. Accumulo is designed to take security labels very seriously. As such, it is not possible to simply turn off the iterator responsible for examining security labels and filtering out key-value pairs whose label logic is not satisfied by the querying user's credentials—even if that user is logged in as the Accumulo *root* user.

What this means for key-value pairs that have incorrect labels is that they simply won't show up in any scan. If a scan over an entire table yields no results when the monitor page indicates that data is, in fact, in there—and when all the known granted labels are being used to scan the table (the default mode of scanning in the shell)— this is a symptom indicating that a table might contain entries with incorrect labels.

If this appears to be happening, a table can be configured to throw exceptions if it is asked to store a key-value pair with a label that can't be satisfied with the writing user's credentials. This way, an incorrect security label shows up before it ever gets written to a table.

This constraint can be added in the shell like this:

```
root@accumulo> constraint -t tableName -a \
        org.apache.accumulo.core.security.VisibilityConstraint
```

If for some reason this and other troubleshooting methods of fixing labels have failed, or other parts of key-value pairs need to be inspected, an administrator with access to read files from HDFS can inspect Accumulo's underlying RFiles to see what the key-value pairs actually are.

 Reading RFiles directly should not be done lightly, because there are no checks in place to ensure that the user has the authorization to see all of the data stored in an Accumulo table. This is the exact reason that access to HDFS must be restricted.

This procedure should only be executed and allowed on development clusters during the debugging phase.

Administrators can dump the contents of an RFile using the following procedure. This procedure should only be executed and allowed on development clusters during the debugging phase:

1. Determine the underlying table ID for the table containing suspected incorrect labels.

   This will allow us to locate the RFiles for the table of interest in HDFS. In the shell, type:

   ```
   root@accumulo> tables -l
   !METADATA       =>          !0
   baseball_stats  =>          17
     wikipedia     =>          18
     wikipedia_index =>          15
   trace           =>          1
   ```

2. List the files in HDFS for one of the tablets in the table of interest. In our example, we'll examine a file in the *default_tablet* of the *wikipedia_index* table with ID 15.

   Exit the shell and run the hadoop fs command:

   ```
   $ hadoop fs -ls /accumulo/tables/15/default_tablet

   Found 7 items
   -rw-r--r--   1 accumulo supergroup   24215993 2013-12-11 05:14
                      /accumulo/tables/15/default_tablet/F0000hy3.rf
   -rw-r--r--   1 accumulo supergroup   18290804 2013-12-11 05:21
                      /accumulo/tables/15/default_tablet/F0000hyk.rf
   -rw-r--r--   1 accumulo supergroup       4515 2013-12-11 09:01
                      /accumulo/tables/15/default_tablet/F0000iab.rf
   -rw-r--r--   1 accumulo supergroup     673682 2013-12-11 09:20
                      /accumulo/tables/15/default_tablet/F0000iax.rf
   ```

```
-rw-r--r--   1 accumulo supergroup   1201112 2013-12-11 09:47
                        /accumulo/tables/15/default_tablet/F0000ibd.rf
-rw-r--r--   1 accumulo supergroup   5282634 2013-12-11 11:17
                        /accumulo/tables/15/default_tablet/F0000idd.rf
-rw-r--r--   1 accumulo supergroup   5631122 2013-12-11 11:24
                        /accumulo/tables/15/default_tablet/F0000ids.rf
```

3. View summary information about an RFile file by using `PrintInfo`.

   To view simple details of the file, use the `PrintInfo` class with only the filename as an argument. This will show statistics from the file as well as the first and last key. These keys may show an example of one of the incorrect labels:

```
$ accumulo rfile-info /accumulo/tables/15/default_tablet/F0000hy3.rf

Locality group       : <DEFAULT>
  Start block        : 0
  Num   blocks       : 665
  Index level 0      : 83,095 bytes  1 blocks
  First key          : 00003138675661000000000205001 :fields [public]
                                     0 false
  Last key           : 00003138675685000000000205001 :fields [prvate]
                                     0 false
  Num entries        : 31,218
  Column families    : []
Meta block     : BCFile.index
      Raw size          : 4 bytes
      Compressed size   : 12 bytes
      Compression type  : gz
Meta block     : RFile.index
      Raw size          : 83,257 bytes
      Compressed size   : 12,992 bytes
      Compression type  : gz
```

In this case, the *prvate* security token probably represents a misspelling of the word *private*. If we scanned the table using the *private* token we would not see the keys with the label *prvate*.

4. View RFile contents using PrintInfo.

   To dump key-value pairs from the file, use the -d option:

```
accumulo rfile-info -d /accumulo/tables/15/default_tablet/F0000hy3.rf
```

The utility will print out the statistics as before, followed by string representations of the key-value pairs in this file.

Performance

One aspect of working with big data is the chance to regularly exercise computer science performance theory. Desktop computers are so powerful that sometimes application developers can get away with inefficient designs without affecting performance to the extent that users notice. When you work with many terabytes of data, performance and efficient design once again become paramount.

Scalable applications that interact with large numbers of users often need to respond to requests very quickly, in under a second. Jakob Nielsen suggests acknowledging time limits (*http://bit.ly/response_time_limits*) that affect how users perceive an application:[1]

> **0.1 second** is about the limit for having the user feel that the system is reacting instantaneously, meaning that no special feedback is necessary except to display the result.

> **1.0 second** is about the limit for the user's flow of thought to stay uninterrupted, even though the user will notice the delay. Normally, no special feedback is necessary during delays of more than 0.1 but less than 1.0 second, but the user does lose the feeling of operating directly on the data.

> **10 seconds** is about the limit for keeping the user's attention focused on the dialogue. For longer delays, users will want to perform other tasks while waiting for the computer to finish, so they should be given feedback indicating when the computer expects to be done. Feedback during the delay is especially important if the response time is likely to be highly variable, since users will then not know what to expect.

Some useful questions with regard to performance include:

---

1 Jakob Nielsen, *Usability Engineering* (Boston: Academic Press, 1993), Chapter 5.

- What performance is acceptable or expected of the application?
- What operations does the application need to perform and how much work is required to do them?
- Can some of the work to answer queries be performed at ingest time rather than query time (precomputation)? How might this affect ingest performance?

The answers to these questions can help guide the application designer to determine how data should be processed and organized so that the required access patterns can be supported in a way that meets the performance requirements and the semantic rules of the application.

Understanding Read Performance

Application designers must understand the capabilities of the hardware and subsystems on which their application must run in order to reason about performance and develop designs to meet performance requirements. As far as understanding hardware is concerned, Google Bigtable author Jeffrey Dean compiled a list (*http://bit.ly/large_dist_sys_advice*) of what he called *Numbers Everyone Should Know*, shown in Table 13-1. Hardware performance may change as technology improves, but these are good order-of-magnitude estimates. Of those, a few are of special interest to Accumulo application developers.

Table 13-1. Some Numbers Everyone Should Know

Main memory reference	0.0001 ms
Send 2K bytes over 1 Gbps network	0.020 ms
Read 1 MB sequentially from memory	0.25 ms
Round trip within same datacenter	0.5 ms
Disk seek	10 ms
Read 1 MB sequentially from network	10 ms
Read 1 MB sequentially from disk	30 ms

To help application designers understand how using Accumulo affects application performance, it is useful to apply the information on how hardware performs to an understanding of how Accumulo operations use hardware.

Accumulo reads, or *scans*, involve doing some lookups in the Accumulo client's cache, then communicating with a tablet server to read out the data requested.

One important thing to note when modeling queries is that in our earlier calculations, the number and size of key-value pairs has a *linear* effect on the time it takes to read data off of disk, sort it in memory, and transfer it over the network—the more data read, the longer it takes. But the total number of key-value pairs in the table has a much smaller effect. The bigger the table, the more servers it will take to store the data. When querying, however, a single scan will usually involve only one tablet server and a small number of files containing the requested data, no matter how big the table gets.

The first step—finding the right tablet server for a scan—requires doing a binary search among tablet extents stored in memory. The time to do this search grows *logarithmically* with the number of tablets. This means that if finding the right tablet among 100 tablets takes 5 microseconds on average, finding the right tablet when there are 1,000 tablets should only take an average of 10 microseconds, not 50. We introduce this concept in depth in "Fast Random Access" on page 7.

Sometimes the blocks referenced as part of a scan will be cached in memory already, because Accumulo employs caching of blocks read from HDFS. However, Accumulo is designed to perform fast scans even when data is not cached and does so by minimizing disk seeks. This design is crucial to scaling to handle large amounts of data in a cost-effective way, because disk is many times cheaper than memory. More information on how Accumulo works is in Chapter 10.

Of course, an application can itself reference memory, disk, other services over the network. Performing back-of-the-envelope calculations about how an application should perform is helpful in determining viable design alternatives.

Understanding Write Performance

When we talk about write performance we often address two things: *throughput* and *latency*, which are sometimes at odds. By *throughput* we mean writing a number of items, or mutations, over time; throughput is the *rate* of writes. We often seek to achieve *high* throughput.

Latency refers to the time between when a write is ready to be written, and when it is available for query. We often seek to achieve *low* latency.

Applications can write data to Accumulo in two ways: by bundling mutations into batches via the `BatchWriter`, or by importing files from HDFS via *bulk import*. These methods allow application developers to balance throughput and latency to meet their requirements.

BatchWriters

High throughput when the `BatchWriter` is used depends on the ability to *amortize* network overhead by grouping mutations together before shipping them to tablet servers. The `BatchWriter` does this by waiting for several mutations to become available so it can group them together and send them all at once. This way, it only has to pay the network overhead for every hundred or thousand or so mutations, rather than every mutation. Seen another way, the network cost of writing a mutation can be reduced by a hundred or a thousand times via batching.

The time the `BatchWriter` spends waiting to gather some number of mutations contributes to latency. If the `BatchWriter` is able to gather 1,000 mutations, throughput will be higher, but latency will also be higher. Applications can choose therefore to configure the `BatchWriter` to send smaller batches of mutations more frequently so that latency is kept low. This configuration allows applications to choose where they want to reside in the spectrum between high throughput and low latency. Applications could choose to optimize for low latency at the cost of throughput by configuring the `BatchWriter` to wait for only a short time to gather a batch of mutations or by explicitly calling `flush()` to immediately send pending mutations. These settings are detailed in "Committing Mutations" on page 93.

Bulk Loading

An alternative to ingesting data via clients using the `BatchWriter` is to prepare key-value pairs into files and *bulk-load* them to Accumulo tables. Using bulk loading to write data to Accumulo tables represents sliding all the way to the high-throughput end of the spectrum. Bulk loading employs the MapReduce framework, which is optimized to process data at very high throughput. The data is only available for query after all the data has been processed and the MapReduce job completes, representing higher latency.

To understand how bulk loading works, it's helpful to know how data for Accumulo tables is stored in HDFS. An Accumulo table consists of a set of files in HDFS and metadata describing which files belong to which tablets and which key ranges each tablet spans. When data is ingested via an Accumulo client, RFiles are created and stored in HDFS as part of the minor compaction process. After tablets are split, they can share RFiles until a major compaction process writes out a separate set of RFiles for each tablet.

Eventually, Accumulo will end up having one or a small number of RFiles for each tablet, and each RFile will only contain data for one tablet. This represents a kind of equilibrium state for Accumulo in which no more compactions are necessary.

Users who want to get data into Accumulo at a very high rate of throughput can use MapReduce to create the RFiles such that they closely resemble the set of RFiles that

Accumulo would create on its own if the data were to be ingested via streaming clients.

Creating RFiles via MapReduce can be faster because a data set can be organized into the optimal set of RFiles in one MapReduce job rather than via several rounds of compaction on intermediate RFiles. The downside of bulk loading is that none of the data is available for query until the entire data set is done being processed by MapReduce. It also requires that all the data to be loaded is staged in HDFS.

Bulk loading is an option for quickly loading a large data set into Accumulo when it is possible to stage the data in HDFS and when the latency requirements are such that the data can be unavailable until the MapReduce job is complete.

"Bulk-loading files from a MapReduce job" on page 448 discusses additional factors to consider when bulk loading, including how to handle key timestamps.

Hardware Selection

Accumulo is designed to run on commodity-class servers. In general, using more-expensive hardware will not dramatically improve Accumulo's performance or reliability and in some cases will work against Accumulo's availability features.

What do we mean by commodity class? Basically *commodity* here refers to servers that are widely available for a large number of uses, such as servers that can be used for serving web pages, handling email, etc. Using these general-purpose machines has several advantages. First, when architecting the first MapReduce and BigTable clusters, Google calculated[1] that it would get the most compute power per dollar using this hardware:

> Combining more than 15,000 commodity-class PCs with fault-tolerant software creates a solution that is more cost-effective than a comparable system built out of a smaller number of high-end servers.

Second, because these types of servers are so widely used, many vendors are competing to sell them, which helps keep prices low and provides enough demand for hardware manufacturers to keep improving performance.

Typical hardware for an Accumulo tablet server is as follows:

CPU
2x 4-core or 6-core CPUs

RAM
16–96 GB RAM

---

1 Luiz André Barroso, Jeffrey Dean, and Urs Hölzle, "Web Search for a Planet: The Google Cluster Architecture" (*http://bit.ly/google_cluster*), *Micro, IEEE*, 23, no. 2, 22–28.

Disks
    2-12x 1–3 TB disks

Networking
    1-2x Gb Ethernet or 10 Gb Ethernet cards

If these servers will also be hosting TaskTrackers for running MapReduce jobs, additional RAM and or CPU cores will come in handy.

Buying hardware with many more CPU cores and much more RAM—*scaling up vertically*—may not result in higher performance, because a single tablet server process is limited in some ways. Accumulo is designed to scale *horizontally*, meaning adding more servers rather than increasing the resources of each server.

Storage Devices

Unlike some databases, Accumulo is designed to keep most of the data managed on disk. As much data as will fit is cached into RAM as data is read from disk, but even reads that request data that is not cached in RAM are designed to be fast, because Accumulo minimizes disk seeks by keeping the data organized and reading fairly large chunks at a time.

Hard disk drives

Because Accumulo relies on HDFS to distribute and replicate blocks of data, it is recommended that storage consist primarily of inexpensive hard disk drives (HDDs), such as 1–3 TB SATA 7,200–15,000 RPM drives, mounted separately (as JBOD, i.e., Just a Bunch of Disks) rather than via RAID. HDFS essentially implements a RAID-1 data redundancy scheme, replicating entire disk blocks rather than using erasure coding, so employing RAID in addition to HDFS replication is unnecessary. The upsides of keeping full replicas are that there is no recovery time when a single hard drive is lost, and any of the replicas can be used for reading the data.

Storage-area networks

Storage-area networks (SANs) are not as well suited to providing storage for Accumulo because the scaling, independence, and failure characteristics are different from the shared-nothing, unreliable hardware Accumulo and HDFS are designed for. SANs provide an abstraction layer that defeats the attempts by HDFS to reason about data locality. If for some reason Accumulo must be run on a SAN, it is preferable that HDFS be configured to keep only one replica of each block, because the SAN will often provide its own replication.

Solid-state disks

Solid-state disks (SSDs) have presented an interesting development for databases in general because many databases require a high number of random-access reads and writes. SSDs provide a much higher number of random reads per second because there is no disk platter to rotate as with HDDs. However, because Accumulo is designed to reduce seeks by performing sequential disk accesses as much as possible, the advantages of SSDs over HDDs are not as pronounced with Accumulo as they would be with databases that perform a high number of seeks per user request. SSDs may work well (*http://bit.ly/fusion-io_accumulo*) in an environment where the ratio of the read request rate to the total stored data is very high, such as 25,000 random reads per second per terabyte of data.

One fact to keep in mind when considering databases to use with SSDs is that random writes can exacerbate an effect known as *write amplification*. Write amplification refers to the case when a single write from an application perspective can result in more physical writes as the SSD attempts to find or create an empty spot in which to write the data. Accumulo's write patterns, which are append-only and sequential, should result in a minimal level of write amplification.

Networking

Accumulo is a networked application and its storage layer, HDFS, is a networked file system. Clients connect directly to tablet servers to read and write data. Tablet servers will try to read data from local disks when possible, avoiding reading data across the network, but will also often end up reading blocks of data from an HDFS DataNode over the network.

Having enough network bandwidth is fairly important to Accumulo. Even data read from disks local to a tablet server must still be transferred over the network to clients on other machines. For most clusters, servers with one or two 1-Gb Ethernet cards are sufficient. If there is more than one network interface card (NIC), they should be bonded in Linux to improve performance and availability. Currently Hadoop cannot utilize more than one NIC (*http://bit.ly/multiple_nifs*). Many clusters' networks consist of a 10 Gb switch atop each rack of servers and a 10 Gb switch connecting a row of racks together.

Virtualization

Accumulo can be run on virtualized hardware, with a few caveats. HDFS makes some assumptions about the physical location of data in order to achieve good performance. If the virtual environment supports access to local disks, then these assumptions can remain valid. If, however, the physical storage of data is abstracted away onto remote media, the efforts by HDFS to reduce network I/O will be pointless. This may or may not be a problem, depending on the total I/O available.

Another consideration is server responsiveness. Accumulo continually attempts to determine the status of its processes. If server response time is highly variable due to unpredictable access to underlying physical resources, Accumulo's timeouts may need to be increased to avoid dropping servers that are alive but don't respond quickly enough. This increases the time that data may be unavailable before Accumulo recovers from a true server failure.

Finally, there is the issue of independence and availability. The shared-nothing architecture Accumulo is built on relies on trying to reduce dependence among hardware components in order to minimize the effect of an individual failure so that the overall system can continue functioning. In a virtual environment, a physical failure may affect more than one virtual server if those virtual servers happen to share any hardware, which can result in less availability than one might expect from separate physical machines. If these issues can be managed, Accumulo can be run successfully in a virtual environment.

Running in a Public Cloud Environment

In Amazon's Elastic Compute Cloud (EC2) environment, for example, it is recommended that tablet server processes be run on instances with *ephemeral* storage, because that allows access to local disks. Some EC2 users recommend picking the largest instance type in a family, because supposedly this means that the virtual instance resources match the physical resources and that there will be only one virtual machine on a particular physical server, which can make access to the physical hardware less variable and services more responsive.

Amazon Elastic Block Store (EBS) volumes are recommended for storing the NameNode's data, preferably across several volumes in a RAID configuration for higher availability, but not for primary HDFS storage because this increases the interdependence between servers. Alternatively, a cluster could utilize multiple NameNodes running in a high-availability (HA) configuration using local ephemeral disk.

Amazon EC2 uses *Security Groups* to restrict network access to specific ports and hosts. See "Network Security" on page 417 for a list of ports that must be open.

Cluster Sizing

Several factors affect how much hardware is required for a particular use of Accumulo.

The best way to gather information on cluster performance starts with gathering empirical measures. Accumulo is designed so that aggregate write and read performance scales with the number of machines participating in the cluster. The perfect theoretical limit is to scale *linearly*, meaning that by doubling the cluster size you get double the aggregate performance. But, as Amdahl's Law describes, because there is some overhead in operations that can't be parallelized, performance increases will be less than perfectly linear.

Informal testing shows that doubling the number of machines in an Accumulo cluster results in roughly an 85 percent increase in aggregate write performance. Several factors contribute to the efficiency of the performance increase seen when the cluster is doubled, including network hardware and application design.

Modeling Required Write Performance

For the purposes of cluster planning using back-of-the-envelope calculations, a good practice is to prototype an application and measure the performance against a single server, and then against two servers, and look for the percentage increase in read and write performance. You may have to write several gigabytes of data or more in order to test the splitting and migration properties of tables before seeing an increase in aggregate write and read rates.

Based on these rates, you can estimate the number of machines required to reach a target number of user requests to read or write application data by multiplying one or two server aggregate rates by 1.85 until the target number of requests is reached.

For example, say we needed to be able to write a million key-value pairs per second, which would allow a theoretical MapReduce job writing to Accumulo to keep up with some reporting requirements.

Testing of an application prototype on some particular hardware reveals that the single-server write rate is 120,000 key-value pairs per second. Multiplying this by 1.85, we get an estimate of 222,000 pairs per second using two servers. We continue to multiply by 1.85 until we reach 1,000,000 writes per second, doubling the number of servers in our cluster each time. At four servers we have a theoretical write rate of 760,000 key-value pairs per second. At eight servers we have a rate of 1.4 million, so we need somewhere in between four and eight servers.

A direct formula for estimating the number of servers required to reach a target write rate is as follows:

$$m = 2^{\log_2(a/s)/0.7655}$$

```
m - estimated number of machines
a - target aggregate write rate in key-value pairs per second
s - measured single server performance in key-value pairs per second
```

On the other hand, if you want to measure the total expected read or write rate of an existing set of servers, you can measure application performance against one or two servers and extrapolate to the size of the cluster to get the aggregate write rate.

For example, if we measure an application as being able to write 5,000 user requests per second against 1 server (where each user request translates into several key-value pairs), and we have 20 servers, we can expect to see an aggregate write rate of about 71,000 key-value pairs on 20 servers, or about 14 times the single-server write rate.

To estimate the aggregate write performance of a cluster given the number of machines and single-server performance, the following formula can be used:

$$a = s \times 0.85^{log_2(m)} \times m$$

```
a - estimated aggregate write rate in key-value pairs per second
s - measured single server write rate in key-value pairs per second
m - number of machines
```

Cluster Planning Example

Let's imagine we are going to set up a Twitter clone that gets just as much traffic. Assume Twitter ingests 500 million tweets a day (*http://bit.ly/tweet_volume*) and each tweet is about 2,500 bytes on average (*http://bit.ly/tweetstream_dist*). That would be about 1.25 terabytes of new data per day. Our incoming data might increase by 100 percent over the year so that by the end we're storing 2.5 terabytes of new data per day. We need to store a year's worth of data online and make it available for queries on this system. Data older than one year old can be deleted because it is stored on another archival system (perhaps another HDFS cluster).

So we expect to have about 685 TB of data over the course of the next year.

Estimated total volume of data

To start, knowing how much data you need to store for a particular period of time can help determine the size of your cluster. Accumulo uses Gzip compression by default. It also compresses sets of keys by using a technique called *relative key encoding* (see "Relative key encoding" on page 370).

These techniques can often result in a 3–4:1 compression ratio. This is convenient because HDFS replicates data by a factor of three by default. So even though HDFS will increase storage requirements by a factor of three, compression brings the amount of storage required for raw data closer to a 1:1 ratio of raw data ingested to data stored on disk.

This means that to store 1 TB of data in Accumulo you will need at least 1 TB of disk space, but usually not 3 TB. But keep in mind that this is before building any secondary index tables, which will require additional space.

For our 685 TB of original data we know we'll need at least that much raw storage.

Types of user requests and indexes required

If your application is designed to do lookups only one way—perhaps taking advantage of a natural hierarchy in the data elements (see "Single-Table Designs" on page 271)—your data can be stored in a single table. In this case the table will likely require about as much space to store the data in an Accumulo table as the storage size of the data in the original format. If additional lookup methods are required, a secondary index table will need to be built.

Typically, a single index table will suffice for any combination of equality expressions ANDed together. Some users will want to query *ranges* of values in multiple fields simultaneously, which can require additional index tables. Depending on your query requirements, knowing the number and type of additional index tables can help you plan to have enough storage. See "Secondary Indexing" on page 275 for details on building secondary indexes.

If users need to be able to query *all* fields, the uncompressed size of the terms in the index would equal that of the original data, and that doesn't include the size of the unique identifiers that the index would use to point to the original data. Accumulo's compression and relative-key encoding are very efficient, so the disk storage needed for a full index might not actually exceed the original data size. However, if you find your indexes are larger than you want, you may want to index only a subset of the fields.

For our example, let's assume that our desired index size is half the size of the original data, adding 50 percent to our storage needs, bringing the total to 1,028 TB, or a little over 1 PB.

Compactions

As new data is ingested into files in HFDS, periodically Accumulo compacts multiple files into a single file to make opening and reading files simpler and faster. During the compaction process, tablet servers copy several files into one new file. The compaction process requires additional temporary storage and I/O resources. Just as with a MapReduce cluster, an Accumulo cluster will need some free space in which to operate. Let's estimate that 20 percent more storage is required for this purpose.

This increases the total to 1,234 TB.

Rate of incoming data

We've estimated the storage required to hold the initial data and the data added each day. To store the data in additional secondary indexes, and to perform compactions, the number of servers we'll need depends on the amount of storage per machine. Modern servers can support 12 or more disks. At 3 TB per disk, a single server can store 36 TB or more. If we buy 2 TB hard drives and can fit 12 drives into each server, in addition to the disks used to support the operating system, we'll eventually need about 52 servers for our 1,234 TB of total data.

But maxing out the storage per server may not be adequate to support the ingest rate of the data. Ingestion depends on having not only enough raw storage, but also enough compute capacity and I/O to sort and manage the data. Let's calculate how many servers are needed to support the ingest rate we require.

For key-value pairs that are about 1 KB in size, a single tablet server on typical hardware can ingest 30,000–100,000 key-value pairs per second or more, depending on the number of CPU cores, the number of drives, the size of the key-value pairs, and how Accumulo is configured. See "Tablet Server Tuning" on page 488 for information on tuning Accumulo for high ingest rates.

You will also have to adjust the number of ingest processes to achieve the best throughput for your system; a single ingest client may not be able to push Accumulo's tablet servers to their highest possible ingest rate.

As the size of the cluster increases, the per-server rate will drop somewhat, simply because clients are forced to split their batches over more and more servers, which increases network overhead. Informal testing indicates that you can increase the aggregate write rate of a cluster by about 85 percent when the cluster hardware is doubled.

Let's estimate how many servers will be needed to support our initial rate of 500 million tweets per day.

Each tweet has about 30 fields (*http://bit.ly/tweet_fields*). Let's imagine that on average about half of those are empty. Just to ingest the data we will be writing 15 x 500 million = 7.5 billion key-value pairs per day, if we store each field as a separate key-value pair in a common row. If we index 10 fields per tweet, including a separate entry for each word of text in the tweet, on average say 15 words, that's roughly another 25 x 500 million = 12.5 billion key-value pairs.

So we'll need to be able to ingest 20 billion key-value pairs per day if we write 40 key-value pairs per tweet. That's an average of 231,500 key-value pairs per second.

Using the formula from "Modeling Required Write Performance" on page 477 we'll need between 3 and 14 servers to get started, depending on whether our per-server write performance is 100,000 or 30,000 writes per second, respectively. If the data arrives nonuniformly throughout the day, and peaks at, say, 2 p.m. at two times the average, we'll need as many as 8 of the higher-end servers to handle peak load. To handle a peak as high as 140,000 tweets per second (*http://bit.ly/tweet_volume*), we might need as many as 192 servers.

If we want to store 1,234 TB by the end of the year, we'll need to add a new server every seven days. If we only buy 10 servers to start with, we'll have to buy more in less than three months.

If we buy half the cluster today, that's 26 machines. We may want to do this, because in six months hardware may be slightly improved and we can get the best performance per dollar.

Age-off strategy

The final consideration in our exercise is how we plan to age-off the data. Aging off old data can reduce our total storage requirements.

We can use Accumulo's `AgeOffIterator` to automatically remove key-value pairs that are over a year old. Accumulo's files are immutable, so to do this we need to make sure we compact the tables periodically to create new files in which the old data is absent, and that we garbage-collect the old files.

This will cause all files to be processed and iterators, such as the `AgeOffIterator`, to be applied in the creation of new files. See "Data Lifecycle" on page 449 for more on managing the data lifecycle.

Analyzing Performance

Accumulo is designed to support high rates of ingest and fast reads across a large number of servers and a large number of user requests. Applications that are designed properly can take advantage of these features, and analyzing performance will reveal whether any design decisions need to be changed.

Using Tracing

Detailed timing information on what Accumulo is doing behind the scenes can be obtained by enabling a process called *tracing*. Tracing is generally only turned on temporarily while analyzing an application's behavior, because it increases the load on Accumulo by generating data that is stored in an Accumulo *trace* table.

Traces can be enabled programmatically in Java or in the Accumulo shell. The Java client code is in the accumulo-core module under `org.apache.accu mulo.core.trace`. Here is an example that uses tracing in Java:

```
DistributedTrace.enable(instance, zooReader, hostname, "someApplication");
Trace scanTrace = Trace.on("descriptiveString");

BatchScanner scanner = conn.createBatchScanner(...);
for (Entry<Key, Value> entry : scanner) {
  ...
}
```

```
long traceId = Trace.currentTrace().traceId();
Trace.off();
```

After running the trace in Java, you can either go to the Recent Traces in the monitor page or scan the *trace* table directory using the `traceId` as the row ID:

```
user@accumulo> scan -t trace -r traceId
```

Note that the *trace* table has the `org.apache.accumulo.core.trace.TraceFormatter` class configured, so the output will be more readable.

Here is an example in the shell, which returns tracing information after a pause when tracing is turned off. You can still use the monitor page or scan the *trace* table directly to retrieve the tracing information:

```
user@accumulo> trace on
user@accumulo> scan -t tablename -r rowId
user@accumulo> trace off
Waiting for trace information
Waiting for trace information

Time  Start  Service@Location       Name
5469+0       shell@hostname shell:root
   1+5          tserver@localhost listLocalUsers
   1+2667       shell@hostname client:getTableConfiguration
   1+2674       tserver@localhost getTableConfiguration
   1+2679       tserver@localhost getTableConfiguration
   1+2686       shell@hostname client:getUserAuthorizations
  82+2723      shell@hostname scan
  41+2723        shell@hostname scan:locateTablet
   3+2743          shell@hostname client:startScan
   2+2746          tserver@localhost startScan
   2+2761          tserver@localhost startScan
   1+2761            tserver@localhost metadata tablets read ahead 4
  41+2764        shell@hostname scan:location
  39+2765          tserver@localhost startScan
  37+2766            tserver@localhost tablet read ahead 9
   1+2767              tserver@localhost open
```

The *time* column of numbers shows the length of a particular operation in milliseconds, and the *start* column shows how many milliseconds elapsed between the start of the entire trace and the start of a particular operation. Note that operations are nested so that the time number for one operation is greater than the sum of the times taken by the operations it initiates, i.e., those nested under it. The nesting is shown by indentation. Tracing is useful for finding operations that are taking longer than expected.

Using the Monitor

The Accumulo monitor is a convenient way to see metrics of cluster performance and diagnose problems. The monitor page shows several graphs of interest to performance analyses. Application designers can check these to see what kind of aggregate performance an application is achieving, and to verify how an application will scale when run against an increasing number of servers. For these graphs to be used effectively, estimates for the theoretical performance of individual hardware components must be known, or else any comparison to empirical performance numbers is meaningless.

In particular, looking at the aggregate ingest rate (Figure 13-1) and aggregate number of scans (Figure 13-2) will provide a good notion of how busy the cluster is.

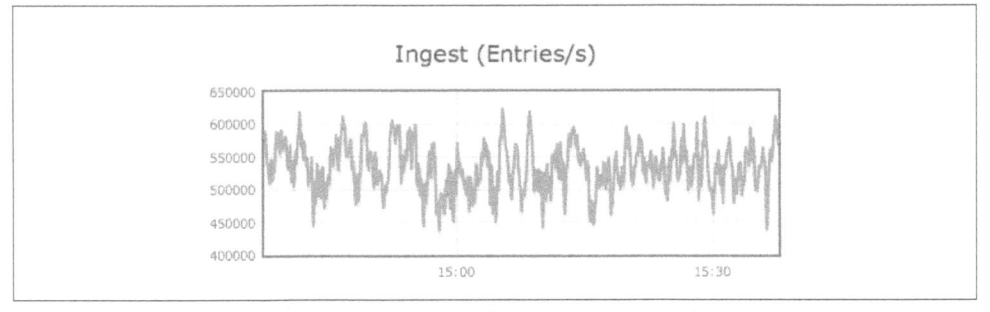

Figure 13-1. Aggregate ingest rate in key-value pairs per second

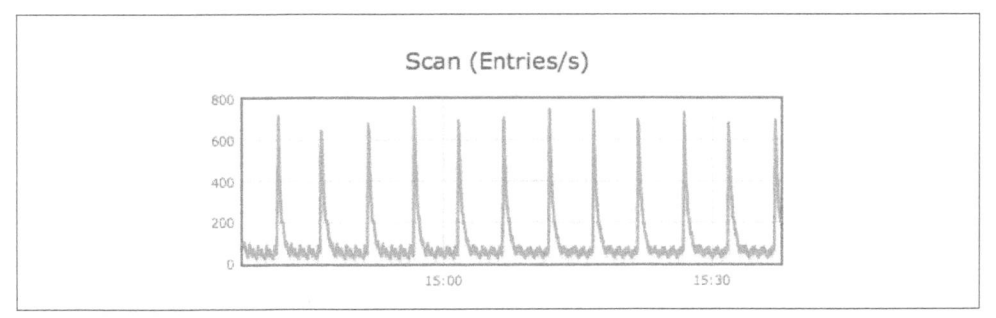

Figure 13-2. Aggregate scan rate in key-value pairs per second

Next most useful are the graphs describing the raw amount of data written or read, in megabytes (Figure 13-3 and Figure 13-4).

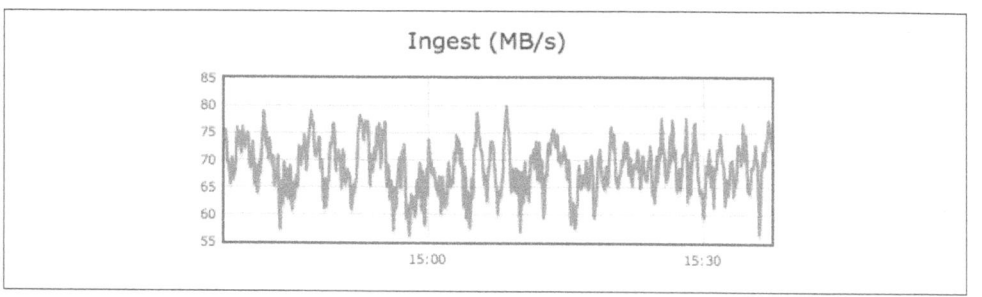

Figure 13-3. Aggregate ingest rate in megabytes of data per second

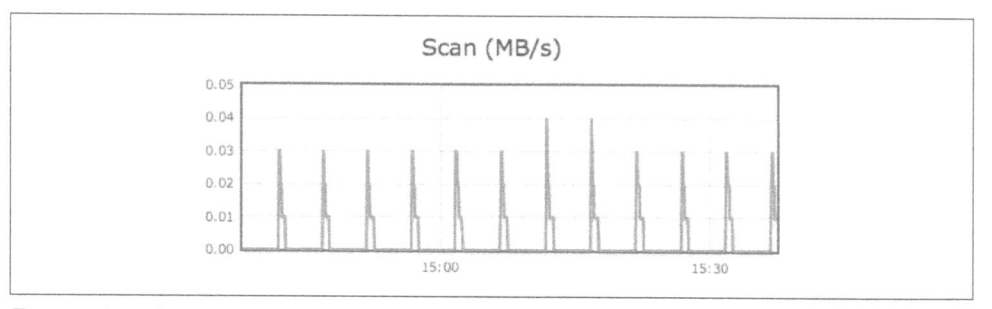

Figure 13-4. Aggregate scan rate in megabytes of data per second

Monitoring CPU load can also be useful in determining how busy the cluster is (Figure 13-5).

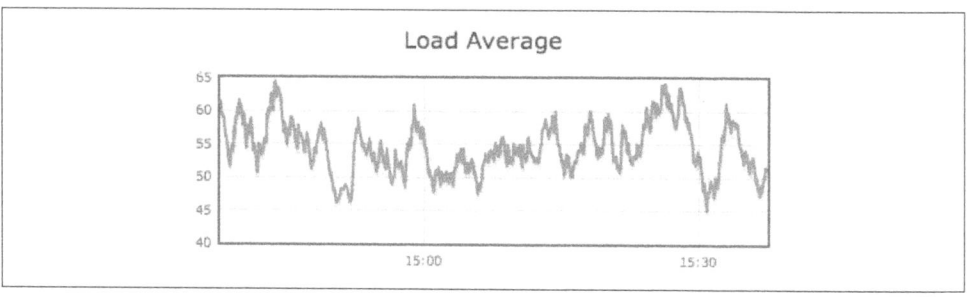

Figure 13-5. Aggregate CPU load

Looking at caching information in the graphs at the bottom of the list is useful for seeing whether index or block caching is having the desired effect (Figure 13-6 and Figure 13-7).

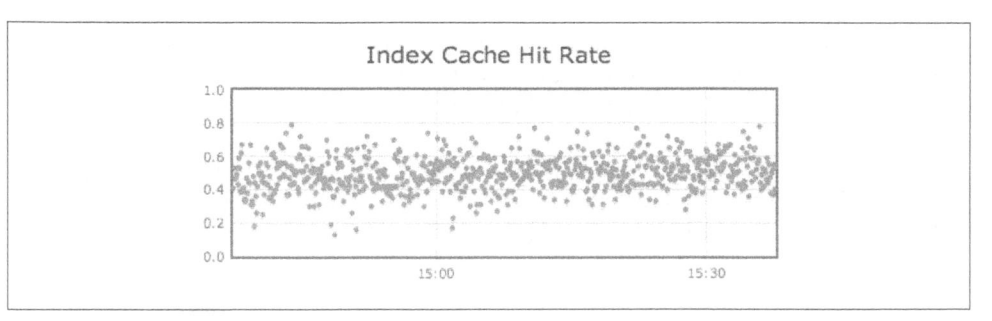

Figure 13-6. Number of index block cache misses (i.e., when Accumulo has to read an index block from HDFS)

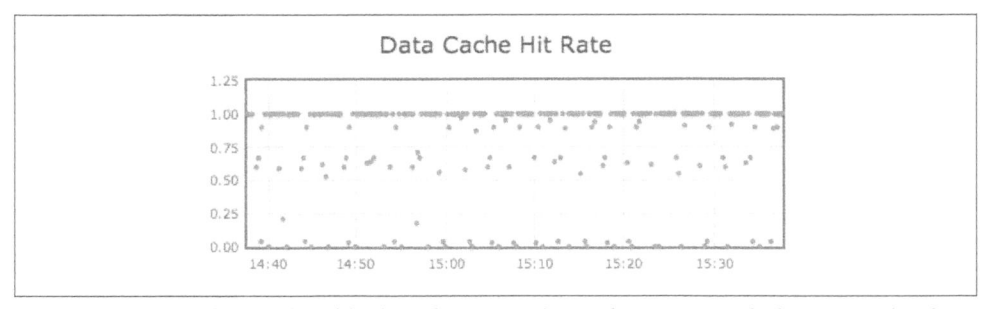

Figure 13-7. Number of data block cache misses (i.e., when Accumulo has to read a data block from HDFS)

In addition, you can measure the number of items that are being processed by Accumulo clients, which may be converting individual user requests into several key-value pairs. Knowing how to convert the number of user write or read requests into the number of key-value pairs or megabytes of data read and written will help verify that the cluster is performing optimally.

For example, if every user request to write a record of application data involves writing the original record as one key-value pair to one table, and several key-value pairs for index entries of individual fields in the record, the ratio of application records to key-value pairs written may be 1 to 10 or more.

Getting familiar with these metrics will help in reasoning about performance and tuning decisions discussed in the next few sections.

We cover the types of exceptions that Accumulo applications can expect and some ways to handle them in "Handling Errors" on page 95. When you troubleshoot an application, it is also important to be able to get information on the health of the tablet servers and master in order to determine whether the application is doing something wrong or simply experiencing issues due to hardware problems or misconfiguration.

Tablet servers forward log messages of severity WARN and above to the Accumulo monitor that displays them in one convenient location (Figure 13-8). Checking these logs can be helpful if a failure occurs within a tablet server.

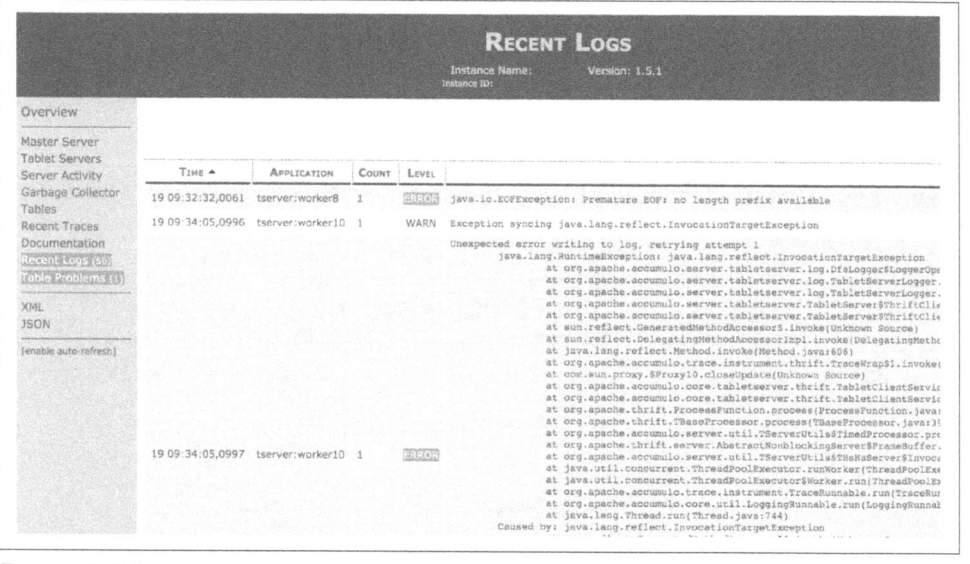

Figure 13-8. Logs in monitor

When you are for hotspots, viewing the page of the monitor that shows the amount of data written or read per server is useful (Figure 13-9). If one or two servers are handling the majority of the reads and writes, versus roughly the same number of reads or writes across most of the servers, it may indicate a hotspot.

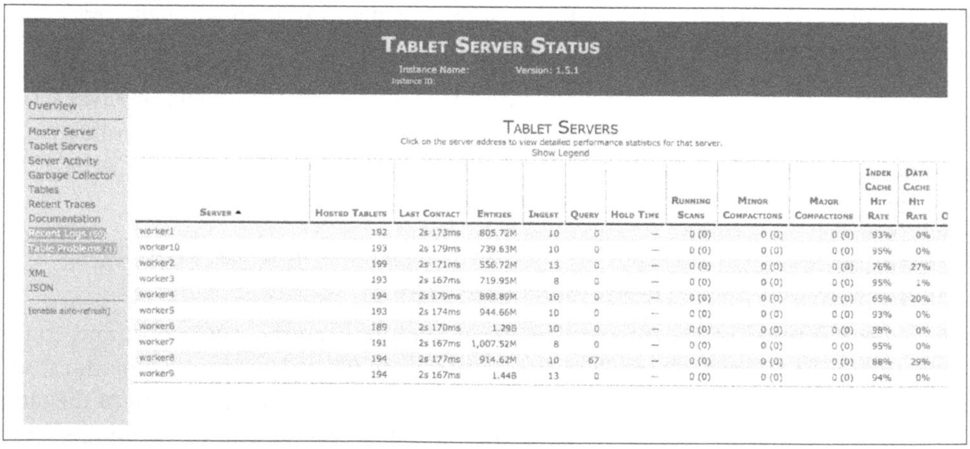

Figure 13-9. Server statistics

Further drilling down into the individual tablets hosted by a server can reveal the range of keys that reads and writes are using (Figure 13-10).

TABLET SERVER STATUS

Instance Name: Version: 1.5.1
Instance ID:

Overview
Master Server
Tablet Servers
Server Activity
Garbage Collector
Tables
Recent Traces
Documentation
Recent Logs (50)
Table Problems (1)
XML
JSON

[enable auto-refresh]

DETAILED CURRENT OPERATIONS
Per-tablet Details

TABLE ▲	TABLET	ENTRIES	INGEST	QUERY	MINOR AVG	MINOR STD DEV	MINOR AVG E/S	MAJOR AVG
record	[mMFqC7SQP1DE/ZxSREs5Ow==]	0	0	0	–	–	–	–
record	[xRr3IgQxx5beGUS/Vodumw==]	0	0	0	–	–	.	–
record	[sRnU3efo12Tk3ZKWGS3Org==]	0	0	0	–	–	–	–
record	[1BjQpHCiM4Avg4KXY6PrTw==]	0	0	0	–	–	–	–
index	[+q8eFoRPOj8tZcRI14Km/Q==]	70.07K	0	0	2s 494ms	2s 285ms	8.57K	–
record	[GS4F31PYxOnHDZZfFgsnzA==]	13.94K	0	0	101ms	16ms	1.52K	–
record	[N6w9J6eHm/0xcka14qoVvw==]	13.93K	0	0	2s 434ms	3s 562ms	635	271ms
record	[u132d3hzhNX1XuKuBNS4Sg==]	13.93K	0	0	3s 1ms	4s 49ms	515	367ms
record	[1BjQpHCiM4Avg4KXY6PrTw==]	13.93K	0	0	2s 849ms	3s 978ms	542	302ms
_index	[WUs6JK7PaDmMCyIWYMzNvQ==]	39.46M	0	0	6s 876ms	1s 408ms	96.69K	1m 45s
_index	[IGDbT21GBZNeUcmtPHRjYQ==]	145.77K	0	0	–	–	–	–
_index	[37y4osMSSOeLREgLzsuJog==]	18.17M	0	0	–	–	.	–
_index	[Tpgvr2TIowSstbLu1+1ghA==]	75.34M	0	0	4s 870ms	2s 968ms	154.37K	44s 343ms
_index	[HXod/Mhe70gJY4I+qEPWyw==]	71.03M	0	0	6s 626ms	2s 161ms	150.88K	1m 10s
_index	[5UHHq6JRdv8sM6VYoiDkzQ==]	46.82M	0	0	6s 986ms	1s 794ms	92.46K	1m 21s
_index	[hjhaUYUex513yKEuf6SbBA==]	146.69M	0	0	902ms	–	289.42K	–
_record	[7X+mCKdv4eZ3UmzP+X3q6Q==]	2.04M	0	0	706ms	396ms	24.74K	5s 731ms
_record	[Fap7oKcAnAAnZCQV1zGkBQ==]	1.29M	0	0	–	–	.	–
_record	[1NOCa/bwYnlQv4GxZTnr4w==]	1.04M	0	0	–	–	–	–

Figure 13-10. Tablet statistics

A hotspot in a particular range of keys can be a feature of some external data being loaded, over which the application has no control, or it can be the result of a deliberate key design.

In the former case, application designers can consider transforming external data into a set of keys that avoids hotspots by using techniques described in "Avoiding Hotspots" on page 305.

For more tips on troubleshooting, see "Troubleshooting" on page 461.

Using Local Logs

In addition to forwarding WARN and ERROR level messages to the monitor, tablet servers write to several logfiles on the local machine, which can include log messages of lower severity that may be useful for debugging. These are typically found in either *$ACCUMULO_HOME/logs* or */var/log/accumulo*.

See "Logging" on page 436 for details on configuring logs.

Tablet Server Tuning

Tablet servers are multithreaded and will take advantage of multiple cores on a server. Additional tuning should be done according to the particular hardware on which tablet servers will run and what other processes are present.

We discuss table-specific properties in depth in "Configuring Table Properties" on page 137 for tuning table behavior. Here we address remaining properties that are specific to tablet server operations.

External Settings

A number of settings external to Accumulo must be configured for Accumulo to work properly. In addition to the settings described in "Kernel Tweaks" on page 384 and "Software Dependencies" on page 386, the following are some settings to examine when you are tuning for performance.

HDFS threads used to transfer data

Depending on your version of HDFS, you may or may not need to increase the number of threads that can be used to transfer data. If the version you are using has the `dfs.datanode.max.transfer.threads` property, which defaults to 4096, you do not need to adjust it. If HDFS is still using `dfs.datanode.max.xcievers`, its value should be increased to 4096:

```
<property>
  <name>dfs.datanode.max.xcievers</name>
  <value>4096</value>
</property>
```

HDFS durable sync

For Accumulo 1.5 and later, HDFS durable sync must be enabled because Accumulo uses HDFS for its write-ahead log. Older versions of Hadoop may need `dfs.sup port.append` set to `true`, but newer versions default `dfs.durable.sync` to `true`, so that value merely needs to remain unchanged. In newer versions of Hadoop, the `dfs.datanode.synconclose` property should also be set to `true` to ensure that data in Accumulo RFiles is synced to disk when the files are closed.

In older versions of Hadoop:

```
<property>
  <name>dfs.support.append</name>
  <value>true</value>
</property>
```

In newer versions:

```
<property>
  <name>dfs.durable.sync</name>
  <value>true</value>
</property>
<property>
  <name>dfs.datanode.synconclose</name>
  <value>true</value>
</property>
```

Memory Settings

Tablet servers are designed to serve data from disk efficiently, but they are also designed to use memory to optimize reads and writes as much as possible. Memory settings are among those that have the most significant performance impact. There are a few things to consider when configuring the amount of memory dedicated to various components of tablet servers.

tserver.memory.maps.max

The in-memory map is where new writes are stored and sorted in memory, in addition to be written to disk in a write-ahead log, until they are flushed to disk in a minor compaction.

The amount of memory that each tablet server reserves for in-memory maps is controlled via the `tserver.memory.maps.max` setting, and increasing this can improve write speed and decrease the number of individual compactions. Memory is divided among all tablets actively receiving writes on the same tablet server, so this property may need to be increased significantly to have a noticeable effect.

If the in-memory map size is increased, the number of write-ahead logfiles should also be adjusted. When a tablet has a given number of write-ahead logs, it will automatically be flushed, even if memory is not full. So, the number of write-ahead logs (`table.compaction.minor.logs.threshold`) times the size of each log (`tserver.walog.max.size`) should be at least as big as the amount of memory given for in-memory maps (`tserver.memory.maps.max`):

> `table.compaction.minor.logs.threshold` × `tserver.walog.max.size` ≥ `tserver.memory.maps.max`

For example, if we are setting `tserver.memory.maps.max` to 12GB, and `tserver.walog.max.size` is set to 4GB, we would want to increase `table.compaction.minor.logs.threshold` to be greater than 3.

Increasing the size of the write-ahead logs via `tserver.walog.max.size` can cause recovery to take longer and should be done with caution.

tserver.memory.maps.native.enabled

In all but trivial testing systems, native in-memory maps should be built, if necessary, and enabled by leaving the `tserver.memory.maps.native.enabled` property set to `true`. See "Building native libraries" on page 400 for details on building native maps.

To ensure that native in-memory maps are being used, make sure the libraries exist in *$ACCUMULO_HOME/lib/native*. If not, they can be built by running the `make` command in *$ACCUMULO_HOME/server/src/main/c++/*.

At startup time, tablet server logs in *$ACCUMULO_HOME/logs/tserver*.log* will show whether native maps are enabled:

```
[server.Accumulo] INFO : tserver.memory.maps.native.enabled = true
```

And whether they were not found:

```
[tabletserver.NativeMap] ERROR: Failed to load native map library ..
```

Cache settings

In general, more memory dedicated to caches will provide better query performance. However, Java garbage collection may then take longer to reclaim memory from objects no longer in use, decreasing tablet server responsiveness and interfering with ZooKeeper's attempts to determine server online status. The cache size properties are `tserver.cache.index.size` and `tserver.cache.data.size` and they govern the amount of memory used to cache RFile index blocks and RFile data blocks, respectively.

Ideally, the index cache size should be chosen so that all index blocks for the tablets hosted by a tablet server fit in memory. To estimate this size, the number of files per tablet and tablets per tablet server must be determined, as well as the average index size per file (see "Inspect RFiles" on page 465 for information on inspecting individual RFiles).

Any amount of memory dedicated to the data cache will be utilized, so its size can be made as large as makes sense for your application and your hardware. The more memory that can be used to hold data blocks in the data cache, the greater the number of disk accesses that can be avoided when Accumulo fetches key-value pairs that were recently accessed or key-value pairs that are sorted close together in a tablet to recently accessed data.

Java heap size

The tablet server heap size is an environment variable, `ACCUMULO_TSERVER_OPTS`, set in the *accumulo-env.sh* file. It should be large enough to cover the total size given to caches, plus some overhead. If native maps are not enabled (which is not recommended), the heap size must also include the size of the in-memory maps. Tablet servers will error out if the memory allocation does not add up when native maps are turned off. The in-memory maps and caches are not the only things the tablet server stores in memory, but they are generally the values that are tuned larger when there is more memory available, and their values therefore are potentially the largest contributors to a tablet server's memory usage.

 Processes other than the tablet server only need sufficient memory to operate and don't benefit from increased memory. A potential exception is the Accumulo garbage collector. If you have a lot of tablets, files, and servers, making the garbage collection memory allocation larger will keep collection efficient. If it can't keep the list of all files that are candidates for deletion in memory, it has to use multiple passes to reclaim files.

tserver.mutation.queue.max

This is the number of bytes of write-ahead log data to store in memory before it is flushed to disk. Setting the value too low reduces Accumulo's throughput, but setting it too high can result in memory exhaustion if there are many concurrent writers. Values of 2M or 4M may be reasonable. (See the ACCUMULO-1905 (*http://bit.ly/ accumulo-1905_jira*) and ACCUMULO-1950 (*http://bit.ly/accumulo-1950_jira*) Jira pages for a more detailed analysis.)

Additional settings are listed in Table 13-2.

Table 13-2. Additional tablet server memory settings

Setting	Description
tserver.default.blocksize	Size of blocks used in caches
tserver.dir.memdump	Local directory to store temporary files used by long-running scans. If an in-memory map is ready to be deleted (its contents having been flushed in HDFS in a minor compaction) but is still being used by a long-running scan, a copy of the data needed by the scan will be stored on a local disk until it is no longer needed. This allows the memory to be freed sooner.
tserver.memory.manager	Implementation of memory manager; default is LargestFirstMemoryManager
tserver.server.message.size.max	Maximum allowable message size a tablet server will accept
tserver.sort.buffer.size	Amount of memory to use when sorting write-ahead logs for recovery

Write-Ahead Log Settings

The write-ahead log currently limits the speed of writes via the BatchWriter because all mutations must be committed in an append-only fashion to the write-ahead log in order to be considered successful. Therefore, tuning the write-ahead log settings is usually worth the effort.

The following are the settings that impact performance the most:

tserver.wal.replication

Write-ahead logs are stored in HDFS as of Accumulo version 1.5, and as such they are replicated for availability should a server fail. By default, write-ahead logs are replicated according to the default policy set for HDFS in *$HADOOP_HOME/conf/ hdfs-site.xml*, but this setting can be overridden for tablet servers in general and specific tables as well.

Reducing the number of replicas for write-ahead logs can increase performance when safety demands allow.

tserver.wal.sync

By default in Accumulo 1.6, tablet servers are configured to use the SYNC_BLOCK flag when closing blocks written to write-ahead logs. In addition, the sync method is called on the underlying filesystem when data is written to a write-ahead log. The particular sync method called depends on the tserver.wal.sync.method in Accumulo 1.6.1 and newer.

tserver.wal.sync.method

When tserver.wal.sync is used as just described, this setting controls the particular sync method used. The default is hsync, which waits until writes are completed to disk. Using the hsync method prevents the loss of data in Accumulo tables even in the event of a sudden power outage.

In environments where uninterruptible power supplies are applied to allow systems to be shut down gracefully in the event of a power outage, this setting can be set to hflush, which does not wait. Using hflush can result in up to a 30 percent increase in write performance.

Note that this setting is only in Accumulo version 1.6.1 and newer.

Table 13-3 contains additional write-ahead log settings.

Table 13-3. Additional tablet server write-ahead log settings

Setting	Description
tserver.archive.walogs	Controls whether to keep copies of write-ahead logs for debugging purposes.
tserver.wal.blocksize	Size of HDFS block used for write-ahead logs.
tserver.walog.max.size	Maximum size for each write-ahead log. Related to `tserver.memory.maps.max`.

Resource Settings

Tablet servers use system resources to respond to client requests and to perform background operations. These resources include open files, threads, and memory. We discuss memory settings specifically in "Memory Settings" on page 489.

The following is a list of settings that control the number of threads dedicated to various tasks. Consider adjusting one of these upward if the particular operation associated appears to be lagging and system resources allow. Changing the number of resources allocated to one activity may require reducing resources allocated to other activities.

tserver.compaction.major.concurrent.max

This setting controls the maximum number of concurrent major compactions that a tablet server will carry out. Because major compactions involve reading multiple files and writing out one new merged file, this setting can impact overall I/O usage. If resources allow and major compactions appear to be queueing up in the tablet server view of the monitor, this setting can be increased.

tserver.compaction.minor.concurrent.max

This controls the maximum number of concurrent minor compactions that a tablet server can execute and determines how much I/O a tablet server is allowed to use for writing new data to disk.

tserver.readahead.concurrent.max

This limits the number of long-running scans a tablet server will support concurrently.

Running Tablet Servers Alongside MapReduce Workers

It is common for Accumulo processes to be deployed on the same servers that are hosting MapReduce worker processes, such as Hadoop TaskTrackers. If this is the case, it is important to make sure that there are enough available hardware resources for each process when all the processes are being utilized.

For example, the number of MapReduce task slots (simultaneous workers) should be multiplied by the amount of RAM allocated for each slot, and added to the RAM required by the Accumulo tablet server and any other running processes to estimate the total required memory. If this amount exceeds the available RAM, processes should each be allocated less RAM, or the number of available MapReduce workers should be decreased to avoid a situation in which pages of RAM will be swapped to disk, which can cause delays that can be interpreted as a failed server and cause tablet servers to be terminated and excluded from the cluster.

The I/O resources of servers will also be shared in this case, and running Accumulo compactions will affect MapReduce performance and vice versa. There is a limit to the number of files Accumulo will allow a tablet to have before forcing a major compaction, in order to keep the number of file resources per scan reasonable. If there is not enough I/O on a server to support the number of compactions required to organize newly written data, compaction tasks will queue up on tablet servers. This can be seen in the monitor on the tablet servers view in the column listing the number of compactions running and queued.

If compactions are queuing up, the resources dedicated to compactions may need to be increased, at the expense of resources dedicated to MapReduce. This can be an indication too that simply more hardware resources are needed.

Additional resources settings are listed in Table 13-4.

Table 13-4. Additional tablet server resource settings

Setting	Description
tserver.bloom.load.concurrent.max	Threads used to load bloom filters in the background
tserver.bulk.assign.threads	Threads used to communicate with other servers during bulk loading
tserver.bulk.process.threads	Threads used to process files for bulk loading
tserver.compaction.major.thread.files.open.max	Number of files that can be opened during major compactions
tserver.recovery.concurrent.max	Threads used for sorting logs during recovery

tserver.scan.files.open.max	Maximum number of open file handles that can be used for scans
tserver.server.threads.minimum	Minimum number of threads for handling requests
tserver.workq.threads	Threads used for copying failed bulk loading files
tserver.metadata.readahead.concurrent.max	Number of metadata scans that can execute
tserver.migrations.concurrent.max	Number of concurrent allowed tablet migrations
tserver.tablet.split.midpoint.files.max	Number of index files to open when looking for a midpoint at which to split a tablet
tserver.monitor.fs	Whether to monitor local filesystems and exit on detecting failure

Timeouts

Tablet servers keep resources around for certain periods of time to allow tasks to reuse them and avoid the overhead of setting up resources anew. These settings control how aggressively tablet servers reclaim those resources. Some of them are used to control how long to wait before determining a failure.

Timeout settings are listed in Table 13-5.

Table 13-5. Tablet server timeout settings

Setting	Description
tserver.bulk.retry.max	Times a server will try to assign a file to a tablet that is migrating or splitting.
tserver.bulk.timeout	Time to wait for a bulk loading task to complete.
tserver.client.timeout	Time to wait for additional scans from a client before closing a session.
tserver.compaction.major.delay	Time to sleep between checking whether major compaction is needed.
tserver.compaction.warn.time	Time before a warning is logged to note a compaction that has not made progress.
tserver.files.open.idle	Time that an open file is left open for future queries before being closed.
tserver.hold.time.max	Time to wait for functional disk I/O after memory is full before exiting. This is used to detect local failures.
tserver.server.threadcheck.time	Time to wait between adjustments to the thread pool.
tserver.session.idle.max	Time to wait before closing an idle session.

Scaling Vertically

Adding more memory and CPU to a single server will help a single tablet server process cope with more concurrent queries and writes. Modern servers can have up to 12 or more disks, which can increase the amount of CPU and RAM required to keep those disks busy.

Write-ahead logs can become a bottleneck for ingest because tablet servers each use one, albeit replicated, write-ahead log. If the ingest rate of a server is dominated by the time spent flushing mutations to the write-ahead log, adding more disks or CPU to each server will not increase the write rate. Adding more RAM and increasing the `tserver.mutation.queue.max` and `tserver.memory.maps.max` will improve performance up to a point. For this reason, it may be more cost effective to have more individual servers, each with fewer resources so that a greater portion of available disks is devoted to write-ahead logs. This is consistent with Accumulo's design to run well on relatively cheap servers.

On individual servers that have extensive resources, including 256 GB of RAM or more and 12 or more disks, it may be possible to improve performance by running multiple tablet server processes on a single physical server. When doing so, it is important that each tablet server listen on a separate set of network ports.

Cluster Tuning

Performance bottlenecks can occur in several places in an Accumulo application. It is important to make sure that Accumulo applications are taking advantage of all the hardware resources available and that each hardware component is being used efficiently.

Potential bottlenecks include:

The number of clients writing or reading data
> If not enough clients are available to ship new data to or scan data from the cluster, tablet servers will be underutilized.

The number of tablets available
> If not enough tablets are available, some tablet servers will be idle, neither accepting writes nor serving queries. If performance is unsatisfactory for a given table and the number of tablets the table is split into is less than the number of available tablet servers, adding additional split points or turning down the split threshold temporarily will cause there to be enough tablets for every server to have one and participate in serving requests for the table.

The number of operations per second that a single HDFS NameNode can support
> At very large scales, the sheer number of filesystem operations can become the bottleneck of a cluster. A single HDFS NameNode is limited to a few thousand update operations per second because each operation is synced to disk.

The throughput of the network
> As clusters grow, the network can become the bottleneck if it isn't scaled up along with the number of servers. In some cases upgrading from Gigabit Ethernet to 10 Gigabit Ethernet or upgrading the switches connecting racks is required to avoid the network becoming a bottleneck.

The distribution of keys being read from or written to in tables (hotspots)
> Even if there are tablets on each server, it may be the case that all of the incoming keys end up going to a small number of tablets, if there are common keys that appear frequently.

The relative amount of CPU, RAM, and hard drives available per server
> For example, servers may have lots of CPU but not enough disks, or vice versa.

The number of servers participating in the cluster
> This is the ideal bottleneck. Performance of the application can be increased by adding more machines.

Cluster tuning will consist of balancing these resources relative to one another. In order to maximize reads and writes, applications should start by considering three numbers:

- The number of tablet servers
- The number of tablets
- The number of client processes writing to tablet servers

Before tablet servers can all participate in servicing requests for a particular table, there have to be at least as many tablets in the table as tablet servers in order for the Accumulo master to be able to assign at least one tablet to each server.

Once each server has at least one tablet from the table to which an application wants to send a request, there must also be enough client processes available to avoid artificially limiting the aggregate read or write rate. If the theoretical limit of the tablet servers in the Accumulo cluster is 1,000,000 writes per second, and if client processes max out at 100,000 writes per second, we'll need at least 10 client processes to reach our cluster maximum.

Once these are roughly balanced, the next things to address are the load-balancing strategy used by the master, and whether we have hotspots in our table, as described in the next few sections.

Splitting Tables

Brand new tables in Accumulo start out as a single tablet. Accumulo automatically splits tablets when they reach a certain threshold known as the `table.split.thresh old` setting in the tablet configuration. We discuss performing tablet splits programmatically in "Tablet Splits" on page 145. Here we discuss splitting tablets using the shell and additional considerations.

Some applications might be bottlenecked by the number of tablets until there are enough tablets for every tablet server to host one or more. You can choose to either wait until there is enough data ingested for the table to split automatically into the desired number of tablets, turn down the split threshold temporarily to cause automatic splits to happen sooner, or presplit the table using a set of known split points.

Lowering the split threshold temporarily has the advantage of allowing Accumulo to still pick the split points uniformly, no matter what kind of distribution of keys exists within a table. This still assumes that the splits that will occur on the initial amount of data ingested are representative of the split points that would have been chosen after all the data is ingested. For example, if we are importing a list of users that has been sorted alphabetically, the initial split points will only occur within the first few letters of the alphabet and will not be representative of how the data would be split after the entire list is imported. Users can try to obtain a representative sample of their data for the purpose of ingesting it and allowing Accumulo to find good split points early.

To lower the split threshold for a table, users can configure the table in the shell like this:

```
config -t tableName -s table.split.threshold=1G
```

 If your application has a table with a small amount of data, consider splitting it as well. Such tables could be filled with lookup information, or generated from another part of your application, and so on. If these tables are on one tablet server, the application is not taking advantage of Accumulo's distributed abilities and may be creating artificial hotspots.

One way to split a small table is the break the range up in one part for every node in your cluster that hosts tablet servers. This may not distribute it very well if data is not evenly distributed by row ID.

Another way is to compact the table and look at the size of the current RFile. Then in the table config, set `table.split.threshold` roughly equal to the RFile size divided by the number of tablet servers. Wait until tablet servers have created the desired number of splits. Be sure to set the `table.split.threshold` back to the original value afterward.

Rather than lowering the split threshold, users can submit a list of split points to Accumulo to use to create multiple tablets. The advantage of this is that the table will be distributed onto more servers before any data is ingested. The onus of picking good split points rests with the user.

To presplit a table from a list of points, the split points should first be put into a text file, with one point per line. For example:

```
e
j
o
t
```

Adding these split points to a single-tablet table would result in five tablets: *(-infinity, e]*, *(e, j]*, *(j, o]*, *(o, t]*, and lastly *(t, infinity)* (Figure 13-11). The special tablet with end point at infinity exists for every table and is called the *default tablet*.

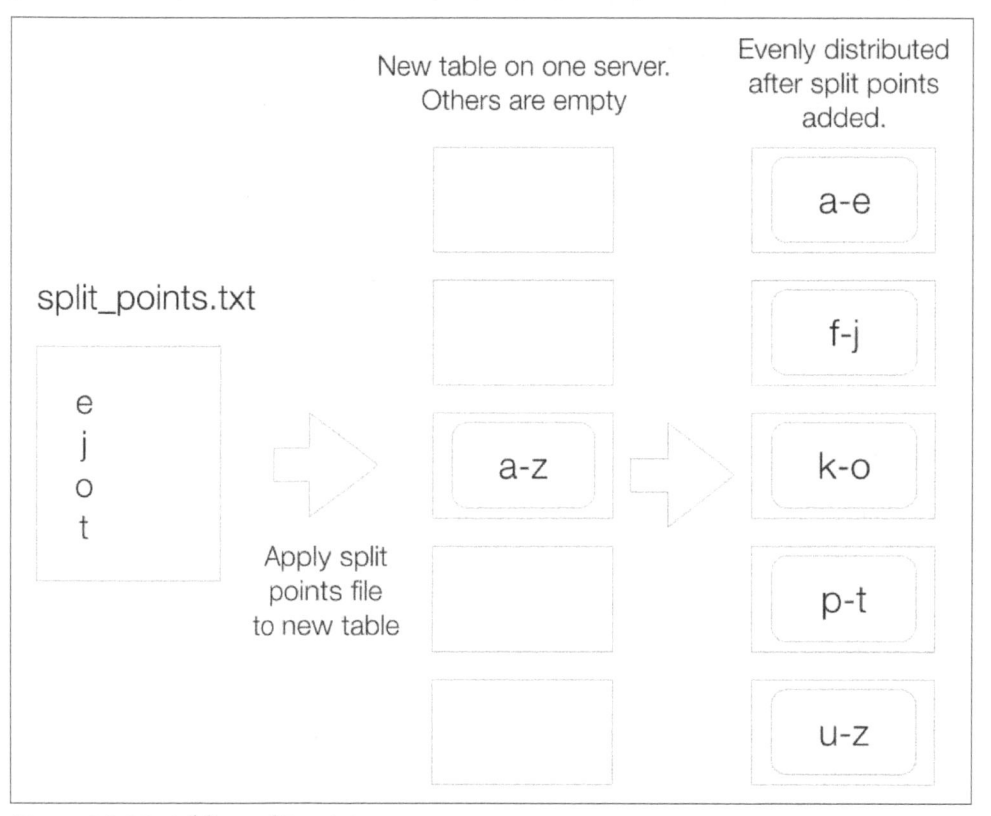

Figure 13-11. Adding split points

Then the split points file can be submitted to Accumulo for splitting via the shell:

```
user@accumulo> addsplits -t tableName -sf fileName
```

A file with split points can also be provided when first creating a table through the shell. To copy the split points from an existing table, use:

```
user@accumulo> createtable myPreSplitTable --copy-splits existingTable
```

To use a file do the following:

```
user@accumulo> createtable myPreSplitTable --splits-file mySplitsFile.txt
```

A small set of specific split points can be added directly in the shell:

```
user@accumulo> addsplits e j o t -t mytable
```

Splits can be added via the Java API as well:

```
ZooKeeperInstance inst = new ZooKeeperInstance(myInstance, zkServers);
Connector conn = inst.getConnector(principal, passwordToken);

SortedSet<Text> splitPoints = new TreeSet<>();
splitPoints.add(new Text("e"));
splitPoints.add(new Text("j"));
splitPoints.add(new Text("o"));
splitPoints.add(new Text("t"));

conn.tableOperations().addSplits("mytable", splitPoints);
```

If a set of split points are to be used to presplit a table from time to time, or to be distributed along with an application for use with multiple sources of data, care should be taken to ensure that the split points used on a table are representative of the distribution of the data to be loaded. The distribution of keys within a data set may change over time, and may not be the same from one data source to another.

Accumulo can also merge tablets, which is covered in "Merging Tablets" on page 453.

Balancing Tablets

Once a table is split into some number of tablets, the Accumulo master can use different load balancers to achieve a good distribution of tablets across tablet servers. By default, each table's tablets are balanced separately and are assigned evenly and randomly to tablet servers. This load balancer will likely suffice for the majority of applications.

However, some applications may require more fine-tuned control over their tablets. Some key design patterns require not only that a table's tablets are distributed evenly, but that specific subsets of tablets are also distributed evenly.

An example might be a table with a row key containing a date. Suppose an application built on top of this table frequently accesses dates falling within the same month at the same time. Using the default load balancer could end up assigning all the tablets for a month to a single server, limiting the insert and query capabilities across that group of tablets. Instead, this table could employ a custom load balancer to ensure that tablets falling within the same month are distributed evenly to tablet servers.

To write a custom load balancer, implement a class that extends `TabletBalancer` as described in "Additional Properties" on page 151. Add a JAR containing the new balancer to Accumulo's CLASSPATH on at least the master nodes, and configure a table to use this balancer by setting the `table.balancer` property for the table.

Balancing Reads and Writes

Accumulo allows users to dedicate system resources to writes or reads as necessary. By default, Accumulo does not throttle writes in order to keep some resources available for reads, so query performance can suffer if clients are using too much of Accumulo's resources for writing.

One method of throttling writes and improving read performance is to decrease the maximum number of files Accumulo is allowed to create per tablet. This is controlled with the per-table setting `table.file.max`, which defaults to 15. When the maximum number of files has been reached for a tablet, Accumulo will merge new data with data from one of the existing files instead of creating a new file for that tablet. The new, merged file will then replace the existing file. This process is called a *merging minor compaction*.

When merging minor compactions are occurring, the overall write rate of the cluster may begin to decrease, because a minor compaction to free up memory for new writes may be waiting for a merging minor compaction to complete. While this is happening, any new writes to the server cannot proceed and clients are told to wait. Increasing the `table.file.max` setting or decreasing the `table.compaction.major.ratio` setting will ensure that enough background compactions occur so that minor compactions will not end up having to wait and block clients.

Data Locality

In MapReduce jobs, the notion of *physical data locality*, in terms of the distance between data to be processed and the CPU and RAM elements in which it will be processed, is extremely important. Many types of MapReduce jobs are run on data that is so large that reading it from some storage medium over a network would limit the performance in an unacceptable way. The primary innovation of MapReduce versus many other types of data processing is that it sends the computation to the data, rather than moving the data to the computation.

When key-value pairs are processed in a MapReduce job, the key-value pairs are read from a local disk by a copy of the map or reduce process that has been sent to the machine holding the data. This allows the overall job to be limited by the aggregate throughput of all the hard drives in the cluster, which is often much higher than the aggregate throughput rate of the network connecting machines in the cluster.

Data for MapReduce jobs is stored beforehand in HDFS, which automatically distributes it over many machines, handles replication, and helps programs find a particular piece of data by exposing the IP address of the physical machine on which it is stored.

For Accumulo, the concept of physical data locality is still important but not paramount. Because Accumulo uses HDFS to store files, each time a tablet server flushes a new file to HDFS as part of the minor compaction process, one copy of that file is stored locally on the machine hosting the tablet server process. Subsequent reads can then simply read from local disk rather than pulling data from a remote machine over a network.

Over time, as the Accumulo master performs load balancing of tablets, some tablets may reference files for which there is no local copy, forcing reads to pull data from a remote machine over the network. But eventually the major compaction process will tend to create new files for each tablet, merging several old files into one new file, which will cause a local copy to be created. Good physical data locality is something Accumulo achieves eventually and asynchronously.

Accumulo has a utility for checking the level of data locality in a cluster. It can be run via the `accumulo` command:

```
accumulo org.apache.accumulo.server.util.LocalityCheck -u root -p secret

Server          %local   total blocks
  10.10.100.1 100.0        7
  10.10.100.2 100.0       10
  10.10.100.3 100.0       10
```

If for some reason a cluster has poor data locality, increasing the frequency of major compactions or scheduling a major compaction can cause files to be rewritten. To compact a table, use the `compact` command from the shell:

```
accumulo@cluster> compact myTable
```

Note that this will completely rewrite all files in a table. When stopping and restarting a cluster, Accumulo tries to reassign tablets to the same tablet servers that were previously hosting them before shutting down, so that physical locality is preserved.

Sharing ZooKeeper

Some other applications running on or close to the Accumulo cluster might also make use of ZooKeeper. In particular, Apache Kafka (*http://kafka.apache.org*) is a popular distributed queue used to stream data to and from applications. Some Accumulo clients can make use of Kafka to stream data to Accumulo or from Accumulo to other applications.

Similarly, Apache Storm (*https://storm.incubator.apache.org*), a popular streaming data processing framework, relies on ZooKeeper for configuration information.

Be cognizant of the load placed on ZooKeeper by these other systems. (See the Zoo-Keeper documentation on monitoring (*http://bit.ly/zookeeper_monitoring*).) Although ZooKeeper itself is a distributed application, one machine of the quorum serves as master, meaning that all writes go to it, whereas reads can go to any member of the quorum. The ZooKeeper quorum master has to handle all writes and replicate those writes synchronously to other members of the quorum, so the scalability of writes isn't improved by adding more machines; rather, it makes each write *more expensive*, reducing the total write throughput of the ZooKeeper instance.

If ZooKeeper can't keep up with operations, Accumulo will not function properly. It is possible to run multiple separate ZooKeeper instances on a cluster, each one consisting of one, three, or five nodes, as long as applications are configured to use different instances.

Shell Commands Quick Reference

Debugging

classpath
    Lists the current files on the classpath.

debug
    Turns debug logging on or off.

listscans
    Lists what scans are currently running in Accumulo. See the `accumulo.core.client.admin.ActiveScan` javadoc for more information about columns.

listcompactions
    Lists what compactions are currently running in Accumulo. See the `accumulo.core.client.admin.ActiveCompaction` javadoc for more information about columns.

trace
    Turns trace logging on or off.

ping
    Ping tablet servers.

Exiting

bye
    Exits the shell.

exit
> Exits the shell.

quit
> Exits the shell.

Help

about
> Displays information about this program.

help
> Provides information about the available commands.

info
> Displays information about this program.

?
> Provides information about the available commands.

Iterator

deleteiter
> Deletes a table-specific iterator.

deletescaniter
> Deletes a table-specific scan iterator so it is no longer used during this shell session.

listiter
> Lists table-specific iterators configured in this shell session.

setiter
> Sets a table-specific iterator.

setscaniter
> Sets a table-specific scan iterator for this shell session.

setshelliter
> Adds an iterator to a profile for this shell session.

listshelliter
> Lists iterator profiles configured in the shell.

deleteshelliter
> Deletes iterator profiles configured in this shell session.

Permissions Administration

grant
> Grants system or table permissions for a user.

revoke
> Revokes system or table permissions from a user.

systempermissions
> Displays a list of valid system permissions.

tablepermissions
> Displays a list of valid table permissions.

userpermissions
> Displays a user's system and table permissions.

Shell Execution

execfile
> Specifies a file containing Accumulo commands to execute.

history
> Generates a list of commands previously executed.

Shell State

authenticate
> Verifies a user's credentials.

cls
> Clears the screen.

clear
> Clears the screen.

notable
> Returns to a tableless shell state.

sleep
> Sleeps for the given number of seconds.

table
> Switches to the specified table.

user
> Switches to the specified user.

whoami
> Reports the current username.

Table Administration

clonetable
> Clones a table.

config
> Prints system properties and table-specific properties.

createtable
> Creates a new table, with optional aggregators and optionally pre-split.

deletetable
> Deletes a table.

droptable
> Deletes a table.

du
> Prints how much space, in bytes, is used by files referenced by a table. When multiple tables are specified it prints how much space, in bytes, is used by files shared between tables, if any.

exporttable
> Exports a table.

importtable
> Imports a table.

offline
> Starts the process of taking a table offline.

online
> Starts the process of putting a table online.

renametable
> Renames a table.

tables
> Displays a list of all existing tables.

Table Control

addsplits
> Adds split points to an existing table.

---

compact
> Sets all tablets for a table to major compact as soon as possible (based on current time).

constraint
> Adds, deletes, or lists constraints for a table.

flush
> Flushes a table's data that is currently in memory to disk.

getgroups
> Gets the locality groups for a given table.

getsplits
> Retrieves the current split points for tablets in the current table.

merge
> Merges tablets in a table.

setgroups
> Sets the locality groups for a given table (for binary or commas, use Java API).

User Administration

addauths
> Adds authorizations to the maximum scan authorizations for a user.

createuser
> Creates a new user.

deleteuser
> Deletes a user.

dropuser
> Deletes a user.

getauths
> Displays the maximum scan authorizations for a user.

passwd
> Changes a user's password.

setauths
> Sets the maximum scan authorizations for a user.

users
> Displays a list of existing users.

Writing, Reading, and Removing Data

delete
> Deletes a record from a table.

deletemany
> Scans a table and deletes the resulting records.

deleterows
> Deletes a range of rows in a table. Note that rows matching the start row are not deleted, but rows matching the end row are deleted.

egrep
> Searches each row, column family, column qualifier, and value, in parallel, on the server side (using a java Matcher, so put .* before and after your term if you're not matching the whole element).

formatter
> Specifies a formatter to use for displaying table entries.

interpreter
> Specifies a scan interpreter to interpret scan range and column arguments.

grep
> Searches each row, column family, column qualifier, and value in a table for a substring (not a regular expression), in parallel, on the server side.

importdirectory
> Bulk-imports an entire directory of data files to the current table. The boolean argument determines if Accumulo sets the time.

insert
> Inserts a record.

maxrow
> Finds the max row in a table within a given range.

scan
> Scans the table and displays the resulting records.

Metadata Table

The metadata table contains a row for every tablet in Accumulo. Tablets are uniquely described by the ID of their table and the last row in the range assigned to the tablet, or *end row*. Table B-1 describes the columns that can appear in a tablet's row in the metadata table, and Table B-2 shows some sample entries from a real metadata table.

In addition to tablet entries, there is a section of the metadata table that records file deletion entries. There is also a section for files that are in the process of being bulk-imported into Accumulo, to assist the garbage collector in not deleting these files prematurely. More about file deletion can be found in "Garbage Collector" on page 376.

Table B-1. Metadata table description

Row	Column family	Column qualifier	Value
table id ; tablet end row	file	*regular data file name*	*size in bytes , number of keys*
table id ; tablet end row	future	*tablet server session id*	*tserver IP : port*
table id ; tablet end row	last	*tablet server session id*	*tserver IP : port*
table id ; tablet end row	loc	*tablet server session id*	*tserver IP : port*
table id ; tablet end row	log	*server / log file name*	*log set	table id*
table id ; tablet end row	scan	*file currently being scanned*	
table id ; tablet end row	srv	compact	*compaction id*
table id ; tablet end row	srv	dir	*tablet directory*

Row	Column family	Column qualifier	Value
table id ; tablet end row	`srv`	`flush`	*flush id*
table id ; tablet end row	`srv`	`lock`	*zookeeper lock location*
table id ; tablet end row	`srv`	`time`	*M or L followed by latest time*
table id ; tablet end row	`~tab`	`~pr`	`0x01` *followed by previous tablet's end row*

Row ID

The row ID for a tablet contains the table ID and the tablet end row separated by a semicolon. For the last tablet in a table, there is no end row. The row for that tablet is the table ID followed by <.

Rows starting with ~del are for deletion entries and rows starting with ~blip are for files that are in the process of being bulk loaded. These entries also contain the name of the file marked for deletion or bulk loading.

There are also entries for problems with loading resources. If the problem involves the metadata table, the information about the problem is written directly to Zoo-Keeper, but problems with other tablets are written to the metadata table. These entries have row ID beginning with ~err and also containing the table name. The column family is either FILE_READ, FILE_WRITE, or TABLET_LOAD, indicating the type of problem, and the column qualifier is the resource name, which is either a filename or a tablet key extent (prev row and end row). The value contains additional information such as the time the problem occurred, the server, and the exception if available.

File Column Family

This column family contains information about a tablet's files. The column qualifier is the name of the file and the value contains information about the file, its size in bytes, and number of keys. Under some conditions these values are estimates. For example, when a tablet is split, the two resulting tablets' file entries will each be assumed to contain about half the bytes and number of keys of the original tablet's files.

The first letter of the filename (the actual file name, not including its path) indicates what type of operation created the file:

F

Minor compaction

C

Major compaction

A

Full major compaction

M

Merging minor compaction

I

Bulk import

Scan Column Family

This column family is used to ensure that files are not deleted while they are being scanned. The column qualifier is the name of a file currently being scanned. The garbage collector takes this information into account when determining which files are still in use and which can be safely deleted.

future, last, and loc Column Families

These column families contain information about where a tablet has been assigned. The *future* column contains the current assignment. The *loc* column contains the current assignment once the tablet has been successfully loaded by the assigned tablet server. The *last* column is the last assignment, used to try to reassign a tablet to the same server to improve data locality.

The column qualifier is the tablet server session ID, and the value is the tablet server location, its IP address, and port. Each tablet server process has a unique session ID, so if the tablet server process is restarted on a machine Accumulo will be able to distinguish between tablets assigned to it before and after it was restarted.

log Column Family

This column family contains information about a tablet's write-ahead logfiles. The column qualifier is the server name and the logfile name separated by a slash. The value is the log set and table ID separated by a pipe. In 1.5.0 and later, the log set is the same as the logfile name.

srv Column Family

The `dir` column qualifier has the tablet's main directory as its value. The tablet can use files outside of this directory, but new files will be created in the directory.

The `compact` column qualifier has the most recent compaction ID as its value. The `flush` column qualifier has the most recent flush ID as its value. These IDs are used to determine whether requested flushes or compactions have successfully completed for all relevant tablets.

The `lock` column qualifier contains the ZooKeeper lock location for a tablet server that is attempting to write to the metadata table. There is a constraint on the metadata table that only accepts writes from tablet servers with currently held ZooKeeper locks.

The `time` column qualifier stores the timestamp of the most recently written data to a tablet. It is preceded by an M indicating that the timestamp is in milliseconds since the epoch, or an L indicating that the timestamp is in logical time (essentially a one-up counter).

~tab:~pr Column

This column contains the end row of the previous tablet, which helps Accumulo keep track of its metadata. The value is `0x01` followed by previous tablet's end row. For the first tablet in a table, there is no previous tablet, so the value is set to `0x00`.

Other Columns

There are a few additional metadata entry types that are ephemeral, such as those written in the process of a tablet split operation. These include a `~tab:oldprevrow` and `~tab:splitRatio` for split operations; `chopped:chopped` for merge operations; `loaded` for bulk import operations; and `!cloned` for table clone operations.

Table B-2. A sample of metadata table contents

Row	Column family:Column qualifier	Value
!0;!0<	srv:dir	/root_tablet
!0;!0<	~tab:~pr	\x00
!0;~	file:/table_info/A0001c8q.rf	965,28
!0;~	last:1409c5a89030283	127.0.0.1:9997
!0;~	loc:1409c5a89030283	127.0.0.1:9997

Row	Column family:Column qualifier	Value
!0;~	srv:compact	10892
!0;~	srv:dir	/table_info
!0;~	srv:flush	10892
!0;~	srv:lock	tservers/127.0.0.1:9997/ zlock-0000000000$1409c5a89030283
!0;~	srv:time	L3523
!0;~	~tab:~pr	\x01!0<
!0<	last:1409c5a89030283	127.0.0.1:9997
!0<	loc:1409c5a89030283	127.0.0.1:9997
!0<	srv:compact	10892
!0<	srv:dir	/default_tablet
!0<	srv:flush	10892
!0<	srv:lock	tservers/127.0.0.1:9997/ zlock-0000000000$1409c5a89030283
!0<	srv:time	L4504
!0<	~tab:~pr	\x01~
1<	file:/default_tablet/ C0000dj7.rf	12617985,527400
1<	file:/default_tablet/ C0000mcw.rf	18999363,790313
1<	file:/default_tablet/ C00013vg.rf	25227499,1035563
1<	file:/default_tablet/ C000191y.rf	7476173,305642
1<	file:/default_tablet/ C0001alv.rf	2239839,91671

Row	Column family:Column qualifier	Value
1<	file:/default_tablet/ C0001boe.rf	1543104,63045
1<	file:/default_tablet/ C0001bzk.rf	452015,18523
1<	file:/default_tablet/ C0001c5h.rf	146692,5864
1<	file:/default_tablet/ F0001c45.rf	95096,3852
1<	file:/default_tablet/ F0001c6j.rf	43762,1750
1<	file:/default_tablet/ F0001c7w.rf	55019,2206
1<	last:1409c5a89030283	127.0.0.1:9997
1<	loc:1409c5a89030283	127.0.0.1:9997
1<	log:127.0.0.1+9997/30d1970a- 3db5-49fc-82d6-8adde36c9453	127.0.0.1+9997/30d1970a- 3db5-49fc-82d6-8adde36c9453:4
1<	srv:compact	0
1<	srv:dir	/default_tablet
1<	srv:flush	0
1<	srv:lock	tservers/127.0.0.1:9997/ zlock-0000000000$1409c5a89030283
1<	srv:time	M1380306759481
1<	~tab:~pr	\x00
3<	file:/default_tablet/ F0000005.rf	186,1
3<	last:1409c5a89030283	127.0.0.1:9997
3<	loc:1409c5a89030283	127.0.0.1:9997

Row	Column family:Column qualifier	Value
3<	srv:dir	/default_tablet
3<	srv:flush	1
3<	srv:lock	tservers/127.0.0.1:9997/ zlock-0000000000$1409c5a89030283
3<	srv:time	M1377020908127
3<	~tab:~pr	\x00
~del/!0/ table_info/ A0001c8l.rf		

Data Stored in ZooKeeper

Under the /accumulo node in ZooKeeper, there is a node for each instance of Accumulo keyed by instance ID. There is also an instances node that contains a node for each Accumulo instance name, with the data for each instance name being the instance ID currently associated with that name.

The following nodes can exist under each instance ID node.

masters, tservers, gc, monitor, and tracers Nodes

These nodes contain the locations of the various Accumulo processes.

The masters/lock node contains an ephemeral sequential master lock whose data is the master location. The masters/goal_state node contains the master's goal state (NORMAL, SAFE_MODE, or CLEAN_STOP).

The tservers/*tablet_server_host:port* nodes contain an ephemeral sequential lock for the specified tablet server. The data for the lock is TSERV_CLIENT=*host:port*.

The gc/lock node contains an ephemeral sequential lock for the garbage collector. The data for the lock is GC_CLIENT=*IP:port*.

The data for the monitor node is the location (IP:port) of the monitor server. There is also a child node monitor/log4j_port, whose data is the port of the monitor server used for collecting error logs from other Accumulo processes.

The data for the tracers/trace-*ID* nodes is the location (IP:port) for the tracer process. The ID is a one-up counter for the tracer processes.

problems/problem_info Nodes

These nodes are created when a problem has occurred with a resource of the metadata table. Problems with nonmetadata resources are stored in the metadata table.

The problem information encoded in the node name includes the table name, problem type (FILE_READ, FILE_WRITE, or TABLET_LOAD), and resource name (either a filename or tablet key extent). The data for the node is additional information about the problem, including the time the problem occurred, the server, and the exception if available.

root_tablet Node

This node has lastlocation, location, future_location, dir, and walogs children. These nodes contain the information that is stored in the metadata table for other tablets: tablet server assignment information, HDFS directory, and write-ahead log files.

tables/table_id Nodes

These nodes contain the following child nodes:

state
: Data is the current state of the table (NEW, ONLINE, OFFLINE, or DELETING).

conf/table_property_name
: Data is the value for the table property.

flush-id
: Data is the ID of the last attempted flush.

compact-id
: Data is the ID of the last attempted compaction followed by an encoding of the iterators used for the compaction.

compact-cancel-id
: Data is the ID of the last canceled compaction.

name
: Data is the name of the table.

config/system_property_name Node

The data for each of these nodes is the value for the specified system property. These property values override what is configured in the *accumulo-site.xml* file.

---

users/username Nodes

Accumulo's user authentication and authorization mechanisms are pluggable. The default authentication implementation is a simple username/password system. The usernames are stored as ZooKeeper nodes whose data is the hash of the user's password. The default authorization implementation stores the Accumulo users' maximum set of authorizations in a child node of the *username* node in ZooKeeper. These authorizations are used along with column visibilities for each key to determine which key-value pairs can be seen by the user.

Other Nodes

hdfs_reservations
: Associates external HDFS directories with a FATE transaction ID when in the process of bulk importing files, importing tables, or exporting tables.

table_locks
: Contains table read and write locks associated with performing some types of table operations.

next_file
: Used for creating unique file and directory names for the lifetime of an Accumulo instance, this stores the current maximum number of names that have been allocated.

bulk_failed_copyq
: Contains tablet server work queue for copying files that failed to bulk import.

recovery
: Contains tablet server work queue for sorting write-ahead logfiles that need to be recovered.

dead/tservers
: Contains tablet servers that have been shut down.

fate/*transaction_id*
: Contains state of in-progress FATE operations.

Index

Q

querying term-partitioned indexes, 279-283
    about, 279
    combining query terms, 281
    specific field, querying for term in, 282

R

random access memory (RAM), 4
random access performance, 7-10
    and hashing vs. sorting data, 9
    with sorted vs. unsorted data, 7
read performance, 470
reading data, 103-113
    and grouping data by rows, 110
    crafting ranges for, 108
    example, 106
    reusing Scanners for, 111
    tuning Scanners for, 112
    with isolated row views, 111
    with Scanners, 103-106
recovery, tablet, 43
relational databases
    Accumulo vs., 46-50
    ACID guarantees in, 47
    approximating properties of, 351-355
    join strategies in Accumulo vs., 353-355
    normalization in, 48-50
    relieving, 57
    schema constraints in, 351
    space-time tradeoff in, 47
    SQL in, 46
    transactions in, 47
relative-key encoding, 45
resource manager, 360-366
    major compaction by, 362
    merging minor compaction by, 364
    minor compaction by, 361
    splitting by, 365
resource settings (tablet server), 493
    and MapReduce workers, 494
    tserver.compaction.major.concurrent.max,
        493
    tserver.compaction.minor.concurrent.max,
        493
    tserver.readahead.concurrent.max, 493
restarting Accumulo, 428
RFile format, 369-372
    bloom filters in, 371
    locality groups in, 370
    optimization of, 369
    relative key encoding in, 370
Riak, 51
Rinaldi, Billie, 12
row IDs, designing, 304-307
    composite row IDs, 304
    consistent updates, designing for, 306
    hotspots, avoiding, 305
    key size and, 305
    Lexicoders and, 304
row-oriented storage, 3
running Accumulo, 425-467
    cluster changes, 438-439
    clusters, stopping, 427
    data lifecycle and, 449-456
    failure recovery in, 456-467
    monitoring system health and usage,
        429-436
    processes, stopping, 427
    restarting after a crash, 428
    starting program, 425
    table operations, 440-449
    tracing operations, 436

S

SAN (storage area network), 4
scalability, of Accumulo, 43
scanner object, 30
search applications, 57
secondary indexing, 275-295
    data types, indexing, 288-295
    document-partitioned indexes, 284-288
    term-partitioned indexes, 276-284
security API, 175-199
    application accounts for multiple users in,
        198
    auditing operations in, 194
    authentication in, 176, 195-197
    authorizations in, 183-193, 195
    disk encryption with, 198
    permissions in, 177-182, 195
    protecting networks with, 198
security features of Accumulo, 416-424
    application permissions, 424
    column visibilities, 416
    encryption of data at rest, 422
    Kerberized Hadoop, 423
    limiting file access to support, 416
    network security, 417-422

security label expression, 22
semantic triples, 329-334
  about, 329
  Freebase API example with, 329-334
server configuration files
  accumulo-env.sh file, 403
  accumulo-site.xml file, 405
  copying, 402
shards, 5
shared-nothing architecture, 4
shared-nothing scaling, 4
shell commands, 505-510
  debugging, 505
  exiting, 505
  for reading data, 510
  for removing data, 510
  for writing data, 510
  help, 506
  iterator, 506
  permissions administration, 507
  related to shell execution, 507
  related to shell state, 507
  table administration, 508
  table control, 508
  user administration, 509
software dependencies, 386
  Apache Hadoop, 386
  Apache ZooKeeper, 387
solid state drives (SSDs), 1
source code, 399
  native libraries from, 400
  tarball distributions from, 399
sparseness, 15
spatial data, 334-337
  open source projects using, 334
  space-filling curves and, 335
SQL databases, 46
  approximating properties in, 351-355
  GROUP BY clause in, 353, 355
  JOIN clause in, 353
  join strategies in Accumulo, 353-355
  ORDER BY clause in, 353, 355
  schema constraints in, 351
  SELECT clause in, 352
  WHERE clause in, 352
SSDs (solid state drives), 1
starting Accumulo, 425
  init.d scripts for, 426
  start-all.sh script for, 425

Stonebraker, Michael, 57
stopping Accumulo
  clusters, stopping, 427
  init.d scripts for, 427
  processes, stopping, 427
  stop-all.sh script for, 427
storage area network (SAN), 4
storage cost, 1
storage devices
  hard disk drives, 474
  solid state disks, 475
  storage area networks, 474

T
table API, 131-173
  alternate compression algorithm, 153
  alternative interpreter, 154
  block replica control, 154
  block size control, 152
  block size for compression, 152
  block size for storage in index, 153
  bloom filters, 142-144
  caching data, 144
  changing file format, 154
  clearing locator cache, 159
  cloning tables, 157
  compacting, 149-151
  creating tables, 131-135
  custom table formatter, 154
  deleting entries returned from a scan, 136
  deleting ranges of rows in tables, 135
  deleting tables, 135
  enabling write-ahead log, 155
  finding disk usage, 160
  ignoring table failures, 152
  importing/exporting tables, 158
  instance operations, 165-173
  locality groups, 138-141
  looking up table IDs, 159
  maximum memory for batching scan
      results, 155
  maximum number of files associated with
      tablets, 153
  memory control, 152
  namespaces, 160-165
  online/offline status, 156
  renaming tables, 135
  setting column visibility to default, 155
  specifying CLASSPATH, 152

V

values, designing, 307-312
  about, 307-310
  human readable vs. binary values/formatters, 311
  large values, 310
  storing files and, 310
versioned data, applications with, 58
vertical scaling, 4, 43
very large-scale clusters, 411-416
  file sizing in, 413
  limits for, 412
  metadata table in, 412
  multiple HDFS volumes in, 413-416
  networking in, 411
  tablet sizing in, 413

W

websites with massive simultaneous users and data, 56
Wikipedia pages example, 84-89
  data in Wikipedia articles, 84
  data modeling, 85-88
  downloading all English articles, 89
  downloading sample pages, 89

obtaining code, 88
worker nodes, 41
write performance, 471-473
  BatchWriters and, 472
  bulk loading and, 472
  modeling, 477
write-ahead log settings (tablet server), 492
  tserver.wal.replication, 492
  tserver.wal.sync, 492
  tserver.wal.sync.method, 492
write-ahead logs
  about, 367
  logfile recovery, 367
writing data, 90-102
  committing mutations for, 93
  example, 97
  handling errors when, 95
  mutation objects for, 90
  to multiple tables, 100-102
  using Lexicoders in, 99
  with strings vs. byte arrays, 92

Z

ZooKeeper (see Apache ZooKeeper)

About the Authors

Aaron Cordova worked as a computer systems researcher at the US National Security Agency, where he started and led the Apache Accumulo project through its first release. He has built large-scale data processing and analysis systems for intelligence, defense, academic research, and web companies. Aaron is a cofounder of Koverse Inc.

From 2008 to 2012, **Billie Rinaldi** was a leader of the National Security Agency computer science research team that implemented Apache Accumulo. Dr. Rinaldi codesigned one of Accumulo's key technical advantages, a customizable server-side programming framework, and made numerous other contributions to the software. Since Accumulo became open source in fall 2011, she has worked to foster the community surrounding it. Dr. Rinaldi was elected the Project Management Committee chair when Accumulo became a top-level Apache project and was subsequently invited to become a member of the Apache Software Foundation. Dr. Rinaldi is a senior member of technical staff at Hortonworks, Inc.

Michael Wall has been using Apache Accumulo since September 2010 and has been involved in all types of development from analytic simulation to a large-scale news aggregation site. After graduating from the US Air Force Academy in 1994, he served on active duty in the US Air Force. Since leaving the military, Mike has worked as a software engineer for the National Security Agency and other government agencies.

Colophon

The animal on the cover of *Accumulo: Application Development, Table Design, and Best Practices* is a yak, an animal well-suited for the higher altitudes and colder temperatures of the mountains and plateaus in Central Asia, where both wild (*Bos mutus*) and domesticated (*Bos grunniens*) varieties still chew cud. Relatively large lungs and hearts permit the bodies of yaks to transport oxygen efficiently, and a larger *rumen*, the first of its four stomach chambers, relative to cattle allows the yak to eat food in larger portions and less frequently. Temperatures approaching 60°F will threaten this animal with dehydration. The yak will more easily accommodate a -40°F winter night in the Himalayas.

Many of the animals on O'Reilly covers are endangered; all of them are important to the world. To learn more about how you can help, go to *animals.oreilly.com*.

The cover image is from *The Royal Natural History*. The cover fonts are URW Typewriter and Guardian Sans. The text font is Adobe Minion Pro; the heading font is Adobe Myriad Condensed; and the code font is Dalton Maag's Ubuntu Mono.

Get even more for your money.

Join the O'Reilly Community, and register the O'Reilly books you own. It's free, and you'll get:

- $4.99 ebook upgrade offer
- 40% upgrade offer on O'Reilly print books
- Membership discounts on books and events
- Free lifetime updates to ebooks and videos
- Multiple ebook formats, DRM FREE
- Participation in the O'Reilly community
- Newsletters
- Account management
- 100% Satisfaction Guarantee

Signing up is easy:

1. Go to: oreilly.com/go/register
2. Create an O'Reilly login.
3. Provide your address.
4. Register your books.

Note: English-language books only

To order books online:
oreilly.com/store

For questions about products or an order:
orders@oreilly.com

To sign up to get topic-specific email announcements and/or news about upcoming books, conferences, special offers, and new technologies:
elists@oreilly.com

For technical questions about book content:
booktech@oreilly.com

To submit new book proposals to our editors:
proposals@oreilly.com

O'Reilly books are available in multiple DRM-free ebook formats. For more information:
oreilly.com/ebooks

O'REILLY®

Ingram Content Group UK Ltd.
Milton Keynes UK
UKHW031127070323
418129UK00009B/901